WHERE COURAGEOUS INQUIRY LEADS
The Emerging Life of Emory University

Emory in Atlanta, 2009

WHERE COURAGEOUS INQUIRY LEADS
The Emerging Life of Emory University

— GARY S. HAUK *and* SALLY WOLFF KING, EDITORS —

WHERE COURAGEOUS INQUIRY LEADS
The Emerging Life of Emory University

Editors: Gary S. Hauk and Sally Wolff King

Editorial Advisory Board
James W. Wagner, President, Emory University
Susan Ashmore, Associate Professor of History, Oxford College, Emory
Virginia Cain (Emory College 1977, Graduate School 1982), Interim Director of Manuscript, Archives, and Rare Book Library, Emory
Rose B. Cannon, Professor of Nursing, Emerita, Woodruff School of Nursing, Emory
Peter W. Dowell, Professor of English, Emeritus, Emory College
Thomas E. Frank, University Associate Professor, Wake Forest University
David Goldsmith, Professor of Chemistry, Emeritus, Emory College
Eric Goldstein (Emory College 1992), Professor of History, Emory College
Leslie M. Harris, Associate Professor of History, Emory College
Irwin Hyatt, Professor of History, Emeritus, Emory College
Consuela Kertz (Emory Law 1975), Professor of Accounting, Goizueta Business School, Emory
Richard M. Levinson, Charles Howard Candler Professor, Rollins School of Public Health, Emory
Clyde Partin Jr. (Emory College 1978, Medicine 1983), Associate Professor of Medicine, Emory School of Medicine
Polly J. Price (Emory College and Graduate School, 1986), Professor of Law, Emory Law School

Copyright 2010 by Emory University, Atlanta, Georgia. All rights reserved. No part of this book may be reproduced or transmitted in any form or by any means, electronic or mechanical, including photocopying, recording, or by any information storage and retrieval system, without permission in writing from Emory University.

ISBN: 978-1-4507-1924-7

All photography in this book is the property of Emory University with the exception of Russell Major, Page 333, courtesy of Blair Rogers Major, and Moses Hadas, Page 277, courtesy of *Classical World* and the Classical Association of the Atlantic States.

Emory University
201 Dowman Drive
Atlanta, Georgia 30322
www.emory.edu

While the content of this book is correct to the best of our knowledge, please note that research is a continual process. We encourage anyone who has relevant information to contact Emory University.

Book Development by
Bookhouse Group, Inc.
Atlanta, Georgia
www.bookhouse.net

Editorial Director: Rob Levin
Project Manager: Renée Peyton
Design and Prepress: Jill Dible
Copy Editor: Bob Land
Indexer: Eric R. Nitschke

Contents

INTRODUCTION
GARY S. HAUK AND SALLY WOLFF KING IX

SECTION 1 STORY AND PLACE IN THE SHAPING OF INSTITUTIONAL CHARACTER

"The Spirits of This Lawn":
Poem commissioned for inauguration of President James Wagner, April 2, 2004
JOHN STONE 1

Chapter 1 "Emory Are Here": *Emory as Place and Story*
MARSHALL P. DUKE 3

Chapter 2 "Dreams Deferred": *African Americans in the History of Old Emory*
MARK AUSLANDER 13

Chapter 3 Lynching, Academic Freedom, and the Old "New South":
President Dickey and the "Sledd Affair"
THOMAS H. JACKSON JR. 23

Chapter 4 National Ambition, Regional Turmoil: *The Desegregation of Emory*
MELISSA F. KEAN 39

Chapter 5 Putting Black Blood and White Blood on the Same Shelf:
The Integration of Grady Hospital
JERRY GENTRY 57

Chapter 6 Lullwater and the Greening of Emory:
Catalyst for a New Environmental Commitment
NANCY SEIDEMAN 71

Chapter 7 Shaped by a Crucible Experience: *The Center for Women at Emory*
ALI P. CROWN AND JAN GLEASON 83

SECTION 2 BUILDING A COMMUNITY OF SCHOLARS

Chapter 8 Catching Up: *The Advance of Emory since World War II*
NANCY DIAMOND 93

Chapter 9 How It Came to Pass: *Oral History of a Half-Century in Emory Arts and Sciences*
Interviews with Former Chancellor Billy E. Frye; Former Emory College Deans David Minter, George Jones, David Bright, and Steven Sanderson; and Former College Senior Associate Deans Irwin Hyatt, Peter Dowell, and Rosemary Magee 113

Chapter 10 Campus Life: *The Interplay of Living and Learning at Emory*
WILLIAM H. FOX 157

Chapter 11 The School of Theology as Prelude: *Candler Conversations* 163
MANFRED HOFFMANN, WILLIAM MALLARD, THEODORE RUNYON, AND THEODORE WEBER

Chapter 12 African American Studies at Emory: *A Model for Change*
DELORES P. ALDRIDGE 173

Chapter 13	"Struck by Theater-Ideas": *Theater as a Site and Mode of Inquiry at Emory University* MICHAEL EVENDEN	187
Chapter 14	"If You Build It, [They] Will Come": *The Birth and Growth of Film Studies at Emory,* DAVID COOK	197
Chapter 15	Guy Redvers Lyle and the Birth of Emory's Research Libraries ERIC NITSCHKE AND MARIE NITSCHKE	209
Chapter 16	Emory Law and the Formation of a University NAT GOZANSKY	215
Chapter 17	Feminist Activism and the Origins of Women's Studies at Emory MARY E. ODEM AND CANDACE COFFMAN	223

SECTION 3 CREATING ENGAGED SCHOLARS

Chapter 18	Adventure as Self-Transcendence: *The Romance of Arthur Evans* RICHARD S. WARD AND MAXIMILIAN AUE	237
Chapter 19	John Howett, Art History, and Cultural Ferment at Emory CATHERINE HOWETT SMITH	245
Chapter 20	Lore Metzger: Pioneer for Women Faculty RALPH FREEDMAN, CAROLE HAHN, PETER DOWELL, MARTINE BROWNLEY, AND GAYATRI CHAKRAVORTY SPIVAK	251
Chapter 21	"Athletics for All Who Wish to Participate": *The Career of Thomas Edwin McDonough Sr.* CLYDE PARTIN SR.	257
Chapter 22	Richard A. Long: *Public Scholarship across Disciplines and Institutions* RUDOLPH P. BYRD AND DANA F. WHITE	265
Chapter 23	A Century of Vitality: *Patricia Collins Butler* MARTHA W. FAGAN	269
Chapter 24	The Osler of the South: *Stewart R. Roberts Sr.* CHARLES STEWART ROBERTS	273
Chapter 25	The Classicist: *Moses Hadas* HERBERT W. BENARIO	277
Chapter 26	Emory Historical Minds and Their Impact GARY S. HAUK	281
Chapter 27	The Charles Howard Candler Professorships GARY S. HAUK AND SALLY WOLFF KING	293
Chapter 28	The Biographer: Elizabeth Stevenson Looked Steadily at Lives and Life BETH DAWKINS BASSETT	303
Chapter 29	Medievalist Extraordinary: *George Peddy Cuttino* IRWIN T. HYATT	311
Chapter 30	Remembering Floyd WILLIAM B. DILLINGHAM AND WILLIAM GRUBER	315

Chapter 31   A Fortunate Life: *William B. Dillingham*
            GREG JOHNSON 325

Chapter 32   Russell Major: *Candler Professor of Renaissance History*
            ALEXIS VICTORIA HAUK 331

Chapter 33   Richard Ellmann at Emory, 1976–1987
            RONALD SCHUCHARD 337

Chapter 34   In Praise of a Legal Polymath: *Harold J. Berman, Emory's First Woodruff Professor of Law*
            JOHN WITTE JR. AND FRANK S. ALEXANDER 343

SECTION 4   RELIGIONS AND THE HUMAN SPIRIT

Chapter 35   Emory and Methodism
            RUSSELL E. RICHEY 351

Chapter 36   Studying Religion at Emory: *Continuing Tradition, New Directions*
            PAUL B. COURTRIGHT 363

Chapter 37   Uniting "The Pair So Long Disjoined": *Science and Religion at Emory*
            ARRI EISEN 369

Chapter 38   The Case for Law and Religion
            APRIL L. BOGLE 379

SECTION 5   FRONTIERS IN SCIENCE AND MEDICINE

Chapter 39   The Making of the Woodruff Health Sciences Center
            SYLVIA WROBEL 395

Chapter 40   Humans and Other Primates: *Yerkes since 1979*
            FREDERICK A. KING AND STUART M. ZOLA 409

Chapter 41   A Legacy of Heart: *The Evolution of Cardiology at Emory*
            J. WILLIS HURST 421

Chapter 42   Pioneering in Radiology: *Heinz Stephen Weens*
            PERRY SPRAWLS 429

Chapter 43   Partnering for Health Care in Tbilisi, Georgia
            H. KENNETH WALKER AND ARCHIL UNDILASHVILI 435

Chapter 44   Looking Back with Boisfeuillet Jones
            BOISFEUILLET JONES 447

ACKNOWLEDGEMENTS 457
CONTRIBUTORS 459
EDITORIAL BOARD 465
NOTES 467
INDEX 505

INTRODUCTION

THE CONCEPT FOR this book took shape about five years ago, as the Emory community began to chart the future of the University by developing a strategic plan. After many months of brainstorming by hundreds of faculty members, and countless hours of deliberation by a core of several dozen faculty and administrators, the strategic plan was hammered out, tempered, burnished, and finally unveiled in the spring of 2005.

The title of the plan, "Where Courageous Inquiry Leads," seemed too good not to use more than once. True, a title alone is not foundation enough on which to build a book, but the double meaning of the title is appealing and suggestive. First, Emory—a "destination university," in the language of its vision statement—is a place *to* which courageous inquiry leads men and women when they boldly follow the logic of their curiosity. Emory also is a place *of* leadership—a place that leads Atlanta, other universities, our nation, and our world—whenever it demonstrates its own kinds of courageous inquiry.

The strategic plan had other attractive features besides the title. The broad themes of the plan—"faculty distinction," "the student experience," "engaging society," "confronting the human condition," "frontiers in science and technology"—also invited reuse for a wider audience. Intended to focus the thinking and energy of Emory people moving into the future, these themes also suggested a way of framing Emory's history. They posed, at least for the editors, compelling questions: In what sense do the aspirations of Emory for the future grow naturally out of its past achievements or disappointments; and, on the other hand, in what sense, if any, do the aspirations of Emory represent a departure from its past? Is the plan a portrait as well as a road map?

With these questions in mind, and with an acute awareness of certain lacunae in published histories of Emory, we set about inviting answers. Knowing that the keepers of the Emory story are many, and that each story keeper witnesses to different scenes and acts of the whole drama, we invited a host of narrators to tell their tales, and we were delighted by the response. This volume brings together the perspectives and voices of more than five dozen men and women. Some of them are longtime members of our community, and some are observers from outside; some are still very active, and some have long retired or (several of them) died. They write about a wide array of scholarly interests in a variety of personal styles with a number of institutional interests. They write about eras, persons, movements, and the daily activities that make up the passage of time at a rapidly changing university.

Organized thematically in sections, this book reflects the current commitments of Emory while ranging freely over some of the activities and plans that Emory has left behind. A few of the essays reach back to the earliest years of Emory College to shed new light on old stories, while broadening our sense of the unusual historical community that is Emory. The overwhelming majority of the essays focus on the latter half of the twentieth century and unfold for the first time in one place a comprehensive narrative of how Emory grew from regional distinction to national excellence: by negotiating the end of its racial exclusivity; by making increasingly effective forays into the higher elevations of research; and, through it all, by demonstrating its true distinctiveness as a place that seeks to blend goodness of heart and greatness of intellect.

Some readers will look for themselves in this book and be disappointed. We could not tell the whole Emory story because of the limits of time and resources—ours as well as those of our collaborators. We regret as much as anyone that not all of the worthy Emory stories have their deserved place here. We hope that other editors and writers will pick up where we leave off.

We do know that these pages reflect the growing interest in the history of Emory over the past decade, an interest that has also borne fruit in many other efforts across our campus and beyond. Over the past few years the Emeritus College has recorded timely and important video interviews of many retired faculty and administrators as part of its oral history project. The Goizueta Business School has produced several video histories leading up to and celebrating its ninetieth anniversary in 2009. The Transforming Community Project—launched in 2005 as an endeavor to understand more fully the racial past of Emory—has created a legacy of groundbreaking historical studies by Emory students, staff members, and faculty members. The Internet has also facilitated the posting of much Emory history online, including the history of the Chemistry Department written by the late Professor Emeritus R. A. Day (http://chemistry.emory.edu/department_info/history/), the more general University history at http://emoryhistory.emory.edu, and even a wiki devoted to Emory at http://wikiemory.emory.edu. The past decade also has brought publication of at least six other books about different facets of Emory history. Most encouraging of all is the growing level of interest in this history among Emory students, alumni, and staff.

Our hope is that this book not only will fill some of the gaps but also will spur still more studies of the life of this remarkable university.

Gary S. Hauk
Sally Wolff King
DECEMBER 2009

SECTION 1

*Story and Place in the
Shaping of Institutional Character*

The Spirits of This Lawn

For let us consider the spirits of this lawn
    who have gathered to speak with us
For the daffodils have flared in fanfare
    the bagpipes have skirled
    the brass and bells have sounded
For this is a high time
For the spirits of this lawn have decided
    that the time is wholly right
    on this quad, this place, this lawn,
    this commons, this yard, this space
For the spirits roam this ground
    scattering their invisible atoms
    as Lucretius knew full well they would
For so do we all scatter our atoms hereabouts
For the Frisbee, wobbling in its orbits,
    has shed its atoms, too,
    over this approving ground
For birds have seen the buildings of this quad
    take shape from the air, time-lapse,
    over decades, like Georgia pyramids
For the Lost Pharaoh, great spirit of Egypt,
    has returned now to his earthly home
For here we have commenced, processed,
    recessed, in these, our best medieval clothes
For in the wings is James W. Dooley—and his cousins
For these are truly our stomping grounds
For I have seen a single jogger, early morning,
    move in circles, one step ahead of solitude
For I have seen this lawn alive in the evening,
    crying with memory candles
For this quad is larger than a whale,
    than a hundred whales
For it swallows me whole, as though I were Jonah
    and disgorges me into art, music, theology,
    history, words, by which I survive
For we have spoken, thought, taught,
    learned under these trees
For the flagpole, center, reminds us that alumni,
    visible and invisible, have gathered here
For during the wars, Emory footfalls made of
    this space a parade ground, a sacred lawn
For the spirits of the lawn honor teachers
    who have taught us to listen completely:
For as it is written, "If you listen carefully, at the end
    you will be someone else."
For the spirits honor those who search:
    the scientists—the biologists, chemists,
    psychologists, the healers, all . . .

For let us take more careful notes about Lucretius.
For the musicians and artists of this city
For the poets, of whom there can never be too many
For the lovers, without whom there would be no poets
For we are mindful always of the need for perspective:
    Van Gogh conferred perspective on his world
    by simply painting a road diagonally
    up and through the fields of wheat,
    letting the crows fly where they would
For perspective may take us a bit longer than Van Gogh:
    But let us walk together into the paintings
    of our lives and talk of what we find there
For everyone comes to the arts too late
For there is the matter of that famous sparrow—
    the one that flew out of a raging storm
    through the great banqueting hall
    in the words of the Venerable Bede
    the sparrow that flew in one door
    and out another, from winter dark
    and back to dark, in an eye's twinkle
For is that flight not like our lives:
    "What there before-goes
    or what there after-follows
    we know not."
For the human quest begets more questions
For the question is at least as important as the answer
    Praise both.
For what matters finally is how the human spirit is spent
In the names, then, of the Genii Loci of this lawn
    the timeless spirits of this commons
    of this humane and mindful city—
In the names, then, of all this lawn's lively spirits,
    some of whom you know already, Mr. President—
    the newest of whom you now most assuredly become.
Welcome.

**Written for the inauguration of James W. Wagner
as president of Emory University, April 2, 2004**

John Stone

CHAPTER 1

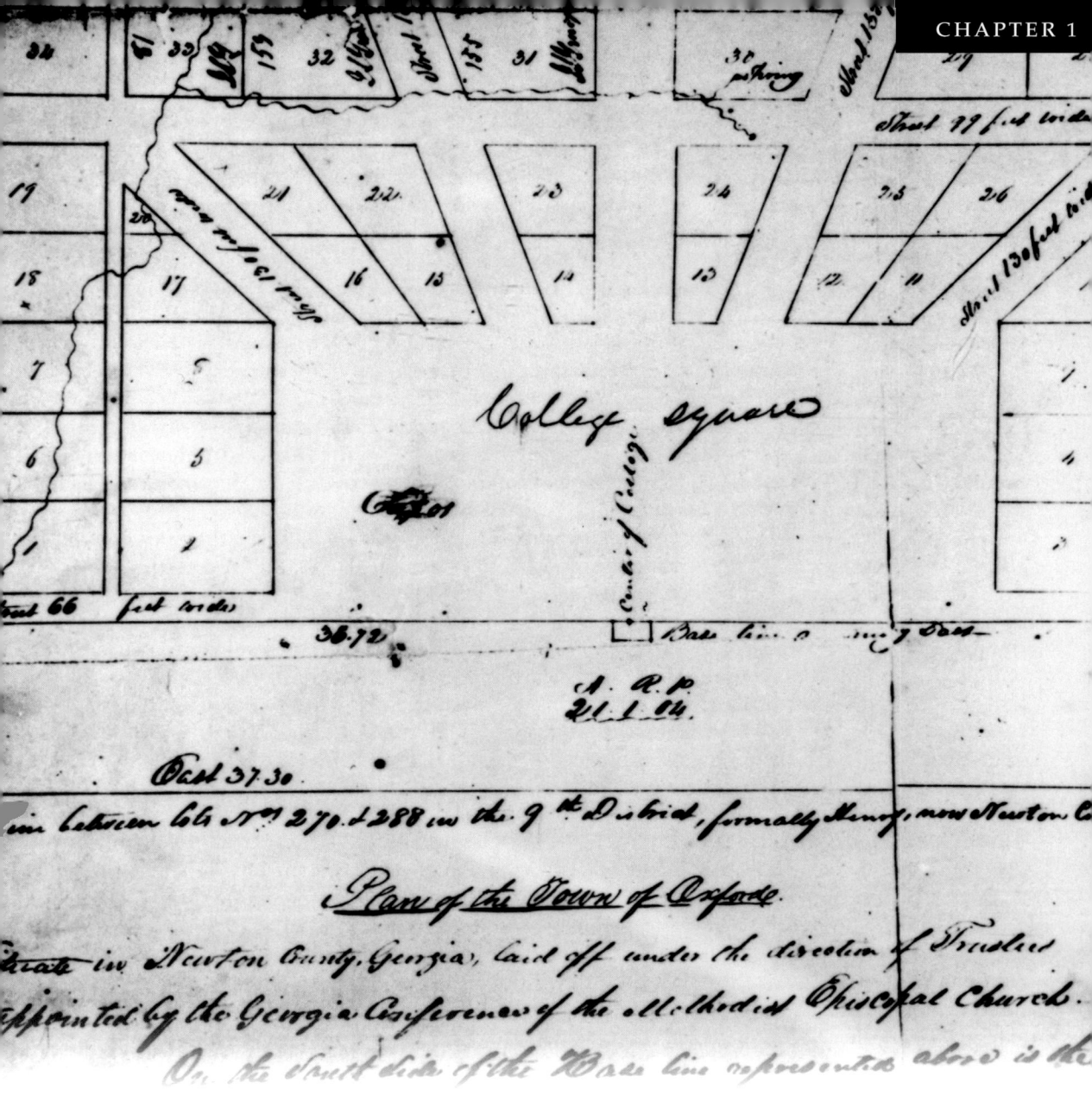

"EMORY ARE HERE"
Emory as Place and Story
— MARSHALL P. DUKE —

With its quaint British use of a plural verb for a group, Marshall Duke's essay title offers a way of illuminating Emory as place. For him, the campus as place—buildings, land, people— is "far more than the sum of its parts" and relies on narrative to define and sustain itself over time. Supported by research into the importance of family storytelling to the long-term resilience of children, Duke embraces the "intergenerationality" that arises from being a part of this community. For Duke, the Emory narrative locates us in the physical university but finally and infinitely resides in our hearts and minds.

IT WAS IN the summer of 1985. Our bus had traveled from Gatwick Airport outside of London to Canterbury, some fifty-five minutes west, and had pulled up in front of the London Guest House, a Victorian-looking bed-and-breakfast that would serve as our group's headquarters for the coming two weeks. On board with me were my colleague Stephen Nowicki, two graduate teaching assistants, and some thirty undergrads from Atlanta, all of us eager to begin our study abroad program gathering data on comparative child development in the County Kent school system. Our innkeeper, Sharon Rockhill, came to the door of the London Guest House as the bus's door opened. She turned, ducked her head into the doorway of the inn, and shouted to her husband, "Emory are here!" It was with this, to-our-ear-quaint, British grammar, which sees group nouns as plurals rather than singulars, that our presence was made known in Canterbury.

Emory "were" indeed there, despite being some four thousand miles from Atlanta. To Sharon Rockhill's eyes, *we* were Emory—not the Quadrangle, not the Administration Building, not then-president James Laney, nor anything or anyone else that we might identify as belonging to the University. To put it another way, where *we* were, Emory was.

This was surely not my first confrontation with the notion that Emory—that any human entity or community that comprises heart and history spanning time and space—was something more than bricks and mortar and fixed location. This was, however, a profoundly and powerfully simple demonstration of the phenomenon, so it is there that I begin my examination of Emory as place—of Emory as story—of Emory as something that, while it is land, buildings, and people, emerges as something far more than the sum of its parts—a force that not only is shaped by those who spend their time here but also shapes them as well. This essay is an attempt to consider Emory as story and to think about the ways in which it has sustained us and itself through its century and three quarters. I begin with one of my favorite moments in the Emory story.

The Great Library Book Turnaround | On an otherwise unremarkable spring day in the mid-1970s, the usual large number of Emory students were studying late into the evening at Emory's Woodruff Library. As the 11 p.m. closing time crept up, most of these students packed up their books and headed to their dormitories. On that particular evening, however, a still-unknown number of them packed up their books and headed for various restroom stalls on the upper floors. It was there that, like a well-trained covert military unit, they waited until the library had closed and all the staff had left for the night. At precisely midnight,[1] they emerged from their hiding places and converged on a particular floor—the humanities collection—and began their night's task. Diligently they walked up and down the stacks, removing every book from its unique Library of Congress classification space and reversing it. Each book remained in its proper place but with its spine turned inward. By sunrise, every book on that floor of the library had been turned around in this manner. When the library reopened, the students once again sequestered themselves in the bathroom stalls, being careful to allow time for the flow of students in and out of the library to resume. Then they joined the flow outward and reunited with their comrades, who had been busily preparing the campus for stage two of this operation.

As the day began and students, staff, and faculty walked across the campus, they beheld an unusual scene on the Quadrangle. The normally hyperpristine enclave was lined with yellow and blue balloons tied to the posts that encircle and purportedly protect the grass. On the Quad and elsewhere, flyers were either posted or distributed saying simply, "Emory beware! Do not turn your backs on the Humanities. They may turn their backs on you!" This, then, was the purpose of the prank: to sound the alarm against the rampant "Me-ism" that had begun to infiltrate Emory and other college campuses across America, where focus on career and financial success drew students away from the liberal arts, which have always been at the heart of an Emory education. Point made, the midnight book turners went on their way. But the library was left with an entire floor of books with their backs turned. Here began the unplanned, but exhilarating happening that resolved the Great Library Book Turnaround.

Faced (or *not* faced) with all of these reversed books, the staff of the library sent out a campuswide call for help. Anyone who could spare a bit of time was asked to come to the library and help undo the work of the pranksters. Within a short time, faculty, staff, and students began to ascend to the humanities collection, and soon everything was made right. Emory as an unseen yet not unfelt force had risen up and righted itself.

This was not the first time that such a thing had happened on this campus, nor would it be the last. In fact, it was just one example of a phenomenon that in so many ways defines the Emory community. I say more about this later, but here I end this library story as an isolated event and reframe it as just one part of a much larger Emory narrative.

In 1999 Emory became the home of the Alfred P. Sloan Center for the Study of Myth and Ritual in American Life—acronymically known as the MARIAL Center. Comprising a broad-ranging interdisciplinary core of faculty, postdocs, and graduate students, MARIAL has focused on ways in which families use rituals and stories to establish and maintain their identities, and on ways in which family stories add to the well-being of family members. The director of the center is Goodrich White Professor of Anthropology Bradd Shore, a campus treasure. Along with my colleague Robyn Fivush, Dobbs Professor of Psychology, I have been part of the MARIAL Family Narratives Project for more than a decade. Much of what I say about Emory as narrative is based on our work at MARIAL, so it is helpful to start with what we have discovered about the stories that families tell and how they tell them.

> *On the Quad and elsewhere, flyers were either posted or distributed saying simply, "Emory beware! Do not turn your backs on the Humanities. They may turn their backs on you!"*

We have interviewed more than a hundred families to examine the nature and effects of family narratives. To describe all that we have found will take several books (we are working on them!), but a few things are particularly relevant to Emory as narrative. First, we have found that strong families tell their stories. They tell them at holiday gatherings, family reunions, birthdays, birth celebrations, and funerals. They describe the good times and the bad. They tell of family heroes and family outcasts. They typically describe histories that have an oscillating pattern; they have been up and they have been down, but they have risen up against adversity and gone on. The stories are told by many people, but usually by the elders (look who was asked to write this essay) and, in families, most often by the grandmothers. One more thing about these narratives: They are not necessarily true or consistent. They are often tailored to fit situations. For example, a child having trouble with math hears about the problems that his or her mother had with math when she was a child. To a different child, struggling in English, the very same mother might be described as having had writing difficulties. Regardless of veracity, the stories have clear purposes. Two appear to be most important.

The first purpose of the family narrative is to establish and maintain a sense of identity and continuity for the family. Each day, as the family comes back together after being out and about in the world, they tell "Today, I . . ." stories. Kids tell about school, Mom and Dad tell about work, and together they incorporate the day as another page in the history of the family. The family dinner continues to be a critical venue for family storytelling and identity maintenance.

A second important outcome of telling family stories is a powerful relationship between how much family members, especially children, know about their families and their psychological and social adjustment. To assess family knowledge we have used a brief questionnaire called the Do You Know (DYK) Scale, which inquires about things such as where grandparents grew up, health history of the family, places lived, and jobs held. We have learned that the more kids know about their families, the higher their self-esteem will be, the lower their rate of problem behavior in school, the higher their level of psychological adjustment, the higher their level of family functioning, the less likely they are to develop social or legal problems, and the better their prognosis in the face of life challenges.

Trying to understand why knowing about family history has such a strong effect, Robyn Fivush and her students developed a concept termed the "intergenerational self." The intergenerational self describes the sense that we exist beyond our actual years—that, for example, as a ten-year-old child, I have connections that stretch back fifty or sixty years, because I know and am part of the stories that I hear from my grandparents. I am part of an entity—my family—that has certain qualities and has had certain experiences. The family's experiences are my own. The intergenerational self decides whether I as a ten-year-old should steal that candy bar or cheat on a test. The question before me as that ten-year-old is not "Do I steal or cheat?" Rather the question—the more powerful question—is "Do people in my family steal? Do they cheat?"

The intergenerational self, arising out of the family narrative, provides us with a way of understanding the importance of the Emory narrative. To reach this understanding, we must move from the family at the dinner table to the University—admittedly a rather large leap, even for an academic. To help bridge the gap, let me tell another MARIAL story.

Each summer, some fifty southern extended families pack up their vans and SUVs and head toward Salem, Georgia, some thirty miles southeast of Atlanta, and take up residence for one week as part of something called the Salem Camp Meeting.[2] Each family attending Salem is multigenerational and lives for the week in sparsely furnished wooden cabins called "tents" (recalling their original form) that these same families have used for many decades. All meals are taken communally, and there are prayer assemblies and other group activities, but the heart of the gathering is the extension and transmission of the family stories from generation to generation.

In addition to long conversations on the tent porches and at the family-style tables in the dining hall, inside the individual family tents are other signs of continuity: family pictures and other treasured objects on display; handprints on the walls, outlined in pencil, with names and dates written below them; a series of prints of the same person ranging from "age 1" through "age 87." Such lifelong representations are not uncommon at Salem, for the same fifty families have been gathering here since 1828—eight years before Emory's founding. This is in fact one of the oldest such gatherings in the United States. No one who was there at the beginning is present now, and yet, because of the rituals and the stories, each living member of the Salem families feels a connection with those who have been part of Salem and have passed on. Though the people are different, the entity called Salem Camp Meeting—an unseen, yet not unfelt force—continues. It is shaped and maintained by those who are living, and they in turn are shaped by those who went before.

In 2005 I had the honor of delivering the welcoming address at the opening convocation for the incoming Emory College Class of 2009. My theme in that address, guided by our work at the MARIAL Center, was that each of the new students not only was about to receive an Emory education but was also going to be given a history. I told the new students the story of the library books; I told them about the pushball competitions and Wonderful Wednesdays and balloons on the Quad; I reminded them about Emory's 1977 NCAA Division I national football championship (that got a rise out of them, too, dear reader). I told them that Emory's stories were now their stories, and that Emory's history now belonged to them. I told them as well that along with this history came an identity as an Emory student with all of the familiar "rights, privileges, and immunities thereunto appertaining."

I also told them, though, that along with this identity and history came a responsibility to be sure that they added to the Emory story, so that when they graduated in 2009, the story would be at once the same and better. I was invoking the notion so often put forward at Emory that we should do well, but we should also do good. That 2005 opening convocation was directed at the students, but the intergenerational Emory story affects all of us. Nowhere can this be seen more clearly than in the multiple manifestations of an unseen yet not unfelt force that transcends us as members of Emory and assures Emory's survival regardless of who is currently living in its tents.

Here is another story. Anyone who has spent any time at a college campus knows that faculty are often lost in their own research, thinking great thoughts, or writing about esoterica. Similarly, most students are too weighted down with work and social activities to worry much about other things. Rarely do faculty and students get worked up about anything, much less the same thing. Yet they did rise up as one in the early 1990s at Emory, when it was announced that the architectural plan for the expansion of the Carlos Museum included a significant structural incursion into the Quadrangle. The thought of one corner of the new building breaking the inviolable rectangle of the Quad resulted in veritable paroxysms. Faculty felt that one simply could not violate the essence of the Quad, the lawn that our late beloved colleague John Stone said held the "spirits" of those who have walked through it over the decades. Students felt that the traditionally most playful part of the campus, where Frisbees flew and friends gathered in the spring sunshine, was being threatened. In a congenial fashion, the architectural plan was changed in short order, and the faculty went back to thinking great thoughts, students returned to their classes and term papers, and peace settled over the heart of the campus.

Why is this event important? Because not one of those faculty members or students was here when the Quad was laid down; not one had a truly and deeply personal reason to see it maintained. What had happened was an example of the Salem Camp Meeting phenomenon—the sense of intergenerationality that arises from being a part of this community had driven these faculty and students to exercise their responsibility to and for Emory, an entity greater than themselves. In a conflict between progress and tradition, a balance was struck; old Emory and new Emory had worked things out.

Emory in many ways harbors a dynamic tension. On one hand is a force driving us toward progress and growth. This force is counterbalanced by a second force seeking to maintain our sense of history and tradition. Neither force will ever win out, but the tension between them is essential to our identity and guides what we may or may not do. There are many examples of these forces playing out in the core Emory conflict between tradition and progress. They represent the manifestations of our connection with our forebears—the Ignatius Fews, the Eléonore Raouls, the Robert Woodruffs, the Floyd Watkinses, the Evangeline Papageorges, the Jim Laneys, and all the others who have come here before us and felt the same way most of us do about this place called Emory.

The first place that Emory occupied was, as most know, in Oxford, Georgia, where Emory College was founded in 1836. From its inauspicious beginnings, Emory grew in size and stature until it was apparent that it needed to move to Atlanta. This move, completed in 1919, was an early manifestation of the conflict between tradition and progress that defines Emory as a place. The oldest buildings on the Atlanta campus date back to 1916, when the grand new Emory began taking shape in the Druid Hills suburb of Atlanta. But even though progress was desirable and inevitable, the advent of the new Emory awakened that tension with the old. In the specific instance of the move to Atlanta, it was not until 1937 that this tension was reconciled through the construction of the now-familiar Haygood-Hopkins Gate at the main entrance to the campus. That it was constructed to retrieve and remember the old Emory is not mere speculation. John D. Thomas documents it in the description of the dedication of the gate:

> On October 8, 1937, Robeson [Linton Robeson, Class of 1886, the man who donated the gate] delivered an address in Glenn Memorial Auditorium in honor of the gateway's dedication. During

his remarks, he said, "In thinking over what I could do to honor these two great and good men, Haygood and Hopkins, and keep their names before the youth of the land, it occurred to me that a gateway at the entrance to the campus of Emory University would be the best thing. *I thought it would serve to bring the "Old Emory" a little closer to Emory University, and to link the two together, and to remind the present and future generations of the fact that Emory is a great institution and has a great history extending back many years before it was moved to Atlanta.* (emphasis added)

The inclusion on the Atticus Haygood pillar of a favorite saying of that past president of Emory further strengthens the connection between the old Emory and the new Emory: "Let us stand by what is good and make it better if we can." Even today, on leaving the Oxford campus one is bid farewell with a sign posting this same inscription.

While the Haygood-Hopkins Gate served as the main entryway for all traffic entering the Druid Hills campus for decades, in 1971 traffic was detoured around the pillars after several incidents in which large trucks damaged the overhead crossbar. In a literal and figurative sense, new Emory had bypassed old Emory. Progress had trumped tradition—at least until 2009, as we shall see.

Other examples of the unseen but not unfelt conflict that defines Emory have appeared over the years. In the 1950s, during the presidency of Goodrich C. White, a proposal was put forward to increase the amount of space in the Candler Library by dividing the majestic twenty-five-foot-high main reading room horizontally, creating two floors, each with twelve-foot ceilings. As described by Guy Lyle, then head of libraries, this was not received well by the old Emory:

No sooner had this proposal reached the architect who originally designed the building, and the critics on the campus who were against all change, than they swarmed over to the President's office to suggest that this meddler was about to ruin the aesthetics of the Asa Griggs Candler Library and ought to quit.

From the new Emory side came Lyle's rationale for the redesign:

The Reading Room divider gave us three-quarters of all usable new space in the building and make [*sic*] possible the creation of a Science Library. . . . We might reasonably expect a hundred percent increase in library use because the two new reading rooms would be air-conditioned and the lighting greatly improved by the reduction in ceiling heights.[3]

As Emory moved forward with the renovation, it appeared once more that progress had won out. But that other unseen but not unfelt force remained. Emory itself seemed not to be comfortable with this decision; something had been lost. This restlessness persisted until the late 1990s when the widow of William Matheson—who had studied history at Emory for but two semesters in 1946–47 and had become a generous donor, thanks to this brief experience with the Emory narrative—came forward with a $1.5 million gift to restore the grand reading room in Candler Library, re-created down to the chandeliers from its original design of 1926. In a concession to modernity, however, the base of each Art Deco–style reading lamp on the long oak tables contains DSL ports and power connections for laptop computers.

But the apology to Emory about the loss of the original Candler Library did not stop with re-creating the reading room. When the building was gutted for reconstruction—down to its bare shell—measures were taken to assure that, amid the new materials of the completely rebuilt space, a bit of the original building would remain. Taking either the right or the left stairway to the second-floor Matheson Reading room, one ascends new marble steps, all with sharp and crisp corners and edges. On close inspection, however, the visitor will see that the edges of the stair landings are not similarly sharp. These marble landings are in fact the 1926 originals, carefully removed, stored, and then put back. Their edges are rounded and uneven, worn by the literally millions of footfalls they have absorbed in the eighty-odd years since they were as new as the steps that now rise to meet therm.

The plaque that stands outside the Candler Library perhaps says it best: "Candler Library—Built 1926. Renovated—1955; Restored—2003." "Restored"—as if to say, "Someone made a mistake, dear Emory. Please forgive us. We have made you right once more." Like those who rose up to protect the Quadrangle from the incursion of the Carlos Museum extension, the people who decided to restore Candler Library were not here when the original stair landings

Asa Griggs Candler Library

were installed; they never saw the original reading room; they never met the Haygoods and the Hopkinses. Yet they were guided by that same intergenerational sense of connection that has always kept Emory, Emory.

There are many other examples of this dynamic tension between the old and the new Emory. The Dobbs University Center (DUC) was built in 1984–85 at the west side of the old Alumni Memorial University Center (AMUC), which dated from 1927. The former main entrance of the AMUC now forms an interior wall of the large open space called the Coca-Cola Commons. Anyone who walks into the Coca-Cola Commons and looks up at the magnificent steps and entrance to the old edifice gasps with simple joy at the idea and realizes all too well what it says about the spirit and values of this University.

Or consider the recently constructed School of Medicine Building, replete with modern glass and wood paneling. Walk down some of its hallways, however, and you come upon exposed brick walls, unfinished and bare to the eye and touch. These are the original bricks of the old Anatomy and Physiology buildings, constructed in 1917 and renovated as the new medical school entrance was created. In place after place, the old coexists with the new, and unseen forces would seem to be at peace. Emory maintains its intergenerational self through such things.

One more example of the dynamic tension between progress and tradition must be mentioned, and it requires a brief return to the story of the Haygood-Hopkins Gate. While it continued to serve as a pedestrian archway since being bypassed by the road in 1971, it seems that the Emory spirit remained disquieted by the gate's having been shunted aside in the name of progress. So it was with a sense of relief, even delight, that the campus witnessed in 2008–09 the restoration of the Haygood-Hopkins Gate as the true entryway to Emory. In a concession to the past, vehicles once again pass through the gate, and in a concession to the new Emory a grand new entrance complex befitting a major, internationally recognized university has been built. This new-old entryway is a quintessential distillation of Emory as a story. Together they say, "Welcome. You are about to enter a major institution of research and teaching that deeply values its past even as it forges courageously toward the future." If ever there was a sense of "Sorry, Emory, we [of 1971] made a mistake, but we [of 2009] have made it right"—here it is!

Emory has emerged as an entity, a being with some sort of self, a place that we apologize to, a place we feel responsible for, a place that speaks to us, guides us, has expectations for us. Emory is clearly more than a group of buildings and a daily gathering of people. But what exactly is this presence that lives among all of us associated with this university? The answer lies in the concept of emergent properties.

An old adage among those in my profession of clinical psychology holds that if one is working with a married couple, there are three entities: he, she, and they. A husband and a wife are very real people with very real feelings and problems. The third entity, "they," is an emergent property, a very real presence that takes form out of the joining together of the spouses. Similar concepts abound. At some point a number of geese become a flock. At some point single sheets of paper placed on top of one another become an emergent property called a stack. When sufficient numbers of people, buildings, and history coexist, what emerges is an institution, a university, Emory.

Even if Emory represents an emergent property, how do we understand the continuing presence of this entity for some 180 years? After all, the Emory campus in Atlanta occupies different space than the campus in Oxford. Further, over the past 90 years the buildings constructed in 1916 have been replaced or joined by other structures. Our student body changes almost entirely every four to six years; the current faculty and staff are totally different from those of fifty years ago and will be totally different again not many years hence. Where is the continuity between those of us here in 2008 and those "here" in 1836? How will those in this community in 2036 connect with us here today?

This question of continuity might be asked of my colleagues in philosophy. If you bought a brand-new Ford Mustang in 1985 and, during the years since, replaced every single part of the original car, is it still the same 1985 Ford Mustang? Most people would say yes, and our philosophy friends would say that we feel this because the essence or identity of the car has remained. The same can be said about Emory.

Though the buildings and people are all different, we are still the same Emory that began in 1836 at Oxford, completed the move to Atlanta in 1919, and now stands among the top universities in the world. A connection exists between those of us here now, those who have gone before, and those who will come after us. That connection both creates the emergent phenomenon called Emory and produces an intergenerational power that transforms all who have ever been a part of this university into a "family" dedicated to simultaneously advancing yet preserving it. *The connection is in the stories we tell of who we are.* These stories are not only told in words about a library prank, or told in books about Emory history. They are told in the ways we steward this place—through the careful restoration of the Candler reading room; the preservation of the original marble landings in Candler Library; the restoration of the Haygood-Hopkins Gate. These stories produce an intergenerational self in all who have ever been and ever will be a part of this place. This intergenerational self assures that new presidents will honor the work of old presidents; that current faculty, staff, and trustees will never forget that they stand in place of and share responsibilities of their forebears; that the new Emory never loses sight of its responsibilities to the old Emory; and that the magnificent tension between the two remains the tradition that we live by. This is the essence of the Emory narrative, a story nearing two hundred years in length with no foreseeable ending.

> *Emory has emerged as an entity, a being with some sort of self, a place that we apologize to, a place we feel responsible for, a place that speaks to us, guides us, has expectations for us.*

Where does Emory actually reside? There will be little argument that Emory exists physically on some seven hundred acres off North Decatur Road in Atlanta and some fifty-six acres in the town of Oxford. To say that this is where Emory is, however, pays insufficient attention to the extent of Emory's impact. Recall the words of our innkeeper in Canterbury, England: "Emory are here." I have remembered this moment so vividly because it represented so much more than the arrival of a busload of Americans. It represented a phenomenon not unique to Emory but one raised to a glorious level in our community.

I experienced the same phenomenon in Jerusalem in 2008, when I was fortunate to attend an awards reception for the worldwide winners of the Jewish Book Awards. One of the award recipients was Professor Eric Goldstein of Emory's History Department, the keynote speaker was Professor Deborah Lipstadt of our Religion Department, and the young coordinator of the event was an Emory graduate and a former student of mine. As the four of us stood and chatted during the reception, I was struck by the feeling that, in addition to us, there was a fifth presence. Emory "were" there.

I have felt the same thing meeting with alumni groups across America or speaking to Emory groups off-campus. Wherever Emory people gather, one emergent presence is added. Emory is there.

In a short story called "The Infinite Lawn," Italian writer Italo Calvino describes a Mr. Palomar, who, like the observatory for which he is named, examines things closely and thinks deeply about them. Mr. Palomar thinks about his lawn and its boundaries. He ponders where the lawn ends and where nonlawn begins. He notes that it is easy to conclude that the center of the lawn is part of it, but as he moves toward the edges, he realizes that although the grass thins out at the edges, there are wisps of new grass growing and extending out into the places where, just days before, they had not been. Mr. Palomar realizes ultimately that in fact the lawn, any lawn, is infinite, because over time it can and will spread everywhere.

The Quadrangle, the heart of the campus, is Emory's own infinite lawn. It is surely a physical entity, but it is a metaphorical presence as well. Physically it is continuous with the earth upon which every building at Emory stands, the soil on which each of us walks, whether on campus or not. Metaphorically it is continuous with every part of the world to which we at Emory travel, every place where Emory graduates live and work, every mind enlightened by knowledge generated here, every life made better by applications of research conducted here, every part of the world—large or small—that is in any way touched by this university.

When our group of students stepped out of that bus in Canterbury in 1985, the infinite lawn of the Quadrangle was beneath our feet. And when our innkeeper called out, "Emory are here," she said the truth. For what had arrived in Canterbury were those thirty-four persons, to be sure; but the thirty-fifth passenger on the bus from Gatwick was Emory itself. This place had traveled with us in the same way that it has traveled with all who have been privileged to be part of its family, some for four years, some for forty, some since 1936, some since 1836. In this instance, despite the odd sound of the British plural verb, the sentiment was accurate. Emory is plural. In Walt Whitman's sense, it "contains multitudes."

Emory are in Atlanta. Emory are in Oxford, Georgia. Emory are in every state of the union. Emory are in nearly every country on earth. No matter where those of us who have been touched by this place may be, Emory is with us, because all of us, in different ways and for different reasons, stand on the same Quadrangle, the same infinite lawn that reaches out and supports our journeys, no matter how far they take us or how long we have been away. Emory as place has no boundaries. Emory as story has no end.

Laying the cornerstone for old Pierce Hall, Oxford, 1903.

"DREAMS DEFERRED"
African Americans in the History of Old Emory
— MARK AUSLANDER —

A former Oxford College professor of anthropology, Mark Auslander unveils difficult truths about the history of interracial relations at Emory in Oxford, Georgia. Using documents that range from minutes of the Emory College board to "diaries, memoirs, letters, probate records, bills of sale," and oral history, Auslander focuses on the thirteen decades of Emory's history before desegregation, from the founding of the College until the 1960s. Among the case studies that shed light on slaves' lives, particularly those with strong bonds to the College community, Auslander reinterprets the story of "Kitty" with the help of stunning new evidence unearthed by diligent research. Kitty's story continues to stimulate controversy and demonstrate the lingering effects of a culture divided.

THIS CHAPTER EXPLORES the important contributions of African Americans to Emory College and Emory-at-Oxford during the roughly 130 years from the College's founding to desegregation. Excluded by law and custom from the ranks of students and faculty, African Americans were nonetheless a vital presence in the institution—in slavery and in freedom. They served as builders and laborers, groundskeepers and cooks, washerwomen and maids, mechanics and carpenters, chauffeurs and caretakers. In a more subtle sense, African Americans functioned as "distant companions" and interlocutors for virtually all the prominent white families and individuals associated with the College from the 1830s onward. In ways that may not have been fully appreciated at the time, ambiguous encounters with Oxford's African American residents functioned to define the institution for generations of white faculty, administrators, and students.

To be sure, African Americans' participation at Emory before the 1960s was complex. Generations of African American employees during the eras of slavery, Reconstruction, and Jim Crow labored for the school with the knowledge that neither they nor their children were allowed to attend Emory as students. They were often subjected to other forms of racial discrimination, including unequal pay. In spite of their qualifications, they were not hired into professional staff or faculty positions. In many instances their contributions to the institution were not properly acknowledged. Nonetheless, through the decades, African Americans were vital participants in the College, contributing with pride and dignity to the education of students and the mission of Emory in innumerable ways.

Slavery, Race, and the Founding of the College

A strong case can be made that the problem of slavery was central to the creation of the College in the 1830s. The institution's founders were, without exception, slaveholders. In seeking to develop a prominent Methodist educational institution in the South, they took it for granted that their students would largely be drawn from southern white families who owned slaves, or for whom slave owning was considered normal. At a time when the struggle over slavery was taking on increasing national importance, those involved in the early years of the College would often find themselves called upon to legitimate the "peculiar institution" of chattel slavery.

In a proximate sense, the decision to name the new college for the recently deceased Methodist Bishop John Emory (1789–1835) was owing to his important contributions as an educator and the role he played presiding over the Washington, Georgia, conference at which the development of a Methodist college in Georgia was proposed. Yet in a more nuanced sense, the naming of the College for Bishop Emory was embedded in the fact that for its white founders, John Emory was emphatically one of their own. He had recently published a powerful tract against abolitionism, came from a prominent Maryland slave-owning family, and was himself a slave owner.[1]

College officials publicly defended the institution of slavery. College president Augustus Longstreet, who played a central role in the great national schism of the Methodist Episcopal Church in the mid-1840s over the issue of slavery, published several impassioned defenses of involuntary servitude, including an 1845 commentary on the scriptural foundations of slavery, *Letters on the Epistle of Paul to Philemon*, and *Letters from Georgia to Massachusetts* (1848), in which he denounced the hypocrisy of northern abolitionists for not attending to the plight of exploited New England mill girls.

In contrast with some prominent Georgia institutions, such as the Georgia Railroad, the College itself never owned slaves. Rather, the College and its predecessor, the Georgia Conference Manual Labor School, at times rented slaves from their owners. For instance, the minutes of the Manual Labor School Board of Trustees for February 9, 1837, state,

> Resolved that the Treasurer be instructed to pay the sum of Fifty Dollars for the hire of a negro woman by the name of Sib for 1836 and to give notes for the hire of the negroes ordered to be

hired for the present year and the following rates, for Sim: $150, for Charles: $150, for Sib and her children: $75.

Slaves and Slave Owners |
The economic fortunes of the men who founded Emory and guided the College in its early years indisputably rested upon the institution of slavery and upon the labor of hundreds of enslaved persons. Most slaves were moved back and forth between farms on the city's outskirts and residences within Oxford itself. Some were rented out as factory laborers and artisans to businesses in Covington or elsewhere in the state.

The nature of slavery has rendered many of these persons anonymous. Yet through diaries, memoirs, letters, probate records, bills of sale, and oral historical research it has been possible to identify by name some of the slaves owned by the College's antebellum leaders; in some instances, through census records we have been able to determine their years of birth or death and the surnames they assumed after emancipation. For example, Bishop James Osgood Andrew, president of the Emory Board of Trustees, in 1850 owned twenty slaves, including Addison, Edward, Elleck, George, Jacob, James, Jefferson, Kitty, Laura, Lillah, Thomas Mitchell, Nick, Orlando, Peter, and Susan.

African Americans were vital participants in the College, contributing with pride and dignity to the education of students and the mission of Emory in innumerable ways.

Iverson Graves, an important College trustee, owned Charley, Lawrence, Leniah, and Nick. Alexander Means, professor of natural sciences and a president of the College, owned Albert (b. 1818), Fanny (b. 1828), Harriet (1852–1861), Iveson (b. 1858), Samuel Means, Henry Robinson (b. 1806), Cornelius Robertson (b. 1836), Ellen Robertson (b. 1835), Milly Robinson (b. 1811), Mildred Robinson Pelham (b. 1836), Thomas Robinson (b. 1850), Troup Robinson (b. 1852), Thaddius, and Anna Tinsely.

Gustavus John Orr, professor of mathematics, owned Charles, Hannah (b. 1833), George W. (b. 1853), Henry, Lizzie, Octavia Hunter (b. c. 1856–57), Peter, Phil, and Walter. A later professor of mathematics, George W. W. Stone Sr., owned Abner, Anna, Caesar, Clinton, Darcus, Duncan, Frank, Hunter, Isaac Stone (b. 1810), Jake, Lucinda, Mary, Louisa Means (c. 1832–1882), Nancy, Phillip, Ruth, Sallie, Silas, Sterling, Tempy, Tony, and Victoria [Carter].

James R. Thomas, the president of the College before and just after the Civil War, owned eight slaves in 1860, including Charity and Dave. Professor George W. Lane owned at least seven slaves, among them Elleck (or Allick) and Aphy.

In some instances, it has been possible to trace the descendants of these enslaved men and women, among whom are African American families whose members have been involved with Emory for generations. Consider, for example, the family of Ellen and Cornelius Robinson, enslaved by Alexander Means. According to their descendants, Cornelius (b. 1836) and Ellen (b. 1835) were married to one another, and were allowed to live in a small house behind the Means mansion, Orna Villa, on present-day Emory Street in Oxford. Cornelius, a Native American, was Means's valet. Ellen was the personal maid of Means's wife. As such, they seemed to have occupied the highest status among all those enslaved in the Means household. After emancipation, Cornelius and Ellen formed an independent household, which by 1870 consisted of their children Cora (b. 1857), George (b. 1859), Sarah (b. 1861), John (b. 1863), and Thaddius (b. 1867). Sarah Robinson married Robert, the son of Thomas Mitchell, who had been enslaved by Bishop Andrew. One of the sons of Robert and Sarah was Henry "Billy" Mitchell, who served as chief janitor of Emory at Oxford for much of the first half of the twentieth century. His daughter, Sarah Francis Mitchell Wise, and grandson Billy Wise were close friends to many faculty and students at Oxford College.

The Enigmatic Case of Kitty | Perhaps no case illustrates the enduring legacies of slavery in Emory University's self-conceptions as sharply as that of the enslaved woman known as Kitty (c. 1822–c. 1854), owned by Bishop Andrew. Standard white accounts hold that according to the terms under which he had inherited Kitty as a girl, Bishop Andrew attempted to emancipate her in 1841 (when she turned nineteen) by offering to send her to Liberia, where many freed slaves had been resettled. According to a legal document produced by Augustus Baldwin Longstreet, then president of the College, Kitty refused to go to Liberia. Bishop Andrew, it is said, then built her a small cabin behind his own, in which she resided, "as free as the laws of Georgia would allow." White authors further state that she married a free black man named "Nathan Shell," had children by him, and continued to live in Oxford until her death in the early 1850s. It is asserted that on her deathbed, Kitty exulted that she would soon see "Miss Amelia," the late first wife of Bishop Andrew, "in the better land."

Bishop Andrew's ownership of Kitty and fifteen other slaves became a matter of national controversy in 1844, when his slave-owning status was publicly debated at the annual conference of the Methodist Episcopal Church, held in New York City that year. Northern abolitionist bishops requested that Andrew resign from the episcopacy, a move denounced by Longstreet and Andrew's other southern supporters, who asserted that Andrew was only involuntarily a slaveholder. The next year, the Methodist Church formally split over the issue of slavery, and was not reunited until 1939.[2]

Oxford's African American residents contest nearly every detail of the above account. Many older residents of the community assert that Miss Kitty was the coerced mistress of Bishop Andrew and that he was the father of her children. They note that the historical record is ambiguous. Although Bishop Andrew repeatedly asserted that he had been "willed" Kitty by a rich woman in Augusta, an exhaustive search of antebellum probate and deed records in Richmond County, Georgia, has failed to unearth any such bequest. Newton County, Georgia, tax records give no record of any antebellum freedman by the name of Nathan or Shell. The identity of Kitty's parents remains unknown; since Kitty was light-skinned and comparatively privileged among Oxford slaves, it is widely assumed that her father was a prominent white man. (Some elderly Oxford African Americans recall their parents and grandparents asserting that Bishop Andrew himself was Kitty's father, rather than her lover.)

In any event, the century and a half since Miss Kitty's passing have seen repeated symbolic struggles over the meaning of her life and her death in Oxford. Buried within the Andrew family plot, she is the only person of color generally acknowledged to be interred within the city's long-segregated white cemetery. In the late 1930s, on the eve of the reunification of the northern and southern denominations of the Methodist Church, the wealthy Atlanta businessman and Emory University trustee H. Y. McCord arranged to transport the former slave cabin from the land once owned by Bishop Andrew to Salem Campground, at the time an all-white religious campground about twelve miles away. McCord simultaneously erected a large stone tablet near Kitty's grave in the Oxford City Cemetery on which was inscribed the standard white account of Kitty's life, emphasizing Bishop Andrew's blamelessness in the matter.[3]

Meanwhile, the old slave quarters, renamed the "Kitty's Cottage Museum," served as a memorial to the Lost Cause of the Confederacy at Salem until it was returned in 1994 to the city of Oxford, where white members of the Oxford Historical Shrine Society labored to restore it. Most Oxford African Americans have refused to enter the cottage, which remains a considerable site of controversy. In 2007 an African American congregation from Lithonia, Georgia, conducted an ancestral walk to the cottage, in which they poured libations and gave Miss Kitty a new name in the West African Ewe language. Some asserted that the spirit of Kitty spoke to them, detailing the sexual assaults she had suffered from white clergymen in antebellum Oxford. These assertions, published in the local newspaper, were deeply upsetting to many of Oxford's white residents. More than a century and a half after her death, the struggles over Kitty remind us that the unresolved legacies of slavery continue to haunt the Emory and Oxford communities.

Other Lives under Slavery: Case Studies | Whatever the ultimate truth of the matter, and for all the profound passions her story still arouses, the case of Kitty is exceptional in many ways. The historical record in most instances provides only fragmentary glimpses into the lives of the enslaved persons owned by Emory's early leaders. In only a few cases is it possible to piece together more detailed pictures of family life under slavery, hinting at the ambiguous connections between white and black families in nineteenth-century Oxford.

Consider, for example, the case of Louisa Means, a woman born around 1832 and held in slavery by the family of George W. W. Stone Sr., Emory's professor of mathematics during the middle third of the nineteenth century. Stone had purchased Louisa on the birth of his daughter Tudie in 1841, when Louisa was about nine years old.

> *In any event, the century and a half since Miss Kitty's passing have seen repeated symbolic struggles over the meaning of her life and her death in Oxford. Buried within the Andrew family plot, she is the only person of color generally acknowledged to be interred within the city's long-segregated white cemetery.*

Louisa was, in a sense, already a "member of the family," for Professor Stone bought her from his brother John. (In significant ways, one might argue, enslaved persons functioned as the social glue that held together extended, elite white families in antebellum Georgia.)

Louisa worked for the Stone family for the rest of her life, in slavery and in freedom, as nurse, cook, and caregiver. In a memoir dictated in the 1930s, G. W. W. Stone Jr., the son of Professor G. W. W. Stone Sr., recalls,

> [Louisa] became our head nurse, washwoman and mammy. We all thought she was one of the best niggers ever born. And we think so yet. She couldn't have loved her own children any more than she did us. And we loved her just like she was kin to us. She married a man named Sam Means. He was a blacksmith and behaved himself until after the surrender. Then he was unkind to Louisa. He became *too free*. When she died in 1882 Father's children put a tombstone over her grave.[4]

To modern readers, the passage seems deeply ironic. The white author is sure that Louisa "couldn't have loved her own children any more than she did us," although he makes no mention of her actual children. Louisa was "like . . . kin to us," but she was buried in the segregated section of the Oxford City Cemetery, hundreds of feet away from the Stone family plot. Although the white author acknowledges that she married Sam Means, the author can never bring himself to refer to her as "Mrs. Means"; a substitute mother figure, she is always "Louisa" to him. The rather ominous figure of Sam Means, whom the white children might have regarded as threatening to alienate the affections of their substitute mother, is dismissed by the telling phrase, "too free."

The 1882 headstone, erected by the adult children of G. W. W. Stone Sr., still stands in the oldest section of the historically African American portion of the Oxford City Cemetery. It is inscribed on its east side, "Louisa. Faithful servant of G. W. W. Stone, Professor of Mathematics. Oxford College." No mention, significantly, is made of her actual children or of her married name; instead she is referred to solely by the name she had in slavery and by which she was known by the white family for the remainder of her life.

Yet Louisa's identity was not exhausted in her relationship as substitute mother to the white children of her master. Even under slavery, her conjugal bond with her husband Sam, a slave of Alexander Means, was sufficiently strong that Means had to take it into account when he rented Sam out for a profit. In December 1861 Means reports in his diary that he had hired out Sam, a skilled carpenter and blacksmith, to a white man in West Point, Georgia, for three hundred dollars a year, "with the privilege of coming home four times per year." (The white renter of Sam was to provide him, as well, with at least three pairs of shoes per annum.) The fact that Means stipulated these visits home in the contract presumably indicates that he recognized Sam's desire to see his wife and family back in Oxford. (To be sure, Means did not assign excessive weight to the conjugal bond between Sam and Louisa; he had no qualms about profiting from their enforced separation, which allowed Sam only four conjugal visits home per year.)

As noted, the headstone placed by the white Stone family for Louisa did not mention her married name. Yet, as some African American residents wryly note, the Stone family did not have the final word in this story. On the west side of the headstone are inscribed—in a different, less professional hand—the words, "Louisa Means." According to oral tradition, her full name was surreptitiously inscribed by her own kin, sometime after the white family had erected the headstone. The diverse facets of her identity—slave and free, unmarried and married, domestic servant and head of family—thus remain juxtaposed on the stone. In death, she is "kin" to at least two families, black and white, yet in some respects was distanced from both.

The complexity of relations between masters and slaves is also hinted at by the experience of another family owned by Alexander Means—Henry and Milly, who, like Cornelius and Ellen, took the name Robinson after emancipation. During the first year of the Civil War, Henry was sent off to the front, as a slave to Means's son, Thomas Alexander Means, who was serving in the Confederate Army of Northern Virginia. Henry returned home to Oxford in November 1861, having served in the first battle of Manassas (a resounding Confederate victory), only to discover that three weeks earlier Dr. Means had sold him along with his wife, Milly, and their three children, Thomas, Troup, and Mildred. They had been sold to a Judge Reynolds in Covington.

A domestic battle ensued. Dr. Means wrote in his diary, "Henry is much distressed and unwilling to go." Over the course of the argument, Means became infuriated at Milly, Henry's wife. He wrote, "Milly's insolence and angry retorts first induced me to think of parting with them." But finally Means relented and convinced Judge Reynolds to release him from the contract, with one exception. Means was so angry at Mildred, the young adult daughter of Henry and Milly, that he insisted on selling her along with her young child. Means wrote, "Mildred much in fault and therefore I sell Mildred who expressed a desire that I should [do] so." Mildred, in turn, was given by Judge Reynolds, evidently as a dowry gift, to his son-in-law Coleman Brown, who had married Fannie Reynolds.[5]

Five years after the Civil War, Henry and Milly's family was reunited. The 1870 Freedmen's Census for Newton County records as living together in Oxford the family of Henry Robinson, with his wife Milly and three children—Thomas, Troup, and Mildred, who gives as her last name "Pelham." Unfortunately, the story may not have had an entirely happy ending. Mildred had been sold in 1861 with her small child, who seems to have disappeared in the meantime: perhaps the child died or was sold off.

What lessons can we draw from these events? First, close family bonds were present among enslaved persons. Second, in spite of the risks, these bonds were openly expressed at times to the master. Henry and Milly were visibly outraged that their family was being sold, and seem to have had enough moral bargaining power that they were able to persuade their owner, Dr. Means, not to sell off the bulk of their family. But there were limits: Henry and Milly were not able to prevent the sale of their daughter Mildred and their grandchild. Finally, we know that whatever strains may have been placed on this family, their bonds were strong enough that, after emancipation, Mildred returned to live with her parents (albeit without her lost child).

Freedmen's Journeys | In some cases, legal emancipation following the Civil War did not make an immediate impact on the economic lives of Oxford's African American families. Take, for example, the case of the ex-slaves of Gustavus J. Orr, professor of mathematics. In August 1865, five months after Appomattox and two and a half years after emancipation, Orr signed a contract with his former slaves, Phillip, Charles, Eliza, and Hannah:

> As slavery has been abolished by the Government of the United States, the undersigned make the following contract. I, G. J. Orr, agree, on my part, to furnish the freedmen whose names appear below, food, clothing, fuel, quarters and medical attention, and pay them one fourth of the corn, fodder, peas, and syrup of sorghum and sweet potatoe [sic] . . . for their services for the whole of the present year. . . . I do furthermore agree that, should Phil. and Charles leave me on the first of December, there shall be no abatement as to the part of the crops they are to receive, and if they stay with me longer than that time, I am to pay them such compensation as we may agree upon.
>
> We, the undersigned freedmen, agree on our part to labor faithfully and diligently, for G. J. Orr, to obey him in all things, pertaining to labor and service and to treat him and his family with proper respect and courtesy.

The document is worth pondering. In many respects, what it offered to Phillip, Charles, Eliza, and Hannah and her children was not so different than what they had experienced, materially, before emancipation: hard work without monetary compensation. But they did, of course, have—in principle at least—the right to leave Orr's property and to make their own lives.

In time, this is just what they did. By 1870 Hannah was living on her own as head of household under the name of Hannah Hunter; her daughter, Octavia, thirteen years old, was attending the newly founded school for free children of color near Oxford's African American church, Rust Chapel. Hannah's seventeen-year-old son, George, was working as a domestic servant. For all the immediate constraints of their first year of freedom, within five years this family had at least been able to move out on their own as wage earners, away from sharecropper status. In this respect, they resembled many of their neighbors in the new free community of Oxford, employed as domestic servants and artisans.

In the late nineteenth and early twentieth centuries, nearly all African Americans in Oxford worked in one way or another for the College, in official or unofficial capacities. Some worked full-time or part-time as groundskeepers, cooks, janitors, masons, or carpenters; others worked in off-campus rooming houses occupied by Emory men. Israel Godfrey (1849–1929), a former slave, was a respected farmer, stonemason, and landowner in the city, and helped build the college chapel in 1875. (An intriguing early-twentieth-century photograph depicts Mr. Godfrey seated at a reunion of the Branham and Candler families in Oxford.) Some Oxford African Americans left the town to work for the newly established Emory University in Atlanta. For instance, John Wesley Graves, who served in Oxford as college chef, moved with Emory College to Atlanta when the Druid Hills campus was established. Other members of the Oxford African American community worked as governesses and chauffeurs for prominent white Atlanta families that had roots in Oxford. Many others moved north and pursued work in factories and the professions.

Prior to the Civil War, enslaved African Americans in Oxford had worshipped in their own church, in a former classroom structure provided by the trustees of Emory College. After the war, the church was torn down and the land used for the expansion of the city's white cemetery. Around this time, the majority of the community's African American families left the Methodist Episcopal Church, South, and joined the northern Methodist Episcopal Church, founding Rust Chapel, named for the Reverend Richard Rust, secretary of the northern church's Freedmen's Aid Society.[6] African American children from Oxford attended a local Rosenwald School as well as Washington Street School in Covington. Many in time attended African American institutions of higher learning, including Clark, Morehouse, Spelman and Payne colleges. Noted African American educators in Oxford included Augustus Wright (1855–1928), the principal of Washington Street High School, and John Pliny Godfrey Sr. (1890–1982), a graduate of Clark and the son of Israel Godfrey. Robert Hammond and William Mitchell, who in turn served as the College's chief janitors and groundskeepers, mentored generations of white Emory students, who routinely sought their wisdom and support at class reunions.

Oxford at Emory on the Eve of the Civil Rights Movement | Many older Oxford African Americans paint an ambiguous portrait of Oxford and Emory at Oxford during the generation before the civil rights movement. On the one hand, they note that within the two square miles of Oxford, African American families were relatively protected from the grosser inequities and racialized violence that characterized the Jim Crow South. African Americans were able to attend public lectures in science and the arts held on the campus of the College, and many were encouraged in their educational pursuits through friendship with faculty and students. Many African Americans recall quiet support for civil rights goals expressed in private by white members of the Emory community in Oxford. Many benefited from the long history of friendship between their families and Emory's leading white families. John Pliny Godfrey Jr., the grandson of Israel Godfrey, for example, recalls that during the 1954–55 school year he had to suspend his studies at Clark College to care for his ill father. The Oxford College dean hired him that year as a janitor; however, "that whole year," Mr. Godfrey recalls, "I never saw a mop or a broom." He was allowed informally to attend college classes, albeit in the rear of the classroom, so that he did not fall behind in his premedical studies. (Forty years later, Mr. Godfrey returned to settle in Oxford and was elected to the city council, where he led successful struggles to desegregate the city's cemetery and its police force.)

During the most dangerous periods of the civil rights movement, the prominent Southern Christian Leadership Conference activist Forrest Sawyer Jr. recalls, he was repeatedly sheltered by Oxford College faculty and students when he was hiding out from the county sheriff's deputies after civil rights marches in nearby Covington.

Nonetheless, the College and Oxford remained embedded in the deep contradictions of this period. Many African Americans recall the deep anxiety that swept through the community when the Ku Klux Klan held processions through Oxford, the terror that followed the horrific lynching of four young African Americans at nearby Moore's Ford in 1946, and the humiliating daily gantlet of racial epithets and stone throwing that black schoolchildren endured when walking home from Washington Street School.

Perhaps no moment captures these contradictions as poignantly as the planting in 1966 of a tree near the central quadrangle of Oxford College, in front of Few Hall, one of Emory's oldest structures. Planted by representatives of the class of 1913 in honor of two of Emory's most celebrated African American employees, the tree is marked at its base by a small plaque:

> The members of the class of 1913
> in loving appreciation
> Dedicate this tree to the memory of
> Bob Hammond
> 1858 to 1923
> and
> Billy Mitchell
> 1886 to 1958

WHO TOGETHER CONTRIBUTED 95 YEARS
OF FAITHFUL AND EFFICIENT SERVICE TO "OLD EMORY"
DEDICATED JUNE 12, 1966

The ironies of the date are well worth pondering. The period immediately after the passage of the Civil Rights Act and the Voting Rights Act saw, in many respects, the intensification of racial discrimination in the region. In 1966 white leaders of the city of Oxford established the Oxford Historical Cemetery Foundation, which for thirty-five years would effectively monopolize city resources to the detriment of African American gravesites. Voting rights for African Americans were severely restricted, the county's school system remained separate and unequal, and African Americans were unable to attain employment in most white-owned businesses in Newton County. Oxford College itself was still two years away from admitting its first African American students, although Emory in Atlanta had graduated two African American students in 1963. In so many important respects, at the moment of the tree planting, the aspiration of African Americans for equality and full inclusion in the Emory community remained, as it had been for so many generations, a dream deferred.[7]

Warren A. Candler

Andrew Warren Sledd

James Edward Dickey

LYNCHING, ACADEMIC FREEDOM, AND THE OLD "NEW SOUTH"
President Dickey and the "Sledd Affair"
— THOMAS H. JACKSON JR. —

Shedding light on the racial tensions of turn-of-the-century Georgia, Thomas Jackson recounts a sensationalized affair involving a visionary professor, the leadership of Emory College, and the Georgia populace. In 1902 Andrew Sledd, outspoken professor of Latin at Emory College, published an article describing a particularly brutal lynching and criticizing the racial attitudes of the white South. The public, led by notorious white supremacist Rebecca Latimer Felton, responded in an uproar and demanded Sledd's dismissal from Emory. The struggle between academic decorum and academic freedom reveals much about institutions of higher learning during the early twentieth century as well as one of the more shameful episodes in Emory's past.

O**N JULY 8, 1902,** James Edward Dickey, age thirty-eight, became the twelfth president of Emory College. The star product of Emory's class of 1891 and a former faculty member, Dickey was the seventh in a series of Emory alumni to hold the office, following Luther M. Smith (Class of 1848), Osborn L. Smith (1842), Atticus G. Haygood (1859), Isaac S. Hopkins (1859), Warren A. Candler (1875), and Charles E. Dowman (1873).[1]

Less than two weeks earlier, the *Atlantic Monthly*, a national journal published in Boston, had run in its July issue an article modestly titled "The Negro: Another View." The author was Andrew Sledd, a Harvard-educated Virginian who had joined the Emory faculty four years earlier. Besides being perhaps the strongest scholar at the little college, he also was its most outspoken.

The coming together of Dickey and Sledd in the summer of 1902 would lead to one of the more memorable and controversial crises in Emory's history.

Dickey could claim more than alumnus kinship to Emory; he was related by blood or marriage to a number of his predecessors, including Emory's first president, Ignatius A. Few; Dickey's mentor, colleague, friend, and confidant Warren Candler; Dickey's brother-in-law, Charles Dowman; and perhaps even presidents James R. Thomas and Isaac Stiles Hopkins.[2] His Few relatives were among the founders of not only Emory but also the University of Georgia and Duke University.[3]

But even with a strong family pedigree, a sterling record as student and teacher, success in the pulpits of the North Georgia Conference of the Methodist Episcopal Church, South, and the support and blessing of the Candler brothers,[4] Dickey could not have been prepared for the crisis that would wash over the institution without warning in the first weeks of his presidency. Nor could those around him have seen it coming. The crisis would sorely test many of those relationships.

Prelude to a Controversy | The foundations of the Sledd affair had been in the making for a number of years. Its elements included the horrific racial climate in the South of the day; the populist capitalization on that climate by the likes of Rebecca Latimer Felton, whose diatribes in the state's newspapers were fueled by personal animosities; the coming of Sledd to Emory in 1897 as professor of Latin; Sledd's boarding in the home of President Candler and falling in love with and marrying Candler's beloved daughter;[5] and Sledd's modernist and judgmental attitude toward the traditionalists at Emory. It probably did not help that Sledd criticized publicly the South's deficits in education and culture, led a faculty vote to discontinue his father-in-law's prized law department, and blocked a faculty vote to grant an honorary doctor of divinity degree to Dickey just four months before Dickey became president.[6]

The precipitating event to which all the foregoing added froth was the happenstance of Sledd's being on a train bound for Covington in 1899—a train that stopped near Palmetto, Georgia, southwest of Atlanta, so the passengers could view (and some participate in) the lynching of Sam Hose, an African American.[7] Subsequently, Sledd wrote for national publication an essay regarding the incident, though the publication trailed the event by some three years.[8]

Even to historians proficient in the period, the racial attitudes and atmosphere of Georgia at the dawn of the twentieth century are almost beyond comprehension in their ferocity and baseness. Any discussion of race began with the assumption on both sides of the argument, liberal and conservative, that "the Negro" was an inferior race. To almost the entire white populace, commingling of the races in public accommodations was unthinkable, and in sexual relations or marriage was abhorrent.

Historian W. Fitzhugh Brundage chronicled nearly five hundred lynchings in the Deep South from 1880 to 1930, a perverse means of maintaining racial hierarchy and white honor. Southern whites were averse to legal authority beyond the least required to maintain "the social organism."[9] Law officers maintained minimal forces, often calling for posses or aid from the state authorities when demands exceeded their resources. At times such posses could become mobs, combining "the fellowship of a hunt with the honor of serving the alleged needs of the community."[10]

It was an atmosphere reveled in and fed by Rebecca Latimer Felton, wife of Methodist minister, former Georgia legislator, and U.S. Congressman Dr. William H. Felton.[11] She thrived on her reputation as a firebrand. She openly defended lynching in her campaign against "the black beast . . . the Negro rapist," most famously in an 1897 address to the State Agricultural Society at Tybee Island: "If it takes lynching to protect woman's dearest possession from the drunken, ravening human beasts, then I say lynch a thousand a week if necessary."[12] Writing in the *Atlanta Journal*, she expanded those remarks to argue that legal trial was unnecessary for a Negro rapist.[13]

> *Even to historians proficient in the period, the racial attitudes and atmosphere of Georgia at the dawn of the twentieth century are almost beyond comprehension in their ferocity and baseness.*

Almost as famously, Mrs. Felton for years carried on a public clash with Emory president, and later Methodist bishop, Warren Candler. Perhaps, as some have alleged, it was rooted in Candler's dismissal of her son from college as "a vagabond and drunkard." She was known to keep lists of enemies and their perceived offenses against her. She carried out her battles with Candler for decades over a wide range of issues. Her prominent stance as a prohibitionist on behalf of the Women's Christian Temperance Union clashed with Candler's belief that women did not belong in the political arena. Felton was a progressive on women's suffrage; Candler opposed it, arguing that women should be spared the travails of politics.[14] Felton's husband, a trustee of the University of Georgia, joined her in a raging feud with Candler—he on the floor of the legislature and she in the pages of the state's newspapers—over public versus denominational colleges, as Candler repeatedly sought to garner for private schools the same state revenues and tuition breaks as the public university had. Editor Harry Hodgson dedicated the 1893 edition of the University of Georgia yearbook, the *Pandora*, to Mrs. Felton. It contained a political cartoon depicting her giving a whipping to "the fat Bishop" across her knee.[15]

Likewise, Felton jousted with Candler over issues in the Methodist Church to which they both belonged, denouncing bishops as "ruling with tyrannical power, giving the best appointments to their toadies and punishing their enemies with small-salaried pastorates in rural areas." As late as 1924 the two were still publicly feuding, this time over her allegation that some preachers were members of the Ku Klux Klan.[16]

Felton was not alone in her rabid public racism. For more than a decade beginning in 1893, *Atlanta Constitution* columnist Bill Arp regularly supported lynching: "As for lynching, I repeat what I have said before, let the good work go on. Lynch em! Hang em! Shoot em! Burn em!"[17] Rural newspaper editors were sometimes even more extreme. The editor of the *Crawfordville Advocate-Democrat* wrote in 1903, "What's the use of forever apologizing for doing something that is necessary and proper?"[18]

Into this social atmosphere arrived Andrew Sledd in January 1898. The graduate of Randolph-Macon College in Virginia had completed a master's degree in Latin at Harvard the previous year. He wrote to Candler seeking a teaching position, but took one first at Vanderbilt University, accepting it on the condition that he could leave if an opening at Emory became available. He was at Vanderbilt for only one term before accepting Candler's offer of the professorship of Latin at Emory. Candler also offered a room in his home as a boarder.

The two did not warm to each other. Candler no doubt disliked the younger man's critical attitude toward the state of Emory affairs. And as time passed, he grew wary of Sledd's budding relationship with Candler's daughter, Florence. Despite the bishop's opposition, Andrew Sledd and Florence Candler married in March 1899.[19]

It was not as if Sledd was a Yankee, come South to teach southerners the errors of their ways. He was a Virginian, born just after the Civil War. He grew up in the traditions of the white South, receiving his early education in Petersburg, Virginia, under a "firely unconquored [sic] captain in the armies of the lost cause." The same southern influences filled his college days at Randolph-Macon College in Ashland, Virginia.[20] After stints as a schoolmaster, first in Mississippi and then in Arkansas, Sledd went to Harvard to earn a graduate degree. There, he was shocked to witness white students fraternizing with blacks, sitting at the same dinner table, and walking across campus together. For much of the first year, he remained "shocked and horrified" by such things, bound by his southern upbringing and experience. Slowly, however, his attitude changed. "I entered the university with very distinct Southern sentiments on all the negro questions, and [experienced] a gradual breaking down of certain of my then views which was taking place, not only without my consent and approval, but even without my knowledge. . . . I went to Harvard a Southerner and left an American."[21]

Sledd later would characterize Emory as "a fairly good school, but intensely narrow-minded and provincial." Candler, who hired him, was "a man of conspicuous gifts and native ability, but without the training and breadth of liberality of view that would come from a larger and more liberal culture." In Sledd's view, while Candler was an able administrator and fostered the material success of the College, "the president's personal lack of scholarship or acquaintance with scholarly men, and the very narrow sectarianism of his views and those of his constituents, naturally militated against a larger culture and a higher life."[22]

Undeterred by being new to the campus, Sledd took on anything that did not fit his precise view of the way Emory should run. He criticized and moved to abolish the Emory law department, which consisted of only one faculty member with three students. But it was President Candler's pet project, and the sole faculty member was his brother, Judge (and Emory trustee) John S. Candler. Notwithstanding the authority and influence of Warren and John Candler in their own rights, their brother, Coca-Cola founder Asa G. Candler, was chair of the trustees' finance committee and the school's major benefactor. In the face of such authority, Sledd had the temerity to call Emory's law program a "fake" department with a "total faculty . . . of one incompetent and inconspicuous so-called judge," and succeeded in having the faculty abolish the law department.[23]

Sledd continued his impolitic actions by next targeting the awarding of honorary degrees. Sledd argued that they should not be awarded solely in gratitude for patronage or fund-raising. In the spring of 1902 he determined to fight the proposed honorary doctor of divinity degree being considered by the faculty for James E. Dickey, a member of the board of trustees since the previous year. Dickey, a favorite of the Candlers, was being positioned to succeed to the Emory presidency, apparently unbeknownst to Sledd. Initially, Sledd alone among the faculty opposed the degree, but his arguments turned around a sufficient number that, in the end, the nomination failed. Nevertheless, within four months Dickey was president and at loggerheads with Sledd.[24]

At age twenty-one, Sledd had taken a position as a schoolteacher in the small Mississippi town of Durant. On his first day in town, as he sat at dinner in the house where he was to board, the eldest son of the family related with lurid excitement that the town sheriff had "just killed a nigger." The lawman reportedly had been trying to arrest the man, when the suspect attacked the sheriff with an ax—and was shot through the heart. Sledd knew well the prevailing southern attitudes toward blacks, "but an awful tragedy of this sort had never come quite so close before," he wrote in his autobiography.[25]

In that same town, he experienced rampant fear among the white population of a rumored black insurrection to be led by a militant black preacher seeking revenge for the killing of a compatriot. White fear was such that armed posses guarded nightly against an uprising. "I did not expect such a thing nearly thirty years after Appomattox," he wrote. One posse eventually confronted the preacher, who fired first, according to Sledd's account, after which the posse shot his body "into an unrecognized mass to make sure that he could never come to life again."[26]

Add to this background the critical incident Sledd witnessed in 1899. On April 12 Coweta County farmer Alfred Crandall was alleged to have been brutally murdered by Sam Hose, an African American, or "negro," as the media and polite society called persons of his race in those days.[27] Mrs. Crandall reported the brutality of the murder and alleged that Hose raped her beside the body of her dead husband. The authorities offered large rewards for Hose's capture; newspapers fanned the flames, leading to a vigilante mentality; posses formed. The *Atlanta Constitution* reported that the nearby town of Woodbury "is practically deserted. Every man and boy able to carry a gun and help in the chase has left home determined to assist in the capture."[28]

> *Coweta County farmer Alfred Crandall was alleged to have been brutally murdered by Sam Hose, an African American. The authorities offered large rewards for Hose's capture; newspapers fanned the flames, leading to a vigilante mentality; posses formed.*

Newspapers reported sensational and lurid details—some almost certainly fabricated—that Crandall had been peaceably eating supper in his home when Hose sneaked up behind him and bashed in his skull with repeated blows from an axe. Hose robbed the house, the newspapers alleged, dragging Mrs. Crandall with him with a pistol to her head, snatching her eight-month-old baby from her arms and throwing it to the floor, inflicting injuries it would not likely survive. He raped the helpless wife twice beside the body of her dead husband, and, as a correspondent reported to Rebecca Felton, "*stripped* her person of every thread and vestige of clothing, there keeping her till time enough had passed to permit him to accomplish his fiendish offense twice more and again." Further, "he was inflicted with loathsome 'Sxxxxxxs' [*sic*—to stand for syphilis] for which *Mr. Crandall was having him treated*."[29]

That the newspapers exaggerated, even fabricated wholesale, the facts of the Crandall murder is likely. Within two months of the incident, the leader of a group of black antilynching activists in Chicago hired a private detective to investigate. His report, widely published in white newspapers of the North and black newspapers of the South, was that Hose was not the "burly black brute" portrayed in the press, but five feet eight inches tall, weighing 140 pounds. The detective's version was that Hose asked Crandall for money to visit his ill mother. Crandall refused, and the two men exchanged harsh words. The next day, as Hose was chopping wood, Crandall resumed the argument to the point of drawing a gun on Hose and threatening to kill him. Hose threw his axe in self-defense, the detective reported, hitting Crandall in the head and killing him instantly, leading Hose to flee in fear.[30]

As a week went by without Hose's capture, the *Atlanta Constitution* ran columns from prominent citizens suggesting ways to put a stop to such brutal crimes. Rebecca Felton repeated and embellished her now-standard answer: "lynch the black fiends by the thousands until the Negro understood that there was a standard punishment for rape and he could not escape it. She urged Horse's [*sic*] pursuers to forget the reward offered for his capture and to shoot him on sight as they would a mad dog."[31]

Ten days after the murder, on April 22, Hose was captured and jailed in Newnan, Georgia, not far from the site of the murder. The next morning, a mob took him from the jail to the countryside, where "he was emasculated and then burned alive. When the fire subsided, men pulled grisly souvenirs from the coals."[32] As this grotesque scene unfolded, the train bearing Professor Andrew Sledd of Emory College happened past and stopped, the passengers being given the opportunity to step from the train to view the horrible sight, or even participate, as they wished.

The Article That Sparked the Firestorm | Moved by the brutal lynching to put pen to paper, Sledd at first could not find a publisher. He sent his article to the New York *Independent* but received a lengthy personal letter of rejection. About the letter, Sledd said, "[A]ll of his criticisms [were] at the first half of the article, which arraigned the northern attitude toward the black man, as I understand it; while he has nothing but cordial commendations for the latter part of the article arraigning the southern attitude and treatment of the negro."

Sledd next submitted his account to the *Southern Methodist Review* of Nashville, "which publisher had uniformly accepted my contributions before that time," but which rejected it without explanation. Sledd continued to shop the piece, finally finding acceptance from Bliss Perry, editor of the *Atlantic Monthly*. The article ran in the July 1902 issue, which appeared the last week of June, less than two weeks before Dickey took office as Emory president.[33]

Under the title, "The Negro: Another View," Sledd undertook to add to the public discussion of "the negro problem in the South," criticizing previous works as both sectional and partisan. He asserted,

> Northern writers, with practically no knowledge or experience of actual conditions, have theorized to meet a condition that they did not understand. . . . Southern writers, on the contrary, remembering the negro as the slave, consider him and his rights from a position of proud and contemptuous superiority, and would deal with him on the ante-bellum basis of his servile state.[34]

Noting that "partisan and sectional discussion cannot fail to be alike bitter and unfruitful," Sledd said the South regarded the issue as a local matter, and "met any suggestions and offers of outside help with a surly invitation to 'mind your own business.' The North, on the other hand . . . has approached it from the side of preformed theories, rather than of actual facts. . . . As is usual in such cases, the truth lies between the two extremes."[35]

Sledd decried those on both sides who offered opinion while ignorant of the facts, and then proceeded to lay out his two fundamental assumptions: "(1) The negro belongs to an inferior race. . . . (2) But the negro has inalienable rights." Sledd asserted that he was not speaking of the "utterly worthless and depraved," of which there were many in both races, but noted that the black man could not expect a white man even to tip his hat while passing on the street, or to share a restaurant or a train car, or to sit in the same section of a church before "the maker of the black man as well as of the white, and invoke the Christ, who died for black and white alike . . . The black man, *because of his blackness*, is put in this lowest place."[36]

In the last decade of the nineteenth century, Sledd continued, "More men met their death by violence at the hands of lynchers than were executed by due process of law," that "seventy to eighty percent" of lynchings occur in the South, that "three quarters of those thus done to death are negroes," and that "the lynching penalty does not attend any single particular crime . . . but murder, rape, arson, barn-burning, theft,—or suspicion of any of these,—may and do furnish the ground for mob violence."[37]

Sledd asserted that officials and newspapers of the South had defended lynching as deserved punishment for the crime of violent rape, but that most lynchings were not connected to rape, and that most lynchings were not in immediate retribution by offended husbands, fathers, or brothers but were acts of calculated mob violence.[38]

Sledd described the lynching scene he had witnessed. His readers may have been aware of the details already, as the lynching of Sam Hose had been reported widely in the regional and national press. "The burning of Sam Hose took place on a Sabbath day. One of our enterprising railroads ran two special trains to the scene. And two train-loads of men and *boys*, crowding from cow-catcher to the tops of the coaches, were found to go to see the indescribable and sickening torture and writhing of a fellow human being. And souvenirs of such scenes are sought,—knee caps, and finger bones, and bloody ears. It is the purest savagery."[39]

Sledd indicted the double standard of the "Southern community": "If the negro criminal may be burned at the stake with the usual accompaniments of fiendish cruelty, a white man guilty of the same crime deserves, and should suffer, the same penalty. There is nothing in a white skin, *or a black*, to nullify this. And yet to the average Southern white man this manifestly just view seems both disloyal and absurd."[40]

Reaction | Sledd's article appalled his northern audience for the brutality it described. He himself recognized that it would be read in the South as "disloyal and absurd," even incendiary and seditious. But the *Atlantic Monthly* was neither widely read nor well respected by most in the South, so it took awhile for word of the publication to spread and for the reaction to set in.

In the same week the article was published at the end of June 1902, Emory president Dowman resigned unexpectedly to accept an appointment by Bishop Candler as presiding elder of the Atlanta district of the Methodist Church. The annual meeting of the Emory trustees during the first week of June had given no indication that a presidential change was imminent.[41]

On July 5, five days after Dowman's letter of resignation and the call of a meeting of the Emory board, J. W. Renfroe, a former state treasurer of Georgia, wrote Rebecca Felton to make her aware of the *Atlantic Monthly* article and the fact that it was written by Professor Andrew Sledd of Emory College. Felton took no apparent action.[42] Three days later, on July 8, the Emory trustees met at Atlanta First Methodist Church, accepting Dowman's resignation and electing Dickey his successor.[43] Three days after that, on July 11, the *Atlanta Constitution* finally tackled the Sledd article, publishing a highly critical editorial. With no direct evidence of how the newspaper learned of the article, but knowing how such things work and knowing Felton's record, one might surmise that Felton or Renfroe prompted the newspaper's editors.

Not revealing that Sledd was on the Emory faculty, the *Constitution* blasted "the southern negro for being incapable of improving his lot and thereby demonstrating his deserving of rights."[44] The editorial continued with the old but popular argument that if they don't like it here, they can leave:

> And as for the complaint of Mr. Sledd and the Boston cult that the negro must ride in second class cars and eat in negro restaurants apart from the whites, we do not accept responsibility for those things. Any northern man who wants to open a restaurant on the bi-colored plan can doubtless obtain a license for the same by paying the cash at the counter of the city clerk of Atlanta, and then get what customers he can. . . . We may also remark that most of our railway lines are now owned and controlled by investors and managers who live in the east and north. There is no law, in Georgia at least, to prevent the railway owners from giving the colored people as fine cars as can be turned out from the Pullman or Wilmington factories. . . . In view of these plain facts, we cannot see that Mr. Sledd has illuminated the race problem in any sense. He has only helped to encourage an old form of northern fool-osophy![45]

The *Constitution*'s vitriol did not immediately stir its readership to action, nor did the regional or national press take up the cause early. Finally, though, on July 29 another state official, Madison Bell, the executive secretary of the Georgia Commission on Statuary Hall, wrote to Rebecca Felton urging her to weigh in, saying she was "the best qualified person to present the facts of this discussion to the Northern people."[46]

Felton came through. She unloaded all guns at Sledd, the son-in-law of her old foe, Bishop Candler, in a diatribe published in the *Constitution* on Sunday, August 3. Not satisfied with what she could print in the pages of the newspaper, she also purchased a card insert for issues delivered in the Covington-Oxford community surrounding Emory. She disingenuously claimed in her column not to know who Sledd was but insisted that "the statements he sets forth in the *Atlantic Monthly* go to show that no more unfriendly writer to the southern people has ever printed a line in a northern magazine. I am, however, comforted in not being acquainted with Mr. Sledd, or his whereabouts or his profession, because the loathing that his article has inspired to my mind has in no wise been the result of any individual dislike or acquaintance with the writer."[47] Perhaps Felton was at least half-truthful that her dislike was not of the writer; it was of his father-in-law.

Felton suggested that if Sledd lived in the South, he should "be politely compelled" to prove his assertions or move to another part of the country—"for his health's sake." She took particular offense at Sledd's notion that blacks in the South were treated as no more than "a beast, with a curse and a kick, and with tortures that even a beast is spared"—an accusation that she called "'rot' . . . vomited into the columns of the *Atlantic Monthly*."[48]

In response to Sledd's description of the lynching of Sam Hose, Felton returned to her long-standing justification of lynching:

> This white man (I presume his color will pass, as he calls this "our" section) has not a single word to say of the fiendish murder of a father and husband, of the outrage inflicted on an agonized wife and mother, who was blood covered beside the body of her dead husband, or of the little girls who witnessed the horrible sights, and his logic is only here applied to condemn the white men who put the beast to death! Every man in Georgia should read this outrageous indictment of southern manhood and then dismiss the writer of it! . . . Now that Andrew Sledd (may God spare me the sight of this maligner of his own color, and perhaps of his own section) has printed his views of southern white men in a Boston magazine, the world outside will be ready to malign the suffering wife still further.[49]

Felton closed with an ominous suggestion: "If left to a vote in Georgia . . . the slanderer would be made to retire, and he may yet be thankful to get off without an extra application of tar and feathers."[50]

Rather than being appalled by Felton's diatribe, the Georgia public in the summer of 1902 applauded. Newspapers around the state as well as the competing Atlanta newspapers, the *Journal* and the *Constitution*, fanned the flames of anger by publishing lurid stories about Sledd and his article every day from August 3 through August 13.

Sledd was horrified by Felton's "tirade and libel." He later wrote that the experience led him to believe "that an expression of unorthodoxy (meaning any difference in opinion from the prevailing opinion in the South) on the negro question is sufficient to jeopardize a man's career, if not his life."[51] Yet in his characteristically uncompromising style, he attempted a response by granting an interview to an *Atlanta Journal* reporter who was an Emory graduate and a former student and fraternity brother of Sledd's. According to Sledd's version of the interview, the reporter had not read the *Atlantic Monthly* article and asked Sledd to recount it. In doing so, Sledd reiterated the premise that had so outraged the public: "that the negro is treated lower than a brute in the South. I believe the average white man in the south would sooner kill a negro than a forty dollar mule."[52] This interview seemed to cause more difficulty than the original article.[53]

The *Constitution* pounded away. The front page on August 5 carried a six-by-nine-inch photo of "Professor Andrew Sledd of Emory College, whose article on the negro question has caused him to be roundly censured." Asserting that Felton's criticism of Sledd "came almost as a thunderclap to the citizens of Covington," the *Constitution* reported that "Professor Sledd has always been very popular here and his best friends were not aware of his antagonistic ideas against the south, his home, and the southern people." Someone identified by the *Constitution* only as "one of the Emory professors" attempted to defend Sledd, saying that Felton had misconstrued things. But the newspaper reported that Sledd retracted nothing.[54]

The *Constitution* sought out Atlanta's leading black clergy for comment. By tradition built on years of intimidation, they were careful in their statements. Bishop Henry M. Turner called Sledd a "humanitarian." R. D. Stinson, identified by the newspaper as "collecting commissioner" for Morris Brown College, "stated that he believes the article has done harm to the negro race and that it was inopportunely written." Bishop J. W. Gaines "preferred not to give any opinion."[55]

Sledd, meanwhile, began receiving letters on both sides of the issue. Those from the North were "generally commendatory," he said, as were clippings from northern newspapers. Some northern writers took a calm and rational approach, he said, while others "were inclined to make a martyr of me, and to be as intemperate in their commendation as the majority of those of the south were in their abuse." Almost without exception, the southern comment Sledd received, both in letters and in the press, was "harshly critical and unfair." Those few southern editors who insisted upon a right of free speech "were drowned in the midst of uproar and denunciation and of intemperate abuse."[56]

In Covington on the evening of August 5, white youths (there is no evidence that they were Emory students) dragged through the streets and then burned on the town square an effigy depicting Sledd hugging a black man. Citizens of Covington disclaimed any part in the street action but circulated a petition of thanks to be presented to Mrs. Felton. Sledd was emphatic that those responsible were not his students: "Several of my students, in fact, wrote me affectionate and touching letters with reference to the matter."[57]

Emory College Responds

In the five days following the publication of Felton's August 3 column, seventeen trustees contacted President Dickey, all calling for Sledd's departure. As Dickey later told Bishop Candler, all believed that Sledd's continued service on the faculty would hurt the College; six said they would not send their sons to Emory while he taught there—if they had had sons. Letters arrived from around the state calling for Sledd's dismissal. Two of the most passionate were from Candler's brothers, Asa and John. The matter clearly was grievous for the Candler family, forcing Warren to choose loyalty to his daughter, and therefore his son-in-law, over his lifelong devotion to his brothers.

As for Dickey, he was inclined to defer to the president of the board of trustees and the unanimous opinion of the board. The trustees included some of Candler's—and Emory's—best friends. "When I was asked therefore as to my opinion concerning Mr. Sledd's remaining at Emory," Dickey wrote to Candler afterward, "I could not arrive at any other conclusion than that his stay would be hurtful to the college."[58]

Sledd clearly did not like nor respect Dickey. He wrote three years later in his unpublished autobiography that Dickey "was a man of amazing ignorance and the intensest bigotry, but he made up for these defects by great pompousness and pretense of manner and of discourse and by an authorodixy [*sic*] of religious opinion which would be ludicrous if it were not so pitiable."[59]

His view of Dickey, written in hindsight after what seemed to him a great wrong, reflected his view of the Emory faculty and administration in general. Sledd gave no quarter to faculty members, including Dickey, who came to their positions from the ministry, referring to them alternately as "incompetent" or "not a scholar." Dickey's airs and pontification certainly chafed against Sledd's critical nature. Their personalities were aligned for a clash.

Dickey met with Sledd in the president's office on the Oxford campus on August 7, when, Sledd reports, "I called at his office to see him about some other matters." The two walked from Dickey's office in Seney Hall, across the green and down Wesley Street toward the president's house several blocks away. The only account of that meeting comes from Sledd's unpublished autobiography, in which he reports that he asked Dickey if he had read the article. Dickey said he had not, and Sledd retorted, "Then it does not seem to me that you have any basis for an opinion." Dickey replied, "The truth of the article is not involved. My ignorance of it is not the question. The press and the people of the state are railing at you; and members of the Board are approaching me upon the subject."

Sledd's account confirms Dickey's own implication that he and the trustees acted not because of what Sledd said but because of the public criticism being heaped upon Emory because of his comments. Sledd asked if Dickey sought his resignation. Dickey replied that he was merely sharing information, "leaving the course of action in your own hands." Sledd told Dickey that he would not resign but would force the board to take formal action. He did not then understand that he would not necessarily have the opportunity to be heard on the question.

Sledd presented other arguments for keeping him on. Others on the faculty had faults: "Bradley preaches Unitarianism in a Methodist college," and "Bonelson is, and has for years, been totally incompetent to fill his chair," and nothing was said to either. Some, he said, were "not above suspicion in moral lines," and nothing was said. Yet, "I have worked here for five years diligently, faithfully, and successfully; I have preached righteousness, and lived righteousness, and now for the supposition of a heresy which you have not done me the justice to verify by a half-hour's perusal of the article, I am called upon to take my wife and my little one and go out in disgrace." Promising to protest throughout Georgia, Sledd vowed, "I shall not tolerate such an injustice." As the two separated, Dickey informed Sledd he would call at his home that evening for his decision.

Despite his readiness for battle, after discussing the matter with Florence, Sledd determined that dignity should be preserved, and that the appropriate course was to resign. He apparently was swayed by Florence's concern that her family—the Candlers—not be further drawn into the fray. Dickey called at the home that evening after tea, and the three of them had further discussion. Dickey informed Sledd that he had just received a wire from the president of the board of trustees, asking, "Has Sledd resigned?" Dickey said this was indicative of the sentiment of the board, and that if Dickey were in Sledd's place he would give it up. Sledd responded that he had reached the same conclusion, but did not know how he would meet his obligations, to which Dickey gave his assurances that the board would be willing to vote for Sledd a considerable portion of his salary for the year. The next morning, Sledd delivered a letter of resignation through English professor W. L. Weber.[60]

Dickey released Sledd's resignation letter to the papers the same day, along with his own written statement: "In justice to Professor Sledd, I submit the full text of his letter to me. His reference to September 15 as the date at which his resignation shall take effect grows out of the fact, I presume, that he is now engaged in preparing pupils for the fall term, and it would be manifestly unfair to drop them at this date. His resignation will go to the executive committee of the board of trustees for action."[61]

The *Constitution* printed Sledd's resignation letter in full, and it was duly recorded in the minutes of the Emory Board of Trustees executive committee meeting of August 12:

Oxford, Ga. Aug. 8, 1902
Rev. Jas. E. Dickey
Prest. Emory College
Atlanta, Ga.
My dear Mr. Dickey,—

You have of course observed the bitter attacks that have been made upon me in certain of the newspapers in consequence of an article of mine upon the negro question. These attacks seem to me to be quite unjust, and my critics have by no means fairly represented my sentiments or my attitude either to this particular question or to our common section. This I presume you know.

It seems to me likely, however, from the attitude that the newspapers and certain of the public have taken in the matter, that our College may suffer some harm, or at least be temporarily embarrassed, by continuing to maintain upon its Faculty a man who is even supposed to entertain such sentiments as have been attributed to me. I am of course responsible for my own utterances; and I am ready to bear anything in the line of misrepresentation or of loss that my utterances may bring upon me. But Emory College is in no sense responsible for anything that I may say or think and it does not seem to me either just or wise to call upon the institution to assume responsibility or suffer loss for utterances that it may not, and doubtless does not endorse.

In view of these facts, it has seemed to me best to tender to you my resignation as Prof. of Latin in Emory College. As to the time such resignation shall go into effect, I should suggest the middle of September, but leave that entirely in your discretion. Permit me to add an expression of my very high esteem, and believe me

Very sincerely yours
Andrew Sledd[62]

On August 8 the *Atlanta Journal* declined to publish another submission on the matter from Rebecca Felton.[63] The *Constitution* continued to pursue the story for several more days, reporting on August 10 that the trustees had not yet taken action but would likely accept Sledd's resignation.[64]

On August 11 the *Constitution* for the first time reprinted from the *Atlantic Monthly* the entire article, "The Negro: Another View." On August 12 a page-seven story previewed the meeting of the executive committee and forecast the committee's acceptance of the resignation.[65] In that same paper, an "about town" commentary column called "The Passing Throng" revealed for the first time to the general public the relationship between Sledd and Warren Candler: "Professor Andrew Sledd, of Emory College, who has recently resigned the chair of Latin language and literature . . . was in Atlanta yesterday at the home of his father in law, Bishop Warren A. Candler. . . . This afternoon he returns to Oxford, where he is now conducting the summer school and has a large number of boys under his instruction."[66]

The evening before the executive committee meeting, Candler sent a handwritten note by "special delivery boy" to Dickey's home, suggesting, "as a trustee of the college," that the executive committee delay acting until the full board meeting in November. Dickey would later imply, though no record exists, that the note also contained the suggestion that Sledd be granted a severance package. Knowing that he already had discussed such a severance package with Sledd, Dickey tore the note up, "fearing that someone else might chance to read it and obtain a false impression." Candler later would express being hurt by Dickey's decision not to respond to that note.[67]

The next day, the newspapers reported dutifully, "Sledd Is to Leave Emory." The article closed with this editorial comment: "The action of the executive committee . . . is final and will doubtless bring to a close the discussion of this unfortunate affair, which has caused Professor Sledd to give up his position and Emory college to lose one of the best men on its faculty."[68]

That same week, Sledd received a letter from Antioch College in Ohio, offering him the presidency of the institution. Sledd declined on the grounds that he was needed "in my own section and with my own people"; that he was not sufficiently prepared to teach history and philosophy, which the Antioch president must do; and that he did not want to give his critics the satisfaction of seeing him move to be with "the Negro lovers of the North."[69]

Candler and Dickey spoke by telephone the evening after the committee met. In a later letter to his mentor, Dickey recounted the conversation as one of warmth and support: "I remember that you bade me not to be depressed, saying that God was not dead, and then, in a spirit of humor, adding that every time lightning struck, a mule was not killed."[70]

If the crisis strained the relationship of Candler with Dickey, the furor had drawn the bishop and his son-in-law closer. Through it, Candler found a new respect for his daughter's husband. He was hurt and bitter at the treatment Sledd had received and at the mistakes he believed had been made by the board, which included his brother Asa and his protégé Dickey. He was embarrassed for Emory College as reaction set in from national media and his contemporaries in the clergy and the episcopacy across the country.

Candler let it rest, publicly, holding his tongue in the press. But privately he expressed to friends and colleagues his bitterness and deep depression at the wrong he felt had been done to him and his son-in-law. At the root of his hurt was the effect on his beloved daughter, Foncie. He wrote many letters seeking work for Sledd. In each, rather than defend Sledd's position, Candler asserted that it had been misrepresented, and that Sledd did not hold the beliefs attributed to him. This may have been wishful thinking on Candler's part, as Sledd more than once in the media defended and restated his position.

Sledd, meanwhile, considered further response to the *Constitution*, but Candler talked him out of it. Bliss Perry, the *Atlantic Monthly* editor, invited Sledd to examine the article's aftermath in a subsequent edition, but Sledd urged him "not to give any undue prominence to the matter in the *Atlantic*. . . . I do not wish to pose as a martyr, or make any capital out of all this disagreeable experience."[71]

By all indications, Dickey determined to set the incident behind him and the College and move on, almost as if ignoring it would make it go away. He showed no inclination to discuss, much less reopen, the case. His first correspondence with Candler following the explosion of the affair was either blithely ignorant of the furor or incredibly hard-nosed, as his attitude was all business and no Sledd. He informed the bishop that the Quillian Lectureship needed just under two hundred dollars to be fully endowed at three thousand dollars, and proposed to nominate Candler to deliver the next series of lectures. He informed Candler of an anonymous fund-raising prospect, and asked the bishop to appoint Fletcher Walton to a half-time pastorate that would free him to serve as assistant to the president. With a bit more news about progress on raising money for the new science hall and for the Lowe fund, and the prospects for fall enrollment of one hundred new boys, the letter closed, "Hoping to hear from you in the matter of the Lectures and of the appointment, I am affectionately yours, James E. Dickey."[72]

In fact, throughout the several months of the crisis, Dickey was apparently determined to maintain a regular schedule and to move College business forward. Just one week after Felton's first letter exposing the Sledd essay appeared in the *Constitution*, Dickey preached the opening sermon at the Atlanta District Conference, on the subject, "The Need of the Spiritual in an Age of Materialism."[73] Despite the upheaval of July and August, regular work continued, in many cases requiring Candler and Dickey to continue their traditional consultation and cooperation.

In a called meeting on September 3, the executive committee approved Dickey's agreement to pay Sledd a thousand dollars in severance pay, Sledd's entire salary for the academic year. (Apparently unaware that Dickey already had agreed to do this, the Emory faculty had met August 14 and urged such a payment.) The executive committee also appointed Professor M. H. Arnold, a Virginian, to succeed Sledd in the Latin chair as a temporary appointment to finish the academic year.[74]

Candler continued his correspondence, seeking a position for Sledd, but Sledd determined to return to Yale to complete his doctorate, apparently underwritten financially by his father-in-law. He wrote from New Haven, "I cannot tell you how much I appreciate your kindness in this matter, or what your attitude and service means to me. I trust that I may be able in some way at some time to show you that I am not heedless of the service that you are doing me. If it suits your convenience, you may just deposit the money to my credit at Third National."[75]

Candler was prone to periods of depression and self-doubt and often required reassurance and praise from colleagues. His biographer reports that Candler would grow moody, would "sulk around the house," and had "periodic episodes of self-flagellation." Over the years on several occasions, he would think "after all I have done" for them and the institution, *they don't appreciate me.* He would proffer a resignation from the presidency or from a board, submitting that he was unworthy for the position. Of course, these resignations were never meant to be accepted. Candler would be unanimously reelected amid great assurances that he was much loved and the man for the job.[76] The Sledd affair touched many of Candler's closest personal relationships—with his daughter and son-in-law, with his brothers, with his protégé, with the church and college so dear to him. It would have been trying on anyone, but in particular, given Candler's temperament, the emotional effect on the bishop was deep.

Only seven years in age separated Dickey from Candler. The two had been close since that day in the spring of 1898 that the twenty-three-year-old freshman walked into the office of the new thirty-year-old president. Under Candler's close tutelage, Dickey had rocketed from freshman to president in fifteen years. All that Dickey knew about issues of politics and administration in the government, the church, and the College, he had learned at Candler's knee. He shared Candler's views on virtually every major issue of the day. It truly was a mentor-protégé relationship, and the Sledd affair placed it under great strain.

> *Candler was prone to periods of depression and self-doubt and often required reassurance and praise from colleagues. . . . Over the years on several occasions, he would think "after all I have done" for them and the institution,* they don't appreciate me.

In the six weeks from the end of November 1902 through early January 1903, Candler and Dickey finally attempted to move beyond the furor that had complicated their long-standing relationship. An exchange of long letters attempted to sort out the story and understand what had happened and why, and where fault lay. At the heart of the matter lay the slight that Candler perceived in not getting a reply to the note he had sent Dickey the night before the August executive committee meeting. Dickey wrote to Candler and recounted that the delivery person left without waiting for a reply, that Dickey had already told Candler a severance package was in the works, and that he destroyed Candler's note about a severance package rather than have posterity read it and misunderstand. "I beg to assure you that no discourtesy was intended. . . . No man ever entertained a more affectionate regard for you than I, and I could not purposely be discourteous to you."[77]

Candler responded much as a father taking a beloved child behind the woodshed: "[I must] be candid. I thought & think you [responded] to my suggestion inconsiderately. I have apologized for it to myself on the ground that a sensation was spinning on you at the outset of your administration and you lost your accustomed sobriety of judgement. I did not and do not think you have any disposition to be offensive to me. But I thought and think the college could have been saved injury if you had not acted so precipitously and with such persistence in pushing Sledd out."[78]

Dickey dispatched a response to Candler, thanking him for his "frank statement," and relating to him the reaction of the seventeen trustees who sought Sledd's ouster, and the determined stance of Candler's own two brothers, Asa and John. He added that the full board of trustees had ratified the action of the executive committee without dissent.[79]

The bishop was not swayed. In the last recorded word between the two on the matter, Candler said he believed that he and his son-in-law had been wronged, and that Emory had made a grievous mistake. He closed his last letter on the matter by underscoring his personal hurt. "But enough," he says—and then goes over the old ground yet again in thirteen sentences, before adding, "Now spare me any further discussion of this matter." At last he finishes by laying a burden on Dickey by majestically retreating into the solitude of suffering: "My pain is my own and need concern no one else. With best wishes for the New Year, I am Yours affectionately, W. A. Candler."[80]

Ralph Reed, writing on the Sledd affair, concluded that the matter grievously damaged the relationship between Candler and Dickey, writing that "an icy silence separated Dickey and Candler for years to come."[81] But the evidence is to the contrary. In their letters, neither man quit the other; they came through it with pain and hurt, much as family members caught up in a serious misunderstanding. But they continued to be colleagues and even warm, dear friends. They sat in numerous meetings of Emory College and University trustees for the next twenty-six years. Dickey remained in the presidency for thirteen years, longer than any of his predecessors including Candler, before being appointed by the bishop as pastor of the largest church in the conference, Atlanta First Methodist. Upon his subsequent election as bishop, Dickey became a close ally of Candler's in the conservative wing of the Council of Bishops. Candler was of such power and authority during those years that Dickey could not have achieved those leading positions without Candler's support.

> *The forced departure of college professors was not, in those days, peculiar to the South, nor solely a matter of racial attitudes.*

Perhaps more telling is the personal closeness the two men and their families maintained. Candler officiated at the weddings of Dickey's two eldest daughters.[82] In later years, the men had homes just three doors apart on North Decatur Road, across the street from Emory's Druid Hills campus, Dickey at 1627 and Candler at 1655. Indeed, Candler wrote a glowing memorial of Dickey on the younger man's unexpected death in 1928, as well as the foreword to Elam F. Dempsey's tribute, *The Life of Bishop Dickey*. Candler's words carried no hint of the feelings he expressed in his letters after the Sledd affair.[83]

Reed also concludes that the Sledd affair had a negative financial impact on the college, echoing a similar assertion made earlier by Henry Y. Warnock.[84] But Emory, like many southern colleges of its day, faced constant financial difficulty, usually running a deficit, and often dependent on the generosity of individual trustees, particularly Asa G. Candler, to help meet its financial obligations. The trustees' minutes reveal that this was the case for years before and after the Sledd affair, and no evidence is apparent that the financial condition was any worse after the incident than before.

Another general conclusion reached by several writers is that the affair was a unique product of the racial attitudes of the turn-of-the-century South. Yes, Bishop Candler was "an avowed and unabashed racist,"[85] and by extension, so was his man Dickey, as were most other whites in the South of the day. W. J. Cash, in his landmark study *The Mind of the South*, counts Sledd among "a growing handful of men" on southern campuses who from the late 1890s turned "directly to examining and criticizing the South." Cash notes the growing tendency at most schools "to back them up in it, or at least to maintain their right to their heresies." But the Emory faculty, "perhaps intimidated by the uproar of the press against him . . . silently acquiesced."[86]

C. Vann Woodward (College 1930) deals with Sledd briefly in his *Origins of the New South*. Woodward praises Trinity College for preserving the position of Professor John Spencer Bassett in a similar case and criticizes Emory for its "unfortunate example."[87]

While it is true that Sledd's position on "the negro question" was the proximate cause of the upheaval at Emory, the root issue was institutional public relations—the matter of an outspoken faculty member embarrassing the institution and being dealt with as a result. Sledd himself acknowledged as much in his autobiography.[88]

Emory was not alone in experiencing an incident harmful to public relations. Several other institutions recorded similar incidents during the years surrounding Emory's Sledd affair. In October 1903, at Trinity College (now Duke University), another Methodist college in the South, Professor Bassett published an article in the *South Atlantic Quarterly* pronouncing, among other things, that Booker T. Washington was the second-ranking citizen of the nineteenth-century

South, second only to Robert E. Lee. As Sledd was to Emory, Bassett was arguably the Trinity faculty's strongest scholar. When Bassett opined that a small group of blacks had made "remarkable progress" and were no longer content with an inferior place in society, the *Raleigh News and Observer* pounced, much as the *Constitution* had done in the Sledd case.[89]

The difference in the Bassett case was the reaction of Trinity officials. Perhaps they had been enlightened by the Sledd affair. As President John C. Kilgo had corresponded with his close friend Candler over the Sledd matter, so now Candler wrote the chairman of Trinity's board of trustees. He disagreed with some of Bassett's positions but urged the Trinity trustees to make it clear that "our faculties do not hold office at the will of irritable and inflammatory people who too easily join in any hue and cry that may be raised."[90]

Trinity College at first remained silent. Kilgo gave Bassett an opportunity to "clarify" his statements, and Bassett did so in the next *Quarterly*, saying that by "equality" of the races he meant economic opportunity, not social equality; and that Booker T. Washington's "greatness" was in overcoming great handicaps.[91] The clarifications and his offer to resign left Kilgo room to offer Bassett support. In fact, he was able to turn trustee Ben Duke toward supporting academic freedom. By the time the full board met on December 1, 1903, they were able to affirm Bassett's clarification and reiterate their confidence in Kilgo. The college officially disagreed with what Bassett had written but defended his right to publish it.[92]

The forced departure of college professors was not, in those days, peculiar to the South, nor solely a matter of racial attitudes.[93] Laurence R. Veysey, in *The Emergence of the American University*, asserts that there was a larger, umbrella concern governing such matters: unfavorable publicity.[94] He cites numerous cases of troublemaking faculty being shown the door for creating ill will and bad publicity: Richard T. Ely at the University of Wisconsin in 1894, Edward W. Bemis at the University of Chicago in 1895, the Andrews case at Brown in 1897, the Herron case at Iowa (Grinnell) College, and the Edward A. Ross dismissal at Stanford in 1900.[95] The "new order of academic freedom" had not yet established itself over the "older order of academic respectability."[96] Other cases included Henry C. Adams at Cornell for a pro-labor speech; George Steel, president of Lawrence College, for leanings toward free trade and greenbacks; and Docent Hourwich at the University of Chicago for participation in a Populist convention.[97]

In those early days of the Progressive Era, the concept of academic freedom was just emerging. The notion of a faculty member as an employee who serves at the pleasure of the employer still held sway, and embarrassing one's president, trustees, and institution bought a quick ticket out the door at any number of institutions. Even in southern schools like Emory and Trinity, where race was the hot-button issue, the underlying concern was the faculty members' violation of institutional image. Emory provides further evidence of this in its historical treatment of the Sledd affair. For a century, the official Emory story was that Sledd had resigned. Bullock's centennial history of Emory College and University, published in 1936, gives the Sledd affair one page. But even in that slight treatment, Bullock recognized public relations as the basis for the issue, as he reported that Sledd "resigned in the summer of 1902 *to protect the College from the antagonism.*"[98]

Not until a 2002 exhibit of lynching photographs came to the Emory campus did the school take the opportunity to acknowledge the Sledd scandal. Emory marked the one hundredth anniversary of the affair with an exhibition at Pitts Theology Library titled *Protesting Racial Violence: Andrew Sledd, Warren Akin Candler, and Lynching Controversies in Early Twentieth-Century Georgia*. The exhibit of photographs, letters, newspaper clippings, and other original materials explored the larger "conversation" about lynching among white and African American scholars and the faith community in Atlanta in the early twentieth century. The keynote address of the symposium was delivered by Professor Emeritus James Hinton Sledd of the University of Texas, Andrew Sledd's son born in Atlanta in 1914, a 1936 Emory graduate and Rhodes scholar, who died in 2003.[99]

And what of the elder Sledd? He departed for Yale in September and completed work on his PhD in nine months. He returned South, joining the faculty of Southern University in Alabama in 1904,[100] and moving soon to become the first president of the University of Florida, from 1904 to 1909. A dispute with the Florida trustees over admission requirements forced his resignation. After a brief stint as pastor of the First Methodist Church of Jacksonville, Sledd returned to Southern University, this time as president, often working without pay when the college could not meet payroll.[101]

In 1914, when his wife's uncle, Asa G. Candler, gave $1 million to transform Emory College into Emory University and build a new campus in the Druid Hills section of Atlanta, his father-in-law, Bishop Candler, became the new university's chancellor. Sledd joined the faculty as professor of Greek and New Testament in the new School of Theology, Candler's first hire. For the next twenty-five years, he wielded significant influence in training a generation of Methodist preachers, inculcating in them a philosophy of racial tolerance and justice. Sledd's long tenure as one of the nation's most respected scholars in his field continued until his death in 1939. The late Bishop Kenneth Goodson, who was Methodist bishop in Alabama when a 1963 church bombing in Birmingham killed four black children, recalls that the small, brave core of his ministers who helped calm the situation by courageously attending an interracial memorial service were "almost to a man, students of Andrew Sledd."[102]

CHAPTER 4

Charles Dudley, first African American graduate of Emory College, 1967.

NATIONAL AMBITION, REGIONAL TURMOIL
The Desegregation of Emory
— MELISSA F. KEAN —

In an essay rich with historical detail and insight, Melissa Kean examines the social factors that led to Emory's 1962 decision to admit African American students. The struggle to this end was closely tied to the communities in which Emory was embedded, in a South still rampant with racial tensions. Postwar University President Goodrich White began the slow march toward change, often caught between the conflicting allegiances of justice and politics. His successor, Walter Martin, continued to play a balancing act as the Georgia public school crisis and tax exemption for segregated schools weighed heavily on the minds of faculty, trustees, and alumni. Mounting internal and external pressures finally led the University to chart a path out of the thicket.

THE IDEA OF THE UNIVERSITY as an oasis set apart from the daily concerns of the world has had a very long life. It still thrives today, along with the image of the absent-minded scholar oblivious to the real world. While these stereotypes may contain an element of truth, in most important ways universities are closely bound to the world around them. All universities, including Emory, evolve as part of their communities. Nowhere is this more evident than in the long and tumultuous run-up to Emory's 1962 decision to admit black students. Beginning in the mid-1940s, Emory struggled to adapt its goals, its traditions, and its very sense of identity to a new and sometimes unclear set of demands. The story of that struggle reveals Emory's profound connections to its local, regional, and national communities.

In the wake of World War II, all those communities were undergoing deep and rapid change. Nationally, the Cold War with the Soviet Union rose to paramount importance, and in the propaganda battle for the loyalties of Africa, Asia, and Latin America, the racial discrimination practiced in the U.S. South was a serious handicap. At the same time, the South itself was being transformed—economically, socially, and demographically—in some ways more thoroughly than it had been by the Civil War. Widespread mechanization of agriculture fed migration from the countryside to the cities (as well as out of the region entirely). Newly created manufacturing jobs and employment opportunities in government and defense contracting enabled growing numbers of blacks and whites to reach middle-class prosperity. Primary and secondary education improved steadily.

Meanwhile, American higher education was undergoing its own transformation. Scientists and engineers, most based in universities, had been crucial to the war effort. The Cold War only deepened the understanding that American national security depended on a strong university research community. A new commitment arose on the part of the federal government to expansion and democratization of universities, mainly through funding of graduate studies, research, and the GI Bill. Private philanthropies such as the Rockefeller, Ford, and Carnegie foundations also took a keener interest in strengthening higher education, especially in the South, which lagged badly behind the rest of the country. The greatly increased flow of money from these sources created a wholly new set of opportunities and pressures.

At Emory, as at other universities in the rapidly changing South, this development, although welcome, was fraught with difficulties. Emory had begun its existence as a small Methodist college in Oxford, Georgia. It was, of course, for whites only. Like almost all southern schools of that era, it focused on teaching a classical curriculum and Christian doctrine to undergraduates. It also served a powerful social purpose, carefully bringing young men (and, in the twentieth century, women) into membership in the society of respectable adults and anchoring them in the region's traditions. After the Methodist Episcopal Church, South, smarting from its acrimonious split with Vanderbilt University, decided to launch a new Methodist institution of higher education, Emory was relocated to Atlanta, given slightly more resources, enlarged by the addition of professional schools, and christened a university. Progress toward true university standing, however, was slow. Building a significant program of graduate studies and research was difficult. Until 1946 Emory offered no work toward the doctorate and limited work at the master's level. At the end of the war it still remained a thoroughly conservative regional school, serving mainly undergraduates from Georgia and Florida, a creature of its time and place.[1]

With the ongoing transformation of traditional southern life, though, and the outpouring of new money for education, change was clearly coming to Emory. The struggle that would occupy its leadership for a decade and a half was how to shape that change, or at least keep it under control. University presidents are never simply free to do what they think best. Even under normal conditions they are answerable to an unreasonably large number of constituencies: trustees, faculty, alumni, politicians, donors, students, neighbors, parents, and more. These groups are often deeply devoted to and passionate about their school, and they often disagree strongly with each other about what is best for it. At Emory in the postwar era, where deeply held beliefs and long-cherished ways of life were eroding, and plans to remake the University were taking shape, the divisions became intense. Opposition based on respect for southern traditions grew in proportion to the scope and pace of change. This intertwined change required two Emory presidents—Goodrich White and Walter Martin—to perform subtle and intricate balancing acts. To navigate forward in the University's best interests they had to cope with factors ranging from national foreign policy to the expectations of philanthropic foundations, to the intricacies of personal relationships with their friends in the Emory community. In particular, the University's response to growing pressures for racial change was shaped in the cauldron of the intense politics of segregation that played out in Georgia in the decades after the war.

Emory's president in the immediate postwar period was Goodrich Cook White, an Emory man through and through. He earned his bachelor's degree from Emory College in 1908, when it was still in Oxford, and spent nearly his entire adult life affiliated with the University. After earning a master's degree in psychology from Columbia University and briefly teaching at two small Methodist colleges, he returned to Emory in 1914 as an associate professor of "mental and moral science." During World War I, White served as a lieutenant in the psychological division of the Army Medical Corps. After the war he completed his doctorate at the University of Chicago and returned to Emory, now in Atlanta, where he proved a stalwart administrator. He assumed increasing responsibility over the years, rising to become Emory's president in 1942.[2]

> *With the ongoing transformation of traditional southern life, though, and the outpouring of new money for education, change was clearly coming to Emory. The struggle that would occupy its leadership for a decade and a half was how to shape that change, or at least keep it under control.*

An affable man and an able administrator, White was strong and stable, deferential to the Emory trustees, and personally conservative. When he took the reins at Emory, civilian male students had all but disappeared from campus, the University's already tight finances became even tighter, and wartime concerns dominated the early years of his administration.

At the end of the war the school was struggling. White understood that Emory was nowhere near as academically advanced as some others in the South, most notably Vanderbilt and Duke. His response to the new funding environment in American higher education was positive, but cautious. Though committed to Emory's improvement and to pursuing national stature for the University, he was not one to rush into major changes.

Emory resumed its master's-level offerings as soon as possible and authorized its first PhD program in 1946, yet growth was methodical rather than explosive. Moreover, Emory was officially and tightly tied to the Methodist Church, whose conservative influence on the board of trustees was strong. Equally strong was the influence of the Atlanta business community, which provided nearly all the rest of Emory's board members. A study of the state's political process done in 1947 concluded that Georgia's large corporate interests, based in Atlanta, had mastered that process so well that they were the de facto rulers of Georgia. A mere handful of people, nearly all businessmen, effectively ran the city itself. These were all rich men, all "white, Anglo-Saxon, Protestant, Atlantan, business-oriented, non-political, moderate, well-bred, well-educated, pragmatic, and dedicated to the betterment of Atlanta."[3]

White's position on the emerging changes in southern race relations was deeply cautious, perhaps unsurprising given his personality and upbringing. He was born in 1889 and spent his boyhood in Griffin, a county seat town in middle Georgia. In a 1959 autobiographical sketch he reminisced about the world of his youth, a world he described as "closer in time to the Georgia of [A.B.] Longstreet's *Georgia Scenes* [1835] than to the Georgia—at least to the

Atlanta—of to-day." It was a world of cotton tenancy and sharecropping, with a mill village across the railroad tracks from town, and Saturdays spent around the courthouse square. White grew up in town, working at a general store and excelling in school. His family life revolved around the Methodist church, where his grandfather was pastor. This was also a world of Jim Crow segregation: "There were Negro schools and Negro churches. That they were any of my concern was never suggested. We saw Negroes every day. They worked in the kitchens and in the yards and gardens; as nursemaids; as porters and waiters in the two small hotels; they drove the drays." Despite White's recollection of a Sunday afternoon lynching that greatly upset his grandfather, for a young boy these arrangements were simply beyond questioning. "The Negroes' status was fixed," he explained, "and as far as I knew there was no 'race problem.'" [4]

Not unreasonably, White feared that rapid changes in these traditional arrangements could set off a violent white backlash. The volatile racial politics that overtook Georgia after the war fed this fear. Long before segregation became an incendiary issue in the politics of other southern states, Georgia's gubernatorial contests revolved around race. The Democratic Party, which controlled the state, supported the rapid economic growth and modernization that followed the war. But it also vigorously resisted any change to the state's traditional social order. This contradictory stance kept race relations at the forefront of politics for decades.[5] Maintaining segregation became a line in the sand for many Georgians who were unhappy that their old world was disappearing before their eyes.

Georgia's county unit election system created a sort of unbalanced state-level electoral college. Each county had two, four, or six votes, determined by population. Those votes were delivered as a unit to the candidate who garnered the most popular votes in the county. This system was designed to prevent urban areas from completely controlling the state, and it did so very effectively. Biased against the most populous counties, it prevented candidates for statewide office from winning by simply courting the powerful commercial interests in Atlanta.[6] Although this support was critical, so were the votes of the rural, traditional, and increasingly unhappy people in the counties of South Georgia. Politicians soon learned that full-out racial demagoguery and a fervid insistence on maintaining "southern traditions" gained votes outside Atlanta. And while sophisticated businessmen in the city may have felt distaste at the vigor and style of this invective, they were not offended by the core of the message and were willing to go along if politicians continued to serve their economic interests.[7]

In 1942 Ellis Arnall made race a gubernatorial campaign issue and defeated incumbent Eugene Talmadge, helped in part by Talmadge's heavy-handed attempts to purge the faculty of the University of Georgia of "integrationists" the year before. Talmadge's actions had cost the state's universities their accreditation and dealt a blow to the state's reputation and to Atlanta's business interests.[8] From this moment forward, the key issue in Georgia politics was segregation. The 1946 Democratic primary—the only election that counted—pitted two progressives against the traditionalist Talmadge in a savage campaign fought largely over white supremacy. Talmadge used a recent Supreme Court decision, *Smith v. Allwright*, which invalidated the white primary, to conjure up images of federal tyranny and black rule. Robert Mizell (College 1911), a longtime Emory administrator and confidant of Coca-Cola president Robert Woodruff, summed up the situation in Atlanta in February 1946: "Not since the Atlanta riots some forty years ago has the race question been such an inflammable issue as now." Talmadge's victory, though followed almost immediately by his death, set the tone for Georgia politics well into the 1960s. His son Herman became governor in 1948, campaigning on a promise to reinstate the white primary. These divisive elections kept racial fears at a boil throughout the 1940s and beyond.[9]

As president of Emory, Goodrich White understood this political reality fully. His own beliefs about race also help explain his reluctance to confront directly the internal and external pressures for racial change that grew during his tenure. White cogently articulated his views when he served on President Truman's Commission on Higher Education, organized in the summer of 1946. Formed amid the changes that swirled in the wake of the war, this group undertook a formal reexamination of the "objectives, methods and facilities" of American higher education "in light of the social role it has to play."[10] In October 1947 the subcommittee on "Equalizing and Expanding Individual Opportunity" presented its draft report to the full commission and called for the complete elimination of segregated higher education in the South. White did not speak up until it was time for the full commission to approve the subcommittee reports, and even then he tried to keep a low profile.[11]

> *Robert Mizell (College 1911), a longtime Emory administrator and confidant of Coca-Cola president Robert Woodruff, summed up the situation in Atlanta in February 1946: "Not since the Atlanta riots some forty years ago has the race question been such an inflammable issue as now."*

In a written dissent and in personal correspondence, White explained why he rejected the group's judgment. The naiveté of the northerners who dominated the commission, White argued, led them to sunder common sense from theory. Their insistence on immediate elimination of segregated higher education amounted to zealotry, the refusal to acknowledge the practical limitations of laudable principles of democracy and equality. Their recommendations, while inspired by "high purpose and theoretical idealism," were "wholly doctrinaire positions which ignore the facts of history and the realities of the present."[12]

White was not insensible to the injustices of segregation. He acknowledged the "gross inequality of opportunity, economic and educational," and urged that "as rapidly as possible conditions should be improved, inequalities removed, and greater opportunity should be provided for all our people." But eliminating segregation at a stroke, he argued, would have the opposite effect than the one desired; it would incite furious opposition to black progress. Only incremental change would produce improvement. "There are men of good will in the South," he wrote, "who are concerned about inequalities and injustice and who are working quietly and persistently . . . to strengthen existing institutions of higher education for Negroes. . . . It is my own conviction that their patient and persistent 'gradualism' is the only way to accomplishment without conflict and tragedy."[13]

White's insistence that the good works of southern whites would eventually solve the problem failed to persuade the other commissioners. Only three (all southerners) out of twenty-seven joined White in his dissent. The rest argued forcefully that the principles of democracy and equality under the law required them to challenge segregation. Failure to do so, they argued, would be "unfair and an insult to the whole of the South—Negro and white." They took the opportunity provided by White's formal dissent to strengthen the report's condemnation of segregation.[14]

In his 1959 memoir White spoke of his regret at the South's failure to confront on its own its problems with race and its relation to its past and to the rest of the country:

> There have been times when I thought—perhaps it was only wishful thinking—that the South was well on the way to mastery of its [race] problem and the attainment of maturity, properly cherishing whatever is admirable in its past but not trying to live *in* it and *on* it, facing the issues of the day as Americans, divided perhaps among ourselves but not always having our positions brought to the test of whether or no they are properly "Southern." But I can no longer delude myself or even cherish the hope. . . . And it is hardest of all to satisfy my conscience and to define the fine line between patience, wisdom and justifiable prudence on the one hand and cowardice on the other.[15]

This fine line was the one that White chose to walk as president of Emory. On one hand, he believed that segregation led to gross injustices. Surrounded by accomplished men and women in Atlanta's black colleges as well as in the city's black business class, he was far from blind to the unfair treatment meted out to them in the name of tradition.[16] On the other hand, he felt constrained by political circumstances, by the heavy weight of tradition, and by demagogues' manipulation of that tradition. White consistently chose a guarded path. Unlike some leaders in southern higher education who pushed for real, if gradual, desegregation, he supported a "fairer" segregation, one that would provide more opportunities for blacks within black institutions. Rather than attempt to break down the color line at Emory, he turned his attention to the improvement of Georgia's segregated institutions. No hypocrite, White served for years on the board of Clark College, a historically black undergraduate college in Atlanta, and worked throughout his adult life with other black institutions. Improving these schools, he believed, was the only racial progress that white Georgians would peacefully accept.[17]

By 1953 the informal presence of a few blacks on campus was generally accepted, and student and faculty contact with their counterparts at the city's black colleges had become rather routine.

Despite White's growing unease, the turmoil in Georgia politics, and the rising pressure from outside the region, the Emory campus itself remained quiet. Still, tiny cracks were beginning to appear. Emory hosted an occasional black speaker, usually at the chapel or the Candler School of Theology.[18] A handful of blacks applied for admission. (The applications were simply returned.)[19] The student newspaper, the *Wheel*, editorialized in favor of changes in race relations, including limited admissions of black students to the University.[20] That there were limits, however, was still quite clear. In February 1948, the Freshman Emory Christian Association invited Rev. Harrison McMains, a local white minister active in interracial church activities, to speak on "The Teachings of Jesus as Applied to Race Relations." This led to an invitation to the dean of Morehouse College, a black economist, to discuss Christianity and labor relations. In the course of that evening, the group agreed that they would like to invite Morehouse students to the next meeting. The sensitivity of a dinner meeting with blacks was apparent even to freshmen, though, and after consultation with several Emory administrators, they dropped the idea.[21]

Amid growing tension over race, however, the mere idea of such a meeting was enough to enrage at least one opponent of change. It isn't clear how he learned of the proposed meeting, but John A. Dunaway (College 1920, Law 1923) sent White a scathing letter, implying that the president was a hypocrite if he allowed mixed meetings on campus. Dunaway also complained to trustee Henry Bowden, who sat on the board's executive committee. Bowden suggested that Dunaway, a lawyer, prepare a synopsis of Georgia segregation law "in order that Emory might conform fully." Interestingly, that law contained nothing that would prevent the sort of meetings that Dunaway found so offensive. (Bowden, a sophisticated and canny attorney, likely knew this already.) Nonetheless, Dunaway accurately insisted that although segregation in Georgia was "not a matter of written law," it was certainly "inherent in our background and training." In the end, after receiving a mild scolding from White's assistant, Boisfeuillet Jones (College 1934, Law 1937), Dunaway backed off, claiming that he had only been concerned with Emory's reputation.[22]

Where students did not mean to upset anyone, White defended their right to hear whatever speakers they chose. He was less patient when they seemed deliberately provocative. At all private southern universities, student support for antisegregationist Henry Wallace's 1948 bid for the presidency was viewed anxiously by the presidents as a magnet for unwanted outside attention. So when, in March 1948, the Emory University Wallace for President Club passed a "Resolution on Discrimination in Education" urging White and the trustees to consider "admission of Negroes to the University on all levels," White responded with a letter meant to cut off debate. He outlined his personal commitment to black progress, citing his service on the boards of black institutions. But he chastised the group for making a public fuss, arguing that "the pressure tactics now being resorted to" made solutions harder to find. Finally, White arrived at the bottom line: "It is obvious that, holding these convictions, I shall not recommend the admission of Negroes to Emory University."[23]

As the 1950s began, the pace of change quickened. The Communist victory in China and the outbreak of war in Korea further undermined the national sense of security and brought the rise of militant anticommunism in American politics. Wide and deep changes continued to spread throughout the South. As manufacturing industries grew, so did southern cities. By 1950 there were thirty with at least 100,000 people; ten had 250,000 or more. The region's population had increased by nearly 4 million since 1940. These changes, though, were erratic. In many small towns and rural areas, life continued much as it always had.[24] Change was also coming to race relations, although much of it simmered beneath the surface of daily life. By the summer of 1951 the five cases that would be consolidated as *Brown v. Board of Education of Topeka* had been filed, and the issue of school segregation suddenly took on much greater importance. At the same time, the desegregation of public graduate and professional schools as the result of NAACP lawsuits continued at a steady pace.[25]

On the Emory campus, energies pent up during the long war effort were released. A building boom remade the campus, and the influx of outside funding began to bear fruit. In 1951 the University received a $7 million grant from the General Education Board of the Rockefeller Foundation that required Emory to raise a $25 million match. Progress was difficult; aggressive fund-raising did not seem to come naturally at Emory. Still, by 1955 nine departments were offering the doctorate, and forty-five PhDs had been granted since the approval of the first program in 1946. This change, however, was not a headlong rush. The University exercised great care in approving new programs, attempting to ensure that every Emory degree would be worthy of respect.

Emory remained thoroughly segregated. Although pressure for desegregation began to build from outside the University, most notably in the academic disciplinary societies and the large private philanthropies, there was little pressure for racial change from within. The *Wheel* did show some interest: on January 27, 1950, the paper editorialized in favor of limited desegregation at Emory. The following fall, with a new editorial staff, it changed its mind and argued against it.[26] President White's formal reports to the board of trustees in the early fifties don't mention race at all, not even when direct pressure came from outside, as when the American Association of Law Schools contemplated a resolution that would force southern law schools to desegregate or face expulsion.

While White's personal views and cautious nature explain some of his reluctance to raise racial issues with the trustees, also critically important was the attitude of Emory's board chair, Charles Howard Candler Sr. (College 1898, Medicine 1902, Honorary 1942). Howard, as he was called, was the son of Asa G. Candler, the founder of Coca-Cola and chairman of Emory University's trustees from 1906 until his death in 1929. Howard was also the nephew of Methodist Bishop Warren Akin Candler, who was instrumental in the creation of Emory University and served as the University's first chief executive. Howard Candler assumed the leadership of the board upon his father's death and held it until his own in 1957. A generous donor to Emory, Candler was a very active chair and ruled the board with an iron hand.[27]

Candler's views on race were deeply traditional. Even the smallest breach of Atlanta's segregation etiquette offended him, and he saw no reason to keep his unhappiness to himself. A conference on "The Churches and World Order" scheduled at Emory's Glenn Memorial Church in April 1953 presented one occasion for Candler's wrath. By 1953 the informal presence of a few blacks on campus was generally accepted, and student and faculty contact with their counterparts at the city's black colleges had become rather routine. The pastor of Atlanta's Wheat Street Baptist Church, Dr. William Holmes Borders, for example, spoke at vesper services in the Alumni Memorial University Center during Brotherhood Week in February. In October, the Emory Wesley Fellowship sponsored a weekend retreat with delegates from six colleges, including Morehouse.[28] It's not clear why Candler would object to the April church conference but not to these other events. Most likely, he simply never became aware of them. But someone took the trouble to send him a brochure announcing the conference, and when he discovered that the organizers planned to welcome "all persons, regardless of race," Candler fired off an angry and threatening letter to Goodrich White, concluding with instructions to cancel the conference and to prevent "any such function" in the future.[29]

White did not cancel the meeting but replied to Candler with barely cloaked irritation: "At present I must say that I cannot, on my own initiative, take any steps looking to the cancellation of this engagement. To precipitate an issue over this meeting would, in my judgment, be unwise, unjustified, and hurtful." Later the same afternoon White drafted a longer letter to Candler, which he apparently did not send, opting instead to raise the matter when the executive committee met on April 16. Defending the conference, which had been scheduled by Dean Burton Trimble of the School of Theology, White noted that it would be "discourteous and embarrassing" for Emory to force the cancellation of the event, which was cosponsored by some of the most prominent and respectable Protestant organizations in the city. He stressed that there was to be no "social intermingling" between blacks and whites at the event—that is, no "housing or meal service" provided.[30]

White claimed that his position on interracial meetings at Emory was "reasonably clear," but it was not. He scrutinized each situation, rejecting some meetings and allowing others, but he never articulated any principles behind those decisions. (One meeting he disallowed was of the Judicial Council of the Methodist Church—the church's "Supreme Court"—because it had a Negro member.) If White had any yardstick, it seemed to be that if contact between blacks and whites would not attract attention or controversy, then it was acceptable. His goal was apparently to avoid alarming or embarrassing anyone.[31]

White clearly hated having to deal with these matters at all. Also clear is his sense of being caught in the middle, drawing criticism for cowardice from some quarters and for going too far from others. He increasingly sat between the growing desire of the faculty and many students for change and the insistence of a traditionalist board on keeping the old ways. What White wanted was the freedom to deal with these unpleasant issues as they arose, with no pressure from either side. He believed that he knew how to make these decisions without public controversy. He was probably right.

Things began to change in 1954. Although the decision was expected, *Brown v. Board of Education* hit Georgia like a bombshell. The failure of President Eisenhower to publicly support the decision gave room for evasion, and the rise of white "massive resistance" transformed the atmosphere in Georgia into one of crisis.[32] Segregation became nearly the only issue in public life. Governor Herman Talmadge was committed to resistance and had already proposed a constitutional amendment to permit state support of segregated schooling through grants to individual students. Many Georgians, concerned about the quality of their children's education, strongly opposed this "private school plan." Many others, more concerned about race mixing, strongly supported it.[33]

The November 1954 election would determine both the fate of the proposed amendment and the governor's seat (Talmadge was prevented by law from another term). The September Democratic primary, the real election, was hotly contested. Of nine candidates, one advocated compliance with the Supreme Court decision and eight offered plans to evade it. The winner was Lieutenant Governor Marvin Griffin, a member of the Talmadge faction, who ran on a platform of preserving both segregation and the county unit system, and whose mandate to do so was strengthened by the easy passage of Talmadge's "private school plan."[34]

As ever, control of Georgia depended on control of the rural base and the cooperation of Atlanta's business community. But as race relations became paramount after *Brown*, the interests of those two groups diverged. In the rural counties, tampering with segregation remained anathema. Atlanta was different. Increasingly dominated by large corporations, the city was also home to several prominent black colleges, powerful black churches, and influential black leaders. The city's large black population had a small but real voice in politics.[35] Relatively smooth race relations prevailed, the product of cooperation between black and white leaders who shared concern for maintaining a stable business environment. Whatever their private opinions on race, Atlanta's leaders valued calm more than segregation, and economic growth and national influence more than the esteem of Georgia crackers.[36]

Emory increasingly shared this desire to participate in the life of the larger nation. As it grew and improved, Emory was drawn out of its regional orbit and into the national mainstream. It was now competing for money and for the best students and faculty with universities across the country. The growing importance of funding from the federal government and a few large foundations also meant that regional distinctiveness eroded as universities all pursued money from the same sources for the same things. By 1954 Emory had made impressive strides in improving the quality of instruction, especially in the graduate school. In addition to the grant from the General Education Board, Emory had begun participating in a program sponsored by the Carnegie Foundation for the Advancement of Teaching that provided funds to increase salaries of outstanding professors in the graduate school and the stipends of promising graduate students.[37] These grants led to greater success in attracting and retaining prominent professors. The subsequent rise in the University's reputation was not without social side effects. As more faculty came to Emory from outside the South, they often brought northern habits of mind along with their research and teaching skills. Even southerners now often identified more with their disciplinary colleagues at other universities than with their neighbors. With segregation growing rare in American universities, Emory faculty became ever more uncomfortable with it.

Classes were still in session when *Brown* was announced, and the *Wheel* quickly opened debate. On May 20 nearly the entire editorial page was devoted to the decision. The editors accepted that segregation was, in effect, finished. They hoped that graceful, gradual integration would be possible. But they also stressed the danger inherent in the decision, echoing the objections that had long been standard fare for white southerners who objected to northern interference. "While progressives are congratulating themselves," they warned, "Southern demagogues will exploit the situation to the fullest, particularly in the rural areas. Truthfully, little exploitation will be needed. In many parts of the South opinion of the Negro has remained the same since the Civil War." The *Wheel* also did informal polling of students and faculty. The faculty members and administrators they interviewed all stressed the rightness of the decision, its "inevitability." Most, however, also focused on the need for more time.[38]

The public reaction of the Emory administration was muted. In a speech to the Phi Beta Kappa chapter on May 21, President White identified the "beginnings of a break-down of racial segregation" as one of the major trends in higher education. Without engaging in any detailed discussion, he made it clear that the issue was not going away.[39] Otherwise, there is little evidence of any internal administrative discussion. In his October report to the board, White never mentioned *Brown*. The issue did come up briefly at the inaugural meeting of the "Committee of One Hundred," a group of Methodist laity headed by trustee Henry Bowden and organized by the University for fund-raising. In a wide-ranging exchange of views about the University's goals and prospects, someone raised the matter of black enrollment. The terse notes briefly mention an issue that would soon come to loom large: "Discussion of Emory's position on admission of Negroes developed the normal objections, as well as the further fact that under the laws of Georgia admission of Negroes would cause the University to lose its tax-free status, which would have a ruinous effect financially."[40]

The best evidence of the University leadership's thinking is probably an October 1954 *Emory Alumnus* editorial. While the magazine's editor, Randy Fort, had an independent streak and was given a fairly free hand in producing the *Alumnus*, it is likely that such an important piece was discussed with the administration. The editorial powerfully suggests the quandary that Emory was in. It weaves between facts that seem to mean that Emory will have to change and facts that seem to mean that it won't, while providing no principle for deciding which sets of facts ought to prevail. While Fort's piece aimed for neutrality, the overriding impression it creates is of paralysis of will.[41]

Fort's tone was calm. He assured readers that the *Brown* decision did not require Emory, a private school, to do anything at all. But he immediately noted that eighty-two previously white schools, including substantially more private than public institutions, had already opened their doors to blacks. When Emory finally faced things, he seemed to imply, the outcome was foreordained. Fort's second point was, again, designed to soothe fears. While presidents and others might recommend courses of action, he explained, "only the trustees make the policy." Those Emory trustees were all "Southerners by birth or rearing, and in almost every case by both." Of the thirty-one current trustees, twenty-five were alumni of the University. Third, Fort observed that Emory's charter never refers to race, but states simply that the purpose of the University is to promote teaching and learning under the auspices of the Methodist Church. Emory could not continue to do this without maintaining its tax-exempt status, and state law allowed exemption only as long as schools that had been "established for white people" remained exclusively white. The issue now was whether *Brown* meant the law was unconstitutional. According to Fort, the consensus of Emory's attorneys was that it was indeed, but that a test case would have to be mounted before blacks could be admitted. A mistake here could have catastrophic results: estimates put Emory's potential tax bill at about half of the University's annual budget. Fort then returned to the relationship between Emory and the Methodist Church. Bound to the church by charter, Emory could not ignore the 1952 *Discipline of the Methodist Church*, which said, "There is no place in the Methodist Church for racial discrimination or racial segregation." After this wandering disquisition Fort concluded, "This is not a problem which will just fade away and leave us, for too many publics—too many institutions, organizations, and individuals—are interestedly watching and asking questions." And it was quite clear that Emory had no answers.[42]

By the late 1950s a steady stream of highly publicized events—the Montgomery bus boycott, the acceptance and then expulsion of Autherine Lucy at the University of Alabama, the mob scenes in Little Rock, the bombing of the high school in Clinton, Tennessee—had the entire South quivering with tension. At the same time, the rest of the nation was growing more willing to apply pressure to bring about segregation's demise. And at quiet Emory, an era was about to end. In March 1955 President White announced that he would retire by September 1, 1957. Uncertainty and division followed. Emory's chronic financial problems worsened significantly. In White's remarks to the board at its November 1955 meeting he stressed that budget cuts, while necessary to avoid continuing deficits, were coming dangerously close to destroying morale on campus. At nearly the same time, Georgia's political leaders threatened to close Atlanta's public schools rather than allow even token desegregation. For the Emory faculty, many of whom had children in these schools, this was profoundly alarming.[43]

Any public discussion of desegregation at Emory now drew fire from some alumni and board members. One example is the reaction to a 1956 editorial in the *Emory Alumnus* about Georgia's plan to close public schools that the federal courts desegregated. This piece, again written by Randy Fort, argued that such action would be disastrous. It meant "Emory's student body would deteriorate in quality, rapidly and steadily." Perhaps more important, the University's faculty would begin to erode. The response to this piece was furious. One irate alumnus copied board chair Howard Candler on his letter of complaint. Candler commended the writer, applauding his anger at "the unjustifiable use of the *Emory Alumnus* as a medium for propaganda." Angry letters, he believed, "will restrain Mr. Fort if he is ever again tempted to publish in our fine magazine his personal opinion of matters which do not properly belong in it."[44]

Fort's point, though, was that Emory could no longer avoid the debate. Events on campus bore him out as student agitation on both sides of the question became common. Throughout 1955–56 the *Wheel* argued for desegregation, also printing a prosegregation column written by former governor Herman Talmadge and a long letter by Georgia's attorney general, Eugene Cook, which kept the issue prominently visible. A Presbyterian student group, the Westminster Fellowship, submitted a statement to the *Wheel* that decried the possibility of closing the public schools in order to prevent desegregation. Officially, Emory continued its refusal to consider change. In a meeting with a student development committee in early 1957, White answered questions about desegregation by declaring it impossible. His explanation was simple: admitting blacks would end Emory's tax exemption, destroying its finances.[45]

> *By the late 1950s a steady stream of highly publicized events—the Montgomery bus boycott, the acceptance and then expulsion of Autherine Lucy at the University of Alabama, the mob scenes in Little Rock, the bombing of the high school in Clinton, Tennessee—had the entire South quivering with tension.... Any public discussion of desegregation at Emory now drew fire from some alumni and board members.*

In the waning days of White's tenure, the dean of the Candler School of Theology, William Ragsdale Cannon, appointed a special faculty committee to consider the changing racial situation. While members of the theology faculty had long been active in promoting better race relations, as a group they had seemed reluctant to press the case, perhaps aware of Howard Candler's views on segregation. A faculty resolution, brief and carefully worded, resulted from this report. It requested that, in line with the urging of the 1956 *Methodist Discipline*, the University conduct a study of the racial policies of the School of Theology, "making sure that these policies and practices are Christian." The faculty also expressed a "willingness and readiness to have [black graduate students] as members of our classes and of the student body." Finally, they assured the trustees that they understood the "complex and delicate nature of the problems involved in this request" and would treat the matter as confidential. Prayers would also be said. In perfect keeping with his long-standing reluctance to press this issue, White sent this resolution on to the trustees with a brief note: "I have no recommendation to make with reference to action by the Board." The board, of course, took no action.[46]

Understandably, the selection of a new president dominated this board meeting. Immediately after adjournment, Chairman Candler announced the election of Dr. S. Walter Martin as the University's fifteenth president. A native of Tifton, Georgia, born in 1911, Martin attended Furman University and trained as a historian at the University of Georgia and the University of North Carolina. He joined the University of Georgia faculty in 1935 and rose steadily in administration. In 1949 he was appointed dean of the College of Arts and Sciences, a position he held until he accepted the presidency at Emory.[47]

Martin was a dedicated and active Methodist layman. His religious commitment, coupled with his success as an administrator, had led several smaller Methodist colleges to try to recruit him as president. Happy in Athens, he always refused. When the search committee from Emory approached him, Martin was swayed for the first time. Howard Candler chaired the committee, which included two Methodist bishops, and he was determined that Emory's next president be someone who would strengthen the University's ties with the church. Martin, nonetheless, was far from certain that moving to Emory was the right thing. He was well regarded at the University of Georgia, his family was established in Athens, and he was comfortable in his church. Assured by Candler that he was needed, though, Martin agreed. He was elected unanimously by the board and agreed to a starting date of September 1, 1957.

The unanimous vote, however, concealed deep fractures. In the seventeen months since Goodrich White had announced his retirement, several internal candidates for the presidency had appeared. These were among the most powerful and able men on campus, and several could reasonably entertain the notion of becoming president. By contrast, when Martin's name leaked out as a possible successor to White, howls of protest went up. Faculty members who could agree on little else agreed that a dean from the University of Georgia—a school they considered a "cow college"—was an inappropriate choice. A group of senior faculty members, most of them department chairs, took the audacious step of writing to Candler with their objections. Claiming "the support of a substantial majority of [their] colleagues," they asserted that Martin did not "incorporate personally or professionally that combination of qualities so essential for vigorous and effective guidance of Emory's future destiny." Candler ignored this letter.[48]

These faculty members were mistaken in many of their judgments about Martin, but in some sense they were correct: Martin and Emory were not a good match. Martin always remained close to his roots, both social and religious. He was uninterested in Atlanta society—unimpressed by his new memberships, provided by Emory, in tony private dining and country clubs, a man more at home at a Methodist church supper than at the Piedmont Driving Club. This lack of interest in being one of the boys in Atlanta's upper crust would hinder Martin throughout his time at Emory.

Hearing of Martin's selection, President G. B. Connell of Mercer University welcomed him to "the aspirin fraternity." Indeed, even apart from the copious fence mending he would need to do, Martin was in for plenty of headaches at Emory.[49] In May, well before he arrived as president, he received an ominous letter from Dean Rusk, then head of the General Education Board of the Rockefeller Foundation. "I am anxious," said Rusk, "to have a long talk with you about the background and future of the General Education Board's grant for the development of graduate studies at Emory." This grant, made in 1951, gave a desperately needed $7 million but required $25 million in matching funds. Emory had not been able to raise it. This embarrassing situation was a harbinger of things to come for Martin. Although he returned from his meeting with Rusk with a check for $1 million and an agreement to let Emory off the hook, Martin would be beset by fund-raising problems. In his first report to the trustees he identified money as the most critical problem facing the University.[50] Martin's troubles expanded exponentially when Howard Candler died only a few months after Martin took office. Candler had most wanted Martin at Emory, and without Candler's dominating presence on the board, Martin was hamstrung.

Like Goodrich White, Martin was no advocate of integration and would never push the Emory board to admit blacks. Still, like White, Martin was not one to give in to pressure to muffle the faculty or students. Contacts with black professors and student groups continued during the late 1950s, and Martin never considered stopping them, despite sometimes furious threats from angry segregationists. Rather, he tried to act as a peacemaker, a moderate who could avoid disaster by keeping outright division at bay. This was an incredibly difficult balancing act, especially in the late 1950s, when rising pressures from all quarters both for and against racial change meant that any day could bring fresh trouble.[51]

Martin was uneasy about change in the South generally. The economic and social transformations since World War II unsettled him, and he feared that prosperity would result in moral decay. Like White, Martin said little publicly about race. In speech after speech to alumni clubs, parents, students, and religious groups, he discussed the changes that swept the South without mentioning blacks or Atlanta's increasing turmoil over race.[52] The city had remained calm for most of the decade, largely because of the business community's desire for stability. Together with Mayor William B. Hartsfield, Atlanta's power brokers had negotiated slow but steady progress in race relations during the 1940s and 1950s.[53] This progress was threatened by the rise of massive resistance after *Brown*. Finally, in January 1958 the NAACP Legal Defense and

Education Fund filed a class-action suit in the northern district of Georgia seeking the desegregation of Atlanta's public schools.[54] The outcome of the case was never in doubt, and most of Atlanta was probably ready to begin token desegregation. Georgia law, however, with its provisions for closing public schools rather than integrating them, stood in the way. The scene was set for several years of intense conflict between Atlanta and the rest of the state.[55]

This threat spurred Emory's faculty to action. In late November 1958 a statement bearing the signatures of the overwhelming majority of Emory professors, including several prominent administrators, was delivered to the *Atlanta Journal and Constitution*. The statement strongly objected to closing the schools, but race was hardly mentioned. Instead, the faculty's arguments focused on the increasingly high cost of resisting change. Echoing the reasoning of the business community, the faculty argued that the loss of industry that would certainly follow closing the schools would harm the economic welfare of the entire state. Any interruption in the educational system would eventually lead to a shortage of trained service providers, from doctors to county agricultural agents. Closing the schools would also allow the Soviet Union to succeed in its "systematic attempt to overtake us educationally."[56]

> *At Emory, Martin had his hands full. A vocal contingent of students and faculty clamored for change. Many trustees and alumni, just as vocal, were unalterably opposed. And Emory was desperately in need of money—a lot of it.*

Far more interesting than the statement was the reaction to it. It is impossible to imagine Howard Candler responding with anything but fury. Indeed, the faculty half expected that there would be consequences.[57] But Candler's successor as chairman of Emory's board, Henry Bowden, was a thoroughly different person. A trial lawyer, Bowden relied on persuasion rather than power. He also shared the perspectives of Atlanta's sophisticated business community, including a reluctance to see the schools closed. Bowden's response to the faculty statement was sanguine. He did not express approval of its contents, but took pains to support the right of the faculty to speak out. He contrasted this with the situation at "tax supported institutions in our State," where professors who wanted to take similar stands were "thwarted by administrations which shuddered at the thought of reduced appropriations, open criticisms from politicians and embarrassing days ahead." This calm response sent an unmistakable signal that a new day had dawned. Bowden would be the one to lead Emory through the difficult terrain ahead.[58]

But Emory's own policies on race relations still did not change. By now, the normally placid campus roiled. A forum held during the annual "Brotherhood Week" in February brought several speakers to campus to discuss the topic, "What Are the Basic Issues of the Racial Crisis?" Dr. Harry Richardson, president of historically black Gammon Theological Seminary, and James M. Dabbs, of the Southern Regional Council of the Presbyterian Church, advocated for open schools and desegregation. A special issue of the *Emory Alumnus*, "Crisis in the Schools," focused on Atlanta's racial problems.[59] Both the speakers and the article quickly drew strong objection from Emory alumni, but this time Emory officials sprang to Randy Fort's defense.[60]

Articles and seminars, however, would not satisfy proponents of integration. In March, the *Wheel* carried a short but portentous story. Twelve members of the Atlanta chapter of the Congress of Racial Equality (CORE), including several Emory students, picketed outside Rich's Department Store in Atlanta. Emory faculty members were also involved with the group, which had staged the demonstrations against the wishes of Atlanta's black leadership.[61] Holding the peace was going to require accommodation.

The new decade opened with the threat of public school closures still hanging over Georgia. Following the federal court's 1959 order for Atlanta's public schools to desegregate, the city's school board submitted a grade-per-year plan, beginning with twelfth grade. Judge Frank A. Hooper approved it but waited for the Georgia General Assembly to meet in January 1960 before he ordered implementation. Mayor Hartsfield asked the legislature to repeal its mandatory school closure law and allow Atlanta to determine its own course. It was unclear what would happen. Governor Ernest Vandiver, though publicly committed to resistance, had no taste for the consequences of closed schools. But most white Georgians would rather have closed the schools than integrate, and most Georgia politicians vocally supported them.[62] In February, tensions began to ease a bit when the General Assembly appointed a commission of prominent Georgians to hold statewide hearings on desegregation and the public schools. Heading the commission was John A. Sibley, president of Atlanta's Trust Company Bank, a partner in the law firm of King and Spalding, and former general counsel for The Coca-Cola Company. While Sibley did not like desegregation, he understood that massive resistance would devastate Atlanta. In complex and subtle ways, his conduct of the hearings during the late winter and spring of 1960 helped avert outright crisis.[63]

Meanwhile, other events contributed to the tense atmosphere. Martin Luther King Jr. returned to Atlanta, worrying many whites. Students from the city's black colleges published a full-page "Appeal for Human Rights" in the *Atlanta Constitution*. Demonstrations continued throughout the spring, and students (including some from Emory) planned a boycott of Rich's department store.[64]

On campus, the uncertainty took a growing toll. At the end of 1959 President Martin told the trustees that the public school situation "was without question an important factor in nearly all [faculty] resignations." Replacing those who left was nearly impossible. The *Emory Alumnus* reported that "Emory has had turndown after turndown from able young teachers it has wanted to employ from colleges in other states. They simply would not bring their children into a climate where the future of public education is uncertain. Nor will many professors now at Emory stay any longer if the situation grows much worse."[65]

Then, a seemingly minor incident galvanized faculty opposition to Emory's racial policies. In early March the board forced Emory's Glee Club to cancel an appearance at Tuskegee Institute, citing the possibility of a violent reaction to a white choir singing—and staying overnight—at a black college. Martin supported the cancellation but sent a conciliatory letter, which William Archie, dean of the College of Arts and Sciences, read to a faculty meeting in mid-March. The letter provoked a wide-ranging discussion of Emory's racial policies. Archie warned the faculty that the time was not "propitious to have the Board confront these issues officially," but they refused to drop the matter. Acting on unanimous vote by the faculty, Archie appointed a committee to meet with Martin and discuss "the Tuskegee episode and related questions of policy with respect to Faculty and student relations with the Negro community." Predictably, the group left that meeting unhappy.[66]

Martin was now truly caught between the faculty and the trustees. Emory professors continued aggressively pushing, inviting students and faculty members from black colleges to the Emory campus, participating alongside students in demonstrations, and drafting resolutions. The board, though led by the consummately practical Bowden, was not pleased about public identification of Emory professors and students with integration.

On March 31 Martin tried to calm tensions with a formal talk to selected faculty members. He warned them that, although they undeniably had the right to participate in community affairs, that right must be exercised appropriately. He argued that Emory had no duty to help lead Georgia through this trouble, and he defended its commitment to segregation:

> Emory University is subject to the customs and laws of Georgia. Some of you may wish that Emory were elsewhere, but it is in the South. We simply cannot get too far out in front of the community in which we live, or else we ruin ourselves. History teaches that; nature teaches that. The climate must be right. I can easily see this University on the road to destruction if we get too far out in front.[67]

It is a measure of how bad things had become that Martin thought this kind of lecture would quiet the faculty. It had, in fact, no discernible effect. On May 6 the College of Arts and Sciences passed a resolution that called "for Emory to make all of its facilities available without reference to race." In a direct challenge to Martin, the resolution stated that "in assessing the possibility of adopting such a policy it should be borne in mind that Emory has a national as well as a local constituency." When the board met the following week, this resolution prompted "lively discussion," but resulted only in a brisk letter from Henry Bowden saying that "the request . . . cannot be granted."[68]

Still the faculty persisted. The University Senate had also been considering Emory's racial policies but had not yet reached firm conclusions. On May 25 the Arts and Sciences representative offered an identical resolution along with a copy of Bowden's dismissive letter. With Martin voting against the resolution, the Senate adopted it by a six-to-five vote. The Arts and Sciences faculty now set up a committee to study ways to implement the resolution and to communicate with the administration and board. The members understood that they needed the cooperation of the trustees and hoped to meet with some of them informally. From Martin's point of view, the best news was probably that the group did not plan to meet over the summer.[69]

By the time classes began in the fall of 1960, Georgia's public school crisis was again acute. The Sibley Commission had issued its report in April, recommending that the state establish "a system of education within the limitations of the Supreme Court decision, yet one which will secure the maximum segregation within the law, which will vest the control of its schools in the people of the community." Although many, especially in rural areas, still insisted that segregation was more important than schools, the Atlanta community largely supported the Sibley Commission recommendations. Judge Hooper postponed implementation of his order until the fall of 1961.[70]

Demonstrations and sit-ins at downtown Atlanta lunch counters also resumed that fall. On October 19 Martin Luther King Jr. was arrested along with fifty-one students for violating trespass laws after being refused service at the restaurant in Rich's department store. Mayor Hartsfield quickly negotiated the students' release from city jails, but it took an appeal from Robert Kennedy to secure King's freedom. Demonstrations stopped until late November.[71]

At Emory, Martin had his hands full. A vocal contingent of students and faculty clamored for change. Many trustees and alumni, just as vocal, were unalterably opposed. And Emory was desperately in need of money—a lot of it. Never really happy at Emory, Martin was by now miserable, regularly receiving angry phone calls and lectures from all sides. Still, doing his best to salvage the situation, he kept communication open and helped create a special committee of faculty, administrators, and trustees to discuss segregation. It was far from clear that this could accomplish anything at all. Then, on January 12, 1961—the day after a mob rioted outside Charlayne Hunter's dorm room when she enrolled at the University of Georgia—Henry Bowden decided to act. He appointed a committee "to study the policy of Emory University relative to the admission of negroes as students, and to recommend to the Executive Committee at its February 1961 meeting such changes, if any, it feels would be proper."

The membership of this committee resembled an Atlanta Chamber of Commerce roster, and Bowden himself attended the meetings.[72] Most of these men may have preferred segregation. Their bottom-line mentality, though, as well as their privileged and insulated social positions, led them to value other things more than racial separation. They would not keep racial restrictions at the cost of prosperity and prestige.[73] From their first meeting, their only real focus was on the threat of losing the Georgia tax exemption for segregated schools. Integration could potentially cost millions of dollars and end Emory's drive for national prominence. On the other hand, federal research grants to segregated schools already were being restricted and the Civil Rights Commission was calling for a total ban, a possibility that could likewise cost Emory millions of dollars and end the drive for national prominence.[74]

Two days later, President Martin sent a note to one of the committee members: "I believe, as most of you do, that desegregation is coming in all of our schools, so we might as well face it now, and in doing so settle it in our own way." This indeed was the committee's general position. Early drafts of an interim report stressed continuity, citing faithfulness to the school's primary goal of academic excellence. This, the report suggested, would never change. The only thing that would be different was that a class of applicants that Emory had not traditionally accepted would now be eligible for admission. Martin strongly preferred gradual desegregation beginning with the graduate programs, fearing a flood of strong applications from Atlanta's black high schools that would overwhelm the College. The trustees, somewhat surprisingly, disagreed, arguing that this would only drag the controversy out.[75]

The tax exemption, though, was a serious sticking point. There was good reason to believe that the state would not revoke it. Several black colleges now admitted whites and retained the tax status, as did the already desegregated public universities. The dean of Emory's law school, Ben Johnson Jr., doubted that the state would "invite such a crisis on their own motion." With state universities now desegregated and Atlanta's public schools about to be, there would seem to be no point in destroying Emory University. Still, it was, after all, a lot to risk.[76]

In late spring 1961 the executive committee approved the final report and directed that it be presented to the full board in May, but for some reason it was not. The campus was expecting an announcement, and when there was none, anger and dismay followed. Martin and Bowden received anxious letters. The College of Arts and Sciences Legislative Council passed a resolution deploring the board's failure to act. To calm the situation, Martin told Dean William Archie that the board would seek a declaratory judgment on the constitutionality of the racial restriction in the tax exemption, possibly as early as November, though he made no promises.[77]

By the fall board meeting, Georgia's political atmosphere was far different than it had been a year earlier. The January showdown over desegregation at the University of Georgia had forced Governor Vandiver to take a stand, and he judiciously chose to accept federal authority. Almost immediately support for keeping the public schools open mushroomed, and lawmakers overturned the massive resistance legislation in a special session. In Atlanta, after meticulous planning by the mayor and civic leaders, the public schools opened peacefully on a (barely) integrated basis. Downtown, relentless boycotts and sit-ins had paralyzed business through February. White merchants were ready to negotiate, and by fall of 1961 the stores were desegregated. Peace had returned.[78] Emory's trustees now felt that they could safely act. The special committee submitted its report, noting that nothing in Emory's charter forbade the admission of blacks and that the University's admissions standards would not change. The board announced that Emory would admit blacks to all programs—"when and if it can do so without jeopardizing constitutional and statutory tax-exemption privileges essential to the maintenance of its educational program and facilities."[79]

Reaction to the announcement was largely favorable. Faculty members were relieved but cast a wary eye at the unresolved legal issues. A handful of alumni objected, making up for their small numbers with their remarkable stridency. The *Atlanta Constitution* praised the decision for moving Emory "a great step forward toward its ultimate position as one of the foremost seats of learning in the nation" and called on the legislature to remove the "punitive restriction" in the tax exemption.[80]

After receiving an application to the dental school from a qualified black student, Emory filed suit on March 21, 1962, carefully arguing that the tax exemption was valid but its racial restriction was not. Bowden and law dean Ben Johnson argued the case, prevailing at the Georgia Supreme Court. The final order was entered in October 1962, and Emory admitted one black part-time graduate student, a teacher in the Decatur public schools, that fall. By spring, two black women were admitted to the graduate program in nursing. The campus received them "without any turmoil or excitement whatsoever."[81]

Although Emory's trustees made the change with relative grace, there is little doubt that they would rather have kept the school white. Henry Bowden told correspondents that he would be happier if Emory could remain segregated, and that he did not want to change because of "pressure from either the government or private donors who threaten to cut us off if we do not integrate." But he also implicitly admitted that this was exactly what had happened. "Whether we like it or not," he acknowledged, "the Federal Government is deeply embedded in private as well as public education. We are of the opinion that in the not too distant future we will find Congress acting to cut off Federal funds from institutions which by charter or rules prohibit negroes from attending. If such is done and we lose this money we could continue to operate as a small ineffective college but not as a major university because our faculty will leave us if they do not have the chance to do research work." In another letter he expanded the list of outside actors who had forced the school's hand, including the foundations and the accrediting agencies. "I resent [this]," he said, "but must learn to live with it."[82]

Others on the board vigorously resisted admitting what had happened. In a letter to Martin, one trustee proclaimed that in spite of his assent to desegregation, he would never support any suggestion that segregation was wrong, or that Emory was giving in to outside pressure.[83] But willing to face it or not, Emory's trustees had most certainly been forced to desegregate. Outside pressures, and internal ones, too, ensured by 1961 that the school could no longer remain both a major university and segregated. The pragmatic response of the Atlanta business leaders to the state's public school crisis meant that the battle to preserve traditional racial relationships in Georgia, or at least in Atlanta, was already lost. There was nothing to be gained by holding out alone. The board, dominated by members of that same Atlanta business community, thus did the practical thing. The demise of segregation meant that Emory could now return its focus to the business at hand, and begin raising the money and recruiting the faculty it would need to build an institution that would grow in size, quality, and reputation throughout the decades ahead.

Grady Memorial Hospital, 1960s.

PUTTING BLACK BLOOD AND WHITE BLOOD ON THE SAME SHELF
The Integration of Grady Hospital
— JERRY GENTRY —

For more than a century and a quarter, faculty members in Atlanta's schools of medicine—largely Emory's medical school and its predecessors but also, since 1978, the Morehouse School of Medicine—have treated patients and taught students at Henry Grady Memorial Hospital, established in 1892 for the care of Atlanta's indigent. Large, complex, and battered by vexing economic forces, this great public hospital also labored for more than half its life under the burden of Jim Crow laws. The struggle to desegregate the hospital, and thereby improve medical care for all of its patients, makes for a compelling story, told here by the author of the book Grady Baby: A Year in the Life of Atlanta's Grady Hospital.[1]

ONE DAY IN 1961 Dr. Roy Bell answered the phone at his Atlanta dentistry office and was told that a "colored" woman had died at Grady Memorial Hospital because she had not been treated. Bell had no proof the story was true, but he believed it. In 1961 Atlanta, the truth of a particular story was not as important as the daily oppressive grind of segregation, which Dr. Bell faced, and despised, every day. "That was the starting point," he recalled years later. "Grady Hospital, to Atlanta, was a very image of the power structure of Georgia. It was just unthinkable. How can something like this be turned around?"[2]

The "it" he referred to was Grady's long history of segregation. Founded in 1892 for the care of Atlanta's indigent, the hospital was named for the renowned editor of the *Atlanta Constitution*, Henry Grady, who had popularized the phrase "The New South" in the 1870s and 1880s, encouraging his home city and state to move into a modern era of economic progress and national harmony promised by the resolution of the Civil War. Three years after his untimely death in 1889, the city's public hospital bearing his name opened its doors on Butler Street, across from the Atlanta Medical College, the forerunner of Emory University's School of Medicine. In that same year, the Southern Medical College, a rival medical school founded on Edgewood Avenue in 1878, relocated next door to the Atlanta Medical College, exacerbating the schools' rivalry, but bringing to Grady additional community doctors who served as faculty members of the two schools.

From the outset, then, Grady was a site for medical education. By the time Emory University was chartered in Atlanta in 1915, precipitating the move of Emory College from Oxford, changes in standards for medical education made it desirable for medical schools to affiliate with universities. In 1915, therefore, the Atlanta Medical College, which remained from the merger between the two older medical colleges, transferred its assets to the new university and became the Emory University School of Medicine. The instruction of medical students continued at Grady, where law and social custom required the treatment of black patients and white patients in separate buildings. Separate but hardly equal, the two facilities became known as "the Gradys." Merely one indication of the nuances inherent in their inequality was the policy, in place for more than two decades, prohibiting medical students from treating white patients; only black patients were suitable for student practice.

Roy Bell was not the first black Atlantan to question Grady's segregation. In 1919 the Atlanta NAACP had written an open letter to the city protesting the exclusion of black doctors from Grady, and black doctors, in countless ways, had noted that a segregated hospital was unwise. But when the "new Grady" was built in the mid-1950s (it is now called "old Grady" since the construction of a newer facility in the 1990s), it would have been illegal to operate it without separate facilities. Shaped like a giant three-dimensional H lying on its back, with two towers rising sixteen floors, Grady Hospital had two emergency rooms, two waiting rooms, two labor and delivery wards, two surgery departments, two registration areas, two of everything—identical, except for the color of their patients. In fact, before the new Grady was built, the hospital had in effect been two Gradys, two wooden buildings facing each other across Butler Street, with a tunnel under the street to cross from the white world to the black world, or vice versa—which is why one might still hear reference to "the Gradys."

By 1961, when Bell received the phone call about Grady, the tremors of opposition to white-imposed segregation were rumbling more and more confidently. The Student Nonviolent Coordinating Committee (SNCC) and other black student groups proposed tactics more radical than those of the older black generation of Atlantans, who had forged a nonconfrontational working relationship with Atlanta's powerful whites. The elder black leaders knew how to get certain things for the black community, in exchange for other things. They knew when to push, when to ask, when to compromise. They had an uneasy relationship with Atlanta's white civic and business leaders that had brought some benefits to the black community without the violence experienced by other southern cities. And they often were put off by militant students who made radical demands.

Bell and other young black professionals in their early forties, who were eager for the end of segregation, lived, chronologically and tactically, between the two generations. Bell's cohorts were more forceful than their seniors but less explosive than the students. Activist college students fiercely, publicly, demanded immediate change; their elders arranged deals in private meetings. Atlanta's public transportation was integrated, for example, after a lawsuit prompted not by a Montgomery-style boycott but by an arrest of black leaders who had boarded a bus and sat defiantly in the whites-only section—a defiance and arrest coordinated by black leaders in meetings with Atlanta's white chief of police. The students, on the other hand, picketed, sat in, boycotted, and demanded the end of segregation, not caring about the cooperation of white leaders. The gulf between the generations was so wide that a Student-Adult Liaison Committee was formed to facilitate communication between the students and the dignified older black leaders. Roy Bell, drawn to his elders by his intellect and savvy, was eventually drawn to the students by his intemperance and impatience.

> *Grady's separate facilities hampered the quality of services for all. By maintaining two hospitals in one, Grady cost taxpayers more than necessary.*

After the disturbing phone call, Bell's target was Grady Memorial Hospital. Bell was an intellectual, reflective man with a precise command of words, but when his anger pinpointed a target, he moved—fast, rash, alone, even if ridiculed by his peers. His tactic was simply to demand to be heard.

Morehouse College student activist Charles Black recalls, "He was one of the few black professionals who was supportive of the students. He knew what he was talking about, but he was very impatient—radical, to say the least. Bell was not of our generation, though he was at least as radical as we were, so he appeared even more radical. . . . His being a dentist identifying with the students was important to us. But he was sometimes not satisfied with [our own slow] pace of things. We had very democratic committees; we'd meet sometimes two or three times a day. There wasn't a place for a maverick like Bell; he wanted to act quickly and on his own."[3]

Jondelle Johnson, a civil rights activist and later director of the Atlanta NAACP, says about Bell, "He had no finesse, at a time when it was dangerous not to. We had problems with the police, the Klan, but he didn't care. He said what he wanted to say and did what he wanted to do. He jeopardized his family and his practice. Most of us feared for our lives, but he went beyond the limits the rest embraced. He would go anywhere. Everybody said he was crazy. There was a *way* of doing things so not to alienate the whites, but Roy did it his way. Quite a few blacks didn't want to associate with him, for fear it would jeopardize what they had." But Johnson also says about him, respectfully, "He was well-read. He was brilliant. He was one of my heroes. I guess he was ahead of his time."[4]

Once Bell determined that Grady Hospital would be desegregated, he was relentless. He might appear anywhere and say anything to bring attention to Grady. He went before the Atlanta City Council and called them killers and murderers for endorsing a policy that discriminated against sick black citizens. He addressed the Georgia legislature, hounded mayoral candidates. He telegrammed the Georgia attorney general, suggesting that, as Emory Hospital was segregated, the attorney general should give an opinion as to whether Emory University's tax-exempt status should be revoked. Bell wrote many letters: to President Kennedy, President Johnson, the Civil Rights Commission, county, city, and state politicians.[5]

In August 1961, before the Fulton County commissioners, he gave a logical, statistically well-researched plea. He said Grady's separate facilities hampered the quality of services for all. By maintaining two hospitals in one, Grady cost taxpayers more than necessary. He pointed out that there were no Negroes among the five hundred visiting medical staff. Atlanta, he said, had 4,000 hospital beds, only 680 of them for Negroes. The three private hospitals for Negroes were not fully accredited. Public funds were used to operate two Grady technical schools, neither of which admitted blacks. He appealed to the county commissioners, the Fulton-DeKalb Hospital Authority (FDHA), which oversaw Grady, and "all responsible humane citizens, Negro and white, to do something immediately about these deplorable conditions" without resorting to court action.[6]

The Atlanta-based regional director of the U.S. Department of Health, Education, and Welfare, Pete Page, recognized that Bell's tactics could be good strategy: "He had a pattern of making some outrageous suggestion about what to do, sometimes making people very angry, which would elicit useful responses from people who would do something a little less explosive and more practical. He was different, but on balance he earned his way. He really did."[7]

Bell decided to picket Grady, and for picketers he turned to the restless, energetic black student activists at Atlanta's historically black colleges. They, however, had heard of the loose cannon Roy Bell and were leery. They were desegregating lunch counters, hotels, restaurants, the state capitol; why include a public hospital in an already hectic schedule—especially if it meant trying to tame Roy Bell?

The hesitant students changed their minds when a small boy was hit by a car a half-block from the office of the student-run Committee on the Appeal for Human Rights (COAHR), a ten-minute drive from Grady. They called the Grady ER and were asked the boy's race. They said Negro and were told there were no Negro ambulances available at the moment. Forty minutes later, an ambulance arrived. The students fumed—and then joined Bell on the Butler Street sidewalks, sometimes picketing eight to ten hours a day, carefully avoiding any interruption of hospital services. More drastic actions were planned but not enacted, such as faking an emergency in the picket line and carrying the black person into the white emergency room. Students visited twenty-five churches to ask for donations and picketers. Charles Black asked Negro citizens to report mistreatment at Grady so they could compile a list for future use, possibly for a lawsuit.

In 1961, with demonstrations occurring all over Atlanta in restaurants and public accommodations, picketing at Grady received little press attention, most of it from the *Atlanta Inquirer*, which was begun by civil rights activists. Bell repeatedly called the *Inquirer*, requesting a reporter to come down to Grady. He held aloft signs that read, "Disease and Death Know No Race Give the Other One-third an Equal Chance to Live" or "Grady Has 75% Negro Patients, 0% Negro Staff Physicians, 0% Negro Interns, 0% Negro Board Members, Why?"[8]

Atlanta Constitution columnist Pat Watters interviewed Bell and wrote that Bell wanted someone with power to listen. He said Bell had been before the county commission, who listened but could not tell the FDHA what to do. The FDHA would not grant him a hearing. Uninvited, Bell went to an FDHA meeting to speak. The FDHA said it would appoint a committee to look into his concerns but gave no date for the committee's report. Thereafter, the entirely white FDHA would respond to questions about desegregating Grady with, "We're working on it." Bell threatened to sue. Bell tried to meet with all five (white) mayoral candidates, but only one responded, while another sent a representative.[9]

Bell also turned to talk radio. For a time he conducted two weekly programs on two black-owned AM stations and occasionally appeared on a talk show called "Open Line" on another. Black and white listeners called and responded to Bell's provocative rhetoric.[10]

But inside Grady, the daily, hourly insults of segregation persisted.

Former Grady nurse Ernestine Kelsey remembers the resentment she felt when black employees received a letter from the Grady administration announcing, "I am happy to announce that your salary has been increased by five dollars a month." Kelsey stresses, "Not a week, a *month*. It wasn't worth the paper it was written on. He made a big deal in those letters about five dollars a month."[11]

The author of those insulting letters, the hospital superintendent, Frank Wilson, was a gregarious man, a University of Georgia graduate, teller of hilarious stories, classic southern backslapper, and a wily maneuverer among Atlanta's powerful whites. Former city councilman, former vice president of a lumber company, member of Druid Hills Baptist Church, he was credited with Grady's growth and impressive national reputation. He served a term as president of the Georgia Hospital Association. Known to favor white suits, a thin black tie, and white Panama hat, he was overheard by Kelsey saying, "I'll die and go to hell before Grady Hospital is integrated."

He was politically astute. Joseph Wilber, a white doctor who served his residency at Grady, tells of Wilson once acceding to the black community: "One night Grady was jammed with people, and a black woman with a stroke was brought in. The policy then was that if someone like that could swallow, you could send them home. They told her family to take her home, feed her, clean her, have her move some to keep up her strength. They were shocked. 'You're not going to let her stay in the hospital?' But there were no beds. We got a call from Frank Wilson at midnight. He said to admit her. I told him there were no beds. 'Find a bed. We don't turn away school principals,' and he hung up on me. She was a black school principal with friends in powerful places. He responded to political pressure from somebody."[12]

In September 1963 a Negro worker at Grady went to the "colored" laborers' cafeteria without her meal ticket. The white supervisor called for a security guard, who roughed up the worker for forgetting her ticket. Almost three hundred workers—maids, porters, housekeepers, kitchen helpers—signed a petition saying they would walk out if nothing were done to make amends. They included a list of grievances, including that most of them made fifty cents an hour, less than half the federal minimum wage of $1.15. They were required to use the basement bathroom, and only at specified times. Dr. C. Miles Smith, president of the Atlanta NAACP, presented the petition to Wilson, who agreed to open all restrooms to all workers and to hire a Negro supervisor for the laborers' cafeteria. Smith reported that Wilson was gracious to him. The security guard was fired. Wilson also said he would submit a pay increase suggestion to the hospital board.[13]

That "colored laborers' cafeteria," which Smith called a "segregated segregated cafeteria," was a cruel insult. A white cafeteria and a colored cafeteria had respective degrees of higher and lower status; below them both was the colored laborers' cafeteria. A small, dingy place, it was the only dining area for the lowest-ranked workers in the hospital. Kelsey, who resented the smaller portions on the colored side, says the laborers' meals were worse: "When they served roast beef, the whites had chunks. We had it thin like sliced bologna. If we got thin roast beef, the laborers' cafeteria got, maybe, grits and collard greens."

Under Wilson's administration, black nurses were addressed by title: "Nurse Kelsey." White nurses were addressed as "Miss," a small but nagging reminder that one counted more than the other. According to Kelsey, during one week of evaluation by a hospital accreditation agency, switchboard operators were instructed, for that week only, to refer to all nurses, regardless of color, as "Miss." The hesitant operators were assured the previous policy would be restored after the evaluation.[14]

A white instructor in the Grady nursing school decided that it was foolish to teach the same class twice, once for white students and again for black students. She combined the two classes, saving time, until two city officials saw the mix of students and demanded that they return to segregated classes.[15]

The *Inquirer* listed these reports from Grady personnel: Blacks had to make arm boards out of plywood, while the white side had custom-made boards. Blacks sometimes had to make chucks out of paper padding. They did not have enough blankets. Doctors still called black patients by their first names; whites they called Mr., Mrs., Miss. Blacks had a shortage of diapers while the whites had extras. Black patients without ready money, who had to wait on someone to bring money before they went home, were put on stretchers in the halls instead of being placed in empty rooms on the white side. Negro student nurses put their laundry in the chute on one day, whites on another. The Grady blood bank even had a shelf for "black" blood and a shelf for "white" blood.

Dr. Joseph Wilber has a gentle voice and a low chuckle. Retired, he lives in the North Georgia mountains, overlooking a small lake. A graduate of Harvard Medical School, he began his residency training at Grady in 1954. He recalls seeing Negro patients brought their food with only a spoon, no fork or knife. He saw Negro women asked to undress in a room full of people and asked to sit, unclothed, on an exam bed and wait.

> "Conditions on the black side were absolutely atrocious," he recalled years later. "The patients were so close together that when they did a procedure they had to pull the patient's bed out into the aisle like a file drawer, then push it back."

Local physicians made rounds at Grady each week—a contribution of time that carried some prestige—with the residents presenting cases to them. Wilber began one such round by describing a case to a visiting local doctor: "Mr. Jones here was brought in last night with a headache and nausea."

"What did you say?" the local doctor asked.

Wilber repeated himself. Three times the doctor asked him the same question, and three times Wilber answered the same way.

"What's your name?" the doctor asked the Negro patient.

"Bill Jones."

"Dr. Wilber, you are no longer in Boston. To you, this man is Bill."

Wilber continued, refusing to disrespect Mr. Jones, "The *patient* came in last night with headache and nausea." The doctor glared at him.[16]

Sometimes insults came in the exclusion of blacks from decisions that affected their lives. In September 1961 the Grady administration announced that a just-completed Negro Grady nursing student dorm would be named "Mississippi Hall." At a time of intense civil rights activity, the new Negro dorm would be named after the most defiantly segregated state in the country, a state whose murderous backlash against desegregation was once referred to as "special savagery,"[17] a state that Martin Luther King Jr.'s friends would later beg him not to visit, for fear of his life. The Grady administration also announced that the already-occupied Negro nursing student dorm would be renamed "Alabama Hall." Local black doctors protested. Grady officials denied that the dorms had been named yet, but when the NAACP president called the Grady switchboard and asked for Mississippi Hall, he was transferred to the new dorm.[18] Grady relented, and the dorms became Piedmont and Armstrong, for the streets next to them.

While marchers walked up and down Butler Street, one person watching them from inside the building was the Reverend Charles Gerkin, head of the Grady chaplaincy and later a professor of pastoral theology at Emory's Candler School of Theology. He had come to Grady in 1957, just before the new building was completed. Gerkin, born and reared in Kansas, asked the search committee if he would be chaplain to the whole hospital, not just the white side. The committee, which included Frank Wilson, assured him that he would minister to all of Grady. Later, Gerkin wished he received that assurance in writing. Soon after Gerkin's arrival at Grady, Wilson summoned him to his office and said, "Them niggers over there don't want you. Stay on the white side of the hospital. Let the Negro preachers take care of them." At that point Grady was still two Gradys, on opposite sides of Butler Street. Ignoring Wilson's instructions and Grady tradition, Gerkin walked freely to the colored side, ministering to patients as they needed him. "Conditions on the black side were absolutely atrocious," he recalled years later. "The patients were so close together that when they did a procedure they had to pull the patient's bed out into the aisle like a file drawer, then push it back."[19]

Gerkin did agree to segregated worship. "I knew I couldn't have integrated services. Part of the agreement I made with the committee was that I would conduct services for blacks in the auditorium and whites in the chapel. But Wilson vetoed it and said I had to get black ministers to conduct services for blacks. So I contracted with a young black minister."

Gerkin once met with black nursing students to answer questions about chaplaincy. After several questions, a young student in the back raised her hand. "This was a real honest question," Gerkin recalled. "She was not a militant girl." He nodded to her, and she asked, "Do you think we're inferior?" He replied, "No, you are one of God's creatures, like everybody else."

Eventually, according to Gerkin, Wilson spoke with some pastors of white churches to see if they could have Gerkin sent back to Kansas. "Fortunately, he approached the wrong ones," Gerkin said. They said they would not vote to fire him. "Over the years, we learned to have a certain respect for each other," Gerkin said of Wilson. "We of course disagreed. One day at lunch he said, 'Chuck, you mean you would like to have these Negroes up here eating in the same dining room as us?' I said, 'Sure,' and he just shook his head. He could not comprehend that."

Gerkin often looked out the window of his office and watched Bell and others marching on Butler Street. His office was furnished with opulent antiques donated by a prominent white Atlanta woman. When Gerkin held meetings with students in that office, an administrator told him he had desecrated the donor's gifts by allowing students to sit on the antique chairs. Amid his fancy furniture, watching the protesters, Gerkin wondered, *Should I be out there?* "My conclusion was that I wouldn't be able to do the job I was brought here to do. And, two, I think I can do more good for integration where I am. I've never been absolutely sure about that."

Charles Black and another student eventually arranged a meeting with William Pinkston, assistant director of Grady. They prepared a presentation of their demands and their justifications for them. Pinkston greeted them warmly and welcomed them into his office, where they saw a surprise guest: Daddy King, Martin Luther King Sr. Daddy King was one of the prominent older black leaders whom the student activists deemed too compromising. It was not uncommon for white leaders who were irritated with students to turn to leaders such as Daddy King for help. Black began explaining why they were protesting and what their demands were. They were interrupted by Daddy King, who told them not to kick a man when he's down. You're being too hard on Mr. Pinkston, he said. He has shown good faith, and he will do what is right. You need to give him time. Pinkston then called on King to say a word of prayer, which he did. The prayer ended the meeting.

"We got nothing accomplished," Black says. "I blame Daddy King for that."[20]

After the meeting many students were demoralized. To push Grady further would require that they regroup and find ways to increase the pressure—in a battle that received little support from the black community and little visibility in the press. Black says, "It was a lonely vigil." And it was a vigil publicly associated with Roy Bell, the fierce man who might embarrass you if you stood next to him. The students returned to other demonstrations, and, from then on, when Bell picketed in front of Grady, he marched alone. The *Inquirer* called Bell a "one-man gang," and "the militant dentist."[21]

Grady was not Bell's only target. The local chapter of the American Dental Association (ADA) was closed to him because of segregation, but membership in the local chapter was a prerequisite to membership in the national body. He and another dentist presented a resolution at the National Dental Association, the association for black dentists, criticizing the granting of federal funds to segregated medical research institutions. They urged nonviolent action at the next ADA national meeting. Black dentists were educated and evaluated by ADA standards while being barred from membership in twelve states. For three years Bell picketed the Hinman Clinic, an annual dentists' scientific conference held in Atlanta, which did not allow black dentists. He and a group of medical students picketed the meeting of the Georgia Dental Association. He traveled to Miami and picketed the national ADA meeting.

Finally, in June 1962 Roy Bell, working with the NAACP Legal Defense and Education Fund, filed suit against Grady Hospital to force Grady to desegregate. Bell filed as a dentist who might potentially practice at Grady. He also put together the team of plaintiffs. One was Dr. Clinton Warner, who asserted he should have the same privileges as other Atlanta MDs. Ruby Doris Smith, a Spelman College student and SNCC activist who had picketed Grady, sued as a potential patient and potential nursing school applicant who would want to attend a nonsegregated school. Five other co-plaintiffs filed as potential patients. They sued not only Frank Wilson and the FDHA, but also the local and state chapters of the AMA and the ADA for barring black members.[22]

> *In a move that stunned student activists, on a Saturday afternoon one hundred black college faculty picketed Grady, and a group of doctors and dentists led a march through downtown Atlanta.*

The Grady defendants responded with a flurry of motions to dismiss the case. The dental association claimed freedom of association: "Private practices, however discriminatory, however repugnant, do not fall within the Constitutional ban on racial discrimination." Grady claimed that the lack of black doctors was Emory's choice, not the hospital's, for Emory supervised the residency program.[23]

The medical associations reported that they had already rescinded a category of membership that had been particularly odious to black doctors: scientific membership. This category was created in 1952 to appease black doctors, who wanted membership in local and state associations less than they wanted access to membership in the national AMA, group malpractice insurance rates, and privileges in Atlanta hospitals. Scientific membership involved no dues or voting privileges; it allowed admittance to "scientific" continuing education sessions but not to regular meetings or social gatherings. You may hear a lecture with us, the category communicated, but you may not sit down to a meal with us or make decisions with us. Invitations were mailed to local black doctors; all declined. They wanted full membership or nothing.[24]

The scientific membership was a branch in a thicket that prevented Atlanta's black doctors from practicing medicine fully. Without membership in the AMA they could have no hospital privileges. But joining as full members required two endorsement signatures from current members. Finding two white doctors willing to sign was a chore. The local medical societies could truthfully claim that no one had submitted a completed form. Similarly, some hospitals required two letters of recommendation with an application for privileges. Emory Hospital, for instance, required doctors to be currently in a practice that already included Emory Hospital doctors—all of whom were white. Some hospitals required donations to a building program. Some required doctors to practice in a certain area—generally not the parts of Atlanta where black doctors were segregated.

In one deposition, Bell was asked if he had spoken with Frank Wilson about hospital privileges. He replied that he had, that Wilson was cordial, but that he said, "Well, let's be frank with one another. I know what you want. You want to have Negro doctors controlling Grady Hospital, and before I'll see Negro doctors down here, I'll die and go to hell." Bell said, "Well, we'll see," and left.[25]

While the suit was being argued, other related actions were taken around the country. The NAACP picketed the national AMA meeting in Atlantic City and the AMA national office in Chicago. President John Kennedy sent a telegram to the American Hospital Association urging it to address discrimination in hospitals. He also directed the Justice Department to associate itself with the NAACP in suits against federally funded hospitals that discriminated. Some AMA chapters began asking the national AMA to revoke the membership of segregated chapters. The Department of Health, Education, and Welfare held an all-day conference on the elimination of hospital segregation.

In early 1963 the local and state AMA chapters were dropped from the lawsuit. They had amended their bylaws to allow membership without regard to race, and they presented to the judge a list of eleven black doctors, including Warner, who had been accepted as full members.

In May, Frank Wilson claimed in a deposition that although Grady Hospital was segregated, no one was discriminated against. About the emergency room, for example, he said the "operation of nondiscriminatory but separate emergency treatment facilities for white patients and Negro patients is in the best interest of the patient care program at Grady Memorial Hospital and designed to preserve said patient care program for the benefit of and in the best interest of the physical and mental health and well being of all patients at Grady Memorial Hospital irrespective of race." The phrase "nondiscriminatory but separate" appeared throughout depositions given on behalf of Grady. Explaining why the emergency room operator would ask for the race of someone needing an ambulance, he said they often called on private ambulance services when theirs were all in use, and those services were segregated, so the Grady operator would need to know the person's race in case a private service was called upon.[26]

Wilson did, after all, have the backing of the national publication of the American Hospital Association. In an issue of *Hospitals*, an administrator from Gary, Indiana, warned about the risks of desegregating hospitals. The professional staffs, he said, would, of course, cause no problems, because they could be depended on to work with skilled people without prejudice. What about Negro trustees? he asked. Since it was uncommon for Negroes to have the status required to be a trustee, there would probably be only one for any given hospital, and it was probable that any discriminatory decisions would be made in informal meetings when the Negro was not present. Prolonged use of this tactic would undermine the board of trustees, and the Negro trustee might become regarded as an Uncle Tom by the Negro community. So desegregating boards would be a problem. And in a hospital room, he warned, an elderly white woman with heart problems lying in an oxygen tent could be roomed with a Negro, and the white woman's husband might complain, "She doesn't like Negroes. She does not live with Negroes, and she does not want to start now. Her emotional condition will be aggravated by the presence of Negroes."

What to do?

"To legislate that physicians and hospital staffs," he wrote, "ignore emotions in patients arising from any cause [would be] to amend the historical right of medicine to make the patient's well-being its most important concern."[27]

In late 1963, upset with slow change in Atlanta, a large group of blacks marched to Hurt Park, where Martin Luther King Jr., James Foreman of SNCC, and others called for better job opportunities, improved schools, a public accommodations law, and desegregation of Grady. The march was coordinated by the Summit Leadership Conference, a coalition of civil rights groups. In spring of 1964, the Summit Leadership Conference organized a "Sacrificial Easter," urging blacks to buy nothing more than food and medicine during Lent, so that white businesses would get the message that change must come soon. In a move that stunned student activists, on a Saturday afternoon one hundred black college faculty picketed Grady, and a group of doctors and dentists led a march through downtown Atlanta.

Judge Frank Hooper ruled against the dental associations' request to dismiss, which they had based on the right of private association. He cited the role given the two associations by the state of Georgia to nominate members of state agencies that regulated dentists. The associations thus were, in his judgment, "under color of law," meaning that they were using authority given to them by the state and therefore were not private organizations. The result was that only white dentists did the appointing and only white dentists were appointed. The action of excluding Negro dentists from its membership was state-authorized action and was a violation of the equal protection clause of the U.S. Constitution.[28]

Atlanta's "white power structure"—the city's most prominent business and political decision makers—saw where the case was going. According to Atlanta black politician Leroy Johnson, these white leaders let Grady's administrators know that theirs was a lost battle.[29] Atlanta had made significant changes peacefully; the power structure would not let a charity hospital ruin the city's image. So Grady began to desegregate piecemeal. First the emergency rooms were made nonracial; a black intern was accepted; black chaplains were accepted; black doctors were accepted to the visiting staff to make rounds with residents; technician training facilities were made nonracial; the chapel became open to all persons at all times; the Grady card application office; then the individual clinics: pediatrics, cardiac, dental, surgery, and so on. "White" and "Colored" signs were removed from all doors. Black and white nurses began to wear the same color uniform and same style cap.

> They said changing Emory would create a ripple emanating out to other Atlanta hospitals. They noted that Emory had no black interns out of twenty, no black residents out of sixty, no black physicians out of four hundred.

Finally, in February 1965 Judge Hooper ruled that Grady must desegregate every aspect of its operation. Only two components remained segregated: patient rooms and nursing school dormitories. Administrators had held until last those places where whites and blacks might lie in beds near one another. Grady proposed that the dorms desegregate the next fall semester, in September, and that all rooms and wards in the hospital be filled without regard to race by December 31. The plaintiffs accepted the dorms proposal and objected to the wards and rooms proposal. It was finally agreed by all to desegregate the wards and rooms by June 1.

When May turned to June, Grady Hospital performed as instructed. Black and white patients were moved so that rooms and wards were no longer segregated. A seminar had been held on how to handle white patients who resisted, but there was little resistance. A few whites checked out, and, one nurse recalls, a female white patient undressed, donned a gown, and, when a black doctor entered the room, screamed and ran down the hall.[30] *Atlanta Inquirer* reporters toured Grady as rooms were desegregated. They observed white and black patients exchanging cordial greetings. They called it "the Tuesday that was" and reported that Pinkston announced, "All phases of Grady are nonracial as of today," but quoted Bell saying, "Since Mr. Pinkston's concept of brotherhood is the same as that of a dollar, I will withhold further comment until I can take a personal inspection tour."[31]

Later in June, the *Inquirer*, through its sources inside Grady, reported that some white doctors had problems with integration. One white woman raised a fuss when placed with a Negro woman; she was moved to another room. Later, another Negro woman was placed in her room, and she requested to be moved, was not moved, and checked out. Chaplain Gerkin had his residents circulate the hospital to defuse any conflict. "I remember going to the ER," he said, "and there were ambulance drivers at a gathering place out there when not out on a call, and I went down to see how they were doing." He remembered that in earlier conversations with them they talked about the "rhesus factor," that blacks were "the way they were" because they came from rhesus monkeys. "But the amazing thing, since integration had become the company line, was they dealt with patients by saying well, this is the way it is. I don't think what they thought privately had changed one iota, but they responded to authority."[32]

In July, Bell conducted his inspection and commended Grady for its progress but said the Negro cafeteria was all Negro, and the white cafeteria had only a sprinkle of Negroes. He also reported that many wards were still segregated among the nurses, whites on one side and Negroes on the other. He said Negro doctors were not employed to their full capacity, and Negro patients still had a "C," for "colored," on their records. He announced that, given the even more segregated condition of Atlanta's private hospitals, perhaps it was time for federal pressure to be applied. That, later, would be his next battle.[33]

In September the nursing school opened for the fall semester, and the school's administrators had decided that, since they had to assign rooms nonracially, they would do so alphabetically.

They announced the policy to the students and said that after six months the students could change roommates if they wanted to. Bernice Dixon, one of those school administrators, tells this story now and adds, with a tinge of sadness and hurt in her voice and on her face, "A few changed, mostly blacks choosing black roommates. . . . The black students were more disturbed and concerned than the white students. They had a tendency to segregate themselves. We continued the separate graduations and yearbooks for two years, for those already there. The black nurses started the Black Grady Nurse Conclave for alumni, which also granted black scholarships. We worked hard to have one alumni association, but they plain segregated themselves again."[34]

Before all that happened, in early 1965—a year and a half before Grady was fully integrated, several months before they began the piecemeal desegregation—Superintendent Frank Wilson, the man who had said he would die and go to hell before Grady would be integrated, had a heart attack and died.

Gerkin called Pinkston, the interim Grady superintendent who would become superintendent, and said, "We're going to have a memorial service for Frank, and I'm not going to have a segregated service."

"There was a good long pause," Gerkin recalled. "Bill is basically a good guy, raised in South Georgia, a good Presbyterian, and value-wise I think his heart was in the right place. Finally, he said, 'Do what you want to do.'"

Gerkin told him he wanted to have two services, one at each shift change. The service would be announced over the hospital-wide intercom, with nothing said about race. "Again there was a long pause, and he said, 'Let's do it.' And that's what happened. The blacks and whites came together, in the chapel on the white side of the hospital. I insisted on that. That was the first integrated worship service we had. You'd think they'd come only if they have a certain respect for the man. If he's dead, there's no penalty in not coming. I never asked them why they came. I thought that was interesting.

"I read scripture and prayed. The key phrase in the prayer, a prayer of thanksgiving, was, 'We thank Thee for all that was good that came from the life of Frank Wilson.' And the ones that knew where I stood and had their own negative feelings about him knew exactly what I meant. It went right over the heads of the others."[35]

Grady Hospital, the local medical society, and the state medical society all desegregated and were released from the lawsuit. Schools, restaurants, and hotels desegregated. Civil rights laws were passed and enforced. The future, it appeared, was clear. The state and local dental societies fought against integration for a while longer, but they eventually opened their membership to all dentists.

Despite these rapid changes, Atlanta's private hospitals still found ways to deny practicing privileges to black doctors. So a group of black doctors decided to go to Washington, see the folks at HEW and in the Congress, and let them know they were spending federal tax dollars on segregated institutions. The doctors put together the Committee on Implementation, which would encourage the implementation of what civil rights laws said should already be happening in private hospitals. The committee comprised Bell and physicians Otis Smith, Albert M. Davis, and J. B. Ellison. Their coordinator was Xernona Clayton, a longtime civil rights activist who worked closely with Coretta Scott King.

In Atlanta the committee helped the regional HEW with spot inspections of hospitals and gathered statistics on black health care and on the limitations black doctors faced when trying to treat patients who needed hospitalization. Hundreds of doctors had their referral patterns tracked to monitor compliance with civil rights laws. Peter Page, regional director of HEW in Atlanta, said, "The in-hospital checks were the only way we could catch the miscreants. Georgia Baptist [now called Atlanta Medical Center] was one of our toughest and Emory Hospital was no less so, though more civil than the Baptists were. Georgia Baptist kept saying, 'It takes time.'" The inspectors would often discover some practice that perpetuated segregation, and the hospital would be told to comply with the law or face loss of federal funds. They found out, for example, of Grady Hospital's practice, even after officially desegregating, of placing a "C" on the Grady cards of its black patients and a "W" on cards of its white patients.[36]

The Committee on Implementation also organized a meeting of doctors from around the Southeast. When Bell spoke he said, "Keep the Negro doctor out and you keep the Negro patient out." He explained that the most common method hospitals used to minimize the presence of blacks was tokenism. After one or two black doctors were accepted, no more would qualify; applications would be misplaced. The doctors heatedly attacked Emory University Hospital, which had received nine applications from black doctors and rejected them all, while Emory received almost as much federal money as all other Atlanta hospitals combined. They said changing Emory would create a ripple emanating out to other Atlanta hospitals. They noted that Emory had no black interns out of twenty, no black residents out of sixty, no black physicians out of four hundred.

Bell insisted, "Emory is morally wrong, but the federal government is worse because they disburse the funds that help Emory carry on its program."

Speakers accused HEW of bad faith for certifying hospitals that had not actually desegregated. The doctors at the meeting passed a resolution calling on HEW to fire any staff member who approved a hospital that operated by the guidelines on paper but not in practice. The resolution also called for firing hospital authorities whose governing policies demonstrated hostile attitudes toward admission of Negro doctors to the staff. An HEW representative who was present promised a reevaluation of certified hospitals and pointed out that the law required nondiscrimination but did not require integration.[37]

Once the team of Clayton and the four doctors had gathered sufficient information and organized it into a compelling presentation of statistics, stories, and observation, they traveled to Washington to confront the men who made policy and either enforced it or didn't. One public health official disregarded their information and said he would have to review his own records, which, unfortunately, were in Baltimore and would not be available until the next day, when, the official regretted to say, the team would be gone. Clayton, who normally remained silent at their meetings, said they would remain an extra day.[38] Later, at the Washington Hilton, after a day of meetings, Clayton blurted to the doctors, "We should see the president. We wrote Johnson a letter, and he never responded." The doctors chuckled, thinking, *That Xernona*. She picked up the phone and called the White House. "I want to speak with the president," she said into the phone. Her call was routed to someone, and she explained who they were, why they were there, and why Johnson should talk to them. Somehow, word of the black doctors talking about civil rights was passed around lower-level White House staff, and someone saw it as an opportunity. Wilbur Cohen, undersecretary of HEW, met with them to assure them the president would personally make sure no hospital receiving federal money would remain segregated. Johnson himself spoke to them for a few moments and said he shared their concerns and would do whatever he could.

Most of the group were satisfied with the meeting, but not Bell. He would have a press conference. Before they left, he went to the White House press room, announced their presence, and said they would take questions after their meeting with the president. Stunned at Bell's audacity, Clayton and the doctors joined him on the podium. The impromptu press conference received national coverage. They told the scribbling reporters that the federal government allowed eighteen Atlanta hospitals to receive federal money without full compliance with the Civil Rights Act. They reported that hospitals continued to keep black doctors out even though most had been ruled in compliance with federal guidelines. They named Emory University as a key institution as it worked with five hospitals and had powerful Washington connections. The doctors requested HEW to withhold funds from Atlanta hospitals pending full compliance, that Negroes be included on compliance review boards, and that HEW visit Atlanta hospitals on a tour hosted by the Negro doctors. Smith said unless something were done soon, there would be demonstrations and sit-ins throughout Atlanta.[39]

When all hospitals had finally desegregated—and segregation was reduced to the sneaky, unspoken manipulations that would plague many institutions and that would perpetuate the privileges ingrained by decades of Jim Crow laws and distorted perceptions of white superiority—the victory was the result of both the local acts of detection and enforcement, and of a much larger act, a new federal program that would change hospitals everywhere: Medicare. Before Medicare was enacted, the U.S. Commission on Civil Rights had recommended to Kennedy that he use federal funds to influence hospitals, deny funds to those that discriminated, and predicate acceptance into Medicare on operating without racial discrimination. That recommendation became policy, and in early 1966, before Medicare began that summer, letters and policy statements were mailed from HEW to all hospitals explaining that compliance with the Civil Rights Act was mandatory for acceptance. Hospital administrators counted their elderly patients and concluded big money was at stake. Huge money. Enormous money.

That was when they became interested in making sure their 441 forms were filled out and signed. Suddenly, black doctors began receiving polite letters from Atlanta's private hospitals. One letter was mailed to the black doctors' association requesting another copy of the association membership list. The letter said the hospital expected to comply with HEW regulations and added it had never excluded any physician from the hospital since its opening in 1954. The administrator said, as a matter of fact, he had served as free consultant for one of Atlanta's black colleges. He concluded, "We would love to have any member of your association come by and visit our hospital any time."[40]

By the end of 1966 there were almost no complaints of discrimination to HEW about Atlanta hospitals, and by the middle of 1967 the issue was resolved. Dr. Smith recalls that as he first walked into one private hospital, low-level black workers pulled him aside and said, "We're glad you're here." The doctors could focus their attention on treating their patients.

CHAPTER 6

THE Emory ALUMNUS

Enrollment Bounces Back
It's at a 10-year peak

The No. 1 Doctor of America
He's Alumnus Louis Orr

NOVEMBER 1958

ROOM TO BREATHE:
The Candler Estate

LULLWATER AND THE GREENING OF EMORY
Catalyst for a New Environmental Commitment
— NANCY SEIDEMAN —

Beginning with lush descriptions of the charm and tranquility of Lullwater, "one of the few remaining natural areas on campus," Nancy Seideman quickly plunges into a broader discussion of the University's reassessment of its environmental stewardship. Reaching back to 1925, when Walter T. Candler (College 1907) bought the land that would become Lullwater, Seideman traces the history of the natural Emory landscape and the work to foster a sense of responsible stewardship. In her telling of this history for the first time, she focuses on a proposed road as the catalyst for a struggle to define environmental principles for Emory.

L**ULLWATER. THE NAME** evokes a sense of peaceful, hazy drift. And that is indeed how you feel, passing through the stone-pillared gateway on noisy Clifton Road into the forested preserve and walking down the gently sloping roadway to the meadow, with the lake just visible on the horizon. The clatter of a kingfisher swooping over the water and cries of red-shouldered hawks gliding above slowly begin to muffle the traffic sounds left at the gate.

The seasons bring change: In summer, emerald and ruby-colored hummingbirds flit among the marsh's jewel-plants. As autumn leaves swirl down, sandhill cranes pass overhead on their way farther south. Gold-leaved beech trees blaze in winter, and the bright sun lures turtles to their favorite rocks even on the most frigid days. The soft spring air conveys the promise of renewal. Tree buds swell, the lavender petals of hepatica lining woodland trails pop open. Dogs strain at their leashes, eager to reach the water. Children struggle out of their strollers to throw loaves of bread at happy geese.

The comfort in being in aptly named Lullwater comes partly from the sense that the preserve is a constant, both for the humans who seek its restorative embrace and for its native inhabitants, which depend on the place for survival. Walking along its paths today, it's difficult to believe that in 1999 Lullwater represented a flash point for the Emory community, as a proposed road along its periphery threatened one of the few remaining natural areas on campus. The resulting controversy was a painful chapter in Emory's history, but the resolution led to a discovery and reexamination of the University's environmental legacy, and a renewed commitment to stewardship of Emory's environmental resources.

The story of Lullwater is the story of how a community divided over issues of growth and preservation ultimately found common ground.

Mud and Marble | Preserving natural areas was not an issue in the second decade of the twentieth century, as Emory relocated from rural Oxford to an "urban" setting six miles northeast of downtown Atlanta, in an area of abundant pines and pastures known as Druid Hills. There was way too much nature.

As Thomas H. English noted in his 1966 semicentennial history of the University:

> The primitive conditions encountered on the new campus have long been the subject of amused and rueful reminiscence. Excavation and grading had exposed great areas of red clay, with consequent clouds of dust in dry weather and morasses of mud in wet weather. There were no paved roads until the mid-twenties. . . . Any extended rainy spell closed the area to auto traffic and reduced the community to slogging through the mud for all occasions.[1]

Community amenities were few, and "For several years it was extremely difficult for the newcomers to realize the conveniences of urban life."[2]

Located about a half-mile from the new campus Quadrangle was the tract of land later known as Lullwater. Appropriated from the Creek Indians in 1821 the Piedmont forest in this part of Georgia had been divided into lots, and the land passed through the hands of various settlers and plantation owners throughout the 1800s and early 1900s. In 1925 Walter T. Candler (College 1907), a son of Asa Candler, bought 250 acres of the densely wooded land and named it Lullwater Farms. As Walter Candler went about breeding horses and overseeing a farm of cattle, hogs, and chickens, the nearby University continued to raise marble buildings from the mud fields. Lullwater would remain Candler's property until 1958, when the University bought it for "breathing room" and to provide a home for Emory's presidents.

Taming the natural environment in the 1920s was not always successful. In 1925, as part of a fund-raising campaign—"Ten Million in Ten Years"—the entire Emory community devoted a day to a student-led project to dredge a proposed Emory Lake in the ground along Peavine Creek, approximately where the Peavine parking deck now stands. Unfortunately the county commissioners had not cleared the creek of sewage, as promised, and when it became apparent that the new lake would eventually become a huge cesspool, the project was abandoned.

Anyway, why the need for man-made nature, when the new community was surrounded by natural riches, lush ravines filled with mosses and ferns, dense groves of old-growth hardwoods—oaks, tulip poplars, hickories—hillsides covered with native azaleas of every hue, the occasional copperhead snake crawling out of the ravines to race across the Quad? Photographs of outside activities throughout the 1920s and 1930s depict an ever-present ring of trees in the background—slender, towering pines standing in the midst of crowds and seemingly attentive to the ceremonies unfolding before them.

The mud and muck were what prompted Woolford B. Baker, who had come to Emory in 1919 as a graduate student, to stay on as a biology professor. He reveled in every ravine, creek, and spring in which he found "every single thing nearly . . . that would attract a biologist. . . . There were small puddles around, and some of the lower sections of the campus now occupied by the athletic fields were always damp and muddy, so that the whole campus was attractive," he said.[3]

Although Baker would have a long and distinguished career as a biology professor, then as first director of the Emory Museum, his greatest legacy is a living one that endures in the native hardwoods that grace the Quadrangle, the flowering shrubs that frame the buildings, and the wildflowers that grow in the few remaining ravines. As Baker noted in a reminiscence captured in an oral history in 1980,

> It did not take me long as a biologist to begin to complain to the President (Harvey Cox) regarding the failure to preserve some of the beautiful things we had. It was not unusual to find somebody, for example, putting in a new telephone line or new light wire or something, to go through the woods and dig a hole and put down a post and there it was, destroying, of course, any of the shrubbery in its path.

Cox, worn down by Baker's constant complaining, finally told him, "From now on, not a thing will be planted on this campus nor anything taken off the campus, not a tree will be cut nor a path laid out unless you o.k. it."

Thus, with the grand sum of $250 a year, Baker became Emory's first official landscaper in the early 1920s. Given the abundance of natural areas, Baker focused on planting around the new buildings (noting the difficulty of selecting the right shrubbery for "these flat buildings with the red top roofs and pink marble"), enriching the soil, and landscaping common areas—adding trees, rhododendrons, and hollies at a ferocious clip, trying to keep pace with the loss of greenery to construction.

But as fierce a protector of the natural areas as he was, Baker could not stand in the way of "progress." He recounted what was gained but also what was lost over the years:

> Of course, through the years several of those trees have had to give way to buildings and so on, and we no longer have the beautiful screen of pine trees that was so attractive. . . . When we had to widen Clifton Road, we lost one of the most beautiful of the English hollies, one with variegated leaves. . . . The little low place down at the entrance to the campus across from the Village was just a little marshy place and the water ran down pretty freely, so I planted a good number of the hollies that grow naturally in swampy places in there. Again, progress demanded that we change the drainage system as we built new roads and changed the whole aspect of the campus, and so most of those are gone. . . . So it has been ever since we started in the development of the campus.

Of course. Nothing—literally—had ever stood in the way of Emory's relentless growth and expansion in its seven decades in Atlanta.

John Gladden (Graduate School 1979), Baker's grandson, recalls, "My grandfather's opinion carried a lot of weight, but he really was out there alone. There weren't a whole lot of faculty pushing preservation of the natural environment back then."

Gladden himself was a biology student who did research in Lullwater and even served as a student representative on the Campus Development Committee. "I didn't win many environmental campaigns," laughs Gladden, recalling one failed initiative to halt the construction of a parking lot because of erosion concerns.[4]

In 1980, at the age of eighty-eight, Baker was a special guest at a meeting of the Emory University Senate Campus Development Committee, during which he reflected on his sixty years of watching the University grow and offered several recommendations, including a proposal to develop the grounds of Lullwater as a kind of environmental showplace of both native and nonnative species. Doubtful that the University would be able to preserve much of the natural habitat still left on the campus, Baker made a plea that his beloved ravine south of what is now Carlos Hall be preserved as an "example of what the campus used to be." The ravine represented for him "the culmination of the growth of materials, undercover plants, as well as tall plants. You can't build a beech forest like that in under a hundred years."

Although most of Emory's ravines by now either have been built over or are essentially ecologically dead, the part of the ravine behind Carlos Hall was renamed the Woolford B. Baker Woodlands in the 1980s and has been the site for many community ivy pulls designed to protect the remaining native species.

"Regrettable Loss of Several Large Trees"

| What is striking is that in decades of considering environmental issues, the Campus Development Committee apparently had never invited Baker, with his vast expertise, to join its deliberations. From its inception in the 1940s, the committee was charged with overseeing basically anything happening out of doors. The committee, comprising at any one time some twenty faculty members, administrators, and students, oversaw environmental aspects of development, but mostly what could be considered "beautification"—many ambitious and important planting projects, lawn and flower bed maintenance, and overall landscaping aesthetics. Not big fans of outdoor art, the committee customarily cited potential safety hazards as the reason for tucking such objects in corners "framed" by shrubs or obscured by a ravine. Fortunately for future generations the committee's abundant caution and use of "safety" as a reason for certain recommendations were not always observed—as when a committee member in the early 1960s suggested that certain big trees be removed because they represented a risk from lightning strikes.

The relentless growth of the University and its medical complex—the addition of new buildings and constant renovations to old, along with the corresponding need for more and more parking—dominated the committee's attention. As early as 1962, it was estimated that twenty to fifty cars were turned away daily from campus owing to lack of parking.[5] About the same time, in an attempt to give some definition to a campus that had grown rather haphazardly over the years, the University's trustees drew a perimeter around 620 acres—a northern boundary at Peachtree Creek, with western, southern, and eastern boundaries roughly following Peavine Creek, Oxford Road, North Decatur Road, Clifton Road, and the Seaboard Railroad tracks east to Clairmont Road. Within these boundaries, building and renovations continued unabated for the next four decades.

From the early 1960s through the late 1970s alone, Cox Hall, the first nursing school building, Woodruff Library, the first sorority lodges, Yerkes Primate Research Center, Gambrell Hall, the Woodruff Health Sciences Administration Building, White Hall, and the Atwood Chemistry Center all were built. Where formerly the Campus Development Committee had been asked to review single building projects, it now gave its attention to multidimensional complexes that required this volunteer group of employees and faculty (with varying levels of development expertise) to assess building design and location, zoning requirements, traffic and parking management, and environmental impact—which at that point still focused heavily on how many trees needed to be cut down.

Although tree planting continued on campus, increasingly the committee's meeting minutes noted the "regrettable loss of several large trees." The committee clearly felt that something irreplaceable was slipping away from the Emory community, and comments were made about the need to protect the natural beauty of the campus. But in the absence of long-range planning and established environmental principles, decisions with enormous impact on the University's few remaining natural areas were made on the basis of expediency, or even the request of one individual.

For example, in 1966 law dean Ben F. Johnson Jr. (Law 1939) determined that the new law school building should not be built in the ravine between its former home (now Carlos Hall) and Glenn Memorial, because he "hoped, along with others, that the ravine could be kept in its natural state, from an aesthetic point of view." Although threatened many years later by expansion of the Carlos Museum, and adversely affected by decades of adjoining construction, that site remains today one of the few wholly natural areas on campus, the Woolford B. Baker Woodlands.

As early as 1962, it was estimated that twenty to fifty cars were turned away daily from campus owing to lack of parking.

The nation's first Earth Day, April 22, 1970, had a major impact on how the Campus Development Committee viewed its charge. Parking still consumed much of the committee's time, but now the parade of campus planning and traffic consultants who came before the committee were questioned about air quality, storm-water runoff, and the impact of projected growth on the natural environment and Emory's character. The committee supported students as they launched recycling and stream cleanup projects. Ecological considerations had emerged as part of the environmental equation.

Helped by the addition of biologists and ecologists to its roster—faculty members Robert B. Platt, Larry Ragsdale, and Donald Shure—the committee explored and recommended a number of initiatives throughout the 1970s (including solar panels on the new Rich Building, an idea rejected because of cost), offered eight pages of energy conservation measures for campus buildings, advocated for a pedestrian campus with traffic and parking pushed to the periphery, lobbied heavily for rapid transit to Emory, and suggested carpools and satellite parking lots with a shuttle service to campus. The committee still had to deal with endless laundry lists of new building projects, but it also pressed the University to develop and implement a long-term strategy to address the use of Emory's natural resources.

Acknowledging the need to integrate the ecological perspective into campus planning, Orie Myers, who as vice president for business and director of the Woodruff Medical Center served as the longtime chair of the Campus Development Committee, asked Platt in 1970 to assess the quality of Emory's natural environment, and to review how these resources were being addressed in the University's recently completed campus master plan. Platt and eight graduate and undergraduate students in advanced ecology conducted a ten-week study of Emory's soils, vegetation, water, and air and produced an extraordinary report. It was laden with practical solutions to problems, as well as a prescient assessment of the likely state of the campus's natural assets twenty years into the future. The report also offered an eloquent reminder: "Our natural environment is a priceless heritage received from past generations, . . . [and] we have the direct responsibility of maintenance and preservation for those generations which follow."

Platt concluded that Emory's stewardship of natural resources was insufficient to prevent further deterioration, much less restore an earlier, higher quality. Taking a swipe at the 1970 Comprehensive Campus Master Plan, which "frequently referred to" the quality of Emory's natural environment but gave it "a decidedly subordinate position," Platt recommended that

Emory undertake "an intensive study" of its natural resources. "Even though natural areas and green open spaces are shown throughout [the plan], the meticulous planning and importance given to other aspects, such as landscaping, art, and campus graphics, have not extended to the natural resources of the campus," he wrote.

Noting that Emory's environmental problems were the result of a half-century's assumption that natural resources were "expendable" and "inexhaustible," Platt blasted the master plan for perpetuating that assumption. In reality, he wrote, the campus's "natural setting is not as beautiful as most people want to believe. Its streams and lakes are for the most part ugly and polluted . . . , its two central ravines . . . largely filled and covered, its original tree canopy . . . drastically altered, its irreplaceable trees of venerable age and great beauty . . . disappearing at an alarming rate." He added that the "highly urbanized" campus was, even then, "one of the major traffic generators in metropolitan Atlanta."

The recently completed Woodruff Library (1969) exemplified the long-term impact of construction. In planning to build the structure in a natural woodland ravine, the University had stipulated that contractors implement ways to minimize the impact on vegetation. Despite these efforts, about half of the sixty-five trees left standing around the project site were dead or dying less than a year later. Of particular concern were the twenty-nine remaining majestic white oaks, of which Platt predicted Emory would lose three-quarters. Where the master plan envisioned a campus covered with hundred-year-old oaks, Platt wondered how many years it would be until actually no trees were left.

The report's assessment of the University's waterways, soils, and air quality was equally blunt and sobering, but Platt and his students offered comprehensive recommendations under every category—including confirmation of action already recommended by the Campus Development Committee, relatively easy steps that could be incorporated in construction projects, and new guidelines for the use of the University's natural areas, including Lullwater. Platt himself drafted a "Comprehensive Master Plan for a Quality Natural Environment" that called for "reordering of priorities and value judgments," and outlined simple steps for enhancing the environment, including development of a long-range maintenance program for natural resources, application of environmental objectives and criteria to new construction, and "appropriate involvement of students, faculty, employees, visitors and other members of the community." Platt's message was simple: if we say we treasure something, we—the entire community—need to take care of it.

Perhaps most important, Platt's study drew a strong connection between a healthy natural environment—clean air and water, trees that provide canopy and a pollution filter, forests that offer a peaceful respite from work and study—and the health and well-being of humans. He could not help pointing out the irony of placing parking decks next to health-care facilities.

Although the Campus Development Committee endorsed the Platt study, it is not clear that action was taken on most of the recommendations. Still, two years after the study, President Sanford Atwood asked the committee—at the request of the board of trustees—to appoint a subcommittee to give "further counsel and advice designed to assure proper environmental consideration in plans for future physical developments on campus." Atwood suggested that the subcommittee base its deliberations "upon a mass of background data," including the Comprehensive Campus Master Plan and the Platt report.

The subcommittee produced a one-page document with two recommendations: that the University implement a new traffic plan, and that a land-use zoning plan be adopted for the campus to "ensure that most of the areas of natural beauty that we have will not be violated." The subcommittee developed a map to help guide future development, dividing the entire campus into areas fitting one of three categories: preserved, limited use, or high density. But in 1975, over the Campus Development Committee's strenuous objections, Emory sold several acres of preserve-designated Lullwater property to the Veterans Administration Hospital, for a surface parking lot. The hospital eventually built a multilevel deck on the land, within feet of South Peachtree Creek.

Discussion about environmental issues continued, but the momentum brought about by Earth Day and the Platt study seemed to be spent, as the University moved into the 1980s, straining at its boundaries, with many ambitious plans on the drawing board.

Lullwater | When Emory bought the 185 acres of Walter Candler's Lullwater estate in 1958, people noted that the University had avoided "land strangulation," and speculated that Emory would soon expand into the new "breathing room." Although various campus plans over the next decades mentioned the possibility of building along Lullwater's borders—and DeKalb County road proposals presented occasional threats—the property remained undisturbed by construction within its boundaries.

Lullwater House, the Elizabethan-style mansion on a hill above the creek at the back of the estate, became the University president's official residence, beginning with the Atwood family in 1963. Despite the need to preserve the privacy of the home itself, the University generously opened the grounds to a delighted Emory community and to the public. Pretty much from dawn to dusk, the expansive grounds below and around the hill were busy with people enjoying a break from work, athletes jogging along the dirt trails, and patients and visitors from the nearby health-care facilities seeking solace amid rolling hillsides, forests, and lake. On weekends Lullwater was filled with picnickers, dog walkers, and Frisbee enthusiasts. In less-trafficked areas, faculty and students used the land and waterways as a living laboratory, studying the rich ecosystem, the wildlife inhabitants, and the diverse vegetation, so much of it unique to the region.

After barely a decade of opening Lullwater's gates to all, the Emory community began to express concern about the deterioration of the property unless protective measures were taken. In the 1970s the Lullwater Study Committee—a subcommittee of the Campus Development Committee prompted by the Emory Student Government Association, among other community members—issued specific recommendations to protect the land, including a prohibition against vehicular traffic and discouragement of adjacent property owners from polluting streams that flowed into Candler Lake. By this time the tremendous development along Clifton and Clairmont roads, with accompanying increases in population, traffic, air pollution, and storm-water runoff, was placing greater stress on Lullwater's ecological health.

In 1986 Candler Lake was dredged, and the silt was dumped behind an artificial dam on the hill south of the lake. Unfortunately the dam breached, sending tons of the silt flowing back down the hill, through the woods, and into the lake and the biology research pond. In the mid-1990s, in a well-publicized cleanup of hazardous materials, the University retrieved toxic chemicals that had been buried in Lullwater twenty years before by the Chemistry Department.

The dredging of the lake—and the sale of five acres of the northeast corner of Lullwater forest to the Southern Association of College and Schools for its new headquarters—led biology professors William Murdy and Eloise Carter to study the dimensions and quality of the "Emory Forest." An additional outcome of these incidents was the formation of the University Senate Committee on the Environment (COE), which for the first time separated environmental campus issues from the purview of the Campus Development Committee.

The Murdy-Carter report, titled "A Report on the Status of Forested Land of Emory University," is a concise, beautifully written narrative that provided an inventory of Emory's "unique, near-pristine hardwood forests with rare and diverse species." Teachers to the core, Murdy and Carter extolled the exceptional learning opportunities the forestland offers to students, noting that "understanding natural systems is essential to the liberal education of those citizens who will make critical societal decisions in the future."[6]

The objective of their report, wrote Murdy and Carter, was to provide information for University administrators who would be called upon to make decisions as stewards of Emory's natural resources. Suggesting a land-use policy, Murdy and Carter proposed that those parts of Emory's hardwood forest that were nearly pristine "should be preserved undisturbed, because they represent a unique and valuable natural resource of scientific, educational and aesthetic value." They also recommended careful environmental assessment of other, mature hardwood forested areas before development. "Mature forests like those at Emory are self-perpetuating, complex associations of living species, the products of millions of years of evolution, and are virtually impossible to replace or re-create if lost."

The COE used the Murdy-Carter report as the basis for its position statement on forest use in 1992, and continued to develop policies and procedures designed to integrate environmental concerns into early stages of campus planning.[7] With construction of research and teaching space steaming ahead, the University was needing to plan carefully how to build on its remain-

The biology research pond in Lullwater, circa 1970.

ing land, and it was clear to those who cared for and understood the value of natural ecosystems that any land that could be imagined as a site for buildings was in jeopardy of being cleared—even Lullwater. Despite successful environmental partnerships and progress in many areas of the University's operation, debate over land use intensified.

In August 1994, when Emory's new president, William Chace, stepped into his office for the first time, one of the issues waiting on his desk was an environmental matter. The University had been planning to build a wellness center in the Harwood-Yerkes forest, along Gatewood Road between Harwood Condominiums and the Yerkes Primate Research Center. But the Murdy-Carter report had recommended that this area be preserved as a protected area. After opposition from COE and other groups, Chace instructed the administration to choose another site for the wellness center.

The next year, a proposed shuttle road through Lullwater, linking the VA Hospital on Clairmont Road with Clifton Road, was rejected by the COE, along with a plan to locate the new Hope Lodge—a facility for long-term cancer recovery—within Lullwater's forest. The COE decision was appealed to the full University Senate, which unanimously supported the committee. In addition to the hazards to the environment posed by Hope Lodge and the shuttle road, one other issue had caused alarm among campus environmentalists. Neither the proposed road nor the Hope Lodge site had involved any consultation. An announcement about the road had been made to the community before the COE had been consulted, and the Hope Lodge site had been presented to the committee as a done deal.

After nearly three decades of reports, policies, and procedures produced by Emory-based, national authorities—all of which were endorsed by University presidents, governing committees, and top administrators—this disconnect between stated commitment and actual outcome was discouraging and puzzling for campus environmentalists—indeed for anyone who understood that quality of life was directly connected to the overall health of the environment.

Now, prompted by concerns about the need for additional construction and a movement to avoid some of the architectural mistakes of the 1960s and 1970s, Emory was about to embark on another comprehensive campus master-planning process. With a renewed focus on environmental concerns, the plan would spark another shuttle road controversy, which itself would represent a turning point in the University's history and a challenge to the community to provide environmental stewardship in both word and action.

The Road through Lullwater

The first sign of controversy was the chalked message that began to appear on sidewalks throughout campus and along Clifton Road in early 1999: "Stop Construction Thru Lullwater." Students from the Emory chapter of the Student Environmental Action Coalition had organized a vigorous protest against a proposed road along the edge of Lullwater. The quarter-mile road was intended as a conduit for shuttle buses from a new parking deck on the Clairmont campus to the core campus; it would skirt the southern edge of Lullwater, following the CSX rail line from the old University Apartments to a new bridge across the tracks behind Druid Hills High School. Highly visible protests to proposed construction rarely occurred in Emory's history, but this time was different. Lullwater was at risk.

The perceived threat to Lullwater's future galvanized the community in a way that the Committee on the Environment—and the Campus Development Committee before it—had not been able to do. Whether students, alumni, faculty, or staff—all cherished the many gifts that Lullwater provided. They realized that the community was on the verge of losing not only something tangible in the sense of forest and waterways, wildlife and rare vegetation, but also a vital part of Emory's identity—perhaps even its heart. Once it was gone, it would be gone forever.

"We are all caretakers of campus resources and what we do will set a precedent," said COE chair and geology professor William Size, whose committee members had decided to take a public stand.

But the debate was not easily divided into us vs. them. The proposed road was part of a new campus master plan rolled out to the community in a series of town hall meetings the year before. The process had involved discussions with more than three thousand students, faculty, staff, and neighbors. The building program was ambitious, calling for a new cancer center, a performing arts center, a new building for the nursing school, a 350,000-square-foot biomedical research building, and new classrooms and laboratories for physical sciences. The Clairmont campus itself would undergo a tremendous transformation, with the demolition of the decades-old University Apartments and construction of new student apartments, an athletics and activities center, tennis courts and an Olympic-size swimming pool, a new day-care center, and a parking deck for eighteen hundred cars. The parking deck heightened controversy over the shuttle road, because the deck would be sited in a wooded area and over a stream.

But this 1998 campus plan also had an environmental focus. It not only aimed to create a pedestrian campus connecting new open spaces with green walkways, but also eliminated vehicular traffic and street parking at the core of the campus, pushing parking to the periphery. A key element in traffic control would be the new Clairmont deck, which would allow students and employees to park more than a mile away and be transported by alternatively fueled vehicles along the new road, which would be open only to shuttles, pedestrians, and bicyclists.

An unprecedented community dialogue on the importance of Emory's natural areas started. President Chace engaged with faculty, staff, and students in a public forum. The *Emory Wheel*, *Emory Report*, and local newspapers covered the debate in news articles and editorials. More than a thousand students, faculty, and staff signed petitions opposing the shuttle road. Those in favor of the road countered by noting that it would significantly cut down traffic on North Decatur Road and reduce both commuting time and pollution.

After what Chace termed a thorough and "healthy debate," the University Cabinet decided to recommend to the board of trustees construction of the shuttle road. Summing up the decision, Chace wrote a letter to the community:

> Lullwater, of course, is our most precious green space. For this reason, as president, I must find a balance between conserving a hallowed area while at the same time doing something that will benefit the community as a whole. . . . Let us remember that Lullwater is not protected by a [dome]—it is being polluted by car exhaust every single day. We must get cars stopped and off the roads. . . . I am also convinced that Lullwater needs to be protected. I have heard your concerns loud and clear: One of them is this: Will the shuttle road just be the beginning of our encroachment on Lullwater?

The shuttle road was opposed by the COE, but supported by other University Senate committees, and ultimately by a slim majority of the full Senate. But no one involved in the issue—environmentalists or the campus planners tasked with building the road—felt any sense of victory. The head of campus planning and construction, Vice President Bob Hascall, had recently arrived from a California institution that had invested in electric vehicles. He did not find Emory at all unified in its approach to environmental concerns. "We came away from the shuttle road experience with the feeling that this just wasn't the way to get things done."

COE members, of course, had felt that way for a long time. John Wegner, lecturer in human and natural ecology, who also had recently joined the University, had been a leader in opposing the road. But now that the project was moving forward, he was determined that environmental standards be maintained every step of the way. The road and bridge design was modified by the COE to help avoid old-growth forest to a greater degree than originally planned, and to mitigate damage caused by the road, since it was known that such an abrupt fragmentation of the natural ecosystem would have a harmful impact on the forests' inhabitants for some distance from the edge of the disturbance.

"Environmental principles moved up quite a few notches after the shuttle road," said Size. Where developers used to "listen politely to what sounded like nice, cozy sentiments, then went ahead and did their own thing, after the road, they acknowledged the value of our contributions, and the importance of healthy ecological systems." Under Wegner's leadership, the COE and campus planners collaborated to the point of serving on each other's committees, so that planning could be approached holistically rather than project by project.

Ideas converged, collaborations formed. At the urging of anthropology professor Peggy Barlett, Hascall and University architect Jen Fabrick attended a Second Nature conference in 2000 that persuaded them to pursue a green building program. In partnership with COE, Hascall won trustee support for seeking Leadership in Energy and Environmental Design (LEED) certification for all future buildings. Emory received silver LEED certification for the first building in the Southeast so designated—the Whitehead Research Building.

In 2001 the University Senate adopted a mission statement affirming the University's commitment to the environment and appointed a University task force to implement that vision, which led to Wegner's appointment as Emory's first chief environmental officer.[8] The construction of the shuttle road—now called Starvine Way, for a rare plant that grows in Lullwater—and the campus conversation about Lullwater's future was the beginning of a recommitment to environmental stewardship and led directly to inclusion of ecological principles in Emory's current vision statement and strategic priorities.

> *The perceived threat to Lullwater's future galvanized the community in a way that the Committee on the Environment—and the Campus Development Committee before it—had not been able to do.*

Environmental stewardship takes many forms—recycling, energy conservation, food gardening, alternative transportation. Emory has made a substantial commitment to all of these. Perhaps the most important manifestation of this commitment, from the perspective of the generations who have cared for and studied and enjoyed the University's forests, has been the commitment that grew out of the Lullwater shuttle road controversy.

In supporting the road, President Chace had voiced the community's biggest fear—was this step just the beginning of a nibbling at Emory's forests until none were left? Chace himself responded to this question by appointing a Lullwater Management Task Force, charged with developing a comprehensive management plan for Lullwater, now referred to as a preserve. A policy of no net tree loss was developed and implemented. With the recommendation of President James Wagner and Executive Vice President Michael Mandl, the board of trustees in November 2005 approved a land-use classification plan designating all University property as either preserved, conserved, restricted, managed, or open to development. More than 50 percent of the University's land now was designated as protected.

The Legacy | It is difficult to review Emory's history without feeling a sense of loss, not only for its natural resources, but also for missed opportunities in making the best use of the University's human resources. An enduring environmental ethic has been passed on through Emory's generations, from Woolford Baker and Robert Platt to Larry Ragsdale and Don Shure, and on to Bill Murdy, Eloise Carter, and John Wegner. This legacy is the conviction that forests give us life, and that we owe them something in return. The collective voice of these environmental stewards now, finally, resonates throughout Emory's vision statements and—perhaps even more important—in development proposals that have a potential impact on the University's natural resources.

Emory has stepped up to its responsibility, says Eloise Carter. "Emory's practice now matches its environmental values. We have a shared vision for making decisions for the land, the natural environment, for the common good."

CHAPTER 7

SHAPED BY A CRUCIBLE EXPERIENCE
The Center for Women at Emory
— ALI P. CROWN *and* JAN GLEASON —

Tracing the establishment and growth of the Center for Women at Emory, Ali Crown and Jan Gleason detail the events and campus climate that brought women's issues to the fore at Emory in the 1970s and the 1980s. Following two serious campus incidents of violence against women, students and others soon called for a women's center. Crown and Gleason describe the progress—sometimes slow and often frustrating—toward creating a "resource for services and programs to support women throughout the University."

A SERIES OF CONTROVERSIAL events involving race and gender in the late 1980s tested Emory to its core and pushed the University to a new understanding of itself as a diverse community. Having expended considerable effort in opening the path to parity in the numbers of women and minorities, Emory now was forced to find ways for them to be supported, heard, valued, and included as full members of the community. These events served as crucible experiences for Emory and led to the creation of the Center for Women at Emory.

By the late 1980s some three and a half decades had passed since women had first been admitted to Emory College as residential students, and the number of women faculty members and students was growing. The Women's Caucus had formed in the early 1970s, and by 1976 its work led President Sanford S. Atwood to establish formally the President's Commission on the Status of Women (PCSW). By the late 1970s the PCSW's annual reports were primarily concerned with Emory's hiring more women as faculty and staff, so that their sheer numbers would increase Emory's attention to their particular issues. The late 1980s also saw increasing activity among women students. Undergraduates formed a feminist group, CHOICES, in 1986, which raised concerns about sexual harassment and was particularly vocal in 1988 about a lewd and graphic T-shirt for a fraternity fundraiser. A Division of Campus Life task force on sexual assault organized Coalition Against Rape at Emory (CARE) in 1990, a group whose student members were trained by professional staff to educate the campus about sexual assault.

By the late 1980s minority students also had been enrolled for a quarter of a century, and their numbers had increased dramatically. Several painful racial incidents had occurred in the 1980s including both students and faculty that, according to historian Stuart Gulley, "called into question the University's commitment to racial equality."[1] In the same year that students were raising issues about racial intolerance, Dr. Sondra O'Neale, a female African American faculty member, charged that Emory's denial of her tenure had been based on racism. Rage about discrimination peaked in the spring of 1990 when Sabrina Collins, a freshman, claimed that she was receiving harassing letters and death threats. Although investigation later showed that Collins created the letters and threats herself, concerns about racism at Emory did not diminish.

The presence of large numbers of women and minorities on campus meant that they had achieved a parity of sorts within the traditionally white, male university, but questions continued to surface about the support and processes for their full inclusion in the community.

By 1989 the PCSW had monitored the progress of women at Emory for more than a decade, and that year the commission published an extensive report that raised concerns about the status of women. These concerns found expression in two major recommendations: first, that Emory hire and promote women staff and faculty with an even more vigorous affirmative-action program; and, second, that Emory develop a comprehensive leave policy to include paid parental leave for faculty and staff. The report, published in a September 1989 issue of *Campus Report*, included President James T. Laney's response: "The report makes a persuasive case that the concerns of the staff of the University are not adequately heard at the highest levels of the various divisions and of the University. It reminds us that women are underrepresented on the faculty."

That same month, the University Priorities Committee, a body of faculty members chaired by Provost Billy E. Frye, laid the foundation for an anticipated fund-raising campaign. The committee noted that a decade of positive development had been under way since the gift of $105 million to Emory by Robert and George Woodruff in 1979: facilities had been expanded; faculty had grown in size and scholarly productivity; sponsored research had increased, and so had student selectivity. The committee's report observed that "Emory has moved quickly from the status of a fine regional university with notable points of distinction to that of an institution poised on the threshold of achieving national and international distinction across the broad spectrum of its programs."

Emory's development of the 1980s had created an ambitious intellectual agenda for the University, but in September 1989 Laney pointed out some of the tensions inherent in this agenda, when he addressed the faculty. "The very growth of the eighties has put strains on our community," he said. Taking stock of Emory's progress, Laney asked a pivotal question: "What kind of university do we want to become? . . . How do we keep Emory humane?"

In answer, he pointed to the "moral authority" in teaching, an endeavor through which "one invests in another life. . . . We want Emory to be a place of intellectual ferment, . . . where the encounter with ideas challenges our most fundamental presuppositions and makes us question our own biases."[2]

The Fire under the Crucible | In a foreshadowing of issues to come, Ali P. Crown—then-chair of the PCSW—wrote on January 23, 1990, to President Laney expressing several concerns: "Among the most pressing concerns we [the PCSW] expressed . . . was our wish to see the University make a strong statement against sexual assault and acquaintance rape. For example, many institutions have a published policy in their handbooks and conduct codes clearly stating their unwillingness to tolerate such offensive behavior."

On February 7, 1990, the front page of the *Emory Wheel* reported on incidents that would become the spark for the creation of the Women's Center: "Two rapes reported on campus," proclaimed the headline; "one student arrested." According to the *Wheel*, both of the alleged rapes had occurred on Fraternity Row [now Eagle Row] on the previous Saturday at two different locations. In both cases, Chief of Police Ed Medlin said the victims were "acquainted" with their attackers, but the circumstances were different. The twenty-one-year-old student who was arrested was charged with raping a woman who did not attend Emory. Medlin said it was a "classic case in which the suspect prevented his victim from leaving the room." The other incident, involving a nineteen-year-old Emory student, was described as "less violent, but nonconsensual." As a result of legal confidentiality requirements, additional factual details about the assaults were not made public at that time.

In an editorial in the same issue, the *Wheel* wrote, "Time to clean up the row . . . . Rape. DUI. Maybe, just maybe, two public drunkenness arrests could have gone without notice. However the problems of Fraternity Row are no longer as simple as people getting drunk and acting stupid. Students are now getting drunk and acting dangerously."[3]

The two rapes set off a tumult of campus activism and activity. President Laney read a statement at a subsequent press briefing announcing that a "special task force" would be appointed "to examine comprehensively the way that the abuse of alcohol and drugs, as well as violent or discriminatory behavior toward individuals and groups, work together to undermine our University community."[4]

Later that month, a group of graduate students weighed in on the issue. In a letter to Laney and William H. Fox, dean of Campus Life, they reiterated the need for immediate action by the administration to "improve our common life," and pressed for the creation of a women's center. The students underscored the need for "more alternative social spaces to accommodate the diverse needs and interests of our community," and they envisioned a women's center "as a locus for information, dialogue, and learning for *all* members of the Emory community." Administratively and physically independent of women's studies, the center would meet "educational, social, political, and cultural needs" not being met through existing structures.

By early March, Laney had appointed twenty-five faculty and staff members, students, and alumni to serve on the Task Force on Security and Responsibility, chaired by Barbara A. B. "Bobbi" Patterson (then associate chaplain, later senior lecturer in religion). Charging the group to find ways to "improve security and ensure responsibility in community life by recognizing and honoring diversity," Laney suggested eight topics for particular focus, including "sensitivity to gender and ethnic diversity."

The task force's report, published in the April 27, 1990, issue of *Emory Report*, covered a broad range of community life. One of the report's twenty-four recommendations called for "Creation of a Women's Resource Center to address women's concerns through social, educational, and support programs for both men and women." The administration responded positively to many of the recommendations, including the proposal to create a women's center. In a May 16, 1990, address to the Board of Visitors, Laney reported,

> The tumult on campus this spring has suggested that the old coordinates by which we measured our life in this community are no longer adequate. . . . I have to confess that, for a long time, in my own kind of simple-minded way, I thought that numbers were what this sort of place was about. You opened the gates of admission to new students and faculty and staff, you increased the numbers of women, increased the numbers of minorities, recruited more international students—and, lo and behold, it all would come together, and you would have the new university. Not so. . . . The leadership that is perceptive and visionary enough to understand the new world aborning has got to be shaped in the crucible of experiences like those that happened this spring at Emory.

Out of the Crucible | With this new personal and institutional understanding that additional support structures would be needed for the full participation of women and minorities in the Emory community, work began to create the women's center. In a July 1990 letter, Patterson wrote to Jan Gleason, the new chair of the PCSW, suggesting that the PCSW take responsibility for creating the center and emphasizing that it not "become 'ghettoized' into a particular interpretive model of feminism." Patterson called for input by a group of diverse individuals to "explore and develop goals and objectives for such a center." Thus began the PCSW's early role in the creation of the women's center.

Paula Washington, one of the Emory's first PhD recipients in women's studies, who graduated in 1995, shared her knowledge of women's centers and suggested resources regarding women's centers at the October 4, 1990, PCSW meeting. She urged the commission to review models of women's centers and think carefully about what Emory needed in a center. As a group of volunteers, however, PCSW members were concerned that they lacked expertise to carry out the responsibility of creating the center. Gleason wrote to Laney later that month to report the commission's recommendation that the University hire a consultant to assist in the development of the center. She added that the commission was anxious to see an advisory committee appointed by the end of October.

As the community became clearer about its vision, it also grew impatient with the slow pace of creating the center. According to the November 20, 1990, *Wheel*, the undergraduate student group CHOICES presented a petition with 672 signatures to Secretary of the University Thomas Bertrand, demanding that a committee to create the center be named immediately. Later that month, Bertrand received another missive, from the PCSW Faculty Concerns Committee, signed by 31 women and men, also expressing urgency. Having gathered input at a series of open forums, they observed,

> A women's center could provide a focal point for addressing ongoing problems, such as violence, in a way that is neither fragmented nor simply reactive. Of equal importance is the center's ability to enrich the campus's intellectual and social life. Attentiveness to women's cultural, aesthetic, intellectual, and social contributions could be greatly expanded by a women's center. Finally, such a center could provide a context for Emory's women to find resources they need because of the peculiar problems they face in the academy and in the world as women.

The letter went on to say that the center should include all of the constituencies of women on campus; provide a central meeting place for women with diverse interests; develop programs in diverse areas, including those focused on health; house a library and resource center; and welcome men. Consensus was clearly developing about a model for a center that would best serve the entire community.

The *Annual Report of the President* published in the January 28, 1991, issue of *Campus Report* contained a summation of the transformation that Emory had undergone the previous year:

> All of this discussion [through the previous spring] showed, among other things, that a University must find appropriate ways to air and deal with conflict. We learned not that the fabric of our common life was in danger of being rent by discord or suspicion, but that the warp and woof of our tapestry was strong. . . . Emory can hold safely in its midst the conflicts typical of close-knit communities. What is more, Emory can transcend these conflicts in creative ways. In a society as pluralistic as the America of the late-twentieth century, we can expect more such tests. American universities must explore new avenues for defining and resolving conflict, and Emory means to lead in this endeavor.

As the spring semester unfolded, progress on the center gained speed. In February, Laney appointed an advisory committee, chaired by Ali P. Crown, associate director of executive programs in the Business School. She had come to Emory in 1980 to direct the move of the Law and Economics Center from the University of Miami to Emory, and quickly had become involved in women's issues. She chaired the PCSW in 1989–90. The advisory committee, charged with studying and formally recommending a model for a women's center, included undergraduate and graduate students, staff, faculty, and ex officio members representing the President's Office, the PCSW, the Task Force on Security and Responsibility, and the Division of Campus Life.

Maria Luisa "Papusa" Molina, director of the Women's Resource and Action Center at the University of Iowa, visited campus on February 21 and led a retreat for the PCSW and the advisory committee. She noted that a women's center, in order to be effective, must be structured and developed to profit from and promote positive relationships with the central administration and other women's constituencies. Further discussions ensued, often in open forums, sponsored by the advisory committee. Along the way, the advisory committee developed a mission statement for the Emory Women's Center, whose "purpose . . . is to provide resources and support for women as they empower themselves and each other in the pursuit of their individual and collective goals. The center strives to create an atmosphere in which all persons are free to affirm and celebrate their differences." The committee envisioned the center as a resource for services and programs to support women throughout the University, as an advocate for "the full participation of women in the community," as a promoter of freedom and openness, and as "a forum for women's cultural, spiritual, aesthetic, intellectual and social life."

The Center Opens | After nearly another year of planning, study, and a national search, the Emory Women's Center opened in September 1992. President Laney appointed Ali Crown as its first director. The origin of the Emory Women's Center, traced to the two 1990 campus date rapes, mirrored the origins of many women's centers. Nationally, their establishment began in the late sixties and early seventies with a growing awareness that the academy had been designed to accommodate men, and that women's particular needs were largely unmet. Frequently, a rape or a legal action by a woman faculty member was the catalyst for a center's creation. Centers were often established to raise awareness about the need for equity and safety and to help women see that the power of their numbers could lead to institutional change. By 1990 there were several hundred women's centers on college campuses in the United States. Today there are more than five hundred, and new ones continue to be established. Their network is strong.

Because Emory's center was designed to represent a wide constituency and a variety of issues, the early plan called for the director to report to the President's Office. But the center's initial physical location was less than presidential. A September 28, 1992, *Wheel* headline announced, "Center opens to empower Emory women"; it was accompanied by a photo of a trailer that would become the center's home, delivered on a flatbed truck and set down behind the Dobbs University Center loading dock, where it remained for the next twelve years. While the trailer was euphemistically referred to as a "modular unit," the center and its staff were frequently referred to as "two women in a trailer."

Inside the front door of the trailer, however, visitors found themselves transformed by its warm, comfortable ambience. Women's poster art filled the walls. The trailer housed two offices, a library, a spacious meeting room, a kitchen, and a small "quiet room," which eventually served many purposes, including use as a lactation space. Students and staff at the center worked with University archivists to create a wall of photos that told the story of significant events in the lives of Emory women, predominantly since the College had become coeducational. Though not appealing on the outside, and by no means majestic within, the trailer became a haven for students, faculty, and staff.

> *"Every good university guarantees its members that certain basic, enabling conditions of work will be met and certain fundamental academic values will be honored."*

By the time the center opened, the reporting line was changed to the Provost's Office. During its first twelve years, its full-time staff included the director and a succession of support persons—almost all of whom were recent Emory College graduates taking a hiatus between college and graduate school. While this was an ideal mentoring model, the practical side of this arrangement, based in slim resources, meant that in the center's first fourteen years, eleven women filled this support position before the center obtained funding for a second career-track person, who eventually became an assistant director for programs. This long-awaited growth of the staff occurred simultaneously with the center's 2004 move to newly renovated space on the third floor of Cox Hall, in the hub of the campus.

Before the opening of the center, its advisory committee had developed a five-year plan, and the center's staff focused energy on following that plan. Along with visits to other women's centers, Crown drew upon constant community input. This community engagement became a notable feature of the center, as the staff worked hard to develop partners for the center and to establish it as an integral part of the Emory community.

As the women's center developed a full complement of programs, it provided a formal mechanism to support women and to let their voices be heard. Emory was listening to those voices and began creating programs and resources in response. But needs change over time, and the center needed to continue evolving. One early feature, however, remained constant: the center did not duplicate services offered elsewhere on campus. Instead, it worked in partnership with other resources to strengthen everybody. Early programs emphasized safety, for example, and the center worked with the director of sexual assault services, also a fairly new position, and the Coalition Against Rape at Emory (CARE), a student group, to develop strong resources. When it became clear that graduate students, postdocs, and staff had no place but bathroom stalls to pump their breasts for infant feeding, the center adapted its quiet room into a lactation space. When nursing moms entered, they put a sign on the doorknob identifying the room as the "nursing nest." For many years it was the only dedicated lactation space on campus and was in constant use.

In 2005 Crown suggested to Susan Carini, a staff member in the Division of Communications and Marketing who was then chairing the PCSW's Staff Concerns Committee, that they work together to seek additional lactation spaces. Carini enthusiastically took on the task. Soon afterward, under the leadership of Lisa Newbern, a committee member from the Yerkes National Primate Research Center, the PCSW developed a lactation policy that the University administration endorsed. Today the campus has thirteen nursing rooms, most adapted from existing spaces, and every new building has a private space for this purpose included in its design.

Students from Goizueta Business School, setting the stage for a 2000 external review of the school, conducted a class project in 1998 to evaluate the center and its need for resources. Their report, quoting a 1994 Emory planning document, "Choices and Responsibility," stated, "Every good university guarantees its members that certain basic, enabling conditions of work will be met and certain fundamental academic values will be honored. . . . Emory's Women's Center has exemplified this vision by overcoming adversity to outperform other schools. . . . By rewarding hard work and bringing the community closer together, Emory has the power to enhance its future."

When Emory developed a new vision statement in 2004 and a strategic plan in 2005 to execute that vision, the Long-Term Planning Committee of the center's advisory board developed a new strategic plan for the center in 2006. The goals and initiatives of the center's strategic plan were focused to state explicitly its contributions to one of Emory's overarching goals: to create a community-engaging society. The plan was informed by the University's Vision Statement but reflected the board's particular passion for women, stating, "During the next decade, the Center for Women at Emory will become a change agent for the University so that women are fully integrated as equal participants in all aspects of University life."

Bridgette Young, senior associate dean of the chapel and religious life, and chair of the advisory board in 2006–07, remarked, "While some refer to the present as 'postfeminist,' we still need the CWE for advocacy, community, and celebration." She continued, "Discrimination may be less blatant and intentional, yet we still must keep our community aware that women's voices, ideas, and contributions are essential. And while Emory has come a long way in terms of representation of women in higher levels of the institution, there are still opportunities to do even more."

After sixteen years of center leadership, Crown retired in August 2008, and Dona Yarbrough, director of the Lesbian Gay Bisexual Transgender Center at Tufts University, was named the new director. Ambitious plans are in place to ensure that women will be heard, and that a welcoming community that addresses women's concerns thrives for generations of women who have yet to arrive at Emory.[5]

SECTION 2

Building a Community of Scholars

CHAPTER 8

Atlanta skyline over the Administration Building, early 1980s.

CATCHING UP
The Advance of Emory since World War II
— NANCY DIAMOND —

Emory University—which had started strongly in Atlanta in 1915 but soon fell behind its southern counterparts in developing as a research university—took off in the last quarter of the twentieth century and achieved membership in the Association of American Universities before the century expired. Nancy Diamond, a distinguished historian of higher education and research associate professor of educational leadership and policy studies at the University of Vermont, examines the impediments to Emory's research enterprise in the first half of the century, the steps that prepared the way for transformation, and the difficult decisions and hard work that led to acceleration into a higher orbit of research.[1]

THE GROWTH OF the American research university system since the Second World War is a recognized success story, one that includes the advance of a new group of rising institutions.[2] In the context of postwar population growth, economic prosperity, and the national expansion of higher education enrollments, many campuses launched ambitious drives to position themselves among the top-ranked research universities. Southern universities, late entrants into the world of graduate education and research, faced unique challenges. This chapter documents the transformation of Emory University and explains the circumstances and decisions that advanced campus research capacity and status in the half-century following the war.

At the beginning of World War II, Emory was a small Methodist university enrolling mostly southern students. In the early 1940s, when Yale historian Howard Lamar was an Emory undergraduate from Tuskegee, Alabama, his classmates were primarily "boys from cities of Savannah and Atlanta as well as small Georgia towns."[3] John Palms, an Emory graduate student in 1959, and later Emory's vice president for academic affairs before becoming president of the University of South Carolina, remembers Emory faculty for their dedication to teaching rather than to research.[4] During the early 1960s an external consultant compared Emory to "a southern Oberlin or Amherst rather than a southern university."[5] Yet, less than thirty years later, Emory had become one of the nation's most respected universities, a major producer of research, and a member of the prestigious Association of American Universities (AAU). What were the circumstances and strategies that led to Emory's rapid advance?

The most often quoted explanation argues that in 1979, Emory received a monumental bequest of Coca-Cola stock with substantial annual earnings that enabled the campus to attract a new group of renowned faculty and talented students. This story is well known and entrenched in campus history as well as national higher-education lore. In fact, however, although the $105 million Woodruff gift was a major factor in Emory's progress, the campus transformation is better explained by the dynamic interaction of external trends and circumstances and internal decisions, policies, and strategies. The post-*Sputnik* national expansion of research and graduate education, the migration of population and industry to Sunbelt regions, and the growth of Atlanta as a metropolitan area were important factors, but campus leadership was crucial to Emory's advancement.

Emory's Southern Legacy and the Growth of Atlanta |

The historical difficulty experienced by the predominantly rural South in establishing major research universities has been well documented.[6] Southern universities developed later than their counterparts around the nation, and comparisons with other regions reflected an insurmountable gap. Prior to 1900 only six of forty-four American doctorate-granting universities were in the South, with fewer than 100 southern doctorates awarded by 1915.[7] By 1925, of nearly 17,000 doctorates awarded in the United States, the eleven doctorate-granting southern universities had produced only 225, half of them from the University of Virginia.[8] Following the Depression, despite a crucial need for university research to address the region's rural problems and stimulate industrial development, southern universities were plagued by a brain drain of scientific talent to other regions and remained far behind in research capacity and achievement. Unless this negative trend were reversed, it was argued, the South would be "forever doom[ed] to mediocrity."[9] While southern campuses generally recognized their obligation to provide graduate research and professional training, "Such ambition called for larger resources than an existing institution alone [could] command."[10] To address these circumstances, the Rockefeller-funded General Education Board (GEB) supported development of strategically located schools and colleges and, in 1938, chose Atlanta as one of five southern centers for research and graduate education.[11]

Identified by President Franklin Roosevelt as "the nation's number one economic problem," the South remained in the early 1940s "a rural, agrarian region in the midst of an urban nation."[12] But World War II brought dramatic changes—the mechanical revolution in southern agriculture, the migration from rural regions to metropolitan areas, and a large infusion of funding as the federal government spent more than one-third of the national military budget on southern facilities.[13] Southern universities, where G.I. Bill recipients rapidly expanded enrollments, experienced many of the postwar changes that affected higher education nationally. Like schools in other regions, many southern campuses without appropriate resources instituted doctoral programs, with the result that graduate education was spread too thinly across too many institutions.[14] Many feared that southern higher education might be "fr[ozen] in a pattern of continuing mediocrity or worse for the next several decades." The region needed "not one great university . . . but three or perhaps four."[15]

> *Recognizing that change was inevitable, Tulane, Rice, Emory, Duke, and Vanderbilt joined their public counterparts from Chapel Hill, Austin, and Charlottesville in 1952 to create the Council of Southern Universities for improving higher education in the South.*

In the years following *Sputnik*, the relative lack of scientific personnel in the South remained "a major stumbling block."[16] As a result, southern campuses could not take full advantage of higher education's so-called golden age, when federal support of university research increased multifold. During the early 1960s southeastern states, with about 21 percent of the population, employed only 11 percent of the nation's scientists and engineers, 13 percent of life scientists, 12 percent of earth scientists, and 9 percent of physical scientists.[17] Nearly half of the thirty-five doctorate-granting southern universities had awarded their first PhD after 1945. The average salary of full professors at southern universities was almost 20 percent below the national average, an extreme statistic even in light of a lower cost of living, and salaries at private universities were especially low.[18] Southern campuses were also far below those in other regions in educational and general expenditures per student.[19] Only 15 percent of the free-choice Woodrow Wilson, National Science Foundation (NSF), and National Defense Education Act (NDEA) fellowship recipients chose to attend selected southern schools.[20]

Not surprisingly, Hayward Keniston's 1959 study of the nation's twenty leading graduate schools did not include a single southern institution. Princeton, the smallest campus in Keniston's study, awarded 227 doctorates a year, nearly three times the number granted by Duke or the University of North Carolina–Chapel Hill.[21] Nor did southern universities figure prominently in the top categories in Bernard Berelson's influential 1960 study of graduate education.[22] This lack of recognition created problems with respect to federal funding as the National Science Foundation's commitment to a "best science" criterion generally ignored most southern universities.[23]

In a series of influential reports, the Southern Regional Education Board (SREB) lobbied for development of research activity at southern universities. "Only where university teaching and research . . . have achieved excellence can there be hope for effective research centers geared to industrial development," one study argued.[24] The SREB called for southern campuses to "cast away forever the traditional double standard according to which Southern institutions are compared only with others in the region," and argued for judging these campuses according to national standards of excellence.[25]

Furthermore, the region's entrenched tradition of segregation "seriously threatened . . . the public school base vital to the development of great southern universities," and served as an obstacle to attracting superior faculties.[26] Legal challenges to the prevailing separate-but-equal doctrine in higher education had been under way since the 1930s, long before the U.S. Supreme Court's momentous decision in *Brown v. Board of Education of Topeka, Kansas*, and by 1951 federal courts had compelled the law schools of state universities in Texas, Oklahoma, Louisiana, and Virginia to admit black students.[27] These decisions, which eventually would lead to the end of Jim Crow arrangements in public institutions, also put private campuses on notice.[28] Recognizing that change was inevitable, Tulane, Rice, Emory, Duke, and Vanderbilt joined their public counterparts from Chapel Hill, Austin, and Charlottesville in 1952 to create the Council of Southern Universities for improving higher education in the South. These schools discussed future enrollment of Negroes at graduate and professional schools but issued no joint declaration.[29]

With desegregation under way by the 1960s, southern universities began to profit from federal programs that supported centers of graduate education and better regional balance for the nation's research economy. In fact, the South was the leading regional beneficiary of the NSF's University Science Development Fund, which awarded funds to thirteen southern schools.[30] In their race to catch up with universities in other regions, southern campuses increased PhD production tenfold and graduated more physicians and lawyers.[31]

The development of higher education was an important part of the region's success, but by the 1970s the South also experienced other important economic and social advances. An international energy crisis, increased leisure time, and more adequate retirement income accelerated migration to Sunbelt regions. In the thirty years following World War II, southern states enjoyed a population growth rate that outdistanced that of the rest of the nation, with Georgia one of the fastest growing states. The gap between southern and national incomes also decreased; by 1976, average income in the South was 90 percent of the national income.[32] These changes accompanied a shift in southern attitudes and lifestyle toward national rather than regional norms, with the "Americanization of Dixie" most evident in cities like Dallas, Houston, New Orleans, Charlotte, and Atlanta.

As a federal administrative center, Atlanta received a boost during and after World War II, when federal patronage of the Bell bomber plant, Coca-Cola, and other industries brought significant profits. By 1959 Atlanta's population had reached 1 million, and by 1970 more than 80 percent of its commercial funding came from outside the South.[33] In just a decade, the city changed from "a somewhat sluggish regional distribution center to a . . . truly national [city]."[34] To enhance Atlanta's growth and productivity, political and business leaders recognized that great benefit would derive from developing a major health center and university in their midst.

Origins of Emory University

Emory's early history, discussed in detail by Henry Morton Bullock, dates from 1834, when the Georgia Methodist Conference established a manual labor school, and from 1836, when the Georgia legislature granted the Emory College charter.[35] The establishment of Emory University seventy-five years later is traced to a 1914 lawsuit that severed ties between Vanderbilt University and the Methodist Episcopal Church, South.[36] When the church sought to establish two new universities, one east and one west of the Mississippi, Southern Methodist University in Dallas was chosen as the western campus. Asa Candler, owner of The Coca-Cola Company and brother of Methodist Bishop Warren Candler, pledged $1 million and a tract of land to bring to Atlanta the type of education that would "be definitely directed to the advancement of sound learning and pure religion."[37] The Methodists accepted Candler's offer.

On August 14, 1914, a site northeast of the city, in Druid Hills, was selected for the campus, and Emory College trustees approved a plan to join the new university. To ensure continued training of candidates for ministry, the Methodists opened the Candler School of Theology in downtown Atlanta. The University's new charter, granted six months later, on January 25, 1915, explicitly stated that "the Methodist Episcopal Church, South, is and shall be always regarded and held as the founder of the university."[38] Board members had to be confirmed by the General Conference of the Methodist Episcopal Church, South, which also had the power to remove them.

In 1915, Asa Candler, who had served since 1906 as chair of the Emory College board, was named chair of the Emory University board, and his brother Warren was named chancellor, the title that Vanderbilt had given to its chief executive. That year, the Schools of Medicine and Law were established. Four years later, as Emory College relocated to Druid Hills, the Graduate School and a School of Economics and Business were founded, to be joined in 1922 by Wesley Memorial Hospital, later renamed Emory Hospital, and its nursing school. The original campus continued as a preparatory academy until 1929, when Oxford College was constituted as a two-year division of the University.

The years following World War I were significant for the new university. The Coca-Cola Company was sold in 1919 to a group of Atlanta businessmen headed by Ernest Woodruff, whose son Robert later would guide the company. During the 1920s Emory continued to develop and change. Harvey Warren Cox, a Harvard-educated philosopher and former dean of the University of Florida Teachers College, began in 1920 his twenty-two-year tenure as Emory's president. When Asa Candler died in 1929, his oldest son, Emory graduate Charles Howard Candler, succeeded him as chair of the University board, a position he would hold for almost thirty years. Before the end of the decade, a Phi Beta Kappa chapter was established.[39]

An important and lasting relationship was strengthened when, in 1935, Robert Woodruff accepted an appointment as an Emory trustee, making formal an existing relationship between Emory, The Coca-Cola Company, and Trust Company Bank, founded by family patriarch Ernest Woodruff, Robert's father. The University was a significant shareholder of Coca-Cola stock, and the bank provided financial services to both the company and the campus. In 1937 Woodruff made his first major gift to Emory to found a clinic for the study of neoplastic diseases, a euphemism at the time for cancer.[40]

Becoming Emory University

Emory's development during the years surrounding World War II was influenced by the need for a first-rate university in the Deep South, the expansion of federal support for research and graduate education, the growth of Atlanta, and the University's own aspirations and goals.[41] Before the war, the munificence of Emory's benefactors had created the image of the institution as the private domain of Methodists and a few wealthy Atlanta families. But wartime changes, especially the influx of veterans, made expansion possible. A wartime navy training program and the G.I. Bill brought students from other sections of the country, and veterans expanded enrollment from 2,045 in the spring of 1946 to almost 3,600 by the fall.[42]

The need for a professionally educated labor force in the South led to establishment or expansion of professional programs.[43] In 1944, the Southern Dental College became Emory's School of Dentistry, and the Hospital's School of Nursing was elevated to collegiate rank. To support the medical complex, brothers Robert and George Woodruff established the Ernest and Emily Woodruff Foundation with the estates of their parents (Emily had died in 1938 and Ernest in 1944); the foundation's funds would provide nearly four hundred thousand dollars annually, and by 1953 the family had committed $5 million to Emory's health sciences.[44] The federal government's 1947 decision to locate the Centers for Disease Control adjacent to Emory provided further opportunity.

Cox's successor, Goodrich C. White, served from 1942 to 1957, and when he retired, he served as chancellor (a largely advisory position by this time) from 1957 until his death in 1979. White, an Emory College alumnus (1908), had been recruited by Cox as dean of Emory College and then dean of the Graduate School. White recognized the value of expanding graduate education. He asked Emory graduate (College 1910) and Jefferson biographer Dumas Malone to analyze campus options for developing graduate studies. Malone responded with an enthusiastic report that claimed, "in the whole tier of states beginning with South Carolina and stretching to the Gulf and the Mississippi," Emory was the most likely to become a university of the highest quality.[45] Research and graduate studies, he advised, should emerge from Emory's strengths, rather than be "superimposed."[46] Malone found that the chemistry and biology departments were sufficiently strong to begin doctoral work.

All the same, Malone noted, "The mere restoration of the faculty to prewar strength [would] be a formidable task," especially in humanities.[47] To attract first-rate faculty, Emory would need adequate laboratory and library facilities, a more reasonable teaching load, and research funds and leaves of absence for those who demonstrated scholarly ability. Malone emphasized the importance of establishing arts and sciences graduate programs of equal strength to those at the School of Medicine, limiting the number of graduate fields, and emphasizing balance in academic pursuits. Following Malone's recommendations, Emory's first PhD in chemistry was conferred in June 1948, almost thirty years after the Graduate School was established.

A timely chance to expand graduate education came in 1951, when the General Education Board (GEB) promised Emory $7 million in matching funds in order "to create a [southern] university of the first rank . . . by national standards." More than any other institution in the Southeast, the GEB argued, Emory "seem[ed] capable of acquiring the resources and providing the leadership necessary for a university of national stature and influence."[48] Emory ranked below Duke, Vanderbilt, and Tulane, but the GEB believed that Emory was making serious effort. The University had strengthened the faculty, raised salaries, and avoided distractions like intercollegiate football. To receive the GEB funds, Emory was required to secure $33 million from other sources, of which $25 million would be for graduate education.

> *The campus endowment increased from $390,000 in 1944 to $1.8 million in 1954.*

As it turned out, Emory officials did not share the view that the campus was ready to be transformed into an important regional graduate center. Responding to the GEB offer, President White asked instead for one-third of the grant to support Emory's professional schools, and two-thirds for undergraduate instruction. Although the GEB was willing to compromise, Emory could not secure the matching funds by December 1957, the date set by the pledge, and the campus formally surrendered hope of receiving all but $2 million.

The 1950s nevertheless brought consolidation and achievement for Emory. Educational and general expenditures increased from just over $1 million in 1944–45 to $4.5 million a decade later.[49] Major construction during White's presidency meant that at the time of his retirement, about half the University had been erected during his administration. Enrollment grew from seven hundred to seventeen hundred. In 1953 a new policy of coeducation stabilized declining enrollment during the Korean War and increased the size, quality, and geographical diversity of the student body, balancing the predominantly male enrollment in preprofessional education with female enrollment in the liberal arts.[50] The campus endowment increased from $390,000 in 1944 to $1.8 million in 1954.[51] Ties with the Methodist Church were strengthened when Emory trustees created the Committee of One Hundred, an advisory group representing the nine-state Southeastern Jurisdiction. Under a Jurisdictional One Percent Fund for Ministerial Education, established in 1955, the School of Theology would receive one-third of the annual funds donated by Methodist congregations for ministerial training.[52]

The campus medical complex grew as Emory moved the medical school from downtown to Druid Hills, expanded its clinical services through acquisition of the Crawford Long Memorial Hospital (now Emory University Hospital Midtown), and the creation of the Emory Clinic in 1952; a new clinic building, made possible through Robert Woodruff's gift of $1 million, opened two years later.[53] A $6 million grant from the Woodruff Foundation in 1954 for the first time allowed the School of Medicine to operate without a deficit. Biomedical research was enhanced when Emory agreed to assume ownership and administrative responsibility for Yale University's Florida-based Yerkes Laboratory of Primate Biology in 1956.[54] That year, Emory also received a $3.9 million Ford Foundation Challenge Grant, of which more than half was allocated to the medical school and the hospitals.[55]

When Goodrich White announced in March 1956 that he would retire after the next academic year, the trustees searched for a new president. They sought a candidate who was "dedicated wholeheartedly to the Christian interpretation of God and Man as manifested in Jesus Christ."[56] Opposed by the faculty but with strong support from the board, Sidney Walter Martin, dean of the College of Arts and Sciences at the University of Georgia, was selected as the president who would lead Emory into the golden age that had already begun.[57]

Slow but Steady Progress in the "Golden Age" | The "golden age" (1958–68) was a time of historic expansion in American higher education, growth fueled by what seemed an unlimited supply of students, generous federal research support, and strong public belief in the value of scientific research.[58] By the time *Sputnik* circled the earth, Emory was a regional Methodist university with aspirations that dovetailed with federal intent to expand the nation's research capacity. The plan was to become a good academic institution measured by national standards with a special responsibility to the Methodist Church, and to continue a commitment of service to the Southeast.[59] Emory planned "to move more actively into the community," providing graduate and professional programs that would help meet the region's need for business and professional leadership.[60]

Unfortunately, University resources did not match University aspirations. In the early 1960s, the Emory faculty was "good but undistinguished."[61] There were no winners of Nobel or Pulitzer prizes or comparable awards, and no officers of national or international professional organizations. Nor did the faculty demonstrate the "uniform and omnipresent dedication to research . . . characteristic of truly great universities."[62] With only a "score of individuals" accounting for the bulk of publications and honors, Emory faculty had achieved academic recognition at a level "just below the top."[63] They were competitive with other southern faculties, but not with great national faculties.

There were serious deterrents to developing a research ethos. During the 1950s President White and the trustees had balanced the budget by increasing the student-faculty ratio, paying low salaries, and "stinting the academic program."[64] In effect, they had imposed the obligations of graduate instruction and scholarship without a corresponding increase in faculty size to support first-rate graduate programs.

Outside evaluators from prestigious universities noted that Emory faculty were still operating under a workload that had been appropriate when there was no graduate school.[65] Faculty in English taught three classes per quarter and averaged twenty-seven students per class.[66] The Biology Department was "singularly understaffed."[67] In physics, teaching responsibilities "simply [did] not permit" faculty to compete successfully for research funding.[68] In comparison with faculty salaries at fourteen public and private southern campuses, Emory ranked near the bottom.[69] The School of Medicine, however, continued to receive generous federal funds for sponsored research. In 1956–57 biomedical researchers gained support of about $1.2 million, 16 percent of the total campus operating expenses; four years later, they won about $3.5 million, or 31 percent of Emory's total.

Southern reluctance to move toward integration of higher education, and the specific threat in the early 1960s that Georgia public schools would be closed, further inhibited Emory's ability to recruit and retain top faculty talent. At the same time, circumstances in Atlanta, "a city too busy to hate," produced different results from those in Birmingham and Little Rock.[70] Corporate leaders, including Robert Woodruff, recognized that attracting new dollars and industry to Atlanta depended on the peaceful integration of public schools.[71] Atlanta's influential citizens thus supported integration.[72]

Although its charter and bylaws had never excluded students on the basis of race, Emory held to an all-white admissions policy in order to comply with state legislation that would revoke the tax exemption of any institution that taught whites and blacks together. In 1961 the trustees

Thomas P. Johnston (College 1940, Graduate 1941) received Emory's first PhD degree (in biochemistry) in 1948.

declared their intent to admit qualified students "without regard to race, color or creed," pending clarification of state laws with respect to the tax exemption of the University.[73] The next year, the Georgia Supreme Court declared unconstitutional all provisions in the state constitution and statutes that denied tax exemption to private campuses that integrated their student bodies. Emory enrolled its first two full-time African American students in the School of Nursing in January 1963, and each received a master's degrees the following December. With Rockefeller Foundation support, eighteen African Americans were enrolled in four divisions during the next year.[74] Since then, Emory has consistently ranked at or near the top in student diversity, with the largest percentage of black students among the nation's top twenty-five highest-ranked universities.[75]

All the same, Emory was at a crossroads. Significant and immediate increases for faculty salaries and funds for plant maintenance were "imperative" at a time when the University was operating at a deficit.[76] In order to compete on a national level, the University had to "diversify its portfolio [and] broaden its base of support." No longer able to rely on the generosity of one or two prominent Atlanta families, Emory would have to "project the image of a public servant to several new constituencies, professional groups, the Methodist Church, alumni, [and the] business and industrial community."[77]

As the University confronted these challenges, President Martin, whose tenure was marred by continuing budget deficits, was pressured to resign after five years of service.[78] During the next year, the University operated without a president, governed instead by a "troika" (the Administration Building had been dubbed "the Kremlin"), comprising Emory insiders Henry Bowden, board chair; Judson "Jake" Ward, vice president and dean of the faculties; and Goodrich White. Although Emory urgently needed additional funds to augment faculty salaries and improve facilities, this was hardly the time to begin a major fund-raising campaign. Such an event would have to wait for a new president, one who could provide leadership for Emory's entrance into the big leagues.

The July 19, 1963, issue of *Time* magazine heralded the news. "Atlanta's ambitious Emory University, which had searched for a year for a new president, last week snagged just the man."[79] Like other southern universities trying to establish national reputations, Emory reached outside the region to hire Sanford S. Atwood, a University of Wisconsin–trained botanist and former Cornell provost, who could further Emory's national aspirations.[80] A radical departure from his predecessors, Atwood—a Yankee, a layman, and a Presbyterian—was unanimously elected by the trustees on July 8, 1963.[81] With enthusiastic assistance from Graduate School dean Charles Lester, Judson Ward, and Henry Bowden, Atwood set out to improve Emory's reach and reputation.

Atwood believed that Emory had "the greatest potential of any private university in the country."[82] Finding faculty morale unspeakably low, he offered a dose of self-esteem: "You people are twice as good as you think you are, whereas Harvard faculty think they are twice as good as they really are."[83] During his presidency, the faculty was strengthened, growing "slowly in size and significantly in quality and prestige."[84] By 1965 the full-time College faculty had increased to 273 (up from 178 ten years earlier), with graduates of Yale, Chicago, and Harvard making up a high percentage of new recruits.[85]

Atwood recognized that to improve campus quality, he first had to establish financial solvency. In 1962–63, basic educational expenditures were almost $7 million, and the campus endowment was $2.2 million.[86] "Dr. Atwood's insistence on fiscal soundness is what helped [Emory] grow," recalled Henry Bowden.[87] Atwood would never accept a budget deficit, and soon paid off the cumulative debt he inherited. He linked admissions policy to the larger goal of securing a place for Emory among the nation's top universities, and raised tuition, which had the perhaps unanticipated consequence of attracting undergraduate applicants from northeastern states, where tuition at private institutions was already high.

During Atwood's tenure, Emory's reputation greatly improved. His style and sophistication also helped to recruit faculty from top universities in other regions.[88] To change the perception that Emory was a small-time Methodist school, Atwood and his wife Betty spent considerable time entertaining Atlanta's social and business elite at Lullwater House, the president's campus residence. But the adjustment of Emory's socially conservative trustees to the new president was not smooth. When they learned that the Atwoods had served wine at a lunch honoring Lady Bird Johnson, the Methodist constituency "went into orbit."[89] Despite their criticism, and confident in his own vision, in October 1965 Atwood inaugurated the University's MERIT (Mobilizing Educational Resources and Ideas for Tomorrow) Campaign with a goal of $25 million, the largest in the school's history and among southern universities.

Positive publicity came unexpectedly from Atwood's 1965 stance in a controversy involving Thomas J. J. Altizer, a young faculty member in the Religion Department and a vocal proponent of the "God is dead" movement.[90] Despite enormous pressure to condemn Altizer's views, the Emory president stood firm in defense of academic freedom. When board members criticized him, Atwood argued that having granted tenure to Altizer, the trustees were obligated to protect his academic freedom.

The Altizer incident was one of the major turning points in Emory's evolution from a regional college with satellite and professional schools to a university of national stature. An article in *Time* identified Atwood and three other southern university presidents who were part of "a real educational renaissance [and who] refused to keep old Southern traditions at the cost of academic quality."[91] When a *New York Times* notice brought further attention to the Altizer controversy, the Ford Foundation, which had previously rejected Emory's application, awarded the University a $6 million Challenge Grant, which set the MERIT campaign off to a dramatic start and spearheaded an expansion of voluntary support.

Nevertheless, during these years Emory did not exhibit the rapid advancement typical of more established campuses. Instead the mid-1960s were characterized by slow movement "from its position as a strong university to an institution of first quality as measured by the most exacting national standards."[92] As at many second-tier universities, expansion of graduate education enhanced institutional stature and access to new revenues. Research support in the amount of $6.8 million came through the NSF's Science Development Program.[93] Funds from the NDEA supported math and physics and, later, new PhD programs across the academic spectrum.[94] More than two hundred doctorates were awarded between 1957 and 1965, compared to a total of twenty-seven before 1957.[95] During these years, Emory ranked forty-eighth nationally in the number of students with free-choice Woodrow Wilson and NSF fellowships.[96]

The School of Medicine continued to attract significant federal research support. The school's operating budget in 1963–64 was $6 million (of a total campus budget of $25 million), almost two-thirds of it from federal funds.[97] That year, the Woodruff Endowment for Medical Education—with assets of more than $11 million—was transferred to full University control. Of the $9 million in federal support awarded to the campus during the mid-1960s, more than $7 million came from the Public Health Service (PHS).[98] Dramatic advances in research potential also came in 1965, when the federally funded Yerkes Primate Research Center was moved from Florida to the Emory campus.[99]

The American Council on Education 1966 Cartter Report offered positive recognition for faculty and graduate programs in six areas (biochemistry, English, history, microbiology, pharmacology, and physiology).[100] Despite these accolades, Emory's progress at mid-decade perhaps was characterized best by Thomas English's 1965 assessment: "If Emory has not yet achieved the highest rank among America's institutions of learning," English wrote, "it has at least made fair progress toward the ultimate goal of usefulness and distinction."[101]

Supporting Research during the Stagnant Years | Sanford Atwood's early years as president of Emory corresponded to a time of historic growth for American higher education. By 1968, however, abrupt changes in the nation's economy, the redirection of federal research

funding to applied projects, and erosion of public trust created a vastly different climate.[102] For southern universities especially, inflation and recurring recessions of the early 1970s threatened progress. Even in the South, "The projection of substantial surpluses of potential faculty had significant consequences for graduate programs [and] for the management of institutions."[103]

Although not exempt from student protests against the war in Vietnam and the harsh economic conditions that confronted the nation's campuses, Emory was able to avoid the disasters that plagued many private institutions.[104] Facing the first budget deficit of his presidency in 1969–70, Atwood initiated a series of stop-gap measures, including a salary freeze and a moratorium on hiring. Faculty vacancies were filled either at lower levels or not at all.[105] Campus officials prepared a balanced budget for the next year by increasing tuition and again eliminating faculty salary increases. This decision, risky in terms of faculty retention and recruitment, was seen as a better alternative to closing programs or operating at a deficit.[106] Integration of the faculty continued, however, as Emory hired its first two black faculty members in 1971: Grant S. Shockley, professor of Christian education at the Candler School, and Delores Aldridge, the first black faculty member in Emory's College.[107]

> *Limited finances during the early 1970s virtually eliminated the possibility of new senior appointments, and departing faculty, often those with national reputations, were replaced by recent PhDs or not replaced at all.*

At the same time, 1971 was a record year for private donations, as $47 million placed Emory first in the nation in total gifts received. While other universities suffered retrenchment, these gifts included $17 million from the Woodruff Foundation that made possible necessary renovation and construction of campus science facilities.[108] Although there were no accumulated reserves at the end of 1972, Emory did not face the large deficits that confronted other private campuses. Where declining enrollments and budget deficits were the national norm, Emory enjoyed a record enrollment and operated in the black.[109]

Yet Emory leaders faced difficult decisions. Although the College enrollment had increased by almost 30 percent, the full-time faculty had grown by only 5 percent.[110] As at many other universities, the administration during the 1960s had made few strategic decisions about expansion. New positions were authorized to meet undergraduate enrollment needs, rather than to strengthen graduate or research programs.[111] Limited finances during the early 1970s virtually eliminated the possibility of new senior appointments, and departing faculty, often those with national reputations, were replaced by recent PhDs or not replaced at all. This strategy, though perhaps necessary, gradually eroded faculty strength.[112]

Lacking infrastructure and salaries to attract the best candidates, Emory could barely compete for qualified faculty. Compared to selected Council of Southern Universities campuses, Emory ranked next-to-last in average salaries.[113] Deteriorating facilities and poor library resources continued as major deterrents. A growing proportion of tenured faculty inhibited recruitment of new talent.[114] Nevertheless, President Atwood argued, with more selective hiring and promotion policies, the Emory faculty could grow in quality. A faculty Committee on Promotion and Tenure, the campus's first, was a crucial addition in 1971. The committee determined that "no member of the faculty [would] be promoted to full professor unless he ha[d] become a leading scholar in his field."[115]

The president professed a commitment to "training individuals at the highest levels," but graduate-school deficits produced serious concerns.[116] A Committee on the Graduate Faculty polled faculty opinion about continuing the graduate program. Three-fourths of the respondents claimed that they would not have accepted Emory appointments had there been no graduate program, and almost 90 percent indicated that they would be receptive to offers from elsewhere if graduate programs were abandoned.[117] The committee concluded that the high-quality programs in biology, chemistry, English, history, mathematics, psychology, and religion must be preserved, but weak programs in classics, geology, and German could be terminated.[118] Complementing their endorsement of graduate education, increased numbers of Emory faculty demonstrated higher levels of research. More than half had received external research grants, and a third had won postdoctoral research fellowships. The 1970 ACE Roose-Andersen evaluation rated thirteen Emory programs at the high end of the scale, compared to six in the 1966 Cartter report; pharmacology ranked eleventh nationally.[119]

With campus research activity centered in biomedical fields, Emory was not adversely affected by changing patterns of federal support during the 1970s. In 1971 almost 90 percent of the basic health sciences faculty received external research funding.[120] Between 1963 and 1972 federal support for biomedical research had produced a 12 percent increase in Emory's share of total federal research funding.[121] However, declining federal support for graduate fellowships caused concern, especially in the basic health sciences, where almost 80 percent of students were supported by external funds.[122]

During the mid-1970s, Emory exhibited what one observer of higher education has called the "social capability to capitalize on distinct conditions of the period."[123] President Atwood believed that Emory had to adjust to difficult conditions rather than be consumed by them. He argued that "a university with a clear set of objectives and a plan of operation . . . had a special advantage in times of uncertainty."[124] Atwood's Five-Year Planning Report submitted to the trustees in November 1976 reflected financial realities. Proposing small increases in enrollment and tuition and a substantial improvement in facilities, the report concluded, "Emory could continue to provide distinctive, privately supported education of the highest caliber, and fulfill its commitment to prepare leadership for metropolitan Atlanta, the state, the region, and the nation."[125] There remained major questions about how the necessary costs would be financed.

Achieving Success in the New Era | The period encompassing the late 1970s to the 1990s has been called "a new era" for American research universities.[126] At Emory, these years were inaugurated with a search for a new president. Sanford Atwood had been candid about his intention to retire at age sixty-five, and in 1977 the trustees began a search for his successor, "a person who would relate effectively to various constituencies, including the Methodist Church." Interested candidates were told, "The search for values must continue to be an important function of this institution."[127] On March 17, 1977, the trustees announced that Emory's next president would be forty-nine-year-old James T. Laney, dean of Emory's Candler School of Theology.[128] An ordained minister with degrees in economics and divinity from Yale, Laney had been recruited to Candler from Vanderbilt in 1969. The new president "combine[d] the abilities of a first-rate scholar with those of a deeply dedicated Christian churchman."[129] As Candler's dean, Laney had led Emory's successful effort to purchase the valuable Hartford Seminary library "right out from under the noses of the prestigious seminaries in the Northeast."[130]

At his first trustees' meeting, Laney articulated several goals: to restore Emory's traditional southern base in the student body and to reclaim Emory's heritage in relation to the church, to enrich the undergraduate experience, and to build graduate programs of distinction.[131] Laney argued that Emory could "make some very real advances if we find ourselves hospitable to research."[132] The new president recognized that the late 1970s was not an auspicious time to launch a major research effort; however, anticipating the Carter administration's growing support of basic research, he convened a University-wide council to address research issues.[133]

Persistent inflation and uncertainty about key federal student aid programs produced a sober challenge for private universities during these years.[134] In the context of troubling financial realities, Laney's early tenure as president was characterized by deliberate reassessment and reorganization, and a continuation of the prudent fiscal approach chartered by Atwood. Like his predecessor, Laney was committed to making Emory "one of the principal universities in this country, one of this society's unassailably distinctive resources."[135] To achieve this goal, Emory needed to enhance its graduate program with "solid research, a top faculty, and the best students." The liberal arts were "very weak" relative to other parts of the University, and there was "no conceivable way to have a great university without a great liberal arts program."[136]

Recognizing that his great ambition could not be realized without considerable effort and expense, Laney asked for and received trustee approval for a five-year, $160 million Campaign for Emory.[137] Unlike many universities that had instituted capital campaigns to meet existing commitments, Emory, with no significant encumbrance, could use the campaign to move ahead. Waiting in the wings, Trustee Emeritus George Woodruff read a letter from his brother Robert that announced a major gift. "Gratified by Emory's progress, its demonstrated capacity to manage its affairs, and its continued commitment to excellence and service to society," the letter stated, assets from the Emily and Ernest Woodruff Fund in excess of $100 million would be transferred to Emory.[138]

While Atwood had accomplished a great deal to strengthen the campus, balance the budget, and establish Emory's reputation, it was Laney who secured the spectacular gift. Presidents Martin and Atwood had visited Robert Woodruff occasionally, but Laney actively cultivated his friendship and became his spiritual adviser.[139] Laney also ensured that the gift was made unrestricted to the University rather than to the medical school, which historically had been the Woodruffs' principal interest.

The largest single donation to an educational institution at the time, the gift thrust Emory into the national spotlight. Its major impact came as much from its psychological lift as from its monetary contribution. (In 1979 Emory's $175 million endowment was already sixteenth-largest in the nation. The bequest raised the total to $280 million and thirteenth-largest.) "The fact is," Laney later recalled, "the endowment made it possible to begin long-range planning and serious building in a way that was almost unprecedented, certainly at Emory."[140]

When the Woodruff Fund was received, the College was in a dismal state. The budget was "pathetic," and the College was accepting nearly 90 percent of its applicants.[141] To avoid having the gift absorbed into the operating budget, the Woodruff funds were kept as a separate endowment. A prudent rule for allocation was announced: the principal was to remain untouched, except by a two-thirds vote of the trustees. The endowment would be committed to Emory's academic programs at the rate of $1 million a year until 60 percent of the net income was being used for that purpose. The remaining 40 percent, earmarked for capital needs, enabled Emory to retire bonds or to leverage future facilities, thus permitting the campus to combat enormous inflationary pressures.[142] Delaying use of the income provided a substantial reserve for much-needed capital improvements.

During the next two years, Laney further tightened financial controls and hired an administrative team that could "bring to Emory an aspiration to be nationally prominent, and at the same time, the experience with which to help measure progress and help set priorities."[143] John Palms was promoted from Emory College dean to vice president for academic affairs.[144] David Minter, a respected English professor from Rice, was appointed dean of the College and vice president for arts and sciences. Billy E. Frye, the Michigan provost who had earned an Emory PhD in biology, returned to become graduate dean in 1986 and, in 1988, Emory's first provost.[145]

President Laney believed that Emory "must husband [the Woodruff] resources with great care and choose our priorities wisely if we are to sustain steady growth in the face of negative indicators in the outside society."[146] To allow time for thoughtful review, the 1980–81 budget was prepared without recourse to the new endowment, and every academic division was directed to undertake a thorough assessment of its programs.[147] The resulting self-studies revealed continuing impediments to development of campus research capacity. In Emory College, for example, an increase in the student-faculty ratio (from about 10-to-1 in 1970–71 to 13-to-1 in 1979–80) imposed teaching responsibilities incompatible with advancement of research.[148]

With the exception of the highly ranked pharmacology program, Emory science faculty demonstrated significantly lower per-capita extramural grants than "model" departments at MIT, Johns Hopkins, and others.[149] Even the School of Medicine needed improvement. Outside evaluators agreed that "biomedical research at Emory [was] simply inadequate," owing to deteriorating facilities, an emphasis on clinical service, and an institutional structure that separated medicine from the rest of the University.[150] Social science departments, where teaching loads were excessively high, were "undistinguished by most of the accepted standards of academic excellence."[151] Humanities faculty, hit hard by elimination of twenty-seven positions during the early 1970s, expressed concern that they were hidden in the shadow of the professional schools.[152]

All the same, Laney believed that Emory was "perhaps the last private university in the United States to have adequate resources to set a new course for graduate education."[153] Favored by geography, climate, and demographic shifts, Emory seemed to be in a position similar to that of Stanford twenty-five years earlier.[154] By the early 1980s, the general health of the University was strong, and faculty in seven divisions were recognized by the 1982 National Research Council (NRC) assessment as important contributors to the advancement of knowledge.[155]

To guide allocation of income from the Woodruff Fund, Laney asked Emory College alumnus (1945, Honorary 1975) and Yale dean Howard Lamar to chair the Emory Visiting Committee for the Arts and Sciences.[156] Using the Woodruff gift–inspired self-studies as a guide, Lamar and a group of prominent faculty from five elite universities endorsed a plan that would influence planning for the next decade. By enlisting participation of faculty with national reputations, Emory both gained recognition in the scholarly community and received sound advice on how to become a university of the first rank.

The Lamar Committee emphasized that "Emory [was] not a multiversity and should not become one," and that the campus should not try to be "a second-rate replica of the 'model' schools."[157] Nevertheless, a concerted effort to improve graduate training and research was "the best present emphasis for [Emory's] expanded opportunities, and the best way to improve all aspects of the University."[158] Perhaps most importantly, the group proposed that the president be given responsibility for distributing the Woodruff funds. This recommendation gave Laney the flexibility and power to shape the institution according to his own priorities, and to centralize decision making within the administration.

The Lamar Committee found that Emory had "remained steadfast to the goal of becoming a truly distinguished national university."[159] The English and history departments provided distinction, and chemistry was "the most likely to achieve national prominence."[160] The Institute of Liberal Arts (ILA), founded in the 1950s, was the key to the development of an interdisciplinary [humanities] focus.[161] At the same time, deteriorating equipment and facilities in biology and physics would have to be upgraded for the departments to advance. The social sciences had the longest way to go to achieve national visibility. Library collections, inadequate for graduate education, would have to be expanded dramatically.[162]

Committee members also endorsed specific proposals. They recommended recruiting the most promising young assistant and associate professors, who "over the long haul . . . [would] carry Emory to its high goals."[163] They urged an interdisciplinary division of biological sciences to "strengthen the graduate school and College rather than starve them, and complement the clinical work of the Medical School rather than be subsumed into it."[164] They identified for development three new areas based on existing University strengths that matched federal funding priorities: a neurosciences division, an immunobiology program, and a comprehensive cancer center.

Despite optimism generated by the Woodruff gift and the Lamar Committee recommendations, in 1983 a candid Southern Association of Colleges and Schools (SACS) accreditation report found that Emory was "suffer[ing] from an irony of riches and mood of deflation born of unrealistic expectations."[165] The SACS report concluded that Emory's high ambitions could only be realized by "a marked improvement" in the faculty through more stringent hiring and promotion procedures that were "ruthlessly enforced." Echoing the Lamar report, the SACS team observed that theology, English, history, philosophy, chemistry, and biology should be emphasized as "towers of excellence," while weaker departments should be expanded to meet undergraduate enrollment needs and to offer master's-level programs. A Woodruff chair in molecular biology would support a field "that must be developed rapidly if Emory is to catch up with its peers."[166] Attention to Emory's "seriously deficient" management information and planning systems was identified as necessary for future success.[167]

> By 1984 more than half of the fifty-four new appointments in Emory College had been made at the senior ranks, and salary increases placed Emory ahead of Vanderbilt, well above Tulane, and only slightly behind Duke.

The SACS assessment complemented Dean David Minter's aggressive effort to raise faculty quality in the arts and sciences. Minter lobbied successfully for higher salaries that would attract more accomplished faculty, implemented new tenure guidelines that emphasized scholarship as well as teaching and service, and recruited new faculty chairs across the board. He also convinced Laney to increase dramatically the undergraduate scholarship budget, an effort that produced a 400 percent increase during the early 1980s, which in turn stabilized enrollment, increased student quality, and established a predictable tuition income.[168]

Fueled with income from the Woodruff gift and continuing medical research support, Emory's advance as a national research university truly began around 1984. That year Laney reported to the trustees about increased support for undergraduate and graduate students, the enhancement of libraries, and the creation of interdisciplinary research centers.[169] In particular, Laney noted new senior faculty. By 1984 more than half of the fifty-four new appointments in Emory College had been made at the senior ranks, and salary increases placed Emory ahead of Vanderbilt, well above Tulane, and only slightly behind Duke.[170] A major coup was the appointment of former U.S. president Jimmy Carter as University Distinguished Professor and formal affiliation between Emory and the Carter Center.[171]

The School of Medicine continued to win support from the coffers of the NIH. Of Emory's external funding, 85 percent, primarily from the NIH, was awarded to the School of Medicine.[172] As a result, Emory demonstrated steady growth in federal R&D awards and moved in the national rankings from sixty-ninth in 1982 to forty-ninth in 1987.[173] Nevertheless, a continuing problem resulted from Emory's historic decentralization that had "allowed the activities of some constituent schools to obscure the public perception of the whole."[174]

The Emory Clinic and hospitals had become financial powerhouses, and, like academic health centers at campuses around the nation, independent from the rest of the University.[175] Medical doctors with Emory clinical appointments treated patients in Emory offices, but paid only a modest fee to the University. Laney addressed this situation by negotiating a controversial formula that would increase the University share of revenues from professional services.[176] These revenues supported a new Graduate Division of Biological and Biomedical Sciences, which combined the resources of basic health sciences departments throughout the University. This consolidation "was crucial" for recruitment of research faculty and more active involvement of the medical school in graduate education.[177]

Despite significant progress, Emory officials learned just how long it takes—and how difficult it is—to join the ranks of the nation's elite. When Howard Lamar addressed a trustee retreat in 1987, he reported that Emory was "being talked about as a new Hopkins or a new Chicago."[178] However, actual comparisons with prestigious campuses suggested more measured progress. When judged against six other schools in the University Athletic Association (UAA) (Carnegie Mellon, Case Western Reserve, Chicago, Johns Hopkins, Rochester, and Washington University) and four private southern institutions (Vanderbilt, Duke, Tulane, and Miami), Emory was near the bottom in most categories.[179] Of this group, Emory ranked next to last (and eighty-sixth nationally) in federal R&D obligations, fifth in alumni gifts, and tenth in the number of doctorates awarded.[180] As would be expected, Emory fared better in the endowment category. While Emory did not have the largest endowment, ranking third behind UAA members Chicago and Rochester, Emory was first with annual endowment income (more than $42 million). In 1987 Emory moved into eighth place in R&D expenditures, ahead of Vanderbilt and Tulane.[181]

Emory's disappointing comparative assessment led Laney to restate an earlier goal: Emory should become one of the nation's dozen "truly distinguished private institutions."[182] He found it particularly irritating that research support in the South still lagged behind that of other regions.[183] To facilitate Emory's advance to national research status, Laney proposed specific numerical goals to be achieved by the year 2000. The campus would aim to double its research base from $50 million to $100 million, triple gift support from $30 million to $90 million, and increase PhDs awarded from fifty or sixty to one hundred per year. Laney further proposed that Emory place two graduate programs and two professional programs (specifically theology and medicine) in the top ten, and two (law and business) in the top twenty.[184] To capitalize on strength in the biomedical sciences, Laney and Vice President for Health Affairs Charles Hatcher determined to expand the medical school faculty with appointees whose primary function would be research. As a result the medical faculty grew from 671 in 1984 to 883 in 1992.[185]

The arts and sciences faculty also increased, from 236 to 328 between 1984 and 1992, with 36 positions supported by the Woodruff endowment.[186] Laney understood that the heart of the University was arts and sciences.[187] He was committed to strengthening the liberal arts even if it meant purchasing a department outright. In a highly publicized move, during the late 1980s Emory successfully recruited the entire French department from Johns Hopkins. This action brought "one of the country's most highly regarded [departments] and . . . helped Emory vault overnight into the front rank of American universities in French literature studies."[188] Another sign of progress was the attempted raiding of Emory faculty by distinguished universities. Dean Minter recalled spending considerable time "trying to persuade faculty that in the long run they [were] better off here than at Stanford or UCLA or Berkeley or Northwestern."[189] All the same, the cost of advancement was enormous. In 1989, only five years after the end of the previous fund-raising campaign, Emory embarked on another campaign to raise $400 million.[190]

In the early 1990s Emory officials endorsed important structural changes that included the establishment of one school and the closing of another. Accompanying the growth of medical research faculty was a tripling of research space in a new $41 million Rollins Research Center.[191] To build on collaborative relationships with the neighboring U.S. Centers for Disease Control and Prevention and the American Cancer Society, the medical school's public health offerings were reorganized into a separate Rollins School of Public Health.[192] The School of Dentistry faced a different fate. When the quality and number of its students declined and increasing University support was required to maintain what was considered an average program, campus officials decided to close the school.[193]

With its late entrance into research and graduate education, Emory's goal of achieving status as a premier research university was not realized until the late 1980s and 1990s.

The campus budget underwent a major transformation between 1977 and 1992. Total current expenditures increased from $153 million to more than $890 million; basic educational and general expenditures grew from $71 to $419 million. The student aid budget—increased dramatically during the 1980s—was raised from just over $6 million to more than $95 million, with 70 percent of Emory students receiving some financial assistance. The endowment grew to $1.8 billion in 1992, the sixth largest in the nation.[194] Despite endowment strength, Emory's revenue base was expanded as much by the huge increase in income from tuition and fees as it was by endowment revenue.[195]

Between 1987 and 1995 Emory's sponsored research increased more than 144 percent to almost $132 million, with federal support (including $76 million from the NIH) providing more than $96 million, or more than 70 percent of the total.[196] In 1997, nine academic departments, most conducting health-related research, each generated at least $5 million in grants.[197] By the mid-1990s researchers at the Yerkes Primate Research Center and the new Rollins School of Public Health were winning more than $20 million annually.[198]

Despite strength in biomedical fields, efforts were taken to ensure that "in case federal funding trends change [Emory could] diversify its research funding portfolio through partnerships with industry."[199] By 1995 the University was generating about $2 million annually through technology transfer projects, and this revenue was expected to increase as faculty and researchers secured additional patents.[200] Corporate-sponsored funding in 1996 provided some $18 million, or 11 percent of the total, and private funding grew to $15 million—7 percent of the total—up from $8 million one year earlier.[201]

Explaining Emory's Advance | While focusing on the changes that enabled Emory to advance, one must not underestimate the forces of continuity that prevail at any institution. A tradition of balanced budgets, a strong program of medical research, the continued support of a major donor, location in a Sunbelt city that was growing in population, economics, and stature—these factors all contributed to Emory's transformation. At the same time, the University expanded its research capacity despite inherent impediments—the later development of research agendas at southern universities, entrenched racial segregation in the region, a conservative Methodist influence, and a resource-consuming commitment to regional service. The $105 million Woodruff gift provided the means for advancement, but other factors produced growth and innovation.

Since the mid-1940s, when Dumas Malone evaluated campus options for graduate and research development, campus officials were determined to achieve national status as a research university. Emory's journey toward national recognition and research excellence stumbled in the 1950s, developed steadily through the 1960s, experienced setbacks in the 1970s, was sustained through the mid-1980s, and advanced beginning in the mid-1980s and continuing through the 1990s. During these latter years, when other universities were forced to cut back on graduate programs, Emory was able to hire top faculty and expand graduate fields. When other campuses were burdened by a surplus of tenured professors, Emory could make cluster appointments of research faculty to build a critical mass of excellence. When other universities were experimenting with innovative programs to attract new audiences, Emory was able to strengthen its commitment to the liberal arts in the College and the Graduate School. Emory officials expanded faculty and associated resources in areas that were already strong.

Emory benefited from effective presidential leadership that moved the campus toward research university status. The process began in the early postwar years with Goodrich White, a former graduate dean, who understood the importance of extending graduate education. With help from an inherited group of dedicated senior administrators, Sanford Atwood elevated Emory faculty and programs to the next level. Believing that Emory could become one of the nation's best universities, Atwood spearheaded an effort to strengthen the faculty and recruit high-quality students. Based on his courageous support of academic freedom during the mid-1960s, Emory won positive national attention as well as Ford Foundation dollars. During his tenure, as one campus official recalled, "We did all we could with what was available."[202]

It fell to James Laney to realize the goals established by his predecessors. Laney hired experienced senior administrators, who recruited with high salaries and bold strategies strong faculty and talented students to the College and Graduate School. Among his most important contributions, Laney cultivated a close personal relationship with Robert Woodruff, Emory's principal benefactor, and convinced him to donate assets without restriction. Laney's efforts also produced a more equitable distribution of clinical fees. Emory's ties with Atlanta's business community were strengthened as Laney served on the boards of Coca-Cola and the Trust Company Bank, and the CEOs of these two companies served as Emory trustees. While the tradition of American research universities had been to jettison religious ties as they advanced in the secular world of research and graduate education, Laney continued to argue that Emory could "play in the big leagues while sustaining a commitment to values."[203]

Emory's success also was grounded in moderate expansion and careful fiscal management during an era when American higher education generally was experiencing rapid, unplanned growth. Adopting a practice of slower growth and a goal of staying relatively small through the late 1970s, trustees insisted on, and presidents from White to Laney were able to produce, balanced budgets even in times of financial constraint. When many campuses faced perilous deficits during the early 1970s, Emory avoided disaster, risking gains and reputation to stay financially solvent. When the value of university endowments declined, the board's investment committee continued to manage the campus portfolio with success.

The continuing strength of its biomedical research was a major factor in Emory's advance. Even before World War II, the School of Medicine was the best-known and most respected Emory division, and the uninterrupted federal support of biomedical research after World War II only enhanced the school's prestige. Yerkes brought increased federal support and recognition. Historically, biomedical research received between two-thirds and three-fourths of the federal R&D funds awarded to the campus, and 85 percent of Emory's external funding came through the medical school. At the same time, the growth and success of the medical complex produced a strained relationship with Emory's other schools and an ambiguous identity in the mission and character of the University.

Emory is one of a number of schools, including Chicago and Rochester, that derived financial support from a primary benefactor. While the Woodruff donation in 1979 enabled Emory to expand research faculty and augment a scholarship budget that attracted talented students, advancement as a result of a major gift was not an isolated circumstance in the campus's history. A generous donation from Coca-Cola founder Asa Candler in 1915 signaled the beginning of Emory's transformation from college to university, and Candler continued to give munificently to Emory until his death. Following World War II, the Woodruff family used increased Coca-Cola earnings to support the growth of Emory's medical complex. Contributions continued throughout the postwar years, and in 1975, trustees of the Emily and Ernest Woodruff Foundation rechartered it to form the Emily and Ernest Woodruff Fund; under the Fund's new charter, 40 percent of the net annual income would be granted to Emory.

The 1979 Woodruff gift thus represented the culmination of almost a half-century of Woodruff support of the medical complex and, later, the University. The unprecedented gift, prudently invested, enabled Emory to hire senior faculty, to offer generous financial aid to undergraduates and competitive stipends to graduate students, and to build a research infrastructure. With these resources, Emory was able to mount an effort to elevate the stature of the arts and sciences to that of the medical school.

Finally, there were intangible elements that characterized Emory's advancement. Among the most important was the role of dedicated and loyal Emory alumni and friends in Atlanta.

Through the 1960s Emory graduates served as campus leaders and trustees, stepping in to fill a presidential leadership void when circumstances required it. Others, including respected academics and alumni (Dumas Malone in the 1940s and Howard Lamar in the 1980s), volunteered their experienced service. Billy Frye, provost at Michigan, returned to his graduate alma mater to serve as the University's chief academic officer and, later, Emory's acting president. Some with no prior association seemed committed to Emory's success. The efforts of Georgia native Jimmy Carter also extended Emory's academic programs and stature.

Writing about turn-of-the-twentieth-century southern progressivism, Dewey Grantham found that "the machinery for social amelioration [in the South] is to a large extent educational."[204] Grantham's assessment of these earlier years might also characterize the post–World War II era, when southern universities found themselves at the center of a southern renaissance. Emory's remarkable advance as a research university thus must be assessed in the context of exceptional development of the South, rather than through a comparison with more traditional elite institutions that developed earlier and under other circumstances. All the same, it must be recognized that Emory has attained national research university status with a very concentrated effort, in a very short period of time.

CHAPTER 9

HOW IT CAME TO PASS
Oral History of a Half-Century in Emory Arts and Sciences

The View from the Office of the First Emory Provost:
An Interview with Billy E. Frye (MS 1954, PhD 1956)

Considered by some to have been the best academic administrator in America in his day, Billy E. Frye had journeyed far from his Georgia mountain boyhood home to become provost at the University of Michigan before returning to his native state and Emory in 1986. On his retirement as Emory's provost—he was the first person to hold that position—he received the University's Thomas Jefferson Award, the highest honor bestowed on someone who has spent a significant portion of his or her career at Emory. In this interview conducted by Gary Hauk and Sally Wolff King, recorded on October 24, 2008, he ranges from his student days in the 1950s to the challenges facing Emory in the 1980s to advance its research programs.

You came to Emory to work on a PhD in biology when the graduate program was still quite young. What was that experience like?

The experience I had as a graduate student at Emory in the fifties was just extraordinary, and the reason for that had to do in part with where I was in my life. I had finished undergraduate college at Piedmont, quite young, and gone off to graduate school at the University of Illinois. I was eighteen or nineteen. I had never been away from home, quite literally, in my life, so by the middle of my first semester there I was so homesick that I was literally sick. About Thanksgiving, I just left and came home. My Piedmont biology professor, who had gotten me into several graduate schools—including Emory—discovered that I had left Illinois, and she came to our house with fire in her eyes. But she took one look at me and forgave me after a brief scolding and came down to Emory and had me readmitted.

So I came in the middle of the year. I've always thought she must have told Bill Burbank, who was the chair of biology at the time, something about my experience and my immaturity. Whatever the reason, the whole department, the faculty and the students, embraced me and built a protective fence around me. I was extraordinarily shy and immature, but under their protection I flourished academically and socially. Whatever the reasons for that, it was a wonderful experience.

It was also wonderful because the faculty were really quite exceptional. We tend to think of Emory at that time as a sort of sleepy, aristocratic, southern institution that has emerged into research prominence only in recent years. But in fact there were a considerable number of faculty in biology and in some other departments, such as biochemistry, that had quite prominent research programs funded through the National Science Foundation and so forth. Half to two-thirds of the faculty in biology were active as publishing scholars. But they were also devoted teachers in the way that we're so proud of at Emory. The courses I took were small, and I was a bottomless pit of learning.

The culture of the department was one of community, in the finest sense. At that time, there may have been two dozen graduate students, including both master's and PhD candidates, and about half that many faculty members. The faculty all seemed to have very good relationships with one another. They were youthful mostly, in their late thirties and forties. Dr. Woolford Baker was by far the oldest member. Almost without exception they were wonderful teachers, devoted to learning and to the scholarly life. That attitude spilled over onto the students. I don't know whether that was characteristic of the whole University then, but there were certainly pockets like that. Chemistry had it, biochemistry and anatomy, religion. There was a self-perception by the faculty that they were among the best in the South, and their intention was to build a strong, respectable department. Not that anyone had any illusions that we were Harvard or Michigan, but in every way it was a fine experience.

I finished my degree, unfortunately, in two and a half years, so I was just in my early twenties when I graduated. I say unfortunately, because I didn't learn enough, didn't do enough—I wasn't deep enough.

You started your career at Piedmont College, and then the University of Virginia.

I had been deferred by my local draft board throughout my studies, from the time I was old enough to be drafted. They deferred me to go to graduate school and then deferred me again, somewhat reluctantly, to do postdoctoral studies at Princeton for a year. I promised them that the next year I would go do my duty in serving our nation.

I was up at Woods Hole Biological Station the final summer of the year I spent at Princeton, and I received a call from the president of Piedmont, James Walters, saying that the college's biology professor—my mentor—had resigned abruptly. He called me, desperate to find a replacement in late summer. I said, "Well, my draft board is expecting me. If you can get them to defer me again, I'll come and teach for you." So he called them, and they deferred me, and that's how I came to teach there for a year. That year I managed to get permanently deferred from the draft because I had to have part of a lung removed. After that my draft board gave up on me!

I also started looking for another job. I never intended to stay at Piedmont. I had gotten the bug for research, so my Emory mentors helped me get into Virginia, where I went for a stint in a program called the National Science Foundation Academic Year Institute. The program allowed high school teachers to return to college for renewal and some advanced study, and I taught the biology courses for that group of students, about twenty or so middle-aged teachers. I did that for three years, then, since it was a temporary position, and the department didn't have an open slot in my field. I began looking for jobs elsewhere.

In those days most universities were still growing rapidly because of the expansion that occurred after World War II. I received a call from the University of Michigan asking if I would be interested in applying for a job. My first reaction was not enthusiastic because I always thought I wanted to be in a small college, and I never expected to live north of the Mason-Dixon Line. I called Dr. Anthony Clement at Emory, one of the most distinguished members of the faculty, who had become a close friend. I said I'd had this call from Michigan and that I didn't know anything about Michigan—should I go interview for the job? There was silence on the phone. He was a man of enormous grace and decorum, but after a minute, he exploded, "Frye, you damned fool! The University of Michigan is one of the top five universities in biology in this country. Of course you shall go to the University of Michigan!"

So I did, and thankfully I took that job and moved to Michigan. I didn't think I would be there very long, imagining that after four or five years I would return to the South. But the University of Michigan, and Ann Arbor, turned out to be a wonderful place, and my wife, Elisa, and I stayed for twenty-five years.

You eventually became provost at Michigan.

I became dean of the College of Literature, Science and the Arts in 1973 and served in that role for six years, after which I was named provost, and held that position until 1986, when I left to come to Emory.

How did your move to Emory come about? Did Jim Laney seek you out?

In a way he did. After I had been dean and provost at Michigan for a dozen years, I was feeling burned out and began to think I couldn't do it much longer. I also felt that I couldn't go back into the classroom; I had let my research slip and didn't know whether I could pick up the thread of it and rebuild a credible research program. To be immodest about it, I had been reasonably successful in the administration at Michigan, but I was

Billy E. Frye

concerned about burning out and becoming a deadweight. My parents were getting older, and over the years I had responded to a few job inquiries from southern institutions that would have enabled us to live closer to them. But I ended up always feeling that I could not bear to leave Michigan. In fact, during that period, Jim Laney offered me a job as dean of Emory College. I gave that extraordinarily serious consideration, but again, I just couldn't leave Michigan. That was how in love I was with the place. At that time Michigan was a huge, wonderful community. The pride we had in the institution! I couldn't imagine giving up the friends I had there, or the institution. So with some embarrassment I finally called Dr. Laney and declined the offer. I thought I would probably never hear from him again.

But a few years later I reached this burnout stage, and I began to make discreet inquiries about jobs in the Southeast. Because of my elderly parents and the notion of possibly coming back to northeast Georgia, I even started looking at some of the small colleges there. Although I had never wanted to be a president, I actually applied for the presidency of one. I didn't get picked, and the head of the search firm called me up one day, and said simply, you scared them; they're not ready for you. I think they thought I would come and try to turn them into a research university.

Anyway, there was a trustee of that school who had some connection to Jim Laney and told Jim about my candidacy there. Jim, of course, remembered me, and I received a phone call from him.

He says, I hear that you might actually be considering leaving Michigan now. I said, well, yeah. I was embarrassed because I thought he had caught me out. He said, well, I don't have anything available right now except the deanship of the Graduate School. Would you come for that? I said I sure would.

I've often wondered what he said to the search committee, but he intervened in some way, and they invited me down for an interview, and in the end I was hired for that job. I didn't have the slightest idea at the time that this might lead to the provostship. But a couple of years later he called me into his office and looked at me with those penetrating eyes. He wanted me to take the job of academic vice president and provost.

You were the first person at Emory to have the title "provost," were you not?

Yes. I don't recall why Jim decided to change it from simply "vice president for academic affairs" to "provost and vice president for academic affairs." I may have suggested that because that was what the position was called at Michigan; if I was going to be the vice president for academic affairs, I wanted to have clear budget authority over the academic program—not financial, but budget authority—as I did at Michigan. To my mind, that was the chief distinction between a vice president for academic affairs and a provost.

In the short two years that you were the graduate dean, what issues and challenges did you confront?

Emory was not, at that time, very strong in graduate education in most fields. We had few nationally ranked programs. [Emory College dean] David Minter still had more to do in bringing the undergraduate program to the fore, especially in building faculty. But that goal of building graduate programs proved to be entirely compatible, so I always felt a tremendous complementarity in our respective goals. My relationship with David was wonderful. He knew as well as I did that any university with the aspirations of Emory had to be strong in graduate education. In an intellectual sense, the graduate school sets the tone of the institution.

What was your priority as dean of the Graduate School?

The first challenge was to make Emory more attractive to top graduate students. The financial support for graduate students was poor, comparatively speaking. We put together a budget that showed what we thought we would really need. I remember meeting with the trustees' executive committee and telling them what it would take to bring Emory to the next step, and it was just an astounding number. Well, Jim Laney made the commitment and accomplished it, by golly! Within a very few years, we began to compete for the best students and to rise in the national rankings. We were able to do this because University revenues were still growing, mainly through growth in undergraduate tuition income, as well as the great Woodruff gift.

So in some ways, the income from the College paid for the growth and strengthening of the Graduate School.

Yes, but most of the benefit flowed back to the College, too. Strong graduate programs are essential to recruit and retain strong faculty, and that redounds to the benefit of the independent programs and to the reputation of the University. In the College discussions about building the graduate programs, I don't recall any resistance, just skepticism that we could really do it. But we did it.

The other big challenge in developing the Graduate School was administrative. Until I became provost, Emory had not distinguished "budget" from "finance." The chief financial officer had more influence over academic priorities than I thought was appropriate, and he was not very enthusiastic about the Graduate School. Later we changed things to make it clear that the provost has primary responsibility for academic priorities, but it took an enormous amount of time and effort to overcome that resistance.

The Graduate School still needed a lot more support, but other opportunities in professional and graduate education needed attention, most obviously the Business School and the about-to-emerge School of Public Health. Why we didn't have a public health school here many years before we did is a mystery to me, given the presence of the United States Centers for Disease Control and Prevention on Emory's doorstep. Bill Foege [Presidential Distinguished Professor Emeritus and former CDC director] was very helpful in pushing that through. Likewise, the business school, because of the strength of the Atlanta business community, was way overdue to move up to the next step.

What was the budget-setting practice when you became provost, and how did it change?

President Laney or [Executive Vice President] John Temple had already established a series of annual budget conferences, in which each dean would present his or her budget. I started working with the deans to evaluate and eventually approve their proposed budgets before they were brought to the University Budget Committee, and hopefully thereby have some influence on them. After that, I began scheduling and chairing an annual budget conference with each dean. It was about that time that I also set up the University Priorities Committee of faculty, because I wanted the faculty to feel more engaged in decision making. I made it a practice to present the budget to them every year and let them react to it before it was final. In this way, the budget setting became a more open process.

This grew out of my experience at the University of Michigan, where I created a committee called the Budget Priorities Committee, which played a major role in helping me evaluate all of the schools and colleges for the purpose of cutting budgets in response to state funding cuts. In some ways I learned that it's easier to cut and set priorities during a budget crisis than it is during perceived plenty, when nobody sees why you need to take from them and give to someone else.

You once said that right after the Woodruff gift, in the early 1980s, you could have spread money just about anywhere at Emory and made a positive difference. At a certain point, though, you need to begin making more selective advances, because the pool of money won't spread as deep and far. How did you begin to sort that out, so that in time it became clear that the Geology Department and the Library School needed to be phased out? What led to the selective strengthening or, in some cases, selective elimination of programs?

No university—not even the wealthiest—can afford to do everything and do it well. While Emory's fortunes were rising dramatically, we were far from the wealthiest! By the time I became provost, the budget was already not growing fast enough to meet the legitimate needs of the schools, especially in the arts and sciences. That included the Graduate School and certain other units, particularly the University libraries. Although our theology library had jumped into the top ranks because of Jim Laney's acquisition of the Hartford Seminary Collection, the Woodruff Library at that point was hardly more than a good liberal arts college library in most areas, surely not a first-class university library. So we had to invest a lot more there. In addition we were on the threshold of having to invest a lot in academic computing, and in the development of some of the professional schools.

It was clear that if we were going to continue to develop in the arts and sciences in the way we wanted, we were going to have to give up some things. We knew we could not excel in everything, and would need to cut back on some areas in order to improve others. So, after careful review, we decided to eliminate the Division of Library Sciences. It was not a bad program. But having been heavily involved in library affairs nationally, I knew something about library schools and knew what it was going to take to become competitive. It was obvious that Emory would never be nationally distinguished in this field unless we invested at least three or four times what we were already investing in that program, and that was not in the cards, given all of our other, higher-priority needs. The same judgment was reached about geology. It is a very important basic science, and we have to have an undergraduate program in it. But it would have taken a large injection of new funds to make that department competitive nationally.

What led to your involvement in the libraries on a national level?

A clever librarian. When I became provost at Michigan, Harold Shapiro, the president, who had preceded me as provost, wanted me to continue his involvement with a library consortium that included Harvard, Yale, Michigan, and Stanford. It comprised librarians and presidents of these and some other major universities, who tried to find ways of cooperating and sharing the cost of things that were rapidly escalating beyond the means of any individual institution. About the same time, the librarian at Michigan, Dick Daugherty, nominated me for a couple of national boards and committees, and I was appointed to them. Later he confided that he did that with malice aforethought, because he felt the more I knew about the libraries, the better off he would be, and he was quite right!

I sometimes think that my work with libraries was the most significant work I did in my whole career, because initially I was among the very few academic officers working with librarians to try to bring about collaboration among them. For reasons that are complicated, they could not make much progress in this regard without the support of their provosts and presidents. I knew, and still know, little or nothing about the actual operations of libraries, but I was able to help keep the potential benefits of collaboration continually before these groups, and perhaps to reassure them that they were not in this alone. I became "Little Johnny-One-Note," repeating on every possible occasion, "We have to share, we must collaborate, we can't go on, each trying to buy all the books in the world." Faculties of great universities are very jealous of their libraries, and change is often resisted and can imperil the careers of librarians. But gradually, things have changed.

When I came to Emory I was on two or three national boards, among them the Commission on Preservation, which I chaired for ten years. The commission successfully lobbied Congress to authorize funding to microfilm one copy of each of a large fraction of the books held in our libraries, which were rapidly crumbling into dust because they had been printed on acidic paper. We also lobbied for a shift to the use of acid-free paper in future publication. Very soon, the emphasis shifted to computers and digital information rather than paper.

Your personal investment and your willingness to invest institutional resources in some ways pushed Emory ahead in the library world.

When I came, I recruited a new head of the libraries, Joan Gotwals. As soon as she came from Penn, I asked her to get involved, and that put us into the council of these elite institutions that I had been involved with. That connection proved to be invaluable, and together with Jim Laney's large investment in the library and later Bill Chace's continued investments, that opened doors and brought us national recognition.

Our ability to move ahead in the library was a consequence of several factors. Foremost, of course, was the outstanding leadership of Joan, the strong connections with the academic library community, and our ability to provide her with adequate funding at a time when others were experiencing major declines in purchasing power. Second, being less burdened with traditional "baggage," such as a commitment to huge purchasing budgets, we were able to invest more in academic computing as a means of accessing information, then were able to move ahead gradually while others were struggling just to keep afloat.

After Jim Laney became the United States ambassador to South Korea, you served for a year as interim president and then continued as provost for part of Bill Chace's presidency.

When I came to Emory my rather vague "plan" was to work for about five years and then retire and go trout fishing! But when Bill Chace came as president, I did not want to walk out and leave him in the lurch, so to speak. Perhaps that sounds a bit arrogant, but I did not want to leave until he had been there a while and had had an opportunity to build his own administrative staff. So, when he asked me to stay on, I agreed, but told him of my intentions to retire soon. After that, for a couple of years I kept reminding him of this occasionally, but he kept asking me to stay on a while. This was flattering, of course, but eventually I wrote him a formal letter of resignation.

I was completely taken by surprise when Bill responded by offering me the position of chancellor. My understanding is that this offer came about because he asked Joe Crooks, then Emory's general counsel, to come up with an arrangement that would give me the option of staying on in an advisory capacity part-time. Joe remembered that the University bylaws contained a provision for the position of chancellor, which had been created by the board of trustees in 1915. After that, the title remained on the books, though it was rarely used [only for retired University presidents like Harvey Cox and Goodrich White]. Joe suggested to Bill that I be named chancellor, and Bill in turn proposed it to the trustees, who approved it. The gesture was exceedingly kind and generous, and I continue to feel grateful for it. I was never made to feel that it was done as a way of putting me out to pasture (which would have been unnecessary in any case, since I was the one who was insisting upon retiring!), and it gave me the chance to continue to be engaged in University affairs, on a more limited, lower-pressure basis. Perhaps it was useful for Emory and President Chace, too, insofar as it gave him a way of using me in an advisory capacity, but I cannot be the judge of that.

In any case it was a kind thing to do, and I appreciated it deeply. But if I am completely honest I have to say that however well intended, I think perhaps it was a mistake in some ways. Among universities, the titles of president and chancellor are sometimes used synonymously, or nearly so, and I felt that the use of both titles at Emory would inevitably result in some confusion, especially on the part of people who were not familiar with our particular history. Since the duties of the position of chancellor are nowhere spelled out, there is an inherent and potentially confusing ambiguity about just what the role of the chancellor is. There really is not a clear job there, and since above all I wanted in no manner to get in the way of the president, it sometimes felt a bit awkward to me. But Bill was always gracious and never gave me any reason for that feeling. We met at least weekly to discuss whatever issues were weighing most heavily on his mind. He asked me to undertake special projects from time to time.

For example, one year I wrote a paper on the pros and cons of affirmative action for him. Another time I chaired the planning committee for "The Year of Reconciliation" on behalf of Provost Rebecca Chopp, and I also began having weekly meetings with her after she was appointed to that position. And thus it went. I formed the impression that for both Bill and Rebecca the most useful part of my job as chancellor was our weekly meetings and discussions—perhaps the opportunity to talk through troublesome issues freely and off the record.

You wrote "Choices and Responsibility," a rather substantial pamphlet subtitled "Shaping Emory's Future," and published in 1994. This turned out to get considerable traction among the community as a statement of the values of the University—balancing teaching and research; building stronger community; encouraging interdisciplinary scholarship; keeping pace with infrastructure needs; and enhancing Emory's external relationships. When you wrote that, were you still provost?

I was acting president. That year, as I recall, I started the faculty discussions that led to "Choices and Responsibility."

That year, 1993–1994, you were acting president as well as provost.

Right. As I told people, if they were looking for the provost I was the president, and if they were looking for the president I was the provost. It worked pretty well.

What was the impetus for "Choices and Responsibility"? Where did it get its genesis?

Jim Laney had become ambassador to Korea and was gone, and with that his strong leadership. We were in a holding pattern, and I felt that we needed to have some sense of direction, lest we go adrift. I also had the strong feeling that we needed to evolve toward greater faculty participation in University governance. Those two things led to this initiative.

The lunchtime conversations that you had with various faculty groups that year provided the fodder.

It was the best way I could think of to get some sense of the faculty's needs and aspiration. At the same time, it seemed to be an opportunity to begin to meld the very disparate, almost factionalized faculty into a more coherent community and promote some sense of shared goals. This process was set up to help us start to see what we next needed at Emory to build on the remarkable Laney years, and for the University to make the whole flourish more.

The piece that followed it, "A Vision for Emory," is a values piece, really. I still firmly believe that the right way to plan is not merely to set budgeting parameters. That kind of plan never lasts. The future is just too uncertain. But what you can decide is what matters most, and then you can have all your deans and department chairs begin to make decisions based upon these understandings. One of the most important things about "Choices and Responsibility," in my mind, was that the deans all voluntarily signed a letter stating that they were party to it. I think people began to get a certain sense of shared purpose. You can push that only so far, of course. But I think it's important and has an impact.

It did seem that the campus picked up the language of "Choices and Responsibility" and began to use it constructively.

It sure did, and thanks should go to Bill Chace for that. He never lost an opportunity to refer to that document. It was just incredible how consistently he did that. He could have squelched it. He did quite the opposite, and I was enormously grateful to him.

It had been a while since the Woodruff gift and the priorities that were set following it, and people were starting to talk about what should come next. Did you have a sense as provost that the University needed not only to reaffirm its values and direction but also to get another financial shot in the arm? Was this document of yours the foundation for a campaign?

I cannot recall whether a capital campaign was a specific part of the motivation behind "Choices and Responsibility." It may have been, because we always need more money, and you have to start your next campaign before the last one is done. But leading a campaign was the remotest thing from my mind.

When you look back on "Choices and Responsibility" and "A Vision for Emory," do you see particular successes that have evolved from them, or particular gaps where the University didn't follow through?

I had a sense that the ideas were being picked up rather widely, but I can't tell you what the actual impact was. At the time I felt very positive about how willingly people seemed to pick it up. I knew there were skeptics who had their doubts about the merit of the exercise. Nonetheless, a lot of people were far more positive and far more hopeful as a result of it.

One last question: The teacher who came to your home to get you—did she live long enough to see you become chancellor of Emory?

Unfortunately, no. Her name was Elizabeth Sawyer. She was a New Englander from Maine, and I sometimes thought she must have come South as a missionary! She received her PhD at the University of Missouri and came to Piedmont the same year I did, almost as if sent by Providence. Her attitude, her outlook, her standards were the very ones I found when I got to fine universities. It was under her tutelage that I learned to think in a scientific way. She didn't just deliver information. She worked through problems, formed and tested hypotheses. She was a wonderful person and a mentor, a motherly figure to me. She died of breast cancer while I was at the University of Virginia. She was a rare lady to whom I have felt indebted all my life.

It's funny how one little thing sets your path, but without her, I never would have pursued this career. Before her, I vaguely thought I wanted to be a horticulturist or a high school teacher. I went to Truett McConnell College in Cleveland, Georgia, as a freshman and sophomore, and came to Piedmont as a junior. A few weeks into classes she called me in and said, "You have to go to graduate school." I had never heard of graduate school. "Have you had French?" "No." "Have you had German?" "No." The little colleges that I attended were just struggling to survive, and to be honest the curricula at that time were very spotty and weak. So she quickly set up a two-year plan to fill in as many gaps in my background as possible, so I could be admitted to some graduate school. Then, in my senior year, she told me to pick some places where I would be interested in doing graduate work, and she would start writing letters. She got me into several, including, as I recall, Cornell and the University of Illinois, as well as Emory. Eventually, after the false start at Illinois, I chose Emory, and I've never regretted the choice!

David Minter Reflects on Years of Growth and Change in Emory College

David Minter served as dean of Emory College and vice president for arts and sciences from 1980 until 1990. Before coming to Emory at the invitation of President James Laney, Minter completed his doctorate at Yale and was professor of English at Rice University. His area of academic specialty is American literature.

Sally Wolff King interviewed him on December 5, 2008, at his home in Houston, Texas.[1]

Before coming to Emory you had established a career as scholar, teacher, and highly respected member of the Rice University community in your home state of Texas. What attracted you to the deanship of Emory College?

I wanted to go where I could make a difference. I thought I could do some good at Emory, and I liked Emory immediately. Emory was not a pretentious place but a very inviting one. I had been at other places where they talked big and did little, but Emory was not like that. Caroline and I felt at home there; I have never regretted the decision.

How were you recruited?

Tom Bertrand [J. Thomas Bertrand, secretary of the University from 1978 to 1991] was the first person to mention me to Jim [Laney]. Jim had been at Yale Divinity School when Caroline and I were there as I was finishing my PhD at Yale. We also had personal connections to Emory. [Former associate dean] Garland Richmond had been at North Texas State University, where I had finished my undergraduate degree. Caroline's father had been born in Georgia, so she had some roots here.

Jim came to Houston and took us to dinner. He was very persuasive! He was determined to make Emory a very fine place, and I felt convinced that he was going to do it. I wanted to be a part of what he was trying to do. Ultimately he gave me a chance to do things I wanted to do but never thought I would do, and that's very inviting.[2]

David Minter

You spent years at Yale and Rice. Did those institutions, which have strong residential college traditions, provide you with collegiate models when you were building Emory College?

Yale had a lot to do with forming me and meant a lot to me, but no, I did not have those schools as models in my mind at that time.

How did you work with President Laney and other members of his senior staff?

It's not always easy for very strong-minded people to work cordially and effectively together, unless they have a lot in common. Jim Laney seemed to have almost immediate respect for and confidence in me. Almost from the start, we understood each other; we found it easy to work together. I learned a lot from him and am proud of what we accomplished. He is maybe the finest person I have ever known in my life.

Jim wanted to do as much as he possibly could do. I learned from him to think about things I wanted to undertake, plan how I would want them done, and know what should be done to accomplish them. Then I would go to him. He listened and was always open-minded. Sometimes we modified the plans.

What did you and Jim Laney have in common?

Faith. That made a lot of difference. By faith, I mean—some of it is religious. My father was a Methodist minister. That made it easier for Jim and me; we spoke the same language. We did not always see eye to eye on everything, but I respected him enormously, and I felt blessed to be working with him overall.

Were there instances in which you and the president disagreed about priorities or directions, and if so, did you try to persuade him to take a different tack?

He was always responsive to the suggestions I made. Of course, I didn't tell him what to do—ever—but he paid attention. He listened to me carefully and respected me. He never made promises he didn't keep.

What was the administrative and governance relationship of the College and the Graduate School? Did you do anything to change it?

We did a lot to change and improve it. Jim and I were on the same wavelength about it. I think we made a lot of progress. Both the College and the Graduate School were the stronger for it. Emory was a local place when I arrived; it was a more national university later. The Woodruff money made it possible for us to do things that we had not done before.

What faculty appointments are you the most proud of?

James Flannery in theater. Bradd Shore in anthropology. Dennis Liotta in chemistry. He's always full of energy and good to work with. His recent accomplishments in helping to discover and patent the leading HIV drug, Emtriva, are remarkable, but I'm not surprised to learn of them. I also hired Betsey Fox-Genovese [the founding director of women's studies] and am proud of that hire and was sorry to learn of her death. I also hired Don Verene [now Candler Professor of Philosophy] and recruited [former Samuel Candler Dobbs Professor of Chemistry] Isiah Warner from Texas A&M.

You were the first dean to be named vice president for arts and sciences.

That title was not given to me when I first came there. Jim gave that title to me after I had done good work on several matters.

What steps did you take to strengthen Emory College?

I gave deliberate attention to two areas. The first was the scholarships fund, which was rebuilt to help redefine the student body. Massive infusions of funds into scholarships enabled Emory College to recruit more diverse and more talented students in an intensely competitive market. We strengthened the regional identity of the College, which then drew 50 percent of its students from the Southeast, and at the same time diversified, with nearly 10 percent of its students from each of the other five regions of the country. Achieving greater ethnic diversity was more difficult, and I could tell that it would require further initiative.

What faculty improvements came about during your tenure as dean?

The College faculty grew by more than a hundred positions.[3] The faculty became more and more able, ambitious, and centered on what they were doing. While I could see that we still had considerable room for growth and improvement, the College when I left it was on the verge of having a faculty of national distinction. Several small departments had achieved distinctiveness, and some of the large departments held a major place nationally.

What other initiatives do you recall from the 1980s?

We upgraded the computer technology of the College from a few dedicated word processors to hundreds of terminals and several labs, all linked by cable network. We established the Freshman Seminar Program [later called Freshman Advising and Mentoring at Emory, or FAME] and instituted new academic programs in women's studies, classical studies, Latin American and Caribbean studies, Soviet and East European studies (now the Center for Russian and East European Studies), film and writing, a new Department of Theater Studies, and the African Studies Institute. We received major grants from the Luce, Hughes, Mellon, and Dana foundations for faculty and program development. Major funding dedicated by the University for program enhancement in the College resulted in enhancement of the Martin Luther King Jr. Scholarship Program, support of new programs in the arts, and equipping major research laboratories in physics and chemistry. The College also assembled some of the strongest faculty in the nation in southern studies.[4]

What was your impression of the students at the time of your departure as dean?

I felt proud of the students. We worked for and saw a rapid rise in Emory's recruiting better and better students. They, in turn, worked harder and harder. They excelled academically. They won forty national fellowships in the last five years of my time at Emory. The graduates took a new pride in the College.

What challenges did you see ahead of Emory at the time of your departure?

First of all, Emory needed to fuel further growth to retain the quality of both faculty and students and to fulfill the promise that faculty had come to expect. Second, Emory College faced difficult choices in establishing priorities for the budget because it needed to decrease dependency on tuition income and establish new sources of income. Third, the University needed to find ways of building the arts and sciences in a coherent way, so that neither the College nor the Graduate School would succeed at the expense of the other, and priorities would be weighed judiciously. The risk was that the College would lose economic viability and institutional integrity.

Why did you decide to leave Emory?

After a time, I felt I had done everything I could do there. [And] I felt uncomfortable teaching there after the deanship.

Wearing Two Hats in the Arts and Sciences: Interview with George H. Jones

George H. Jones joined the Emory faculty in 1989 as dean of the Graduate School and vice president for research. Previously he had served as dean of the Rackham Graduate School at the University of Michigan. During the 1990–91 academic year he served also as interim dean of Emory College. He has also served as chair of the Biology Department and currently holds the position of Goodrich C. White Professor of Biology. His research interests include the biochemistry and evolution of RNA processes.[5]

Your first year as dean of the Graduate School and vice president for research was also David Minter's last year as dean of Emory College, and the following year you were asked to serve simultaneously as interim dean of the College while a search was on for a new College dean. How did you manage that double load?

I would spend three days one week in the College and two days in the Graduate School, and then two days the next week in the College and three days in the Graduate School. I did that for a year. I was also vice president for research during that time.

That was a new position.

It was. I really was the vice president for research in the arts and sciences, because I had very little contact with or influence over the medical school or any of the other professional schools. So to the extent that I was vice president for research, it primarily was the College and Graduate School that I had responsibility for.

What was that responsibility?

One of the major responsibilities was that the Office of Sponsored Programs, some of whose activities included the medical school, was under my oversight. One thing we were clearly trying to do during that time was to increase Emory's research capacity, primarily in garnering additional extramural funding. It was during those years that we first topped the $100 million mark in extramural resources.

That was one of the targets established by President Laney in his "Emory 2000" address of 1987.

That's right, and we actually reached that landmark well before 2000.

What did you see as your charge and your goals in that interim year as College dean?

There were several things apparent to me. As you say, there had been tremendous growth in the College, but there was also a fair amount of anxiety among many College faculty because of what they perceived as a change in the mission of the College, away from primarily teaching, to teaching and research. A number of people felt they had been brought here under one set of conditions and now were expected to meet a different set of criteria.

So one thing that I felt I needed to do during that year was allay some of those concerns and to try to make people feel that they were valued for their contributions—that in fact the environment might be changing, but that didn't mean that they were any less important to the College and to their departments. One way that I tried to do that was by a series of luncheons that brought people together from across departments in the College, so that they could talk to each other and get some sense of their shared anxieties, their shared aspirations, some sense that we valued what they were doing.

It was also an opportunity for them to sound out to you, because you were part of the luncheon conversations.

That's right, I was. One of the other major things that we did during that year was primarily with the assistance of Irwin Hyatt and Rosemary Magee. We started to take a hard look at faculty salaries, and it was reasonably clear that there were some significant inequities. Although we weren't able to address all of those within that year, we began to make some significant headway.

George H. Jones

Were they gender inequities, rank inequities, inequities among disciplines, or salaries below the market?

Essentially all of the above. There were problems within departments, there were problems across departments; faculty who had been at the University for the same period of time, had essentially the same records qualitatively, who were making significantly more or less than someone in another department who looked the same. We tried to deal with some of those issues during that year, and I think we made some progress.

One year is a very quick time to make that up, but from your perspective as graduate dean for another five years or so, did you see some of those inequities begin to close?

I think so. David Bright continued to address those issues once he became dean. One of the other strong supporters for doing those things was Billy Frye. Billy was very interested in what was going on in the College. When I first came to Emory I wanted to meet with the faculty in every department in the Graduate School. Billy went with me to most of those meetings, and that was the first time he had met with faculty in some departments. I remember very clearly when we met with theater studies, and Billy knew those people—Alice Benston and Jim Flannery and others—but he had never really met with them as a faculty. Billy came away from that meeting with a much more positive feeling for the quality of the people in the department, the quality of their program, and the quality of the contribution they were making to the College. That translated into support from Billy when I came to him as dean of the College and said we need to do something to bring up faculty salaries in theater studies.

Did you have leverage or authority as interim dean of the College that you wouldn't have had as graduate dean solely?

Yes, because, of course, as graduate dean I didn't hire or fire any faculty. Even as interim dean of the College I was in position to make decisions on faculty hiring. The year that I was interim dean we hired something like twenty or twenty-five new faculty.

Any hires you are particularly proud of?

If I remember correctly, our first shot at Walter Melion was during my year as interim dean. Another strong hire during that year was Carlos Alonso, in Spanish.

Was there any anxiety among the faculty about having the dean of the Graduate School serve as interim dean of the College?

I don't remember any anxiety about my wearing both hats. I tried to communicate to all of the constituencies that I was going to try to be as fair as possible, whichever hat I might be wearing at the time. What there was anxiety about was the simple issue of what was going to happen with regard to leadership in the College. There were times when I needed to make decisions when faculty felt that maybe those decisions should be postponed until there was somebody in position who didn't have "interim" in front of their name. My feeling was that as long as I was dean of the College, I was supposed to be able to do whatever a dean needed to do in those circumstances. For example, one of the things I had to do during that year was to remove at least one person from a chair's position. That was a responsibility I had as dean of the College, interim or not. At no point did I feel that I was just a caretaker. Of course, until the ultimate decision was made, there was always at least the formal possibility that I might have become a candidate for the position permanently.

If you had done that, do you imagine that the president and the provost might have considered bringing the two arts and sciences deanships into one?

There was never any discussion of that, interestingly enough, despite the fact that I wore both hats for a year. I would have opposed combining the deanships permanently then, I think, in the same way that I opposed it subsequently. I would have been concerned that even a well-meaning "super dean" would not have been able to give the Graduate School the kind of attention it needed if it was going to grow and develop.

In your year of interim deanship, did you bring the two staffs together at any time?
We did. We would meet together, maybe once or twice a month. It was as much as anything so that people could know what was happening on the other side of the plaza. But we didn't really accomplish very much in terms of integration of the College and the Graduate School as a result of trying to do that.

What was your mode of setting priorities, establishing the goals during that interim year, and communicating with the faculty?
It was my sense that we needed to make some strategic choices in building departments and programs. That wouldn't necessarily mean that we wouldn't have a department of underwater basket weaving, but it would mean that it would not get the same sort of attention that English would get, or biology or chemistry. That has to be true where the size of the pie is finite. Not everybody will or should get the same-size slice. There was concern in some people that they weren't going to get anything at all, that they basically were going to be just left to flounder, and if they succeeded by using their own devices, that would be fine, but if they didn't, nobody really cared. I had to try to allay people's fears that at least during the time I was at the helm, that wasn't going to be the case.

To give you an example, we had a chairs retreat, and at the end of it I asked people to pick three departments into which they would invest resources, but they couldn't choose their own department. This was after they had actually heard the reports of the other chairs. It was really gratifying to see the chairs respond in ways that at least suggested that, based upon the kind of information that they had been given, they were able to appreciate the contributions that other departments, sometimes departments very different from theirs, could make to the College.

Did that help to inform the way you actually constructed the budget?
It did. What I tried to do, again, was, within our constraints, to provide the kind of resources that would help people feel they were making a valuable contribution to the College while we also invested in areas where we had the best chance of growing to national stature.

Were there any programs you started in the College during that interim year?
We started our first Asian languages class—I think it was Japanese. That was something we needed to do.

Any things that you're particularly proud of in terms of both of your deanships?
I'm very proud of starting the TATTO program[6] as graduate dean. One thing I was able to do during the year I was wearing both hats was to learn a lot not only about Emory but about how universities work. So one thing I think I was able to do, during that year and thereafter, was to foster the growth of departments and programs in terms of their undergraduate mission and in terms of graduate education. People were valued not only for their undergraduate teaching but also for their contributions to graduate education, and those contributions were going to pay dividends in an increase in quality of the graduate programs and their ability to attract very strong graduate students. They were also going add visibility to Emory as a locus for intellectual activities. We were able, as a result, to do some things that led to

achieving those objectives. For example, one of the factors that contributed to Emory being elected to the Association of American Universities was the increase in the quality and visibility of our graduate programs.

I never felt that graduate and undergraduate education were in conflict, but I had a better sense of the ways in which both the Graduate School and the College needed to act and react to the departments and programs to make sure that they didn't feel that way either.

Did your experience in that year inform your later work with David Bright?

David and I had a very good working relationship. There were certainly issues that came up during his time as dean of the College and my time as dean of the Graduate School where our cooperation was not only desirable but absolutely necessary.

Can you give an example?

One was a situation in women's studies that arose from some conflicts in terms of leadership. Women's studies was a College department, but I had made some appointments in women's studies using resources in the Graduate School. So the issue needed to be resolved by both deans. And while not everybody agreed with our resolution, we ultimately did resolve the situation in a fashion that I think left people reasonably unscarred.

At the same time you were dean, you were a vice president and therefore part of the president's senior staff. Did that inform your perspective?

It certainly did, but I think the most important outcome of my being a vice president and being able to sit with the president's staff was that I was able to keep the interests of the Graduate School on the table. Although Jim Laney and Billy Frye were committed to the growth and development of graduate education at Emory, I'm not sure that there were a whole lot of other people who shared that vision, at least not without some additional prodding. Over time, other people around the table did come to share it. Charlie Hatcher [executive vice president for health affairs], for example. That really helped in terms of our being able to get the kind of resources, both human and fiscal, that were necessary to move the Graduate School forward.

One anecdote to support that notion, on one of the trustees' retreats Coleman Budd [Business 1950, former alumni trustee] asked all of the deans to name something that didn't cost money that the trustees could do to assist the deans in discharging our responsibilities. I remember clearly that I wasn't prepared for that question, and I didn't answer it very effectively, but the year that I stepped down as dean, I asked Bill Chace to allow me to meet with the Executive Committee of the board, and I told that story. I said, I'm prepared to give you a better answer now. The answer is that the value of the Graduate School at Emory needs to continue to be appreciated by all in the community, including the board of trustees. And graduate education, as an enterprise that contributes to the quality of this intellectual environment, needs to continue to be high on the list of Emory's priorities.

Since 1990 the scope of PhD programs has grown well beyond arts and sciences, into nursing, public health, and business. As the Graduate School grew and developed during your deanship, did the staff in the graduate school keep pace, or did you feel stretched? Were the resources there to build administratively?

I think that we had more than a reasonable number of staff to do the kinds of things that we needed to do in the Graduate School, particularly in terms of the deanery. During all my time as dean there were at least three assistant or associate deans, and I was able, therefore, to divide the various responsibilities among those people in ways that allowed us to get all the day-to-day administrative things done but also allowed us to do some of the more intellectual kinds of things that I thought we were primarily to be about as a graduate school: things like organizing workshops and symposia. Putting TATTO together, for example, was a responsibility shared by essentially all the people in the deanery at that point. All of those things I was able to do because of both the quality and the quantity of the staff that I had.

Is there any way in which your perspective on your deanship has deepened or been enriched after going back into the College as a regular faculty member?

It is certainly the case, beyond a shadow of a questionable doubt, that my time as a faculty member, my time as chair of biology, was made easier as a result of the knowledge I gained during my time in the College and Graduate School administration. I learned a lot about how not only Emory but other universities work, and that has been extremely helpful to me as both a faculty member and a chair. Knowing what buttons to push, but also knowing what buttons not to push. We lived in an environment for a number of years when, if you wanted something as a faculty member, you went to the top, to the president. That's just not the way you do it, and I think you have to understand, in order to be successful ultimately, not only what buttons to push but also what buttons not to push.

Overall, what is your impression of the progress of the College at this point?

I'm very pleased about where we appear to be right now. I think we have a reasonable and viable vision for the University. Nevertheless, I am concerned that within the last decade or so we missed some opportunities and, having missed those, are not as far along as a university, as a college, or a graduate school, as we might be. We should have started another capital campaign a long time ago, as soon as we finished the previous one in 1995.

Have we missed intellectual opportunities apart from what might have been possible with additional funding? Are there people we missed out on hiring, or programs that we should have gotten under way sooner, partnerships that we let slip?

We certainly missed some hiring opportunities; as to whether or not, had we been able to attract those people, it would have made a significant difference, it's hard to know. There are probably a lot of other institutions that are going to say the same thing, so I'm not sure that that makes us any worse off than anybody else.

On the other hand, we've made some fairly spectacular hires as well, so that's something we can be proud of and gratified by. To give you just an anecdote, my first year as chair of biology, the dean authorized two searches, one in computational neuroscience and the other in evolutionary genetics. I was happy that he was willing to do that, so we went through the regular search process and advertised and beat the bushes and brought people in. We have a stunning—absolutely stunning—set of candidates, so that out of the half dozen or so people we brought in, we would have been thrilled to have gotten any one of them. I called the dean and said we have a real chance to move forward; you've authorized us to fill two positions, one in each area; I'd like to bring in two people in each of those areas. He said yes. Unfortunately, we were only able to bring in two in one of those two areas, but those two people were Astrid Prince and Robert Liu, both of whom have gotten off to a running start.

I'm happy that we have taken another look at the curriculum. Unlike many other faculty who hoped that we would chisel those rules in stone and never have to look at them again, my feeling was that it was not only desirable to look at them again, it was necessary. As times change, our curriculum is going to have to change, too, and we're going to have to revisit these changes every few years.

I'm also very pleased that the University has continued to provide the resources to allow the College faculty to grow. It has been the case for a number of years that our faculty was too small to accomplish all the things we needed to accomplish to be a top-twenty-five university. Continued faculty growth is tremendous and exactly the thing that we need.

But let me tell you something that I'm concerned about in terms of the College. I made the argument over a decade ago that Emory was, probably unconsciously, committed to becoming a more diverse institution primarily by becoming more international. I think we continue to see evidence of that, so I am concerned that there are as few minority faculty as there are in Emory College, and that there are as few minority undergraduates as there are in Emory College. That's something I think we still have a ways to go to address.

We still don't have Division I basketball, but there's nothing I can do about that.

Bright Years

David F. Bright is professor of classics and comparative literature, emeritus. A native of Canada, he earned a BA degree from the University of Manitoba in 1962 and completed his MA (1963) and PhD (1967) at the University of Cincinnati. An award-winning teacher and classics scholar, he came to Emory with more than a decade of administrative experience and served as vice president for arts and sciences and dean of Emory College for six years. After concluding his work as dean, he returned to the classroom but later stepped back into his administrative harness for terms as chair of the Department of Classics and codirector of the Comparative Literature Program. In 2006 Emory awarded him the George P. Cuttino Medal for Distinction in Mentoring.

You arrived at Emory in 1991, as vice president of arts and sciences and dean of Emory College. At that point, George Jones, who was dean of the Graduate School, also had been acting dean of the College for the second year of the search.

Yes. He and I were the Bobbsey twins of arts and sciences for those first few years. I had been at the University of Illinois for nearly two decades, and in my last year there I had been the interim dean of arts and sciences on the Urbana-Champaign campus. Then in 1989 I became dean of the College of Liberal Arts and Sciences at Iowa State and served there until I came to Atlanta in 1991.

So a lot of your career before coming to Emory had been at state institutions.

That's correct. I did my graduate work at the University of Cincinnati. I taught at Williams College for three years, so my career had been at four very different sorts of places, in both size and mission.

The transition to Emory from the perspective of both size and resources must have been an inviting challenge.

It was. The scale of the campus is just about a third the size of the Urbana campus. But on the other hand, there were still resources available to be deployed, whereas in the giant public institutions, the crunch had already begun. Then, too, so much of the scientific side of the Urbana campus is distinguished. There was great pressure to preserve eminence rather than either achieve it for the first time or regain it where it had slipped. So that left a very delicate balancing act in terms of where we could put resources.

On the other hand, it gave me a much clearer idea of what an emergency looks like, and that turned out to be helpful in several ways. So when I came to Emory, the scale of the operation was smaller and the sense of ambition was quite strong, but the definition of that ambition was very hazy. It was a bit like a general Olympic motto: higher, faster, stronger. But in what? And with what? Everything that David Minter had achieved in the eighties, which was the Sutter's Mill moment of the University, had changed the landscape and the rules, so I wasn't stepping into the job he had had. But it was not yet clear what job I was stepping into. Part of the job was to define it and then do it. I had to set my own exam and then take it and do well in both setting and taking, which really did make it an enormously attractive prospect.

Into that mix, the personal involvement of President Laney and his sense of the role of the arts and sciences as the heart of the institution meant that there was an appreciation of the importance of getting things done. That fit into both a sense of responsibility and, within limits, a sense of empowerment. Billy Frye shared that notion of where the arts and sciences were going.

You had the title of vice president for arts and sciences as well as dean of the College. Did that make any difference in your relationship to the Graduate School or in what you felt empowered to do?

Not really. There was one advantage to it, which was that I sat in on meetings of the trustees and in some cases contributed to those meetings, which meant that I was perhaps more conversant with what was happening, and why. It gave a context in which to assess a problem or opportunity. The other very valuable thing under Jim Laney was the Arts and Sciences Council, which met every week or two—the president, the provost, the dean of the College, and the dean of the Graduate School.

That meant that I could meet with the president regularly and shape, refine, and define where the arts and sciences were in terms of institutional intentions and the view from the top.

When you came, there had been tremendous growth—many faculty appointments, a larger student body.

That's correct. And the issue of faculty growth and assignment of resources was one of the key issues in the time I was dean.

How did you establish priorities and determine where the areas of development and strengthening would be and why?

The Arts and Sciences Council was certainly a place to which I would take ideas on a large scale. Within the College, there were at least three sources of advice. One was the senior staff of the College, that is, the three associate deans and three assistant deans. They were able to give perspectives on size, the faculty, the curriculum, and the students. One key question that emerged was the quality of advising, which in some departments was hindered because of too many majors for the number of faculty.

One solution to that supply-and-demand problem is to take fewer majors, and the other one is get more faculty. You can imagine which the faculty opted for. From the faculty point of view, there was a real shift, as the definition of faculty responsibility focused more and more on published research. That has always been a piece of the expectation, but the center of gravity shifted quite strikingly in those years. As one faculty member famously said to me, how am I supposed to get anything done if I have to talk to students?

Of course that translates into issues of research leave and teaching load. The teaching expectations were still felt to have been inherited from a simpler time, when teaching was job one and research job two. Now those

David F. Bright

roles had essentially been reversed in terms of selecting whom to recruit and where merit raises went, and how departments were assessed.

It's not that faculty don't want to teach. Most faculty do want to teach. That's the problem. One of the best teachers on this entire campus was due for some time off. I said, "I'll tell you what. I'll reduce you to one course in the spring, and you'll have the fall off, and that's close to a year off." She said, "Don't do that; if I have one course, I'm a teacher, and I will put twice as much energy into that single course because I'm teaching. I love teaching, but I need time free to work on research."

So the yin and yang of teaching and research really was a tussle. In some departments—religion, history, psychology, for instance—research was an established fact and had been for a while. But they realized that the horizon is constantly receding, and so they needed to put more into it. But those are three great teaching departments as well. So they didn't want to give up on the one, but they had to do the other, and it was just agonizing. It was even harder in departments entirely populated by faculty who had come in with 80 percent teaching, 19 percent student advising, and 1 percent research. They weren't large enough to justify giving them more faculty lines at the expense of political science, where they were getting sixty students in their 400-level seminars.

This was the resource problem: do we pull a weak department up to strength, or do we protect at whatever cost the premier departments of the college? We don't have enough to do both. In the eighties at Emory, there were enough resources that you could play both games at once; in the nineties, there weren't. That shift had already occurred when I arrived here. So setting priorities became trickier from day one.

Faculty were mixed in their view of how it should happen and who should decide. So to come back to your question, one source of advice was the dean's staff, one was the department chairs, and one—when I was feeling particularly in the mood for a bruising—were the faculty meetings. There was also the executive committee of the College. But it had reshaped its bylaws just the year before I arrived there, for a post-Minter world, to make sure that the dean did not have any effective power over the governance of the College from the faculty's point of view. For example, it rested with the faculty and not with the dean to set the agenda for faculty meetings. I could call a meeting, but I could not set the agenda. They were quite open that the reason they had done this was that Dean Minter had had a rather more autocratic style for reasons that I can perfectly understand. His charge was, "Make a difference, make it now." If it takes ten years to get change approved at all the levels of the community, you will not make that difference.

After you had gathered advice, how did you set priorities and implement them?

I sat down with my associate deans and said, okay, you have feedback on your respective areas, you know everything that's out there as well as I do, you are yourselves among the senior faculty. Here's what you think we should do, here's what I think we should do, and when we found common ground, that's what went into the strategies and the budget. When the smoke clears and the dust settles, the dean has to send something to the president with his or her signature on it. That meant, of course, that the more opinions you invite, the more people's opinions will not eventually be followed, and that has consequences as well.

An interview of you appeared in Emory Magazine *a year after you had come. In it you outlined three areas of development you felt Emory College needed: internationalization, the fine arts and performing arts, and environmental studies.*

Those certainly were on the short list. A fourth area was curricular reform. The General Education Requirements [GERs] loomed from the day I arrived here, and one of the things I took most satisfaction in was getting a reform of the GERs. Ironically, it is also the one thing that has caused most problems since then, because of the way everything else has evolved and because of the way it finally was shaped up by faculty governance. But that the faculty moved at all was very gratifying.

The curriculum recently has been refined again.

Right. You wear the shoes for a while and find out where they hurt. Most of the curricular changes moved along fine. There was a real crunch on resources, though, and with relatively few courses that would meet the GERs, the faculty were finding themselves teaching courses they didn't really want to teach. But the students had to take them. It is the constant evolution of expectations and possibilities, but that's true of every college. Berkeley a few years ago announced that it was almost impossible for a student to graduate in four years, because the courses they would need for almost any major wouldn't all be given in any given four-year period.

We had other kinds of difficulties, some related to more aggressive and successful pursuit of external support, which took people out on research leave. Even if you had a replacement, the chances that they would be able to do your specialty course might be small. So it was a stronger faculty, a more diversified faculty, a more active faculty, but a more pressed faculty in terms of playing the traditional role of strong undergraduate education and accessibility to students.

Any faculty hires that you're particularly proud of?

A lot. Frances Foster [in English] comes to mind as maybe the franchise player of those that came and stayed. David Lynn [in chemistry]. Rudolph Byrd [in African American studies] was a significant arrival in matching the direction and fortunes of the College. As, for that matter, was Dwight Andrews [in music].

So much of that depended on the acuity, the geniality, the reliability, the perceptions of [Associate Dean] Irwin Hyatt, because his was the office to which all the candidates came. I talked to them if they were a final prospect for tenure, but he devoted a chunk of his time every year to French candidate number three, physics candidate number eleven, and so on.

To come back to those three priorities—internationalization. One of the acorns that I was able to stick in the ground that has come out rather nicely was the whole study-abroad enterprise. When I arrived here, there was essentially nothing available during the year, and only a couple of programs over the summer, and while we thought it was a fine idea, most students didn't feel either permitted or really encouraged to spend a semester away. A lot of course paths were sequential—fall and spring semester—so students ended up going during the summers, which really was not what they wanted. Or they went under the aegis of other institutions of varying quality and reliability, from which they received only the haziest of credit. So developing institutional allies out there, where you can use your passport and get credit back home for this course, solved this issue. Now the number of students abroad in a given year is many times what it was when we first started the Center for International Programs Abroad.

Was there a need to shore up or redefine area studies programs—Latin American and Caribbean studies, for instance, and Russian and East European studies?

That was an area of fairly intense tussling, because spending a semester in a location is not the same thing as being a major in a field related to the location. You may go to London because it's the easiest way for you to do Japanese studies in a language you understand. If you go to Rome, you might work at John Cabot University in modern Italian, but it's not the same thing as the Italian studies program here. Our area studies programs wanted to be able to redefine their mission to be driven by or drive the activities of the students who went to that country. Students, though, just wanted to get on a plane and go to Rome and not come back to discover that it doesn't count toward graduation. CIPA was able to divorce those two questions in a way that we hadn't been able to do before.

The other impact that internationalization had was a sharp increase in the number of faculty members whose portfolio was international and multidisciplinary—so, not just someone who teaches French literature, but someone like Geoff Bennington, who teaches French thought and spills over into comp lit and philosophy and history and so on. It drove the diversity of the faculty.

This meant, however, that when the History Department received an appointment, it didn't necessarily give them four more courses in history, traditionally defined; it gave them a really exciting colleague, part of whose attention was in another part of the College. That sets up more interesting dynamics. So part of the growth of the faculty went into people who didn't fit the usual verticalities of a department. They went into the horizontal linkage that took you across departments. They still were located vertically, but the students didn't understand—and for good reason don't appreciate—the verticality. A twenty-first-century student does not want a university whose departments are named after books by Aristotle: physics, poetics, politics. That's not how the world is working. Don't give me departments. Give me an education. That turned out to be the largest single question that was started while I was dean, but it had to get resolved by subsequent deans.

Was that move toward horizontal connections deliberate or something that you just found developing?

A bit of both. The faculty whom we interviewed tended to be coming out of premier programs where that's the way the world was working. We were behind the curve in academic structure and course definition. We were still a traditionally shaped institution hiring people from places that had turned that corner already.

Another factor was that I became increasingly involved over the decade in the Council of Colleges of Arts and Sciences, the national organization of deans in the arts and sciences. That was where you went to hear what's out there. It was tremendously helpful to hear why some places were struggling and others were doing well. It gave me a better idea of which way the train was headed, and I could bring that back. As with curricular reform, so with intellectual mapping—there was a real tussle from the traditionalists. The short form of the advice I received was, don't bring in untenured people with untraditional portfolios, because they're not going to get tenure. You will have wasted the appointment and their time.

I think we're over that hump now. We want that kind of diversity and linkage now. The three most inherently "multi" programs in the College were women's studies, African American studies, and comparative literature, all now departments. So we've solved it by agreeing that it wasn't a problem after all, rather than finding a clever solution. We discovered you could have a committee deciding tenure with people from three different departments representing those specialties. It was seen at the time as a watering down of quality control, but now it is seen as an asset.

The priority of environmental studies, again, was the same. It was very timely. There was only halting progress on that while I was dean. The College was very fortunate that it was one of Steve Sanderson's central interests when he followed me as dean. He had the gravitas, coming out of political science and political policy and, therefore, what other people used as the point of entry. He was the right dean at the right time.

What about the arts?

Fine and performing arts were an instance of going from "not there" to "there" to a spectacular failure to trying again. It cost us $5 million to make the mistake of planning an aborted arts center designed by Peter Eisenman in the early 1990s. What would the next mistake cost? One member of the board of trustees said the Eisenman model looked like an aerial view of a crash between two semis on I-285. He had a point. The role that Rosemary Magee played in salvaging that is incalculable. We needed more time to rethink and redefine the challenge, and if there's a Nobel Prize in making a silk purse out of a sow's ear, she should get it.

But it was not just a matter of developing a center; the programs needed work as well.
  Yes. For example, the first person ever to get tenure in the College in the performing arts was Sally Radell, in dance. You may do theater studies, but you also come up as a book-writing type. But how do you adjudicate a performing art? How do you document it? Are you willing to say this is an academic pursuit for which we give the same kind of status, seniority, credit that we do in political science or chemistry?
  You had to make the case that the academy is where you not only define the limits of temerity but also provide the support to do something that is worth doing for someone who does it very well. Tenure isn't just First Amendment protection. Tenure is an academic commitment, a positive rather than a protective thing. The same was true of African American studies or women's studies, particularly when most of the faculty who came in those days received their PhD in English or political science or history. Why don't they then just do that? Why do they have to do something else in which they don't have a PhD? So it was part and parcel of arguing for academic evolution.

After you left the deanship, the administration was reorganized and the vice presidency for arts and sciences eliminated. What has been the effect of that change?
  One regrettable feature was that the health sciences side continued its access and its role with the trustees, while the arts and sciences have not had that. The shift, symbolic though it was, had practical results. A representation of the arts and sciences in that next level of discussion and planning remains a good idea.

Can the provost carry that responsibility?
  Yes, but if the next provost is out of the health sciences, you really would not have that voice from arts and sciences. In fact, the sciences within the arts and sciences felt a little left out when everybody above their department heads was someone in the humanities. We had a College dean from the ILA, a provost from theology, and a president in English; the scientists wondered whether anybody up there understood what scientists were talking about.

Would you reflect on the relationship between the College and the Division of Campus Life?
  I would say that the College administration saw itself as engaged in the academic enterprise, and saw Campus Life as responsible for the other-than-academic dimensions of students, preponderantly for undergraduates. It really boiled down to the distinction between "academic" and "other-than-academic." My former colleague Frances Lucas-Tauchar, who was vice president for Campus Life at the time, certainly thought the distinction was overrated. She rejected the term "extracurricular," because in her view nothing is outside the student's reason for being here to study. The term she liked was "cocurricular." But in reality, from Campus Life's perspective there was *in* the classroom, and then everything else, and they thought of themselves as running everything else. So the interaction between those two offices was difficult and became more so.

Did you teach while you were deaning?
  I did not, except single performances. There has been an enormous shift in the job description of a dean from the eighties to the nineties to this decade. There used to be room for the dean to do that, when the dean was a senior academic person. The dean is now a corporate dean, and job one is administrative. So there really wasn't room for teaching, let alone—most particularly—guaranteeing that I could be available at 10 o'clock Monday, Wednesday, Friday.

Did you spend a lot of time in fund-raising?
  That curve was rising very sharply at the end of my term. When I started, there were deans who would grumble that fund-raising was using up sometimes as much as 25 percent

of their time. Today a dean would kill to have it occupy only 50 percent of her time. That obviously has an impact on who wants to be a dean and whom you will most want to be the dean. That also has implications for the organizational structure of the College and University administration.

I'm struck by the evolution of the job. In my ten years as dean at three different colleges, the notion of what a dean was evolved dramatically. In those early days deans were senior scholars, operating out of a sense of noblesse oblige, from within the ranks. If you had your druthers, you would pick somebody who was ready for the job on day one. That evolved over ten years into a more complex job, because so many of the pieces that had been defined in a comfortable and familiar way for a hundred years were changing—the skill set, the resources, the market, and so on. Eventually, there were so many pieces changing that it was hard to say what, at a particular moment, a dean should be, because by the time you finished hiring, it had already changed.

What it takes to be a dean in this place has changed dramatically again just in the years since I left the dean's office, and it will continue to do so. That has an implication for longevity in office. Twenty-five years ago the average time in office for a dean was ten to fifteen years, and then that shrank to about five, about the same as for presidents and provosts.

It used to be that you left a deanship either to a bigger deanship or up to a provostship. Now, it is likely that people can't or won't do this for more than five years, or that the situation will have changed enough that the institution needs you to do something different than when you started. So with burnout, job change, a host of things, the average time in the deanship is likely to grow shorter, and the requirements on any given dean search are going to be more idiosyncratic and temporary. We have something on our plate, and if we can get four years out of a dean addressing the things that we can see now, we'll probably be ready for somebody else after that period, and you'll probably be glad to get paroled. It's become more of a specialty job. That certainly happened to the presidency twenty years ago and is now happening to the provostship more and more.

The problem is that there's a learning curve.

Exactly. I had one advantage in that I had been dean at two other places before I came to Emory. The disadvantage was that they were two *other* places. On Monday I thought I knew the job, but by Tuesday I realized I didn't, and by Wednesday I realized maybe nobody does. The learning curve can be shortened by getting somebody who's already been a dean elsewhere, but that carries its own risks. The disconnect between the dean and the faculty will be large and permanent. Again, take the shift after David Minter: what they were looking for was a faculty member–style dean. By the time I was done, they wanted somebody who would be, you know, more decisive: "Who cares what the damn faculty think? Get it done." Steve Sanderson brought a managerial style that fit very well with the campus wanting things to work. The pendulum went there, and then when he left, there was a sense that it really wouldn't be a bad idea to get one of the most experienced faculty members on the entire campus.

One of our own.

There's that sort of tick-tock, tick-tock. The implication is that we're right on schedule to bring in a techno dean who will address these issues and rely even more extensively on the associate deans in crucial area roles. So I do see the deanship becoming more technically described. The job description will evolve much more rapidly, and the real risk is that the dean will be seen as a remote figure from the faculty as well as from the students.

That's where I think the deanship is going within research universities. Freestanding arts and science colleges always blur the president and the dean because they do each other's roles in many ways. A place like Davidson College is totally different from Emory. But now that we are in the major, major research university league, that's a tiger we can't get off, and the more we emphasize the college or school dean as participating in that research enterprise, the greater the gap will be with the role of individual faculty. That is probably the riskiest thing that the University faces in the next generation.

From the Wilds of College Life to the Wildlife Society: Interview with Steve Sanderson

Steven Sanderson served as vice president for arts and sciences and dean of Emory College from 1997 to 2001. He received his PhD in political science from Stanford University. He left Emory to become president and chief executive officer of the Wildlife Conservation Society in New York and a member of the Council on Foreign Relations.[7]

Tell us about your decision to come to Emory.

I came to Emory from the University of Florida in 1997. I had gotten pulled into the world of deans by Cornell University, when I was asked to apply for a deanship there. I had never considered the possibility but went through that process. It was an enriching experience, because as a faculty member I had never looked certain issues in the eye—what you would do if you were trying to advance the cause of the college and the university instead of just your own academic work. I had played a minor role in being chair of a department, and I had created a big program in tropical conservation and development, but I was just a regular old faculty member. My wife, Rosalie, said, well, you ought to continue to look at this sort of position, because it might be interesting. So I did.

When the Emory position came open, I was involved at the same time in the search for the Vanderbilt deanship. It was fascinating to compare the two opportunities. I was able to see side-by-side the difference between the two universities. Emory had so much more effervescence and a more diverse community and was so much more aggressive toward its mission than Vanderbilt. Within twenty-four hours, I was offered both jobs. There just wasn't any question that I wanted to come here because of that vibe that was really good.

I'm no good to anybody as a leader if the job is simply "steady as she goes." What I'm interested in is change, and this place wanted change.

There was one question in my interview with President Bill Chace. I had fifteen minutes with him. He said, "Well, are you a leader of men?" That was a good question! He didn't say, "Are you an administrator," or "What do you think about faculty governance," or anything else. His question to me, whatever he made of the answer, was whether I was interested in leading. I think that's what we were trying to do.

What were some of the changes you heard suggested by the people interviewing you, and what were some of the things you had in mind when you arrived here?

Steve Sanderson

There were certain touchstones for everybody. The first was people. The first message I received from the faculty was that this place cares about its undergraduate teaching. This commitment was exemplified by the beginnings of the Center for Teaching and Curriculum. There was a lot of attention to try and have graduate students learn how to teach before they taught. And then I came just as the curriculum reform was about 80 percent complete, and in the fall, my first challenge was to get the faculty together to mark it up. Of course, being a curricular reform, it attracted strong opinions, and there were at least four hundred of them. We went through a really organized, intense process, meeting every week until we had it all marked up. The process was an affirmation of the devotion of the faculty to teaching.

People not only had strong opinions about the body of learning and the habits of mind that they wanted to convey but they also were willing to commit themselves to those goals, including a consensus that only ranked faculty could teach the new freshman seminars. They weren't creating a freshman requirement and then handing it off to TAs. The faculty wanted it; they loved it.

Another thing that people felt very strongly, and I share the feeling, is that the arts and sciences are the heart and soul of the University. Evidence of that feeling was clear: my associate deans were completely committed to Emory College as a center for teaching and scholarship. Rosemary Magee, Irwin Hyatt, and Peter Dowell embodied the College as a sacred place with students and faculty at its core. They and their colleagues taught me and held me to high standards. Not only are the arts and sciences the biggest educational budget unit, but they really are what the University is about, and then it is surrounded by refinements such as the Graduate School and the professional schools. What every university has to produce is a really first-rate arts and sciences corpus. It was my job to represent that to the University and make the College a leader in the University.

Some changes that I felt were necessary we made some progress in. One of the great challenges of any university is to focus. Universities don't focus. They don't decide what they're *not* going to do as much as they decide what they *are* going to do. But you can't do everything, and you end up diluting your effort.

This particular university has great strengths historically and ethically and collegially, and it has weaknesses as well. For instance, in languages we taught a lot, but we were putting effort into languages that nobody wanted or nobody took.

People had ambitions for things that didn't make any sense at Emory or that had made sense at one time and then no longer made sense. For instance, we had our own versions of high-energy physics, which was quite the thing until the end of the Cold War, and then it became quite not the thing. My feeling was that we had to do physics in a way that interacted with other departments to create positive multipliers. So biophysics was a good idea, because we had strong biology and strong chemistry. We did some physical chemistry to unify the two, and then we tied our basic sciences to the applied sciences in the academic health center. All of that was by way of focusing and making our science effort more effective.

Did you lead the development of Science 2000? That was the notion that the science departments, which were housed almost literally at the farthest remove from each other on different corners of the campus, should be brought into closer physical alignment as well as programmatic alignment.

I'm sheepish about claiming anything, but I owe a lot to [medical dean] Thomas Lawley and [public health dean] James Curran, the former EVP for health affairs Mike Johns, and Dennis Liotta, who was vice president for research at the time. I said, look, we would like to join forces with you and open the door to the applied sciences. We know how hard that is, but there are great gains to be had if we share equipment and share appointments where possible, and recruit to best effect. It also extended to psychology and psychiatry and so forth. They supported that, and we worked together to produce protocols for equipment sharing and time costs and grantsmanship, and Dennis and Lanny Liebeskind [Dobbs Professor of Chemistry] were great at pounding on that until we got it right. The point was that we could be better unified.

Before then, everybody in the College had said that the great shadow of a medical center loomed over them and got all the money. It turned out, of course, not to be true. Their life was just as hard as ours, and we were just as big as everybody else, so why not figure how to work together? It did come to a good result for Science 2000, and it helped us identify a larger strategy in science.

The big question was what we could reasonably expect of a university built like us in this time. You have a few choices, and you bet on those. Chemistry really [took advantage of that opportunity], as one would expect, because they have very good research records and are real leaders. We also recruited David Lynn, another great collaborative type, and Les Real in biology. We built some senior leadership based on people at the intersection of things.

Any other hires that you're particularly proud of?

Not a hire, but we brought Eleanor Main back from the Graduate School to the College. The Educational Studies Department was in an odd position in the College and didn't have a sense of where it wanted to go. They were really good people, but we could not for the life of us figure out a coherent, compelling direction. So I asked Eleanor to take the lead, and she was perfect.

Economics was also in rough shape. They would ask for commitments that were just not possible. I took the department into receivership, and we had a little interim arrangement. Then Bob Chirinko and Hashem Dezhbaksh became the leadership core over there, and Hashem has really been not only a great teacher but also a great colleague and outstanding chair.

One of the programs you moved into a different position was environmental studies.

It was actually created during my tenure as dean. The faculty wanted something like that, and I had thought a lot about the subject because I had worked with a team to create a kind of "college without walls" at the University of Florida, an interdisciplinary college of faculty on natural resources and environment.

I agreed that we would move forward on a department proposal if the faculty came up with one. The only thing I insisted on was that it be science-strong, because so many environmental studies programs are just feeling good about being green. This had to be rigorous. It's been slow to build a significant faculty base, but I think it's done well in its way.

One thing I did that was big and different was to change study abroad. When I came we had roughly sixty undergraduate students a year studying abroad, and almost all of them were on other schools' programs. The year I left, we had six hundred, and they were almost all in our programs.

Bill Chace genuinely wanted to internationalize the curriculum. He himself studied literature outside this country and cared for the foreign experience, felt that it was enriching to undergraduates, as I did. I knew that that experience had shaped me, and I think every student should go outside the borders of the United States for some purpose. It shouldn't just be with the family to Paris.

We did several things. We invested a lot in a study-abroad program, and we created an international center. I took all of the dean's money that went to faculty research and student activities abroad, and I put those funds in the hands of the steering committee of the international center. The center's first director, Howard Rollins [professor of psychology], and the faculty who were in that mix did a great job. Nobody could come to me and ask for money; I didn't have the money anymore. The faculty had it. They were deciding on a basis of peer review. That worked well, and Howard was a great asset.

Howard and I also established good relationships in the sciences with Imperial College in London and with the University of Cape Town and the University of Western Cape, in South Africa. We also deepened our relationship with the University of St. Andrews, which is a really good one.

What was the College's relationship with the Graduate School?

We had good relations, and Eleanor Main was a big part of it. Don Stein was the graduate dean while I was here, and was a good colleague and a good friend. He's a serious scientist and a bridge builder. He is a psychologist but really a neuropsychologist, so he knew the sciences. He knew the funding streams. But I had all the faculty in the arts and sciences. He had faculty and graduate students who weren't in the arts and sciences. There's not a way to clean that up, so you need a good relationship, and I think we had that.

Were there initiatives with Campus Life that offered opportunities for collaboration?

Frances Lucas-Tauchar was the dean for Campus Life, except for my last year, when she left to become president of Millsaps College. We worked very well together. Campus Life is a resource, but it's also a sink in the sense that the College gets taxed for Campus Life, and the judgments about what Campus Life ought to be delivering to the students are not made by the academic tax providers. Some of the things that Frances gave priority to, legitimately, were not things I would have put at the top of my list. But how do you figure out how much to spend on counseling and on improvement in sports? I can't say I have any great difference of opinion on what they did, because she was good and really cared about students. But it could have been deeper and richer.

When I came, the faculty was so anti-fun. The faculty would make long speeches about Campus Life, as if it were a pox. I never felt that way. [Frances] and I actually worked well together.

You were a member of the president's senior staff, or cabinet.

Well, here is one of the things that I regret about my time at Emory. I learned something from it, so I'm not going to blame anybody. I should have done differently than I did. Here's my narrative.

I came as vice president for arts and sciences as well as dean of Emory College. About two or three years into my experience, they were recruiting Marla Salmon as dean of nursing, and she wanted to be a vice president, too. That didn't make any sense as far as anybody could tell. But instead of saying, look, the College is a different case, they said, well, Steve, we don't think it makes sense for you to be the only academic dean who is also a vice president.

I didn't care personally if I had this label on the front of my name. It was the same mug in the mirror in the morning. But I should have defended my institutional prerogative and said no, because my faculty colleagues in the College saw it as a blow. It didn't change anything in the way I spent my day, but it did change a little bit of the valence that was assigned to the College.

Did it change the role that you played in making decisions about the budget?

It didn't. The way Emory's budget was built, there were two big units, the academic health enterprise and the arts and sciences. The revenue stream for arts and sciences all flows through the College.

I always had access to John Temple [former EVP for finance and administration], and I always had a fair hearing from him. He really cared about the success of the College. But there was never a point in the process where the College was anything other than a really big revenue center.

How did you determine the priorities and strategic choices for the College? Who were your main conversation partners in setting directions?

The chairs certainly were. I had active, good relations with the chairs, and I met with them a lot. I went out to the departments all the time. I visited all the departments in the first semester I was here. Gradually people saw that I really listened to what they were saying. There was a lot of interaction. My simple rule was that you could say anything you wanted to in a meeting that was professionally responsible, but you couldn't not say what you had to say in a meeting and then come up to me afterward to voice an opinion out of the earshot of other legitimate stakeholders. If you had something to say, say it in the meeting.

Then I worked with the Tenure and Promotion Committee through Irwin Hyatt and through the faculty as people rotated on and off. I talked with people I really admired. Micheal Giles, professor of political science, was so serious about his responsibilities—never about himself but always about making a strong decisions. That's how I came to know Lanny Liebeskind, who was chair of the Chemistry Department. I would come across these very strong figures, always very responsible and willing to come to the meeting and do the work.

All institutions grow by accretion, so what you have to do is to watch and not accrete so much. I announced that all space belonged to the College and not to the departments, and all positions belonged to the College and not the department, so that when there was a faculty vacancy, it devolved to the College. You could petition to have a restoration, but it was not a cinch.

Basically, in the give-and-take, the faculty piece of the job was serious. I was much harder on tenure. The year I came, the success rate was 90 percent, and the year after I came, it was 50. That was a shock.

Did it stay at about that rate?

It did. We did better on the front end [of the retention process]. We began giving more research support money to junior faculty, especially in the humanities. If we hired a junior scientist, we gave her a quarter-of-a-million dollars to set up a lab. But if we hired a humanist, we were not giving him anything, even though the scientist has a lot better chance of getting a grant than a humanist. So right away, everybody whom we hired in the humanities we funded. If we hired a young English professor, we would give that person a pot of money to advance that person's research. It wasn't a lot of money, maybe twenty thousand dollars. They could use that to make their research case for tenure. These steps helped us improve the rate of success at tenure by the time I left. But it never went back to where it had been.

Departments would make recommendations, and if I turned them down, I would hold an open meeting with the tenured faculty in the spring. I wouldn't say anything about particular cases. I would talk about our standards and how we were trying to meet them, and ask the faculty whether there was something that we could do to enhance our chances to help people succeed.

Did you bring that standard with you to the institution, or was there something from the president or the provost that was decreeing that there needed to be stiffer standards of tenure?

There was nothing from above. It was my feeling. To be honest—and this was nothing I ever really articulated or acted on—I don't think that tenure serves the university. There are ways to give the right protections and a good employment contract to people without tenure. But that's neither here nor there. We did put in place with our lecturers and senior lecturers very good contracts, good wages, good promotion processes, and so forth. We valued their work.

In any event, I felt that the tenure system was built upside down. People wanted to make generous judgments on the front end and regret them for twenty-five years afterward. What I wanted was to give each person the best chance of succeeding, but if they didn't, not regret sending them off.

The other thing I wanted was to avoid any possibility that the University would overturn a decision, because the academic integrity of a college resides in the college, and the provost and the trustees should basically see a terrific case each time or see a rejection. A couple of cases were contested but not more than that.

Is there anything you regret or miss about your time as dean, now that you've moved out of academia?

The best thing about being a dean was that I quit being a political scientist altogether, and I really did read in the fields that I represented. Even though I wouldn't claim any expertise, I would read as much as I could in the particular tenure cases—everything the candidate had produced.

That was just due diligence on my part, but I really enjoyed being part of an arts and sciences community. I don't know much about the dance program, but I enjoyed learning about it and talking to people who lived and breathed dance. I had an affection for Russian language and literature, but I don't speak it and don't know the literature, yet I was always taken with what they cared about. The best thing about my professional life is that I've stayed in school all these years. That's what was greatest as dean. I was a generalist who was able to dine out on everybody's scholarship.

You said earlier that Emory had strengths and weaknesses. What do you think they are?

The greatest thing about Emory is that it really is an ethical place. This university is a good place, and it believes in being a good place, and when it's not a good place, it gets embarrassed about itself. Its whole institutional narrative is about being good, whether it's service or leadership. That's really wonderful, and it's not true of every place by any means.

It is also all about teaching and learning. I think of all the conversations I've had here with people from eight to eighty who are eager to learn, eager for a richer life of the mind? Why don't we read together, and why don't we sit down on the lawn? That kind of positive anxiety about learning and doing and thinking and protecting knowledge and nurturing students— that's very rich here relative to other places.

Emory works hard at being self-conscious as an institution, sometimes bordering on neurotic. I used to do a dean's dinner sign-up. I'd go over to the DUC and have one of those lovely buffets, and there'd be about twelve kids, and I would say, "If you could wave your wand and change one thing about Emory, what would you change?" The kids would say they want better race relations or want to know other kinds of people or want to see more of the world. It was heartfelt. The kind of student we were recruiting married well with the institutional anxiety about being part of a world that's doing better than it was yesterday. That's wonderful.

It's hard to recognize every day how unique Emory is in that regard; other universities are not like this. They don't have the same feeling, the same kind of kids coming out.

What took you off to New York and out of academia?

I had left academic life before and had really thought about staying out when I went to Brazil for the Ford Foundation. So that wasn't foreign to me.

There was a conjuncture for me. I was coming up to the fifth year of a five-year term, and, to be honest, the president and the provost would not give any signals as to what their intentions were after the fifth year. In fact, the deans generally didn't get annual evaluations in those days. My first year, I received this little-bitty letter from the administration saying that I was getting a salary increase, but there was no performance review. I wrote back and said I want to know how my performance was; here's my annual activities report. So they started a serious evaluation.

But you never knew where you were, and some basic things had changed. I supported a change in the way instruction was done, both technologically and in the freshman seminar that was really the heart of the new curriculum. But personally I didn't feel well suited to that style of teaching. I had a long record of successful teaching, and I love to teach, and I think I was a good teacher. But I was an old-fashioned teacher. I prepared lectures, and I'm a storyteller. But I didn't like the democratization of the classroom. I didn't think that they knew what they needed to know, and I didn't want to have a debate about what they didn't know. If somebody didn't know what the United Nations was, I didn't want to hear their opinion about it. I had to get across what it was in the first place. So when I looked at the prospect of reentering the faculty and teaching again, I didn't like it. I had a sweet taste in my mouth from my teaching and didn't want to risk that.

So I didn't know whether I was going to be deaning for another five years, and I didn't think I could go back to teaching. I knew I didn't want to be a provost: the job description was awful. It was like being the executive officer on a ship: you have all the problems and none of the scrambled eggs with your ham.

Not that anybody was inviting me to, but I didn't want to be a president of a university with an academic health center, because at the time they were all in the soup. I didn't want to be the president of a university without one either, because it shrank the mission so much without those wonderful science and clinical services.

So that gave me some clear cross-offs in my career path. I was motoring along minding my own business when two things happened. One was that the Wildlife Conservation Society started to recruit me, and then my father died. I mean within days, those two things came together. So it was a combination of having done about what I thought I could do and not seeing my academic vocation proceed in a way that was clear to me, and then having this extraordinary opportunity. The clarity came with the process.

Any questions we haven't asked? Anything that you have been burning to share?
Poetry.

What about it?
We started Poetry Fest—in April of 1998, I think. There were a few faculty around interested in poetry, and I said, "Well, gosh, what would we do if we had a little walking-around money for poetry?" They all came together and noodled over it, and started the Poetry Month celebrations on the Quad. I still have my "Poetry Matters" T-shirt. We worked at bringing poets here and supporting poetry in the English Department, and now Emory is a great repository and a center of influence.

You know, it takes on kind of a sweet taste over time, even the stuff that was hard. In my experience, being dean is an absolutely deadly job. I worked all the time, many weeks a hundred hours. It was suffocating. But now that's not so vivid in my mind as the fun and the collegial effort that we all put into it, and the friendships that you end up making. Everybody here all the time tried as hard as they could to do the right thing, and I never, ever felt done in by another dean. When I tell people that, they can't believe it, but it's true. There was a scrape here and there, but nothing low-down or devious. The leadership here really is good.

The Long View:
Interview with Peter Dowell and Irwin Hyatt

Peter W. Dowell, who taught American literature, African American literature, and American studies for forty-five years at Emory, is professor of English, emeritus. His teaching and research interests spanned American literature and culture from the late nineteenth century through the 1950s and, in recent years, turned especially to baseball and American culture. He served as senior associate dean for undergraduate education in Emory College for fifteen years and earned the George P. Cuttino Medal for Distinction in Mentoring in 2000.

Irwin Hyatt is professor of history, emeritus, and taught East Asian history at Emory for thirty-six years. He served as senior associate dean for faculty development for thirteen years before retiring in 2002. Upon his retirement, the University honored him with the Thomas Jefferson Award for his significant service and leadership. Hyatt earned his BA degree from Emory University, and after completing his doctoral work at Harvard he became the first Asian studies faculty member in Emory College.[8]

Peter, when did you first come to Emory College, and in what capacity?
I came to Emory in 1963, officially as an assistant professor in English, but they were just developing an American studies program in the Graduate Institute of Liberal Arts, and it was understood that I would teach one course a year in the ILA. I began by teaching the introduction to American studies. It was sort of funny, because I hadn't finished my PhD yet, and I was teaching a graduate course.

Irwin, you came as a student in what year?
I was here as an undergraduate from 1953 through 1958, and then came back to teach in 1966. As a lot of people did, I came as an instructor and then finished the PhD and became an assistant professor. I've been here more or less continuously, with a few times off for leave, since 1966.

A lot has happened in that time. Are there particular anecdotes that would suggest some of the changes you have experienced over the last forty-five years?
Dowell: One event I remember from my first year of teaching was in the middle of the spring. I was teaching in the second floor of what's now Callaway South [formerly the Physics Building], overlooking the Quadrangle. All of a sudden I heard this enormous screaming and yelling and hollering. We all arose up and we went and looked out the window, and here was a whole group of young men charging across from the Administration Building toward Candler Library. I later found out that it was the birthday of the Kappa Alpha fraternity (KA), and on the birthday of KA they reenacted Pickett's Charge on the Quadrangle. That was about the last time they did it, but I still remember seeing that and wondering what the hell was going on.
Hyatt: They used to wear Confederate uniforms!

Peter Dowell

Have you noticed a change in Greek life and its influence on the campus in your time?
Hyatt: I think in some ways it's the same, but it seems to me now that fraternities are more interested in the academic side of things and really have emphasized that.

A smaller percentage of the male student body belongs to fraternities than was the case in the old days. I mean in the 1950s virtually everybody belonged to one. If you didn't, you wouldn't have a social life. Of course, it hasn't been like that in a long time now.
Dowell: In the first year I was teaching here, I was asked to be the faculty monitor of a fraternity party up on Lake Lanier. I agreed to do that, and then I talked to somebody in Campus Life, and they said, well, that meant I was supposed to keep the alcoholic consumption down. When I arose up there, one of the young men

from the fraternity said you don't need to pay any attention to alcohol, which I didn't.

Hyatt: I was asked one time to be a judge of the Dooley's lawn displays. They used to have skits out on the lawns [of the fraternity houses], and the judges would go around and sit at a little table that each fraternity would have out on the lawn. The brothers would come out and, making no bones about it, just make you a drink, put a tumbler out and fill it up with bourbon. A student did that in front of one of the fraternities, and I said if I actually drank that I wouldn't be able to proceed.

In terms of the quality of the students, the SATs have been going up, the GPAs have been going up, the College has become much more selective over the years. Have you experienced in your teaching an impact from that increase in the quality of the student body?

Hyatt: Peter knows more about that than I guess anybody alive, because he chaired the Emory Scholars Committee for so many years.

Dowell: Garland Richmond was actually the associate dean who chaired the scholars program initially. I think something of that idea

Irwin Hyatt

of the scholars becoming a kind of yeast within the student body had some effect. I'm not sure if today's students are that much smarter than some of the earlier ones, but we have all these testing programs that they've been put through, and they know more about jumping hurdles. Maybe the quality is a little bit better across the board, but we had some awfully good students who I wouldn't say have been replaced by superior ones now. I suspect it's at the middle where quality has risen. I used to think the average student here was a B-minus; now maybe they're B, B-pluses, though again, how much of that is grade inflation and how much of that is really that the students are better, I'm not sure.

Has the experience in the classroom changed over the years?

Dowell: The classroom activities are more varied. In the early days it was pretty much lecture with some question-and-answer discussion, writing of papers. Now you have oral projects, you have students going out and doing independent projects, and you have classes going to places in the city. That kind of variation and activity is one of the most pronounced changes.

The major changes were in the curriculum. When I first came we were on the quarter system. Students took three courses, and each course met five days a week. So every day there was class. Then when Jack Stephens was dean, fairly early after I arose here, he brought the faculty together and proposed Wonderful Wednesday. Classes would not occur on Wednesday and would only meet four times a week. Everyone would be off on Wednesday. That obviously changed things. When we converted to the semester system, during Jim Laney's presidency, that was an even bigger change.

You mentioned John Stephens, who was College dean in the 1960s.
Hyatt: Yes. He was kind of an old-school dean. I remember one group of young professors describing department budget hearings with Dean Stephens. The story was that he had done all his figuring on slips of paper that he would produce from various pockets at appropriate moments. It all looked handwritten and very amateurish to the young professors.

The administration was much leaner than now.
Dowell: Oh yes. The only other administrators in the College were a dean in charge of juniors and seniors, and a dean in charge of sophomores and freshmen.
Hyatt: John Palms followed Stephens. Palms was the last of the old-school deans. His idea of the way the College budget would be done included a meeting of department chairs at an impressive off-campus place like the Omni. We'd all sit around a table, and every College chair would have to defend or at least explain the budget requests that he had submitted to the dean. That was an old style of doing business that became less common as Emory became bigger. The discussion kind of meeting was fun, incidentally, and you did learn something about what other people were up to.
Dowell: When Palms first came in, a lot of the people in English and some of the other humanities departments were leery that this physicist was going to just underwrite Emory's emphasis on the sciences. He didn't do that, however. He was pretty good at working with all the departments.

How did each of you move into administrative positions?
Dowell: David Minter arrived as dean in 1980, and he brought us over to the administration in 1988. He left Emory about two years later.

Did either Palms or Minter enlarge the administration of the College?
Dowell: Minter certainly did. He had first hired [psychology professor] Howard Rollins, and then [political science professor] Eleanor Main, as his chief assistant dean. He also hired a dean for the study abroad programs, Carol Thigpen. Study abroad is indicative of the way the College was expanding. Study abroad had been virtually nonexistent. A handful of undergraduates would talk to their faculty and say they wanted to study abroad and find places to go, but there was no real College input into getting students to do it.

The Oxford, England, summer program was one of the early formal programs.
Dowell: One of the big pushers of it was [Professor] Ron Schuchard, along with [Professor] Jerry Beatty, in the English Department. Initially we didn't have the tie-in with Oxford. In those days we were simply in a place called Manchester College, which isn't a college of the University of Oxford, but an old religious college that happened to be in Oxford. It was only later that the arrangement with University College grew up and Oxford became the center of the trip.

How has the national distribution of students changed?
Dowell: For a long while, the South and the middle-Atlantic [region] were the core of our student body. While I was in the [administration], the three largest home states for College students were Georgia, Florida, and New York. That held up pretty well even as it's grown out to a more national outreach.
Hyatt: Emory was almost exclusively a southern or a deep-southeastern school through the 1950s, when I was here as a student. When I came back to teach in the sixties, I couldn't tell much difference the first year I was here. It seemed like it was about the same kind of people I'd gone to school with, in the way they talked and the way they acted. It was a real change by the time I came back in 1969 from being on leave for two years; we had a lot more students from up East.

Did that change the nature of the teaching or the academic engagement in the classroom at all?
Hyatt: Probably not. The students from up East were much more willing to speak up and talk in class. Southern students were more attuned to letting the professor talk. They weren't as used to give-and-take. In those days, so much of [what affected the classroom experience] was just the spirit of the times. There was a lot of crazy stuff going on.
Dowell: I suppose the major change in the curriculum during this time was a student-led movement, with a number of faculty involved, to take ROTC off the campus. We finally did eliminate it, but not because it was ROTC. The faculty objected to granting academic credit for it and giving grades and treating it like another course. Of course the air force—the military service in general—insisted that they wouldn't allow us to have a unit if we didn't make it a regular subject and give credit for it.

Surely the Vietnam War entered into the reasoning as well.
Hyatt: Oh, certainly. Nobody ever gave it a thought until Vietnam came along.

We talked a little bit about the geographic provenance of the students changing. Did you see similar change in where the faculty were coming from—different universities, different regions of the country?
Hyatt: Well, the old faculty was like the students, mostly southern, though never as heavily as the student body. It's been many years since I was aware of any regional flavor in the faculty. When our departments went out and recruited, they sought the best individuals they could get, period.
Dowell: When I came, the English Department was pretty much either from southern schools or from Ivy League schools.
Hyatt: Some of the southern professors, like Floyd Watkins and George Cuttino, were prominent in representing the Emory faculty nationally, yet what could they possibly be but southern? They did emphasize the southern character of Emory.

As the College moved from Palms to Minter to Bright and Sanderson, with Jones as interim dean during the year after Minter left, what sort of changes in focus or priorities did you see?
Dowell: Each one brought strengths. Minter, of course, had been given the idea that he should be changing things. He was the first College dean who hadn't already been an Emory faculty person. So some people may have thought of him as an outsider. He was very active in recruiting faculty, and he would find people he thought ought to be faculty candidates and would try to sell them to the department. Of course that would upset the faculty, who thought that they were supposed to initiate searches and find these people, and then the dean was supposed to approve them. The dean wasn't supposed to be out there recruiting faculty.

When I arrived to the College administration for his last two years as dean, I remember he brought in a few documents to deans' meetings that he'd written to the University administration about the faculty. I was struck at what an advocate he was for the faculty point of view. The faculty had not really seen this side of David Minter.

What changes came about as a result of his efforts?
Hyatt: His chief focus was on raising the quality of the faculty. He wanted to raise the quality of the students, too, generally, and the Emory Scholars Program was one initiative along that line. But I don't know of anything that he thought more about or that seemed to engage him more than building the faculty. He was the first dean in my experience who used the term "interdisciplinary." He would be talking about how if Emory brought this person here in Eng-

lish, there would be people in the romance languages or in history who would interact with them. He really thought in those terms.
Dowell: He was an American studies PhD, so he had that interdisciplinary kind of stamp.
Hyatt: I'm still impressed when I think about the degree to which, as a humanist, he could understand what scientists did. He could apply the same kinds of perspectives and vision related to the field of science as he did to things in humanities and social sciences.

Were there changes in focus, priority, budgeting practice between Minter's administration and Bright's?
Hyatt: I don't remember David Bright setting out to change things the way David Minter did. Minter was such a builder; perhaps by Bright's time there wasn't as much need for that. They were both good, honest men and effective leaders.
Dowell: Bright was more willing to listen to arguments from groups of faculty about new programs, rather than coming up with a program and then trying to sell it to the faculty.
Hyatt: Bright, of course, inherited a number of people who had been brought in by Minter, and who had then begun to build their own structures and to aspire to bigger and better things. So it was a different ball game in a way. He had more to juggle than Minter did.

There has always been the double-duty of teaching undergraduates as well as graduate students. How has the relationship between the College and the Graduate School fared over the years?
Dowell: A lot of the graduate programs were just developing when we first came here. The founding of the ILA, in the mid-1950s, was one indicator. One reason the ILA was founded was that we didn't have many graduate programs, and it was going to be difficult to have PhD programs in all the different departments. Various senior faculty were interested in teaching graduate students, so the idea of an institute where faculty in different departments could have graduate students was a major impetus behind the ILA.
Hyatt: The relationship between the College and the Graduate School generally was okay. But the Graduate School seemed to me not to have much money of its own. Their faculty held appointment in Emory College or one of the professional schools, and it's the schools that pay the salaries. How the College and Graduate School got along was largely a function of how well the dean of the College got along with whoever the dean of the Graduate School was at the given time.

The dean of the Graduate School for many years was Charlie Lester, an old Emory faculty type who understood the limited aspirations the Graduate School could have. I always had the feeling, however, that the later deans would sooner or later get tired of the second-tier status of the Graduate School.

Dowell: Lester was one of the best administrators I ever saw. He had an ability to overcome some of this problem of the Graduate School being the stepchild of the College.

A lot of the growth of the Graduate School occurred under him. He managed to help engineer all of that rather well. Of course, the other change was a kind of change within the faculty. When we first came here this place was really thought of as an undergraduate college. I was going to get to teach some graduate students, but I didn't really think that that was the big thing. We've moved to the point now where that's basically what most of the new faculty think: that whom they are supposed to be teaching is graduate students. The undergraduates are somehow there to teach, too, but the faculty think graduate education is what is important somehow.

Even in the spirit of the faculty—talk about changes. We used to have lots of faculty meetings in the sixties and seventies. My sense of the senior faculty at Emory was that they were very College oriented. The present faculty teach in the College, but they're not College oriented.

They are oriented to their own academic field. The whole way they construct their faculty identity is very different from that older Emory faculty.

Hyatt: Lester was like Jake Ward [former dean of the faculties and, later, dean of alumni, Judson C. Ward] in that he must have done at some time or other virtually everything. Charles Lester was never acting president, but he was just about everything else.

He used to run faculty meetings as if he didn't know anything much about parliamentary procedure. I think he just didn't want to be bothered with it. Some faculty members acted insulted by that. But the meetings were moving, I presume, as Dean Lester wanted them to, and the business all was concluded pretty well.

Speaking of faculty meetings, has there been some change in the way the faculty meet or the way the faculty thinks of itself as a collegium over the years?

Dowell: We used to have more meetings, and most of the faculty came, and there was a real engagement. We might meet every other week. It was just frequent. Now, of course, they have them at most once a month. The attendance is very poor. There are certain groups of faculty who do it, and the rest don't.

What is your sense of how the College and Campus Life have worked together over the years?

Hyatt: Campus Life as such didn't exist before 1979. I always think of Bill Fox as having been the person who really started Campus Life. He was the one who came to provide all kinds of services and direction for the students. He embodied a feeling that Emory is getting to be a bigger place, we have students coming here from all over. Here's this guy who really cares about the students and exudes a warm approach.

We did get exasperated sometimes with some of the things that Campus Life did. Some of the cooperative things, like freshman orientation, which both the College and Campus Life were involved in, gave us the sense that those things needed to be better balanced.

Dowell: It was largely things that someone in the College office felt should have been checked with the College before Campus Life did them.

Hyatt: There was more student social activity in the 1950s and sixties than we might imagine, but it was student originated largely. A lot of it was heavily fraternity and sorority. There weren't a lot of organized activities for the student body as a whole, apart from music with the glee club, and theater. Then Campus Life came and started things like big rock concerts on McDonough Field.

Dowell: I was the [associate] dean who probably worked most closely with Campus Life, because I was in charge of student affairs for the College. There were specific issues where the faculty and Campus Life might disagree. For instance, it took a long time for us to deal with learning disabilities. There was a strong feeling for a long time among the faculty that you brought the students in, and if they could make it, great, but if they couldn't, too bad. The faculty was not particularly interested in creating certain kinds of programs to give students special aid. That had to grow up gradually to get it put in.

Do you sense that Emory was behind the curve on those things, since there were other institutions nationally that were leading in those areas?

Dowell: Yes. When we started looking at people to work in disabilities, we had candidates coming from places that really had well-developed programs already, and our program was really difficult to get moving. Part of the problem was that the administration put the disabilities program in the Office of Equal Opportunity Programs, where it was housed along with staff and faculty protests of various kinds, as well as sexual harassment case adjudication. The only rationale for the placement of this office—the one common denominator between these entities—was that they were all federally mandated programs, but they didn't have much relationship to one another. For the longest time we kept fighting this [arrangement] in the College. Finally, under Steve Sanderson, we made the appointment of Wendy Newby as assistant dean for inclusive instruction. We seated her office partly in the College, so that it would not always be the most junior appointment in the EOP office.

How have faculty promotion and tenure changed over the years?
Hyatt: It's become a good deal more formal, with a lot more rules and regulations and procedures. Emory is just part of a trend nationally in that respect. David Minter was important in that. He really believed very strongly in the system that they had at Rice, where the Faculty Council, as it was called there, not only handled promotion and tenure but apparently played much more of a role in faculty governance than was the case at Emory. Rice is smaller and oriented a bit differently.

What I constantly hear from people in the History Department now is that there is not the sense of camaraderie or fellowship that was the case when my cohort was coming through. But that's probably the times also. Simply in growing, some sense of closeness is going to be lost.
Dowell: The process became more systematic. The president became a more active part of it when Bill Chace set up the President's Advisory Council [to review all tenure and promotion files and regularize the process across the University].

Both of your departments have grown.
Hyatt: Substantially, yes. When I came there were fifteen people in the History Department, and now there are twice that number.
Dowell: English is over thirty now.
Hyatt: So many things have changed in our department. It used to be the faculty were all in either American or European history, and whichever of the two they were in, they knew something about the other. Now you have people spread all over the place, and methodologically they do different things.

In the History Department as it was constituted when I came, virtually everybody was from the South. It was a different era in a lot of ways. One difference is simply size, and some of this applies to the student body. The class of 1958 had been so small that you would have known by name a great deal more of the people in your class than would be the case now.

Your departments were very strong even in your first years on the faculty.
Dowell: At one point, trying to build up the graduate programs, Emory decided to focus on six [or seven] departments to be the chief ones with graduate programs. English and history were two of them; chemistry was one; psychology was one; and biology. [The other two were anatomy and biochemistry.] They had obviously decided to say, okay, what are already the best or strongest departments here, and let's focus graduate development on those.

Who are some of the graduate students who went on to academic careers out of history or English?
Dowell: Linda Ray [PhD 1971] was brought back here for an alumni award a few years ago. She had been at the University of Nebraska and worked her way up from faculty to being some kind of administrative person. There was a Joan Hall [PhD 1976], who worked with [Professor Emeritus] Lee Pederson, and of course his graduate students were distinctive because they worked with him on the linguistic atlas of the Gulf States, and we didn't have any other linguistic types. She's a major lexicographer now and runs one of the linguistic dictionaries.
Hyatt: Two comparable history PhDs are James Robertson and James Wood, who have held endowed chairs at Virginia Tech and Williams College, respectively. There are a number of others who are also distinguished.

Dowell: One interesting aspect that we haven't talked about, and obviously it's major, was the coming of African American students and the development of black studies, which was a major effort here beginning in the 1960s and then growing after that. In 1970 Delores Aldridge was hired, and the African American Studies Program was launched. [See chapter 12.]

When I came in the 1960s, some of the people in American literature, particularly [Professor] Al Stone, created a course in African American literature. The first three or four years, different people from Morehouse [College] taught it. At one point I decided I'd like to teach it, and that's how I really arose into African American materials. I think my case was typical. The simple fact is none of us had any training in it. I'd never had any African American literature in undergraduate or graduate school, and I had to teach it to myself as I went along and taught it to students.

A number of people who were interested in this, like Al Stone, like me, like [professor of history] Harvey Young were in the ILA. So that became one of the tracks in the ILA—an African American studies PhD. I had something like a half a dozen PhDs in African American literature over the years.

At one point, in the mid- to late sixties, [Professor and ILA director] Jimmy Smith helped engineer a joint program with Atlanta University. Dana White was initially brought here as a faculty member connected to Clark Atlanta University but was going to teach on both campuses. Dana finally was recruited to Emory College.

One of the people very involved at Atlanta University was Richard Long, and later he came here as a faculty member. [See chapter 22.]

So the African-American Studies Department is one of the major changes over the course of time here.

The Art of Creative Administration: Interview with Rosemary M. Magee

Rosemary Magee was appointed vice president and secretary of Emory University in January 2005. In addition to her work with the Emory Board of Trustees, she served as a member of the Strategic Implementation Committee, as cochair of the Work-Life Initiative, and as chair of the Creativity and Arts Initiative of the University Strategic Plan. Before her advancement to the vice presidency, she served as a senior associate dean of Emory College. The University honored her with the Thomas Jefferson award in 2008.[9]

How did you first encounter the Emory administration?

I came to Emory as a graduate student in 1977. I had the honor of being elected president of the Graduate Student Council one year. My most memorable recollection of that era is that Saunders Hall was going to be converted to another purpose than graduate student housing, and there was great consternation. Graduate students really liked the location, near the dental school building, and it was an inexpensive place to live. I was asked to head up a petition to the administration to continue to use that for graduate student housing until alternatives were identified. I presented the petition to the assistant dean for Campus Life responsible for housing, who was Joe Moon [later dean of Campus Life at Oxford College]. They did delay the change for a year, and that was my first real experience with the Emory administration.

I then served on the search committee for the dean of the Graduate School, which led to my being hired as assistant dean in Emory College in August of 1983. David Minter was the dean; I was hired by Garland Richmond and Howard Rollins, the two associate deans. I did some work in student academic affairs for Garland and also worked for Howard, the budget dean, overseeing summer school and eventually incorporating summer study abroad into my portfolio.

David Minter was a very ambitious and demanding dean. He demanded a lot of the University, he demanded a lot of the faculty, he demanded a lot of the students, and he demanded a lot of his staff. It was very clear to those of us on his staff that he was in charge and making the decisions, but once you established a relationship with him it became more reciprocal, and he became open to your ideas. I was asked to develop a program advising students working on proposals for Rhodes and Marshall scholarships and the like. David was certain that this emphasis would help bring a whole new caliber of students to Emory, and we needed to make sure that they had these special kinds of opportunities.

The Lamar Committee[10] had already delivered its recommendations by the time I was hired. As a result of its report, Minter, in consultation with President Laney and others, decided that faculty pay and faculty raises would be limited that year, and that the highest priority for funds would be student financial aid—need-based aid and merit scholarships. Other agenda items were also going to be important, but they were going to be deferred because student quality would be the driver of

Rosemary M. Magee

the new educational agenda and model. David received a lot of criticism for that, but that was just the starting point for his vision. Again, I'm sure he did this very much in tandem with President Laney to lay the groundwork for the next phase of a strategy for faculty recruitment and development.

The second thing that I remember as very controversial back then was the so-called star system—hiring a William Arrowsmith or a Richard Ellmann [the first two Robert W. Woodruff professors], either as full-time regular faculty members or visiting professors. That approach still is controversial. People receive relatively large salaries while not teaching as much as their colleagues on the faculty. Dean Minter believed that we needed to raise the academic profile of the institution. Those two issues—student financial aid and recruiting highly visible faculty—were hot-button items during his administration, but he was not easily deterred from what he wanted to accomplish to enhance Emory's standing.

What was your role in reshaping study abroad?

At that time, all Emory study-abroad programs were scheduled during the summer; we didn't have any academic-year study-abroad programs. David Minter had a lot of trouble with a financial model that would defer Emory tuition dollars or place them in other institutions. He didn't see how we could sustain that approach; he was going to need all of the resources to do the things he needed to do for Emory to grow in strength and reputation.

The summer study-abroad model was fairly easy for people to accept, and we expanded those programs. We had a summer program in Russia with the Pushkin Institute that Juliette [Stapanian] Apkarian started. We had art history; we had the Vienna program and the French program and the British studies program. We gradually expanded those to include a program in Salamanca, Spain. Judy Raggi-Moore [senior lecturer in Italian studies] started the Italian program. But we didn't have a good way to do the academic year abroad.

These programs were growing in small ways until Howard Rollins returned from a leave after serving as chair of psychology. Upon his return, David Bright asked him to lead an environmental studies initiative. Howard said, "I don't know anything about environmental studies, but I'd really like to put something together for international programs."

By that time I was in the job that Howard had previously had as the budget officer. Carlos Alonso, who was the chair of the Spanish Department, asked to pilot a program in Salamanca in the academic year. We had a place there; we had other foundations to build on there. So Howard I worked with Carlos to establish the Salamanca program as a pilot for academic-year study abroad, with a financial model that we thought would work. It was very successful.

Howard and I then worked to take that initial Salamanca idea and expand it into a larger program. He came up with the idea of establishing the Center for International Programs Abroad. He figured out how to make the dollars and cents work. Then the Institute for Comparative and International Studies was added, so that the area studies programs all were pulled out of the departments to report to ICIS, and Howard led that for a while. All of this developed incrementally over a lot of time, spanning the deanships of David Minter, David Bright, and Steve Sanderson.

At a certain point you moved into College budgetary work. What did that entail?

Eleanor Main had been overseeing the budget, and then was asked to be acting dean of the Graduate School. When a new dean of the Graduate School was hired—George Jones—Eleanor became the associate dean there. While George was also the acting dean of the College, he asked me if I would do the College budget work. I thought, *It can't be that hard, can it?* Of course, I had no idea how to use Lotus or Excel or any of those programs, but I took on that responsibility, based on my earlier budgetary experience with summer school and study abroad. Over time, I grew to enjoy it.

Ron Johnson, professor of chemistry (now emeritus), was an associate dean at the time overseeing space planning, but he was stepping down, and I ended up doing both the budget and the facilities part of the job. It was a great moment for Emory College in terms of expansion and resources. I found it very challenging and creative work.

A huge issue at the time, especially during David Bright's administration, was a lot of energetic discourse, shall we say, around the College and Campus Life. The growth of the Campus Life Division added costs to the College. Many of these discussions had to do with the role of the faculty around advising, governance, curriculum, and admissions.

More recently, there's been a lot of professionalization of all of those areas (admissions, student support, advising, etc.), which I think has some benefits and also some drawbacks. But a big part of that shift had to do with the drive toward a research faculty.

It sounds like there were actually pulls in two different directions. One was a shift towards research faculty, and the other was a pull toward the professionalization of student advising or student activities, Campus Life as a whole separate division.

Right. Of course, Bill Fox had a lot of those ideas and dreams that were really needed—to strengthen the sense of community on campus. Once that occurred, some people felt that the student services areas became too large.

What other significant academic transformations do you recall?

David Bright established the Center for Teaching and Curriculum. Our original idea for something like the CTC was to call it CREATE—Curriculum, Research, Education, and Teaching at Emory. David loved acronyms, and he especially loved clever ones. He invited Walt Reed [professor of English] to be the director of it. Walt went into the meeting with David, and he came out and had a cheerful smile on his face, and David was quite cheerful because Walt agreed on the spot to do it. But Walt does not believe in acronyms that spell out words. So he said it should be the Center for Teaching and Curriculum, and Walt led that program for quite a while.

CTC was a College center and remained a College center all those years, although it was very open to people from other disciplines participating and sometimes sponsoring programs. Now we have the University-wide Center for Faculty Development and Excellence that Laurie Patton [Charles Howard Candler Professor of Religion] is leading through the provost's office, and the CTC has been absorbed into it. Some of this reflects shifts in the relationship in the centers of gravity over the course of time.

Two initiatives stand out as critical developments in the late 1990s—Science 2000 and the "Arts Commons."
Sometime in the mid-nineties the science chairs had started meeting—Dennis Liotta in chemistry, Krishan Bajaj in physics, John Lucchesi in biology, and Dwight Duffus in mathematics and computer science. They invited me to participate in those meetings, and we came up with the Science 2000 proposal. Some important things came out of that in terms of faculty and research support, start-up funding, and the facilities. Those plans eventually led to the construction of Cherry Logan Emerson Hall and the Mathematics and Science Center, as well as renovations in the Rollins Research Center and the Dental School Building.

We actually had a presentation called "Art and Science," and we were told over and over that if we were going to make progress the College had to choose either moving forward with the arts or moving forward with the sciences. We refused to choose, because we really needed to make progress on both of these fronts.

In the arts, a committee met in the late 1980s that led to the selection of Peter Eisenman as the architect of a proposed arts center. Max Anderson [former director of the Michael C. Carlos Museum] was chair of that group. Near the end of the process it became clear that there was little trustee support for the design, and that fund-raising would be difficult. I went to a meeting of the arts faculty with President Bill Chace and Provost Billy Frye and Dean David Bright, where basically they said this project is going to be put on a shelf. The University had already spent $3 million on design, but the administration said we're going to put it on a shelf, and if somebody comes along and offers $50 million, then we'll build it. But the arts were living in Annex B [a former barracks on the site of the present Goizueta Foundation Center of the Business School], and in the basement of what previously the Physics Building [now Callaway South]; the conditions were deplorable.

I went to David Bright and laid out how I thought we might move beyond where we were. I felt that saying we're just going to put this on a shelf and wait for $50 million was a sign that we weren't going to do anything at all.

We assembled a new planning committee—myself and Ben Arnold in music, Sally Radell in dance, David Cook in film studies, and Vinnie Murphy, Michael Evenden, and Alice Benston in theater. We got in a van and drove to various places, from Spivey Hall [in Clayton County] to Clemson University. People visited Vassar and other places on their breaks, and we put together a report that listed what we thought the highest priorities were. By that time Steve Sanderson had become dean, and he said, "Wow, this is really interesting. Let's go out and try to raise some money for it."

With my colleague Randy Fullerton, I put together a presentation for Steve to give, and we went to New York. The people who we thought were potential big donors didn't come to the event, so we saw this as a trial run. At the last minute he asked me to give the presentation, since I had done the report. William Ransom played the piano at the home of an Emory alumnus, Bill Cohen. The next day Donna and Marvin Schwartz made a commitment for a naming gift. It was incredible. Then we went out and identified an architect.

We tried to put together all the resources we had and then house as much as we could in the new Schwartz Center, which was intended as the first phase of a two-phase project. Later, as the project moved along, we hired Michael Dennis as the architect. I met with the Real Estate, Buildings, and Grounds Committee to show some designs, and they challenged me about the project because, of course, they felt really burned by the Eisenman project. The next day I received calls from three of the trustees inviting us to come back with Michael Dennis. What I learned was that if you have a good idea, or if it's something the University needs, then maybe there will be an opportunity, a way to do this, and you just have to keep working at it.

What was the order of development? Was it that the arts departments had grown and really needed the space, or that we built new space and the departments set about filling it?

It works both ways. The process was enormously complicated. Of course, we didn't meet everybody's needs. Even if we'd built both phases of the arts project, we would not have met everybody's desires. But we accomplished a lot. One big decision was the size of the concert hall. Some people thought it should be big enough for the entire freshman class, but if we'd done that it still wouldn't be big enough for the whole freshman class now. Still other people thought it should just be a very intimate place. I actually think it was the right size, so that you can use it for intimate concerts or student recitals as well as the New York Philharmonic.

The whole issue around theater was problematic. Phase two is where we hope to have more traditional theater space. Dance had grown and was gaining some independence from the Physical Education Department, so they needed some space. They had no faculty offices. Visual arts had been in really horrible conditions. Theater in some ways was the most robust. The Music Department needed both traditional musicology rooms and performance space. But there were also more traditional student needs that we haven't fully met even today—Ad Hoc, No Strings Attached, and different groups.

It met the needs that we saw at the time as being the most important, and every member of that committee signed on to that report. That's how we got it through—that kind of consensus.

Talk about the fund-raising for the arts center.

Our trustee Laura Hardman [College 1967] was extremely persistent. She had us meeting over breakfast, lunch, and dinner with the Loridans Foundation, the Woodruff Foundation, and the Kresge Foundation. She made those calls personally and placed us in front of people to make a presentation and ask for support. We had to show 100 percent trustee participation, and she called each board member. We ended up with gifts ranging in size from ten dollars to $10 million—from students, faculty, staff, alumni, and friends—when all was said and done, which was quite an accomplishment.

CHAPTER 10

CAMPUS LIFE
The Interplay of Living and Learning at Emory

William H. Fox came to Emory in 1971 in pursuit of the doctoral degree in religion and literature in the Institute of Liberal Arts. He became the first dean of Campus Life and then was promoted to vice president. In 1991 he became vice president for institutional advancement (now the Division of Development and Alumni Relations) and raised more than a billion dollars for the University during his tenure. Named senior vice president for external affairs in 2003, he retired in 2005.[1]

Tell us briefly about when and why you came to Emory.

I chose Emory for my PhD by going to a library at Southern Methodist University, where I was in the dean of students' office and teaching, to look up PhD programs to see what I might be interested in. I did not want to study English or religion per se, but I had heard of the field of religion and theology. I found three or four programs, and the one that fit best was Emory. I didn't know Emory well and had never been on its campus, so I flew to Atlanta and visited the ILA [Institute of Liberal Arts], which at that time was in Thomson Hall, the old dormitory. James Smith was the director, and I met with [professors] David Hesla and Bob Detweiler. I left convinced that this was the right place for me. When I was accepted, my wife, Carol, got a job here, and that was the beginning of our Emory and Atlanta years. That was in 1971.

The first two years I essentially was a graduate student. My third year, in the fall, Smith died quite suddenly of a heart attack. Detweiler was appointed acting director, and he said he would take the job if he could have a full-time administrator to work with him. Bob was aware that I had done administration at SMU for about seven years, so he asked me. I took that job in January of 1974, and it was exciting, it was fun. I did a lot of the paperwork, we had a great secretary, and she and I ran the ILA—not the academic program, but admissions, financial aid, interviewing students. I grew very fond of Emory.

They also began to let me teach in what then was called the Humanities Department. Some of us had an idea to start a major in interdisciplinary studies, and with the support of the faculty of the ILA, I began that project and went through all the steps to create a new major. That was a great experience. It was exciting intellectually and personally.

This of course delayed a less-than-brilliant person from finishing his PhD, so I did not finish until 1979. When I did finish I received a faculty position in the ILA and became director of the undergraduate major in interdisciplinary studies. By then, we had several majors and a number of courses, and we asked people from across the University to teach things that were interdisciplinary, but which they had never had the chance to teach.

Along the way—in 1977—Jim Laney became president, and in fall of 1979 Robert and George Woodruff made their dramatic gift to Emory.

That's right. Actually I had already been asked to be acting dean of Campus Life before the Woodruff gift. After Jim Laney became president he appointed a University-wide strategic planning committee, and I served on that. I was assigned to the subcommittee on student life. It was almost like destiny at work. So when I went to Campus Life as acting dean, I didn't go empty-handed. I had already heard from across the University—we talked to faculty, we went to Oxford, we talked to students, we talked to trustees. I had presented a report on the priorities as they had appeared, so I didn't go to Campus Life with a blank slate.

One bright October morning in 1979 I was preparing for class. I was head of interdisciplinary studies, assistant director of the ILA, and teaching. I was sitting in the library preparing, and someone tapped on my shoulder. It was [then–University Secretary] Tom Bertrand, and he said, "The president needs to see you." Well, I did not know the president well. I thought I was in trouble.

The president said he would like for me to consider serving as interim dean of Campus Life while Emory did a national search. I was thrilled to death and thought it would be fun. But I said, if I leave the ILA now I'm going to need a job when a dean is chosen, and he said, we'll guarantee you a job at no less salary if you will do this for us. So within a week I was in a new office, as interim dean of Campus Life.

I must admit that I never acted "interim." I just took over. I had dreams. I had a platform. I had a whole agenda. Then the Woodruff gift was announced, and some of those dreams that I had worked on for two years we now had funds to realize.

The top priority for the University regarding community life was the physical education center. With the Woodruff backing and Clyde Partin [former athletics director Clyde "Doc" Partin Sr.] and others begging, Jim Laney let us move ahead. That became the first major capital project in student life. We never saw the P.E. center exclusively as a student area. We always saw it as a community area, although students would certainly have a major role. But we planned a faculty locker room and staff space. There were very few places for this community to even gather, and suddenly we had this possibility.

This first capital project was followed quickly by desperate need for more housing. So the P.E. center was followed quickly by the Turman Residential Center.

What we call "campus life" I always considered a University-wide division. The largest, most important clientele we had were undergraduates, but Campus Life was for the community. We tried to plan activities that would involve students, faculty, and staff in the same places at the same time. The P.E. center realized that quickly, and in Turman Residential Center we built faculty apartments. Our greatest mission was the one that every institution has, and that was the life of the community. We suddenly had opportunity with the infusion of funds and a president who put as one of his top two or three priorities the improvement of community life at Emory.

When did the job become no longer "interim"?

They did a national search. I know nothing about that, except that I did have an interview, and I was told two or three days later that I had been chosen—would I like the position? By that time, I was absolutely enthralled with the possibilities of the job and wanted it so badly that I said yes, thank you, and left before they could take it back.

Some of the priorities were laid out by the strategic planning document that you had helped to craft. What other priorities did you bring to those early years?

I remember walking out of a class I was teaching and talking to a young man who was a student leader at Emory. He was a senior. I asked, "How do you like Emory?" He said, "Well, I think I received a good academic education, but this isn't a great place to be a student unless the only thing you want is an education. I don't feel it's a very caring place; I don't feel any real sense of community with the larger body."

I never forgot that, and I carried that conversation with me to the Campus Life office the first day. My number-one intention was to see what we could do about making a community. A related passion was for this to be a caring place. The sense of caring, of compassion, of realizing that we were here to serve and care for our students—those were my overriding passions.

Were there things you wanted to do in Campus Life but were not able to do because of budgetary or cultural reasons?

We would be asked every three or four years to submit a priority statement. Each time I put the arts center first, even though I was representing Campus Life. That's how much an adequate arts center meant to me. I love the arts, am passionate about the arts.

I also wanted Emory to have an international award—something that stood for the very best of what we are and what we promote. It would probably take, I figured, a $2 million endowment: the winner would receive fifty thousand dollars from the annual payout, and the other fifty thousand dollars would support our putting on an event. Every time Columbia University has its Pulitzer Prize activity, the whole world pays attention.

I also wanted to have a requirement that 100 percent of undergraduates live on campus, with exceptions only for those who were married or had some kind of severe medical need or lived at home with their parents. I thought a fully residential campus would be the answer to the question of community. The Clairmont Campus has come a long way in that direction.

I wanted a campus pub really badly, but state laws forbid that, and I finally quit putting it on my list.

I wanted more all-University events that would cost money. I suggested one time that the Monday before Thanksgiving we have an all-University Thanksgiving dinner in the Dobbs University Center [the DUC], on all levels, and everyone could come for free, and someone would get up and talk about our blessings. When I was a student here we had a kind of Thanksgiving potluck in the old gym. You couldn't say it was anything luxurious, but it had a spirit to it. The Heritage Ball started through Campus Life. One time we had it down at Colony Square, and it was packed, with faculty as well as students.

What were some of the most challenging moments?

The Sabrina Collins incident was the hardest moment in my professional life.[2] Jim Laney and I met every morning for two months to review what was happening. We knew a month before the public did what was the truth, and we had to sit on it and live with it. I had television trucks outside my home waiting for me to leave in the morning, and the telephone rang all night.

One of the things that I had done on being appointed to Campus Life was to promote everything without any discrimination. I had chaired a College committee for improving our racial mix. I demanded that there be in the residence halls a program every fall about civil rights and equal rights. And then this thing was happening under my administration. I can't tell you how many tears I shed. One night a local black political leader came on TV, and he said that if she did it herself, the environment at Emory drove her to it.

That hurt. We had the highest percentage of faculty members who were African Americans, the highest percentage of African American students, an office devoted entirely to multicultural affairs, with a good staff and programs and money. We had tried so hard, and then for someone to say this "racist" place was what made her do it was so untrue and heartbreaking.

You had this position in Campus Life for thirteen years or fourteen years?

Well, thirteen, and then the fourteenth I was still head of Campus Life while taking on a new role as senior vice president for institutional advancement. I did both jobs one year. And I asked Bobbi [Barbara A. B.] Patterson, who was then the associate chaplain, to help out as interim dean of students, and Todd Schill and Ron Taylor carried a lot of water as associate vice presidents.

Did you view the move from Campus Life to advancement as an exciting challenge that you were ready to take on?

When the opportunity first was presented to me I said no—the first time I guess I'd ever said no to Jim Laney. I loved Campus Life so much I didn't want to leave it. So I said, Jim, I just don't want to do fund-raising. I don't know how to do that. Then on Memorial Day [in 1991] he called and said, this is a critical moment, and I need you. So I said, yes, sir.

Then I became excited as I began to think of opportunities. I had so many friends who were alums that I'd get to see again. By the time I started I was enthusiastic. There were times I missed the wonderful people with whom I worked in Campus Life, and I came to discover that I would not know many students. But I never wished I had made a different decision.

What do you see as the biggest accomplishments in your time in institutional advancement?

We did the best reconnection with alumni in Emory's history. I gave a lot of attention to that and traveled a whole lot for that. In my first year or two I would go to an alumni event and hope for 10 or 12 people; now there's 120. I wish I'd had a little more program money, but we did build an alumni house. That was a high priority for me. That was a priority before I came along, but I'm very proud of the way we ended up doing it.

Moorehouse College President Benjamin Mays, Bill Fox, and religion professor Jack Boozer

I'm also proud of the money we raised. In those twelve or so years that I was in institutional advancement, we raised more than $1.5 billion. We were blessed that the Woodruff Foundation gave to us. But we had to reach out beyond that. We started reaching out much more nationally. The [whole] organization deserves credit for that—people like Jack Gilbert and many others.

Both of the divisions that you inherited you expanded, especially Campus Life. When you stepped into that role, there were maybe a dozen staff members. And by the time you left?

Four hundred professional staff—everybody from assistant and associate deans to food servers. Jim Laney made a decision to put food service under Campus Life, and that was fun actually, hard but fun. We made changes, and bless her heart, [food services liaison] Helen Jenkins went along with it. She needs to have a statue in the middle of the Quad. This woman kept us fed for fifty-seven years.

Other things that I'm really proud of? I helped form the University Athletic Association. That has proved to be successful. Jim Laney supported me, and without his support it might have gone down the tube.

I take enormous pride in the Counseling Center, in little things like the Humanitarian Award, in the Center for Lesbian, Gay, Bisexual, and Transgender Life. We were the first school south of the Mason-Dixon Line to have such a center. I had a lot to do with the purchase of University Apartments, which provided space two decades later for the Clairmont Campus. There was some resistance about spending the money for it, but we had to have it for the long-term future.

Were you also instrumental in developing the Magnolia League?

When I first came to Campus Life I made visits to campuses that had similarities to Emory—Duke, Vanderbilt, Miami, Tulane. I didn't go to SMU because I knew it backwards and forwards, and by the way, SMU had some good student life programs that I was proud to incorporate here, including a much better residential program. The whole sophomore adviser program that I created here with Joe Moon's help I got from them. We [now] have a great residential program, and Joe Moon deserves more credit than I do there.

Of all the Campus Life programs, the one I liked the best was Duke's. I kept in touch with my counterpart at Duke, who is a gem of a man. He and I began talking about how much we learned from each other, and we got in touch with other vice presidents, from private schools with very similar student bodies and faculties and missions, and we formed what we called the Magnolia League. I was in some other associations, but none as important as that. We were open, we didn't try to promote ourselves. It was very helpful. You left knowing you weren't the only one with problems, and you weren't the only one with solutions and new ideas.

The Durham Chapel, now the reference room of Pitts Theology Library.

THE SCHOOL OF THEOLOGY AS PRELUDE
Candler Conversations
— MANFRED HOFFMANN, WILLIAM MALLARD,

THEODORE RUNYON *and* THEODORE WEBER —

In September 1914, before Emory University itself had even received its charter (which would be signed on January 25, 1915), the Candler School of Theology opened its doors (although the name "Candler," in honor of its founding family, would not be attached to it until the following February). In this and in many other ways the Theology School has served as a forerunner for the rest of the University. This conversation among emeritus faculty members of the school touches on many of the "preludes" played by the school—in race relations, in research, in curricular reform, and even in fund-raising.

Manfred Hoffmann is professor of historical theology, emeritus; William Mallard is professor of theology, emeritus; Theodore Runyon is professor of theology, emeritus; and Theodore Weber is professor of social ethics, emeritus.[1]

T**HE CANDLER SCHOOL** of Theology made great strides as a scholarly community, in addition to being a ministerial seminary, during the administration of William Ragsdale Cannon, who served as dean from 1953 until his election as a bishop of the United Methodist Church in 1968. What stands out about his leadership?

Mallard: Dean Cannon brought me to the Candler faculty in 1957, and I say that advisably, because it was his interview alone that mattered.

He was an interesting dean. He did not consistently show a scholarly mind, which is odd since he was the first dean of Candler with a PhD and later became known as the "scholar bishop" of the United Methodist Church. His *History of Christianity in the Middle Ages* is a summary of known materials concerning that history rather than a new reading of primary sources. Some of the things he did for Candler were to help build the foundations for development. He strengthened what Dean [Burton] Trimble had started as "The One Percent Plan," encouraging Methodist churches across the Southeast to give 1 percent of their annual budget to theological education.

Weber: Duke and other Methodist theology schools came into the plan after Emory started it.

Mallard: Dean Cannon also had a very strong logical mind. In those years Emory faced the question of racial desegregation and the question whether students would be admitted to the University regardless of race. I recall a faculty meeting when our faculty voted to request the dean to take word to the central administration that we were open to admitting students without regard to race. That occurred while Atlanta was going through remarkable tensions over the question of public education. There was a drawing together of black and white clergy and the Atlanta newspapers and the mayor and the business interests to keep the public schools open.

In those days Candler had two kinds of reputations across the national Methodist Church. One was that we were a southeastern pietistic seminary that particularly emphasized producing preachers for the pastorates. The other, through the Deep South, was that we were Communists, because we declared ourselves open to admission without regard to race.

There was a waffle shop at the edge of the campus in those years. I was in there one day. They had a sign on the cash register that said, "Cash Checks up to $10 for Emory Students Only." I said to the gentleman, "You cash them I guess for Emory faculty members," and an elderly gentleman sitting on the stool near me said, "He will as long as you're not from the School of Theology." I turned to him and said, "But I *am* from the School of Theology."

Well, he didn't know what to do, and he left the shop very quickly. But that was a tense and interesting time, and one in which I think the school acquitted itself well in looking toward the future. Is that a fair thing to say?

Weber: It certainly is. There were two petitions on the issue of integrating the public schools. One, in 1957, the year that you came, was signed by about eighty local clergy. I don't know whether it made its way to the School of Theology, but you may have signed it. One of the leaders of that group was [alumnus] Bevel Jones, later bishop, and then later vice chair of the Emory Board of Trustees. The next year another petition was signed by 311 Emory faculty members, including three of us who are here and almost all of the faculty of the Candler School of Theology.

Of course, many things happened on the way to the desegregation of the University and, indeed, in the South. We talked in the faculty about the possibility of having some exchange with the faculty of the Interdenominational Theological Center, which was primarily African American.

We had to get permission from the president, so the dean appointed a committee of three—Earl Brewer, Clinton Gardner, and me—and we met with the president's assistant, Robert Whitaker. He stonewalled us the whole time. We kept asking him whether we could do this, and he never said a mumbling word—nothing —and finally broke up the meeting.

Afterward, somehow, we were able to have a luncheon in our seminar room, with boxed lunches, and that was the first concession that the administration made, until finally the walls were broken down a little later.

We did have some interracial meetings before formal desegregation, through the interseminary movement. The students themselves were very concerned that there be a way of demonstrating their openness to their fellow students from Interdenominational Theological Center, and that led to a combination of Candler School of Theology, Columbia Theological Seminary, and the Interdenominational Theological Center. The Atlanta Theological Association came out of that.

Mallard: Ted, was it during that time that you were going to a meeting of black and white seminarians, and the drivers refused to tell you where [they were taking you]?

Weber: Yes. Franklin Littell came on the faculty in 1958, when Ted Runyon and I came. Two other persons came at that time. One was Immanuel Ben-Dor, who was Israeli and a world-class archaeologist and the only Jew on our faculty until recently. The other was [Robert] Funk, in New Testament.

> *In those days Candler had two kinds of reputations. . . . One was that we were a southeastern pietistic seminary that particularly emphasized producing preachers for the pastorates. The other, through the Deep South, was that we were Communists.*

Littell took the lead in organizing this interaction of Candler students with ITC students and faculty, and on one occasion we drove to Ebenezer Baptist Church and got out of our cars and got into cars driven by black students. Every so often, they would stop and make a telephone call. We'd say, where are we going? They'd say, well, we'll get there, don't worry about it.

Ultimately, we showed up at the parsonage of Martin Luther King Sr. Everybody in the King family was there except Martin Jr. Coretta was there and Daddy King and A. D. King and the children. That was my first meeting with that [interseminary] group, and the group lasted basically only so long as Frank was on the faculty, only two years. He left for SMU, and the meetings fell apart.

Mallard: People forget now the strange sense that folk had of crossing barriers in meeting together racially. It's hard to get your imagination back into that, but that was a very self-conscious move, and people were very alert toward such matters.

I remember in February 1958, I was then a volunteer teacher of a Sunday school class at St. Mark United Methodist Church in downtown Atlanta, where Dow Kirkpatrick was the preacher. February included what the Methodist Church had then as "Race Relations Sunday," and that Sunday I was present when Dow preached the sermon.

He preached on the topic, "You Have to Be Taught to Hate," and he took his lead from the musical *South Pacific*. "You have to be carefully taught." He concluded the sermon simply by saying that whatever comes of our issues over racial relationships in this city, we are obligated to look at it from a Christian standpoint. When he finished his sermon and started to announce the last hymn, a member down in front stood up and began to make his own speech and said, from the floor of the sanctuary, that if the *Atlanta Journal* and *Constitution* are here this morning, I want them to know that not everybody in this congregation agrees with the sermon they have heard today.

Now all they had heard was that we have to be Christian in all relationships. But he cited his background and his pedigree and said that he did not share the view of the pastor. When he sat down, another man stood up and declared he was from a Deep South state and [agreed with the previous speaker]. By that time, there were about half a dozen people trying to get the floor and make their impassioned speeches, and in the midst of that confusion, Dr. Kirkpatrick announced the last hymn.

As the hymn was being sung, I would estimate a third of the congregation marched out of the sanctuary in protest [against Kirkpatrick's sermon] and came up the aisle with that sort of sweet glassy-eyed smile, you know—"They're not going to move us!" It was a crucial day for the church and for Dr. Kirkpatrick. Of course, it turned out to move in the direction of new openness and understanding, but in the meantime it was extremely tense, difficult.

Bishop Cannon was strengthening the academic tenor of Candler, and you all were part of that.

Hoffmann: I was appointed in 1960 really by correspondence. I was in Heidelberg finishing my doctorate, and William Cannon appointed me as the assistant professor of church history sight unseen. At the time, the red carpet was extended from the United States to the old country, Central Europe. We called it a brain drain, even though I did not really think that I belonged to the brainy people. But I came, and he didn't even want a photograph.

Weber: And we all concluded that you did belong to the brain drain.

Hoffmann: I came, thanks to the decision to develop a graduate program. I came particularly [to teach in] the Graduate Division of Religion, but also taught in the School of Theology. The major question was how to bring academic rigor and the education of ministers in the church together, a practical approach and the classic academic approach. Throughout my life at the school, I was more oriented toward the academic side, until under Dean [Jim] Waits and my good friend [Professor] Jim Hopewell, the question of the education of ministry became so urgent that we—and I particularly—were drawn into this question. I think that characterizes the school.

Weber: The biggest change came in 1958, when the graduate program in religion was instituted. Five of us hired in 1958 were hired partly as replacements but partly also to expand the faculty so that it could carry a graduate program and have stronger representation in various fields. That was not only the initiation of the program, it was the beginning of a change in emphasis within the school from preacher education to much more in-depth and critical study in the field of religion. Since that time, there has been a tension between the two emphases, and on the part of many of the faculty there has been more weight on the academic side than on the church side, which has caused considerable distress to a number of people.

Hoffmann: From the beginning, the graduate program in religion was interdisciplinary. We had a common seminar, called Common Program 400, that engaged philosophers and historians and so on. We went beyond the disciplines.

Runyon: We were in conversation with each other during those years to a much greater extent than was true later; that is, we met weekly for two-hour seminars, and we developed a common theme or topic which we spoke to from various angles. It was unique in the study of theology and religion.

Mallard: And it helped the PhD program in religion prove itself.

Hoffmann: Earlier, I had the impression that the School of Theology was kind of looked down upon as a preacher mill. But within the University, the reputation rose more and more until our friends in other disciplines realized that we are indeed competent in our own discipline.

Runyon: The kind of operation that Dean Cannon developed at that time was much more casual than has become the case later, so that just as Manfred was hired sight unseen, so was I. I was doing my doctorate in Goettingen, in Germany, and Cannon had a couple of references from my former teachers at Drew University. Other than that, he had no notion of who I was. So apart from some letters back and forth, I was hired sight unseen as part of Cannon's effort to develop a genuine graduate program that would take into account the best of current knowledge worldwide. Germany was at that time the center of theological education, so he was eager to get persons [who had] trained there.

Mallard: And to have a diversified faculty. Dean Cannon was very serious about it.

Weber: Manfred, what role did Jack Wilson [a graduate student] play in your being hired?

Hoffmann: It was a little odd. I was at the University of Heidelberg. One of the graduate students at Emory studied for a time in Heidelberg, and we became close friends. He said one time, there's an opening in church history at the School of Theology, and I kind of chuckled because in Germany, you don't simply apply for a professorship. But within a week or so I received a letter from Dean Cannon asking for credentials. I sent off [my application], and I thought I [would be] number thirteen on a list of thirteen. But within six weeks or so I received an invitation to teach church history. This is in my case something of a miracle, that I suddenly am transported from a central academic place in Germany into the South of America. It was a culture shock. I mistook people. . . . I mistook Bill Mallard for Dean Cannon, and the language was a problem. So I thought okay—I'll serve my year and then back to the Elysian Fields.

> *This is one of the most important things about Candler across these years. Somehow or other there was a strong sense of collegiality that has since gone on over into the faculty in general and still continues.*

So, yes—I was hired on the recommendation of a graduate student! That still is some kind of puzzle to me, but I'm here. People like these three colleagues and Hendrik Boers, who is not with us anymore, created a kind of community in which I felt at home.

Runyon: Cannon was able to combine his academic concerns with a kind of rapport with the church. He was a southerner, he was a favorite son of Georgia, so he was able to retain the loyalty of the church, on the one hand. At the same time, he had the commitment to the quality of Yale, where he had done his work, so that he was concerned that we ought to launch a graduate program that would be competitive with the best in the nation. That's what really promoted in his own mind the necessity to expand the horizons of the school.

Mallard: I have a comment that bears on this, at least indirectly. I've already noted that he did not consistently show a scholarly mind; however, he developed the finances of the school. He wanted and brought a diversified faculty. At the same time, there were very significant tensions during the sixties. I found myself being asked to write a statement of my theological views, which then would be reviewed by the administration and the full professors of the school, seeking out whether they felt that I appropriately had a place in the faculty and in the teaching of the school. I produced that statement and met with the administration and faculty for something like six hours with a dinner break one day. This was in winter/spring of 1966. That conversation explored my theological position quite thoroughly. All of that concluded with the decision that I would have a place on the faculty and be part of the school. That's important, because it clarified that the school was genuinely open to a variety of approaches, interests, and concerns respecting the academic exploration of theology and associated disciplines.

In those days the four of us, plus one or two others, but most particularly Professor Boers—one day at the cafeteria he said to two or three of us, we have to hold together in these circumstances. We did, and that group of half a dozen or so, including the four of us, read each other's papers, had conversations, talked about the future of the school. That formed a core of collegiality that carried over into the seventies and eighties.

Dr. Leander Keck came and was head of graduate studies and professor of New Testament. When he left seven years later, at his farewell lunch he said that when he first came here, he asked where were the factions in this faculty. Somebody said there aren't any. He said, oh, well, I'll find them out myself. But then he said, "After seven years, I say to you they're right—there are not factions in this faculty." Everybody sort of moves according to their best judgment, and there's a collegiality holding the thing together.

This is one of the most important things about Candler across these years. Somehow or other there was a strong sense of collegiality that has since gone on over into the faculty in general and still continues. It avoided infighting or factional divisions, and the students picked up on that sense of harmony. That's one of Candler's most important contributions across these years from the sixties until now.

Runyon: That's certainly true. Theological faculties have the reputation of having great controversies within them because, of course, they represent different theological points of view and, therefore, tend to be at odds with each other. That has never been the case here, and it was not even the case when we were the young Turks on the faculty. It's true that we represented the more open and liberal position in our theological orientation, but we were able to maintain a rapport with the senior faculty, those who were longtime churchmen in the South and who might otherwise have formed a contingent over against us. But as a matter of fact we worked together as genuine colleagues.

Hoffmann: The difference of opinion without rancor, I would say. The difference of opinion was an academic thing, never personal; it was in the pursuit of truth.

What we also did was to lay the groundwork for change in the School of Theology's administration and therefore for the future. That is also a thing that kept me in America. We had a change in administration to the better.

Mallard: For example, with the coming of Dean James Laney, now of course President Emeritus Laney, there was no longer a committee [limited to] full professors that sat and met in and of itself. Everybody was welcome around the table, and that was part of the fresh air that came with Dean Laney's administration.

Weber: The question earlier was what Dean Cannon was like, and I think that through the threads of what has been said we can see some things. One thing I recall about Cannon was that he looked like a simple person, but he was complicated. He presented to the church an appearance of a very conservative man, whereas on the inside, we knew that he wanted academic excellence, and that would come at the cost of some surrender of conservatism, and he was willing to pay that price.

He also created the impression of being very naïve, but we knew indeed he was a very shrewd man. He knew what was going on, and he knew how to make decisions, and sometimes we were a bit wary of that.

There were, in fact—I don't know if we'd call them factions, but by the 1970s they had disappeared. They had disappeared because people had moved on. Cannon had been elected bishop in 1968. Associate Dean Mack Stokes was elected bishop in 1972. Others had retired or died, so the four of us had emerged as a leading group, having been the young ones in opposition. Part of the reason why we developed that early collegiality that Bill has talked about was that we saw ourselves as different in important respects and over against some of the others who were there. So it was a kind of friction, a kind of alternative presence in the faculty and the school that encouraged us in part to develop the way that we did.

Hoffmann: Cannon had a tendency toward, I would say, Catholicism. He was at the Second Vatican Council. He really liked the pomp and circumstances and the power of the bishops. His good friend was Cardinal Brown. I remember standing with Bishop Cannon in front of the Castel Sant'Angelo, and I said, pretty rashly, you know, this river will flow long after the church is gone. He said, no, the church will be there long after this river has dried out. He had the sense of the church as a real unity and institution that is dominant in a culture.

Mallard: You see all of this by further contrast with the coming of Dean Laney in 1969. Laney offered in such a genial way the opportunity for all faculty, senior and junior, to gather around the table and chart the future for the school. By the end of that first year Dean Laney had already appointed more than a dozen new faces on the faculty and staff. That was partly because of deaths and retirements, but nevertheless it gave a fresh new stimulus.

Dean Laney was also very much interested in what the School of Theology could say to the church. He was academically sophisticated and had fine judgment about those he brought to the school. At the same time, he was keen on service to the church and instituted, or encouraged the faculty to institute, a program of ministry that we called, in those days, supervised ministry. In this program all of the faculty, regardless of discipline, would participate in ministry formation. This was quite unheard of! The systematicians, the historians, the sociologists would combine with those who were in homiletics and pastoral disciplines to form and shape ministry. That was a turn in which Dean Laney instituted a very important look toward the future of theological education.

> *Laney offered in such a genial way the opportunity for all faculty, senior and junior, to gather around the table and chart the future for the school.*

Weber: A lot of the credit there belongs to Chuck Gerkin.

Mallard: Yes, Dean Laney brought Charles Gerkin to the faculty from his position as chaplain at Grady Hospital. Gerkin later became a very widely affirmed, authoritative figure in the whole area of pastoral psychology.

Hoffmann: His aim was to expose students to actual ministry in the hospital. I always felt that the ministry in the congregations and in other contexts was somewhat neglected, but there was no structure in those places, so we concentrated on the CPE movement—clinical pastoral education.

Runyon: This became a model adopted by theological seminaries all across the nation. It gained us a reputation, a way in which Laney's leadership and also Candler School of Theology became well known in theological circles throughout the nation.

Hoffmann: Also important was the presence of Jim Hopewell [professor of world religions until his death from cancer in 1984]. He did a lot in instituting a new way of looking at congregations by congregational analysis. To analyze a congregation with sociological, theological, and historical means was a new way for the seminary to serve the church.

Mallard: So the turn in the future of Candler was the coming of James T. Laney as dean. I mean, when he was first introduced as a possible candidate, he was an assistant professor of ethics at Vanderbilt Divinity School. The comment was, well, he's young and doesn't have any administrative experience really. These people were talking about the person who would, after a few years, become president of Emory University.

Weber: He'd been pastor of a church, and he'd been a missionary in Korea, so he had a richness of experience. But I resist the idea that it was Laney and a moment in time that made everything happen. Those of us who were already here, and some other people, made it possible for Laney to come.

Mallard: I agree with that.

Weber: As you know, there was a succession prepared after Cannon, and that didn't work. It didn't work because we stopped it and hired somebody else. Those of us here and a few others —most of them have died—said, we're going to have a different future for this school. We acquired candidates who would be of that type. Laney came because things were prepared for him to come.

Mallard: That's absolutely right. Laney was sort of the wonderful fruition of a way of preparation.

Hoffmann: And Ted Weber needs the kudos for floating the name of Laney.

Weber: I went up to Connecticut to visit my in-laws, and while I was there I went to Yale Divinity School to see who was still there whom I had studied with or whom I knew. Jim Gustafson was there, who later joined the Emory faculty under the invitation of Jim Laney as president. We talked, and at that time the dean search was on. He said, why don't you consider Jim Laney? He's a Methodist, and he was number two on our list for Yale Divinity School, and some of us wished we had chosen him. I thought, wow, Jim Laney. I knew him in 1950 when he came to seminary, but I never thought of him as a dean. I went downstairs and talked with

Raymond Morris, the Yale Divinity librarian, who was a Methodist layman. Without my saying anything to him about what Gustafson had said, Morris said, you really ought to take a look at Jim Laney, because he would be a good dean for a Methodist seminary. So I came back and talked with the committee, and I said the people at Yale say we ought to look at Jim Laney.

We had some advantages in that search committee. One was that Earl Hunt was the bishop appointed as the adjunct member of our committee. Hunt knew Laney and was very impressed by him. That was a plus, because the bishops had been very suspicious of what we were doing. But when Hunt went to them and said this guy is okay, that was all right. Then Professor Gordon Thompson did a lot also, because he had seen Laney in action somewhere, and [Gordon] was respected by the church and came from the church to the faculty. So some things were working together.

Even so, it was not a slam dunk. It was still a fight. But we fought, and we won, and the faculty vote to accept Laney was thirteen to eight. Laney phoned me, and he said, I'm worried about that vote; that means I'm going to have a lot of opposition. I said, don't worry about it, they're voting for the other candidate who was the chosen successor, and some of [them] will immediately slide over to your side as soon as you become dean. And they did.

Mallard: When Dr. Laney came down to receive the offer for the deanship, the president of Emory, Dr. Atwood, showed him a number of telegrams from the bishops in the Southeast. One of them said, I am praying that you, Dr. Atwood, will not make a mistake—meaning, don't go in this new, untried direction. Then when Laney went back to Nashville to think over the offer. Some of us here got together and sent him a telegram saying, we are praying you will not make a mistake. Signed, the Holy Club. And lo and behold, he came. And it's just as Ted is saying. What had been building in the school as a new look toward the future found fruition in Laney's being hired.

Hoffmann: Whenever I went to Laney with some request, I always [found] open doors. That says it for me. The concern for the church did not diminish the academic effort and emphasis. The struggle was how to handle these two sides together.

The school really exploded in growth.

Hoffmann: There was a new spirit.
Weber: Growth more in quality than in numbers of students. The student body was fairly large, and we did add some students as well as faculty. But certainly the school grew in prestige. At one point it was ranked among the top five theological seminaries in the United States, and I suppose would still hold that ranking. That came shortly after Laney moved into place.
Runyon: Another development was the aftermath of the Second Vatican Council and the impact that had on us. It opened up the possibilities of a much more ecumenical approach. One thing we inaugurated at that time was the "Interseminary Seminar," which included not only students from our three Atlanta seminaries—ITC, Columbia, and Candler—but also brothers from the Monastery of the Holy Spirit in Conyers, which, of course, is a Trappist monastery. Every year we met during the spring term for weekly seminar sessions. At first those were at Columbia, but then the abbot of the monastery decided that since they had a vow of stability, the brothers had to stay in the monastery. So all the rest agreed that we would go out to the monastery for those sessions, and our students were able to participate in the ecumenical developments that took place as a result of the Second Vatican Council.
Mallard: The early Laney years were also years when the number of women in the student body began a significant increase [because of the decision of several major denominations to ordain women]. This has been a very important change in the culture and the strength of the school. The first three women [master of divinity] students that I recall were the Reverend Nelia Kimbrough, who is now one of the leaders in the Open Door Community on Ponce de Leon Avenue in Atlanta; Reverend Toni White of the South Carolina Conference; and the Rev-

erend Diane Mosley of the South Carolina Conference. In Nelia's senior year, Dr. Laney appointed her to be an assistant dean. She was a part of the administration before she even graduated, and, her husband, Calvin, was head of the media center his last year here. So this was a fresh turn and emphasized the presence and the strength and the ability of the women who have come through Candler.
Hoffmann: The arrangement with the Episcopal Church brought a number of women into the student body, too. The percentage of black students increased, even though most of them went to ITC.
Weber: Now about 24 percent of the student body are minorities. When we came, the only black people on campus were maids and kitchen workers and furniture movers. Now the provost of the University is an African American, and the former dean of the Graduate School was, and quite a sizeable number of faculty members, and many students, some of them in strong leadership positions.

We've talked about a number of other changes. The difference between the informality at the beginning, when most of us were hired without interviews—these elaborate mechanisms for seeking out faculty members and running them through the hoops are different. The bureaucracy has multiplied. Back then you had the dean and the associate dean who also was a full-time teacher and who also was the director of the graduate program, and an assistant dean. Now, we have a dean and four associate deans. Very few women at the beginning, and now women run the place. These are major changes. Still, the tension between service to the church and acknowledgment of the academy remains very strong.
Mallard: That is a strong tension, but very strong progress has been made. The faculty of all disciplines sit with students and clinical trainers to theologize about the pastoral experiences they are having. That's exciting, and that has been strengthened over the years.
Hoffmann: We should also name Dean Waits, who was the successor of Dean Laney. Jim Waits basically continued the direction of the seminary that Laney had instituted, and strengthened it. The Waits years were practically an elongation and improvement on the direction that we had started.
Runyon: One thing we ought to emphasize is how our students have gone on to play major leadership roles in the church. Larry Goodpastor, for instance, is a bishop now in Florida and Alabama, but he will be the president of the Council of Bishops as of 2010. Susan Henry-Crowe, one of our early women students, is now the head of the United Methodist Church Judicial Council. That is the "supreme court" of Methodism; she will be playing a very strategic role in that office over the next few years.
Weber: She's also the dean of the chapel at Emory now.

Would you have believed when you started here that Candler would look like it looks now, that it would be the force that it is now?

Weber: No.
Mallard: I don't think so.
Runyon: No.
Weber: We were trying to survive, for one thing. Not only were we trying to survive, but after the initiation of the graduate program, some of the people who had planned the graduate program left immediately and went off to other schools. Candler had brought in this fresh batch of PhDs, and we had just come out of graduate school ourselves. So in a sense, they said, okay, you run it. We were chairing major committees and directing dissertations, to a large extent not really knowing what we were doing. There was a lot of dealing with immediate tasks that grasped our perspective at the time. So we weren't looking ahead to what the school might look like fifty years later.

CHAPTER 12

May 1969 protest at Cox Hall.

AFRICAN AMERICAN STUDIES AT EMORY
A Model for Change
— DELORES P. ALDRIDGE —

Less than a decade after the admission of the first African American students to Emory, the University was forced to recognize the inadequacy of its curriculum with regard to a whole dimension of American experience—the dimension shaped by the lives of African Americans. Delores Aldridge, the Grace Towns Hamilton Professor of Sociology and African American Studies, recounts the arduous effort to create the first program in African American studies at a major southern university and then to build it into a strong department of the first rank.

History and Context | African American studies, Afro-American studies, black studies, Africana studies, Pan-African studies, African diasporic studies, and Afro-Caribbean studies—all are but different names for academic disciplines that focus on the systematic investigation of people of African descent in their contacts with Europeans, their dispersal throughout the world, and their experience of and resistance to racism and oppression.

As an interdisciplinary field, African American studies largely concerns the analysis of race and institutional distributions of power of persons of African descent in the American context; a critique of the scholarship on persons of African descent produced in various disciplines that inform the field; and the creation of appropriate research methodologies that advance the mission of the field: academic excellence and social responsibility. Although the long intellectual tradition in African American studies focuses on the political and geographical boundaries of the United States, it is diasporic in scope, examining connections between African Americans and the peoples of Africa, Europe, the Caribbean, and Central and South America.

The analysis of race as a product of history and culture serves as the point of departure from which to examine the dynamics of racism, slavery, imperialism, segregation, emancipation, self-determination, and institutional transformation. So, too, issues of gender, class, sexuality, region, language, and religious practice serve as overlapping categories of analysis and further inform the interdisciplinary dimensions of the field. Equally important, and complementarily, African American studies invokes and advances an activist tradition that emphasizes social responsibility: the interdependent relationship between the academy and African American communities emphasizes commitment to social and political progress.

Black Studies/African American Studies at Emory: Its Beginnings | The development of the black studies program at Emory University provides a revealing example of the crucial role of the discipline as a resource for study of the black experience. The program has also been a significant vehicle for students, faculty, and staff to advocate for peoples whose cultural and historical experiences have been ignored and maligned. Black studies at Emory served as a forerunner to other new interdisciplinary programs and paved the way for greater University commitment to addressing the culturally specific needs and concerns of students of varied racial, ethnic, and gender minorities. In meeting the challenges of these endeavors, the program has bridged the distance between peoples by reminding them of their commonalities and the strengths that lie in understanding and respecting human difference.

Although many universities outside of the South had admitted and graduated black students since the turn of the twentieth century or earlier, most historically white southern universities remained segregated into the 1960s. Emory University did not admit its first black student until the fall of 1962. Significantly, the continuing institutional and societal racism that limited the numbers of blacks on predominantly white college campuses, coupled with a relative lack of commitment to providing support for black students, provided the impetus for a revolution within institutions of higher learning—one that called for the development of black studies programs. By the end of the 1960s, black students at Emory, whose consciousness had been sharpened by the protest ideology of the civil rights movement, were demanding a relevant education that included a systematic study of what was termed the black experience. Unlike any other discipline in the academy, African American studies arose as the intellectual arm of a social protest movement—the civil rights movement. Compelling intellectual and social stimuli prompted the assembling of a faculty in African American studies that would create courses focusing on the history, cultures, and traditions of persons of African descent, and that would develop coherent and rigorous curricula to serve the intellectual development of students and foster the continued liberation of black communities.

Confrontations between Emory faculty, students, and administration occurred throughout 1968 and 1969. The newly formed Black Student Alliance (BSA) charged that the low number of black students and the absence of black faculty and administrators and black history courses, as well as insensitivity of white faculty to the needs of black students, contributed to what they described as a hostile environment for nonwhite students. Subsequently, at a meeting on April 24, 1969, the Curriculum Committee of Emory College authorized the appointment of a Subcommittee on Afro-American Studies, charged initially to consider whether Emory should have a black studies program. Black students, however, continued to pressure the University to commit to change. On May 25, 1969, the BSA presented a list of demands to University President Sanford Atwood, stating,

> Emory, out of ignorance, has not understood fully the implications of admitting black students. Emory admitted black students, and concomitant with this admission were certain responsibilities which Emory should have fulfilled in behalf of these students. These responsibilities are in the four main areas of campus life: social, academic, psychological, and financial.

The students asked that an Afro-American studies department offering a degree in Afro-American studies be established at Emory, and that the charge of the subcommittee be changed to consider "What direction should an Afro-American Studies Department take and how should it be developed?"

In response, the subcommittee met on May 28, 1969, and strongly urged the president to make a priority of allocating funds "for scholarships and tutorial services for culturally distinct students and for the operation of a quality Afro-American studies program." After the meeting, the Afro-American Studies Subcommittee, headed by professor of mathematics Henry Sharp, devoted its attention primarily to the type of program to be recommended rather than to the rationale for such a program. In an April 1970 Curriculum Committee Report on black studies, the following observation was discussed and considered worthwhile:

> The black man's experience in this country . . . has been unique. This uniqueness has impinged on practically every facet of the American experience. The black man is an essential part of the American experience. Yet non-blacks have never bothered, in an ordered sort of way, to understand either the black man or his impact on the non-black majority in this country. The Program that we propose is an attempt at least to make a beginning.

The subcommittee (which included, in addition to Sharp, Peter Dowell from English, John Fenton from religion, John Howett from art history, and E. Phil Morgan from political science) recommended that because of the interdisciplinary nature of the proposed program, a division of black studies (rather than a department) be established. The University began a national search for a director of the program, and in the fall of 1971, Emory University hired me, the first African American to hold a tenure-track position in Emory College, to direct the newly approved Black Studies Program.

Arriving at Emory in 1971 I became the founding director of black studies, which later became African American and African studies. Later still this program was separated into African studies and African American studies, and finally the Department of African American Studies was formed in 2003, with African studies continuing as a program.

My return to Atlanta was a homecoming of sorts. I came to Emory from a position as executive director of the Greater Lafayette (Indiana) Community Centers Inc., but I had earned a BA in sociology and Spanish from Clark College in 1963 and a master of social work degree from Atlanta University in 1966. (The two schools merged to become Clark Atlanta University in 1988, at which time I was invited to serve on the board of trustees of the new institution.)

Having just completed a doctorate in sociology from Purdue University in June 1971 I faced the task of conceptualizing and developing a brand-new undergraduate black studies program.

The obstacles seemed insurmountable. I was not only the first black female faculty member but also the first black female at an institution traditionally dominated by white men and located in the conservative South. At the same time, few black studies programs in the United States could serve as a model for the interdisciplinary program that I had been charged with inaugurating. Students who interviewed me queried, "On which side will you be when the stuff goes down? On which side will you be when we have to fight the administration?" To which I answered, "I will be on the right side of whatever issues come up." I also recall a faculty member telling me on the first day of my arrival, "You aren't wanted here. You should be across town." I responded, "And I love you, too."

Of course, Emory was not then the institution it is today. The introduction of a new program raised questions in the minds of some whether this new program would grow at the expense or loss of other positions in longer-standing academic units. Despite the novelty of the situation, the Black Studies Program at Emory quickly became the first degree-granting program of its kind at a major private institution in the South.

In September 1971 I introduced an outline of the general philosophy of the new program. The outline stated:

- that course content relating to the black experience is a valid and necessary part of the curricula of institutions of higher education;
- that black courses are appropriate in a number of disciplines, and content should be intensified wherever possible in existing courses;
- that the offerings in black studies overlap and should be related to urban blacks through practicums;
- that the content of black courses should be oriented to preparing students for life in a racially integrated society; and
- that black faculty members should teach black courses wherever feasible, but that the preparation of the faculty member and not the color of the skin in the final analysis is what is relevant.

I had developed and received approval for a course titled "Dynamics of the Black Community" prior to my arrival on campus; thus I was running before I even hit the ground. I also developed a course titled "Social Welfare of the Black Experience," and by the end of the academic year achieved approval for two additional courses that involved directed readings and discussion of selected topics. From the outset, I intended to include internships or practicums in the program to give students firsthand experience in dealing with problems in the black community. The internship/practicums, initiated during the second year of the program, required that students on the junior/senior level obtain a position allowing field experience related to their area of concentration in a traditional field. Black studies became only the second program in the College (after political science) to offer an integrative internship for academic credit.

The internship offered a viable link between the Emory community and academic, social, religious, political, and cultural institutions within Atlanta's African American community, such as the Atlanta NAACP, the Atlanta Urban League, the Institute of the Black World, Planned Parenthood, the Atlanta Community Development Services, and the Martin Luther King Center for Non-Violent Social Change. The practicum was especially useful for white and other nonblack students, who attained a broader understanding of black people through contacts beyond the immediate campus.

The inception of a study-abroad program in West Africa during the 1973–74 academic year broadened the horizons of the Black Studies Program still further. Led by Professor Kenneth Baer, whose fields were anthropology and educational studies, the six-week program was among the first to offer study in Africa or the Caribbean and was only the second study-abroad program at Emory, after the one offered by the Art History Department. For the first time, Emory students could experience and observe life and culture in West Africa while receiving academic credit.

Although the Black Studies Program graduated its first two majors, Gloria Bowden and Bennie Hammonds, in 1974, the financial challenges that characterized the first years continued to limit the program's potential. The biggest obstacle in setting up an undergraduate black studies program was not getting qualified personnel but finding the resources to afford them. Despite limited financial support, the program added "The History of Jazz" to the growing core curriculum and received a gift of a sizeable African art collection in the spring.

The program sponsored seven guest lectures in its third year, more than any other department in the College. Speakers included Clarence Bacote, Luther Weems, Edward Sweat, Basil Matthews, George Napper (author of *Blacker Than Thou*), Adrian Leftwich (from the University of York, England), and Alvin Poussaint, the well-known Harvard psychiatrist and author of *Why Blacks Kill Blacks*. Two one-day seminars titled "Blacks and the Communication Media" and "Black Psychologists and the Black Community" took place that spring as well.

Delores Aldridge

Insufficient funding continued to remain a problem for hiring full-time faculty. In my 1973–74 year-end report, I described my salary allotted to the program secretary as "meager" and "exploitative." The annual library allowance of twenty-three hundred dollars could not adequately supplement a deficient number of periodical holdings in Caribbean literature, black scholarly journals, and magazines. I even painted my office and purchased draperies from personal funds. Financial concerns were dire enough that I decided to leave if certain recommendations were not addressed. In a 1974 letter to the board of trustees, I argued that "the Black Studies Program should be totally dismantled and eliminated or should be revamped to effectively compete with any other academic discipline within Emory College." The program could not continue to function as a "token offering."

Several concrete recommendations for improvement included: (1) an independent black studies budget similar to those for other major departments; (2) addition of at least one full-time or two part-time faculty members; (3) a budgetary increase for visiting lecturers or professors; (4) graduate teaching assistants; (5) staff to meet student interest and enrollment; (6) sponsorship of seminars and workshops; and (7) greater emphasis on the African American presence in traditional departments.

In the wake of these recommendations, the College established a Black Studies Ad Hoc Review Committee, composed of six white males and one white female, Dr. Dora H. Skypek, an educational studies professor, who served as committee chair. The committee rejected the notion of eliminating the program; however, it also concluded that the proposed expansion of the program was questionable, because it would mean

Elevating . . . an interdisciplinary area of study to the status of department. Black studies is not a discipline. To separate the program from an interdepartmental structure will lead to a duplicating of courses in the departments of history, sociology, political science, literature, and music.

The committee suggested that in lieu of a major in black studies, interested students should complete majors in "traditional" disciplines with a "focus" on black studies. The committee failed to perceive a contradiction, however, in justifying the continued existence of the program based on its uniqueness, yet denying its expansion because of a purported duplication of traditional course offerings.

Importantly, the ad hoc committee did recommend additional faculty support services to assist the director, whom they described as "Herculean" in building the program. The committee added that the program had never received the commitment, in spirit or money, that it needed from the University in order to survive successfully, yet it had remained and grown. This continued growth was owing to the competent and talented academicians, lecturers, and graduate students (from Emory and the Atlanta University Center), as well as visiting scholars from throughout the nation, who shared their time and talent out of friendship with the director, because monetary reward was often unavailable. In one instance, Ojeda Penn, an adjunct professor from the Atlanta University Center, taught a course initially without pay to assist the struggling program. Black studies would nonetheless witness no considerable increase in its financial and faculty resources, and Emory College would not hire another full-time black faculty member until the arrival of Margaret Spencer, a psychology professor, in 1977.

During the 1976–77 academic year, my faculty line had been placed in the budget of the Institute of Liberal Arts (ILA), where I was the ILA's first and only black faculty member. The College administration decided that only half my time should be devoted to the Black Studies Program. Despite my being solely responsible for the groundbreaking of a nontraditional field, my promotion and tenure would depend on my performance in the ILA. With no new faculty at the time, I taught four courses in the fall and two in the spring, and my responsibilities to the ILA required serving on thirteen doctoral dissertation and master's thesis committees. Despite this excessive workload, the program did not receive funds for expansion, and black studies began to settle into its position as an understaffed, underfunded interdisciplinary program.

The annual report of the program for the 1976–77 academic year was devoid of the recommendations for improvement and change that characterized reports from earlier years. This complacency was not a sign of contentment but the result of fatigue. The pressure of my role as the focal point for black student concerns began to take its toll. The program also functioned as a resource center for black staff members. By the fall of 1978 the frustrated program staff felt it necessary to disseminate an information sheet reminding students, faculty, and staff that the Black Studies Program was separate from the Black Student Alliance and from the Caucus of Emory Black Alumni Association, although much of the impetus for the Caucus had come out of the program. These responsibilities as well as my increasingly multifaceted role as program director, student adviser, University committee member, Martin Luther King Scholarship coordinator, instructor, and community liaison would continue to accrue until the creation of a minority student affairs office (later the Office of Multicultural Programs and Services) that reflected a wider reach to an increasingly diverse student body.

Student enrollment in black studies courses neither declined nor increased after the first six years of the program. Two reasons were that students could not take black studies courses to fulfill College distribution or departmental requirements, and students were reluctant to take courses from a host of unfamiliar professors and visiting lecturers. After seven years, I was still the only full-time black faculty member in the program. Consequently, the coordination of extracurricular activities related to the program fell to me and the secretary. While the faculty roster of affiliated faculty members had increased to thirty-two, these professors taught only occasional courses in related fields and were housed in other departments. Affiliation did not necessarily translate into a strong commitment to black studies, since working that was not their single obligation.

In the midst of these challenges, the program outgrew its space in Candler Library. One office and two smaller rooms housed both the secretary and me. Visiting lecturers had no space, nor did we have space for general office supplies. Limited space did not curtail achievement, however. Two majors graduated in the spring of 1978, and library acquisitions related to the black experience increased in quality and quantity. The program sponsored a film series that included *Hallelujah*, *The Emperor Jones*, *Stormy Weather*, *Carmen Jones*, and *Mandingo*. The series was associated with a newly initiated course on black film. The program also hosted an awards dinner for the Black Student Alliance's theatrical production of *River Niger*, as well as two faculty-staff-student receptions to encourage black-white dialogue. Bobby Seale, founder of the Black Panthers, presented a lecture on "Political Climate and the Survival of Black People."

> *On March 6, 1980, black studies became the African American and African Studies Program (AAAS), a move that demonstrated efforts to maintain a strong ideological and practical connection with a dynamic black community.*

In the fall of 1978 the Black Studies Program launched a newsletter, the *Black Voice*. The first issue focused on national, local, and campus concerns related to the black community. Topics included the resurgence of KKK activities and the lagging Emory black student enrollment. The newsletter sought to publicize activities and discuss concerns involving blacks on campus and in the black community at large, but would ultimately cease publication, largely because of uneven quality of contributions.

Nevertheless, throughout the 1978–79 academic year, the program strove to increase its visibility on campus and in Atlanta. The program sponsored a luncheon seminar in black studies for the University custodial staff, collaborated with the Psychology Department and the Minority Women's Recruitment Bureau to present workshops for minority women, and initiated a bus tour of the black community during freshman orientation week. Importantly, visibility of the program increased on a national level when I was elected to the executive board of the National Council for Black Studies (NCBS).

Such heightened visibility and increased recognition still did not translate into sufficiently increased support from the University. Limited funds were allocated for the hiring of five part-time black studies instructors. After eight years, we still did not have an office copier; the secretary had to travel across campus to carry out office duties. Despite insufficient administrative support, the program pressed onward and upward.

At the end of the 1978–79 school year, I outlined new, modest goals for the next five years, and some of these goals became realities by the following year. To increase enrollment, the first goal was approval of at least three black studies courses as options for fulfilling College distribution requirements. Other objectives included having at least five students declare black studies as part of their joint major, hiring more faculty and staff, developing greater outreach activities on the campus and in the black community, developing a stronger national image, adding a full-time assistant to the director, maintaining independent status in the College, and acquiring a budget that would allow for a high-quality program.

Two courses, "Dynamics of the Black Community" and "Twentieth-Century Southern Black Life," received Educational Policy Committee approval as options for uniform requirements in the College. Additionally the History Department approved "History of Afro-Americans: African Origins to 1865" and "History of Afro-Americans: Emancipation to Present" for credit toward completing a history major. Two undergraduates selected black studies as part of a dual-major concentration. Mary E. Billingslea joined the program as a full-time black affairs development specialist to assist the director and the secretary in disseminating information to the black communities of Atlanta and Emory. Student activities in various practicums, coupled with the newsletter, contributed to greater visibility at Emory and the community at-large. My professional involvement in the NCBS, as well as the activities of other black studies faculty members, increased program recognition on the national level.

Although the problem of space remained intractable, by fall of 1979 the program gained access to a small office behind the African-American Reading Room in Candler Library. Despite success in achieving certain goals, the administration did not grant funds for one more permanent faculty member nor substantially increase the budget of the program. Among the most significant revisions in the program was a decision to change its name. On March 6, 1980, black studies became the African American and African Studies Program (AAAS), a move that demonstrated efforts to maintain a strong ideological and practical connection with a dynamic black community.

The activities of AAAS within the Atlanta black community and at Emory increased substantially during 1980–81: planning sundry cultural events, advising local universities on their own AAAS programs and departments, assisting DeKalb County in planning its Black History Month activities, and planning for the Conference on the Life and History of Black Georgians.

While I was on leave that year, Peter Dowell, of the English Department, served as part-time acting director. In January the program cosponsored with the Emory Black Caucus the first lecture in the Black Family Colloquium Series, which featured Nathan Hare (founder of the first black studies program in the United States), author James Baldwin, and family psychologist Alyce Gullattee. A symposium on "Black Literature and Art" brought together many well-known southern writers and critics to plan a major conference for the fall of 1981.

Two new courses, "Black Southern Writers" and "Courting and Marriage in Africa in the West," made good contributions to the core curriculum. Another course, "Art and Architecture of Black Africa," reflected the new emphasis on the African dimension of the program. Our program growth did not hinder us from assisting other departments in the University in our effort to transform the Emory community. We researched information on the black elderly for a course in the Sociology Department, located a native Haitian to speak in the modern languages and Classics Department, researched health statistics on black Americans for a course in nursing, sponsored a lecture by Jontyle Robinson of the Art History Department on African American art, developed a recruiting brochure for black students for the Equal Opportunity and Affirmative Action Office, and cosponsored Community Law Day with the Law School.

Despite an increase in activities as well as additions to the curriculum, the facilities remained the same. Limited working area provided little or no privacy for phone conversations, interviews, and consultations. The African American Reading Room needed refurbishing. Office duplicating equipment was insufficient. Dowell suggested that in light of the impending change from the quarter system to a semester system the following year, and the recent admission of the largest number of black freshmen in the University's history, Emory had a unique opportunity to reexamine its curriculum and commitment to the AAAS program.

Continued Movement against the Odds | In fall of 1981, after a decade of steady progress, I returned from a year on leave to find that not only must I start over but I must do it alone. The dean had terminated the secretary, student assistant, and black affairs specialist. Furthermore, the last position had been placed in moratorium. Consequently I spent much of the first quarter recruiting staff and developing documents to assess the past and make cogent projections for the future. I developed a comprehensive report titled *A Decade of Struggle*, which included detailed assessments of the staff, curriculum, and budgeting concerns, as well as a five-year plan.

Looking to the future, the ILA faculty and I drafted a memorandum to the dean of the College, recommending, among other things, that the ILA be authorized to fill its vacant position, that the AAAS Program be upgraded to departmental status on the model of the Religion Department and Graduate Division of Religion, and that appointments of faculty with AAAS expertise be strongly encouraged in traditional departments. Disappointingly, Dean David Minter indicated that the program would not be upgraded to a department and would need to continue to draw on adjunct faculty from the Atlanta community.

In November 1981 the program cosponsored "A Conference of Black South Writers and Artists," which included Jerry Ward, Charles Rowell, actress Ruby Dee, Atlanta mayor Andrew Young, poet Toni Cade Bambara, Margaret Walker (author of *Jubilee*), and Alice Walker. Additionally, AAAS participated in the development of activities related to the National Black Studies Curriculum Development Project, based at the Institute of Black World in Atlanta. The program also sponsored a film/lecture series in the spring that featured budding director Shelton "Spike" Lee, who presented two of his films, *The Answer* and *Sarah*.

The beginning of the 1982–83 academic year brought encouragement, and consequently expectations and enthusiasm increased. The College administration made several commitments and promises aimed at strengthening the program: (1) establishment of AAAS as a separate structure in the University, (2) a full-time director for AAAS who would have tenure in his/her field of study and responsibilities only to the program, (3) continuing use of adjunct faculty from the Atlanta academic community, (4) a full-time member on tenure track with expertise in the social sciences, and (5) a full-time tenured or tenure-track faculty member with expertise in the humanities.

A national search began to bring additional faculty to the University in the following year. Improvement in the program was also characterized by increases in enrollment, the declaration of five new majors, and curriculum advancement. In 1981 NCBS published guidelines for undergraduate studies, and the program at Emory needed only one additional course to meet those guidelines.

Although the program showed significant growth, inadequate office space remained a problem. Still, with new majors, new courses in the curriculum, additional courses meeting uniform college requirements, and the hiring of two African American resource librarians in Woodruff Library, the program instilled us with hope for its future and the belief that it could not only survive but continue the trajectory forward.

The optimism that characterized the beginning of the twelfth year of the program yielded to disappointment, however. The search committee had spent a year looking for an African American historian and had finally made its recommendation. The College dean, however, did not offer a position to the individual recommended by the committee. The AAAS faculty nonetheless was determined to see its number increased in the coming year; after yet another yearlong search, a new African American historian accepted an appointment with primary responsibility in the AAAS program. Five students declared majors in 1983, and in May 1984 one major graduated. I served the first term of an unprecedented two-term position as chair of NCBS and received the outstanding teacher of the year award from the Emory Senior Council.

The program also progressed in other arenas, cosponsoring seven lectures throughout the year on topics ranging from the black experience in America, to relationships of black men and women, to theology in French-speaking Africa. Service projects continued both nationally and locally. Additionally we reactivated the summer study-abroad program in Haiti and Jamaica.

The annual report for 1983–84 included a definitive five-year plan that illustrated the philosophy, goals, and objectives of the program. The philosophy remained the same as in 1971—strengthening of the program within the arts and sciences of Emory College. Objectives included adding one new faculty member, modifying the curriculum, refurbishing physical space, reassessing needs, and acquiring library materials during the forthcoming year. Although the program had met some of its objectives, it fell short of a few others, including efforts to upgrade the program to departmental status and to secure adequate office equipment.

In 1985–86 AAAS celebrated its fifteenth anniversary, but jubilation was tempered by two administrative decisions, one of which placed two of the three tenure-lined faculty in moratorium. That decision jeopardized a crucial tenet of the five-year-plan. The College administration determined that a joint appointment between AAAS and the Art History Department would not be made because of a lack of consensus between the department and the program. The administration promised to create a joint appointment with the Music Department, but the question remained what would happen if, again, we could not achieve consensus.

> *The Grace Towns Hamilton Chair was the first in the nation named for a living African American woman.*

With support from other departments, units, and individuals from the University, more than forty events took place during the year to mark achievements of black studies scholars affiliated with Emory. Events included an international bazaar focusing on Jamaican, Haitian, and African goods; a premiere film presentation of "History of Afro-Americans at Emory 1836–1984"; installation of a permanent art exhibit in the reading room; a black film festival; an art exhibit in Schatten Gallery titled "Lest We Forget . . . Images from the Black Civil Rights Movement"; a black excellence awards banquet; more than fifteen lectures; and a play, a seminar, and two concerts.

Significant achievements by AAAS faculty added to the festivity of the anniversary. I was elected to a second term as chair of NCBS and received the W. E. B. Du Bois Award from the Association of Social and Behavioral Scientists. Jontyle Robinson received an American art visiting faculty fellowship from the Smithsonian Institution, and Elsa Barkley Brown was appointed to the National Advisory Board of the Center for Research on Women at Memphis State University.

Our determination led us to strive for what we could accomplish without adequate administrative support. We began refining the curriculum and examining it to access more adequately the African American content in the program. We added two courses, "Ethnomusicology" and "Apartheid and South African Society." We prepared a booklet on the AAAS program at Emory. The number of declared majors rose to four, and the minors to fifteen. The program sponsored an essay contest exploring the question, "Are White Academic Institutions Producing Black Leaders?" and hosted an international bazaar, a black film festival, Black Alumni Weekend, and a lecture by Lerone Bennett Jr., senior editor of *Ebony*.

Social unrest permeated 1987–88. Conflicts involved dissemination of racially offensive flyers, denial of tenure for black English/AAAS professor Sondra O'Neal, sexist fraternity T-shirts, and charges of racial discrimination in the promotion process in the Department of Public Safety (now Emory Police Department). These events culminated in campus-wide protests and meetings among students, faculty, and staff throughout November. Responding to charges of institutional racism and questionable commitment to AAAS, President James T. Laney contended in a November 21 open letter to the Emory community,

> In 1980, 23 out of 949 members of the faculty were Black. Today there are 41 Black faculty out of a total of 1022. Just within the last six months two prominent Black scholars have been made the recipients of endowed chairs, one of whom is a renowned authority in Afro-American and African culture. These developments contradict the claim that Emory has reduced its commitment to equal opportunity and minimized Afro-American Studies.

Despite continuing debate over charges of sexism and academic racism, the AAAS program made substantial contributions to both the academic and social life of the University. The curriculum was supplemented by three new courses, "Afrocentric Health Care Systems," "Black Images in Media," and Black Child Development." In an effort to respond to recent tensions, the program cosponsored a workshop on "Unlearning Racism." The international focus of the program led to a visit by South African Archbishop Desmond Tutu, who delivered the Commencement address and received an honorary degree in May 1988.

In 1988 I began to direct a three-year effort to advance black studies throughout the nation. The project was funded by a three-hundred-thousand-dollar grant from the Ford Foundation through NCBS and focused on three main areas: training scholars and administrators of African American and African studies, collection of data on existing black studies curricula and development of model curricula, and creation of a centralized database that has provided a profile of black studies faculty nationwide. Further, I was promoted to full professor, the first African American in the history of the University to move through the ranks from assistant professor to full professor, and, later, to a distinguished chair named for Grace Towns Hamilton, the first African American woman Georgia legislator. The chair was significant because it was the first in the nation named for a living African American woman. (Earlier, an annual lecture had been named for Mrs. Hamilton.)

Ending the eighties, AAAS became associated with the editing of the Martin Luther King Jr. papers. Importantly, too, Emory formalized the tie between Atlanta Public Schools and Emory's M. L. King Jr. Scholarships as a result of discussions between Dr. Alonzo Crim, the schools superintendent, and President Laney. This meant that a scholarship managed by AAAS would now be significantly funded and centrally located in the College office.

Moving Forward | After twenty years, in 1992 I stepped down as program director, the longest-serving director of an African American studies program in the nation at the time. The African American Studies Program continued to grow under the leadership of a new director, Dr. Rudolph P. Byrd. At Commencement that year I received Emory's premier award, the Thomas Jefferson Award, presented by President Laney. Byrd garnered support from a new College administration and was able to bring new full-time faculty on board but eliminated the adjunct faculty such as Dr. Marcellus Barksdale of Morehouse College, who had so strongly supported the program in the past.

The new full-time faculty facilitated an increase in curriculum offerings and greater outreach to students. Further contributing to changes in the program was its separation into two programs, African American studies and African studies. Importantly, a number of impressive cultural and academic initiatives continued. The Hamilton Lecture brought to campus stellar lecturers such as Randall Robinson of TransAfrica; Dr. Mary Frances Berry, chair of the United States Civil Rights Commission; and former Ambassador Andrew Young. Symposia featuring Nobel laureates and subsequently the attraction of Nobel Literature Laureate Wole Soyinka to the faculty as a Visiting Woodruff Professor further enhanced efforts, as did new ties with a university in South Africa and one in the Caribbean. A series of luncheon lectures was resurrected as Black Tower Lectures, and the Race and Gender Lecture initiated with the Institute of Women's Studies (now Department of Women's Studies) engaged lecturers Kathleen Cleaver and Elaine Browne. Randall Burkett came to Emory to expand our African American collections, which now include major archives of the Southern Christian Leadership Conference, the papers of Carter G. Woodson, the archives of the Association of African American Life and History, and novelist Alice Walker, among others.

Continued Positive Moves | Two new directors took leadership roles during the first decade of the new millennium, Dr. Mark Sanders (2000–04) and Dr. Leslie Harris (2005–08). Sanders led the program into departmental status. In response to the spring 2001 invitation of the College and University administrations and the long-term discussions of our faculty, the program put forth a proposal for it to be designated a department in Emory College by fall 2003.

Offering the major and minor, the department would no longer offer courses taught by a faculty whose appointments, training, research, and pedagogic interests were not primarily focused on African American experiences. Though claiming no dogmatic adherence to any theoretical construct, the department emphasizes that experiences of African peoples are central, not peripheral, to analysis in African American studies. As a department, African American studies would now make decisions and recommendations about faculty appointments, tenure, promotion, and salary. The department retained most of its current administrative structure and programs, including joint faculty appointments, associated faculty, and visiting professors, but it would need several new senior appointments to replace four distinguished professors affiliated with the program (Johnnetta Cole, Wole Soyinka, Richard Long, and Richard Joseph) recently lost to retirement or departures. The formal designation of African American studies as a department became effective in fall 2003. This and the move into newly renovated and expanded space in Candler Library were major accomplishments under Mark Sanders's leadership. AAS also observed its thirtieth anniversary. A miniconference on the history of AAS featured a number of original architects of the field as well as promising new voices.

During the tenure of Harris and again under Sanders (2008–), significant strides were made toward a graduate program. In 2004 Emory also welcomed the new University provost, Earl Lewis, as a professor with joint appointment in history and AAS. He was the senior-most African American appointed by the University to that date. Growth continued during Harris's administration with hires in art history, history, and journalism, the primary appointments for whom are in AAS.

The Committee for Departmental Status contended, in 2001, that the Program in African American Studies had pursued examination of African American life and history through curricular and scholarly excellence for more than thirty years. Through its existence, the program had provided important courses and an essential major to the College curriculum. In addition, members of the African American studies faculty produced scholarship that gained national recognition within the field and in each of the longer-established disciplines represented in the program. With real strengths in faculty and curriculum, a growing national reputation (based on faculty publications), the development and expansion of a general library collection, and creation and growth of the African American Collections in Emory's Manuscript, Archives, and Rare Book Library (MARBL), AAS is well positioned to provide leadership in the University.

Looking Backward: Looking Forward | Emory's program was in the vanguard of
the black/Africana studies movement in higher education in the late sixties and garnered national and international respect as the first degree-granting program in the South. The founding director of the program was also the first African American faculty member at Emory College. Since that time, the program has grown in both African American and non–African American faculty and has acquired departmental status. The highly qualified and respected faculty members excel in teaching and scholarship both in the departments where members are jointly appointed and in various other University programs. Moreover, members of our faculty are deeply committed to community outreach, as reflected in the creation of the first internship program Emory offered in Atlanta, in 1972, a program that over the decades has served as a model for other departments, programs, and centers.

African American studies faculty members have been recruited to lead other Emory programs and committees and have participated in local, national, and international efforts to advance the field. As a result, African American studies faculty members have garnered numerous awards for teaching, scholarship, and service. Thus, the department functions at the center of intellectual leadership and service for the University and larger academic community. Having begun as a meager attempt to comply with the Georgia Supreme Court's decision to open the doors of white private colleges and universities to blacks, Emory's black studies program is now an established unit within the institution.

CHAPTER 13

The White Devil being performed in the Black Rose Theater.

"STRUCK BY THEATER-IDEAS"
Theater as a Site and Mode of Inquiry at Emory University
— MICHAEL EVENDEN —

Michael Evenden's essay describes the experimental nature of theater studies at Emory and affirms foremost "the priority of theater itself as the wellspring of an academic program." Begun in 1982 and representing "the intersection of theater practice, liberal arts education, and research inquiry," Theater Emory encourages scrupulous academic study and theatrical innovation among professional and student artists in collaboration with the Department of Theater Studies. For Evenden, the community of scholars and the community of players are inseparable.

> *[Theater] is always on the move, always engrossed in its own course, overspilling individual experience, nomadically evading responsibility. It is self-transporting, serially across experience.*
> —Brian Massumi, A Shock to Thought (2002)

> *As imagination may extend the power of research and scholarship, by its very presence shaking off stuffiness, it is possible to conceive of a theater on a campus which is locally dissident, clarion, substanced by ideas born of hard solitude in other disciplines, challenged by the criticism of colleagues worthy of respect, and in turn testing those ideas and weighing criticisms in the open, unscholarly, but not less exacting forum of the stage.*
> —Herbert Blau, The Impossible Theater: A Manifesto (1964)

> *Our stated commitment with Theater Emory is to create a theater of intellectual excitement, a theater in which significant ideas are expressed imaginatively. Our concern is not only entertainment, but also entertainment of a very special order in which the audience is moved by a poetic convergence of subject and form. Our ultimate aim is to provide Emory and Atlanta with a living library of the masterpieces of dramatic literature performed side-by-side with the best in contemporary drama, including original works. In all of these ambitions Theater Emory will strive to become a public manifestation of those values treasured by the University itself.*
> —James W. Flannery, "High Expectations, Responsibilities, Opportunities, and Choices: A Prospectus for Theater Emory" (1983)

THEATER EMORY AND the Department of Theater Studies, a combined entity, has dedicated itself from the first to the intersection of theater practice, liberal arts education, and research inquiry. Combining academically rigorous study with hands-on learning at a professional level across the many subdisciplines of theater (criticism, playwriting, performance, technology, design, dramaturgy, and administration), we ask students and professional artist/teachers to think, question, and create beyond the received limits of commercial theater and specialized skill sets of, for instance, "acting" or "design" or "directing." We seek to open larger questions by bridging the divisions of theory and practice, experiment and expertise, demonstration and proof, thus inviting a local reimagining of theater and education and research. For us, this has meant above all investing in theater—a practical activity, including planning, rehearsal, production—as a site and indeed a distinct *mode* of inquiry that has its (productively unsettled) place in a research university and a liberal arts college. This essay is a recounting of some of the forms of theatrical experiment, inquiry, and outreach that have marked the path.

Founded in 1982 with the support of Emory College dean David Minter, Theater Emory was shaped at first by the recommendations of James W. Flannery of the University of Rhode Island, who came to Emory as a consultant for the creation of a theater department and was invited to stay to inaugurate his vision of "a professional theater *out of which* we will then develop a solid academic program in theater studies" (emphasis added). The priority of theater itself as the wellspring of an academic program is central to the continuing vision of theater education at Emory: we believe that academic study of the field is incomplete and ungrounded without engaging the practical and creative challenges of informed, rigorous, and forward-thinking theater work. The Department of Theater Studies, therefore, pursues all the traditional forms of pedagogical and scholarly excellence, but with this difference: we begin with the discipline of theatrical collaboration at Theater Emory; that is our distinctive mode of inquiry.

Witness a scene set in the Dobbs University Center in the 1990s:

In "The Black Rose," a painstaking reconstruction of a Jacobean indoor theater from the days of Shakespeare, resident actor Tim McDonough, who has been playing Prospero in this production of Shakespeare's *Tempest*, emerges onto the empty stage at the end of the performance, and looks around—first below, then at eye level, then above—at the assembled audience, who, in authentic period practice, are as fully-lit as he and surround, and potentially overwhelm, him. "Draw near to me," he says to them, and the audience, standing or seated together in benches (rather than separate, padded seats) surge forward in an unexpectedly direct physical response; many are now close enough to touch him. He descends into the trapdoor on the stage, and, hidden to the waist, delivers Prospero's epilogue with new immediacy, directly soliciting the audience's applause that will signal his freedom to leave the theater and join the world outside. The audience's answering applause, hesitant, then exultant, is transformed from a conventional gesture into a form of new and immediate communication between actor, character, and community. The actor disappears through the stage.

This vision of active artistic research has sustained and provoked theater at Emory through a quarter-century of growth and many changes in structure, personnel, and physical facilities, from its original constitution in 1982–83 as a two-member faculty (including a single academic chair/artistic director) plus five affiliate artists teaching a newly approved academic minor in theater studies, through a period in which the department combined with film studies (now an independent department), and into its present formation: a resident professional theater and a full academic department offering a major, a minor, and a co-major with creative writing, sharing faculty and staff as resident artist/teachers. Today each unit, the theater and the department, is headed respectively by an artistic director or department chair, each with a limited term; together, these peer leaders support twelve full-time faculty, three faculty-equivalent staff, and five part-time faculty artists, all teaching, practicing, and conducting research through an annual theater season of three fully staged productions and a varying number of smaller projects (uniting student and professional artists in each), while over forty majors and twenty minors join some seven hundred other students in over ninety academic, studio, and laboratory courses.

Innovative Teaching as a Site of Inquiry | The imperative to make theater a site of inquiry, of refusing to settle for the familiar even in a collective and public art, of simultaneously exploring and violating traditions, has required questioning both academic and theatrical business as usual. Innovative efforts in teaching, artistic work, and their combination have emerged. Learning experiences offered in Emory theater courses are unprecedented and original to this faculty and their willingness to invent.

A signal effort has been to tear down the traditional wall of distrust between literary/historical scholarship and the creative processes of acting and directing. A series of intensive seminars in the drama of Henrik Ibsen, George Bernard Shaw, the English Restoration theater, and Samuel Beckett, each taught by a team of a senior-level scholar and a senior-level acting teacher, constitutes an ongoing experiment in creating acting exercises and methods directly out of the textual questions raised by literary scholarship. The Shakespeare seminar has become a regular feature and a prized experience for Emory students, and these advanced seminars lead in every case to public workshops and full productions at Theater Emory, sometimes incorporating several related productions or even several theatrical seasons into an overarching exploration.

Witness a classroom experience in theater studies:

In a team-taught class uniting scholarly analysis and acting style, teaching artist Tim McDonough finds a passage in Ibsen's little-known *Love's Comedy* that seems to literalize Kierkegaard's famous formulation of the leap of (or, rather, to) faith (especially interesting because Ibsen resisted any acknowledgment that he was directly influenced by Kierkegaard, although the influence is widely inferred—and here, perhaps concretized). This spontaneous, in-class discovery, building on his coteacher Alice Benston's exploration of the philosophical theme, prompts him to develop an original and specific acting exercise in which the metaphoric leap is made physical and incorporated into realistic stage behavior. Many of the students involved in this class will continue in these explorations and apply these lessons in a series of Ibsen productions at Theater Emory under professional directors.

A sampling of teaching innovations would include: a section of "Introduction to the Theater" that makes students contemplate and artistically express the social and natural landscapes of their own childhoods; a freshman seminar taught across "Theater, Dance, Music, and Creative Writing on Creativity and Collaboration"; "Creating New Works," a course in theatrical adaptation of nontheatrical materials, which has led to strikingly original staging experiments by students who have gone on to professional directing careers; and a textbook, *Acting Narrative Speeches: The Actor as Storyteller* by Tim McDonough, which has emerged from a distinctive course called "Acting: Speeches and Monologues," focused on the fundamental acting task of telling a story and conveying an alternate reality. Add to these a course, "Creating a Role," that directly addresses the besetting limitation of acting classes everywhere (there is only time in class to work at the microlevel, on scenes and moments, but never to construct a coherent overall performance); this course has enabled several students to define honors theses based on this particular artistic challenge, explored in a professional context at Theater Emory. The department also stands out from other theater programs nationwide in offering courses in theater management, which has launched a number of students into administrative careers and provided a kind of umbrella training for new theater groups forming in Atlanta, including Out-of-Hand Theater and Le Théâtre du Rêve, both currently headed by Emory graduates.

> By general agreement, one of the most onerous assignments in Pat Miller's course in Theater Administration is the planning of a season budget for a theater of the student's imagining. But when one student (whose primary focus is not administration) submits the assignment, he does so with the enthusiasm of unexpected discovery: "This budgeting isn't about numbers—it's about values." This encapsulates the difference between a liberal arts and a conservatory approach to the field: the specific question of theater practice—the what and the how—opens up larger questions of why art exists, and, thus, how its purposes might newly be realized.

The teaching adventure has also been significantly shaped by a tradition of tutorials—individual and group—for ambitious students with particular interests; for example, this possibility encouraged Emory scholar Mark Blankenship (College 2001)—now a theater reporter for the *New York Times*, an occasional columnist for the *Huffington Post*, and creator of the blog *The Critical Condition*—to request a formative series of tutorials in critical writing and in theater applied to social problems. With the establishing of departmental standards for honors in theater in 1995, the way was prepared for exceptional students to cap their growth with independent artistic explorations, wedded to critical and historical research and critical self-reflection. This has led to some extraordinary student artistic research, including productions directed at Theater Emory with professional designers and actors working under student leadership—for example, contemporary British playwright Peter Barnes's *Red Noses*, directed by David Garrett (College 1992), now an independent filmmaker; Ibsen's rarely produced *Pillars of Society*, directed by Ariel de Man (College 1998), now artistic producing director of Out-of Hand Theater, a nationally recognized Atlanta theater company; design projects such as Holly J. Morris's (College 1997) surreal costume design for Megan Terry's phantasmagoric biography of Simone Weill, *Remembering Simone*; and two memorable environmental theater projects produced independently of Theater Emory: a multiple-location staging of Maria Irene Fornes's *Fefu and Her Friends*, directed by Matt Huff (College 1997), now a freelance director in Atlanta and Houston; and a site-specific staging by Snehal Desai (College 2002, now a freelance director and performer in New York and Atlanta) of José Rivera's *Marisol*, a magical-realist play reimagined to draw on the Emory Briarcliff campus's history as a mental hospital, so that Desai's audience was led through scenes in the confining spaces of the abandoned hospital and outside to gather around fires and finally to hold hands under the open sky for the play's concluding, apocalyptic vision. This open portal between class work and production, between scholarly and critical rigor and imaginative experiment, is at the core of our educative vision.

Inquiry through Theater: Breaking the Received Forms | Outside the classroom, many academic theater programs, particularly in undergraduate colleges, function in pale imitation of commercial theater, with repertory mirroring contemporary Broadway seasons. More high-minded programs perform more classics; occasional guest professional artists are not uncommon. In the case of conservatory or graduate professional programs (highly specialized preprofessional skill-training aimed at fitting students into the existing professional theater as efficiently as possible), these features can be more fully developed—more professionals, more challenging repertory—so that a theater program's offering effectively become those of a regional theater that is also a teaching theater for young professionals.

Theater Emory stands apart from these models in two particulars: first, rather than jobbed-in professionals, Theater Emory maintains a sustained resident company of artist/teachers who maintain professional careers beyond their teaching and their work in residence; and, second, it addresses itself educationally to *undergraduates*—liberal arts students whose training with us will be, in keeping with the spirit of such education, broad-based as opposed to focused on narrow skill acquisition, and directed toward educating the whole person regardless of career plans. (A statistically impressive number of Emory's theater students have maintained artistic careers and lives after graduation, but our program is equally committed to the education of doctors or engineers or lawyers or chemists.) To the best of our investigation, we have found no other undergraduate theater program that frames itself exactly this way, and these emphases require a special open-mindedness and a willingness to ask larger questions and seek unprecedented forms of expression, extending our discipline by breaking its boundaries.

Beyond the Conventional Repertory
Even in production work that is more conventional—classical plays presented with various forms of audience education such as meet-the-artist forums, talkback sessions, extensive program commentary, and the like—we have felt free to be adventurous. Few theaters in the United States can boast a classical repertory that includes Shaw's *Back to Methuselah* (a sequence of five plays performed in two adjoining theaters across two evenings, taking an itinerant audience from the Garden of Eden to the end of human possibility), the regional premiere of Ödön von Horváth's rebarbative *Don Juan Comes Back from the War*, Ibsen rarities like the early verse masterpieces *Peer Gynt* and *Brand* as well as *Pillars of Society* and *Lady from the Sea*, William Butler Yeats's mythopoeic *A Full Moon in March*, paired with an interracial treatment of Strindberg's naturalistic tragedy *Miss Julie*, an evening of Bertolt Brecht's youthful poetry and songs, an adaptation of Brecht's *Schweyk in the Second World War*, Heiner Müller's postmodern *Despoiled Shore Medeamaterial Landscape with Argonauts*, Albert Camus's *Caligula*, and Irwin Shaw's rarely performed antiwar drama *Bury the Dead*. By asserting the freedom to explore the repertory this broadly, Theater Emory has dedicated itself from the first to bold artistic inquiry.

Having built "The Black Rose" in 1996, Theater Emory sought to explore the relation of Renaissance dramatic literature to this theatrical architecture: one experiment was a public workshop in 1998 (attended by Patrick Spottiswoode, educational director of Shakespeare's Globe in London), about performing the drama of Shakespeare's near-contemporary, the Spaniard Pedro Calderòn de la Barca. In the midst of a variety of experiments—passages performed in Spanish, comparison of English translations, "original practices" staging, and improvisations that exceed those strictures—the director asked the audience to join the experiment by dividing, in the manner of the Spanish playhouses, so that the women sit above and the men below to hear certain scenes from Calderon's masterpiece *Life Is a Dream*. The spatial arrangement unexpectedly begins to connect to and intensify the effect of the poetic imagery: actors discover that certain gendered images can be played to separate parts of the now-gender-divided space, masculine imagery tied to base impulses and a lower physical position, feminine to idealized values and a loftier space, or, in another passage, where the heroine defines herself as symbolically uniting male and female in one, the cultural resonance of such a dissonant figure gains a somatically reinforced power. A fundamental resonance in the text is revealed with new force. (At the conclusion of the workshop, Spottiswoode confides enthusiastically that this is the kind of open-ended experiment that the London Globe needs to find the courage to do.)

Beyond the Isolated Production and Beyond Emory

But even with such striking freedom in choosing repertory, Theater Emory has chosen to expand from the model of isolated productions, each a closed and self-referential exploration, in a number of ways. Thematically related plays have been performed in rotating repertory (e.g., Shakespeare's *Midsummer Night's Dream* with Michael Gow's *Away*); entire theater seasons have been linked by thematic questions (e.g., a season devoted to "War" in 2007–8, or to "Self and Other" in 2008–9); explorations of particular playwrights (e.g., Henrik Ibsen and George Bernard Shaw) have extended across multiple seasons; and plays explored at Emory have been taken up by other theaters in shared productions—such as a workshop production of Shakespeare's *Measure for Measure* that led to a full staging at the Georgia Shakespeare Festival, or an adaptation of Beckett's short story *Enough* that traveled to the International Beckett Festival in Holland. Most ambitiously of all, Theater Emory twice initiated festivals engaging theaters across the city celebrating a living playwright in residence: the internationally regarded South African playwright Athol Fugard (1992–93) and, later, the rising American playwright Naomi Wallace (2001–2), elevating the level of theatrical ambition and collaborative communication across the city and drawing national attention to Atlanta's theater scene.

Beyond the Established Playtext: New Plays

The inauguration of the Playwriting Center of Theater Emory in 1988 opened a whole new dimension in the Theater's research. Focused on open-ended new play development (as opposed to driving the writing process toward a conventional and commercially viable conclusion), the various workshop processes range from one-day, in-progress public readings to fully rehearsed, semistaged treatments, to full productions, depending on the playwright's sense of the journey the play needs to take to its final form. Offering playwrights the resources of actors, dramaturgs, directors, designers, composers, and research specialists, in collaborative consultation, improvisation, and rehearsal of various kinds, with no pressure except to explore, the Playwriting Center not only reinvigorates and encourages playwrights—it also enriches students and audiences with new experiences that reenvision the dramatic text, not as a fixed, copyrighted object, but as a dynamic response to creative impulses, pressures, and opportunities. Pulitzer Prize–winning playwright Robert Schenkkan, long professionally diverted into screenwriting, returned to playwriting with the encouragement of Vincent Murphy, then head of the Playwriting Center. In 1998 *Handler*, Schenkkan's abandoned script centering on the metaphor of Appalachian snake-handlers, a piece that had stalled after a reading at the Sundance Playwriting Lab, found new life and new direction at Theater Emory's Playwriting Center, and later, in a premiere production at Actor's Express Theater in Atlanta. OBIE-winning playwright and director Robert O'Hara developed his *Antebellum*, a tense and angry exploration of oppositions in race, gender, and sexual orientation in an Atlanta setting, in workshops and then a professionally staged reading with design elements; the play premiered in its final form in 2009 at the Woolly Mammoth Theatre in Washington D.C. During academic year 2001–2, Arthur Kopit, internationally recognized American playwright, developed in readings and full production at Emory *The Discovery of America*, singled out by *New Yorker* critic John Lahr as one of the most exciting new scripts (still in development) that he had encountered in 2008.

> Having taken advantage of the Playwriting Center's open-ended workshop values, playwright Robert Schenkkan, returning to *Handler*, an unfinished script, and boldly throwing out half of the existing version, is at an impasse in imagining the second half of his hero's journey. At a pause in rehearsal, he looks across the room and sees an undergraduate student actress in conversation. His imagination begins to work, and a new scene occurs to him in which the hero meets a wild child—a woodland girl who is physically deformed. Improvisation and exploratory writing follow. By the end of the workshop, it is this child who escorts the protagonist on an almost mythic meeting with spiritual darkness that in time becomes the new climax of the drama.

Beyond the Established Playtext: When Inquiry Reassembles the Drama

Beyond developing new plays, processes of inquiry are also permitted to reshape and recontextualize canonical writings: anthology productions addressing various themes, authors, periods, and modes of theatricality have been mounted—exploring through a collection of contrasting scenes the drama of George Bernard Shaw; testing for connections between the pioneering women playwrights Roswitha of Gandersheim (tenth-century Saxony) and Gertrude Stein (twentieth-century Paris); staging a celebration of the drama, theater, and dramatic criticism of the English Restoration (a project that arose from a department faculty seminar); or distilling a compendium of the clown scenes in Shakespeare. All of these projects were devoted to using theatrical performance not as a substitute for scholarly analysis but as its own critical method, a mode suited to the discovery of what the philosopher Alain Badiou has called "theater-ideas":

> Theater is . . . the assemblage of extremely disparate components, both material and ideal, whose only existence lies in performance, in the act of theatrical representation. These components (a text, a place, some bodies, voices, costumes, lights, a public . . .) are gathered together in an event [that] directly produces . . . *theater-ideas*. . . . This means they cannot be produced in any other place or by any other means. It also means that none of the components taken separately is capable of producing theater-ideas, not even the text. The idea arises in and by performance. . . . The idea is irreducibly theatrical and does not exist before its arrival "on stage." (*A Handbook of Inaesthetics*, 1998)

Beyond the Established Playtext: Adaptation of Dramatic and Nondramatic Sources

Such dedication to the ideas produced *only* in performance can unseat the sealed-off sanctity of the text. Theater Emory has experimented with various forms of theatrical adaptations of great plays: British novelist, playwright, and dramaturg A. C. H. Smith in 1987 contributed a substantial body of new dialogue to the production of Shakespeare and Wilkins's imperfectly preserved play *Pericles*; audiences arriving for Brecht's *Schweyk* in spring of 1988 saw gigantic puppets portraying not Hitler and his cronies but Ronald Reagan and Oliver North; an adaptation of Goldsmith's classic comedy *She Stoops to Conquer* in 2006 featured not only a newly written prologue and epilogue devised for and addressed directly to the Emory audience, but gave the servant characters in the shadows of the original play an opportunity to comment skeptically on the principal action through period work-songs, drinking songs, patriotic anthems, and hymns. A new translation of Ibsen's *The Master Builder* in 1999 was devised as a collaboration between the turn-of-the-twentieth-century Norwegian playwright, an Emory dramaturg, and a prominent Atlanta playwright, Steve Murray.

Just as new plays in process have found further development at Theater Emory, so nondramatic texts have invoked theater-ideas in new theatrical adaptations. Nondramatic works by James Baldwin, Athol Fugard's journals, Marjorie Shostak's pivotal anthropological study of an African bushwoman, *Nisa*, and a sociological study of an American family struggling with mourning and child neglect, *Georgie Nobody* (based on a book titled *Pathways to Madness*, by Jules Henry), have all found theatrical life at Theater Emory, often in unexpected theatrical forms, incorporating music, choral reading, audience movement, or larger-than-life puppets.

In an off-site presentation of *Dreaming with an AIDS Patient*, and adaptation of a case study by Robert Bosnack, a group of hospitalized patients with advanced HIV/AIDS sit, stirring uneasily, their eyes darting in poignant anxiety and anticipation as if a secret were being told openly: an actor is recounting in words and dancelike movement a dream of a cowboy with the disease who envisions a lariat that suddenly spins and glows into a serpentine, scarlet image of his own embattled immune system. The unexpected power of the image is more than aesthetic.

Theatrical Inquiry beyond the Theater
Site-Specific and Emory-Themed Productions

Such processes of adaptation, letting theatrical form follow the compelling specifics of the source material, also has the potential to break apart the standard expectations of dramatic form or the ordinary exchange of a production with its audience. Theater Emory has invented productions that weave themselves specifically into their Emory setting: not only in site-specific productions of plays as such—such as a series of scenes from *Hamlet* that erupted in 1995 at unannounced times across campus (from Lullwater Park to the tennis courts) to suggest a theater without walls, or, in 2004, an itinerant production of Bernard-Marie Koltès's *Roberto Zucco* in the Michael Street parking deck, where the open space and impersonality of the parking structure became a manifestation of the antihero's existential isolation and nausea—but the principle has been taken further, too, in adaptations that respond specifically to Emory locations, history, and events.

A museum exhibition of classical statuary from the Louvre (an exhibition on the theme of ancient Rome in Africa) is enlivened with a production of Terence's *The Mother-in-Law* that begins in the Carlos Museum's lecture hall and proceeds through the exhibit, stopping to add to both the play and the exhibit historical commentary and questions about Terence's nearly hidden history as an assimilated African slave in the ancient Roman world. In 2005 a site-specific adaptation of Aristophanes' *Frogs*, an ancient Greek satirical comedy, turned to the question of whether theater can address ecology—the performance beginning in the Schwartz Theater Lab and concluding on the bridge over the Baker Woodlands, a preserved campus green space, where actors stood below the bridge among the trees and played a variety of poets and playwrights of the past, vying for the opportunity to voice ecological concerns in theatrical form. (Another site-specific performance project attempted to recover the Emory history—and the pre-Emory history—of the Baker Woodlands itself.) *30 Below*, a project developed in cooperation with Out-of-Hand Theater in 2003, featured a series of pieces, many of them student-authored, about coming-of-age issues in college life; these short pieces were performed both in the Mary Gray Monroe Theater in the Dobbs University Center and, alternatively, in a variety of adjacent campus spaces—open-air processionals, restrooms, and cars parked outside the building—unexpected encounters, heartfelt conversations, and youthful epiphanies, intimate issues played out in intimate settings.

> In a rehearsal for *What I Heard about Iraq*, a documentary theater piece about the causes of the American military campaign, an Iraqi immigrant who has been volunteering help with Arabic pronunciation for the play has agreed to answer questions by the all-student cast about his wartime experiences. (The students include two practicing Muslims, one from Chicago and one from Pakistan; a student from Mumbai; and several students of conservative backgrounds from rural Georgia. The text of the production has been altered to allow the students to add their own perspectives on current history.) When the guest describes his experience of torture at the hands of a local militia, his translator cannot go on, but breaks down and cries. Knowing the cast needs time to absorb and respect the experience that has been shared, the director instructs the cast, in silence, to collaborate in drawing a chalk outline of Iraq on the black-painted floor of the rehearsal hall; when the outline is complete, each student is invited to contemplate it and leave in her own time, ready to bring her own thoughts to the next rehearsal. This action is incorporated into the production.

Theatrical Inquiry beyond Theater

Perhaps the ultimate test of theater as a mode of inquiry would be to see theatrical methods used beyond the boundaries of theater—theatrical methods applied to other fields of inquiry. Two productions exemplify this theater-beyond-theater. One, *The Van Gogh Gallery*, positioned a variety of interdisciplinary and free-form performative expressions of the life and paintings of Vincent van Gogh as if they were exhibits in an art gallery—audience members wandered according to their individual trajectories from piece to piece, including three-dimensional stagings of famous paintings that the audience member was free to step into (in one, Van Gogh's painting of his own room, one would encounter Vincent's exasperated lover and then the artist's brother, Theo, both of whom would address the patron/audience member as van Gogh himself and reflect with him on the necessity of painting), or find dancers in specially colored costumes forming and disincorporating elements of Van Gogh's *Starry Night* (here reproduced as a dance floor), or enter a confession booth in which one might ask questions of a concealed actor playing van Gogh; and all the while one actor on a high platform recited memorized passages from van Gogh's journals as the artist's various self-portraits were projected onto her face. It was a multifaceted dialogue of history, biography, and art, and of painting with dance, performance art, and theater—new, innovative forms born of unbridled inquiry, exploration, and reflection.

For a second, and final, example of extratheatrical experiment, consider the *Family Project*, an innovative collaboration between Emory's MARIAL Center (a Sloan Foundation–funded endeavor to consider Myth and Ritual in American Life) and Theater Emory, to consider, through a scholarly conference, American theater as a chronicler of the American family: for one evening, actors (professional and student) performed ten scenes from ten different plays reflecting on the American family, each respectively representing a different decade of the twentieth century; on the next evening, with the aid of a panel of experts of various disciplines, the conference community reflected on the family through its dramatic representation. And, in a grand improvisation, the actors were invited to replay pivotal moments in their scenes with characters from different scenes, different plays, different decades intervening to talk with, aid, argue with each other, which in turn gave way to a final, richly energetic, metareflection from experts and audience.

This example—original enough to have no precedent in my experience—of using and respecting theater as a source of its own ideas and truths, while breaking the theater's own customary modes of presentation and creating innovative dialogue with other disciplines and forms, may serve as a summary example of the distinguishing, transformative vision of Theater Emory and theater studies. These adventures of burst boundaries have become the way for theater at Emory to manifest the teaching and research values of Emory itself in disciplinarily rooted yet unanticipated ways. Emory is, in this sense, reviving theater as a site of play, but a boundary-dissolving, nomadic play of the mind, always on the move across experience and disciplines:

> The public comes to the theatre to be struck. Struck by theatre-ideas. It does not leave the theatre cultivated, but stunned, fatigued (thought is tiring), pensive. Even in the loudest laughter, it has not encountered any satisfaction. It has encountered ideas whose existence it hitherto did not suspect. (Badiou, *Inaesthetics*, 1998)

CHAPTER 14

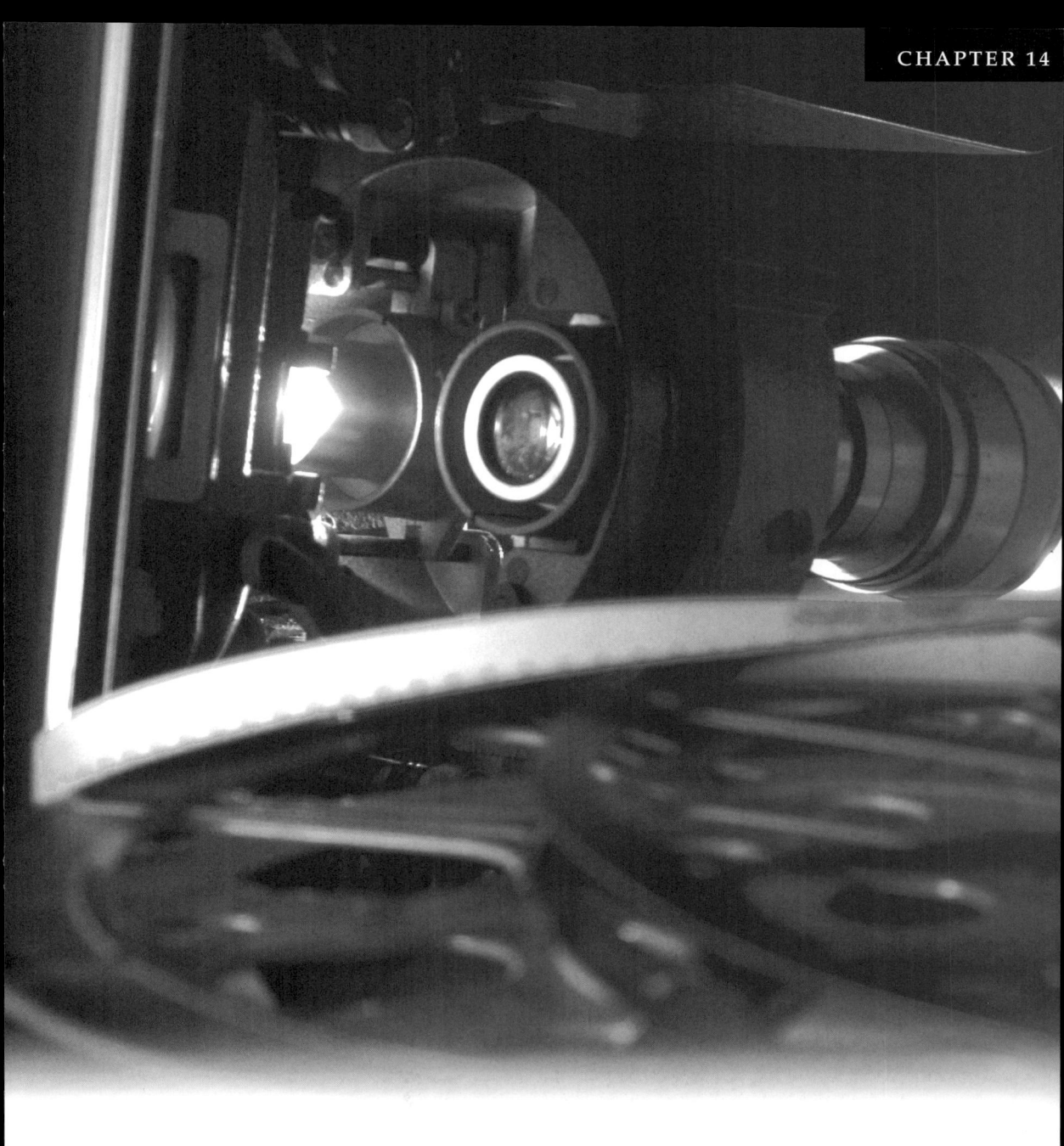

"IF YOU BUILD IT, [THEY] WILL COME"
The Birth and Growth of Film Studies at Emory
— DAVID COOK —

In another tale of building an academic department from the bottom up, David Cook describes the evolution of the Emory film studies program from its inception in the 1970s to its achieving departmental status thirty years later. Cook's promotion to full professor in 1986 brought deserved recognition, but development of the mature program required years of painstaking work. Cook ultimately reveals how even the smallest community of scholars can accomplish the seemingly insurmountable.

It's not cathartic.
Nothing ever is unless you're Sophocles.
—TERENCE DAVIES on his autobiographical documentary
Of Time and the City (2008)

THE HISTORY OF the Film Studies Department at Emory is the history of a series of migrations among three departments from 1973 to 2003, when the Emory Board of Trustees finally voted to give film studies departmental status. Highly conflicted, this history suggests both the tenuousness of a program's existence and the difficulty of creating a new, full-fledged department.

Many people, even faculty, do not understand that a program differs significantly from a department. A program is not just a small department. The real distinction is that a program exists at the discretion of the dean and the chair of the department of which it is part. Only the board of trustees has the authority to create or disband a department, but a program can be relocated, restructured, or removed on a whim. Moreover, in Emory College faculty tenure lines run through departments, and faculty cannot be tenured in a program. Departmental status can help to ensure the permanence of an academic unit, but a program exists at the mercy of more local forces. If these forces are benign, the program prospers. If they are not, the program must survive by nimbleness and wit. That was the case with film studies at Emory.

Sojourning in the English Department, 1973–86[1] | The study of film at Emory began innocuously enough but led to a long skirmish between me and the English Department, beginning in 1973. That was the year I was recruited by Emory's English Department from Purdue University, where I had been teaching in the English Department for two years. At Emory I was supposed to teach modern and Victorian literature (my fields at the University of Virginia, where I had earned my PhD) as well as one film course. At Purdue I had been teaching a film history course that I took over from Albert Fulton, a retiring English professor who had pioneered the course—incredibly—in the midst of World War II. Fulton had in fact written one of the first film history textbooks in English (*Motion Pictures: The Development of an Art from Silent Films to the Age of Television*, 1960) and had used it in his course ever since. It was good but out of date, so I started writing one of my own. This was in the form of handwritten lecture notes when I arrived at Emory, and I used them in my classes.

Everything in the Emory department seemed fine at first, but, as is often the case in academe, there was a skeleton in the closet: I replaced an assistant professor who had been denied tenure because his interests had drifted from eighteenth-century poetry to film. (This individual found another job immediately and went on to write the best-selling introduction-to-film textbook in the United States, currently in its tenth edition.) I also discovered a hostility toward film studies among the faculty who ran the department (i.e., those who had tenure). By November I was sufficiently panicked to start writing letters of inquiry to get out of what was beginning to look like an untenable (and untenurable) job. But fate intervened to save me and ensure that film studies would have at least a short-term future.

The South Atlantic Modern Language Association (SAMLA) was having its annual conference that November at the Biltmore Hotel in Midtown Atlanta, and I went to see if I could find anyone I knew from past lives. That did not happen, but I did run into a colleague from Emory, who introduced me to his editor at W. W. Norton & Company, where two other English Department colleagues had also published. I talked to the editor about my idea for a film history textbook based on my lecture notes, and within a month I had a contract for the book that would eventually become *A History of Narrative Film*, now in its fourth edition and, to date, the best-selling film history textbook in the United States, Canada, and the European Union. Having signed with a publisher who was also publishing three other tenured members of the Emory English Department—even though my book pushed me irrevocably into the arms of film studies—I was briefly protected by my publishing link to three of the department's power brokers. This meant that when I came up for tenure in 1976, the quality of my manuscript (or, at least, my publisher) could not be challenged. Nor was it. I was recommended for promotion and tenure by the only unanimous decision anyone in the department could remember. This glory, however, did not last.

The First Leak in the Levee | From 1977 to 1979 I held a fellowship from the John and Mary R. Markle Foundation to do research for a cultural history of television. The English Department conducted a national search for someone to replace me for two years, with the possibility of a permanent appointment for that person. Naturally, I was on the search committee. Our front-running finalist was a man whose C.V. showed that he had a PhD in English and film studies from the University of Maryland. When he came to Atlanta for his interview, he had laryngitis and was clearly laboring physically to answer standard interview questions, so we politely stopped asking them. In those days, credentials were not checked very closely, so no one thought to request a transcript.

The candidate from Maryland was offered the job, and in the fall of 1977 he came to relieve me of my courses. He arrived in September with a U-haul trailer and no place to live, so my family put him up for a couple of weeks while he looked for an apartment. He stored his furniture temporarily in our basement, later retrieving all of it but three chairs, one of which I am sitting on as I write this. The reason I have his chair is this: by mid-semester he was having problems teaching his classes, and by the end of the semester his students were furious at his incompetence. But since students are always upset about something, the warning signs were ignored. Then, just before classes began in fall 1978, he disappeared, leaving an open copy of Melville's *Bartleby the Scrivener* on the desk in his apartment. Much was made of this in the cover story in the *Atlanta Constitution* Sunday magazine several months later. In fact, the cover photograph showed a collection of Melville's short stories open on a desk, presumably as his had been, to the page in *Bartleby* where the title character first says to his employer, "I would prefer not to." The *Constitution*'s story characterized this temporary faculty member as something of an existential hero who had refused to conform to the "system" and courageously, if mysteriously, opted out of it. We learned, though, that he was not a hero at all but a good old-fashioned imposter. His credentials were faked, and the reason he could not answer our interview questions was not because he had laryngitis but because he did not have the answers. Understandably this incident further soured the English Department on film studies, which it had always thought of as fraudulent work. Now they had a real fraud to prove it.

In fairness I must say that not everyone in the English Department was hostile to film studies. With two of my tenured colleagues, for example, I cotaught courses in "Shakespeare and Film" and "Nineteenth-Century Fiction and Film." The Shakespeare course was especially significant, first because it was written up in a long article in the *Atlanta Constitution*, and second because John Palms, then the dean of Emory College, funded film rental for the course in the amount of one thousand dollars.

The Cost of the Show | Such funding was a not-insignificant issue for film courses during the 1970s and much of the 1980s. No films were available on videotape, laserdisc, or DVD, because those technologies had yet to be introduced. (The first videotape recorder, the Sony Betamax, was initially marketed to consumers in 1976; laserdisc appeared in 1989; DVD in 1997.) Films for institutional use had to be rented in 16mm gauge from companies like Films Inc., which had national distribution chains and could charge steep rental fees. The cost of a

single film course could easily exceed a thousand dollars and had to be raised from extradepartmental sources. After film studies had officially become a program, the College built rental funds into our budget starting in 1988, but before that film courses had to be funded ad hoc. There was, however, one alternative—purchasing 16mm films outright. This was quite difficult, because 16mm distributors did not like to sell their product and, in effect, compete with themselves. If they could be induced to sell at all, distributors often demanded fifteen hundred dollars to twenty-five hundred dollars a print.

In a 1975 meeting with Charles Lester, dean of the Graduate School, I explained this situation, and he offered to let me use funds left in his budget at the end of the fiscal year to buy 16mm prints for Emory. (I usually had a two-week window in which to do this, and it resulted in the acquisition of some pretty exotic films, since distributors would part with only their least-rented titles.) This arrangement lasted for three years, until I went on leave under the Markle Foundation grant, and I was able to buy twenty-two prints, now stored in the Candler Library and still (if rarely) used in classes today. Dean Lester was thus the first major administrative benefactor of film studies at Emory. He once told me that he believed in the importance of studying media because he had grown up in a small South Georgia town during the Depression, when the only access to the outside world was radio.

To research my television book, I had moved in 1978 to Los Angeles for a year. Within a year of my return, the first edition of *A History of Narrative Film* (1981) appeared, and I was able to use it as a textbook in the only film courses offered by the English Department—"Film History to 1938" and "Film History 1938 to the Present." I wanted to propose a two-semester film theory sequence, but the leadership of the department refused to support this on the grounds that, if approved, the courses would fall to me, making my entire course load film. This would never do in an English department.

But while the senior members of the department would not support new film courses, they refused to put ceilings on enrollments in the existing ones. The department was happy to have the numbers but did not want the academic stigma of offering too many film courses. During this time, Emory's film history classes typically had enrollments of over 75 students (and no teaching assistants). At one point, my "History of Television" course drew 185 students in the White Hall auditorium (I did have three TAs for this one, who mainly served for crowd control). As a matter of survival I began to use multiple-choice tests in these large courses, only confirming departmental suspicions that film studies was low-grade work.

While I could feel pleased with my work by the early 1980s—I had been granted tenure, had earned a two-year fellowship, had published a well-received book, and was teaching the English Department's largest courses—film studies at Emory was hardly secure. Some senior colleagues told me that I was overreaching. Although I felt that I had earned a chance to be considered for promotion to full professor, it seemed to me that the way was blocked until other, more senior associate professors had been considered first. So I exercised my right

David Cook

to put myself up for review in 1984 and was rejected by a vote of seven to two. The reason given was that my outside letters were insufficient. I learned, however, that all six of those letters supported my case, and I was given copies of them at the annual conference of the Society for Cinema Studies (now the Society for Cinema and Media Studies, or SCMS) in Madison, Wisconsin, later that year. This alone was grounds for an appeal to the Faculty Council, which was in charge of these matters during the 1980s and 1990s. But because the vote had been so lopsided I was advised instead to request another review. This time the vote was five to five, another full professor having joined the ranks of the department in fall 1985 (the eminent postcolonial theorist Gayatri Chakravorty Spivak, who was uniquely attuned to issues of marginalization). The dean interpreted the vote as negative so that it could be appealed to the Faculty Council. In November 1985 the council returned my case to the department, indicating that it contained procedural irregularities requiring a new vote. This produced a six-to-four majority, and I was promoted to full professor.

On January 28, 1986, the day of the space shuttle *Challenger* explosion, the dean called me into his office to inform me that I had been promoted. (Through leaks, I already knew; confidentiality is, by and large, an academic fairy tale.) The process had been so acrimonious, however, that he felt he could not put me back into the English Department, so he did what I had suggested more than a year before. With unceremonious haste he took me out of the English Department and put me into the recently established Department of Theater Studies, adding "and Film" to its name. To give film studies the nominal heft of an actual program he pulled an additional tenure-track faculty line from the English Department budget and transferred it into the new Department of Theater and Film Studies. He told me that, as far as he was concerned, the Film Studies Program would be a two-person operation for the duration.

The Department of Theater and Film Studies, 1986–92 | The abruptness of the dean's decision was underscored by the fact that he had not yet informed the chair of theater studies about it. In fact, as I was leaving the dean's office, I bumped into this person (Professor James Flannery) on his way in, where the dean informed him of my transfer, without giving him any choice in the matter. (He was subsequently heard to remark on several occasions that film studies had been "parachuted" into his department against his will, which was undeniably true.) Flannery pretty much left the program alone, though, because of issues in theater studies to distract him.

Nevertheless, film studies was eventually caught in the crossfire. That was because Geoffrey Reeves, the artistic director of Theater Emory, was a fanatical *cinéaste*—that is, he loved movies, and art films in particular. He had grown up in a suburb of London at the high-water mark of *Cahiers du Cinéma* and the British New Cinema movement, and he wanted to see 35mm (i.e., theatrical-gauge) movies at Emory. In the spring of 1987 he proposed that we go to the dean and ask for twenty-four thousand dollars to buy two used projectors at seven thousand dollars apiece, with the remaining ten thousand dollars as the first installment of an eventual hundred thousand dollars to purchase 35mm prints. With these resources, we could start a very respectable film society that would benefit us both.

I was dubious about the idea, given the penny-pinching of all the deans I had ever known, but we went and asked anyway. Amazingly Dean David Minter agreed to give us the money almost as soon as the words were out of our mouths. I will never know exactly why, except that he had a particularly high opinion of Geoffrey's talents, but, in any case, this is how the two 35mm projectors came to be placed in White Hall 205, where they support film series to this day.

A year later, in the spring of 1988 Geoffrey fell from grace, and without tenure he was let go. The dean explained that he had made this decision because the personal antagonisms within the department were undermining its effectiveness. The dean also decommissioned the department chair and appointed in his place an untenured associate dean of the Graduate School. *Sic transit gloria*.

In 1987 the Department of Theater and Film Studies had conducted a national search to fill the second film studies line that Dean Minter had transferred to the department. Because I was a film historian, the new person had to be a film theorist for balance. Any academically respectable film studies program must have a strong history and a strong theory component; everything else—criticism, screenplay writing, and even production—are add-ons to these essentials. At the end of the search, we were able to recruit Gaylyn Studlar, a newly minted PhD from the University of Southern California (she had already taught for a year at North Texas State University), whose work challenging the theoretical position of Laura Mulvey had recently caused quite a stir among film and feminist scholars.[2]

Studlar was quite a catch for a two-person program that had existed as an academic unit for only a year, and she knew it. By the end of her first year, she had become so disgruntled with the program's lack of prominence and power that she began to consider leaving, and in fact had another job offer. We were able to retain her by going to the dean to request a third faculty line, which he eventually granted, so that we began another national search in the fall of 1988, this time for a more specialized film historian with a PhD, like Studlar's, in cinema studies. We ended up hiring Matthew Bernstein, an economic film historian whose dissertation at the University of Wisconsin, later the book *Hollywood Independent* (1994), had been a critical biography of Hollywood producer Walter Wanger. Like Studlar, Bernstein was a dedicated and accomplished teacher, and he brought to us the perspective of one of the best PhD programs in the country. To no one's surprise, Studlar was promoted to associate professor and tenured in the Department of Theater and Film Studies in 1992, and Bernstein in the Institute of Liberal Arts in 1995.

A Collector Possessed | Robert Troutman was an outrageously successful real estate speculator married to a cousin of Emory alumnus, trustee, and benefactor Pollard Turman (Law 1943, Honorary 1973). Troutman had a passion for collecting, and by far his most extensive collection was an archive of the world's greatest films on videotape. This collection was categorized by genre and sorted into a database for cross-referencing by titles, actors, production years, and so on. He had begun the collection in the late 1970s, before films on VHS became widely available through retailers like Blockbuster, and many of the tapes were of poor quality; some were barely legible. But for research this was an extremely valuable archive, and Troutman dangled it in front of us (i.e., Emory in general and film studies in particular).

My relationship with Robert Troutman began in 1985, while I was still in the English Department, and continued through 1988, when he let us copy some of his films to create our own archives. Ostensibly, Troutman wanted to donate his entire collection to Emory, in exchange for which the University would construct a building, or at least devote part of an existing building, to house it. I spent many Saturday afternoons at his house on West Wesley Road chatting with him and giving him advice about the collection—for instance, which films fit which genres. I was encouraged to do this by Turman, with whom I had several meetings at his foundation offices downtown, and by Dean Minter.

Eventually, in spring 1989, Troutman and Emory reached an agreement that the films would be housed on the fourth floor of the Candler Library, and vans were dispatched to his house to pick up the tapes. When the vans arrived, he refused to surrender the tapes, claiming that Emory had misrepresented its intentions to store them properly. We later learned that he had negotiated a better deal with the University of Southern California, where they are stored today in a climate-controlled archive specially built for the purpose—and are virtually worthless. Maybe all he ever really wanted was a distinctive resting place for all those tapes, understanding their transitory value. Since he died unexpectedly in 1990, we will never know for sure, but the publicity surrounding the botched donation attracted the attention of another collector, whose films were stored on a much more viable medium.

This was John Croaker, owner of Laserdisc of Smyrna, the largest distributor of laserdiscs in the southeastern United States. Film studies had bought a significant number of titles from Laserdisc of Smyrna, because they were more user-friendly in class than tapes, in terms of both accessibility and image quality. Croaker knew about us from these transactions, but the catalyst for his donation was gratitude: his wife had been saved from an unspecified life-threatening situation at Emory University Hospital in 1991, and he wanted to return the favor. So, with us in mind, he donated over ten thousand film titles on laserdisc to the Candler Library, together with state-of-the-art electronics equipment to create a dedicated screening space in Candler (the Croaker Room), where students and faculty can watch and study films. His donation included every title available in the United States and Canada at the time, so by fall of 1991, film studies had access to the Croaker Collection for all of its teaching needs and the tapes that Troutman had lent to us for research. All we needed now was a rationalized curriculum.

> *I worried at first that our MA graduates would have trouble finding jobs, but their placement rate was nearly 100 percent—they worked for advertising agencies, public relations firms, film festivals, and nonprofit film centers like IMAGE; some entered PhD programs and law schools.*

Building Curriculum | We already had a minor in film studies, and we had a handful of graduate students from the ILA. The next step involved proposing a major to the Curriculum Committee, but we needed a fourth faculty position to staff a major. The College did not want to give us a full-time, tenure-track line this time, but we were able to shake loose a two-year postdoctoral Mellon Fellowship. After a national competition, we selected Robin Blaetz, who had just finished her PhD in cinema studies at New York University. She came to teach avant-garde and experimental cinema, as well as courses in Latin American and other national/regional cinemas. We now had one faculty member representing each of the three major cinema studies PhD-granting institutions in the country—USC, Wisconsin, and NYU. (At this point, the irony of my position within the program began to emerge. As program director, I wanted to hire only the best people with the best training and best degrees in film studies, and I did. But these same people tended to look at me as "undertrained" because my PhD was in English. At some level, the perspective of my colleagues that I was an outsider never quite disappeared.)

In 1991, shortly after Robin arrived, the department proposed a major concentration in film studies, which, after some tinkering, was approved. Then, in response to demand from students in the ILA who had come to Emory expecting to study film at the graduate level, we proposed an MA program. By this time David Minter had stepped down as dean of Emory College and had been temporarily replaced by George Jones as acting dean, while a national search was conducted for a "permanent" replacement. George was also dean of the Graduate School, and both the College and the Graduate School seemed sympathetic to us. At any rate, our proposal for the MA program made it clear that we conceived of it as the first step toward a PhD program, but we were advised that because of our small faculty we should test the MA program first.

Our proposal for the MA program specified stipends for the candidates we admitted, at the rate of six a year. It was a two-year program, so we would have twelve students in residence in any given year once we started. The program was approved without stipends in 1992, but with the understanding that these would be forthcoming in future years, and that, as we intended, the MA program would be an entrée to a film studies PhD (The Graduate School did let us give our students tuition waivers). As it turned out, none of these commitments were kept, and we became one of a handful of programs in the Graduate School granting only the master's degree, and the only one that did not offer its candidates stipends. So while our MA students did not have to pay tuition, they had to support themselves through part-time jobs, loans, spousal generosity, or some combination of these.

Under these conditions, it amazed me that anyone would apply to us at all, but in fact our MA program became a lesson in the truth of the cliché—from a movie, of course (*Field of Dreams*, 1989)—"If you build it, he will come." From 1993 on we never had fewer than twelve MA candidates in residence, usually more; add to that the number of PhD dissertations we were directing for the ILA, and we averaged twenty graduate students in our ranks each year. I worried at first that our MA graduates would have trouble finding jobs, but their placement rate was nearly 100 percent—they worked for advertising agencies, public relations firms, film festivals, and nonprofit film centers like IMAGE; some entered PhD programs and law schools. By 1995 we also had the eighth-highest number of undergraduate humanities majors in the College, and we taught a significant number of elective students. I used to chart the flow of students through our courses year by year; by the end of the 1990s we averaged over 560 annually and had, on average, 50 to 60 majors. I thought we had arrived.

The Graduate Institute for Liberal Arts (ILA), 1992–2003

To back up slightly: in spring 1992 a fourth-year review was scheduled for a member of the Department of Theater and Film Studies, of which I was acting chair—the chair having gone on a semester's leave. The subject of this review was a person on the theater side of the department. The review committee was dominated by the film studies faculty, however, because, in a bizarre set of circumstances, we were the only tenured people in the department, with the exception of Jim Flannery, who also sat on the committee. (At this point, even the department chair herself, Alice Benston, was not tenured.) For us, there was no issue of preference involved: we evaluated the candidate's credentials scrupulously and reached a determination that he could never get through Emory's rigorous tenure process, so we voted to terminate him at the end of his fourth year. We saw this as fair for both the individual and the University, and we sent our recommendation to the Faculty Council in the form of a five-page letter. The letter, which I wrote and then rewrote four more times, presented an open-and-shut case, but the Faculty Council kept returning it to us, demanding more information, until there was finally no more information to give. This dance stretched through much of the spring semester of 1992, at the end of which the Faculty Council refused to accept our recommendation, returning it to us without apparent recourse. It went forward to the provost and president and trustees, so that the candidate was permitted to stay on the faculty and proceed toward tenure.

Less than two weeks later, David Bright, who had become dean of Emory College in fall 1991, telephoned to inform me that effective immediately film studies would be separated from theater studies and "transferred administratively" to the ILA. (We were also moved physically, from the site of our former department in the World War II–era temporary building Annex B, into the ILA's premises on the third floor of the Humanities Building, now the Callaway Center North.) There had been no prior discussion about this transfer with either film studies or the ILA, and neither party was given a choice in the matter. Things had been arranged so that we could never be involved in a theater studies promotion case again.

Our transfer into the ILA meant that we no longer had departmental status and the protection that comes with it. This was not a problem so long as Dana White was acting director of the ILA, because his own historical research included film and television. Over the summer he and I put together a memorandum of agreement clearly stating the program's relationship with the ILA, which he and I and Dean Bright signed in fall 1992, after the ILA faculty had also agreed to the terms.

A year later, a new director came to the ILA. Though a scholar, he had also been a federal government bureaucrat for ten years and possessed all the skills required for governmental infighting. He declared our memorandum of agreement to be merely "a document of the moment," and with the dean's approval the agreement was set aside. In his view our MA program had no place in the ILA, nor could the film studies faculty alone evaluate our own colleagues for promotion and tenure; this would be done by all tenured professors of the ILA. The dean heard that we would not allow other ILA faculty to teach film (a ridiculous rumor, because half of the ILA was on our associate faculty list). In short, the director's low opinion of film studies undermined faculty morale and soon drove Gaylyn Studlar to accept another job at the University of Michigan.

Fortunately, at this point film studies came under the beneficent interest of a member of the College administration. There were two key benefits to this. One was the physical removal of our offices from the ILA's main site into the World War II–era temporary building Annex C, where we would be out of the ILA's sight, if not mind. The other was to associate film studies gradually with the performing arts as part of a new initiative to build a performing arts center, pulling us away from the orbit of the ILA. We still served on ILA committees, went to ILA faculty meetings, and so on, but we were slowly drifting away.

> *We prided ourselves that we did not yet have rifts and cleavages like other departments, but we also knew that this situation could not last forever. I knew that we had become a full-fledged academic unit when we had our first nasty battle over tenure.*

There was soon another problem to address, however: when Studlar left, the program lost her personnel line until we could prove that we needed a film theorist. This would be comparable to asking the History Department to prove that it needed a specialist in American history, or for the English Department to prove that it needed a Shakespearean. We had forty majors at the time in a concentration whose core required them to take a two-sequence theory course. The program could not exist without a full-time person to teach theory, but somehow the College (and, it turned out, the Graduate School) thought that this "person" could be cobbled together from the faculty of other departments.

Challenged to prove that we could not find people already on the payroll to teach these courses, we interviewed everyone with the slightest qualifications during the spring of 1996. We then completed a self-study, bringing in outside evaluators who told us what we already knew: film studies could not exist without a full-time theorist. (They also said that our program was the best of its kind in the country.) In one of his last acts as dean, at the end of 1996 David Bright restored the line, yielding to the logic of keeping intact what was now deemed to be a prestigious program. After this experience, all of my strategic efforts went toward achieving departmental status for film studies.

With the restored line, we hired a film theorist, Angela Dalle Vacche, who had taught at Yale for ten years. She had published one important book (*The Body in the Mirror: Shapes of History in Italian Cinema*, 1992) and had another one forthcoming (*Cinema and Painting: How Art Is Used in Film*, 1996), and she interviewed well, so for a while things went along very nicely. One of the great things about film studies (and also its weakness), as both a program and a department, is its small size. We were so small, in fact, and our offices so close together, that we could have meetings in the hall or on the phone (and, later, by email). We had conventional meetings only twice a year, when we would gather, usually for about three hours, to set our schedule. We prided ourselves that we did not yet have rifts and cleavages like other departments, but we also knew that this situation could not last forever.

I knew that we had become a full-fledged academic unit when we had our first nasty battle over tenure, even though we were still a satrapy of the ILA. In 1999 an assistant professor of film studies, Robin Blaetz, came up for tenure and received a weak positive vote, because the manuscript on which her hopes were pinned had been inexplicably rejected by SUNY-Albany Press, just two weeks before her decision. I thought this highly suspect, because I had seen a letter from her editor, dated a month before, authorizing her to select and caption illustrations for the book. I will never know what forces intervened to ruin this person's chances, but ruined they were. Arguing her case before an ill-disposed Faculty Council, I staked my reputation on the faith that her manuscript, which I regarded highly, would find another, better publisher within the year. (It did: the University of Virginia Press published it the following year as *Visions of the Maid: Joan of Arc in American Film and Culture*, and it was named a CHOICE Outstanding Academic Title.) The Faculty Council rejected her candidacy almost unanimously. She appealed the decision, unsuccessfully, and soon left for Mount Holyoke College, where she is currently an associate professor and chair of the film studies program.

The bad feelings created by this process healed over time, and the faculty was able to reach agreement over the major issues facing the program in the early years of this century. For example, in 2001 we were able to replace Blaetz with Nina Martin, a new PhD from Northwestern University, which has one of the best graduate film studies programs in the country. Nina came to us as a specialist in avant-garde experimental cinema and women's film, and she became an excellent teacher during her first five years. On the other hand, our hire from Yale turned out to be a problematic teacher and colleague, and we had to deny her tenure, a long, painful process that no one felt good about. Yet she went on to become an associate professor of literature, communication, and culture at the Georgia Institute of Technology, where she has since published three more books.

To replace her in the theory position, we were able to hire Karla Oeler in 2002, a graduate of Yale, whose PhD was in comparative literature. Although she was not in cinema studies per se (her dissertation was on the novels of Dostoyevsky), her theoretical sophistication and the experience of assisting/teaching film courses at Yale made her more than qualified for the job. She turned into a great teacher and wrote a book extending the focus of her dissertation from literature to film (*A Grammar of Murder: Violent Scenes and Film Form*).

Meanwhile, Martin lost her bid for tenure in 2005. Even though she was about to publish a book with the University of Illinois Press (*Sexy Thrills: Undressing the Erotic Thriller*, 2006) and was unanimously recommended for promotion by the film studies faculty, the College Promotion and Tenure Committee rejected her, and the following year she left to become director of the film studies program at Connecticut College. She was the third woman in a row to be denied tenure in film studies, and this began to look like a pattern of discrimination. In truth it was more a combination of bad judgment on several levels, and it was mitigated when Karla Oeler earned tenure in 2007.

The last part of this story begins with Steven Sanderson, who replaced David Bright as dean of Emory College after a national search. Sanderson was a political scientist by training with a deep appreciation of film, and he helped us to raise our profile three ways. First, when I explained to him our need to move from programmatic to departmental status, he asked me to prepare a proposal that he could present to the board of trustees. The proposal was, I thought, persuasive and asked for no new resources. It was nevertheless rejected by the board, to be revisited at some future date.

The second thing that Dean Sanderson did was to fund a 35mm film series of international festival winners, which was so successful that it became a regular part of the College budget. For the next six years, I programmed a variably themed 35mm series each semester, introducing the films and holding discussion sessions afterward.

The third thing he did for film studies was quite inadvertent (or maybe not). Shortly before he resigned as dean to become president and CEO of the Wildlife Conservation Society in New York City, in 2001 he recommended tenure for a faculty member in the Institute for Women's

Studies, which, like film studies and African American studies, was a program rather than a department. According to College bylaws, this was "illegal," so Robert Paul, who succeeded Sanderson as dean, and Acting Provost Howard (Woody) Hunter had to legalize it somehow. Their solution was to propose to the trustees that departmental status be granted to all three programs, and this worked. In fall 2003 Dean Paul wrote to inform me that our proposal to become a department had been approved. This was something we had been fighting for since 1991. If, in the end, we became a department by default, that was good enough for me.

But I could never escape the lingering sense that we were not really welcome, because we had created ourselves out of whole cloth. Other programs that had become departments over time—Jewish studies, African American studies, women's studies—had been mandated originally by the administration. We had not. We began as one person in the English Department in 1973 and by 2003 had grown into a full-fledged department, with four full-time faculty members, six adjunct faculty, numerous teaching assistants, an administrative assistant (named, appropriately, Annie Hall), and a secretary. We had a thriving major concentration and MA program, both with generous budgets, and we occupied the front ground floor of a building (Rich Memorial) with some of the best views on campus. And we had done this ourselves—not without occasional help and encouragement from the College and University—in the face of both personal and institutional opposition. I will always be proud of what we accomplished. There would be no Film Studies Department at Emory today but for the sheer will of a handful of people, without much power, who just would not let the idea go away.

GUY REDVERS LYLE AND THE BIRTH OF RESEARCH LIBRARIES AT EMORY

— ERIC NITSCHKE *and* MARIE NITSCHKE —

Coauthors and retired husband-and-wife librarians Eric and Marie Nitschke present an articulate, professional, and personal biography of Guy Redvers Lyle, the director of libraries at Emory from 1954 to 1973. Born in 1907 to parents who had traversed the Atlantic from Great Britain to Canada, Lyle followed family tradition when he pioneered changes in library structure and focus that ultimately outlasted his own remarkable life. Among his many contributions to Emory during his nearly two-decade tenure, Lyle oversaw the addition of more than seven hundred thousand volumes to the Emory collections and led the proposal for an advanced studies library, the ten-story Robert W. Woodruff Library that opened in 1969.

WHEN GUY LYLE came to Emory in 1954, the University library was housed in an attractive but unimposing structure, the 1926-vintage Asa Griggs Candler Library, at the east end of the Quadrangle. It shared this space with University administrative offices and the Library School. The collection was small, fewer than 275,000 volumes.[1] With Lyle's arrival, the library's modest presence on campus began to change. By the time of his retirement two decades later, the library had expanded into a towering new building overlooking the Quadrangle. Its outlook had changed, too. No longer primarily a college library paying the greatest attention to the education of the undergraduates, it now aimed to be a research library focusing on the scholarly interests of all its constituents.

Lyle was forty-six years old when he accepted the position at Emory. He was already well known in the library profession for his numerous articles and books, his work in library professional organizations, and his thought-provoking public speeches, delivered with charm and wit in his native Canadian accent. Tall and lean, with the craggy good looks of an outdoorsman, he did not fit the stereotypical image of a librarian.

As director of libraries, he had as his major responsibility the management of the Asa Griggs Candler Library, the main library on campus at the time. He was also expected to serve "in an advisory capacity to the deans and directors" of the other libraries in the University including the library at Oxford, and the libraries in all of the professional schools. As he suggested in his autobiography, "University Librarian" might have been a more appropriate title for his position since each of the other libraries retained its independence.

Soon after he arrived Lyle made an inventory of "library needs" that he had discovered in the Candler Library. "Increased book funds" were at the top of his list. "Additional stack space" was next, followed by space for a variety of purposes, including recordings, newspapers, periodicals, typing, and reserve readings for classes. He wanted the stacks to be opened to library users, and the building to be air-conditioned. A larger staff would be required to handle all this, along with additional space where they could work.[2]

The timing of Lyle's arrival and planning was fortunate. The administrative offices were scheduled to move from the Candler Library into the new Administration Building as soon as construction on it was completed in 1955. Lyle wanted to make sure that the best use was made of the new space for the library. President Goodrich White appointed a committee to visit leading university libraries in the East and come up with a plan. Meanwhile, Lyle was busy building support for the library, first with a report to the faculty, then with articles in the student newspaper and the alumni magazine.[3] The following May, the board of trustees approved the plan for "remodeling and refurnishing the Asa Griggs Candler Library."[4] The final plan included "a proposal to divide the thirty-two-foot-high Reading Room . . . by installing a new floor at midpoint all the way across the room." It was not a happy choice aesthetically, but it provided "three-quarters of all the usable new space" in the renovation.[5] Emory used its own work crews for the renovation, which meant that workers were often called away to handle emergencies elsewhere on campus,[6] delaying work. Finally, however, on November 15, 1957, an open house was held to celebrate the completion of the remodeling. Despite the happy achievement, Lyle and others knew that this building would soon be outgrown.

He began cultivating friends for the library among influential figures in the community, through a series of informal book talks in the newly refurbished Candler Room in the library.[7] Trustee Henry Bowden was among these. Newly elected as chair of the board after the death of his predecessor Charles Howard Candler Sr., Bowden had also been a member of the committee appointed by President White to make plans for the Candler renovation, and soon he would become a part of the "Troika" that temporarily headed the University between President Walter Martin's resignation in 1962 and the appointment of President Sanford Atwood in 1963. Once again the circumstances were favorable for the library. Bowden had seen the libraries at Princeton and Harvard, and "learned that a research library can be a great service to the public as well as the world of learning."[8]

There had been some talk of building an addition on to the back (the east side) of the Candler Library to relieve the space crunch, but Lyle had a different vision. Harvard had built an undergraduate library in the late forties, incorporating some eight thousand volumes from the main library and making them available in user-friendly areas for the undergraduates.[9] Other universities began to follow this pattern of building a new undergraduate library. Lyle thought the Candler Library was ideally suited to be an undergraduate library, and proposed that a new library for advanced studies be built instead of merely expanding Candler. The undergraduate library would "meet the need of the beginning general education courses where the student is *dependent upon teaching*," while the library for advanced studies would offer research materials for students and scholars.[10] In the six years since Lyle's arrival, the number of departments offering the PhD degree had increased from seven to fourteen. Lyle made the case that a strong research library was "vital" to support this growing graduate program. In November 1962 the board of trustees gave its approval, and Bowden appointed a committee to begin work on the plans.[11]

The resulting ten-story Robert W. Woodruff Library for Advanced Studies was completed by the beginning of the 1969 fall term. At the dedication ceremony on October 31 that year, George Healey, curator of rare books at Cornell University, said, "One cannot doubt that this library is Emory's highest pinnacle. But it is also, and at the same time, its deepest foundation."[12] Structurally, it was impressive, but Lyle recognized its shortcomings.

In his final annual report before retirement, Lyle noted that Emory had acquired its millionth volume, an occasion for celebration. He pointed out, however, that the "accomplishment says nothing about the quality of the library, nothing about how well the library is keeping abreast of current teaching and research needs; neither does it afford a clue as to the use made of the library." He emphasized "the library's financial need" in order "to realize its potential of service to the faculty and students as well as to the scholarly community at large." Unfortunately, he reported "the library's situation has taken a turn for the worse," by which he meant that the University could no longer easily afford the "high-cost research materials upon which the long-term quality of a university library depends." He felt that a new director with "more financial punch" would be able to make a difference,[13] and in time, new directors were able to do that; but he had laid the foundation. The research library's new commanding presence just off the Quadrangle could no longer be overlooked.

In 1964, when plans for the new library were being finalized, Lyle had been invited to give Emory's summer Commencement address. He spoke then about the "great new library" that would soon be "rising on the Emory campus." He anticipated not only the research collection that it would house but also the uses to which its collection and services would be put:

[The library] . . . will stand as a symbol of what Emory has tried to offer you in the way of an education:
A vision of your cultural inheritance but an awareness that it combines both wisdom and myth;
A personal philosophy of life which obligates you to think things out by yourself instead of accepting whatever happens to be the prevailing pattern of belief;
A knowledge of the tools which will enable you to acquire and test facts;
And finally, what has been expressed by another more simply and forcibly than I can state it, "a sense of morality," which will help you to direct what you learn "in favor of humanity and not against it."[14]

While at Emory, Lyle continued to contribute to professional journals, publish books,[15] accept speaking engagements, and actively participate in library organizations. His role as a

Where Courageous Inquiry Leads: *The Emerging Life of Emory University*

Robert W. Woodruff Library

founder of the Association of Southeastern Research Libraries (ASERL) in 1956 is especially noteworthy. He also returned to the classroom several times, teaching summer semesters in the library schools at Keio University in Japan (1957) and at the University of California, Berkeley (1968), and beginning his retirement as a professor during the winter semester of 1973 at the University of Puerto Rico. Among the many honors he received, the Joseph W. Lippincott award from the American Library Association, presented to him at the time of his retirement, provided good testimony to his achievements when it recognized him

> for devotion to the improvement of libraries and librarianship, for excellence and versatility, and for being a successful library administrator, inspiring library educator and a dedicated and active participant in all levels of professional organizations.[16]

In a section titled "Aspirations," in Lyle's last annual report, he called attention to the work of an ASERL committee investigating the establishment of a computerized bibliographic network in the Southeast. The following year, ASERL established SOLINET, the Southeastern Library Network, which revolutionized bibliographic verification, shared cataloging, and interlibrary loan, as he had anticipated that it would. Few on campus remember him now, but the central place that he created for the library at Emory endures.

Life before and after Emory[17] | A Canadian by birth, Lyle was the son of Barr Colony settlers who had migrated from Great Britain to Saskatchewan in 1903. Lyle was born there, in the town of Lloydminster, on October 30, 1907. His father, a prominent citizen, served on the town council, as mayor, and in the provincial Legislative Assembly, but he was greatly changed by his service in World War I. Upon his return from the war, he began drinking heavily, became abusive to Lyle's mother, and they separated. In 1921 Lyle's mother moved with her children to Edmonton, in the neighboring province of Alberta, during Lyle's second year of high school. The only teacher he remembered "with any degree of appreciation" from high school was his history teacher, Walter E. Edmonds, who prophetically gave him a graduation gift of Edmonds's writings titled "In a College Library." Lyle was accepted at the University of Alberta and took a part-time job in a branch library of the Edmonton Public Library. He was influenced by his classics professor, William Hardy Alexander, from whom he received "some comprehension of what real education is all about," but none of his university courses, including Professor Alexander's, required use of the library.

The work in the public library provided financial support for Lyle while he was a student, and appealed to his love of books and reading, but he did not think of it as a career. Soon after graduating from the university, he took a job overseeing cattle being shipped on a freight train from Edmonton to Montreal with the hope of getting a working passage to London from there. Along the way, a conductor talked him into trying his luck in New York instead. Once there, a letter of introduction from the librarian of the Edmonton Public Library provided his entrée into the New York Public Library and the beginning of what would become an illustrious career in librarianship.

Robert W. Henderson, chief of the stack division, was Lyle's supervisor at New York Public and encouraged Lyle to enroll in Columbia University's School of Library Service. Lyle graduated in 1929 with a BS degree in library science, the standard professional degree for librarians at the time. A month later, he was hired as the librarian of Antioch College in Yellow Springs, Ohio. Antioch's curriculum of "self-directed study" was tailor-made for promoting good library use, turning the library into "a kind of laboratory or workshop for practically all courses." Lyle's experience here "determined" his "thinking about the purpose and administration of college libraries" ever after.

While at Antioch, Lyle began his activities with the American Library Association and published his first articles and books. At his initial ALA meeting, he had the good fortune to meet Margaret Elizabeth White of Nashville, who became his wife on November 27, 1930. In the summers of 1930 through 1932, he returned to Columbia to earn his MS degree in library science. The first of the Lyles' four children was born during the Antioch years also.

In 1935 Lyle accepted a position teaching in the Library School at the University of Illinois, which brought in a better income for his growing family. While he did not find teaching to be his forte, a project he directed in his library administration class was considered so innovative at the time that it rated an article in the *Christian Science Monitor*.[18] He asked six of his students to produce a film that would show freshmen how the library could be used intelligently to prepare for their classes and produce their term papers. The American Library Association, recognizing the potential of this medium for library instruction, asked to make it available for rent to other libraries.

After a year in the classroom, Lyle moved back to the work that he liked best, library administration. He became librarian at the Women's College of the University of North Carolina in Greensboro in 1936. In the happy and productive years that followed, Lyle received strong support from the college administration enabling him to improve the library's collection, increase the size and salaries of its staff, and provide better services and facilities. A substantial grant from the Carnegie Corporation buttressed these efforts. Professionally Lyle became a prominent figure, writing a regular column for the *Wilson Library Bulletin*,[19] and serving as chair of the College Library Advisory Board (predecessor of the Association of College and Research Libraries), member of the Council of the American Library Association, president of the North Carolina Library Association, and chair of the ACRL Publications Committee. For two summers he taught again in library schools, first at Louisiana State University, then at the University of North Carolina. In 1941–42, he took leave from the Women's College to teach for another year at the University of Illinois, and while there he took graduate courses in American literature. During these years, he also began to write his best-known book, *The Administration of the College Library*, which would become the standard text in the field.

In October 1944 Louisiana State University invited Lyle to become director of libraries, and he accepted. In his ten years there, he was able to strengthen the staff and collections, while also taking the lead in planning and obtaining support for a new library building. Lyle's *Administration of the College Library*[20] came out soon after his arrival at LSU, and he published two more books while he was there: *A Bibliography of Christopher Morley*[21] and *I Am Happy to Present*.[22] He continued his participation in state and national professional organizations, chairing the Reference Section of the Louisiana Library Association and the University Libraries Section of ACRL, then moving on to the presidency of ACRL. In addition to these activities, Lyle's reputation as a public speaker grew during these years, and he was in demand on the lecture circuit.

Lyle moved to Emory before LSU's new library was begun. At Emory, he would again be challenged to plan a new building, and this time he would be able to see it through to completion.

After his retirement, he continued to receive invitations to teach and speak, but as time went on, he accepted fewer of these. In 1981 he published his autobiography, *Beyond My Expectation*, which included a last chapter, "L'envoi," about the pleasures of retirement. There was more time to spend with family and friends, to read, to garden, and also to indulge his passion for sporting activities, developed in his youth, especially horseback riding.[23]

Lyle's beloved wife Margaret died in 1983. In 1986 he married Vena Wren, and the two of them spent many happy hours together riding down rural trails in Georgia until the early nineties, when the onset of Alzheimer's made these rides too difficult for him. He died on July 20, 1994.

CHAPTER 16

Original Law Building, now Carlos Hall.

EMORY LAW AND THE FORMATION OF A UNIVERSITY

— NAT GOZANSKY —

Longest-serving member of the law faculty, Nathaniel Gozansky eloquently crafts the winding history of Emory Law School, which emerged out of the L. Q. C. Lamar School of Law, formed during the earliest days of the Druid Hills campus. One of the three professional schools (the others were theology and medicine) founded with Emory University in 1915, the law school has achieved many firsts and distinctions. Emory's first officially enrolled woman, Eléonore Raoul, graduated from the law school in 1920; the school's dean helped lead Emory's 1962 legal battle against the state of Georgia to permit integrated private schools to retain tax-exempt status; the school soon became a model for the national program known as CLEO, or the Council on Legal Educational Opportunity for underrepresented minorities.

WHEN THE DECISION was made in 1915 to move Emory College to Druid Hills and expand it into a university, the seeds were planted for the establishment of a law school. The "re-founders" of Emory felt that a true university needed at least three professional schools—theology, medicine, and law. So from the very beginning of the planning and fundraising for the expanded Emory, a law school was contemplated, and plans for the school to be housed on the new campus were in the making.

The original law school building (now Carlos Hall, part of the Michael C. Carlos Museum) was one of the original buildings on the Emory Quadrangle, constructed in 1916. With its graceful central staircase and Georgia marble façade, the building was designed by the highly regarded Beaux Arts architect Henry Hornbostel. The structure reflected the ambition for the school to have office space for the dean and six full-time faculty, and sufficient classroom and other space for one hundred students.

It is difficult to discern the trustees' criteria for a dean of the law school at that time. Correspondence from early 1916 suggests that the hope was to attract an established and respected legal educator. The first person hired to serve on the law faculty was a young man who had received his education at Yale, Herschel W. Arant, who effectively served as the founding leader of the new enterprise.

Professor Arant and Bishop Warren A. Candler, the chancellor of the University, appear to have been of a like mind in their aspirations for the new law school. To implement the goal of having a school that would be in league with the law schools of Harvard, Yale, Columbia, and similar nationally recognized universities, Arant and Candler agreed that the admissions requirements should be, by standards of the time, demanding. Initially two years of college were required—considerably more than the fourteen credit hours of college required by other schools in the South. In addition, Arant and Candler hoped to recruit their faculty among graduates of the very schools that Emory hoped to be identified with.[1]

The Emory Board of Trustees determined to name the new enterprise the L. Q. C. Lamar School of Law. Lamar had graduated from Emory College in 1845 and had a distinguished career as a statesman, scholar, and lawyer, including serving in the cabinet of President Grover Cleveland and as a justice on the U.S. Supreme Court. His distinguished career was thought of as a role model for the future graduates of the new school.

In March 1916 Bishop Candler wrote to Paul E. Bryan, another Yale Law graduate, offering him a faculty position.[2] In the letter to Bryan, an existing endowment for the law school in the amount of twenty-five thousand dollars is referenced. The projected yield from the endowment was to provide Bryan with compensation of fifteen hundred dollars for the year. Reference is also made to the need to have a "large library" to support the planned case method of instruction. The plan was to enroll the first class in September 1916, limiting the new students to the first-year curriculum—that is, the class would include no transfers from other law schools and could be adequately served by two full-time faculty members, possibly augmented by adjunct faculty recruited from the local bar association.[3] Twenty-eight students enrolled in the fall of 1916.[4] They apparently were offered a total of twenty courses, a remarkable array for a new school.

In fact, when the semester began there may have been four full-time faculty. In addition to Arant and Bryan, William Danner Thomson (College 1895, Atlanta attorney, and Emory trustee) was acting dean, and Robert Troutman was another professor.[5] Arant, who played such an instrumental role in the strategic planning for the new school, apparently departed Emory in 1921.[6] Troutman left in 1925, but Thomson would serve until 1941, and Bryan until 1953.[7]

The next three decades would prove challenging to the new enterprise. The year after the school's opening, the United States entered World War I, and as a result enrollment in the fall of 1917 plummeted to only fourteen, three of whom were first-year students.[8] In 1918 enrollment dropped still further, to eight, with no first-year students.[9] (Among those three new students in 1917 was Eléonore Raoul, the first woman to enroll officially at Emory, and the first woman to graduate from the law school—in 1920, as it happened, the year American women were first given the right to vote in federal elections.)

In 1919 the law school hired its first dean, Samuel C. Williams.[10] By an interesting twist he had served on the Tennessee Supreme Court when that body in 1914 decided the lawsuit between the Methodist Episcopal Church, South, and Vanderbilt University—a decision that led directly to the rechartering of Emory as a university in 1915. Williams would serve for five years. During this postwar period, enrollment increased; the full-time faculty grew to five, and the adjunct faculty stabilized at five.[11] Henry Milton Quillian, who joined the faculty in 1921, would serve for another forty years until his retirement.[12]

In 1924 Professor Bryan served as interim dean, and E. Smythe Gambrell joined the adjunct faculty.[13] Gambrell, a South Carolinian, had recently graduated from Harvard Law School; he served on the faculty until the eve of World War II and later provided the gift that enabled the construction of the present law school building—Gambrell Hall, named in memory of his parents.

> *After two successful summers, adding over twenty black students to the student population of the school, the Emory concept became the model for a national program, the Council on Legal Education Opportunity (CLEO).*

During Dean Williams's leadership the law school was the first in Georgia to be admitted to membership in the Association of American Law Schools. In 1923 the American Bar Association classified Emory as a "Class A" school, joining Emory with the University of Virginia and Washington and Lee as the only schools in the Southeast to be so honored.[14]

Charles Joseph Hilkey left the deanship at Drake University and assumed the Emory deanship in 1925,[15] leading the school through the challenges of the Depression and World War II before stepping down from the deanship in 1948. In 1951, at age seventy-two, he joined the Stetson Law School faculty in DeLand, Florida.

Dean Hilkey's stewardship of the law school is marked by several accomplishments. Most of the faculty took a year's leave to work on earning an S.J.D. degree or at least a year's research leave at Harvard or other elite schools.[16] A placement program for graduates was begun in 1927.[17] In 1931 he instituted a minimum publication requirement for the faculty (one article and one book review per year).[18] Students began to do projects of interest to the practicing bar and ultimately became contributors to the *Georgia Bar Journal* and the *Georgia Restatement of Conflict of Laws*.[19] In 1936, as an alternative to the LLB degree, the school offered college graduates who met certain academic performance requirements the JD degree.[20] In 1938 the law school offered its first continuing legal education program, on the newly enacted federal rules of civil procedure. Two years later a similar program was offered on federal taxation.[21]

Enrollment leading up to World War II ranged from approximately sixty to eighty students. While not all students were southerners, the overwhelming majority were. The goal of being a nationally recognized school had not been realized, but Emory's presence as a regional leader was undisputed.

Despite terrible financial pressure, the University determined not to close the law school during World War II. Instead, the law school, with the permission of the American Bar Association, shifted to an evening part-time program with only two full-time professors.[22] The remaining members of the faculty assumed government positions supporting the war effort. Enrollment plunged; however, the part-time evening program positioned the school to meet the dramatic increase in demand for a legal education following the end of the war. The school continued the evening program while reinstituting a full-time day program in 1946.

That same year, the faculty began to grow. Ben F. Johnson Jr. and William Agnor joined the faculty in 1946 (G. Stanley Joslin and Robert Hall joined two years later).[23] W. D. Thomson served again as acting dean for the academic year 1948–49.[24] Maurice Culp served as acting dean for half of the 1949–50 academic year.[25]

William M. Hepburn joined the faculty as dean in 1950,[26] and at least two additional faculty were appointed that same year, bringing the total full-time faculty to at least ten. By this time the existing building had clearly been outgrown. Creative renovations were done to accommodate the space requirements of the growing law school community. The first written comment on the need for a new building appeared in Interim Dean Culp's annual report for 1949, and the need became a recurring theme throughout Dean Hepburn's stewardship.[27]

In 1960 Dean Hepburn suffered a fatal heart attack, and Professor Joslin became interim dean. The following year Ben F. Johnson Jr. assumed the deanship, the first time the deanship went to an existing member of the faculty. Dean Johnson's twelve years as dean proved to be a dynamic time that moved the law school into national prominence.

Shortly after assuming the deanship, Johnson and the chair of the board of trustees, Henry L. Bowden (College 1932, Law 1934), led Emory's successful suit against the state of Georgia to overturn a state constitutional provision that prohibited private schools from integrating without losing their tax exemption.[28] With that barrier gone, Johnson received Field Foundation support to embark upon a summer program designed to identify and recruit African American college graduates to the law school. A new faculty member, Michael Devito, accepted the dean's invitation to design and manage this program.[29] After two successful summers, adding over twenty black students to the student population of the school, the Emory concept became the model for a national program, the Council on Legal Education Opportunity (CLEO). CLEO was funded by the federal government and served students from disadvantaged backgrounds nationally. Another member of the Emory law faculty, Nathaniel E. Gozansky, became a pivotal contributor to the early success of CLEO, owing in part to Dean Johnson's support for time release to make his work with CLEO possible.[30]

In 1967 the law school accepted a grant from the OEO Office of Legal Services to establish two neighborhood law offices that would provide civil legal services to the area poor. These offices provided students an opportunity to have a supervised clinical experience while providing a socially significant community service. Several years after the establishment of the program, the funds and the neighborhood offices were transferred to the Atlanta Legal Aid program sponsored by the local bar association. To this day, Emory students as well as those from other law schools intern at one or more of the legal aid offices in the metropolitan Atlanta area.[31]

By the late sixties, even though the faculty had grown to nearly twenty, the burden of maintaining both a full-time and a part-time program weighed heavily on the resources of the school. While the day division attracted students from all over the country, albeit predominantly from the South and Northeast, the evening program was exclusively serving a local population. Georgia State University, in downtown Atlanta, was seeking authority to establish a law school. It was believed that if Emory would cease operating the evening division, resistance in the legislature would dissipate and the new law school would be approved. The faculty voted, and the Emory trustees approved the phaseout of the evening division in 1970. Politics being what they are, it would not be until 1981 that Georgia State University was approved to establish its law school. One of the early supporters of this new venture, Dean Johnson, left his beloved Emory to serve as the founding dean of that new school.

By the mid-sixties the original law building had become completely inadequate for the needs of the school. Faculty offices were jury-rigged throughout the building, with several in the basement; classrooms were antiquated and inadequate in number; technology as simple as individual phones for faculty was unavailable; and maintenance was bordering on ineffective.

Dean Johnson, who had done so much to lead the school through faculty growth, innovative programs, and national exposure, focused his attention on the pressing brick-and-mortar needs of the school. He turned to his old teacher and friend E. Smythe Gambrell, who responded with a million-dollar gift to kick off the campaign for a new building. In 1972 one of Johnson's last official acts as dean was the dedication of the new building at the corner of Clifton and North Decatur roads.

In 1973 L. Ray Patterson, a distinguished member of the Vanderbilt faculty, became the law school's fifth dean. Patterson assumed the leadership of the school just after it had moved into its new building. He would be challenged to manage a near doubling of the student body without compromising quality. His six-year term was not marked by academic innovation. Rather, he focused his energies on expanding and professionalizing the administration, adding faculty, and developing strategies for recruiting students from across the country. This last strategy involved deploying faculty to many of America's elite colleges and universities, with a view to establishing relationships with prelaw advisers. During his six years as dean, twelve new faculty members were hired.

> *Of more than a dozen faculty recruited during Dean Hunter's stewardship, five were women, five persons of color or ethnic diversity, one an internationally renowned scholar of conflicts of law, and two internationally recognized human rights scholars/activists.*

Professor Harold Marquis served as interim dean for the 1979–80 academic year. Interim deans generally try to merely keep things from sliding backward. With faculty support, however, during that one year two new faculty members were appointed, including Professor Richard Doernberg, who joined Professor Thomas Marr in building a nationally recognized LLM. program in taxation. In addition, major technological advances were made in the law library.

Thomas D. Morgan assumed the deanship in July 1980. Owing in part to the Woodruff gift to the University the previous November, his deanship proved to be one of academic expansion and renewal. In his first year as dean he succeeded in bringing Professor Abe Ordover from Hofstra University, and with him came the establishment of the award-winning Trial Techniques Program. He also lured from the University of Miami the nationally recognized Law and Economics Program, headed by Professor Henry Manne. In addition he led the faculty through a comprehensive curricular revision that dramatically altered the content of the curriculum. Building on Patterson's efforts to expand and professionalize the administration in order to relieve the faculty of administrative burdens, Morgan moved the emphasis on faculty scholarship to the forefront.

The *Emory Law Journal* (originally named the *Journal of Public Law*) had begun in 1952. In the final year of Morgan's tenure as dean, the law school started a second journal—the *Bankruptcy Developments Journal*. It was followed two years later by a third journal, *International Law*. This last was no doubt influenced by the hiring of two internationally renowned scholars.

In 1983 the law school was allocated one of four new Woodruff chairs and was able to recruit Harold Berman from Harvard Law School to fill the chair. Berman was, among other things, a leading authority on Russian law. The following year Thomas Buergenthal, a Holocaust survivor and leading human rights scholar, also joined the faculty. Buergenthal remained at Emory for a few years, but in that period of time he built the LLM program into a leading vehicle for attracting foreign scholars to the law school.

Professor Berman remained at Emory as an active member of the faculty until his death in 2007. Space for this chapter does not allow a full telling of his contributions (see chapter 34). Under Berman's influence, however, and with the active leadership of Professor Frank

Alexander, the Law and Religion Program was launched. Professor Berman then brought John Witte Jr. to the law school as a research assistant, and Witte was appointed to the tenure track in 1988. Through Professor Witte's efforts the Center for the Study of Law and Religion was founded and grew into a major locus of scholarship (see chapter 38). Professor Berman's good works, prolific scholarship, and many lectures delivered all over the world brought international attention to the law school. His fame became Emory's fame.

The seventh dean arrived in 1984: David G. Epstein, a scholar in the field of bankruptcy and a remarkable teacher. The latter skill endeared him to students, but his administration confronted several challenges. One was low student morale; another was disaffected alumni. In addition, the law library had long since outgrown its space in Gambrell Hall, and an addition or new building was a pressing need. Raising money required a supportive alumni base. Epstein increased the law school's Office of Development and embarked on an ambitious effort to engage and reengage alumni in being involved in and supportive of the law school. Those efforts would reach fruition in the years following his administration. He also engaged the staff and faculty to conduct their activities in a more student-friendly manner. Everyone rallied to the charge, and a period of student satisfaction emerged, with the number of disaffected students dwindling to insignificance. Throughout his tenure he continued Morgan's emphasis on faculty scholarly productivity. In 1988 Dean Epstein left the deanship to join a law firm in Atlanta.

Howard O. "Woody" Hunter assumed the interim deanship in the summer of 1988. Eighteen months later, with faculty support, the president of the University appointed Hunter the eighth dean of the law school. He served until 2001, when he stepped down from the deanship to serve the University as interim provost for two years. During his tenure as dean a successful campaign led to the construction of the Hugh F. MacMillan Law Library. Of more than a dozen faculty recruited during Hunter's stewardship, five were women, five persons of color or ethnic diversity, one an internationally renowned scholar of conflicts of law, and two internationally recognized human rights scholars/activists. Curricular offerings increased dramatically, and a number of activities were initiated to support faculty scholarship. The faculty's publishing frequency and quality led to national recognition from peer schools.

In addition, with Hunter's support, students started the Emory Public Interest Committee (EPIC), which raises funds to support summer public-interest internships. As a complement to EPIC, the law school also established a loan repayment assistance program that facilitates graduates' accepting low-paying public-interest jobs in spite of their student loan debt. Clinical opportunities became available through the establishment of the Turner Environmental Clinic and the Barton Child Law and Policy Clinic. As if to underscore the dynamic times, the school's moot court team in January 1990 swept the National Moot Court competition in New York, winning every possible award except for second place.

In 2001 Professor Peter Hay accepted the task of serving as interim dean while a national search was conducted to find a successor to Hunter. The law school's ninth dean was the third dean to come from the faculty. Professor Thomas Arthur, who had served as associate dean during a portion of the Hunter administration, was chosen to lead the enterprise.

While Arthur's administration was only three years long, it was productive on a number of fronts. The University allocated two Woodruff chairs to the law school, allowing the school to recruit a constitutional scholar, Michael Perry, and a feminist legal theorist, Martha Fineman. Professor Fineman brought with her the Feminist Legal Theory Project, a program that attracts international scholars for periods of a month to a full academic year and sponsors a variety of workshops and programs both in and beyond the United States.

In addition, in anticipation of a University-wide fund-raising campaign, Arthur spearheaded the development of a strategic plan that has defined the agenda for the development of the law school in the years ahead. In a period of aggressive hiring, five female professors and two minority professors joined the faculty, so that diversity in the student body is increasingly mirrored in the faculty composition.

As it became clear to Dean Arthur that the fund-raising campaign would begin later and last longer than originally thought, he felt that it would be necessary for whoever was dean to be in place throughout the campaign, and he decided to return to the faculty. Professor Frank Alexander assumed the interim deanship for the 2005–6 academic year while a national search was instituted. That search resulted in the appointment of David Partlett, who left the deanship at Washington and Lee University School of Law to come to Emory and lead the school through the capital campaign. In anticipation of the campaign, the strategic plan was revised, and several centers were established: the Center for Transactional Law and Practice, which has had a marked impact on the curriculum; the Center for International and Comparative Law; and the Center for Federalism and Intersystemic Governance. A comprehensive review of the curriculum has also been instituted.

Current faculty (as of January 2010) who have been at the law school for twenty-five or more years include:

NATHANIEL E. GOZANSKY	1967
FRANK J. VANDALL	1970
GARY SMITH	1971
WILLIAM T. MAYTON	1974
CHARLES SHANOR	1974
TIMOTHY TERRELL	1975
WILLIAM J. CARNEY	1977
THOMAS ARTHUR	1981
FRANK ALEXANDER	1981
HOWARD ABRAMS	1982
MORGAN CLOUD	1982
RICHARD FREER	1982

Lioness and spiral stairway in Carlos Hall

FEMINIST ACTIVISM AND THE ORIGINS OF WOMEN'S STUDIES AT EMORY

— MARY E. ODEM *and* CANDACE COFFMAN —

Mary Odem, who holds a joint appointment in women's studies and history, collaborates with her former student, Candace Coffman (College 2009) to document the growth of feminist activism and scholarship at Emory, from the formation of the Emory Women's Caucus in 1974, through the creation of the Institute for Women's Studies under the leadership of nationally renowned historian Elizabeth Fox-Genovese in 1986, to the achievement of full departmental status in 2003. The program's accomplishments along the way include catching up after a late start, establishing the nation's first doctoral program in women's studies, and achieving recognition as the top program of its kind in the country.

Introduction | Emory's Women's Studies Department is recognized as one of the premier programs in the country for the interdisciplinary study of women and gender. Given its current status, it may surprise some to learn that Emory's program was a latecomer to the academic world. The first women's studies programs in the United States were established in the early 1970s. By 1981 there were more than 350 programs in colleges and universities across the country, yet it was not until 1986 that Emory created a program in women's studies.[1]

The Institute for Women's Studies, as it was initially called, made up for its late start under the leadership of a dynamic first director, Elizabeth Fox-Genovese, and with the support of dedicated faculty members and future directors. A decade after its founding, the institute had seven core faculty members, a wide network of more than thirty associated faulty, a thriving undergraduate program, and a nationally recognized graduate program—the first in the country to offer a PhD in women's studies. The creation and future success of the Women's Studies Department could not have occurred without the organizing efforts of women faculty in the 1970s, the vision of its directors, the support of key administrators, and the contributions of its core and associated faculty members. The path was not smooth but involved political and philosophical struggles over the meaning of feminist scholarship and the very place of women's studies in the academy.

The Emory Women's Caucus and the Struggle against Sex Discrimination

| The movement to create a women's studies program at Emory grew out of the activism of the first generation of women faculty members at the University. Like other institutions of higher education, Emory began slowly to increase its small number of women faculty in the late 1960s and early 1970s in the wake of feminist challenges to employment discrimination in male-dominated professions and occupations. By the mid-1970s a cadre of women had joined the faculties in Emory College and the professional schools of law, medicine, and theology. Yet while departments and schools had increased the number of women in faculty positions, they had not altered discriminatory attitudes and practices that made the University an unwelcoming place for women. Women faculty members from that era describe the environment they encountered in the 1970s as "isolating" and "paternalistic." Donna Brogan, hired by the Emory School of Medicine to teach biostatistics in 1971, explained, "I was the only woman out of seven department members." She recalled, "My boss used to say that our department was overrepresented with women, since I represented 14 percent of the department, and the average was 8 or 9 percent."[2]

When Martine (Tina) Brownley, now the Goodrich C. White Professor of English and founding director of the Fox Center for Humanistic Inquiry, arrived at Emory University as an assistant professor of English in 1975, she was one of only six women professors in the College. She recalled the difficulties of that position in an oral interview in 2008. "We were just freaks," she conceded. "I remember how students used to call the [male professors] Doctor and [female professors] Miss or Mrs."[3] Peggy Barlett, who joined the Sociology and Anthropology Department in 1976, described a similar sense of alienation:

> I didn't feel particularly welcome.... Right before school started I was taken out to lunch by my department chair, which is a common thing that happens. As we got in the car and drove away from campus he said, "Well, I am a member of two golf clubs. Normally I would take you to the Druid Hills Golf Club for lunch but they don't allow women in the dining room so I'm going to take you to my other golf club."[4]

Beyond feeling unwelcome at the University, women faculty encountered real material inequities in salary, benefits, and promotion. The process of hiring and advancement resembled an "old boys' network" with no clear, established guidelines and procedures. According to

Dora Skypek, a pioneering woman professor in the Division of Educational Studies, Emory was a "revolving door" for women. They tended to have nontenure, temporary appointments; even those on tenure-track lines could be terminated with little explanation and no process for appeal. Lore Metzger, the first woman with the rank of full professor in Emory College (in English), said that there was "idiosyncratic decision-making, and no processes that ensured equal and just treatment."[5]

In 1974 a small group of women faculty began to meet over lunch to discuss the problems of gender discrimination on campus and how to address it. The group, which included Gwen Kennedy Neville (sociology and anthropology), Carole Hahn (educational studies), and Skypek, Metzger, and Nelia Kimbrough (a Candler theology student), decided to call an open meeting for women faculty and staff across the University to find out what their concerns were. Hahn recalled the meeting as "electrifying." "We had no idea if anyone would come," she explained, "but the room was packed. . . . From the law school, medical school, theology, and the College—all across the board, women met people they had never known before."[6] The meeting resulted in the formation of the Emory Women's Caucus (EWC), the first feminist organization acting on behalf of women faculty and staff at Emory. Over the next decade, the Women's Caucus spearheaded efforts to challenge gender inequalities at the University and called on the administration to develop an affirmative action plan that addressed the multiple forms of discrimination women encountered.

One of the first issues taken up by the EWC was the abrupt firing of the popular dean for women, Peggy Ziegler, who at the time was the only woman in an administrative position at the University. In a letter to President Sanford Atwood and the board of trustees in September 1974, caucus members complained about the "abuse of administrative power," "the questionable procedures followed in making the decision," and the "adverse effect" the firing would have on female students.[7] The administration refused to reconsider Ziegler's termination but agreed to appoint Dr. Sarah Healy to serve as acting dean of women and to chair a committee for the selection of a new dean. After meeting for several months, Healy's committee recommended the creation of a University-wide commission on the status of women that would serve as a nucleus for women's concerns at Emory. When the recommendation went unheeded, the women's caucus kept up pressure on the administration until President Atwood authorized the creation of the President's Commission on the Status of Women (PCSW) in February 1976.[8]

Initially chaired by Dr. Margaret Drummond, a member of the Microbiology Department and an active member of the ECW, the commission embarked on an in-depth study of the status of women staff, students, and faculty at Emory. The PCSW's first report (1977) identified the difficulties encountered by women faculty: "The available information shows women to be few in number, low

Dora Helen Skypek played a crucial role in the development of women's studies at Emory.

in rank, with poor representation among those with tenure or continuous appointment, and with lower salaries."[9] The poor representation of women faculty was especially notable in Emory College, which had only 6 women at the associate professor rank or above, out of a total of 133 at this rank. Ten departments in the College had no women faculty members, and not one woman hired at the rank of assistant professor had been promoted through the ranks to professor.[10]

The concern about sex discrimination in hiring and promotion came to a head when Gwen Kennedy Neville was fired from her position as assistant professor in the Sociology and Anthropology Department in the summer of 1976, the year she was to come up for tenure. An effective teacher with a solid publication record, Neville had received positive evaluations from her department up to that point. During the previous two years, she had also been one of the leading activists in the women's caucus, and, according to Peggy Barlett, many people "saw this as an effort get rid of the troublemaker."[11] Neville decided to appeal the department's decision; because there was no appeals procedure in place at Emory, the College dean, John Palms, created an ad-hoc appeals committee of seven faculty members to review the decision. After a year of hearings and meetings, the committee reported that it found no grounds for overturning the decision to terminate Kennedy; the report was subsequently reviewed and approved by President James Laney.[12]

With the support and encouragement of the ECW, Neville filed a complaint of sex discrimination against Emory University with the federal Equal Employment Opportunity Commission. Over the next eighteen months, the EEOC held legal hearings to investigate the complaint, and the ECW organized to raise money and support for Neville's legal defense.[13] The case made it to the front page of the *Atlanta Journal-Constitution,* which reported that discrimination in the hiring and promotion of female faculty made Emory a "bad place for women."[14] Not long after the appearance of the article, the University agreed to settle the case.

The struggle over Neville's case led to significant changes at Emory in the interest of women and minority faculty. The administration completed a University-wide affirmative action plan that addressed gender discrimination, and Emory's first affirmative action officer was appointed to oversee its implementation. As part of this plan, the College and professional schools created standardized procedures for hiring, promotion, and tenure, including the requirement of national searches and open advertisement of faculty positions, and the formation of affirmative action committees to oversee hiring.

While the case marked a victory for women's equality at Emory, it came at high personal cost for Neville. According to Barlett, the two years Neville spent challenging her termination were "tremendously damaging to her psyche and her ability to function."[15] Although she was given a position in the Candler School of Theology, Neville was not allowed to return to the College as a faculty member in the Sociology and Anthropology Department as she desired. A year later she left Emory to take an endowed chair in the sociology and anthropology department at Georgetown University in Texas. According to Barlett, "She wanted to stay at Emory. It was painful to her that she fought her case and won but didn't get to stay."[16]

The Creation of a Women's Studies Program
In the course of challenging gender inequality, women faculty began to discuss the burgeoning of feminist scholarship in the academy and how they could further the development of women's studies at Emory. A survey conducted by the PCSW found growing faculty and student interest in the new interdisciplinary area of study. Between 1972 and 1977, ten women's studies courses were offered in the College and an equal number in the theology school. With titles such as "Religion and Sexuality," "Women and Politics," "The Feminist Movement as Social Critique," "The Female Voice in English Literature," and "Women in Antiquity," the courses had strong enrollments, but most were not part of the regular course offerings.[17]

At the suggestion of Lore Metzger, the Emory Women's Caucus organized an informal reading group of faculty to study feminist scholarship and to discuss ways of making it more central to the teaching and research that took place at Emory. From these gatherings, participants became convinced of the need for a "feminist studies program" at Emory. They submitted a proposal to Dean David Minter in January 1984 that outlined the rationale for such a program and called for a firm commitment of resources from Emory College. "The state of feminist scholarship in most disciplines has now reached maturity, and its validity has been established," read the proposal. "Emory can no longer afford to ignore feminist studies; it must be incorporated into our established curriculum."[18]

Dean Minter responded the following year by appointing a committee, chaired by Peggy Barlett, to "study the advisability of establishing an interdisciplinary undergraduate program in Women's Studies/Feminist Studies."[19] In May 1985, after numerous meetings and much research, the committee produced a proposal that strongly recommended the creation of such a program: "Virtually all of the schools with which Emory compares itself, and with which we compete for students, currently have such programs. . . . Given the vigor and importance of the field, its absence at Emory is noticeable and disturbing."[20] In the course of developing both proposals, faculty debated what constitutes women's studies as a field. Their debates reflected the larger conversation taking place in universities across the country about the meaning and place of feminist studies in the academy.

> *A key concern of Emory faculty was to avoid the marginalization that numerous women's studies programs had encountered in their academic institutions.*

The faculty made a distinction between a program based simply on women as a subject matter, and one based on a feminist theoretical perspective. An important "aspect of the intellectual vigor of the Women's Studies Program," stated the 1985 proposal, "is the theoretical approach of feminist analysis that arises out of the questioning of the previous exclusion of women, women's experience, and the female perspective. Feminist analysis examines the role of gender in the shaping, legitimation, and dissemination of knowledge."[21] Faculty also debated the political implications of calling the program "feminist studies" or "women's studies" when Dean Minter raised concerns that the former could be seen as exclusionary. At Minter's urging, the committee agreed to call the program "women's studies" in order to appeal to a wider group of faculty and students, but still insisted on a program informed by feminist analysis.[22]

Another debate revolved around the best structure for the program—whether it should be a separate academic department or a program with faculty who had joint appointments in other departments. A key concern of Emory faculty was to avoid the marginalization that numerous women's studies programs had encountered in their academic institutions. As Carole Hahn explained, the problem stemmed from the fact that "all the women's studies people [were] in the same department. Then everybody else could say we've taken care of that. . . . And the women's studies people just talked to [other] women's studies [people] and they didn't have much influence on the other departments."[23] In an effort to prevent the marginalization of women's studies at Emory, the committee recommended the creation of a program made up of jointly appointed faculty connected to other academic departments. To develop a wide network of women's studies' scholars and teachers on campus, the committee also recommended forming an associated faculty who would teach cross-listed courses and serve on committees.

The proposal for a women's studies program encountered fierce objections from some professors. In an editorial published in the *Emory Wheel*, George Cuttino, Candler Professor of Medieval History, attacked the proposal: "Dear Mr. Woodruff must be turning in his grave like barbecue on a spit! And what will alumni, alumnae, and parents think of a university that underwrites pseudo-academic avant-garde rubbish instead of buttressing proven academic disciplines."[24] Cuttino complained that the proposal was written by "a cozy little group of four females and two males, all of them feminists and most of them simply tiresome Marxists." The editorial sparked a lively debate over the next several weeks in the pages of the *Emory Wheel*. Undergraduate history major Polly Price (College 1986, Graduate School 1986, later professor of law at Emory) challenged Cuttino's "narrow and reactionary" views: "I am not of the 'offended gaggle' mentioned by Dr. Cuttino simply because I believe the Old Guard views expressed by this professor are on their way out. I am hopeful that the Emory leadership will carefully consider this much-needed program."[25] In a letter to the editor, Dobbs Professor Melvin Konner, then-chair of the Anthropology Department, also took Cuttino to task. One can appreciate his reluctance," Konner wrote. "He (like most men in academic and other professional walks of life) has profited greatly from the traditional exclusion of women, and he would not like to see the rise of a legitimate field of study which will cast a harsh light on such traditions."[26]

Ultimately the arguments in support of a women's studies program proved more persuasive. Emory faculty approved the proposal, and the following year a search committee was formed to hire the first director of the newly established Institute for Women's Studies.

The Institute for Women's Studies and its First Director | In 1986 Elizabeth Fox-Genovese joined the Emory College faculty as the founding director of the Institute for Women's Studies. She had impressed the hiring committee both with the quality of her scholarship and with her broadly conceived vision for the program. Trained as an eighteenth-century French historian, Fox-Genovese had published two books on European history informed by a Marxist analysis, including *Fruits of Merchant Capital: Slavery and Bourgeois Property in the Rise and Expansion of Capitalism* (1983), which she coauthored with her husband, Eugene Genovese, a well-known historian of American slavery. In the late 1970s she and her husband founded the journal *Marxist Perspectives*. When she came to Emory, Fox-Genovese was writing a major historical study of women and slavery in the American South that brought a feminist lens to the analysis of the political economy of slavery. *Within the Plantation Household: Black and White Women of the Old South* was published in 1988 to widespread critical acclaim and established her as a leading scholar in southern and U.S. women's history. In one review, Mechal Sobel wrote that Fox-Genovese succeeded brilliantly at the "enormous tasks she undertakes of telling the life stories of the last generation of black and white women of the Old South, and of analyzing the meanings of these interconnected stories as a way of illuminating both Southern and women's history."[27] With this book and the numerous articles she wrote before and after its publication, Fox-Genovese advanced the theoretical and conceptual sophistication of women's and southern history.

When she arrived at Emory, Fox-Genovese faced the daunting task of creating a women's studies program from scratch. According to the department's 1992 self-study, Fox-Genovese's September 1986 proposal for the program included an interdisciplinary approach and "the creation of an Institute which would provide a campus focus for intellectual work on women through academic courses, lectures, workshops, a film series, conferences, and ultimately a series of publications."[28] During her tenure, Fox-Genovese reached many of these goals and added even more depth to the program. Her conceptual plan evolved into the Institute for Women's Studies. The program offered undergraduate courses beginning in 1987, with the addition of a women's studies minor the same year.[29] She established a colloquium series for the presentation of academic research in order to, in her words, "anchor an intellectual community" at Emory.[30] That same year she launched a forum on women's issues for faculty, students, and staff.[31]

In the academic year 1988–89, the undergraduate major, graduate certificate, and PhD program (through the Institute for Liberal Arts) came to fruition.[32] The first women's studies graduate students enrolled in 1989, and application to the program more than doubled the following year.[33] The quality of applicants increased along with quantity. Course offerings swelled with the growth in enrollment, paving the way for core faculty appointments to the program.

In 1989, three new faculty members had joined the program as assistant professors with joint appointments in English (Julie Abraham) and history (Mary Odem and Cynthia Patterson). The joint appointments located tenure in the home department, and professors divided their teaching and service equally between the home department and women's studies.[34] Over the next several years Fox-Genovese hired additional women's studies faculty with joint appointments in philosophy (Pam Hall, now in the Religion Department), political science (Beth Reingold), sociology (Irene Browne), and anthropology (Carla Freeman). Her key concern was to build a core faculty of strong scholars and teachers who brought a range of different intellectual and methodological approaches to women's studies. The program relied as well on the contributions of associated faculty members who served on committees, advised students, and taught cross-listed courses to help enrich and expand the women's studies curriculum.

Fox-Genovese added to the teaching environment at Emory another component whose tradition continues today. At the conception of the program, she envisioned an interactive network between Emory University and other colleges in the Atlanta area, and a special bond developed with Spelman College, the historically black liberal arts college for women located approximately eight miles southwest of Emory, near the Atlanta University Center. Each year at least one women's studies course is taught by a distinguished faculty member from Spelman. Known as the Enhanced Educational Community/Opportunity Professor, past professors have included eminent scholars such as Beverly Guy-Sheftall (PhD 1984) and Johnnetta Cole (Honorary Degree 1996).[35] The Women's Studies Program values its ongoing relationship with Spelman, which ranked first among Historically Black Colleges and Universities in the 2009 and 2010 *U.S. News & World Report* rankings.[36]

Another significant milestone in the development of women's studies at Emory during Fox-Genovese's tenure was the appointment of former first lady Rosalynn Carter as distinguished fellow of the Institute for Women's Studies.[37] Beginning this appointment in 1990, Carter worked in conjunction with the institute to develop a series of programs in public policy, central to which was the Rosalynn Carter Distinguished Lecture in Public Policy. The first person to deliver this lecture was Sarah Weddington, the attorney who represented "Jane Roe" before the U.S. Supreme Court in the landmark *Roe v. Wade* case (1973) that established a woman's right to abortion. Along with Carter's appointment, the institute created an honorary fellows program that honored three women a year as Rosalynn Carter Fellows in Public Policy. Other significant additions to the program in the 1990 academic year included an undergraduate honors program in women's studies as well as Mellon dissertation fellowships for graduate students.[38]

Martine Brownley, the second director of women's studies at Emory, described Fox-Genovese's vision as "beautifully conceived."[39] "It was like an explorer coming to a new continent, and they don't lay out a town, they lay out a whole capital,"[40] Brownley remarked. By focusing on a comprehensive, well-rounded program including colloquia together with academic programs consisting of an undergraduate major and minor and a doctoral program, women's studies at Emory grew to include ten core faculty, forty-five associated faculty, and twenty-two undergraduate courses by the time of Fox-Genovese's resignation.[41]

To the surprise of many, Fox-Genovese submitted her resignation as director of the Institute for Women's Studies in January 1992. The resignation occurred amid complaints about her governance of the program. In the fall of 1991 a group of associated faculty members, including some who were instrumental in the creation of the program, met with David Bright, the newly appointed dean of Emory College, to complain about the absence of collaborative decision-making in the program. "It's a very simple issue in terms of academic governance," said Emilia

Navarro, a professor in the Spanish Department and associated faculty member in women's studies. Navarro continued, "Basically Fox-Genovese does not believe, in practice, in the collaborative nature of a program."[42] The associated faculty members who had served on the advisory committee felt they had been excluded from the decision-making process. Fox-Genovese responded to the complaints by submitting her resignation, calling the actions of the faculty who met with Dean Bright a "political power play."[43]

At the same time that conflicts over her academic governance surfaced, Fox-Genovese demonstrated a conservative shift in politics and scholarship. She had just completed the book *Feminism without Illusions: A Critique of Individualism*, in which she criticized the women's movement for reflecting too narrowly the concerns of middle-class white women. Her attendance at a "Feminists for Life" rally in New York in the fall of 1991 also reflected her shifting political perspective and critique of liberal feminism.[44] In the summer following her resignation, Fox-Genovese suggested in an interview with *Academic Questions* that "people were beginning to feel that I was simply too conservative to be director of the program."[45] Brownley reflected that although Fox-Genovese's emergent conservatism may have raised some eyebrows, in general, faculty within the Women's Studies Program respected her right to free speech and personal opinion.

As the tensions mounted with disgruntled faculty and Fox-Genovese's own frustration grew with what she saw as the increasing politicization of women's studies, she resigned. In addition to these complications, a lawsuit surfaced from the former associate director of the program, Virginia Gould, alleging sexual discrimination and harassment. Gould charged that Fox-Genovese required her to carry out duties that would not have been required of a male employee, such as arranging parties. The suit, which was settled out of court in 1996 with both sides claiming victory, further strained Fox-Genovese's relationship with the Emory faculty and administration.

In their 2006 self-study the women's studies faculty noted that the spring of 1992 demonstrated "a period of upheaval in the program."[46] Fox-Genovese's unanticipated resignation certainly left the program in a state of shock, but under the leadership of Tina Brownley, and with the support of a dedicated group of core and associated faculty members, women's studies withstood the crisis and continued the development of intellectually vibrant programs of undergraduate and graduate study. Fox-Genovese's abiding legacy is not the publicity surrounding her abrupt departure, but rather the broad intellectual vision she brought to the program and the strong institutional foundation she put in place. By establishing a program based on academic excellence and diverse approaches to women's studies, Fox-Genovese laid the groundwork for the future growth and success of women's studies at Emory. Her vision was taken up by future directors, faculty members, and engaged students of the program.

Expansion and Challenges, 1992–99 | In February 1992 Brownley, who was part of the associated faculty and a member of the executive committee in women's studies, accepted the request of Dean David Bright to serve as interim director of the program while the College conducted a nationwide search. At the end of the spring semester, the search did not produce an acceptable candidate, and Brownley agreed to remain as permanent director. A highly regarded teacher and scholar, in her academic interests Brownley ranged from eighteenth-century fiction to literary criticism, contemporary women novelists, and politics. One of her most impressive works of feminist scholarship is *Deferral of Domain: Contemporary Women Novelists and the State* (2000).

When Brownley accepted the position as director, her first priority was to establish clear procedures and rules for running the program. The executive committee and faculty "met incessantly" during those first few months, focusing on the development of procedures to create a clear system of governance and stability in the program. She recalled, "I did nothing but convene committees for a couple of years to write rules."[47]

The Women's Studies Program continued to grow and mature under Brownley's tenure. Like Fox-Genovese, she emphasized intellectual rigor in teaching and scholarship. A major concern was building the doctoral program, which had been transferred from the ILA to women's studies exclusively. This significant development, which Fox-Genovese had initiated, allowed Brownley and the women's studies faculty to expand the doctoral program and shape its organization and intellectual content. The number of PhD students grew steadily over the next four years. From two students in 1992, the doctoral program was accepting six graduate students a year by 1996. Emory was the first university in North America to establish a free-standing PhD program in women's studies. Numerous other institutions followed suit over the next few years. The strength, size, and intellectual range of the faculty, both core and associated, along with strong institutional support, established its reputation as a leader in the field of graduate education in women's studies.[48]

"It was a fun time," Brownley reflected on her tenure as director. Of the first crop of doctoral students, she wrote, "I am very proud of some of those people who are now anchoring women's studies programs across the nation."[49] The first PhD graduates included Vivian M. May, later associate professor of women's and gender studies at Syracuse University, and Allison Kimmich, later the executive director of the National Women's Studies Association.

After stepping down from directing women's studies, Brownley continued to contribute to the growth of the scholarly excellence at Emory. As the Goodrich C. White Professor of English, she was selected to serve as the founding director of the Bill and Carol Fox Center for Humanistic Inquiry, which opened at Emory in 2002. Because of her leadership and accomplishments in this position, she was a recipient of Georgia's 2009 Governor's Award in the Humanities, which honors "individuals and organizations who build community, character, and citizenship in Georgia through public humanities education."[50]

The next faculty member to serve as director of women's studies was Robyn Fivush, the Samuel Candler Dobbs Professor of Psychology. Fivush first came to Emory in 1984 as an assistant professor, one of three women in a department of twenty-two faculty members. In her second year, she was asked by Dean Minter to serve on the search committee for the director of the new women's studies program. Her response was "one of surprise," she remembered, as she "simply assumed that Emory had a women's studies program" by that time. She accepted Dean Minter's request and made a commitment to support the new program to encourage feminist scholarship and "to make the College more hospitable to women."[51] After her stint on the search committee, Fivush stayed actively involved with the program, serving as a member of the executive committee during Brownley's tenure.

As director of women's studies from 1996 to 1999, Fivush found the experience both satisfying and challenging, especially because of the dedication and hard work of the faculty. "Everyone wanted women's studies to work and be vibrant,"[52] she recalled. Still, the program faced numerous challenges. One of the greatest was inadequate faculty resources. The institute was running a thriving undergraduate and graduate program with the equivalent of four faculty members (a director and seven faculty with joint appointments). While joint appointments promoted better integration of women's studies into the life of Emory College, they also created a difficult balancing act for the core faculty members. Hired as assistant professors, they were stretched between the demands of two departments in terms of teaching, committee assignments, and administrative work. They carried a heavier service load than was typical for assistant professors, but still faced the same research and publication requirements for tenure. Still, in spite of the hurdles, all of the six junior professors hired by women's studies during its first decade were promoted to the rank of associate professor and gained recognition in their respective fields for their scholarly work: Odem in history, Abraham in English, Hall in philosophy and religion, Reingold in political science, Browne in sociology, and Freeman in anthropology.

In addition to supporting junior faculty on the road to tenure, Fivush also focused on strengthening the doctoral program. During her time as director, the faculty and graduate students engaged in intense discussions about the direction, purpose, and structure of the graduate program. They addressed such questions as the purpose of a PhD in women's studies, how best to train scholars in the interdisciplinary field of women's studies, and how to prepare students for a job market unfamiliar with and perhaps resistant to the idea of a degree in women's studies. With a multilayered approach to these questions, the program achieved, according to Fivush, an "excellent record" of placing its doctoral students.[53]

Another source of pride during her tenure was the Rosalynn Carter Distinguished Lecture program. Together Mrs. Carter and Professor Fivush brought to the Emory campus three of the most accomplished American women in public policy positions: former surgeon general Dr. Joycelyn Elders, former attorney general Janet Reno, and former secretary of state Madeleine Albright. Fivush describes her participation in this program as "the highlight of my personal experience with women's studies."[54]

Women's Studies at the Oxford Campus

As faculty and directors built the women's studies program at Emory College, a similar program took shape at the Oxford campus. Inspired by the developments at Emory and encouraged by Fox-Genovese, Patricia Owen-Smith, then an assistant professor of psychology at Oxford, decided to develop an introductory women's studies course for approval by the Oxford faculty.[55] Untenured at the time, Owen-Smith worried about faculty resistance to the idea at what she perceived as a somewhat more conservative campus environment at Oxford. History professor Ted Davis proved to be her biggest supporter and guided Owen-Smith on how to "sell" women's studies to the faculty. The Oxford faculty accepted Owen-Smith's proposal during the first meeting in which it was discussed.[56]

A talented and committed teacher, Owen-Smith attracted a growing number of students to women's studies. A key component of the program was Theory Practice Service Learning (TPSL), which Owen-Smith developed in an effort to integrate classroom learning with real-world situations. Students in the introductory women's studies course, in addition to attending class, also volunteered at various community organizations, such as a local Girl Scout troop, a battered women's shelter, and a home for at-risk adolescent girls. Students wrote final papers that integrated the knowledge gained from service experiences with that gained from course readings in feminist scholarship. Still a part of the introductory course, service learning, according to Owen-Smith, enables students to see how gender inequality "plays out in the community and how we can address this."[57]

The program at Oxford evolved to include three women's studies courses taught by Owen-Smith and Professor Pat del Ray, the former director of women's studies at the University of Georgia, as well as cross-listed courses taught by faculty in other departments, including English professor Adrienne Ivey and sociology professor Valerie Singer. Over the years, many Oxford students, inspired by Owen-Smith, Del Ray, and other faculty, made the decisions to major or minor in women's studies when they continued at the Atlanta campus. Some of the most talented and enthusiastic women's studies undergraduates at Emory began their academic journeys at Oxford College.

From Program to Department, 1999–2009

In 1999 Professor Frances Foster became the fourth director of the women's studies program at Emory. A leading scholar of African American and women's literature, Foster came to Emory from the University of San Diego in 1994 with a joint appointment in English and women's studies. Her arrival greatly enhanced Emory's reputation as a center for the study of African American literature and culture. The author of *Witnessing Slavery: The Development of the Antebellum Slave Narrative*

(1979) and *Written by Herself: Literary Production by African American Women, 1746–1892* (1993), Foster also edited and published a number of important collections of African American writings, including *A Brighter, Coming Day: A Frances Ellen Watkins Harper Reader* (1990) and *The Oxford Companion to African American Literature* (1997), which she coedited with others. In recognition of her scholarly accomplishments she was awarded a Charles Howard Candler Professorship by Emory in 1996 and two years later accepted the position as director of women's studies.

Foster brought new energy and ideas to women's studies as she worked to nurture intellectual and social community among undergraduates, graduates, and core and associated faculty. With the Student-to-Scholar Program, she created opportunities for undergraduates to meet and converse with visiting scholars and lecturers in women's studies. During her first year, she organized a colloquium series to address current debates about the direction of women's studies, bringing renowned and provocative speakers to campus. Her efforts gained praise from graduate students who commented in a letter, "Under your direction, 'Speaking of Women's Studies' has demonstrated the best of what the colloquium series can be: an exciting opportunity for scholarly, professional dialogue—with the added benefit of some food."[58] Throughout her tenure Foster sought ways to bring faculty and students together in intellectual dialogue and to recognize the hard work and accomplishments of women's studies faculty. She started the practice at the institute of holding readings and book parties for those with new publications, beginning with the celebration for Carla Freeman's book, *High Tech and High Heels in the Global Economy* (2000).

> *The department conducted an external review in 2005–06 and was acknowledged by outside reviewers to be the leading women's studies department in the country.*

Like directors before her, Foster devoted much time and thought to the development and direction of the graduate program. At her initiative, Emory hosted in October 2001 the first National Conference on the Ph.D. in Women's Studies, which brought together faculty members and directors from more than ten programs in the United States and Canada for two days of intense discussions about the challenges and future direction of doctoral education in women's studies. That conference established the basis for cooperation and constructive dialogue among doctoral programs and heightened Emory's national and international visibility in women's studies education.

Under Foster's leadership, women's studies gained three additional faculty members. Kimberly Wallace Sanders, a scholar of African American culture, was hired as an assistant professor with a joint appointment in the Institute for Liberal Arts, along with Julie Shayne, who joined the faculty as an assistant professor of gender and development in Latin America, with a joint appointment in the Sociology Department. In a significant development, women's studies hired Associate Professor Rosemarie Garland-Thompson in spring 2002 as the first faculty member with a sole appointment in women's studies. A leading figure in the emerging field of disability studies, Garland-Thompson impressed faculty and students with her scholarship on feminist theory and informed by disability. Her key works are *Extraordinary Bodies: Figuring Physical Disability in American Literature and Culture* (1997) and, as editor, *Freakery: Cultural Spectacles of the Extraordinary Body* (1996). She is the author, most recently, of *Staring: How We Look* (2009).

Garland-Thompson's appointment anticipated a major development in women's studies at Emory—the shift from a program to a free-standing department. The Institute for Women's Studies became the Department of Women's Studies in fall 2003, a process begun during Foster's tenure and completed soon after Carla Freeman took over as director. The change, which was strongly supported by Dean Steven Sanderson, followed long discussions among the faculty about the advantages and disadvantages of departmental status. One of the greatest advantages was the ability to hire and tenure faculty within women's studies, which enabled the director and faculty to make decisions about hiring and promotion in accordance with the needs and goals of the discipline alone, without regard to the needs of other departments. Over the next four years, the department hired two new faculty members with sole appointments in women's studies—Lynne Huffer, a scholar of feminist theory and queer theory, and Holloway Sparks, a political theorist. A third faculty member, Pamela Scully, was hired with a joint appointment in African studies, but her tenure home was women's studies.

Since acquiring departmental status, women's studies has continued to consolidate its reputation nationally, internationally, and at Emory. The department conducted an external review in 2005–06 and was acknowledged by outside reviewers to be the leading women's studies department in the country. This assessment was confirmed in 2007 with the department's number-one ranking by Academic Analytics. In fall 2007 women's studies celebrated its twentieth anniversary at Emory with a two-day symposium. Also recognizing the thirtieth anniversary of the President's Commission on the Status of Women and the fifteenth anniversary of the Emory Center for Women, this event publicly marked the decades-long collaborative efforts at Emory in behalf of women.

With twelve core faculty members—including four full-time and eight joint appointments—and more than sixty associated faculty, the department enjoys consistent support from the University administration and continues to grow. Its most recent hires in feminist science studies, Elizabeth Wilson and Deboleena Roy, demonstrate the ongoing commitment to building bridges with other parts of the University, including the Neuroscience Initiative, the Psychoanalytic Studies Program, and the Rollins School of Public Health. The department continues to offer a vibrant undergraduate major and minor, an increasingly popular graduate certificate, and a PhD program that sets the benchmark for the nation.

SECTION 3

Creating Engaged Scholars

CHAPTER 18

ADVENTURE AS SELF-TRANSCENDENCE
The Romance of Arthur Evans
— RICHARD S. WARD *and* MAXIMILIAN AUE —

Arthur Robert Evans joined the Emory faculty in 1966, after establishing himself as a scholar of distinction at the University of Notre Dame. Appointed to the Romance Language Department to teach French, he collaborated in scholarship with his wife, Catherine "Tass" Evans, and published on a wide range of topics in literature, art, and history. Born in Wisconsin in 1925 he was educated at the College of St. Thomas in St. Paul, Minnesota, and earned an MA degree in cultural history from the University of Chicago and a PhD degree in French from the University of Minnesota. At Emory he earned the Scholar/Teacher Award. These two reminiscences by colleagues and friends of Evans capture the spirit of a gentle man who helped shape the scholarly ethos during a dynamic period of Emory's life.

Richard S. Ward

THIS REMINISCENCE IS only a small window on the life and work of a remarkable scholar and a gentle, yet passionate, man. That I should ever have had an opportunity to experience and enjoy Arthur Evans as a teacher seems in retrospect to be something of an accident.

He had been at Emory only since 1966, as a professor of French in the Romance Language Department, yet he was already sought after by discerning graduate students because of the qualities he showed in his teaching relationships with them. I had little reason to know anything about this. I was not a graduate student, not even a registered student at all, and was some five years older than Arthur. I was a faculty member in the School of Medicine who had been at Emory since 1960 as a professor of psychiatry, teaching the basic course in psychiatry to medical students, while developing the training program in child psychiatry and laying the basis for a psychoanalytic institute. I had plenty of work to do.

In the summers, though, I liked to take advantage of living so close to campus that I could audit an occasional course—for example, a course in Italian grammar, and one in modern Italian literature with Walter Strauss, of the Institute for Liberal Arts, who departed afterward for Case Western Reserve University; I deny the charge that it was I who drove him away.

The emphasis on Italian was because of my wife, or, more precisely, my wife's family. Just before coming to Atlanta and Emory I had remarried, to someone whose family had a Sicilian background. My in-laws asked frequently, "Why does Richard know French and Spanish but doesn't learn Italian?"

My wife's grandfather, a dignified old Italian gentleman who had been a merchant both in the south of Italy and then in New York, could quote sections of the *Divina Commedia* from memory, and he frequently did. It was from him that I felt some pressure to make an effort in learning the Italian language, and so I did, in odd moments, working away with tape recordings and a couple of used textbooks. When Emory happened to come up with a short course in beginning Italian, it made sense to try to sit in.

My grandfather-in-law responded to all this one day by unloading on me two massive volumes of that great Sicilian epic, Luigi Natoli's *I Beati Pauli* (a narrative of resistance against Spanish oppression in the seventeenth century, a kind of Sicilian Robin Hood story). He had raised the ante. I would read this long tale before going to sleep at night, the heavy Cambridge Italian-English dictionary on the bed beside me, for looking up unfamiliar words. It was a wonderful adventure. I read with the rapt credulity of a child, engulfed in the emotions of triumph and despair, heroism and treachery, and I frequently read long after midnight, pushing on to translate yet another page because I couldn't wait to find out what happened next. I am convinced that it is the slowness of reading in a foreign language that brings back a childlike willingness to believe the story you are told; it's like walking or bicycling through a countryside absorbed in all the details you would miss by driving a car through it.

Then, in the spring of 1967, on a trip to Europe that included both work and a few days of vacation in Sicily, I was able to hold my own in conversations with relatives who spoke little or no English, although it was exhausting for me to keep it up for very long.

It was with this background in Italian that I heard about Arthur Evans, who was said to be considering leading a seminar on Dante and the *Divina Commedia*. I jumped at finding some way to join in; among other things, I thought it would be a fitting gesture of respect to my wife's beloved grandfather, now failing in health, and who would soon die of laryngeal cancer, in 1971.

The details of how I met Arthur and how the sessions on Dante came under way are lost for me in the mists of memory. Surely, if a seminar had indeed been planned, what actually developed was nothing like one in any conventional sense, and I rather doubt that anything ever was listed in official records of the Romance Language Department, because from the start I turned out to be the only student. For me it became like reading with a tutor, as if I were enrolled at Oxford or Cambridge. The failure to get any other students to come never seemed to bother Arthur. Though he perhaps had thought of teaching a group of graduate students, when it didn't work that way, he simply decided to go ahead with me. Much later Arthur did eventually give a real seminar on Dante, one attended by an appropriate number of graduate students, that was several years away. My sessions with Arthur were still going on then, but we had long since moved on to Ariosto.

Back near the beginning, other people seemed to find out about our Dante meetings. We would get a rare drop-in from a graduate student. Such visitors never stayed for more than a session or two, and I can understand why. We were reading Dante at a very leisurely pace. We used the John Sinclair edition, with translations on facing pages, but we worked almost entirely in Italian, reading it out loud and using our own words for translations. We took a year to read *Inferno*, a year for *Purgatorio*, and so on—scarcely the kind of schedule that would meet the needs of a graduate student intent on getting credits for graduation. The chair of the Romance Language Department, a charming lady named Emilia Navarro, would sometimes join in our readings, but she may have come in her official capacity, to check on what Arthur was doing, and she didn't come at all regularly.

> *His style was that of a shared exploration; he read a page, I read a page, we talked about items that interested us, we covered one canto of the poem each week.*

Moreover the "seminar" was held in my office, not in the Romance Language Department. At some point near the start of things, Arthur had seen my office and had reached the astute judgment that it was a great deal quieter and more comfortable than anything he could find in the Romance Language Department across campus. This is one of those little injustices in university life; medical offices (in this case, psychiatric) have to be suitable for seeing patients (i.e., paying customers) and so get more space and better furnishing. My office, in a former incarnation, had been the dining room of the house originally owned by Emory's first contractor, Arthur Tufts, a house now redecorated as a children's psychiatric clinic. The office not only was large but came complete with a pantry next to it, now refitted as a library, and a kitchen beyond; it was perfect for meetings and was quiet and comfortable for patients. Best of all, there was plenty of parking in the backyard, a priceless bonus at any university.

So this is how we started and how we continued for the next six or seven years. Studying with Arthur was for me an entrance into a wholly different world of educational experience. Arthur never taught in the conventional sense, certainly never lectured or pontificated. His style was that of a shared exploration; he read a page, I read a page, we talked about items that interested us, we covered one canto of the poem each week. Arthur was precise without being fussy, and he was interested in the details of words without being pedantic. Dante's vocabulary is at the interface with Latin, so that some of his expressions are language in the process of linguistic change; Arthur was intensely interested in this. His pace was always unhurried, his delight in the language infectious, and I had the experience not only of watching a scholar at work, but also being allowed to accompany him in the work in progress.

Arthur liked to find and bring in items that he thought added to our discussion. These were of great variety: photocopies from texts or scholarly articles, clips from the *New York Times*, or notes from his own past studies. At this distance it is hard for me to remember most of these. One that does stand out is the story of the man—Swiss, I think—who undertook to memorize the entire *Divina Commedia*. We marveled at such an undertaking. That fellow, apparently, was able to master *Inferno* with some ease in a couple of years, but then found that *Purgatorio* took much longer because he had to spend so much time reviewing the earlier sections to keep them in memory. Then, the problem was doubled or tripled when he added *Paradiso* to the load. Supposedly that next step took him more than an additional twenty years.

After all that, of course, he would have to keep on practicing, so as not to lose his hard-won accomplishment, and when and to whom would he recite the whole thing; who would have the patience to listen to it all?

Of course, this was in the days before computers and the Internet. Now you can go to Google, or Wikipedia, and easily find many of the things that Arthur had to expend labor to search out in order to add to his stores of information. For Arthur back then, however, knowing where to look for these bites of knowledge was part of his expertise, and at our sessions he was almost always coming up with something. The items themselves were not uniformly of great significance, but what was charming was Arthur's evident enjoyment in finding and presenting them. Maybe these things were an alternative to the usual long list of readings most seminar leaders assign to their students. Arthur didn't assign anything. His style was to suggest as we went along some sources that I could dip into, if I had the time and inclination. One that made the most lasting impression on me was Erich Auerbach's *Mimesis: The Representation of Reality in Western Literature*.

> *Though it took a full three years, there came a point when we had finished the* Divina Commedia. . . . *I don't believe there was any suggestion that we would stop reading together; the question was what we were going to read next.*

Over six or seven years of weekly meetings together, I should have learned more about Arthur himself than I did. In retrospect I find it somewhat remarkable that throughout our sessions together we were mostly occupied with the subject matter before us—the poetic texts. We did not spend much time talking about other matters. I learned little or nothing about his family, though I had met his wife, Tass, at least once, and my wife had known her in a different context. He did not inquire much about my family. I knew even less about his other faculty activities at Emory, and he did not ask about mine. I have since wondered if this was mostly his professionalism: he was, after all, the teacher, in these sessions. Or it may have been partly a consequence of the fact that we were both so busy. For my part, though I had a high level of control over my schedule, taking extra time out of it was at a price. I suffered, like most university professors, from the chronic guilt trip, since there always was more that needed to be done than could ever be realistically accomplished.

I am more inclined to think a larger factor in my not learning more about him was Arthur's innate modesty and reserve. He had no trace of showmanship or exhibitionism, and in fact he did not talk easily about himself. He was certainly friendly and warm. I can picture him in his customary gray cardigan sweater; I can picture his quick smile, which was quite endearing. In thinking about it, I have the feeling that that smile of Arthur's often had a hint of embarrassment in it and seemed to come at times when he had expressed himself more unguardedly than usual. This restraint was part of his courteous style and his habitual considerateness, which were also endearing, partly because they were really genuine, and partly because they were refreshingly old-fashioned, for that tumultuous era of student protests, the free speech movement, and the harshness of the Vietnam War conflicts.

One area in which Arthur did allow more of himself to show was tennis. Arthur played tennis, and was a tennis fan, especially a fan of Rod Laver, the Australian tennis star, about whom he would sometimes indulge in enthusiastic talk. These were the years of Laver's ascendancy, his Grand Slams, and, in a sense, the last of the grand old (wooden-racket) style of tennis. Apparently, though Arthur was relatively indifferent to the fads of popular culture, and especially those of television, he did watch tennis matches, the only television he allowed himself to watch.

I remember, at some point during these conversations about tennis, Arthur complained that he had some difficulty in finding people to play with. That led me to make a somewhat abrupt decision. I had come to Atlanta eager to play golf. Escaping from the concrete surfaces of Manhattan I loved the golf course because of its open air, green grass, trees, and blue sky. But ten or so years of life in Atlanta had worn down that special reason for golf. I was ready to change to a sport with better exercise and more companionship. I decided to take up tennis to be able to play with Arthur; at least that was the reason I remember as prompting the decision.

His personality as a tennis player was consistent with the rest. He did not carry his admiration of Laver to the point of imitating Laver's hard-charging net game. He was a pretty good intermediate player, with somewhat stylish strokes (which you couldn't say about mine) and was content to stay in the backcourt most of the time. He was always a gentleman and a good sport, in victory or defeat. I enjoyed playing tennis with Arthur, and treasure the memory of those few years when we played a fair amount together. I saw another, though not very different, side of his personality, but it did not lead to any particularly enhanced intimacy between us.

Though it took a full three years, there came a point when we had finished the *Divina Commedia*. I have only a dim memory of the discussions that followed, about what we were going to do. I don't believe there was any suggestion that we would stop reading together; the question was what we were going to read next. The clear vision that I do have of Arthur at that time is of his sitting in his favorite chair in that child psychiatry office at the moment when he told me of his preferred choice, which was to continue reading in Italian, reading the *Orlando Furioso* of Ludovico Ariosto.

Our "seminar" then turned to the study of the *Orlando Furioso*, to be interrupted by Arthur's thirteen-month sabbatical, during which he took his family to Europe, and to be resumed, after he came back. Arthur had explained that he preferred to stay with Italian rather than shift to Spanish, which we would have had to do if he followed my suggestion of Cervantes and *Don Quixote*. How grateful I feel, looking back, for that decision of his. Without it I never would have experienced the beauties of Ariosto's poetry, or the endless variety of the stories of the Paladins, Orlando (Roland), Rinaldo, Ruggiero, Bradamante, and others, that provided the plots for so many operas in the eighteenth century, but seem mostly forgotten today. *Orlando Furioso* is 38,736 lines long—one of the longest poems in European literature, and Arthur delighted in its twists and turns. How long we might have continued reading it together I cannot guess, but our "seminar" came to a close for tragic reasons.

Sometime in 1974 Arthur discovered that he had Parkinson's disease. The story as I later heard it was that he happened to stumble once while walking on campus, and a stranger sat him down on a bench to rest and told him that he showed signs of Parkinsonism. Of course, Arthur did not tell me about this, nor share his troubles with me. He had come back from his sabbatical in good health and probably was able to keep his impairments to himself for several years. I guess this was part of his being a private person, although I am sure that at that time I was never as perceptive as that walker on the campus had been. In later years I had vivid exposures to the personal tragedy that Parkinsonism brings to its victims, but in 1974 I had not yet had the experiences that would make me sensitive to the issue of the fatigue that is such a crippling part of Parkinson's disease. I was not able to be of much help to Arthur, nor did he ask me for help, or really allow me to share any of this with him. Sometime in 1976 he informed me that we would have to stop our readings altogether, that he had Parkinsonism, and was just too tired in the evenings; he needed to conserve his strength for his regular teaching work. I was surprised and disappointed, of course. I offered alternatives, to come to him, and to try to make it as easy as I could for him to continue, but Arthur was firm, and his decision included not encouraging any visiting. In retrospect, I see this as part of his courage in the face of what lay ahead and his refusal to accept sympathy for it; at the time, I missed him and felt cut off.

So we never finished the Orlando *Furioso*. We had reached something like a midpoint, and I kept on going by myself to the end. It seemed like a way of paying respect to Arthur.

I lost touch with Arthur over the next years but saw him a couple of times from a distance, as he was out walking in the neighborhood that we shared. His jerky movements and awkward postures gave sad testimony to the ravages of Parkinsonism. It is one of the tragedies of that disease that, though the mind may remain active and alert, speech becomes more difficult, and typing almost impossible. Communicating with others becomes more and more difficult, and increasingly one is shut up in a prison of isolation from which there is no escape. I was not a witness to this in Arthur; it must have been almost unbearable for those around Arthur, and who loved him, to watch the process of his decline. That is to say nothing of what it was like for Arthur himself.

One of my favorite lines in the *Orlando Furioso* seems apropos. It comes right at the beginning, verse 2, line 5; and goes like this "che 'l poco ingegno ad or ad or mi lima" (that the small talent [I have] from hour to hour she wears down [literally, "files" away]). Ariosto is complaining about his frustrations with his mistress, which he likens to those Orlando had with Angelica that drove the knight to madness, and is the central theme of the poem. He fears that she won't leave him with enough strength to finish his task (the writing of the poem). In a most cruel way, the line applies to Arthur, dealing with his harsh mistress, Parkinsonism, which so inexorably wore down just those faculties of his that were crucial to what he found enjoyment in and that had been such a vital part of his life.

Arthur retired from Emory in 1985 and died in 1992. A festschrift organized in his honor was published in 1993. I have read some of the beautiful things spoken and written about Arthur around his retirement and later at his funeral mass. I am made very aware that so many others admired and loved him and that they had so much broader a knowledge of him than I did, and that knowledge sharply limits the testimony that I can give tribute to him.

I retired from Emory in 1986, at the conventional age of sixty-five, but did not retire from my work as a psychiatrist. I, too, had a retirement party and a kind of book prepared for me, not a festschrift, but just a loose-leaf collection of comments from colleagues and former students. Somehow Arthur learned of this occasion and insisted on making a contribution to that collection. His piece occupies pride of first place in that folder. It is by far the longest contribution, more than three full pages of tightly handwritten script, the handwriting distorted by Parkinsonism but so carefully done that it is quite decipherable. I cannot imagine the cost to Arthur of the effort and labor that required. Seeing it, I was moved almost to tears. That he would make the effort to do that was somehow quintessentially Arthur.

As I said in the beginning I had only a small window into the life of this remarkable man, but what came through that window made an indelible imprint, and the store of fond memories I have of Arthur will stay with me as long as I am allowed to live.

Maximilian Aue

WHEN ASKED TO SAY a few words about Arthur Evans at his retirement, I felt honored and accepted gladly. But I should have been wary, for it was truly impossible to come close to doing Professor Evans justice in that context. What I had to say was incomplete at best, a mere indication of the range of Arthur Evans's impact on Emory.

I should like to start with a symptom: When I checked in the departmental office to refresh my memory on his publications, there was not a list to be found in the entire departmental files. The carefully compiled, annotated, and dated lists of publications, the very essence of academic existence, jealously treasured and meticulously kept up to date by most faculty members, were simply not there. Instead, after listing his books on Eugene Fromentin and *Four Modern Humanists*, he had simply written: "Articles on French, Italian, and German literature; on the interrelationship of the arts; on art history; on cultural history; translations." One and a half lines.

This seemingly small act illustrates why Arthur Evans's presence at Emory left its mark, and why his absence leaves a gap not easily filled, for both the range of expertise indicated in the statement just quoted and the matter-of-fact way in which it is described—indeed the sense of embarrassment at having to put it to paper at all—are rare indeed and are qualities I think it fit to remember and celebrate.

Arthur Evans's appointment was in French, but he never allowed this fact to limit him to national or linguistic boundaries. What interested him was the life of the mind and the senses, in whatever language or form of expression he might encounter it. Thus (after doing some detective work) we find articles on Balzac and his significance for modern painting; on Curzio Malaparte and Ernst Jünger; on Giuseppe Tomasi di Lampedusa; on Benito Mussolini's march on Rome; on Pieter Brueghel and John Berryman; on Dante, Paul Claudel, Erich Auerbach, Stefan George, and Max Beckmann. In each of these, sensitivity to detail and analysis enter into dialectic relationship, strengthening and refining one another and imparting a deeper understanding and greater sense of respect for the work of art. For this was what Arthur wanted: to have the work of art admired, rather than his own cleverness in analyzing it.

> *For Arthur, gentleness meant "gentilitas," the relationship of those who belong to the same "gens," the human gens; it meant the art of civilized and humane relationships between people.*

In a sense, Professor Evans's publications give us only an incomplete picture of his impact on the university he served for so many years. They say nothing about his many other interests, about the fact that, for years, his courses were the only place one could find Italian literature at Emory; about his contributions to the course titled "Europe between the Wars"; or about his findings concerning the late-nineteenth-century language crisis, including fine lectures on Flaubert, Mallarmé, Rimbaud, Rilke, and Georg Trakl. For him, more than for anybody I have known in a very long time, scholarship was not something to be expressed in publications and then more or less set aside in order to make room for the various demands of real life. For him the life of the mind was to be lived and shared, and not only written about. One was just as likely to come across an important insight while talking with him over coffee or dinner or at a party as in the context of a scholarly meeting. He rarely forgot such conversations. Even after a rather prolonged evening, one could expect a note from him the next day, continuing the conversation in some way, challenging one to think further, not just letting the matter die as so much small talk. The number of people he reached out to in this way is huge, and if we had always followed up, we would be much the richer for it.

Arthur Evans was a gentle man; someone first meeting him might be misled into believing that he was withdrawn or bookish and that his gentleness was in some way a sign of not wishing to cope with the world. Upon getting to know Arthur Evans better, this person would have had a surprise in store. For Arthur, gentleness meant "gentilitas," the relationship of those who belong to the same "gens," the human gens; it meant the art of civilized and humane relationships between people. Wherever he encountered violations of this mode of interaction—in coercion of any kind either by the carrot or the stick—he showed a resolve and strength that took one by surprise. Because he believed so strongly in the value of the whole human being, he frequently found himself at odds with processes that attempt to reduce human beings to the quantifiable—which, as we know all too well, can occur in the periodic evaluation processes that punctuate even the academic existence. Countless letters of support for colleagues at critical points in their career, some successful, some not, testify to his dedication to his belief that a university, of all places, ought to be concerned with human beings, and not just with CVs.

Thus it is perhaps appropriate that I close by referring to an entry on the slip of paper that he submitted in place of a CV. Under "Current Research" he writes, "adventure as mode of self-transcendence." I submit that this entry is not only a description of his research but a call to us: to embark on such an adventure, on a journey ever beyond our current limitations.

CHAPTER 19

JOHN HOWETT, ART HISTORY, AND CULTURAL FERMENT AT EMORY

— CATHERINE HOWETT SMITH —

Just before his death in April 2009, at the age of eighty-two, John Howett received word that he would be honored with the Woolford B. Baker Award for lifelong service to the arts. It was one of many awards he received during his career. Among the contributions to Emory for which John Howett will be remembered, the University will always count his four daughters, all of whom earned degrees at Emory, and three of whom were employed at Emory as of the publication of this book. In this chapter, one of those daughters pays tribute to the beloved scholar, teacher, mentor, and community servant who nurtured the arts at Emory with so much passion.

WHEN JOHN HOWETT came to Emory University in 1966 from the University of Notre Dame, he left a position as curator of a large art collection, housed in a new climate-controlled museum building, to join a fledgling department of art history installed in a house that had previously been a faculty residence on an edge of Emory's campus. The dining room of this modest building served as the departmental office; classes were held in the living room; the beginnings of a slide collection were stored in the kitchen; upstairs bedrooms became faculty offices; and the attic accommodated a photography studio. The program in art history had been inaugurated barely a year earlier under Professor William Crelly, who drew on his experience of teaching art history at Yale University in designing the first course offerings, attracting a small group of students. Emory had no program in studio art, and the only art objects available for study were part of an "archaeological" collection, housed in the basement of Bishops Hall, the home of the School of Theology, that included some authentic and useful examples of Egyptian art (brought to Emory in 1920 by Professor William Shelton) buried among a miscellany of stuffed birds, minerals, and such curious items as a nineteenth-century circuit rider's saddle and a chunk of salt labeled "Lot's Wife."

Nevertheless, Howett was excited by the prospect of teaching art history full-time in a major university and by the ambitious plans outlined for him by the dean of Emory College, John Stephens, who envisioned a much-enlarged program in art history, courses in studio art, and an expanded art and archaeology museum. In addition to professors Crelly and Howett, Emory provided a graduate teaching assistant, Anthony Cutler, a doctoral student in the Institute of the Liberal Arts (ILA), who subsequently pursued a distinguished career as a scholar of Byzantine studies at Pennsylvania State University. A wonderful staff at the Candler Library—then the main library on campus—worked to increase the art history holdings, and in the following year the new Woodruff Library was under construction, presaging an accelerating rate of physical growth of both the campus and the arts over more than four decades.

In 1968 Thomas Lyman, a former classmate and friend of Howett's at the University of Chicago, came from Southern Illinois State University to teach medieval art history. Howett taught subjects in the art of the Renaissance, and Crelly covered the seventeenth century. All three men participated in team-teaching an introductory survey of art history as well as a course in contemporary American art, forming the nucleus of the program during the years in which additional faculty were being recruited to broaden course offerings in other periods of art and culture. The Art History Department was the first at Emory to have equivalent representation of women and men on its faculty.

In desperate need of more space for a growing program, the department moved early in the 1970s into an equally unglamorous, rambling, one-story frame structure—"Annex B"—a former World War II army barrack that had been moved to the campus after the war (and located approximately where Patterson Green separates the Schwartz Center from the Goizueta Foundation Center). New faculty needing offices now included several working artists from the Atlanta area hired to teach a range of courses in studio art. At the outset it had been determined that all majors in art history should acquire some knowledge of art making, and the new departmental home soon accommodated classes in painting and drawing, photography, weaving, and pottery. Pottery was fired with sawdust in a makeshift kiln behind Annex B. Everyone, students and faculty alike, became adept at scrounging to make things work, and increasing enrollment in the program reflected that enthusiasm on campus. Emory's Visual Arts Department, now housed in its own building, had its beginnings in these years.

The faculty also wanted art history majors to experience actual works of art at close hand, rather than relying exclusively on slides and reproductions. As a former curator Howett recognized the formidable obstacles posed by limitations of space and, especially, funding, and recommended development of a study collection limited to works on paper—prints, drawings, and photographs. Over the years this collection grew slowly but steadily, through departmental funding, private donations, and the help of good relationships with a few dealers specializing in works on paper. The long central corridor of Annex B became a gallery space for exhibiting the collection as well as the work of students in the studio art program. The collection became an important instructional aid, complementing the availability of the best artifacts in the archaeological collection, which had been relocated from Bishops Hall to the old law building (now Carlos Hall) on the Quadrangle. The works-on-paper collection later became one of the core collections at Emory's museum and is now displayed in the John Howett Works on Paper Gallery.

It was during these early years, too, that the Art History Department initiated both a master's program to augment the interdisciplinary doctoral degree offered by the ILA, and a summer study-abroad program to further enhance students' firsthand experience of art and culture. Faculty and students familiar with this painstaking but very hopeful strengthening and expansion of opportunities over the years could hardly have imagined the splendid resources that would ultimately become available to the entire University community—as well as to scholars and the general public—through the collections represented in today's Michael C. Carlos Museum, all of it made possible through the generosity of the Carlos family and other donors, the dedicated efforts of President James T. Laney and Dr. Monique B. Seefried, and the tireless work of faculty members, curators, and museum staff.

> *One of Howett's principal concerns when coming to Emory was to reach out to the arts communities of Atlanta and the Southeast.*

The story of the establishment and growth of Emory's Art History Department throughout the sixties and seventies would be incomplete without recalling that all of these positive developments took place against a background of political and societal turmoil prompted by the war in Vietnam, civil rights protests, the assassinations of Martin Luther King and John and Robert Kennedy, and a host of other volatile public events and issues. Increasingly, university campuses across the country served as catalysts for vigorous debate of the most divisive questions facing individual citizens and the country as a whole; in some instances, serious—even violent and unlawful—confrontations took place, involving administrators, faculty, students, and law enforcement authorities.

At Emory the growing tension created by increasingly angry antiwar demonstrations came to a head on the day—May 4, 1970—that brought news of the tragedy at Kent State University, where protesting students were fired on by troops of the Ohio National Guard. The outpouring of anger and grief that followed the announcement of student deaths was creatively channeled on Emory's campus that evening by a participatory performance on the Quadrangle. Under the auspices of the Emory theater program, Peter Schumann's Bread and Puppet Theatre, a company nationally famous for its use of ten- to fifteen-foot-high puppets, expressed with stirring visual eloquence its opposition to war and violence of all kinds. A group of faculty that included John Howett had meanwhile won the full support of President Sanford Atwood in their appeal to the administration to resist the use of force in suppressing antiwar protests.

Another outcome of this period was the successful effort to make the by-laws governing the College faculty more democratic by allowing the participation of every faculty member, rather than just elected representatives. Subsequently the faculty, led by Howett, challenged the Emory ROTC to follow the same procedures as other departments in faculty selection and curriculum development, which were the responsibility of tenured faculty; the ROTC chose to withdraw from the University rather to conform. Elsewhere in the country, the presence of ROTC on a campus had provoked dangerous kinds of antiwar protests.

There were, in fact, many positive and enduring initiatives from this era of revolutionary change, when so much creative energy found expression in political action. Tom Lyman of the Art History Department participated in the highly contentious Democratic Party national convention of 1968 as part of an alternative delegation challenging the seating of the Georgia delegation appointed by segregationist Governor Lester Maddox, at the same time that Howett represented a group of Georgians filing suit against the governor, demanding democratic election of delegates. While unsuccessful at the time, this change was effected by the 1972 presidential convention.

Within the University, a greater sense of community, collegiality, and shared responsibility emerged from the new activism. Important new courses and programs requested by students and faculty—black studies, women's studies, environmental studies, for instance—breathed new life into academic discourse, eroding traditional disciplinary divisions. A group of art history students interested in environmental issues at both the global and local levels organized a University-wide celebration of the work of the visionary architect, designer, and futurist Buckminster Fuller. For his visit to campus, volunteers hand-painted a large reproduction of Fuller's "Dymaxion Air Ocean Map" on a wall of Annex B overlooking the Woodruff Library terrace, where a student rock band performed and a free meal of vegetarian soup and fresh-baked bread was distributed to one and all. Fuller lectured that evening to a packed house on his ideas of synergy in a global society.

In 1979, as the University prepared to celebrate the fiftieth anniversary of its Phi Beta Kappa chapter with a major symposium on "Intellect and Imagination," Clark Poling, one of the earliest members of the Art History Department faculty, proposed two of the participants for the symposium. The first was art historian Leo Steinberg, who presented a paper on Michelangelo's *Last Judgment*. The other was an artist, George Trakas, who was commissioned to build a three-part site-specific sculptural complex, representative of the "land art" movement that had become so important during the preceding decade.

In consultation with retired professor of biology Woolford Baker, who had many years earlier added native trees and shrubs to the ravine between the Quadrangle and Glenn Memorial, Trakas decided to install two narrow walkways that would allow visitors to descend the slope to the stream meandering below. The purpose of this part of Trakas's work, which he called "Source Route," was to refocus attention on the natural beauty and symbolic importance of a part of the campus that had become invisible to most people, a "wasted" opportunity for an experience of nature mediated by art. "Source Route" was left in place after the Phi Beta Kappa event and became a popular destination for visitors, with its atmosphere of quiet retreat; the ravine was dedicated as the "Woolford B. Baker Woodlands" in 1980. In 1985 a matching grant from the National Endowment for the Arts allowed Trakas to return to campus to stabilize and improve his sculptural walks, and John Howett's wife, Catherine, a landscape architect, to provide guidelines for managing the vegetation in the ravine. The work of caring for the woodland, its stream, and its important sculptural feature is now part of an ongoing environmental restoration project.

In 1985 the Art History Department moved to splendid new quarters in one of the original early-twentieth-century buildings on the Quadrangle designed by Henry Hornbostel. The former law school building, now renamed in honor of Atlanta philanthropist Michael C. Carlos, had been sensitively adapted to serve the needs of the department as well as the art and archaeology collections by the architectural firm of Michael Graves. John Howett had advised President Laney on the selection of Graves, as well as the earlier selection of architect Paul Rudolph to design Cannon Chapel, and represented Emory when the Graves design was given an Award of Excellence by the American Institute of Architects (AIA).

One of Howett's principal concerns when coming to Emory was to reach out to the arts communities of Atlanta and the Southeast. He was elected to the boards of several art institutions during his years at Emory, including the High Museum of Art, the Atlanta College of Art (where he delivered the commencement address in 1976), the Nexus Art Center, the Museum of Contemporary Art in Georgia, and the Brenau University Galleries. He also frequently lectured or served as visiting critic or juror at academic institutions around the state—Georgia Tech, the University of Georgia, Georgia State, Spelman College, Oglethorpe University, Clayton College, Reinhardt College, LaGrange College—and elsewhere in the region. He joined colleagues from Georgia Tech in organizing the first southeastern chapter of the Society of Architectural Historians, serving as the first chapter president in 1983–84.

A highlight of Howett's twenty-year service on the board of directors of the High Museum of Art was his chairmanship of the committee that chose Richard Meier as architect of a new museum building, completed in 1983; he represented the committee when the AIA gave Meier's firm an Award of Excellence for the design. He sustained his professional involvement with museum work over the course of many years by serving as guest curator for several exhibitions at Emory and the High Museum, including *Italian Renaissance Manuscript Illuminations* at the High in 1976 and *The Woodcuts of Albrecht Durer* at the Carlos in 1986. Two High Museum exhibitions tracing the origins of contemporary developments—*The Modern Image* in 1972 and *The New Image* in 1975—were funded by grants from the National Endowment for the Arts. In 1984 Atlanta's Heath Gallery mounted an exhibition of works by representatives of Atlanta's avant-garde in Howett's honor.

The Emory community of students and colleagues to which he committed himself in 1966 honored him as well over the thirty years of his teaching career. In 1980 he was chosen to deliver the University's Opening Convocation Address; he received the Senior Council Teaching Award in 1982, the Williams Award for Teaching in the Humanities in 1993, and the Arts and Sciences Award of Distinction in 2002. This last award summed up John Howett's contributions as "Teacher, Scholar, Curator, and Citizen of the University" with the following encomium:

> *We have been honored to witness almost your entire professional career as a scholar of Italian Renaissance and Contemporary American art, spanning thirty years at Emory University. You pioneered the creation of the Art History Department and later the Studio Art Program, serving seven years as Department Chair. Your efforts led to the rebirth of the Michael C. Carlos Museum, where your impact was so great that a room was named in your honor and an endowment established in your name. Your role as beloved teacher and mentor earned you the Emory Williams Award for Teaching in humanities. Your reach into the art world has extended far beyond Emory, as nearly every art institution in Atlanta has been touched by your wisdom, vision, and support. In the highest compliment that any practical man could hope to receive, Gudmund Vigtel, former director of the High Museum, said simply, "People have to listen to what he says because it makes good sense." Your record of achievement and your loyalty to Emory University forever distinguish you as one of our most valued faculty members.*

CHAPTER 20

LORE METZGER
Pioneer for Women Faculty

— RALPH FREEDMAN, CAROLE HAHN, PETER DOWELL,
MARTINE BROWNLEY *and* GAYATRI CHAKRAVORTY SPIVAK —

When Lore Metzger was appointed to the English Department in 1968, she became the first woman to hold the rank of full professor in Emory College—more than half a century after the first woman student had enrolled in the University. In the following reminiscences, her Emory colleagues and friends Carole Hahn, Peter Dowell, and Martine Brownley, her partner Ralph Freedman, and her friend and former colleague Gayatri Chakravorty Spivak, of Columbia University, recall the impact of her teaching and scholarship on Emory and the discipline of comparative literature.

Ralph Freedman

ON JANUARY 31, 1997, at 10:45 in the morning, at her home, Lore Metzger left herself and her world, surrounded by her books, her paintings, her music. The last we saw before she went was her beatific smile—the silent version of her vibrant laugh. Her physician, calling to express her sorrow at Lore's death, said that of all the patients she had had to see die, she had never known anyone "who died so much at peace with herself and her destiny."

This was Lore in death as she was in life: belligerent, even scrappy in her struggle for life and justice, but serene in her great integrity, giving of herself; impatient with fake authority while accepting the only true authority she recognized: humanity. Her devotion to those needing help, especially women, was exemplary. She was a bearer of friendship.

As a young girl Lore had been a refugee. Born in Frankfurt in 1925, she and her family fled from Nazi Germany to Switzerland and eventually to New York. She long since had ceased to be a victim of injustice, but like many others who had been victims, the adult Lore devoted her emotional and intellectual energy to others less fortunate than herself—whatever their origin. And she did so while retaining her clear head and superb sense of irony.

Being a refugee made her very determined. She used to tell an anecdote about her early schooling in the United States. She was twelve or so when she fled to Switzerland, and she must have been sixteen or seventeen when she arrived in the States. They were asked in school what profession they wanted to pursue. She said she wanted to be an English teacher. Her teacher said, "You can't, your accent is too bad. You could never be an English teacher." But that motivated her.

Lore was a creative scholar, a much-admired teacher. From her doctoral work on Goethe's *Faust* at Columbia in the 1950s and her decades of consultation in the editing of Coleridge's *Notebooks* as part of the massive project at Princeton University Press, to her teaching and writing, culminating in her book *One Foot in Eden* on the English romantic pastoral, Lore established herself as an innovative scholar in English and European romanticism. In recent years she widened her sphere to interpretations and reinterpretations of texts in the light of their meaning to women and issues of particular concern to women, focusing, among her many topics, on the novel from Jane Austen to Margaret Atwood.

From a small college like Mount Holyoke to large universities like the University of Washington and Michigan State, until finally settling at Emory, Lore consistently squared her service as an academic citizen with her intense devotion to those she taught. For her students—especially, but by no means exclusively, women—she was the quintessential role model.

Teaching spilled over into action. Lore fought for the recognition of women, helping to found the Emory University Women's Caucus in 1974 and to bring women's studies to Emory a decade later. She extended this commitment to professional organizations in her field, through service, for instance, to the International Comparative Literature Association, and as president of the Emory chapter of the American Association of University Professors, the University Senate, and the Faculty Council. From this activism emerged the role that Lore carved out for herself after retiring in 1992. She joined an Atlanta law firm that specialized in antidiscrimination suits. Though ostensibly a part-time volunteer, she immersed herself completely in this new occupation as a second career for the remaining four years of her life. At the same time, Lore joined the Atlanta Pro-Choice Action Committee and conscientiously gave over early morning hours to escort patients at abortion clinics and involving herself passionately in fund raising for the protection of the mentally and physically disabled. She completed an evolution from literature to advocacy that had long been coming.

Lore's courageous death underscored this dual commitment. Toward the end, an extraordinary moment of clarity, of humor—of intellectual presence—defined this remarkable woman. Already partly unconscious from lack of air the day before she died, she turned to my daughter-in-law, who touched her foot regularly to call her to consciousness. "This reminds me of the Third Voyage in Swift's *Gulliver's Travels*," she said, smiling at us as the inveterate teacher she was, "of those pompous philosophers in Laputa who can't attend to reality without being roused to action by the flappers."

She taught us about reality, about distance, about shaping and sharing a moment. Lore was an artist of life, of knowledge, of friendship, and love. She lives on.

Carole Hahn

I FIRST MET LORE in the spring of 1974. At the time she was president of the Association of American University Professors chapter at Emory, and she had appointed Gwen Kennedy Neville (then an assistant professor of anthropology in the Sociology Department) to chair the new Committee W (for issues related to women). Gwen invited Lore, me, and Nelia Kimbrough (a theology student) to a lunch meeting in the old upstairs of Cox Hall. We decided to hold an open meeting of women faculty to see what their concerns were. We put up posters on campus, but had no idea how many would come. On the day of the meeting, the room was packed! Women came from all over campus—the College, the medical school, the law school, and the theology school. Many issues were raised, including the fact that the University's affirmative action plan addressed only racial inequities but not gender. We decided to meet regularly the following year, and soon came up with the name Emory Women's Caucus.[1]

The caucus decided not to have a formal structure or officers. Yet Lore was a leader in everything the Emory Women's Caucus did to improve policies and practices affecting women in those early years. Lore was especially a champion for individual women who had experienced discrimination. Lore and Dora Helen Skypek, along with key women in the medical school (Margaret Drummond, Betty Edwards, Kay Edwards, Charlotte Deinhard), and across campus (Julianne Daffin, Carol Burns, Emilia Navarro, Delores Aldridge, Gwen Neville, Jo Taylor, myself, and many others) wrote numerous letters and petitions to the administration: to include women in the affirmative action plan, to appoint a University and College affirmative action committee, to establish the President's Commission on the Status of Women, to equalize pay, to join a case suing TIAA-CREF for discrimination against women, to provide child care at Emory, and to investigate the firing of Dean of Women Peggy Zeigler and the decision not to bring Gwen Neville up for tenure and promotion.

I became particularly close to Lore as we fought for Gwen to be treated with due process and nondiscrimination. Lore established a fund to which we could contribute to pay some of Gwen's legal fees. Lore helped Gwen and her lawyer, Maryanne Oakley, strategize as a series of administrators and committees agreed she had a case, but would not override a department and grant tenure. Throughout the two- or three-year battle Lore remained rational and determined and maintained her sense of humor. Over the years, Lore took up the cause, provided moral support, and gave valuable advice to many women and African American faculty whom she felt had been mistreated in employment, tenure, and promotion.

Lore was a leader not only in improving policies and procedures that affected women, but also in the development of women's studies at Emory. About 1984 she started a reading group. She invited about ten women faculty in the College who had an interest in feminist scholarship to come together and meet in each other's homes monthly to share readings reflecting the new feminism in their respective fields. The group included Lore, Emilia Navarro, Tina Brownley, Bonna Wescoat, Juliette Stapanian (later Apkarian), Peggy Barlett, Dora Helen Skypek, myself, and others. After several months we realized that there was so much happening nationally, and such strong interest at Emory, that it was time to lobby for feminist or women's studies at

Emory. Lore led our petition effort to Deans David Minter [of Emory College] and Ellen Mickiewicz [of the Graduate School].

Lore was an outstanding University citizen. She was on every imaginable committee—including chairing the University Senate, the University Research Committee, and the Emory chapter of AAUP; serving two terms on the College tenure and promotion committee; and serving on numerous search committees, and ad hoc committees to investigate particular issues and cases, as well as being director of graduate studies in the English Department and serving on committees in both English and women's studies. One year she told me she was serving on thirteen committees! She would spend long hours reading everything in a tenure and promotion file, including the candidate's publications. And she would have a huge stack of such folders to read each week. Yet she never complained about being overloaded with service. She just thought that's what a good citizen did.

I recall when she was invited to give the Convocation address to new students—the first time I remember a woman giving it. She based her talk on the writings of Hannah Arendt and encouraged students to become active citizens and to take a stand for causes they believed in. Lore practiced what she preached and respected others who were willing to stand up for social justice.

Many of her friends were like-minded, strong women. Lore, Do [Skypek], and Emilia individually were feisty. Together, they were a formidable force.

Lore never expected or sought accolades. When President Laney's secretary called her to come to the president's office, she wanted to know what it was about (it always irritated her that administrators had to know what we wanted to see them about, but never the reverse). She was frustrated not to be told and went to the office reluctantly. She was quite surprised when the president said the purpose of the meeting with Lore and two other individuals was to tell them they were being named Candler professors. Lore did not expect such an honor, although she epitomized a Candler professor—scholar, teacher, and leading University citizen.

Finally, Lore was serious—but she was also a lot of fun. She gave great parties, and she had a wonderful, warm laugh. She also enjoyed life. She and I used to go hiking in the North Georgia mountains, talking and laughing all the way. We also met weekly to swim at the Emory pool—but first we sat on the side of the pool and debriefed the week's issues, and then did the sidestroke so we could keep up our conversation.

Emory is a better place because of her commitment and tireless efforts on behalf of others.

Peter Dowell

I ACTUALLY REMEMBER the English Department interviewing Lore when she came as a candidate in 1968. She stood out that day and had things to say and said them well, but was relaxed and not worried about putting on some kind of pose. What struck me then and always afterward was she was her own person first and foremost. She had friends, she was genial and generous, but nonetheless she was her own person. If she believed in certain things, she wanted to stand for those.

My best experience of getting to know Lore was a rather weird situation in the department. A graduate student was doing a thesis on Flannery O'Connor, and her adviser decided that she was plagiarizing marginalia from books in O'Connor's personal library, which was housed at Georgia College and State University in Milledgeville. The student insisted that she wasn't plagiarizing. This went back and forth, and finally the chair of the department asked Lore and me to go to Milledgeville and read through these books and decide whether plagiarism was happening or not.

We did that, and for both of us, since neither of us had spent a lot of time in the rural South, just getting the sense of the South as we drove there was quite interesting. We ate at a little rustic place for lunch. Milledgeville was still pretty small. We finally decided there really wasn't enough evidence for a plagiarism case. O'Connor wrote so many marginalia, it was amazing. I sat there with her copy of Dante, and there were one or two notions or comments on practically every page.

Here was this professor who had grown up in Europe and New York and had gone to Michigan State and Columbia, and then chose to come South. It was a choice she felt comfortable with, because of the kind of openness she had. In that trip to Milledgeville, I think she felt she was seeing the South for the first time. Where we were was, of course, Flannery O'Connor's alma mater, which at that point was still the Georgia State College for Women, and I suspect that's something that impressed her: here was this supposedly conservative southern town, but home to the Georgia State College for Women and the great woman writer Flannery O'Connor.

She always looked for good graduate students and wanted to mentor them. That was her main strength in teaching, working with graduate students and really establishing a personal relationship with them. I never saw her in the classroom, but my sense is that she excelled in presenting material to students and getting them to understand it beyond the superficial level.

One thing that she did among many things was to campaign for an undergraduate major in literature. She didn't want to call it comparative literature; she wanted it just to be literature. She didn't want the students necessarily to train in another language the way you would in a comparative literature program. She wanted a major that would broaden out literature, and she influenced the English Department and the College to pass that major. It lasted for several years, until the people who were comp-lit wanted something labeled comp-lit in the undergraduate area. Graduate students were always particularly attached to her; she had a way with graduate students. The undergraduates felt she had high standards but she was interested in undergraduates who were interested in reading literature.

Martine Brownley

LORE WAS ONE OF the great intellectual presences at Emory, not just in the English Department but across the University. A superb Romanticist by training, in her reading she ranged far and wide. Whenever I became interested in an author or a genre, the next time I was at her place I'd notice that my latest discovery was well represented in her bookcases.

She was a superb role model and mentor for women faculty at all levels. Her generosity to all of us was unstinting. She taught us how important it was to understand how universities actually functioned, particularly emphasizing the crucial role of proper procedures in ensuring fair treatment to everyone in the academy, whatever their status. She always leaped eagerly to the defense of any underdog. She worked tirelessly to see that Emory hired and tenured more women and African Americans. She did everything she could to clear the path for others.

Lore was an unparalleled intellectual mentor. Whenever I hit a snag in my research, I'd discuss it with her, and even though our areas of work were very different, she could always ask the right questions to get me back on track. She loved intellectual engagement with anything on any level, and she excelled at it.

Gayatri Chakravorty Spivak

MEETING LORE METZGER gave a different meaning to "love," to "courage," to the idea of an examined life. I met her in 1982. She hosted a meal to welcome me to the Emory feminist community. When I came the next time, to negotiate [an appointment], I stayed in her place. Even my mother said that I had gained a sister. When I came to live in Atlanta in 1983, with a job at Emory, Lore and I were natural allies.

I left Emory for the University of Pittsburgh in 1986. Until her death in 1997 we spoke to each other at least once, and usually more than once, every day. In 1987 I started a lifelong commitment to training teachers in subaltern groups in rural West Bengal. The first fifteen years or so I hardly spoke about these efforts. I felt that they were nothing but records of mistakes, and, also, that whatever was happening was altogether too fragile, and perhaps would not and could not last. Yet whenever I saw Lore, words would start pouring out, I would talk Tristram Shandy–fashion, about "what had happened" in the schools—no analysis, just talk. And she listened silently, just a few words here and there. At her death in 1997 I found out that she had left ten thousand dollars for my efforts at rural education. I invested the money in my parents' name and established a nonprofit foundation.

Lore and my mother had become friends in their own right. This, too, was unusual. I have been teaching now for forty-five years. Not one of my colleagues had understood that my mother was a person of great intelligence and idealism—except for Lore, and she brought Ralph with her into this realization.

I do not now remember the year Lore retired; I only remember that she went looking for ways to be socially useful. She told me many times that she had been inspired by my example. And yet, as I told her repeatedly, [it was] she who gave meaning to my elementary efforts, first efforts, at rural education. Isn't that how it should be between friends? Each thinking the other's gift.

First she campaigned for a woman candidate for state office from the Democratic Party. Democracy was her primary interest. She went next to doing heavy-duty paralegal work for unions. Socialism undergirded democracy. Finally, when cancer hit her, she moved to advocacy for the disabled. The body held all principles together. The final move was to use her authority as a terminally ill person to persuade people into support for the cause. A story of tremendous courage.

I told her many times that she was my Mahaguru (a great teacher) as she walked her way with unshakable courage toward death. I was in Delhi in January 1997. (She died on the thirty-first.) I called sometime in the second week of the month. I said, Lore, please stay alive until the end of the month, until I go back to New York, teach my first class of the semester, and come to Atlanta to see you. And so she did. I will never forget our last conversation, her eyes brilliant with affection, intelligence, and the knowledge that her journey was at an end.

What's still valuable, I asked her. And she said, without hesitation, teaching.

CHAPTER 21

"ATHLETICS FOR ALL WHO WISH TO PARTICIPATE"
The Career of Thomas Edwin McDonough Sr.
— CLYDE PARTIN SR. —

In 1919, when Emory College moved to Atlanta, track was the only intercollegiate program allowed by the board of trustees. In time, a few other intercollegiate sports entered the picture, and in 1946 the board began to ease off its restrictive policy. Key to the transformation was the vision of Tom McDonough, chair of the Division of Physical Education and Athletics, who set the pace for a more prominent intercollegiate program that would reach fruition in the 1980s.

THOMAS EDWIN MCDONOUGH SR. was born in 1898, in Lacrosse, Wisconsin, to a railroad engineer and a woman who was descended from Roger Taney, the fifth Chief Justice of the United States. Growing up in humble circumstances, Tom worked after school hours as a printer's devil, a shoeshine boy, a newspaper deliverer, and a foundry laborer. After his parents divorced he moved into a YMCA and took a full-time job. Interested in medicine, in the fall of 1924 he entered Columbia University with a medical career in mind. While there, he befriended Nicholas Murray Butler, Columbia's president, who so impressed McDonough that he decided to go into teaching instead of medicine. Transferring to George Peabody College in Nashville, he received the BS degree in 1927 and an MA degree in 1928. It was here, too, that he met Ophelia Jakes, whom he married in Nashville on May 6, 1928.

That fall, Dr. Herman Lee Donovan was appointed to a faculty position at Peabody, where he met Tom McDonough. When Donovan was later appointed president of Eastern Kentucky State Teachers College, he took McDonough with him to be director of physical education at Eastern. Donovan's wife recalled McDonough as "a dashing, well balanced graduate student directing many activities on the Peabody campus in Nashville, Tennessee. He won faculty attention and approval. The young women students looked at him admiringly."[1] For McDonough, the tenure at Eastern was one of the happiest periods of his life, and it was there that he developed a reputation as a master teacher.

In the meantime, the Atlanta campus of Emory was growing slowly out of the mud of Druid Hills and the slough of the Great Depression. The need for an attractive array of campus activities was becoming as great as the need for stronger academic offerings. When Goodrich C. White became president of Emory in 1942, the first full professor he recruited was McDonough. As head of the Division of Physical Education and Athletics, McDonough replaced Jeff McCord, a friend of McDonough's who had been head of the division since 1931 and had done an excellent job, even putting his own money into the program. But McCord was not a professional physical educator, and White wanted a professional to lead the division. McCord recommended McDonough.

"McCord," said McDonough, "invited me and Mrs. McDonough to his home on Lullwater Road, near Emory, and then over to Dr. White's office." White offered McDonough the position, but McDonough turned it down because it paid four hundred dollars less than he was earning at Eastern Kentucky. White would not take him to see the physical education facilities because, as White later said, he was ashamed of them. Shortly after returning to Kentucky, however, McDonough received a call from McCord asking him to revisit Emory. McDonough did return and talked to Dr. White, who commented that Emory still could not match his Eastern Kentucky salary, which was more than any professor on campus was being paid; but when White again offered McDonough the job, McDonough accepted the challenge. He recalled later that he told the president, "We can go forward if I get your backing and the backing of the board."

The physical facilities that McDonough inherited included an old wooden building constructed in 1923, which had one nonregulation basketball court and a pot-bellied stove in the corner for heat. There was also a small, nonregulation swimming pool, built in 1927 as an outdoor pool and enclosed in 1932 (McDonough called it the black hole of Calcutta). There was also limited space in the basement of Winship Hall, one of the original residence halls (razed in 1984), consisting of a small office and a somewhat larger room that served as a gymnasium, boasting a punching bag, a wrestling mat, and other small pieces of equipment.

This was the situation in which McDonough found himself for his first few years at Emory. He had already distinguished himself in physical education before coming to Emory. As director of physical education at Bluffton, Indiana, he had introduced physical education to the elementary and secondary schools. In Milwaukee he had supervised physical education in the elementary schools, working with twenty-two schools in the Polish section of the city where children could not speak English. For four summers he was a camp counselor for inner-city children in New York City, where he befriended the author Robert Benchley. He also taught at Columbia's Horace Mann Elementary School at the same time he was assistant manager of the Columbia football team under coaches Perry Houghten and Lou Little. At Eastern Kentucky, he had overseen construction of excellent facilities, including a six-thousand-seat stadium in a concave design from top to bottom, the first stadium of this type in the United States. He had developed a four-year major curriculum of health and physical education and required all coaches to teach one or more courses. At the same time, he had continued to officiate football and basketball games from high school to college to the professional ranks. He had served briefly as a visiting professor at Louisiana State University, where he was an assistant coach of football and later assistant director of athletics. While in Kentucky he was president of the Kentucky Association for Health, Physical Education, and Recreation and president of the Southern District of the

Thomas McDonough

American Association for Health, Physical Education, and Recreation. A year after arriving in Georgia, he became president of the Georgia Association.

There was no question that he was the right man for Emory. His philosophy was "out of the grandstand and onto the playing field." He believed in playing, not watching, and his thinking was exactly the same as President White's. The University, under White, recognized that "the direction and control" of athletics was one of the educational functions of the University, to be administered and financed in the same way as other educational functions. With the backing of the administration and funding from the University budget, McDonough emphasized the "education" in physical education, making it a requirement for freshmen and sophomores.

McDonough's advent to Emory coincided with that of the V-12 Program of the United States Navy and Marine Corps during World War II. As part of the war effort to train medical doctors for service, the program brought 650 trainees to the campus. McDonough found that most of them were in poor shape. He put them all through tests to determine their fitness and separated them into three groups based on ability. Then they were put through a regimen of exercises, led usually by theology students who had been hired for that purpose. This initiative impressed the officials in charge of the navy V-12 Unit, and they requested that he take charge of this unit. McDonough begged off, because he was not a soldier or sailor. But the navy persisted, and McDonough took over the unit with great success.

The December 1, 1944, "Report of the President" to the board by White reaffirmed Emory's stand on intercollegiate athletics but stated that a more affirmative position of intramurals was needed.

> I am more than ever convinced of the wisdom of Emory's long established policy with reference to intercollegiate athletics. I think, however, that we have in the past, of necessity, taken too

negative a position; and I think we have not, again of necessity, provided adequately for intramural sports and games as part of our total program of physical education. We are in position now to make adequate provision and to adopt a more positive attitude. Thus, we may capitalize on our defined policy and demonstrate what can be done with an intramural program and rigidly limited intercollegiate competition.

This 1944 report went on to lament the lack of adequate athletic facilities, especially a gymnasium, which greatly hampered an effective intramural program. The report concluded that the board of trustees should do two things: (1) reaffirm its policy of nonparticipation in intercollegiate football, and (2) authorize the president to appoint a special committee to draft an adequate restatement of the University's policy on athletic competition, both intramural and intercollegiate.

The work of this committee led to the board's adoption, on October 16, 1945, of a "Statement of Policy on Athletics and Physical Education." The statement underscored Emory's view of athletics "as an integral part of a well ordered program of physical education," while it reiterated the University's aversion to those competitive sports that require elaborate and expensive facilities for public entertainment. "Competition in football, baseball, and basketball will, therefore, be limited to intramural contests." The crux of the statement was that Emory athletics was intended for the physical and mental betterment of all the students, not for the public's amusement. While McDonough heartily approved this position, he liked even more the board's decision to "proceed with the erection of a gymnasium as soon as consistent with present building plans in order to make the athletic program more effective."

McDonough wanted to emphasize physical education classes instead of the tradition that had grown up at Emory, of games between classes and schools. In 1944–45, McDonough hired graduate or professional students, principally from the theology school, to implement his plan. They were put in charge of classes built around touch football, basketball, and other sports.

In his early years at Emory, McDonough found that half the students were being excused for medical reasons. He persuaded a friend from Eastern Kentucky State to come to Emory as school physician. With Dr. Jacob D. Farris on hand, McDonough wrote to each physician who had excused a student explaining the aims of Emory's Physical Education Program. As a result, he achieved almost 100 percent participation among freshmen and sophomores. Classes were elective, except for swimming, which was required of all students.

In the October 1946 edition of the *Journal of Health and Physical Education*, McDonough published an article titled, "The College Intramural Program." Here he outlined "nine malpractices that physical education departments sponsoring intramurals should not succumb to." With this list at its foundation, the *1952 Bulletin of Emory University* listed guiding principles for the University's intramural program. These principles emphasized intramurals as a "positive good" rather than a mere substitute for intercollegiate athletics; noted the consonance between Emory's intramural program and the University's larger aims; promoted participation without regard to awards, but for the sake of fostering "larger values"; linked the program to the instructional budget rather than to gate receipts and concessions; called for expansion of offerings to meet the needs and preferences of students; and underscored the importance of laying a foundation for "total fitness" for life. Like his predecessors, McDonough believed that intercollegiate contests should be limited to sports that have proven "carry over value" for postcollegiate life—sports like golf, tennis, swimming, and running.

Under McDonough's leadership, Emory's intramural athletic program prospered. He gave it purpose, direction, and goals. He carefully drew the plans of Emory's field house for maximum use and efficiency.

Emory's intramural sports program had been born in the 1890s with the aid of Frank Clyde Brown, when Emory was at Oxford. The program grew in Atlanta under the able leadership of Ray K. Smathers, James G. Lester, Ralph L. Fitts, and Jeff D. McCord. It received a tremendous boost when the Athletics Department was absorbed into the University educational curriculum in 1942. With the completion of a field house in 1948, under the guidance of McDonough, the program continued to mature.

The 1946–47 year saw the largest coaching staff in Emory's history, with eight coaches and four student managers. That year, too, a significant change took place in the intercollegiate program. Athletic contests, formerly limited to events on the Emory campus, were changed to allow Emory teams to travel. Interfraternity play increased. Intercampus events among Emory's campuses in Oxford, Emory, and Valdosta began.

In early 1947 McDonough wrote a letter to President White saying that the programs had reached their capacity without a new gymnasium. He personally showed White and the board chair, Charles Howard Candler, a spot next to the current McDonough Field and told them what he wanted. Both of them recoiled at the size and cost, but finally they consented to the site. McDonough's solution for the building was to plead with George Mew, the business manager of the University, who wasted no time in arranging to go to Oklahoma City and buy a surplus airplane hangar.

> *Emory boasted of having more students take part in sports than any other school, with five hundred men playing on four tackle football teams and thirty-six touch football squads.*

The hangar had been built for military aircraft, so of course changes had to be made. But to McDonough's delight, the building, when shipped to Atlanta and assembled, totaled approximately forty thousand square feet, enough space to hold, in time, four handball courts (one lined for squash), a swimming pool (ninety by forty-five feet), a locker room and shower area, three volleyball courts, five badminton courts, a small weight room, office space, a women's locker room, and four tower spaces for storage or offices. McDonough's gym had everything he had asked for. The Field House, as it was called, was opened in the fall of 1948.

In the fall of 1949, McDonough hosted a seminar in conjunction with a formal dedication of the Field House. The seminar was a working conference on health, physical education, and recreation. Twenty-two states were represented. McDonough received assistance from the Emory Education Department as well as College dean Judson C. Ward, and health education leaders throughout the country. These included Dr. Jay B. Nash, director of the Department of Physical Education at New York University, Dr. Delbert Oberteuffer from The Ohio State University, and Jackson Sharman from the University of Alabama, all of whom led seminars.

The following year, McDonough introduced the Emory Chapter of Sigma Delta Psi, sometimes called the Phi Beta Kappa of sports. Members were required to pass a difficult series of tests. Early in its existence, only two schools in the country had more students qualify than Emory.

In 1951, because of basketball scandals at several colleges and a furor about football at West Point, national attention again focused on the different model of Emory's athletic program. A reporter for the *Kansas City Times* wrote that Emory fielded ten completely equipped football teams and forty basketball teams, and that organized competition was held in every popular major and minor sport. "The college plays regular intercollegiate schedules in golf, tennis, swimming, and track and field. It has nine full-time coaches and twelve assistants," the reporter noted. Another writer, Willard Neal, said Emory boasted of having more students take part in sports than any other school, with five hundred men playing on four tackle football teams and thirty-six touch football squads. He quoted President White as saying that he "was envied by a good many college presidents."

"While nearly everybody at Emory played one game or another," wrote Neal, "hardly anybody watches."

Although McDonough had a few intercollegiate teams, his main interest was in teaching physical education and further developing the intramural program. When asked what pleased him most about his years at Emory, McDonough reminisced later in life, "I was pleased that the administration went along with me on a physical education program. There was constant pressure for intercollegiate competition. I thought that this was the most unique physical education program in the country." While expanding the intercollegiate program by introducing wrestling as an intercollegiate sport in 1950 McDonough continued to emphasize the education work of his program by also sponsoring wrestling clinics for high school coaches. In 1958 he added soccer to the intercollegiate program and held clinics for high school coaches. Under swimming coach Ed Shea, and later coach Ed Smyke, Emory held high school swimming and diving meets annually, with some four hundred to five hundred swimmers each year.

For McDonough, Emory was the only university in the country that fit his philosophy, which not only gave priority to academics over athletics but also valued involving all the students in athletics all the time.

Emory's intramural athletics policy became deeply ingrained in the University. Geared for the ability and skills of the entire student body, it afforded competition for all types of individuals—the talented and the untalented. Then, as now, it was not characterized by the features of varsity sports, including their commercial focus, high costs, large numbers of spectators, and considerable publicity. Moreover, it encompassed all divisions of the Emory University community—undergraduate students, graduate students, and, for many years, faculty.

In 1952 the American Academy of Physical Education cited Emory's Physical Education Department for "commendable policies and practices," an award that placed a capstone on McDonough's first decade in Atlanta. The changes in ten years had been miraculous, including the completion of the gymnasium, the swimming pool, and three three-acre playing fields. President White spoke happily of "modern and adequate facilities and a highly competent staff," expressing pride in the development of "what may well be a model program in this field." The department also offered an intramural program for women (from the nursing school, Graduate School, and faculty and staff) and a summer program for the Emory community.

In cooperation with the Education Department, McDonough offered courses leading to the master of education degree. He also provided consultative services to groups ranging from elementary and secondary schools to private clubs. He made courses available to public school teachers through the Atlanta Area Teacher Education Service and encouraged Boy Scouts and Girl Scouts to use the Emory facilities to further their testing and merit badge work.

When Emory College became coeducational in 1953 McDonough's staff had to adjust to accommodate a large number of undergraduate women with no increase in facilities. A partial solution lay in McDonough's attitude. "They will have to live together in the future," he said. "Why can't they play together today?" Men and women began taking classes together in such sports as survival swimming, tennis, golf, and gymnastics. Women became reserve members of the varsity tennis and golf teams, although in the end they had no opportunity to play in any intercollegiate matches.

The Department of Physical Education and Athletics was always flexible in meeting students' interests. When students lost interest in a sport, it was abandoned, and another sport was found to replace it. Tackle football, long an important feature in intramural contests, was discontinued in 1956 along with intercollegiate golf. The only tackle football on campus after that was the annual Duck Bowl game traditionally played by Sigma Nu and Pi Kappa Alpha fraternities (since 1931), with the losers providing a duck dinner. In 1957, for one year Chi Phi replaced the Pikes, who were unable to field a team.

At least once each decade Emory saw a great surge of support for major intercollegiate competition, usually centered on basketball. True to custom, in 1957 the student newspaper promoted intercollegiate basketball. Students voted for it two to one, but only a fourth of them took part in the polling. Asked about the plan, McDonough said what Emory officials had been saying since 1891—that sports requiring elaborate and expensive facilities for "public entertainment" did not fit the educational priorities of the University.

The gymnasium, which seemed to fill all needs in 1948, was already overcrowded ten years later. President S. Walter Martin, who succeeded White in 1957, listed a gymnasium annex as a major need in his first report in 1961. The original building, constructed before Emory became coeducational, was now inadequate.

The youth and vigor of President John F. Kennedy brought a new emphasis on physical fitness to the national scene in the early 1960s. Enthusiasm for fitness touched college campuses across the country and gave Emory's program added significance. As a national leader in the physical education field, McDonough served as a member of the President's Youth Fitness Committee and was cochair of the Georgia Governor's Council on Physical Fitness, charged with organizing the physical fitness program for the state. He also served as visiting professor at many schools, including the University of Chicago and the University of Rome, Italy. One of McDonough's last accomplishments at Emory came about through his friendship with Walter Candler, a son of Asa Candler. Walter Candler gave the money to carve out three new athletic fields in an area of the campus north of Eagle Row now called Candler Fields.

As McDonough's career neared its peak he received the Creative Award of the American Academy of Physical Education and the first distinguished alumnus award given by George Peabody College (1966). His retirement in 1967 was recognized with a major dinner at Emory, where he was presented many gifts, including a portrait and a trip to Mexico for the Olympic Games. Eastern Kentucky University presented him with an honorary doctorate and named one of their intramural fields for him; a decade after his retirement, the University of Wisconsin at Lacrosse recognized him and Howard Munford Jones with the school's first distinguished alumnus awards. McDonough gave the Emory idea of "athletics for all" a new luster and national distinction.

After being at Emory for twenty-five years McDonough retired in 1967 and worked for a time with the Georgia Department of Education until 1975. After his wife's death in 1984 "Mr. Mac" moved to Wesley Woods, where he died in 1989 at age ninety-one.

References

Arey, Norman. "Emory's Way—How to Succeed in Sports without Cash for a Program." *Atlanta Journal*, May 23, 1973.

Bulletin of Emory University Physical Education and Athletics 38, no. 22 (December 1, 1956): 1–16.

Cleveland, Carol. "The Life of Thomas Edwin McDonough Sr. and His Contributions to the Area of Health, Physical Education, and Athletics." Atlanta: Emory University, 1969.

Dedication Ceremony of Thomas E. McDonough Sr. Field, Emory University. August 5, 1985.

Hackensmith, C. W. "Dr. Thomas E. McDonough: Mr. Physical Education." *Georgia Association for Health, Physical Education and Recreation* (Fall 1973): 6–9.

"He Gives Everybody a Chance to Play." *Emory Reports*, March 1956.

Klatsky, Fred M. "The History of Intramural Sports and Emory University (1890–1950)." Thesis in partial fulfillment of the requirements of the Honors History Program, Emory University, 1973.

Lee, David. "Emory Honors McDonough." *Emory Wheel*, May 25, 1967. 8.

Partin, William Clyde, Sr. *Athletics for All. A History of Health, Physical Education, Athletics and Recreation at Emory University 1836–2005*. Atlanta, GA: Emory University, 2006.

———. Interview with Thomas Edwin McDonough Sr. May 12, 1982.

"That Splendiferous Gymnasium." *Emory Alumnus Magazine*, April 1949. 2–7.

"Thomas Edwin McDonough: A Household Word." *Emory Magazine*, July–August 1957. 12–13.

CHAPTER 22

RICHARD A. LONG
Public Scholarship across Disciplines and Institutions
— RUDOLPH P. BYRD *and* DANA F. WHITE —

In this appreciative essay of Richard A. Long, Emory's Atticus Haygood Professor Emeritus of Interdisciplinary Studies in the Graduate Institute of the Liberal Arts, Professors Rudolph Byrd and Dana White limn an extraordinary and long career spanning many fields and touching countless lives. Trained as a medievalist, Long has been a pioneering scholar and teacher with both a national and international reputation in African American studies, art history, comparative literature, dance, English, foreign languages, music, and philology. His historic restored home in Atlanta's Inman Park has served as a way station for renowned scholars, artists, and writers.

SINCE THE 1990s scholars both inside and outside of the academy have placed great importance upon what has come to be known as public scholarship—that is, scholarship that serves the public good and, in the process, strengthens our democracy and inculcates within the public a deeper awareness of our national history and heritage. As a public intellectual, Richard Long has been engaged in this vital form of teaching and scholarship—which for him takes place within the context of the academy, the museum, and arts festivals—since 1946, when he became a member of Philadelphia's Les Beaux Arts, a circle of African Americans involved in the arts under the patronage of the poet Bessie Calhoun Bird.

As far back as 1955, following his first trip to Haiti, Long organized an exhibition and symposium on Haitian art at Morgan State University and at the Barnett-Aden Gallery in Washington, D.C. In many ways, this marked the beginning of an illustrious career as a curator. Long curated and organized several landmark exhibitions and symposia between 1956 and 1987. In 1968 he organized the Symposium on Traditional African Art at Hampton University, which subsequently became the Triennial Symposium on African Art.

In honor of his friend and colleague Alain Locke, philosopher, art historian, and literary critic, in 1970 Long curated "Homage to Alain Locke: An Art Exhibition" at the New York City headquarters of the United Negro College Fund, which featured the work of such artists as Aaron Douglass, Beauford Delaney, Romare Bearden, Palmer Hayden, Hale Woodruff, and Alma Thomas. This highly acclaimed exhibition was followed three years later with another, titled "Highlights from the Atlanta University Collection of Afro-American Art," a collaboration with Atlanta's High Museum.

Perhaps Long's most celebrated project in the arts is Festival under the Sun, a collaboration with Nanette and Romare Bearden. Taking place in St. Martin, Festival under the Sun drew such artists as Cledie Taylor and Jonathan Green. Concurrent with his curatorial work, Long established the New World Festivals of the African Diaspora. Taking place in Salvador da Bahia and Rio de Janeiro, Brazil (1978); Port-au-Prince, Haiti (1979); and Paramaribo, Suriname (1982), these festivals provided the context for a rich and stimulating dialogue between artists and intellectuals of the African diaspora.

Born in Philadelphia, Pennsylvania, on February 9, 1927, Long attended Temple University, where he earned his baccalaureate and master's degrees between 1942 and 1948. Following postgraduate studies at the University of Pennsylvania, Oxford University, the University of Paris, and the University of Poitiers, where he was a Fulbright Scholar, he earned his doctorate from Poitiers in 1965. During this period he launched a distinguished career in the academy that began with an appointment in English at West Virginia State College and Morgan State College. In subsequent years Long held faculty appointments at Hampton University, Harvard, the University of North Carolina at Chapel Hill, and institutions in West Africa, Central Africa, South Africa, and India.

From 1968 to 1987 he was a member of the faculty at Atlanta University, where, through his teaching, scholarship, and leadership in African American studies as well as the visual and performing arts, he brought great distinction to that university. In 1973 he was appointed adjunct professor in Emory's Graduate Institute of the Liberal Arts, and in 1987 he joined the faculty of Emory University full-time as the Atticus Haygood Professor of Interdisciplinary Studies.

Long's scholarship is exemplary not only for its high quality, but also for his rigorous interdisciplinary approach to questions related to identity, race, culture, and the arts in both a national and global context. In the area of literary studies Long has influenced the manner in which major figures and periods are framed, through such works as *Negritude: Essays and Studies* (1967) with Albert H. Berrian; *Black Writers and the American Civil War* (1988), an anthology; *Afro-American Writing: An Anthology of Prose and Poetry* (1972; 1985), edited with Eugenia W. Collier; *Grown Deep: Essays on the Harlem Renaissance* (1998); and *One More Time: Harlem Renaissance History and Historicism* (2006).

Long is a literary critic who is also a poet. His collection *Ascending: Poems* (1975) is dedicated to the painter Beauford Delaney. In the field of African American studies, Long's *Black Americana* (1985) is a touchstone for all who are interested in African American history and culture from the colonial era to the present. In *African Americans: A Portrait* (1993), with a foreword by his friend, the poet and writer Maya Angelou, Long expands the scope of *Black Americana* to include an analysis of landmark events in politics, the media, and the arts. With the publication of *The Black Tradition in Dance* (1989), Long documented a rich and dynamic tradition in African, African American, and Caribbean dance that includes such dancers and choreographers as Katherine Dunham, Alvin Ailey, Rex Nettleford, and Judith Jamison.

As an art historian, Long has published widely, and his *Beauford Delaney: A Retrospective* (1978), a catalogue for a retrospective at the Studio Museum of Harlem, marks the death and commemorates the achievements of his friend and artist Beauford Delaney. It is representative of Long's pathbreaking contributions to the study of the visual arts.

As a public intellectual, Long's original, creative, and influential work has led him to assume important leadership roles within and beyond the academy. While a faculty member at Atlanta University, he established the annual conference sponsored by the Center for African and African American Studies. Long also served as president of the College Language Association as well as the Southeastern Conference on Linguistics, as well as on the boards of the National Museum of African Art, the High Museum of Art, and the curatorial council of the Studio Museum of Harlem.

A dedicated teacher, Long counts among his students some of the most respected scholars in art history including Amalia Amaki, Jean Billingslea-Brown, Akua McDonald, Tina Dunkley, Judy L. Larson, and Richard Powell. In a special issue of the *International Review of African American Art* titled "Being Richard A. Long: The Life, The Odyssey," Amalia Amaki concludes her essay on Long's many contributions as scholar, public intellectual, and teacher with this observation: "Richard Long continues to balance intellect, humor, and the common touch in ways privileged to a very few. He is still fascinated with adventure, still writing and publishing, still feeding his curiosity . . . and still ascending."[1]

A Bridge between Atlanta's Academic Communities |

Over the past four decades Long has established himself as a singular presence in Atlanta's life, arts, and letters. In the fall of 1968 he joined the faculty of Atlanta University—at that time the sole member institution of the Atlanta University Center offering graduate degrees—as professor of English and Afro-American studies. During that same academic year he participated in planning a projected graduate program in urban social change and black-white relations that would be jointly administered by Atlanta University and Emory University. Initiated in the fall of 1969, this program received multiyear funding from the National Endowment for the Humanities beginning in 1970 and marked the beginning of Long's enduring association with Emory.

The Interinstitutional Program in Social Change set out four major goals. The first was to initiate within the academic community an ongoing dialogue about race among students, faculty, and administrators. The second goal was to apply insights and skills in the humanities and social sciences to those major issues in American life that had become increasingly urban-focused. A third was to promote greater academic involvement in Atlanta itself by including local citizens as participants in program activities and by encouraging research projects vital to the metropolitan area. The final goal was to strengthen existing programs in related fields at both universities so as to promote uninterrupted academic development through the pooling of institutional resources.

At Emory the Interinstitutional Program was situated within the ILA; at Atlanta University it was housed in the Department of History and the Afro-American Studies Program. Senior historian and civil rights activist Clarence A. Bacote brought to the program his expertise in black Atlanta history and his experience in the field. Long's wide-ranging expertise in literature, as well as in the visual and performing arts, neatly complemented Bacote's in history and the social sciences. Together with colleagues throughout the Atlanta University Center, these two highly regarded campus leaders were in a position to direct students in the Interinstitutional Program to courses in cooperating departments on both campuses, as well as to faculty members from both institutions who might serve as advisers.

Ten fellowships were awarded each year, four master's-level at Atlanta University, six doctoral at Emory. Increasingly over the years, students completing the MA at Atlanta University would enter the PhD program at Emory. The Interinstitutional Program also attracted the interest of junior faculty at Atlanta University Center schools—Morehouse, Spelman, Morris Brown, and Clark (later Clark Atlanta University)—in Emory's doctoral program. Over the years, consequently, long-lasting ties among the institutions were established and, thereby, informal recruiting expanded.

By the time it came to a close during the early 1980s the Interinstitutional Program in Social Change stood in the top rank nationally in numbers of scholars trained in race studies. Its outreach in Atlanta, moreover, extended well beyond Emory and the Atlanta University Center institutions to include faculty, staff, and administrators at Georgia State University, Agnes Scott College, and Oglethorpe University. Its graduates would also be found in local museums, libraries, and businesses, as well as in state and municipal government. The program's range reflected its leadership—most especially that of Long.

In 1987 Long accepted the appointment of Atticus Haygood Professor of Interdisciplinary Studies in the Graduate Institute of the Liberal Arts, a position that he held until his retirement in 2001. Since then, while enjoying emeritus status at Emory, he has remained active in campus activities, most especially his contributions to the Woodruff Library's Manuscripts, Archives, and Rare Book Library (MARBL). Throughout his distinguished academic career, Long has reached out beyond the walls of the academy to serve as public intellectual, civic influential, urban pioneer, and patron or, better still, ambassador of the arts.

One of Emory's best-known and most-traveled citizens, Long has lectured, studied, and conferred on six continents. Closer to home, he participated in the initial wave of urban pioneers who, during the early 1970s, reclaimed and integrated Atlanta's first suburb, Inman Park, and shaped it into a vital community, a force in the municipality. As citizen, he has contributed to advancing the common good: in his support of public institutions—schools, libraries, galleries, and museums; by endorsing responsible political leadership; and most visibly, by championing the arts in Atlanta—written, performed, and displayed.

His friend Maya Angelou, in her essay on "Loving Learning," has written,

> There are smart alecks who feel comfortable speaking long and loudly about a multiplicity of subjects with no evidence that they know what they are talking about. Then there are those who do know a little about a lot of things and speak judiciously about what they know. And finally, that rarity, the polymath who knows a great deal about everything.
>
> I have met only three such persons in my life. One . . . is Dr. Richard Long . . . at Emory University.[2]

CHAPTER 23

A CENTURY OF VITALITY
Patricia Collins Butler
— MARTHA W. FAGAN —

Reflecting the changing ways in which women would contribute to American society, Patricia Butler's life spanned a century and more. Martha Fagan had the good fortune of getting to know Butler while working in Emory's law school. In this essay Fagan captures both Butler's spirit and the times she helped to change.

PATRICIA COLLINS ANDRETTA Dwinnell Butler (Law 1931) was born in New York City in 1907, during the administration of President Theodore Roosevelt.[1] Horses and buggies were giving way to streetcars and automobiles, women were pressing for the vote in Europe, and a record number of immigrants poured into the United States.

Her parents had immigrated from Newfoundland, where her father, a journalist, had covered Marconi's historic wireless transmission between Cornwall, England, and Newfoundland. The couple moved to Atlanta when Pat was in her early teens, and she attended Sacred Heart High School. The only child of a father who harbored an unrealized ambition to be an attorney and a mother who was, herself, a businesswoman, Butler was encouraged in her education, and in her father's dream for her to attend law school and to prepare to be independent. At the same time she was shaped by her mother's insistence that she not "be too independent—don't be too masculine." To the end of her life, Butler talked about this duality and how, in her working life, she was told that she "talked like a woman—and thought like a man."

Following her graduation from Agnes Scott College in 1928, Butler enrolled in Emory School of Law, one of only two women in her class. Among her classmates were Harlee Branch (Law 1931), who became the president and chairman of the board of Georgia Power Company; George Lawson (Law 1931), former general counsel of The Coca-Cola Company; and John S. Candler Jr. (Law 1931), of the Coca-Cola Candlers. Butler was in school at the same time that the inimitable Robert Tyre "Bobby" Jones (Law 1929) studied at Emory Law. Among her professors were Granger Hansell (College 1922, Law 1924), for whom a reading room is named in the law school's MacMillan Law Library, and Smythe Gambrell, who was the lead donor for Emory Law's Gambrell Hall, named for his parents.

According to Butler, she found law school awkward at first. "Discussions were foreign to me. Then it just happened. I made friends, and it was better. My dad let me have a car, and I started giving the guys rides in Atlanta—then I started studying with them." Her academic experience must have been a success, because at graduation Butler was ranked second in her class of thirty. Seven decades later she still spoke warmly about her law school classmates, and she remained friendly with Harlee Branch and George Lawson, in particular, until their deaths.

While her academic experience at Emory Law might have been successful, finding a job practicing law was much more difficult. Butler was successful in finding a volunteer position at Atlanta Legal Aid Society and at research projects on a grant from the American Law Institute while she looked for paying employment. She had a great champion in Smythe Gambrell, who took it upon himself to try to find a job for this smart female graduate, introducing her to many firms. Butler remembered interviewing with Bobby Jones's father, a senior partner at a law firm, who told Gambrell that, as much as he would like to, "We couldn't possibly meet our clients and tell them that we were spending money out of the law firm to pay a woman law school graduate."

She continued working at Atlanta Legal Aid, gaining experience and confidence in her legal abilities. The head of the society was impressed with her and went to the society's board of directors to ask for forty dollars a month to help pay for gasoline for her car and her lunches. The chairman of the board was so appalled at the idea of paying a woman that he stood up, put on his hat, and walked out—never to return.

Meanwhile, Gambrell never gave up on his quest to find an open door for this talented young woman. He often was in Washington as an attorney for several big clients. One of his friends was Ashley Sellers, then with the U.S. Department of Justice. One Christmas, while in Canada, Butler received a message to stop in Washington on her way home for an interview with the Department of Justice. After waiting patiently for two days, she interviewed with Assistant Attorney General Harold M. Stephens in the Antitrust Division, and about a month later she received a letter asking her to report to Washington and to the department.

In 1935 Butler was hired to put the antitrust library together in the Justice Department's new building. She organized the library, worked on research related to Indian law, and assisted Carl Swisher by helping him finish his history of the Department of Justice, *Federal Justice*. For years, Butler had few female colleagues. Her work in organizing the cases, legislation, and other documents coming out of the federal government during the New Deal led to the establishment of the field of law now known as administrative law. Butler was the founding secretary of the American Bar Association's section on administrative law and founding editor of what is now the *Federal Register*. Because of research she had done during the New Deal era on "alien enemies" in World War I, Butler was asked to help with research leading up to World War II. Most of this research was highly confidential, working on drafts of war proclamations that went into effect after Butler was called to the White House following Pearl Harbor. President Roosevelt involved her in research relating to his "court-packing" plan. While she disagreed with the plan, she enjoyed working with the Roosevelts and especially admired Eleanor Roosevelt.

> *Former attorney general Janet Reno once called Butler a "pioneer among women at the Department of Justice," but, as Butler put it, "I think women were bound to come into their own no matter what. Nothing could stop them."*

Butler was asked by then–attorney general Robert H. Jackson, who went on to be tapped for the U.S. Supreme Court, to work on the legal staff in the Office of the Attorney General, where she remained and worked for every attorney general from the Roosevelt administration through the Nixon era, including Robert F. Kennedy, for whom she professed a great deal of respect and fondness. She worked at the Department of Justice for nearly four decades, serving under the administrations of six presidents and sixteen attorneys general.

Pat Butler met her first husband, Salvador Andretta, the first week she moved to Washington. Andretta, also new to the Department of Justice, was a colleague in the department who later became its chief budget officer. Years later, after World War II, the two became better acquainted and, in 1948, the couple wed, despite her hesitations about combining a high-powered career with marriage. "I had thought when I started my career that I probably never would be married. I didn't particularly want to be," says Butler. "But then that man came along and changed my mind."

In 1949 Andretta encouraged her to argue an immigration case, *Johnson v. Shaughnessy*, before the U.S. Supreme Court on behalf of the Office of the Solicitor. Butler took over the case unexpectedly when the man who was to try the case was called to Europe. Despite having only ten days to prepare, she prevailed before the court, even undergoing a vigorous exchange with Justice Felix Frankfurter, who had recently joined the court.

Shortly thereafter, Butler was the first woman appointed to the quasi-judicial body of five members on the Board of Immigration Appeals, where she held the title of "judge." She served there for approximately two years before returning to the Office of Legal Counsel of the Justice Department, where she worked for twenty-five more years until retirement. During that time, she saw great upheavals, including the civil rights movement and the emergence of the women's movement. When asked about the role of women in the legal profession, Butler talked about the fact that the Second World War made a big difference for women, as—by necessity—women came into their own. Former attorney general Janet Reno once called Butler a "pioneer among women at the Department of Justice," but, as Butler put it, "I think women were bound to come into their own no matter what. Nothing could stop them."

During her tenure in the Department of Justice, Butler became friends with future Chief Justice Warren Burger, then an assistant attorney general, and his wife, Elvera Burger. Following his appointment to the Supreme Court, Burger invited her to tea in 1974 and asked her to help him start the Supreme Court Historical Society. Butler put together the first bylaws, and today the society has its own building and staff, a roster of more than sixty-four hundred members, and a nearly $3 million budget devoted to the collection and preservation of the history of the U.S. Supreme Court through educational programs, historical research, publications, and the collection of antiques and artifacts relating to the court's history. She served on the board of trustees and executive committee of that organization from its founding until her death.

Following the death of her first husband, Sal Andretta, she devoted herself to her work in the Department of Justice and, in addition to her legal work, represented the attorney general on the National Trust for Historic Preservation. While in that capacity Butler met and, in 1974, married Bill Dwinnell, who persuaded her to retire and move to LaJolla, California. As exciting as her new life in California was, she maintained her interest in and connection to Washington for many years, continuing on the board of the U.S. Supreme Court Historical Society. Throughout her eighties and nineties, she routinely flew across the country to attend meetings and events in Washington and the opera in New York, and maintained an apartment in Georgetown. Following the death of Dwinnell, she continued to live in LaJolla, where she met and married her third husband, Frank Butler, a retired diplomat. Following their wedding in 1989 the couple remained actively engaged in San Diego charitable and philanthropic causes, including the Scripps Hospital, and Butler served on the board of trustees of the Neurosciences Institute and the Centers for Disease Control and Prevention Advisory Board.

Throughout her career and into her retirement, Butler made room in her life for the two academic institutions that most deeply shaped her life and career opportunities. A devoted alumna of Agnes Scott College in Decatur, Georgia, she established the Patricia Collins Butler Endowment to support outstanding writing and public speaking and created the Patricia Collins Butler Center in the campus center for commuting students. In 1976 she was named an Outstanding Alumna for her distinguished career at the college.

At Emory, Butler was engaged while in Washington with the D.C. Emory Club, was named a Distinguished Law Alumna in 1997, and received the Emory Medal in 2000. Butler spoke to Emory Law alumni in Washington, including a talk in conjunction with the first Emory Law swearing-in ceremony at the Supreme Court. She made visits to Atlanta to meet with students at Emory Law and Agnes Scott, including a trip as recently as 2008 when she was 100 years old. In 1998 Butler created a bequest to Emory Law to fund an enduring legacy of scholarships for promising students.

Until the age of 101 Butler continued to live in the home she had shared first with Bill Dwinnell and then with Frank Butler, and remained engaged with family and friends and with the charities that interested her. She was a devoted stepmother, charming and engaging friend, a dedicated historic preservationist, a loyal alumna of both Agnes Scott College and Emory Law, and a passionate volunteer on behalf of health and healing. At her death in June 2009 the legal community—and Emory—lost a great treasure.

CHAPTER 24

THE OSLER OF THE SOUTH
Stewart R. Roberts Sr.

— CHARLES STEWART ROBERTS —

Notable in Emory's history are the families whose Emory alumni span several generations. One such family is that of Stewart R. Roberts Sr., who not only added to the University's alumni rolls but also broke new ground in medical care in Georgia as a faculty member at his alma mater. This essay is written by his grandson Charles (Medicine 1986).

BORN AND RAISED in Oxford, Georgia, Dr. Stewart R. Roberts Sr. (1878–1941) became the first heart specialist in Georgia. As a prolific author and clinical teacher at Emory he achieved national prominence in academic medicine, serving as president of the Southern Medical Association in 1924 and president of the American Heart Association in 1933–34.

Stewart Roberts came into the world with an Emory heritage. His father was James William Roberts, D.D., who graduated first in his class at Emory College in 1877. He entered the Methodist ministry in Georgia and later served as president of Wesleyan Female College in Macon from 1898 to 1903. Stewart's mother was Clifford Rebecca Stewart Roberts, who had five children and died during the last childbirth in Oxford. Her father, Joseph Spencer Stewart, was a teacher and businessman who had graduated from Emory College in 1849. He and his wife, Rebeccah Hannah Starr, provided a college education to all six of their children and aided no fewer than forty students through college at Emory, including James William Roberts, by providing tuition or room and board at the Stewart home in Oxford.

Young Stewart Roberts began at Emory College at the age of fifteen, in 1894, and led his class the first two years. Believing that his son was overworked, however, his father withdrew him and later sent him to the Atlanta College of Physicians and Surgeons, where he graduated in 1900 after a two-year course. Stewart then returned to Emory College, where he graduated first in his class in 1902. He earned a master's degree in zoology from the University of Chicago in 1904, with a dissertation titled, "A Comparison of the Cervical and Brachial Plexuses in Certain Reptiles."

After completing his education Roberts settled in Atlanta in 1905 and started in the private practice of internal medicine. From 1906 to 1915 he served on the part-time faculty of various medical schools in Atlanta, until the formation of the Emory University School of Medicine in 1915 through the merger of Atlanta Medical College with the new university. That same year he became professor of clinical medicine at Emory, and he remained with his alma mater until his death in 1941. After an interlude as commanding officer of the base hospital at Fort Jackson, in Columbia, South Carolina, during World War I, he returned to Atlanta and established the Roberts Clinic on Juniper Street in 1919, associating with several physicians over the years.

Always driven by curiosity toward research, in addition to carrying out his clinical practice Roberts took an early interest in pellagra. In the early twentieth century the cause of this disease was unknown, though it particularly afflicted poor southerners. In preparation for a book, Roberts traveled to Italy, where the disease was also prevalent. When he published *Pellagra: History, Distribution, Diagnosis, Prognosis, Treatment, Etiology* in 1912, the etiology of pellagra was still unknown to him and to the world. Roberts emphasized the characteristic clinical presentation of the disease, which included skin rashes, mouth sores, and diarrhea, with possible mental deterioration over time. It would not be until three years later that Joseph Goldberger, of the United States Public Health Service, determined that pellagra resulted from poor diet, and it would take another two decades for the link to be made between pellagra and a deficiency in niacin (vitamin B3).[1]

Neurology and psychiatry were also of keen interest to Roberts, and over the years he wrote twelve papers on these disciplines. One of his favorite authors was William James, the Harvard philosopher and psychologist, brother of Henry James, and author of the pioneering psychological study of religion, *The Varieties of Religious Experience*. "Probably in no calling is there as much opportunity afforded for the study of psychology as in medicine," wrote Roberts; "nowhere is psychology more needed and nowhere is it more neglected."

Cardiovascular disease, however, became the field in which Roberts specialized. Coronary thrombosis (later called "heart attack" by the lay press) was first described by James Herrick of Chicago in 1912. Roberts wrote his first paper on angina pectoris in 1916, one of twenty papers he published on cardiovascular disease. Among them was one bearing the title, "The Nervous and Mental Influences in Angina Pectoris," which appeared in the *American Heart*

Journal in 1931. In a 1935 paper, "The Relation of the Heart to Surgery," Roberts predicted, accurately, that "Coronary artery sclerosis without angina is probably the most overlooked disease of the circulation after fifty."

He made the first electrocardiogram in Atlanta, at the Roberts Clinic.

Physician creeds or oaths have been written by many authors across the history of medicine, and Stewart R. Roberts, MD, was author of one such oath. "An Ideal of Modern Medicine" was privately published in 1916 and later reprinted by his son, William Clifford Roberts, MD, in the *Annals of Internal Medicine* in 1969. His commencement address to the graduating class of 1927 included a section that came to be known for a time as the "Emory Creed."[2]

Books in general and the history of medicine in particular were lifelong pursuits. Roberts published essays on Jean-Martin Charcot of Paris (the "father of neurology"); the great Canadian clinician and teacher Sir William Osler; Benjamin Franklin; William Charles Wells of Charleston and London; William C. Gorgas of Alabama; and the Renaissance anatomist Vesalius. Roberts's writings are sprinkled with historical and literary references. Though their paths did not cross, Roberts called Osler the "wise friend of my clinical life, unseen consultant with my patients, the Abou Ben Adam of my spirit," in reference to the poem by Leigh Hunt that begins, "Abou Ben Adam (may his tribe increase!)." Attaching similar importance to the art of bedside medicine, Roberts was occasionally called "the Osler of the South," in tribute to the teaching skills and humanistic interests shared by both men.

Two sons of Stewart R. Roberts Sr. chose medicine as a career, as did one grandson, this author, all of whom graduated from Emory Medical School. His published writings in all numbered more than a hundred articles, in addition to the book on pellagra. He was devoted to Georgia and to the South, and his loyalty to Emory was supreme.

> *Roberts wrote his first paper on angina pectoris in 1916, one of twenty papers he published on cardiovascular disease.*

THE CLASSICIST
Moses Hadas
— HERBERT W. BENARIO —

Harking back to a time when the classics formed the core of a college curriculum, the story of alumnus Moses Hadas also exemplifies the degree to which Emory has contributed outstanding scholars and teachers to the American professoriate. In this essay Herbert W. Benario, professor emeritus of classics in Emory College, recalls the career of Hadas, which was "classic" in every way.

MOSES HADAS WAS born in Atlanta on June 25, 1900; grew up in what was then a distant suburb, Buckhead (which became part of Atlanta by annexation in 1952); and attended the city's public schools.[1] He then enrolled in Emory College, which was slowly growing on its new campus in northeastern Atlanta after the establishment of the University in 1915 and the removal of the College from Oxford, Georgia, to the state's largest city. He was among the first to spend his entire undergraduate career on this metropolitan, although simple, campus, and he was easily able to maintain his religious contacts with home. This was important, for his religion was different from that of most of the students at the new Methodist university; he was Jewish, deeply devoted, and learned.

At Emory he studied Latin and Greek, so that it could be said of him, as Ennius, the early Latin poet, had said of himself, that he had *tria corda*, "three hearts"—Latin, Greek, and Hebrew. This blend of languages and cultures remained the focus of his teaching and research for the remainder of his life, well more than two score years, until his death on August 17, 1966.

Study of the classics had long been a staple of the South; the vibrancy of the classical languages perhaps survived longer in that region than in the more "advanced" sections of the nation. With his learning he also displayed a gentleness, courtesy, and *humanitas*, which had their roots in his southern birth and upbringing. The passage of years brought honors and increase of reputation, but his concern for people and his marked interest in the young never changed. He was a "gentleman" in the best and old senses of the word.

After Emory he departed for New York, which became his new home. He attended both the Jewish Theological Seminary, where he gained his rabbinical degree in 1926, and Columbia University, which awarded him a doctorate in Greek and Latin in 1930. He rose slowly through the academic *cursus honorum* at Columbia during the difficult years of the Great Depression, facing in addition the anti-Semitism that was endemic in academe.

During World War II, from 1943 to 1946, he served in the OSS in Greece and North Africa and headed the Greek desk in research and administration in Alexandria.[2] Academic advancement came more quickly after his return to Columbia, until he reached a professorship in 1953, and soon thereafter, in 1956, was honored with the Jay Professorship of Greek.

I first met Hadas in 1949, when I was a graduate student at Columbia, although I never had him in class. When I returned to Columbia as an instructor in 1953, and for the *lustrum* following, he was an awe-inspiring mentor and colleague, particularly supportive when I needed encouragement in teaching the "Humanities" course, for which Columbia was famous, and which Hadas helped establish in 1937. I still vividly recall when I had just moved into my office and he walked in and said, in his deep voice, "Call me Moses." Not every senior member of the department invited use of his first name by junior faculty.

I last saw him in the mid-sixties, when he and his wife were guests in my home. He had not long to live; he had become physically frail, but his outlook on life and people remained as lustrous as it had ever been. It was his concern for individuals that was so striking; when he had become one of Columbia's luminaries with many graduate and university obligations, he continued to insist upon teaching the required freshman course in humanities, and for some years was the senior person among about three dozen in what tended more and more to become an enterprise for younger faculty. He was able to open eyes and minds with his vast learning and to inspire with his gentle Socraticism.

He was an extraordinary teacher and received appropriate recognition from Columbia for his eminence. His alma mater, Emory, honored him and herself by the award of an honorary doctor of letters degree in 1956. The citation reads in part,

> Author and editor of numerous books and papers which have contributed notably to the vital interest in and to the understanding of our literary heritage from the great days of Greece and Rome. Your career has been a source of pride and deep satisfaction to your Alma Mater, for we

like to believe that here at Emory were first aroused the intellectual interests and that here were established the disciplined habits of mind in which are rooted and grounded your distinguished achievements as scholar and educator.

What set Hadas apart from most of his classical peers was his deep knowledge of another intellectual and religious tradition. Although he wrote and translated much that was strictly classical, his interests and uniqueness are best exemplified by two books that appeared late in his life: *Hellenistic Culture, Fusion and Diffusion* (1959) and *Humanism* (1960). Each in different ways represents a culmination of his scholarly career.

The latter attempts to explain the importance of Greek thought for a wide audience. He takes as his theme Protagoras' dictum, "Man is the measure of all things." It is humanity, not God, upon whom Hadas focuses. The former book combines two of the three *corda* mentioned above and examines in a very personal way the relationship of Greek and Jewish cultures. Given the challenges he set for himself, it may not be surprising that many critics faulted Hadas on one point or another. More meaningful, I think, are judgments such as these: from a distinguished British theologian, Henry Chadwick, "It is the work of a fertile and alert mind, writing pleasantly for an educated general public";[3] from the eminent American Semiticist and biblical archaeologist William Foxwell Albright, "Professor Hadas is well known for the breadth of his learning, the wide scope of his interests, and the felicity of his style. In the present volume all three characteristics are again combined to delight the reader and to instruct the student";[4] and from the brilliant Italian ancient historian and student of historiography Arnaldo Momigliano, "Ha vaste conoscenze e curiosità in tutto il mondo greco-romano. Egli tocca una straordinaria varietà di argomenti, dalla filosofia all'arte, dal diritto alla letteratura erotica, e ha qualcosa di non commune da dire su ciascuno di essi"[5] (He possesses extensive knowledge and curiosity in the entire Greco-Roman world. He touches upon an extraordinary variety of subjects, from philosophy to art, from law to erotic literature, and has something out of the ordinary to say on each of these [my translation]).

> *His translations reveal his enormous breadth—books dealing with a wide range of Jewish subjects, with Roman history, with Goethe, with the Homeric gods, and classical authors such as Julius Caesar and Seneca.*

His publications were extensive. When one considers his teaching load until the end of his career, his university service, and his devotion to his family, one wonders how he was able to accomplish so much—and this was in an era when the typewriter was the most sophisticated instrument for scholarly labors. But Hadas did not use a typewriter; I recall him sitting at his desk and writing steadily with a pencil upon a pad of yellow paper. The departmental secretary then deciphered his difficult script and typed the manuscript.

The subjects of his scholarly labors fall neatly into three categories, so that one might say, slightly changing Caesar's introduction to the *Gallic War*, "Opera eius sunt omnia divisa in partes tres." These three categories are his own writings, his many translations of works ancient and modern, and his editing of others' translations, often with introduction and other ancillary material.

Among the first category there stand out books that present antiquity to a wider audience than the classical profession. His dissertation, on *Sextus Pompey*, was published immediately after he had received his doctorate in 1930 and was reprinted in 1966. It has remained a standard work on its subject for more than three-quarters of a century. He published *A History of Greek Literature* in 1950, *A History of Latin Literature* in 1952, and *Ancilla to Classical Reading* in 1954, three volumes that neatly constitute a trilogy. In addition to the two volumes on Hellenistic culture and humanism, two others in a similar vein were *Old Wine, New Bottles: A Humanist Teacher at Work* (1962) and *Introduction to Classical Drama* (1966).

His translations reveal his enormous breadth—books dealing with a wide range of Jewish subjects, with Roman history, with Goethe, with the Homeric gods, and classical authors such as Julius Caesar and Seneca. In one of the last volumes to appear in his lifetime, jointly done with Frank O. Copley of the University of Michigan, the prefaces that each wrote to his share of the book laid out the two differing philosophies of translation that still dominate the art today.

The title is *Roman Drama*, part of "The Library of Liberal Arts."[6] Copley dealt with Plautus and Terence, Hadas with Seneca. Copley wrote, "I have attempted to translate ideas and situations rather than words. I kept one question constantly before me: If this character were speaking contemporary American English, how would he have expressed the idea he has in mind? It will be immediately obvious that this principle is bound, on occasion, to lead to an English version that bears little resemblance, on the purely verbal level, to the orginal Latin."

In contrast, Hadas noted that "The present translations . . . do not attempt to make Seneca a contemporary but deliberately seek to reflect his own rhetorical virtuosity in vocabulary and syntax. Rhetoric is as important in Senecan tragedy as music in an operatic libretto, and to efface it would strip the plays of what makes them moving and meaningful, and leave only a bare framework of frightfulness."

I read these divergent views at an important time in my career. I was working on a translation of the minor works of the Roman historian Tacitus, whose language is often contorted and difficult, vastly different from what is often considered "the Ciceronian norm." I was attempting to retain as much as I could of Tacitus' peculiarities of style and vocabulary. With Hadas's exemplar before me, I chose to produce a translation sometimes harsh and "un-Englishlike," which some reviewers castigated, but I have continued in this fashion to the present day. Tacitus should not read as a modern American, nor should Seneca. How many other readers did Hadas, in this way and others, influence and educate?[7]

Moses Hadas was a learned man, a kindly man, who took the qualities of a southern upbringing to the intellectual capital of this country, New York, where he molded the minds of thousands of students and colleagues. He could have said, in the words of Terence, the Roman writer of comedy, *Homo sum: humani nil a me alienum puto*: "I am a human being and think nothing which concerns a human being unimportant to myself." As a southerner, he knew the psychology of a defeated people; as a Jew, he knew the feeling of standing apart from the majority. The results were understanding of humanity (*sunt lacrimae rerum*, in Vergil's fine expression) and compassion, which combined with deep and joyful learning to produce one of the great teachers of the twentieth century.

Dumas Malone (College 1910 far right) received an honorary degree at the Emory Centennial celebration.

EMORY HISTORICAL MINDS AND THEIR IMPACT

— GARY S. HAUK —

When Emory University launched its first doctoral programs in 1948, the History Department, to no one's surprise, joined those of English, biology, and chemistry as one of the four most ready to recruit and prepare a new generation of scholars. After all, for two decades the History Department had distinguished itself as the home of some of the more able faculty members at Emory. These included Edgar H. Johnson (College 1891), who served as professor of history and political economy while the College was at Oxford, and who went on to serve as the first dean of the business school; Theodore H. Jack, professor of history, who would later serve as dean of the Graduate School and the first vice president at Emory, before becoming president of Randolph-Macon Women's College; and Cullen B. Gosnell, who, in addition to teaching history, founded Emory's Political Science Department and served as vice president of the American Political Science Association.

More remarkable, perhaps, than the strength of the faculty members who had built up the department through the 1930s and 1940s was the legacy they created through their students. Three of them educated on the Atlanta campus—C. Vann Woodward (College 1930), David M. Potter (College 1932), and Louis R. Harlan (College 1943)—would win the Pulitzer Prize and help to transform historiography about the American South of the nineteenth century. A fourth alumnus, who studied under professors Johnson and Jack at Oxford before Emory College moved to Atlanta, also would win the Pulitzer Prize: Dumas Malone (College 1910). Moreover, by the second year of the doctoral program, 1949, the faculty at Emory would be joined by yet another distinguished historian, Bell Irvin Wiley, whose career at Emory would lift the department to still greater distinction through his writings on the Civil War.[1]

C. Vann Woodward, the Revisionist Southerner | From the scant documentary evidence that might shed light on C. Vann Woodward's course work at Emory from 1928 to 1930, one cannot know for certain which Emory professor presided over the "one dull term's course"[2] that nearly killed Woodward's career as a historian before it could even take wing. The choices of subject matter at the time were few—a couple of offerings in American history, several about Europe, and none on Asia and Africa. The History Department at the time was small: four faculty members, including two full professors who had reputations as good classroom instructors. At any rate, in Woodward's memoir *Thinking Back*, published more than half a century after he had suffered through his single course of history at Emory, the most influential historian of the second half of the twentieth century felt compelled to comment on the experience with still-fresh distaste.

To be fair, it may not have been the fault of any one teacher or syllabus that gave the future Pulitzer Prize winner such an uninspiring introduction to historiography. A few years later, while working on an MA degree at Chapel Hill and laying the foundation for his doctorate from the University of North Carolina, Woodward found himself slogging with despair through the standard survey volumes of American history. The experience led him to "wonder if I had ever encountered prose so pedestrian, pages so dull, chapters so devoid of ideas, whole volumes so wrongheaded or so lacking in point."[3]

With such an inauspicious start to a career, one might wonder how Woodward became what his biographer called "the most significant historian of our age."[4] In truth, his early commitments and fondest pursuits suggested that some other, quite different lifetime preoccupation might have been his destiny.

The son of a school administrator and a book-loving mother, Woodward came early to intellectual discourse. His father, Hugh (called "Jack" all his life by his friends), had graduated from Emory College with honors in 1901 and attracted to himself a regular procession of interesting conversation partners. Visitors to the Woodward home in Arkadelphia, Arkansas, included activist-intellectuals who would leave an enduring imprint on Vann's thinking—leaders like Governor Charles Hillman Brough, a Baptist churchman with a PhD in economics from Johns Hopkins, who as governor of Arkansas instituted suffrage for women and spoke out against lynching; Charles Pipkin, a Rhodes scholar from Morrilton, Arkansas, who as a professor at Louisiana State University advocated for world peace and worked for economic development in the depressed South; and the scholar Rupert Vance, who had grown up in Woodward's hometown and inspired young Woodward by his determination to reform the economic and racial landscape of the South. Independently, too, Woodward read widely, so that while family discussions of social ethics channeled his mental energy, literature ignited his imagination.

That intellectual energy carried over to his first two years of college, which he spent at tiny, Methodist-affiliated Henderson-Brown College in Arkadelphia. While the college itself had barely the resources of faculty and library to challenge a student of Woodward's restless capacity, it did add further discipline to his growing strength as a master of the word—a mastery that would distinguish him among practitioners of his craft into his tenth decade of life. He became an adept debater and an ardent student of the southern literary renaissance then under way (Robert Penn Warren would become a great friend later).

Aspiring to a world and life beyond Arkansas, Woodward had the further good luck of a family that deeply shaped his life and schooling. Besides his father and mother, perhaps the most significant figure in Vann's life was his father's older brother, Comer Woodward (College 1900), for whom C. Vann was named. A Methodist clergyman, Comer Woodward earned a doctorate from the University of Chicago and stood, in his nephew's eyes, as the epitome of the scholar who both possessed great learning and applied his powerful intelligence to understanding the dilemmas and perplexities of contemporary society.

When Comer Woodward took the position of dean of students at the relatively new Emory University in Atlanta, in 1924, he saw an opportunity for his precocious nephew as well. In the summer of 1928, ready to stretch beyond the limits of Henderson-Brown College and Arkadelphia, Vann Woodward moved to Druid Hills with an eye to completing his education at Emory. The following year, his parents moved to Oxford, where his father, Hugh, became dean of the junior college that had been launched after the move of Emory College to Atlanta.

> *Son and nephew of Emory alumni, Vann Woodward would write his own place in the Emory book of legends.*

If the coursework in history failed to excite him at Emory, Vann found inspiration elsewhere in the faculty. The young philosophy professor Leroy Loemker was just at the beginning of his long, distinguished career at the University. In time he would become one of the foremost American scholars wrestling with the need for theory to have an impact in life—for *Theorie*, in the old nomenclature, to be balanced by and inform *Lebens*, and vice versa: life and theory, theory and life working together in a kind of instruction that would become formalized decades later at Emory as "theory-praxis learning."[5]

More formative still were friendships he developed in and out of the classroom, relationships that would prove critical to the direction of Woodward's life and the contours of his thought and scholarship. They included a close bond with David Potter, who shared that one course of history that Woodward took at Emory. Potter himself would go on to eminence as a historian of the antebellum period and the Civil War, as well as distinguished professorships at Yale and Stanford, and would win his own Pulitzer Prize for *The Impending Crisis, 1848–1861*. Potter also would become one of Woodward's principal intellectual conversation partners and would serve as a sounding board and, sometimes, corrective, for many of Woodward's ideas. Fittingly, after Potter left the Sterling Professorship at Yale to become chair of the history department at Stanford in 1961, Yale recruited Woodward to succeed him.

Like many Emory students since, Woodward expended as much energy and found as much purpose beyond the gates of the campus as on the campus itself. The campus in those years harbored a courteousness and civility that prevails to the present but was exacerbated by a Methodist propriety presided over by the eminence of Bishop Warren A. Candler (College 1875), former president of Emory and, in Woodward's day, the retired chancellor of the University who still lived in Druid Hills, just across North Decatur Road from the campus. With social life revolving around the game of pushball, fraternities, and various frivolities associated with humiliation of freshmen, the campus no doubt felt even more remote from the realities of Atlanta than was suggested by the six-mile streetcar line to Five Points. Woodward opted for the streetcar and the possibility of reforming the big city.

His partners in activism were two classmates, Glenn Weddington Rainey (College 1926) and Ernest Hartsock (College 1930). Woodward shared with them a devotion to "truth and beauty" that expressed itself in literary output and social engagement. An accomplished poet, who won first prize from the American Poetry Society in 1929, Hartsock unfortunately did not live long past his graduation from Emory and died of pernicious anemia in December 1931. Woodward was at Hartsock's side when he died.

The third member of the trio, Rainey, majored in literature but was motivated by a reformist spirit. Distinctly more liberal—even more radical—than what typically passed for liberalism in the South in those days, Rainey searched the lessons of history for prophetic examples to lead his society out of moral darkness. This expectation that the past might serve as a resource for moral guidance of the present generation left an impression on Woodward, who as a professional historian sought to mine the past for its usefulness without distorting the reality of an earlier age.

Rainey's influence had an even more practical effect on Woodward. Slightly older than Woodward, Rainey began his career by teaching English at Georgia Tech while continuing graduate studies at Emory. Through his friendship with Rainey, Woodward himself landed a position teaching English at Georgia Tech after graduating from Emory. During the next two years he would establish other friendships that would profoundly affect his determination to help transform not only a general understanding of the South but even the very mores and laws of the region—a rare feat for a historian.

Disenchantment with progressive reform arrived in the form of a legal proceeding. Angelo Herndon, an African American member of the Communist Party from Ohio, was arrested in July 1932 for trying to organize black support for the party, campaigning for the party's presidential candidate, and protesting Atlanta's welfare cuts. All of these activities led to a charge against him for violating an antebellum law against insurrection, which had been designed to suppress abolitionists and rebellious blacks. It was serious business and could have meant the death penalty if Herndon were convicted. Woodward, through his associations with Rainey and others, joined efforts to raise money for Herndon's defense. Although Woodward was then employed by Tech, he—and thus Emory—became closely identified with the case of the Communist from the North. As one of Woodward's biographers puts it,

> The courtroom did produce occasional moments of comic relief from the pathos of the obviously impending death sentence. For one, [Professor] Mercer Evans of Emory attempted to testify that the materials found in Herndon's room were not subversive and in fact were available at the Candler Library. . . . The corpus delecti included the *Nation*, the *New Republic*, . . . and some standard translations from Karl Marx's *Das Kapital*. Unfortunately for Evans's plan, the Candler Library did not then have these materials; but Evans, not to be outdone by circumstances, slipped into the library with the intention of putting his own books and journals on the shelves. Caught out by a diligent librarian, Evans could only concede defeat: Angelo Herndon surely did have in his possession books of unusual thought not to be found at a decent school like Emory.[6]

The prosecutor in the case blasted Evans and his fellow professor Troy Cauley as "renegades" and proclaimed Emory "a hotbed of iniquity."

Before Herndon went on trial, Woodward was abandoned in his efforts and left disillusioned by the shifting allegiances of his compatriots. In the wake of the affair, he departed for New York to earn a master's degree at Columbia University, and then traveled throughout Germany and Russia. Unbeguiled by the Soviet Union, he nevertheless took to heart the critique he heard there of American racism. More sobering still, while living with a Jewish family in Berlin he witnessed firsthand the pernicious beginnings of racial policies that would lead to the Holocaust.

Returning to the States, he set his sights on a doctorate at the University of North Carolina, where he began to doubt the received historical interpretation of Reconstruction and the New South. This then-standard view—first formulated by Charles Beard and shared early in the twentieth century by such eminent historians as Ulrich Phillips at Yale and Woodward's own dissertation adviser, Howard Beale—held that the southern experience following the Civil War had been one of corrupt Southern politicians buying African American votes and colluding with punitive northerners to extract retribution from the wayward region. According to this perspective, the end of Reconstruction brought to power a "redeeming" class of southern leaders, bred of the old agrarian South, with experience as defenders of the Confederacy, but eager to turn to a new future, building a "New South," which would rise from defeat by developing ties with the industrial North and emulating its forms of economic progress.

Woodward took as his dissertation topic the biography of Tom Watson, a legendary Georgian who in many ways stood at the confluence of all the swirling currents of the period that followed Reconstruction. A populist with sympathy for southern farmers, Watson opposed the vast giveaways of land by state governments to corporations and railroads, the influence of northern capital on southern business, and the tax burdens felt by both black and white sharecroppers as well as by other poor farmers. He denounced men like *Atlanta Constitution* editor Henry Grady and Georgia Governor Alfred Colquitt—proponents of the "New South"—as greedy and self-seeking "new Southerners," who had no ties to the Old South but eulogized it for its sentimental leverage, while allying themselves with a new class of robber barons.

Woodward's biography of Watson undermined New South notions of "progress, prosperity, peace, consensus, white solidarity, black contentment, sectional reconciliation, and the overarching themes of unity, continuity, and nationalism."[7] It also exposed Henry Grady and his allies as "crass and materialistic" scorners of the little people they professed to be aiding. Grady thought of the New South as continuous with the Old South, but under better conditions. Woodward pointed out the degree to which a new breed of southern leaders had simply taken over the North's colonial treatment of the South.

> *As the 1950s opened, with its air of American triumphalism after the victories of World War II and the nation's move to the center of the world stage, Woodward felt called to a more public scholarship that would question the country's air of economic and military invincibility.*

Woodward earned his doctorate at North Carolina in 1937 and published his dissertation the following year as *Tom Watson, Agrarian Rebel*. Over the next ten years he would teach peripatetically at the University of Florida, the University of Virginia, and Scripps College in Claremont, California, followed by service in the navy during World War II. After the war, he landed at The Johns Hopkins University, where he settled in to overturn the standard version of post–Civil War history.

In 1951 Woodward published two works that established his reputation as perhaps the most influential American historian of the second half of the twentieth century. The first, *Reunion and Reaction: The Compromise of 1877 and the End of Reconstruction*, broke new ground in many ways. His exhaustive research had led to documentary proof that the resolution of the Hayes-Tilden election of 1876 owed its outcome not to the desire of southern leaders to get federal troops out of their states but to the machinations of a few capitalist interests to open a railroad between Texas and California.

He followed this work in the same year with his magnum opus, *Origins of the New South 1877–1913*, which developed his understanding first outlined in the Watson book. Together *Origins* and *Reunion* firmly set aside the myths that had permeated much American understanding of Reconstruction and its aftermath. While later historians would refine this perspective and correct some of the details of the new picture through specialized research and monographs, the fundamental narrative developed by Woodward remains unchanged more than half a century later.

As the 1950s opened, with its air of American triumphalism after the victories of World War II and the nation's move to the center of the world stage, Woodward felt called to a more public scholarship that would question the country's air of economic and military invincibility. He recognized in the work of theologian Reinhold Niebuhr a compatible spirit, which looked skeptically at American "myths of innocence."[8] For in the history of the South, Woodward found the platform he needed from which to puncture American hubris in a stream of essays published throughout the decade. The South stood as the exception to "American exceptionalism"; the South was a region that had experienced defeat and devastation, and a people who had struggled to rise from poverty in a nation of unparalleled plenty. The South's "collective experience of the past," expressed to the world through a historical consciousness wrought in the southern literary renaissance, stood as a prophetic indictment against a nation that had become wealthy and powerful while harboring racism, committing genocide against Native Americans, and expanding its borders through imperialism. By the late 1960s—as the civil rights movement, the American Indian movement, the women's movement, and the errors of Vietnam had stripped away much of the nation's illusion—Woodward could say that "history has begun to catch up with Americans."[9]

In this context of "public intellectual," Woodward published the volume that brought him his greatest renown. *The Strange Career of Jim Crow* began as a series of invited lectures delivered at the University of Virginia in October 1954, just months after the U.S. Supreme Court's landmark decision in *Brown v. Board of Education*. Woodward summed up the book's thesis: "Briefly stated, the thesis was, first, that racial segregation in the South in the rigid and universal form it had taken by 1954 did not appear with the end of slavery, but toward the end of the century and later; and second, that before it appeared in this form there occurred an era of experiment and variety in race relations of the South in which segregation was not the invariable rule."[10] The book did not suggest that there had ever been a "golden age" of harmony between the races, but it did explode the prevailing assumption throughout the South that the apartheid-like laws then in place had always been the racial code.

The full impact of the lectures when they appeared in book form in 1955 was not immediate. But as the struggle for desegregation intensified, with powerful resistance from southern elected officials at all levels, nationwide sales of the book took off. Martin Luther King Jr. would call the book "the historical Bible of the civil rights movement."[11] Woodward was quoted everywhere. The work suffered from the kind of misreading and misuse that made him cringe. "The carefully noted exception, the guarded qualification, the unstated assumption, the cautionary warning was often overlooked or brushed aside." Nevertheless, the book spawned a wide-ranging public discourse about segregation as well as a generation of monographs that sought to test Woodward's thesis, his evidence, and his conclusions. The general outlines of Woodward's argument remain secure half a century later.

In 1962 Yale University called on Woodward to move from Johns Hopkins and accept the Sterling Professorship that had been vacated that year by his good friend David Potter. Woodward concluded his career at Yale but remained active. In perhaps his last visit to Emory, in the early 1990s he took the University to task for adopting a nonharassment policy that he believed constituted a "speech code" and an abridgement of academic freedom. (The policy was later revised to obviate that objection.) He died in 1999, having lived most of the twentieth century.

David Potter, Pastmaster | Like his lifelong friend Vann Woodward, David Potter must have drunk directly from the cup of the muse of history somewhere on the Emory campus in the late 1920s.

In 1969 Harper and Row brought out a volume of essays on American historians, titled *Pastmasters*, which included chapters on such immortals as Francis Parkman, Henry Adams, Perry Miller, Richard Hofstadter, and Frederick Jackson Turner. Limiting their "masters" to those American historians who wrote about American history, the editors noted only three other criteria: the "weight" or magnitude of the historian's oeuvre; continuing "influence" over generations of students and other historians; and "representativeness" of major schools of thought or historiography. Also important was a high level of readability and clarity of interpretation.[12] So while these "pastmasters" would be groundbreaking scholars with academic impact, they would also write history that would engage general readers.

Significantly, of the thirteen historians profiled, eight were born in the twentieth century, and two of them graduated from Emory. One of these—Potter—wrote the essay about the other, Woodward. (In a similar work, *Clio's Favorites: Leading Historians of the United States*,

1945–2000, the Yale historian Howard R. Lamar [College 1945, Honorary 1975] would be included as well in a unique hat trick along with Woodward and Potter.)

Potter and Woodward met as undergraduates in a class taught by an unknown one of the three Emory professors. Two years younger than Woodward, Potter would quickly become the professional equal of his friend. Like Woodward, Potter grew up in the South (his home was Augusta, Georgia), and like Woodward he would spend most of his career beyond his native region. Following graduation from Emory in 1932 he enrolled in the doctoral program at Yale, where he studied under the dean of historians about the South, Ulrich B. Phillips, and completed his dissertation under the guidance of Ralph H. Gabriel, whose work focused on American intellectual history.

Even before earning his PhD from Yale in 1940 Potter had begun teaching, first at the University of Mississippi, and then at Rice University. The year 1942 was a watershed in his career and marked the start of his tenure at Yale as well as the publication of his first book. This work—*Lincoln and His Party in the Secession Crisis*—was a revision of Potter's dissertation and has been ranked among the best doctoral dissertations in modern American historiography.

David Potter

Exhaustively researched and written in the graceful prose for which Potter would become envied, the book brought a fresh interpretation to the burdens of decision borne by Lincoln and others in the months leading to the Civil War. The British historian Sir Denis Brogan commented that "the fact that the dissertation has been continually reprinted and was issued in 1962 in a new paperback edition with an important revisionary preface shows that the impression made by Potter's work was durable."[13]

Perhaps self-evident now, Potter's approach assumed none of the inevitability that in his day characterized much of the writing about the period before the Civil War—and, indeed, much history still being written on a host of subjects. The great temptation for historians is what Brogan calls "the suspect and insidious nature of hindsight,"[14] viewing everything with the benefit of knowing the outcome, so later events appear to be the ineluctable conclusion of everything that preceded them, as though no other result had been possible. Potter resisted this temptation in everything he wrote, and never more brilliantly than in *Lincoln and His Party*. Taking his cues from the statements and actions and documents of the historical actors about whom he is writing, he always keeps in view the moment of decision and the determination of choice. In a sense, the historian must pay as much attention to what did *not* happen as to what did.

This habit of mind led Potter to look afresh at many of the truisms of American history, including the hoary "frontier thesis" of Frederick Jackson Turner (which overstated the independence of the frontiersman's thinking, in Potter's view); the conception of the Civil War as pitting an agrarian South against an industrial North (both regions shared both characteristics in varying degrees); and the notion that the American character could be summed up in terms of "can-do" inventiveness (in Potter's view this character was shaped as much by the abundance of the continent as by the capacity of people to exploit it).

In addition to creating a body of historical writing that has placed him among the greatest American historians of the last century, Potter was renowned as a teacher whose elegantly crafted lectures exemplified his command of English as well as of vast and complicated material. Potter spent his last decade at Stanford University, which recruited him in 1962 as the Coe Professor and chair of the History Department. (Potter also spent a year at the University of Oxford as the Harmsworth Professor and fellow in Queen's College.) Both at Yale, where he was the Sterling Professor of History, and at Stanford, his graduate students found in him a mentor.

Potter's stature is perhaps best demonstrated by his having been elected simultaneously to the presidency of the American Historical Association and the Organization of American Historians, the two most eminent historical guilds in the United States. Diagnosed with cancer several years earlier, he passed away in 1971 before he could deliver his two presidential addresses. Yet his work would continue to triumph posthumously. His Stanford colleagues Carl Degler and Don E. Fehrenbacher gathered some of his lectures and essays into two volumes published after his death, and Fehrenbacher completed the manuscript that was published as *The Impending Crisis 1848–1861*. This superlative study of the decade and a half leading to the Civil War won Potter the Pulitzer Prize, awarded posthumously in 1977.

Mr. Jefferson's Biographer, Dumas Malone

Two other Emory graduates would win Pulitzer Prizes in the decade following Potter's, and both of them would win in the category of biography. Louis R. Harlan (College 1943), who spent most of his career teaching at the University of Maryland, wrote the definitive biography of Booker T. Washington, in two volumes. The second of these, *Booker T. Washington: The Wizard of Tuskegee*, received the Pulitzer for biography in 1984.

Dumas Malone (College 1910) produced what is widely regarded as the definitive biography of Thomas Jefferson—a mammoth undertaking whose first volume—*Jefferson the Virginian*—appeared in 1948, and whose sixth and final volume—*The Sage of Monticello*—appeared in 1981, Malone's ninety-first year. The appearance of the fifth volume in 1973 earned Malone the Pulitzer Prize for history for the first five.

Born into an academic family in Coldwater, Mississippi, in 1892, and reared in rural Georgia, Dumas Malone followed his older brother, Kemp (College 1907) to Oxford, Georgia, and Emory College. (Kemp Malone himself would go on to a distinguished career as a medieval philologist and literary scholar at Johns Hopkins University, where he taught Chaucer and Middle English literature.) Dumas's own biographer, Merrill D. Peterson, recounts that Malone would later recall Emory, in an unfinished memoir, as "a citadel of orthodoxy" but "a modest home of humane learning."

Graduating at eighteen as the youngest member of his class, Dumas taught school for several years and then enrolled at Yale Divinity School, where he not only earned his divinity degree (in 1916) but also shucked off the parochial orthodoxies of his upbringing. "In the free air of a great university," he wrote later, "I gained intellectual independence."

From Yale he returned south to teach Bible at Randolph-Macon Woman's College in Virginia, with the intention of going back to Yale eventually for a doctorate in religion. (His mother apparently instilled in each of her seven children the goal of earning a PhD degree, and all of them did so.) His plans were interrupted, however, by World War I. Enlisting in the Marine Corps he was commissioned a second lieutenant and assigned duties stateside. The war turned his attention to politics, national affairs, and history, while diminishing his interest in religion. With the Armistice, he returned to Yale and earned an MA in history in 1921, followed by his PhD in 1923, and served as an instructor in American history in Yale College.

His initial preparation behind him, he began a long association with the University of Virginia, where he first found the impetus to write about Jefferson. The sesquicentennial of the Declaration of Independence and the centennial of Jefferson's death, both occurring in 1926, brought an avalanche of publications on Jefferson, and having already written a brief essay on Jefferson, Malone decided to attempt a much bigger project.

In the meantime, however, other duties would call. In 1929 he received an invitation from Allen Johnson, editor of the mammoth *Dictionary of American Biography* (*DAB*), to join him in Washington, DC, as coeditor. Offered the additional carrot of writing the *Dictionary* entry on Jefferson, Malone accepted. As fate would have it, Johnson was struck and killed by an automobile while walking in Washington in 1931, and Malone carried forward the *DAB* project. His article on Jefferson, completed the following year, exceeded fifteen thousand words, one of only five articles in the *DAB* that surpassed the standard maximum of ten thousand (the others were on Washington, Franklin, Lincoln, and Wilson). Astonishingly, Malone brought the entire project in almost on schedule, completing it in 1936.

The timing was auspicious, as Harvard University prepared to celebrate its tercentennial. Conceiving a more significant role for Harvard's press, President James Bryant Conant recruited Malone to direct its operations, a task he undertook with great success over seven years, never losing sight of his intention to write a large biography of Jefferson. As early as 1938 he contracted with Little, Brown, and Company to produce a four-volume biography, despite the consuming work of building Harvard University Press in the face of the Depression and impending war. Resigning from Harvard in 1943—which, coincidentally, marked the two hundredth anniversary of Jefferson's birth and the dedication of the Jefferson Memorial in the nation's capital—Malone undertook his life's project with the aid of a Rockefeller grant, working with materials housed at the University of Virginia and the Library of Congress.

The conclusion of World War II offered new opportunities in the academy, and Malone was recruited to a professorship at Columbia University in 1945. Teaching half-time, and with support from the Rockefeller Foundation, he published the first volume of his biography, *Jefferson the Virginian*, to critical and commercial success in 1948. *Jefferson and the Rights of Man* followed in 1951. The demands of teaching and the call of other duties—editing the *Political Quarterly Review*, writing for monthly magazines like *Harper's* and the *Atlantic Monthly*, coauthoring a two-volume textbook—slowed progress on volume 3. With the aid of a Guggenheim Fellowship, Malone took leave from Columbia in 1958 and, the following year, accepted a faculty chair at Virginia, where he would spend the rest of his career. With publication of his third volume, *Jefferson and the Ordeal of Liberty*, in 1962, at the age of seventy, Malone retired from teaching and was named the university's biographer-in-residence. Now able to devote full-time to the labor on Jefferson, Malone waded into the complexities of Jefferson's two presidential terms, devoting a volume to each and anticipating that his four-volume project would have to expand to six.

In an appendix to the volume on Jefferson's first term, Malone took up the controversial question of what he titled "The Miscegenation Legend"—the long-rumored liaison between Jefferson and the slave Sally Hemings. This rumor, prompted by a disgruntled office seeker, had started early in Jefferson's presidency. Malone, like other leading Jefferson scholars of his day, discounted the rumors. The rumor would receive its widest circulation in *Thomas Jefferson: An Intimate History*, published by Fawn Brodie in 1974, the same year in which Malone received the Pulitzer Prize for the first five volumes of *Jefferson and His Time*.

Despite his disagreement with Brodie's thesis, Malone himself had discovered some of the facts that led to her conclusion. For instance, in studying Jefferson's comings and goings closely, Malone had learned that Jefferson was in residence at Monticello nine months before each of Hemings's children was born, and that otherwise Hemings had not given birth to any other children.[15]

Undaunted by controversy and unfazed by the Pulitzer, Malone pressed on to complete his work, which would stand as a monument not only to Jefferson but also to the extraordinary scholarship and literary efforts of its author. Increasingly frail, growing blind, and slowed by accumulating years, Malone soldiered on in good humor with the aid of his research assistant, Steven Hochman (later a member of the Emory faculty and director of research at the Carter Center), and his secretary, Katherine Sargeant, as well as with the aid of mechanical readers to magnify text and audiotapes on which Hochman read results of his research. The final volume, *The Sage of Monticello*, at last came forth in 1981, just shy of Malone's ninetieth birthday.

Much honored and beloved, Malone died in 1986, two weeks before his ninety-fifth birthday. His friend and fellow Jefferson biographer Merrill D. Peterson summed up the man as he summed up the man's work:

> In his humanism, in his liberal values, in his graciousness and sensibility, in the touch of philosophy, the felicity of style, the workmanlike dedication, the methodical discipline of fact, the dominant sense of order, form, and proportion given to his life, above all in his ability to conduct himself as a democrat while practicing the manners of a highly civilized human being—in all this Dumas Malone sensitively reflected the mind and temperament of Thomas Jefferson.[16]

Chronicler of Johnny Reb and Billy Yank—Bell Irvin Wiley | Among the historians who received their training elsewhere but spent the preponderance of their careers at Emory, probably the first to earn international reputation was Bell Irvin Wiley. Born in 1906 in rural Tennessee, one of eleven children in the family to survive infancy, Wiley worked the cotton fields of his parents' farm as a boy, surrounded by a dying generation of Civil War veterans. His maternal grandmother was a Confederate widow, and neighbor men had fought on opposite sides during the war. He once remarked, "I grew up in the midst of Civil War history."[17]

Completing his undergraduate degree at Asbury College, Wiley earned a master's degree in English at the University of Kentucky, then went off to Yale to work on a doctorate at the age of twenty-five. Provincial and very much of his time and provenance in racial views, Wiley underwent a profound transformation at Yale, befriending black scholars and, for one assignment, spending two hours interviewing George Washington Carver. In later years he would become one of the first group of faculty members to push for integration at Emory, incurring hate mail in the process. He remarked that his experience with African American friends in New Haven was "the most important single influence in helping me break away from the pattern of segregation and achieving emancipation of my own."

One reason for these formative friendships was that Wiley chose to write his dissertation about African Americans during the Civil War. The study won the admiration of the editor of the Yale Historical Publications series, who agreed to publish it. Wiley's friend and biographer, Henry T. Malone, recounts that Wiley had meanwhile entered the manuscript in a competition for an award from the United Daughters of the Confederacy, the prize for which would be five hundred dollars in cash and five hundred dollars to subvene publication costs. The only stipulation of the UDC prize committee, however, was that the title be changed from *Southern Negroes during the Civil War*. The new title should be *Southern Negroes during the War between the States*. Wiley gave it some thought, but when the book appeared it bore the title *Southern Negroes, 1861–1865*.[18]

Doctorate in hand, Wiley accepted a teaching position at Mississippi State College for Women (now the University of Southern Mississippi), where he spent four years before being appointed professor and head of the History Department at the University of Mississippi. By that time he had married, and he and his wife, Mary Frances (who would later serve as his principal research assistant and editor), settled into life in this university town. Busy as a scholar and teacher, Wiley nevertheless also found time to enjoy hunting and fishing with his neighbor, William Faulkner.

Following military service from 1943 to 1946, during which Wiley worked as military historical consultant to the Joint Chiefs of Staff, the Wileys moved to Louisiana State University, where Bell taught until being invited to join the faculty at Emory in 1949. By that time Wiley had added two more groundbreaking books to the Civil War bookshelf—*The Plain People of the Confederacy* (1943) and *The Life of Johnny Reb* (1943). The third volume of this trilogy, *The Life of Billy Yank*, appeared in 1952. Together these three books illuminated in a way never before attempted a topic that had come to absorb Wiley's interests—the lives of the common men and women who experienced camp life, the battlefields, and the home front during the years of war. Traveling some twenty-three thousand miles through twenty-four states, Wiley combed through troves of unpublished letters, diaries, and reports as well as published documents to develop a comprehensive picture of unheralded and often forgotten lives.[19] (By one estimate he pored over some thirty thousand letters of Northern and Southern soldiers.)

In many ways his work both anticipated and encouraged the move toward a more socially focused history that would send academic and popular historical writing in new directions in the second half of the century. Interested less in national leaders, commanding personalities, and the movements of armies, this history revealed instead the rhythms, concerns, and habits of daily life among lower and middle classes, slave and free—"the faceless masses of the 1860s."[20] Wiley also edited eight volumes of letters and reminiscences that had never before been published. As much as anyone writing during this period, he helped to turn attention toward the history of women in the middle of the nineteenth century.

As the centennial observance of the Civil War approached in 1961, it was natural that Wiley, ranked among America's leading Civil War historians, should help shape that observance. In 1957 President Eisenhower appointed him and nine other "citizens-at-large" to serve with four congressmen and four senators on the U.S. Civil War Centennial Commission; Wiley was the only southerner among the citizens-at-large. He soon became chair of the commission's executive committee. At the same time he kept up a steady pace of activity in national historical organizations and served as adviser on the publication of the papers of Ulysses S. Grant and Jefferson Davis, lectured throughout the country, and served for a year as visiting professor at the University of Oxford.

Wiley's reputation at Emory rested not only on the distinction of his scholarship but, perhaps most of all, on his skill and dedication as a teacher. His commitment to his graduate students was legendary, and although he was tough on them, they recalled his exceedingly high standards with appreciation in later years. One remarked, "During my days at Emory, I supported my family by working in a local funeral home. Yet in four years I never

Bell Irvin Wiley

saw anything any bloodier than one of my dissertation chapters after Dr. Wiley's red pencil had done its work!"[21]

At some point in the 1960s Wiley began the practice of offering to take his students on a tour of the Shiloh battlefield; that they would give up a Thanksgiving holiday to do so suggests the power of this special tour guide's narrative. In the last year of his teaching, more than three hundred undergraduates enrolled in his course on the Civil War—about half the senior class in those days. A profile of Wiley in the *Emory Magazine* noted,

> [He] was beloved by undergrads. Even the [un]interested became spellbound. He asked students to sit in the same place each day, and composed elaborate charts with students' names and photos. Even in large seminars (his last attracted more than three hundred at registration, a record at Emory), Wiley called each student by name.[22]

No doubt some of the affection the students felt for this genial scholar arose from the sight of him pedaling between campus and his home on East Clifton Road on a large English policeman's bicycle.

An inveterate book collector Wiley amassed a huge personal collection that filled not only his own office but also those of colleagues in the History Building (now Bowden Hall), and he was instrumental in building the library's collections of Confederate material and Civil War history.

As he approached retirement from Emory in 1974, after a quarter-century of teaching in Druid Hills and four decades as a professional historian, Wiley was invited by President Sanford Atwood to deliver the University's Commencement address, and with a fitting valedictory he left with some of the students whom he had devoted himself to teaching for three decades.

Other distinguished historians came along in succeeding decades to carry on the brilliant legacy of the History Department. Beginning in 1962, the first year that Emory presented the Thomas Jefferson Award for extraordinary service to the University, five members of the department received that honor—George Cuttino, Harvey Young, Irwin Hyatt, Russell Major, and Tom Burns. One, Dan Carter, received the University Scholar/Teacher Award, and at least nine have earned recognition through the University's highest teaching honor, the Emory Williams Award, since its inception in 1973. Clearly the department has proven itself over the long haul as one of the brightest-burning stars in Emory's constellation.

THE CHARLES HOWARD CANDLER PROFESSORSHIPS

— GARY S. HAUK *and* SALLY WOLFF KING —

At their annual meeting in November 1959 the Emory University Board of Trustees paid tribute to the late Charles Howard Candler Sr. (College 1898, Medicine 1902, Honorary 1942), who had succeeded his father, Asa Griggs Candler, as chair of the Emory University Board of Trustees when his father died in 1929. Howard Candler, as he was known, also died in office, in 1957, after chairing the board for nearly thirty years and guiding the appointment of S. Walter Martin as president to succeed Goodrich C. White. Martin took office just months before Howard Candler's death.

Like his father, Howard Candler was a major benefactor of Emory. He and his wife, Flora Glenn Candler, gave the money to erect Glenn Memorial Church in 1931, in memory of her Methodist clergyman father, Wilbur Fisk Glenn (College 1861). In 1954 Howard also funded construction of the Administration Building, at the opposite end of the Quadrangle from the library named for his father, who had funded the library's construction in 1926. When Howard Candler died, his widow proposed to give to Emory their magnificent home on Briarcliff Road, Callanwolde. Unable to imagine what to make of the magnificent Tudor-style residence and twenty-seven beautiful acres around it, only a mile and a half distant from the main Druid Hills campus, the administration sought from Mrs. Candler, instead, the monetary equivalent to endow distinguished professorships named for Mr. Candler.

The professorships were intended to recognize faculty members who had achieved significant scholarship, mastery of the art of teaching, and service to Emory. In a formal ceremony on May 30, 1960, the first twenty Candler Professors were honored. Henry L. Bowden, who had succeeded Howard Candler as chair of the board, recalled his predecessor as "a generous benefactor, a warm friend, and a wise administrator. . . . Working with three Emory presidents, he helped establish the University on a sound footing in its early days, brought it through a great depression and a world war, and set its feet upon the path to first rank among America's fine private institutions."[1] Candler contributed more than $13 million to the University in his lifetime.

President Martin added, "Emory believes that good teaching is the first obligation of a university. . . . Since the caliber of its faculty is the most important factor in the life of a university, these memorial professorships are an appropriate tribute to the man whose life-long devotion to his alma mater enables Emory University to serve more fully the community and the region."[2]

Over the next two decades, as the original Candler Professors retired, died, or left Emory, an additional thirteen Candler Professors were named on September 25, 1980. In appointing the second set of professorships, President James T. Laney noted that the Charles Howard Candler Professorships "have long represented the highest standards of excellence in the University's faculties."

To underscore the impact of distinguished teaching and scholarship on Emory, this chapter presents brief profiles of those original Candler Professors along with some others who have retired or are deceased.

The 1960 Candler Professors
Jacob H. Goldstein, PhD, Chemistry
Goldstein, one of the most productive physical chemists in the country, was a native of Atlanta. He received his BA (College 1943) and MS degrees (Graduate School 1945) at Emory, and after earning his PhD at Harvard, where he was a national research fellow, he returned to Emory in 1949 as an assistant professor. Promoted to professor in 1957, he was a member of Phi Beta Kappa, the American Chemical and Physical Societies, and Sigma Xi. His work in molecular spectroscopy, which he developed into a well-recognized program of research at Emory, was internationally renowned. His leadership enabled Emory to offer the PhD degree in physical chemistry.

Chauncey G. Goodchild, PhD, Biology
Goodchild, who served as chair and professor of the Biology Department, was a native of Pennsylvania. He received his BS degree from Westminster College and his PhD degree from New York University, where he was a Sandham Fellow. He won nationwide recognition for his work in physiological parasitology. By 1960 he had already published widely and received research grants totaling nearly four hundred thousand dollars.

A born teacher, who created an aura of excitement and expectation in the classroom, he was said to have a "razor-sharp English mind with Scotch-Irish warmth" and was known to "write as well as he speaks, . . . handle a TV show, construct a telescope, suture like a surgeon." He was also proficient in art and photography.

Coming to Emory in 1952 as associate professor and promoted to professor in 1955 he was a member of Sigma Xi and a special consultant to the National Institutes of Health.

Charles Hartshorne, PhD, Philosophy

A pioneer in philosophy, Hartshorne came to Emory in 1955 from the University of Chicago, where he had been professor of philosophy for twenty-seven years. Prior to that he had taught at Harvard for three years. He added luster to the reputation of Emory through the recognition he earned as one of the nation's best-known and most distinguished philosophers.

A native of Pennsylvania, he was educated at Haverford and Harvard. He was a Fulbright lecturer in Australia and Japan and a visiting professor or lecturer at Yale, Stanford, and the University of Washington, as well as at universities in Japan, Germany, and Australia.

He was the founder of the International Philosophical Association and a member of Phi Beta Kappa, the author of six books and one hundred articles, and editor of the *Collected Papers of Charles Peirce*. In addition to his remarkable career as a philosopher, he established his renown as an ornithologist, publishing several books in that field. He left Emory in 1962 for the University of Texas, from which he retired.

G. Ray Jordan, DD, Homiletics

Jordan was professor of homiletics and a nationally distinguished teacher of the art of preaching. He published 17 books and was the author of more than 200 articles, 250 book reviews, and contributions to 15 volumes, such as the *American Pulpit Series*.

A native of North Carolina, he was educated at Duke, where he received his AB degree and an honorary DD degree. He earned his BD degree at Emory and his AM degree at Yale. He was a member of Phi Beta Kappa, Theta Phi, and Omicron Delta Kappa honorary societies, and was a delegate to five general conferences of the Methodist Church.

Ranked among the best homileticians in the nation, Jordan joined the Emory faculty in 1945. He was a member of the Peace Commission of the Methodist Church for eight years, a member of the Board of Education of the Methodist Church for ten years, and editor of two national religious journals.

Stanley Joslin, LLM, Law

Stanley Joslin was chiefly responsible for developing an outstanding program in corporate law in Emory's School of Law during the 1950s. With a national reputation as a teacher and scholar, he specialized in divorce law and legal restrictions on charities as well as in corporate law. He chaired the bankruptcy committee of the Association of American Law Schools and published widely on topics ranging from alimony to the regulation of utility companies.

Born in 1911 in Wisconsin, Joslin received his AB degree from Cornell College (Iowa), his LLB from Wisconsin, and his LLM from Michigan. He practiced law for three years and taught at the University of Kentucky before coming to Emory as an assistant professor of law in 1947. He was promoted to associate professor in 1951 and professor in 1954, and served as acting dean of the law school in 1960–61.

James G. Lester, PhD, Geology

Born in Covington, Georgia, in 1897 Lester earned BS and MS degrees from Emory and an MS in civil engineering from Georgia Tech, then garnered his PhD degree in geology from the University of Colorado.

Lester came to Emory in 1919 as an instructor in engineering and was already associate professor of engineering when the University asked him to develop a geology department in

1940. He built a reputation for stimulating lectures in the classroom and for his commitment as a mentor to hundreds of students.

As professor and chair of geology, he was principally responsible for building the Geology Department at Emory. The Geology Building (now called the Anthropology Building), constructed in 1951, and geology field camps in North Georgia sprang from his inspiration and devotion. Lester was a major force in developing the science of geology in the Southeast. He was a member of Phi Beta Kappa, Sigma Xi, and Omicron Delta Kappa, and he was a fellow in the Geological Society of America.

Leroy Loemker, PhD, Philosophy

Leroy Loemker served as professor in the Department of Philosophy for more than fifty years, chairing the department from 1946 until his retirement in 1969. A leading authority on Gottfried Wilhelm von Leibniz, the German philosopher whose papers and letters Loemker translated, edited, and published in two volumes, he was widely regarded as the founder of North American scholarship on Leibniz.

Loemker served as dean of the Emory University Graduate School from 1946 to 1952, a period when Emory was just launching its Ph.D. programs and strengthening the entire Graduate School. He was considered one of the strongest intellectual influences at Emory, a gifted teacher, and a fresh and original thinker. His scholarship won recognition far beyond the region, including Rosenwald, Guggenheim, and Fulbright fellowships.

Born in 1900 in Wisconsin, Loemker received AB and LLD degrees from the University of Dubuque (Iowa) and STB and PhD degrees from Boston University. He came to Emory as an assistant professor in 1931, rose to associate professor in 1934, and became chair of the Philosophy Department in 1946. He was a leading figure of the Southern Society for Philosophy and Psychology and president of the Southern Society for Philosophy of Religion, as well as a member of the American Philosophical Association, Phi Beta Kappa, Omicron Delta Kappa, and other academic societies.

Joseph J. Mathews, PhD, History

Joe Mathews earned wide recognition in the field of modern European diplomatic history, authoring several books, including *Reporting the Wars*. As chair of the History Department from 1948 to 1958, he guided the development of the department's national reputation for excellence.

Born in Kentucky in 1908, he received AB and AM degrees from Duke University, and his PhD from the University of Pennsylvania. Before coming to Emory in 1946 he taught at the University of Chattanooga, the University of Pennsylvania, Duke, and the University of Mississippi. During World War II, he served as a U.S. naval officer.

In addition to receiving a Fulbright scholarship and a Guggenheim fellowship, Matthews was a member of the American Historical Association, the Southern Historical Association, the Society of French History, and Phi Beta Kappa.

Dr. H. Stephen Weems, MD, Radiology

A complete narrative of influence is found in chapter 43.

W. Tate Whitman, PhD, Economics

Tate Whitman had a special interest in the history of economic thought and public economic policy. He earned praise from the business community for numerous articles on finance in professional and scholarly journals and for two authoritative books, one on investment and the other on corporate earning power and market valuations. Whitman served as president of the Emory University Senate and was, for several years, chair of the University Educational Policy

Committee. Graduating classes of the Business School consistently voted him the school's outstanding teacher.

Born in Alabama in 1909 Whitman received AB, AM, and PhD degrees from Duke University, then taught at Duke and the Citadel before joining the Emory faculty as an associate professor in 1947. He became professor in 1951. Whitman was a member of Beta Gamma Sigma, Alpha Kappa Psi, the American Economics Association, the Southern Economics Association, and the Industrial Relations Research Association.

Bell I. Wiley, PhD, History
For a fuller account of Wiley's career and his place at Emory, see pages 290–292.

Alfred E. Wilhelmi, DPhil, Biochemistry
Professor and chair of biochemistry, Alfred Wilhelmi was widely known for his groundbreaking study of growth hormones in different animals. More than thirty-five of his articles appeared in professional journals, many of them written in collaboration with his wife, the distinguished scientist Dr. Jane A. Russell, associate professor of biochemistry at Emory. Wilhelmi completed a term as chair of the Endocrinology Study Section, National Institutes of Health, and was director of its Pituitary Hormone Distribution Program.

He was born in Ohio in 1910, and after earning the AB degree from Adelphi College he went to England as a Rhodes scholar and earned BA and DPhil degrees from Oxford. He taught physiological chemistry for twelve years at Yale University School of Medicine before coming to Emory in 1950 as a professor and chair of biochemistry. He was a member of Phi Beta Kappa, Sigma Xi, the Georgia and the New York academies of sciences, the American Zoological Society, the American Society of Biological Chemists, and (as an honorary member) the Canadian Physiological Society. He was an associate editor of the *Canadian Journal of Biochemistry and Physiology*, and a member of the editorial board of *Endocrinology*.

Later Candler Professors
William A. Beardslee, PhD, Charles Howard Candler Professor of Religion
A perceptive scholar of the New Testament, Will Beardslee published two major books—*Literary Criticism of the New Testament* (1970) and *A House for Hope: A Study in Process and Biblical Thought* (1972) and numerous articles in *Biblical Studies*. His application of the tools and resources of many fields to probe the depths of his own discipline brought him wide acclaim.

After arriving at Emory in 1947 Beardslee served as director of the Graduate Institute of the Liberal Arts from 1957 to 1961 and later as acting dean of Emory College, president of the University Senate, and chair of the Department of Religion.

Born in Michigan in 1916, Beardslee received the AB degree from Harvard, the BD from New Brunswick Theological Seminary, an MA from Columbia University, and a PhD from the University of Chicago. During 1935–36, he studied at Lingnan University in Canton, China. A member of Phi Beta Kappa, he was a Fulbright scholar, a fellow of the Institute of Ecumenical and Cultural Research, and a research grant recipient from the Society of Biblical Literature.

Earl D. C. Brewer, PhD, Charles Howard Candler Professor of Sociology and Religion, School of Theology
Brewer was a pioneer in the effort to relate the study of religion to other aspects of human social life. His numerous works included a study of religion in southern Appalachia, analyses of Methodism, and investigations into the role of theological education.

He was born in North Carolina in 1914 and received both his BPh and BD degrees from Emory. After earning his MA from Duke University and PhD from the University of North

Carolina he returned to Emory as a faculty member in 1946. For a decade (1958–68) he was the director of religious research while also actively participating in other University and seminary affairs.

Brewer was president of the Religious Research Association, contributing editor of *Review of Religious Research*, director of research for the National Council of Churches, visiting professor at the Graduate Theological Union, and director of research in religion of southern Appalachian studies under a Ford Foundation grant. His commitment to social issues, however, extended far beyond purely academic pursuits and encompassed distinguished contributions to the United Methodist Church and in the areas of race relations, prisoner rehabilitation, and gerontology.

George P. Cuttino, DPhil, Charles Howard Candler Professor of Medieval History
A full narrative of Cuttino's life and work is found in chapter 29.

Michael E. Fritz, DDS, PhD, Charles Howard Candler Professor of Periodontology, School of Dentistry
As chair of the Department of Periodontology from 1967 until the closing of the Emory School of Dentistry in 1990, Fritz built the department and its highly respected postgraduate program. In recognition of his contributions to his field, the Swedish Medical Research Council in 1973–74 awarded him an International Research Fellowship at the University of Lund, Sweden.

Fritz was born in Boston, Massachusetts, in 1938 and received his DDS, MS, and PhD degrees from the University of Pennsylvania. He joined the faculty of Emory as associate professor in 1967 and enjoyed continuous research support from the National Institute of Dental Research. Among his areas of research was the biology of orofacial herpes simplex virus infection.

J. Willis Hurst, MD, Charles Howard Candler Professor of Medicine
In addition to writing 20 medical books and more than 150 articles, Willis Hurst was editor-in-chief of *The Heart*, one of the primary textbooks for cardiology, now in its eleventh edition and translated into six foreign languages. Chair of the Department of Medicine for three decades, he also served as physician-in-chief at Emory University Hospital, the Emory Clinic, and Grady Memorial Hospital, and is remembered as President Lyndon Johnson's cardiologist.

A native of Carrolton, Georgia, he received his BS degree from the University of Georgia and MD degree from the Medical College of Georgia, where he also served his residency in internal medicine. From 1947 to 1949 Hurst was a fellow in cardiology at the Massachusetts General Hospital, affiliated with Harvard University, and in the mid-1950s was chief of cardiology at the U.S. Naval Hospital in Bethesda, Maryland, where he met then-senator Johnson.

Hurst served as president of both the Georgia Heart Association and the American Heart Association; in 1974 the AHA presented him with the Gold Heart Award. In 1968 he was honored by the Medical Association of Georgia with the Hardman Award for contributions to medicine in Georgia. He was elected both fellow and master by the American College of Physicians, and twice received the Gifted Teacher Award from the American College of Cardiology.

In addition to his many professional publications, in retirement Hurst published a history of the Department of Medicine and, with his son as coauthor, a murder mystery.

Jacqueline Jordan Irvine, Charles Howard Candler Professor of Urban Education
Scholar, teacher, counselor, and community leader, Irvine joined the Emory faculty in 1979 and retired in 2006. During that time, she served on more than forty University committees, including a presidential search committee and the Commission on Teaching. She has forged

effective means of improving education, served meals to the elderly and homeless, cradled in her arms babies born prematurely and with AIDS, and was a model of passionate dedication to the formation of students and personal virtue exercised for the public good.

Irvine received her BA and MA degrees from Howard University and the PhD from Georgia State University in Educational Leadership. Specializing in multicultural education and urban education, with a particular focus on the education of African Americans, her research included examinations of "race, gender, class, and culture in schools and . . . effective instructional strategies to address increasing student diversity in elementary and middle schools."[3] Irvine's extraordinary public service is matched by her nationally prominent scholarship in multicultural education and her consistently superb teaching and mentoring. In 1999, she delivered the Distinguished Faculty Lecture at Emory and was a member of the committee that planned the university-wide Year of Reconciliation. The University awarded her the Thomas Jefferson Award in 2000.

Her book *Black Students and School Failure* received two national awards. Other books by Irvine include *Growing Up African American in Catholic Schools*, *Critical Knowledge for Diverse Students*, and *In Search of Wholeness, Culturally Responsive Teaching, and Seeing with a Cultural Eye*.

Lucy S. McGough, JD, Charles Howard Candler Professor of Law

Lucy S. McGough has attained national recognition for her work in family law and the rights of juveniles. She is the author of *Georgia Juvenile Court Practices* (1980) and the coauthor (with Frank T. Read) of *Let Them Be Judged: The Judicial Integration of the Deep South* (1978). The latter book is a history of the U.S. Court of Appeals for the Fifth Circuit during the major civil rights struggles and was nominated for the Triennial Awards of the Order of the Coif, one of the most prestigious awards offered for legal scholarship.

Born in Indiana in 1941, McGough grew up in Kentucky and moved to Atlanta to attend Agnes Scott College as an undergraduate. She earned a BA in English and, unsatisfied by work in the secretarial pool, set her sights on Emory Law. She matriculated by the dean's special permission without taking the LSAT and soon discovered that law was her forte. After receiving her degree in 1966 McGough spent three years in practice at the Emory Neighborhood Law Office.

A pioneer for women law faculty, she returned to teach at Emory in 1970, after spending time at Harvard on a Ford fellowship. In a time when equality for women was still a hot issue, McGough's ability and ambition to teach in a field dominated by men opened the doors for aspiring women lawyers. In 1980, when she was appointed as a Candler Professor, she was not only the youngest recipient but also the only female and the only law faculty member among the Candler Professors. While at Emory, McGough was actively involved in developing the Emory University Legal Service program and served as a consultant to the attorney general of Georgia.

McGough left Emory to accept a position at Louisiana State University Law School as the Vinson and Elkins Professor of Law.

Leon Mandel, PhD, Charles Howard Candler Professor of Organic Chemistry

Leon Mandel made outstanding contributions to the field of synthetic organic chemistry. Under his chairmanship the Chemistry Department at Emory enjoyed phenomenal growth and gained widespread recognition, in large part owing to his resourceful and industrious spirit.

He was born in the Bronx, New York, in 1927 and received his PhD from Harvard University in 1951. Joining the faculty of Emory in 1955, he was highly successful in securing grants to support his own work, and that of the department, from the National Science Foundation, the Petroleum Research Fund, and the National Institutes of Health. Mandel published more than forty-five research articles and was coauthor of *Organic Chemistry: A Concise Approach* (1974).

He also devoted himself to the art of teaching. Winner of the national E. Harris Harbison Award, given by the Danforth Foundation for distinguished teaching, he was recognized by his students and colleagues at Emory with the Emory Williams Distinguished Teaching Award in 1978. He was a member of Phi Beta Kappa, Omicron Delta Kappa, Sigma Xi, and the American Chemical Society.

J. Russell Major, PhD, Charles Howard Candler Professor of Renaissance History

A narrative of Russell Major's life and scholarship is found in chapter 32.

Neil C. Moran, MD, Charles Howard Candler Professor of Pharmacology, School of Medicine

Chair of the Department of Pharmacology from 1962 to 1992, Moran was an outstanding specialist in cardiovascular pharmacology. As an early investigator into beta-adrenergic blocking drugs, now widely used to treat hypertension and angina pectoris, he wrote some of the landmark research publications in the field.

He was born in Phoenix, Arizona, in 1924 and received both his AB and MD degrees from Stanford University, where he was the Irving Fellow in Physiology and received a senior research fellowship and a research career development award from the National Institutes of Health.

An exemplary and dedicated teacher, he was selected by the graduating classes of the Emory School of Medicine in 1968—and for the next seven years—as the best basic sciences professor. His achievements included the American Heart Association Citation for Distinguished Service to Research and the Georgia Heart Association Silver Medal for Meritorious Service to Research.

Moran served on the editorial boards of *Circulation* and the *Journal of Cardiovascular Pharmacology*, and was a member of the American Society of Pharmacology and Experimental Therapeutics, the National Institute of General Medical Sciences, and the National Heart, Lung and Blood Institute.

Carlos Rojas, PhD, Charles Howard Candler Professor of Spanish Literature

Carlos Rojas is an internationally renowned figure in the literary world and a leading authority in modern Spanish literature. His extensive publications include fifteen novels, numerous short stories, and distinctive critical and historical texts, of which sixteen are scholarly books and two are textbooks, in addition to translations, articles, reviews, and other writings. He was named to the Candler Professorship in 1980.

Rojas has received some of the most prestigious awards offered in Spain. His novel *El Ingenioso Hidalgo y Poeta Federico Garcia Lorca asciende a los Infiernos* received the highly coveted Premio Nadal for 1979. Other distinguished literary honors bestowed on him include the Premio Ateneo de Sevilla (1977), Premio Planeta (1973), and Premio Nacional de Literature (1968). Lecturing frequently throughout the world on Spanish literature and history throughout the world, he has also gained increasing attention as a visual artist.

Rojas's novels are an original mixture of fiction, biography, and historical sources. His literary interpretations focus on some of the key artistic and political figures of Spain: Cervantes, Goya, Picasso, Dali, Manuel Azaña, members of the Bourbon royal family, Primo de Rivera, Garcia Lorca, and Charles II—the last of the Spanish Habsburgs. One colleague describes him as an exile from the Franco regime who stayed in the United States but spiritually and intellectually lives in Spain. Rojas is also a great conversationalist who regales his friends with wit, wisdom, and the occasional recitation of poetry.

Born in 1928 in Barcelona, he did graduate work at the Universidad de Barcelona and the University of Glasgow, Scotland. He received his PhD from the Universidad Central, Madrid, in 1955. Rojas taught at Emory from 1960 until his retirement in 1996. Emory recognized his dedicated and conscientious teaching and work by awarding him the University Scholar/Teacher Award in 1987.

Jerome Sutin, PhD, Charles Howard Candler Professor of Anatomy, School of Medicine

Jerome Sutin, chair of the Department of Anatomy and Cell Biology from 1966 to 1996, specialized in studying regions of the brain that regulate behaviors. His work examined the effects of drug-induced degeneration of brain systems on movement control centers of the brain. He was the author of more than twenty-five research publications.

Born in Albany, New York, in 1930, he received both his MS and PhD degrees from the University of Minnesota. In 1955–56 he was a National Foundation for Infantile Paralysis fellow at the University of California Medical Center in Los Angeles. Before arriving at Emory in 1966 he was director of graduate studies for the department of anatomy at the Yale University School of Medicine.

In 1970 Sutin received a NATO Senior Scientist fellowship and served as a visiting professor in the Institute of Psychiatry at the University of London. He was active in many professional organizations and held offices in the Cajal Club, the Association of Anatomy Chairmen, and the American Association of Anatomists.

Dr. Floyd C. Watkins, PhD, Charles Howard Candler Professor of American Literature

Floyd Watkins served on the Emory faculty nearly four decades; his story is told in chapter 30.

J. Harvey Young, PhD, Candler Professor of American Social History

A medical history review article said in 1979 that James Harvey Young was perhaps the most widely read and influential medical historian alive. His best-known books, *The Toadstool Millionaires* (Princeton, 1961) and *The Medical Messiahs* (Princeton, 1967) sold in the tens of thousands, were reissued again and again, and had established Young as the leading authority on American medical quackery. The value of these books lay not simply in the technical merits of their meticulous research, but in Young's unusual approach: a subject that in other hands had always been exploited as a joke or horror story, a *New York Times* review suggested, had been identified by Young as a social phenomenon of genuine, continuing importance in American life. Young had a good sense of humor and could present case studies as good stories. But his purpose was always serious—to "explain the grievous imposition quackery places upon society's well-being," and particularly to show how "health deception demands continuing pursuit."

Young published nine books altogether and almost one-hundred fifty articles of various types, before retiring in 1984. By that time, he had received two honorary degrees, many fellowships and endowed lectureships, and the highest awards in medical and pharmaceutical history. His capstone publication, *Pure Food: Securing the Federal Food and Drugs Act of 1906* (Princeton, 1989), concluded years of research on the history of regulatory efforts to protect American health. This research drew him into time-consuming public service, including work for the National Library of Medicine and for a 1969 White House conference on food and nutritional problems and tasks undertaken for the National Institutes of Health and the FDA (National Food and Drug Advisory Council).

Known as an extraordinary teacher of undergraduates, Young also had a remarkable record as a graduate history teacher and pioneer of interdisciplinary scholarship at Emory. In his years in the History Department he had more graduate students than anyone else, and in 1976 he became the first Emory College faculty member to receive an Emory Williams Teaching Award for graduate teaching. He was interdisciplinary before the word was invented— a founding member of the Graduate Institute of Liberal Arts and director of twelve dissertations (out of the thirty-eight total that he directed) done by ILA students, not by graduate students of history.

Born in Brooklyn, New York, in 1915, he received both his MA and PhD degrees from the University of Illinois. He came to Emory in 1941 and served as chair of the History Department from 1958 to 1966. A member of Phi Beta Kappa, Sigma Xi, and Phi Kappa Phi, he received the Thomas Jefferson Award in 1969 in recognition of his service to Emory, and the Emory Williams Distinguished Teaching Award in 1976 for his teaching in the Graduate School. He was also the recipient of two honorary degrees.

THE BIOGRAPHER
Elizabeth Stevenson Looked Steadily at Lives and at Life
— BETH DAWKINS BASSETT —

The route to Emory for Elizabeth Stevenson was long and circuitous, but the journey ended quite successfully. Born in the Panama Canal Zone in 1919, she moved with her family to Montana and then to Atlanta, where she attended Atlanta Girls High School. During this time Elizabeth's mother was secretary to George Woodruff at Trust Company Bank. So impressed was he with Mrs. Stevenson's daughters that he financed the education of all three girls at Agnes Scott College, where Elizabeth graduated in 1941 magna cum laude.

She then began a career-long association with people who held PhDs, and although she never earned that degree herself, she would eventually hold a Candler Professorship at Emory University. Elizabeth Stevenson retired from Emory in 1989 and died in her Decatur home in 1999. Reprinted here is an article that appeared in Emory Magazine *in 1987.*

WHEN SHE WAS twenty-five years old, Elizabeth Stevenson decided to write a book. Such a resolve is not unusual; many people, even those newly enjoying adulthood, feel a similar urge. What was unusual was the kind of first book she wanted to produce. Having only recently graduated from Agnes Scott College with a bachelor's degree in English and history, she set out to write a scholarly work, a critical study of Henry James.

Stevenson had read James's early work during her freshman year in college, and shortly after her graduation in 1941 she began to read his more difficult writings. She liked his work, and didn't like what other people had written about him. "I said, 'I'll just go ahead and write one myself,'" she remembered, "and I did."

In 1945, determined that she would not consult authorities on James but would confine herself to his fiction, his memoirs, and the memoirs of his family and friends, she began seriously to study the author. Although she worked full-time as a clerk in a government agency and studied and wrote only at night and on weekends—a regimen she would continue for nearly thirty years—her manuscript was completed by 1948. She submitted it to four publishing houses in succession. One, Scribner's, kept the book a year, then decided against printing it. They asked, however, to be able to consider it again the following year. Stevenson said no. The fourth publisher, Macmillan, accepted it, and *The Crooked Corridor: A Study of Henry James* appeared in 1949 to favorable national reviews.

That a thirty-year-old audit clerk with "no advanced degrees and only meager resources for scholarship" had produced a definitive biography, said *Atlanta* magazine several years later, was a "literary miracle."

The Crooked Corridor was not a flash in the pan. In the years after the James study, Stevenson published *Henry Adams: A Biography* (Macmillan, 1955); *A Henry Adams Reader* (Doubleday, 1958); *Lafcadio Hearn* (Macmillan, 1961); *Babbitts & Bohemians: The American 1920s* (Macmillan, 1967); *Park Maker: A Life of Frederick Law Olmsted* (Macmillan, 1977); and *Figures in a Western Landscape* (Johns Hopkins University Press, 1994), a book that chronicles through biography the historical development of Montana. She received two Guggenheim fellowships, a Rockefeller Fellowship, five Emory research grants, a stipend from the National Endowment for the Humanities, and an award for research from the American Council of Learned Societies. Her work was nominated for both the Pulitzer Prize and the National Book Award, and in 1956 she was awarded the Bancroft Prize for *Henry Adams: A Biography*—the first woman so honored.

Like Stevenson's first book, each of the others was written while she held down full-time jobs, chiefly clerical and secretarial. In 1974, however, she left her last nonacademic job, assistant to the dean of Emory College, to become a research associate in the Graduate Institute of the Liberal Arts. In 1977 she was named to an associate professorship in the ILA. Five years later she was made a full professor, and in 1984 she was appointed Charles Howard Candler Professor of American Studies. When she retired from Emory in 1987 her only formal academic degree was still the BA she had received from Agnes Scott.

Most of the modest houses facing the street on which Stevenson lived in Decatur for forty years sit among oaks and pines risen to great heights and magnolias that are wide-girthed columns of thick, shiny leaves, deeply, richly green. Her house is red brick. Its front windows are shaded by red awnings, and its concrete stoop is flanked by the filigree leaves of nandinas and by large, spreading azaleas.

Inside the house are a great many books—books in the room Stevenson's mother occupied until her death in 1979, books in Stevenson's bedroom, books in the living room. In her bedroom her own works stand side by side on a shelf, and there, too, under a window that faces her side yard, is the simple wooden desk at which she writes.

With Stevenson live two cats—Tammy, coal black, svelte, and standoffish, and George, tabby-colored, substantial, and sociable. When their mistress takes her seat in the high-backed rocker in her living room, George jumps into her lap and makes himself comfortable. Tammy sits on a low bookshelf beneath the windows and gazes at the sun-dappled yard.

It is summer, and summer is the time when Stevenson returns to Montana. Her departure is imminent. "I go," she says, "and sit on the edge of the wilderness."

Montana exerts a strong pull. Although her parents were Georgians, as were their ancestors for generations, her family and six families of Georgia relatives moved west in 1920, when Stevenson was nine months old, and set up a business, the pioneer drilling and refining of the oil of the Kevin-Sunburst field near Great Falls, Montana. For all of the little enclave, the years in the Northwest had a romantic cast. In a draft of the preface to her book about Montana, she wrote,

> We were a colony of six related families transplanted from Georgia. . . . I know that my uncles as well as my father took rather lightly the weekday life of the family company and spent as much time as possible in the joys of camping, fishing, and hunting, and since they were southerners, of talking and visiting.
>
> My father was intoxicated with beauty. He showed us tiny, hidden shooting-stars in the early spring prairie grass. He pointed out strange growths on trees when we walked through the woods. He joined us in rolling down grass banks in childlike ecstasy. Camping, which was his idea, found the five of us in a small, square bell-tent gazing up in July at snow on the tent-top, or noticing the etched edging of ice on a trout stream in October.

The Montana sojourn ended abruptly in 1932, when the oil business failed. Stevenson's family headed back to Georgia. "On the last day of August 1932," she wrote, "when the first snow powdered the tops of the mountains east of Great Falls, Montana, a family of five loaded their tent, bed rolls, camp stove, and other belongings onto an already old square-bodied Studebaker and set out to go, not on a pleasant camping trip as they had done before, but to flee eastward and southward. . . . I was thirteen, the oldest of three children, all girls, and I have remembered that eleven-day trip as a dividing point in my life. All that I had known of childhood was severed from all that I was to know afterwards."

She adjusted with difficulty and with, she wrote, "some damage," but adjusted nonetheless. "Slowly, very slowly, I found myself there: in school, in work, in learning about the depths and heights of this South, the old intractable land."

By the time Stevenson went to college she knew vaguely that she wanted to write, and she thought at first she wanted to be a journalist. After graduation from Agnes Scott she went to work for Southern Bell but also approached Ralph McGill about a job at the *Atlanta Constitution*. When he advised her that there was more security with the telephone company, she just went on reading, writing, and working at jobs that gave her money on which to live. Year after year the genre that steadily fascinated her was biography. In a 1961 essay she wrote,

> In order to write biography a writer does not have to invent a plot. A simple and terrible story offers itself . . . : birth, aging, death. It is a story with a firm structure—a beginning, a middle, and an end. Death, the final event, secures attention even in an awkward telling. No life seen in this perspective can be unimportant, and even obscure existences have pathos. It is the biographer's function to make the reader look steadily at life as defined by time. . . . The rash might conclude that this is a quite simple business. One locates the facts, adds a little color here and there, and sets down sequences. However, . . . facts are the most deceptive of materials. . . . Even the gift given the biographer, the structure of life itself, is very easy to ruin.

During part of the writing of the book about James, Stevenson worked at the Atlanta Public Library as a clerk typist (according to a newspaper clipping from 1949, she experienced, she said, "the thrill of a lifetime" typing the library order for her own book). Except for one year, when she lived on a Guggenheim Fellowship, the entire Adams biography—five years in the making—was written while she was at the library. She had never heard of the Bancroft Prize until the day her editor called to congratulate her for having won it for *Henry Adams*.

By the time she finished the book on Hearn, Stevenson had five dollars left in her savings account. Her search of the want ads led her to Emory College.

By then she was already at work on the Hearn book. She became interested in the nineteenth-century journalist when she turned to his writing to check the accuracy of Adams's observations about Japan. Hearn, who had spent the last years of his life there, wrote extensive firsthand accounts of the country. As she read Hearn's writing, she thought he seemed delightful—"eager and curious as a terrier," she later wrote, "married to a Japanese and thoroughly installed in the Japanese life, yet observant with an alien's eyes." She decided she wanted to write about him. "He was someone I could stick with."

As she began her preliminary research—reading books already printed about Hearn (which she found to be blatantly inaccurate) and reading the journalist's own letters and writings—she began to uncover a man not simple and whole, as he had first appeared, but complicated and emotion-twisted. She began to lay aside her first impressions, a process that, she later wrote, is an unavoidable part of the mental journey the biographer undertakes: "Early work in biography, the first weeks and months of reading, note-taking, and writing, is a heart-breaking discouragement. Misconceptions dissolve, important contradictions arise, even one's initial notion about the subject, without which there is no use even to begin, cracks and sags under the strain."

Hearn's life had been difficult and strange. He was born in 1849 to Irish-Greek parents on Sappho's Isle of Leucadia, or Lefkada (for which he was named). His parents abandoned him, and at the age of six he was taken into the home of a wealthy aunt in Dublin, Ireland, who was interested not in the boy but in fulfilling her husband's dying wish for an heir. At sixteen, Hearn, already nearsighted, completely lost the sight in his left eye in an accident. Thereafter, he so abused his good eye reading and writing that it became enlarged and protruded from its socket in a way other people found alarming. When he was eighteen his aunt suffered financial setbacks and sent him to London to live with one of her former maids, where he suffered terrible aloneness and found refuge in books. At nineteen the dwarfish, abnormally shy boy was sent away permanently, to Cincinnati, where he was to contact an in-law for help. The contact was uninterested in the boy. Penniless and alone, Hearn suffered near-starvation before finding employment as a reporter on the *Cincinnati Enquirer*. There he became locally famous writing sensational journalism about what he called "the Odd, the Queer, the Strange, the Exotic, and the Monstrous."

After eight years in Ohio, he began a nomadic existence, moving first to New Orleans, where his stories of Creole life made him nationally known, then to Martinique, and then to New York City.

In 1890 *Harper's* magazine commissioned Hearn to go to Japan and write a series of articles. He soon came to disagreement with *Harper's* over the terms of his employment and severed his relationship with the magazine. Still, the decision to go to Japan proved a good one. There, writing his impressions of the country, rewriting Japanese folktales in English, and pursuing a career as a teacher and then college professor of English literature, he found a contentment he had not previously known. He entered into an arranged marriage with Setsu Koisumi, a Japanese woman of aristocratic descent, and four children were born to the couple. While in Japan he perfected a simpler style and produced the best work of his life. At his death in 1904 he held the chair of English literature at the Imperial University in Tokyo.

Stevenson's journey toward knowledge of Hearn's life took her to the American cities in which he had lived and finally to Japan. In each location she read whatever the libraries had to offer on the journalist and tried to get the feel of the locality and how Hearn must have responded to it. In the course of her work she received Guggenheim and Rockefeller fellowships.

She researched until, she said, she "felt up to her ears and about to spill over." Talking with the *Atlanta Constitution* following completion of the book, she said, "I have to get into a complete mess . . . utter despair . . . choked with impressions, and then all of a sudden an idea will make [the subject] come clear. . . . I enjoy it, but it's gruesome enjoyment."

At some point she arrived at sureness. "I knew Hearn," she wrote.

> Here I was on the most dangerous yet necessary ground for the would-be biographer. My confidence could make me blind as well as acute. Yet it is this kind of irrational confidence that a biographer needs, in plodding on through documents, in and out of libraries, through museums, historic shrines, monuments—all the places where dust gathers on the vitality of a once hurtful existence. I had to restore that hurt to life, as well as a particular courage, impudence, and enduringness that had once made [Hearn] friends and enemies from Ireland to Ohio, from Louisiana to Martinique, from New York to Tokyo.
>
> This is the contradiction inherent in the art of biography (not a science at all, and not a pure art either, but an impure one, full of interest and entertainment): a queer organization of facts and intuitions about facts.

She grew fond of Hearn (biographers like "strange birds," she says), finding that in spite of his oddness he possessed "integrity and sweetness" that "existed as a core within layers of bitterness, mistrust, and fear." He was, she says, "a genuine human being," whose writing "was a lonely effort to construct a personal universe in a dirty shambles of a world."

The biography of Hearn ends with a simple account of his death. He was buried near Tokyo under tall trees where he had walked with his family, and his posthumous name, according to Buddhist custom, was placed over the grave, as was a flowery quote. He would have liked better, Stevenson wrote, the familiar inscription carved upon another memorial marker, in a village he had often visited with his children:

> "In commemoration of the place where sang Professor Yakumo Koizumi [Hearn's Japanese name]." The people of the village recalled the [man of letters] joining his children in singing in the sunset each evening, "Yu-yake! Ko-yake! . . . Evening burning! Little burning! Weather, be fair tomorrow!"

Of the several biographies of Hearn, said the *New York Times Book Review*, Stevenson's is "certainly the most complete and comprehensive." "It has remained for Miss Stevenson," said *Saturday Review*, "to provide this careful, objective study, the product of formidable research, what will probably be the final account of [Hearn's] fantastic life and summary of critical opinion of his work."

During part of the writing of the Hearn biography, Stevenson lived solely on money from a Guggenheim Fellowship. But by 1960, when she completed the book, she had stretched the funds to their limit. She had five dollars left in her savings account. Although her books had been critical successes, none had been a financial success.

She began to read the want ads and saw that the dean of Emory College needed a secretary. John C. Stephens Jr., who was then dean, hired "Miss Elizabeth," said Charles T. Lester, who became acting dean when Stephens subsequently left the office. (Lester later served as dean of the Graduate School, vice president, executive vice president, and dean of faculties.) "It didn't take Jack long to realize what a gem he had," Lester remembered. "He made her a sort of administrative assistant." She worked at the job for fourteen years, during which time she researched and wrote the book on the twenties and set out to research and write her biography of Olmsted.

Each book involved considerable research and travel. For *Babbitts & Bohemians* she repeatedly visited the Library of Congress and the New York Public Library, where she had also done research on Adams, and she traveled to Paris and London in an effort to understand the world of expatriates of the twenties.

During the nearly ten years she worked on *Park Maker*, she made twenty five-day visits to the Library of Congress in the course of examining fifty boxes of Olmsted manuscripts. She also studied materials at the New York Public Library and libraries at the University of California–Berkeley, Gallaudet College, and Harvard, Yale, Cornell, Stanford, and Emory universities. In addition, she viewed Olmsted's parks in New York, Chicago, St. Louis, and California.

Although Stevenson's working arrangement at Emory was satisfactory and she had no plans to change it, her job was threatened in 1973, when Stephens left the deanship of the College. John M. Palms was appointed to the post, and he planned that the secretary with whom he had worked for some years would move with him into the office.

Lester, who by then was acting dean, did not want Stevenson to leave the University. He knew the quality of her scholarship, and he thought there might be a place for her on the faculty. He approached the director of the ILA, and that faculty voted to invite her to join the institute.

Stevenson went to the ILA in 1974 as a research associate and eventually taught there, although she wasn't sure at first that she wanted to teach. "I was scared to death of it," she says. "I had taken in college enough credits to get what they called a temporary teacher's certificate, and I never went down to pick it up because I didn't want to teach. I don't like authoritarian roles." When she did begin to teach, she was, she says, "scared enough each time [a new class began] to take to the woods." Still, she began increasingly to enjoy watching her students grow and to relish the times when "ideas in a class began to explode and effervesce like champagne."

Former director of athletics and recreation Gerald B. Lowrey, who earned his PhD degree from the ILA in 1981, never noticed Stevenson's trepidation. "When I first saw her, she had graying hair and looked like an erudite senior professor, distinguished, calm, centered, self-assured, modest," he recalled.

Lowrey did not feel, either, that her lack of advanced degrees affected the quality of her teaching. "Her teaching and research were first-rate and an example to others," he said. "Scholarship and love of teaching and caring for students is not necessarily engendered by a degree. If you have it you have it, and she had it.

"I think she followed a nontraditional path to prominence. For a lot of women, there weren't too many traditional paths. She found a way to express her talents in an unorthodox route but proved her abilities beyond question."

Gone now is the writing schedule Stevenson maintained for so long. Now she writes in prime time, in the morning hours. "I do my morning chores first," she says, "washing the dishes, feeding the cats, filling my bird feeders. Then I sit down to write for several hours.

"Then I get restless and I go out and buy groceries or do something different. In the afternoon I try to read some. By evening I sit and watch TV," she says and laughs. "I'm not good at all-day work. I get too tired. The real work is exhausting, the actual composing."

The Montana book began in 1979, when Stevenson, alone following the death of her mother, returned to Great Falls for the first extended visit since she left it in early adolescence. She went in large part because of a desire to knit into the fabric of her adult life the lost world of her childhood.

"I was setting out to mend the break," she wrote in a preface to the book. "I had acquired certain sets of ideas . . . about politics, books, habits of living. In addition to an inescapable load of personal feelings, I had acquired objective feelings and curiosities. I would try to exercise them on a new-old scene. I would travel, I hoped, with a wide-open mind."

Yet she knew, too, that objectivity would not erase the part of her that was a product of her western childhood and of Great Falls in particular. Some lessons were an indelible part of her life. About the city she wrote,

> Within the regularly laid out blocks and streets and houses, life attempted to be rational and sensible. Flowers in gardens and parks bloomed fiercely all summer long, but the bitter blowing winds of winter blizzards reminded us of another world outside the boundaries of green which the early settlers had created on a sandy plain bordering the five waterfalls of a great river. And these proper people were perversely proud of the nearness of the wild. Nothing, they said, held the wind back but a barbed wire between here and the North Pole. The city was safety, but the most delicious part of life was beyond. . . . I think I learned without knowing it what is part of every westerner's emotional equipment: that life is divided into two parts, of comfort and of freedom, and that we need both.

She initially composed the book as a first-person travel narrative to be called *Return to Montana*. The form was perhaps cathartic for her but was not, she found, publishable. She set it aside and began again, integrating some of the early material into a history of the state seen through biography. Biography is, after all, the form with which she feels most at home.

"Biography," she wrote, "is one of the enduring art forms of the Western world. . . . One finds no biography in the East at all, and that gives one pause. Biography is a special product of the West. As long as the single human being has meaning, so long 'lives' will be written."

CHAPTER 29

MEDIEVALIST EXTRAORDINARY
George Peddy Cuttino
— IRWIN T. HYATT —

In response to a tough assignment, Irwin Hyatt, onetime a student of Professor George Cuttino and later his longtime friend and Emory colleague, describes "Cuttino the man." This would be a challenge for anyone, but Hyatt here rises to the task beautifully.[1]

A**NYONE WHO KNEW** George Cuttino knows we are dealing with a great scholar and a most remarkable individual.

George Peddy Cuttino was born in Newnan, Georgia, on (as he would insist on writing it) 9 March 1914. Newnan is today virtually a suburb of Atlanta, so in a strictly geographic sense he spent most of his life close to home. The Newnan in which George grew up, however, was a long way from today's Atlanta. It was still very close, really, to the South evoked in *Saddle Bag and Spinning Wheel*, George's 1981 edition of the Civil War letters of his maternal grandparents. From that world he kept important things like the Georgia Piedmont sound of his voice, his love for hound dogs and barbecue, and probably his predilection for classifying people as "types"—which typically means either as friends or as obstructionist dolts. The friends are very many and are always charming and brilliant; the others are graceless but happily are fewer.

George's life as a scholar started at Swarthmore College in Professor Mary Albertson's honors seminar on England to 1603. He had gone to Swarthmore in 1931 to study political science, with a view to entering the foreign service. But Professor Albertson changed all that by communicating to him her love for English history and her sense of teaching it as a high calling. George graduated from Swarthmore with highest honors, and after a year of graduate study at Iowa State University he went to Oxford in 1936 as a Rhodes Scholar.

At Oxford he studied under V. H. Galbraith, at the time University Reader in Diplomatic, and F. M. Powicke, Regius Professor of Modern History. Vivian Galbraith was a particularly strong influence. George began work with Galbraith that bore fruit in 1940 in George's first book, which established him as a rising authority in medieval English diplomatic history and administration. He became a Fellow of the Royal Historical Society that same year.

George Cuttino went on to publish nine books and more than a hundred articles and reviews. The consistency of this scholarly effort is suggested by the fact that he published at least one item every year save two, from 1939 until his retirement in 1984. In addition to the many items in his major field, he translated the *ballades* of François Villon, coauthored a multivolume textbook for undergraduates, and wrote two books of family history. George's most important single accomplishment, however, will no doubt remain the *Gascon Register A (Series of 1318–1319)*. Published in three volumes in 1975–76, this work won the 1979 Haskins Medal for outstanding scholarship in medieval history. In its report to the Medieval Academy of America, the Haskins award committee called the *Gascon Register* "a model of accuracy, precise information, and lucidity . . . a splendid achievement, the culmination of a lifetime of research."

Many other honors came to George Cuttino. Of particular note were his election as a Fellow of the Society of Antiquaries of London and of the Medieval Academy of America, and as a corresponding member of the Académie Européene D'Histoire. Twice a Guggenheim Fellow, he served as a consultant for the Guggenheim Foundation as well as for the National Endowment for the Humanities. A number of George's honors in fact required significant work on his part. As a former Rhodes Scholar, for instance, he served for years as a trustee of the Oriel College Development Trust and as a member of the editorial board of the *American Oxonian*, while also working on various Rhodes selection committees. Similarly, he served on the Council of the Medieval Academy and advisory board of *Speculum*, and repeatedly as a consultant to four different American colleges.

George's service to Emory University was truly remarkable for its breadth and diversity and for its intensity of commitment. In his forty-four years of teaching at Emory he so immersed himself, as a colleague puts it, in "virtually the totality of college and university life" that we now can scarcely imagine George or Emory without each other. (For the record, he once taught at three other institutions, Iowa State, Swarthmore, and Bryn Mawr.) In his earliest years at Emory he was moreover preoccupied with launching the Institute of Liberal Arts, a pioneer interdisciplinary enterprise at the graduate level. From the mid-1950s to his retirement from full-time teaching, however, George was involved at one time or another with practically every governance body of any significance at all. At one point (1970–73) he was chair of the History Department while serving simultaneously as president of the University Senate, vice chair of both the College Honors Committee and the Freshman Advisory Committee, and president of the Phi Beta Kappa chapter. At Emory these are all working positions, or they were when George held them.

For labors of this sort George received every service award Emory University bestows, including several devised just for him. He did not give himself so fully, of course, for awards or because he had to. He had for years what seemed an almost parental sense of responsibility for seeing that certain things were done right at the University, and the list lengthened as the years went on. Some important features of Emory life would indeed not exist had George not adopted them as personal avocations. The flourishing undergraduate honors program is one example. Another is Emory's "ceremonial tradition," which to tell the truth is almost entirely George Cuttino's invention. As chair of the old Ceremonies Committee and later as University Chief Marshal, George created a veritable treasure house for Emory: coats of arms (authorized by the College of Heralds), gonfalons, gowns and tunics, maces and batons, school ties, and even ballpoint pens. He was forever threatening to do things like sneak a "bedpan rampant" onto the coat of arms of the School of Nursing. George delighted in his dabbling into heraldry, and Emory is much richer for it.

> *As a teacher George was regarded with a respect bordering on awe, for his erudition, rigorous standards, and sometimes menacing mien. At the same time, it would be difficult to name anyone who gave more of himself to his students for so many years and in so many ways.*

As a faculty leader George's style was first of all to hold meetings as seldom as possible and to keep speeches brief. At the same time he was always concerned with many issues and had strong opinions on almost all of them. Usually quite traditional in his views on academic matters, he sometimes found it difficult—as one colleague delicately phrased it—to "conceal his scorn for dubious enterprises others considered stylishly innovative and progressive." As a consequence of all this George was prone to act by executive decision when in charge, and in meetings he sometimes spoke with a colorful bluntness that very much exceeded his true feelings. Yet he seldom really offended anybody. His sense of humor, his lack of any meanness at all, and his complete devotion to the interests of the University contributed to this. Basically he always had deep affection for his colleagues, including most of the wrongheaded ones, and people knew this and responded in kind.

Among Emory's students and alumni he had a unique reputation. As a teacher George was regarded with a respect bordering on awe, for his erudition, rigorous standards, and sometimes menacing mien. At the same time, it would be difficult to name anyone who gave more of himself to his students for so many years and in so many ways. George long served as faculty adviser to numerous undergraduate service organizations, honor societies, publications, and social groups. Purely as a teacher, he guided the dissertations of eleven Emory PhD recipients and offered a variety of courses, from paleography to freshman seminars, that were demanding and stimulating at every academic level. His senior colloquium on English common law may not invariably have been "the most rigorous nonscience course at Emory," as George was known to assert, but it was tough enough to scare off all but the very dedicated.

Nothing I can say, however, captures what George Peddy Cuttino meant to literally hundreds of Emory students whose lives he deeply touched. There are, of course, certain common themes in what these people say. The typical story begins in a freshman survey course, where an eighteen-year-old of conventional southern upbringing hears Professor Cuttino state, probably on the first day, that the three great mistakes in history have been the Apostle Paul, the Protestant Reformation, and the American Revolution. A "culture test" is distributed, demanding information on everything from thermodynamics to grand opera, Asian religions to Latin prose. Most of the class fails miserably. It is not like that every day, however. By the time of the first hour exam most of the students have decided that they can pass the course if they try, and that Professor Cuttino is still outrageous but also the most learned, entertaining, appealingly unusual teacher they have ever seen.

Annually for over thirty years George would pick out certain ones of the new Emory young people, or they would somehow gravitate to him, and these would become his cherished friends as well as his students. They were by no means all top students or southern or even enrolled in his class—at least initially. All would spend many Atlanta evenings, however, at 1270 University Drive, George's home on a snakey little street just off campus. Here they would be introduced to dry martinis and French cuisine (George was a superb cook), and after dinner there would be bourbon or brandy and conversation. Often at some point there would be music. Sometimes it was Elisabeth Schwarzkopf, sometimes a scratchy Stephen Collins Foster record, sometimes GPC himself singing "Amazing Grace" or, if overly encouraged, something like Bach's "St. John's Passion." Always there was talk, often far into the night. George did not exactly try to dominate, but he was the star. A typical evening would open with stories about characters from Newnan or Oxford days, then a few World War II army tales, and maybe next a bizarre death experienced by some unwary medieval monarch. Current events meant stories about new buffoonery among the faculty, or perhaps about the threat to civil liberties posed by some evangelist.

This was all obviously great fun. It was also highly educational; George really did teach people about food and music and sophisticated conversation and the value and pleasure of thinking for oneself. Most important, he taught about adult friendship. Generous to a fault with his time and concern, he never stopped adding new Emory students to his circle, nor did I ever know him to forget an old member of the group. It did not matter how many years had passed; all you had to do was call or show up on University Drive at martini time, and it was as though you had never been away. I never encountered a teacher anywhere who counted so many lifelong friends among his former students, or who so made himself in their eyes the very symbol of his university and profession and of many of their own happiest days.

CHAPTER 30

Floyd Watkins

REMEMBERING FLOYD
— WILLIAM B. DILLINGHAM *and* WILLIAM GRUBER —

Irreverent, irascible, but finally a classroom presence and a mentor beyond the classroom who was beloved by his students and deeply respected by his colleagues, Floyd Watkins requires, in memoriam, two exquisite essays by two of Emory's finest prose craftsmen, Candler Professor Emeritus Bill Dillingham and Professor Bill Gruber.

"An Eclectic and Extra-Socratic Scholar/Teacher," by William B. Dillingham

The history of a university includes a large and varied cast of characters. At Emory University one of the most memorable was Floyd C. Watkins, who resisted being anyone's disciple even from his earliest experiences in academe, so that he could retain, in the words of Herman Melville, "the open independence of [his] sea," who was a traditionalist not afraid of change, and who loved the university where he had once been a student, and where he taught for his entire career, but who never failed to point out to its officials where he thought it was straying.

Born in Ball Ground, Georgia, in 1920, he made his way to Emory through a rather circuitous route: public schools in Cherokee County, Georgia; undergraduate study at Georgia Southern College; a brief period of teaching in a public school in Pitts, Georgia; and service in World War II as an Army Air Corps cryptographer in the Aleutian Islands. He came to Emory in 1946 as a first-year graduate student keenly experiencing a sense of his own inadequacy but at the same time feeling pronouncedly self-confident. This odd combination of attitudes characterized him throughout his life. He always considered himself less well read and less enriched by the "finer things of life"—classical music and art—than many of his fellow students and later his colleagues, but that gnawing suspicion of his inferiority was accompanied by a conviction that he was blessed with an unusual ability to see what was important and with a rare talent for expressing those insights with apparently inexhaustible energy.

Watkins impressed his professors at Emory, especially Edwin T. Martin, the university's only tenured specialist in American literature. He completed his master's degree at Emory in 1947 and moved on to Vanderbilt University, where he was in residence working on a PhD degree in American literature until 1949. At that time he was hired at Emory as an instructor, juggling his heavy course load with completing his dissertation at Vanderbilt. By the time he was awarded the PhD degree in 1952, he was already well on his way to becoming a published scholar. He rapidly rose through the ranks at Emory from instructor to that of Charles Howard Candler Professor of American Literature. He retired in 1988 after a career of startling brilliance.

During that extended period, he won nearly every honor and distinction that Emory could give, including the one considered the most prestigious, the Thomas Jefferson Award, bestowed on those whose contribution to the University has been both unselfish and extensive. In time he was tapped for both Phi Beta Kappa and Omicron Delta Kappa as a faculty member. He was given the Emory Williams Award for Distinguished Teaching in 1972, and he was named Scholar-Teacher of the Year for 1984. Several months after his death in 2000, he was posthumously honored with the Emory University Award of Distinction. Outside his own university, his eminence in scholarly research and writing was recognized with a Guggenheim Fellowship and a grant from the National Endowment for the Humanities. His first book, *Thomas Wolfe's Characters* (1957), won for him the Thomas Wolfe Memorial Trophy.

To comprehend the extent of Floyd Watkins's contribution to the history of Emory University, one must first understand the intellectual milieu into which he was introduced during his early days in the English Department. In the 1940s, American literature had not yet fully emerged as distinctive from British literature. A long, lingering cloud of relative insignificance still hung over it, and American authors were often taught along with their more important British counterparts. Students could choose a survey course in American literature, but more specialized courses in the field were yet to be offered. Watkins was instrumental in bringing about at Emory the change that was also taking place in universities across the land. He initiated courses such as that in the American novel, and he championed with genuine conviction and persuasive argument the cause of giving American literature the position it deserved in a modern curriculum.

Perhaps even more important than his role in placing a new focus on and insisting upon a new respect for American literature at Emory was the way in which he taught classes in that field and the other courses he was assigned. Teaching tends to be a fashion, like styles in dress. We wear what is in style, what our models in attire wear, and teachers generally follow the style of instruction that they were exposed to in their own professors. When Watkins joined the faculty of the English Department at Emory, he knew many of the professors since he had studied under several of them. He admired them and marveled at the eloquence of a few of them. Yet he was destined to break away from the way most of them—and, indeed, most professors in the country—were teaching. Not only was the lecture method in vogue (with some exceptions), but also literary works were as a rule examined as reflections of the times in which they were written and placed in certain categories or "movements," such as romanticism, realism, local color, naturalism, and so forth. Students were responsible for memorizing the characteristics of such literary movements (as professors had duly delivered them from their lecture notes) and were expected to be able to explain on examinations how a given literary work reflected those traits. In other words, this was—as it had been for many years—the era of literary history in the English Department of Emory University, and it was taught, more frequently than not, by lecture.

> *The discussion proceeded with such swiftness as to bewilder some in the class and alarm others, but it proceeded and on his terms, not theirs, tightly controlled and skillfully guided.*

Watkins himself did lecture, but only on occasion. There always came a point in his courses when he determined that he must deliver certain background information, when he must define certain terms, when he needed to pull together the points that had previously been stressed in class discussion. His students welcomed such an occasional lecture because it gave them a reprieve from being "interrogated" (as one student put it), but they also looked forward to Watkins's rare lectures because without exception they were characterized by the eloquence of practicality: no fat, no pretentiousness, no droning monotonal challenge to wakefulness. Whatever he said was something they could use, something they knew to be important—they could readily determine that. They listened. It all made sense. When he delivered scholarly papers at such meetings as those of the national Modern Language Association and the regional South Atlantic Modern Language Association, where his reputation and prestige grew steadily, he exhibited the same grace born of a keen sense of the practical. Salted here and there with humor that surprised and supplied the flavor of his southern roots, his talks were marked by a masterful sense of timing and by conclusions that were never trivial but frequently of high interest to those who endured the crowded rooms in order to hear him. He was never dull, and that fact was widely appreciated at such gatherings.

In the classroom, his general method of teaching was what might be called extra-Socratic. Armed with a series of points to be covered and conclusions to be reached, he asked relevant questions, sometimes allowing volunteers to answer, frequently calling on students by name. The discussion proceeded with such swiftness as to bewilder some in the class and alarm others, but it proceeded and on his terms, not theirs, tightly controlled and skillfully guided. He never permitted any student to elaborate excessively but would mercilessly cut short a response in order to move on to another person. In almost every class, then and now, appear certain students, sometimes genuinely bright and sometimes bright only in their own minds, who repeatedly volunteer to answer professors' questions and to deliver their responses with wandering (and sometimes wondrous) verbosity. Watkins allowed no such virtuoso performances. Appearing rude was not one of his fears. His were fast-paced and highly organized classes. He owed it to his students, he felt, to conduct a class that way.

Students previously exposed to the lecture method and to the consideration of works of literature as examples of certain movements in literary history were likely to be startled to find that most of the time Watkins neither lectured nor paid much attention to literary "isms."

He insisted that his students examine the poem or short story or novel not for what it reflected of the times or even the author's life but primarily for what it was in itself. The method was called "New Criticism," the consideration of literature for its own sake with careful attention to the craft of artistic creation. At Emory, Watkins was in the forefront of this way of reading literature, a method that was being introduced into the writing and teaching of English department professors (especially young ones) all over the country.

Floyd Watkins was not, however, a typical New Critic. When asked with what theory or movement he associated himself, he would answer "none." When asked what kind of literary critic he considered himself, he would say "eclectic." In his teaching he insisted on concentrating closely on the literary work itself rather than on its context, not merely because such a focus had become the vogue. He would probably have been a kind of new critic had there never been something called the "New Criticism," simply because of his cast of mind. He taught as he did, not because of excitement over a new philosophy of education, but because of adherence to an old philosophy of life: concentrate on what is most important. It was a matter of practicality. This way paid off more, infinitely more. It trained the mind; it honed the perception. If a great work of literature was anything, it was, in his estimation, a thing of wonder, full of truth and beauty. He wished to find that beauty and truth and to lead his students in their discovery of the same qualities. For him, that was what the study of literature was all about. The reward was immense. In this pursuit he was not following a trend but his own personal proclivities.

He was, then, an original. When he walked into the classroom, looked at his audience, and started speaking, Emory students knew immediately that he was something different, a professor out of the ordinary, intense, quick of mind and manner, impatient, and devoid—totally devoid—of affectation. Those who had been led to believe that anyone with a small-town southern accent was likely to be somewhat backward and therefore amusing to sophisticates like themselves were soon shocked into recognition that they were going to have to swim for their intellectual lives in this maelstrom of constant probing and questioning that characterized the courses of Professor Floyd C. Watkins. Those who were not able to keep afloat amid the fast moving and imperiling current soon changed to less turbulent waters or discovered through this catalyst of self-discovery that they were not the Olympic swimmers they had imagined themselves to be and—jarred but made better for their new awareness of themselves—settled for a grade lower than those to which they were accustomed.

Others, however, found themselves buoyed up by this professor's attitude toward what he was teaching, that is, the seriousness with which he held the literary work under discussion. That work, whether it was a poem by Robert Frost or a novel by Robert Penn Warren, was evidently something of importance, extreme importance, something worthy of their attention for its intrinsic value, not just for some vague historic or cultural significance. This man, to whom the pose was not only foreign but also abhorrent, caught them up in his enthusiasm for what one of his great heroes, William Faulkner, called the "old verities" and led them to see how those truths could be conveyed through the medium not of dull didacticism but of exciting art. Those countless students never forgot Floyd Watkins. He had turned up in their young lives at a crucial time, forcing them into deep and turbulent waters as if dead-bent upon drowning them, but then not only teaching them to swim better after carrying them further out than they had ever been before but generously furnishing them with a life preserver whenever they needed it. The result was that many of these young swimmers later became lifeguards themselves, never forgetting their experiences with this son of Ball Ground in the North Georgia hill country.

His interest in his students became legendary. He was as inventive and innovative in dealing with them outside the classroom as he was in teaching them in the classroom. During his entire career he refused to keep "office hours." That is, he would not set aside a few hours during selected days of the week when he would be available in his office to students who wished to confer with him. Instead, he was in his office with the door open every day of the week when he was not in class and even on Saturday morning. Students dropped in wherever they wished, and he treated each with kindness tempered with a demand for honesty, especially self-honesty.

Certain perennial types of undergraduates—those wanting privately to impress the professor with their chatty brilliance, those wishing to complain about imagined unfairness in grading, those who simply had nothing else to do and wanted to kill a little time—found him probing their souls to a degree they found unconducive to a lengthy visit and soon departed. Others, those who needed special help or more information dealing with the material under examination in the class, those who were troubled about something entirely unrelated to the subject being studied, those who needed advice professionally or personally—these students were handled with the wisdom, generosity, and caring of a cherished relative whose attitude was never patronizing (though not always uncritical) and whose interest was deep and genuine.

> *It is simply inestimable how much Watkins's unselfish attention to his students' writing helped them, how much it contributed to the future of many of them who went on to become accomplished writers.*

It was not unusual for students who were not even enrolled in his classes to come by to see him, often troubled and in need of caring straight talk. He provided them with that. He listened intently, really listened, to their problems; he encouraged them when they needed encouragement; he told them when he felt that they had potential and thus opened up new horizons for them; but he also pointed out to them where they were wrong and suggested ways in which they needed to alter their thinking. He had a strong sense of duty to them and to his profession. He was, though this truth was seldom obvious, an idealist.

He had little patience, however, with vague and abstract idealism. Fuzzy thinking and writing he found abhorrent. Clarity and concreteness were always uppermost in his philosophy of composition. He taught these virtues in his own courses in English composition—"freshman English," as it was called—with insistent enthusiasm. He wanted his students in these beginning writing classes to observe carefully what was going on around them and to write about those things, describing them pointedly but imaginatively. Above all, he wanted them to write. There was no substitute for the actual act of writing. In whatever course he conducted, writing was an essential ingredient. No student will ever forget what his or her essay looked like when Floyd Watkins returned it, which he always did with amazing, astounding promptness (he dropped everything else to get papers and examinations marked and returned). Nothing escaped his eye; nothing was spared his pen. His extensive corrections and comments affected the student like the sword suspended above his head affected Damocles. Suddenly all was not well. Such markings were not made to intimidate or manifest authority but to establish a point of embarkation, to show students in plain and practical terms, truthfully and conscientiously, what their weaknesses were and how they could become better writers. It is simply inestimable how much Watkins's unselfish attention to his students' writing helped them, how much it contributed to the future of many of them who went on to become accomplished writers. When students' writing improved, he not only congratulated them but he rewarded them tangibly as later papers revealed their progress.

Instructors in writing courses at Emory in the late 1950s used the same textbook, a handbook of freshman composition that was widely adopted in America. Watkins found himself less and less satisfied with it as time went on, and when the publisher, Houghton Mifflin Company, happened to ask him as a user of the book to give his opinion of it (a new edition was being planned), he did so extensively and with the same brutal honesty that was so much a part of his personality. What he charged, essentially, was that the book under review was not truly practical, that is, it was not as much real help to the student as it could be. It was too wordy and in places too vague. It seemed to have been written for the instructor rather than for the student. Such a book, Watkins concluded, should tell the young writer what to do in precepts rather than explain what is generally done. The editor of the college division was so impressed with arguments that Watkins offered and with the extensive detail he furnished to support those points that he asked this brash critic if he would himself write a handbook for Houghton Mifflin oriented along the lines he had outlined in his report.

He did so with memorable results. After contemplating the offer he went to his old professor and current colleague, Edwin T. Martin, to ask if he would be willing to become the coauthor. Martin accepted, and the collaboration began. It should come as no surprise that this book, destined to be one of the all-time best sellers in the freshman English market of college texts (in its eleventh edition as this is being written), would be titled *Practical English Handbook*. It remains a tribute to Watkins's genius for innovation and a monument to his belief that practicality engenders learning. Of all the precepts (or as students commonly call them, "rules") for writing in the *Practical English Handbook*, Watkins's favorite was one that he did not himself write but one contributed by his collaborator, Ed Martin, namely, "Stick to the Point" (precept 39g).

With the inauguration of a doctoral program in the Department of English in the 1950s, Watkins soon became the principal director of dissertations in American literature. As the years passed, he attracted more and more doctoral students, drawn to him by his own increasing prestige in the field and by his reputation at Emory for devoting close individual attention to his graduate students and for constantly encouraging them (some would say pushing them) to complete their degrees. He did not believe in a long and leisurely pursuit of a graduate degree. He considered such indulgence damaging in both a personal and professional sense. The pressure that he applied to his graduate students to finish their work they often decried at the time but deeply appreciated later.

What his graduate students were most grateful for, however, was the sense that Watkins conveyed of being on their side. As long they proved to him that they were worthy of his advocacy (which was not easy), they could count on him to provide it. Many of them who found themselves cornered by puzzling questions from a faculty member during doctoral oral examinations—questions Watkins considered vague or somewhat unreasonable—expressed quiet sighs of relief and gratitude when their director came to their defense, either giving them a hint about how to answer the question or boldly pointing out to the faculty member who asked the question that it was a bit outside of this particular student's area of study and then moving on. He was something of a champion to this host of candidates for advanced degrees, many of whom later distinguished themselves in colleges and universities across America. He was, as they deeply appreciated, a formidable ally.

To a great extent, universities are judged by the quality and quantity of research and writing of their faculty members. As Emory developed from a respected regional institution to a nationally recognized and admired university, Floyd Watkins was in the forefront of its scholarly productivity. His numerous articles and books, consistently excellent in quality and astounding in number, not only shot him to the very front rank of specialists in American literature (especially southern literature) but also beamed a laser spotlight on his university. Emory's transition to eminence was the period of Watkins's tenure, and his contribution to that change through his scholarly publications was immeasurable.

His focus in several of those publications was on the analysis of poems, novels, and short stories as one would expect from his mode of teaching, that is, explication of the text. In many of his writings, however, he revealed a broader scholarly concern that was somewhat at variance with the tenets of New Criticism: an interest in the sources of artistic creation. He uncovered with enlightening results the real people upon which such authors as Thomas Wolfe,

William Faulkner, and Robert Penn Warren based their fictional characters. He was intrigued with the way in which the mind and imagination of the great writer converts reality into art. He pursued this interest with vigor, seeking out for the Woodruff Library of Emory University the notes and manuscripts by leading southern authors that would help biographers and scholars understand how the sea change from experience to art comes about. This impressive and invaluable archival material now carries the designation of the Floyd C. Watkins American Literary Manuscript Collection.

More often than not, as Watkins poignantly recognized, the attempt to create art from real life is not successful. What passes for art but is not was sometimes the object of his ireful attention. When he grew weary of the constant praise, even reverence he suspected, for Margaret Mitchell's *Gone with the Wind*, a novel he considered lacking in the true craft of fiction and shallow in reflecting the complexity of life, he published an article titled "*Gone with the Wind* as Vulgar Literature," which expressed his views and which consequently brought down on him a flood of protest from certain segments of the public. He handled it all with good humor but gave not an inch. Invited to present the prestigious Lamar Lectures at Mercer University in the fall of 1969, he took aim at modern southern novelists who were so enraptured by the desire to bring about social change that they wrote what was essentially propaganda. Such was not, he claimed, the stuff of art. In 1970 those lectures were published as *The Death of Art*, a title that clearly revealed his dissatisfaction with these particular contemporary southern novelists who had, he believed, sold out art to certain "causes," resulting in their fiction becoming melodramatic, preachy, and simplistic. In such work, he insisted with blistering evidence, the complexity of human relationships and "the truth of the human heart" (one of his favorite phrases, derived from Nathaniel Hawthorne) were being reduced to predictable situations and to sermons on the necessity for social change. The problem, he concluded, was at least in part the result of the novelists' alienation from their southern heritage, their roots.

Nothing was more important to this man of blunt eloquence than roots. One could not be in his company for long without realizing that fact. One of the first questions he asked students was where they came from, what their roots were, and how they felt about their heritage. He tried to show them how deeply those aspects of blood and experience affect character and how important they are in forming a healthy sense of identity, which he saw as widely and sadly lacking in the modern world. He revealed his own humble heritage and his deep respect for it in a book about the people and mores of the North Georgia hill country at an earlier time, *Yesterday in the Hills*, which he composed with the memory help of his father. The book, like its author, appeals to those who cherish the best of tradition, who recognize the real thing when they see it, who can enjoy that variety of earthiness that might well offend those who pride themselves on having what they consider refined and sensitive taste, and who never underestimate the importance of place and time in one's upbringing. It is to the credit of Emory University that it nurtured, appreciated, and rewarded in a variety of ways this man, Floyd C. Watkins, who possessed an unusual combination of talents and characteristics and who in turn added richly to the development of the institution.

"His Sprawling, Irreverent Spirit," by William Gruber | His nickname for me was "Old Windbreaker," and each morning when I turned the key in my door I heard the slow, raspy drawl: "Hello, Old Windbreaker!" Floyd Watkins had the office across the hall from mine on the third floor of what is now North Callaway, and no matter how early I arrived at the office after I'd dropped off my two daughters at school, Floyd was there before me, typewriter clattering. But his door was always open, and so for all the years I was an assistant professor my workday began by hearing the most powerful member of the Department of English insult me—a gesture that I soon came to understand was actually his way of inviting me to pop in to say hello.

Floyd knew his own mind and was not afraid to speak it. He was fiercely opposed to what he sensed was the backsliding of literary scholars away from their true role as servants of art and artists. He thought that the profession had been corrupted by identity politics, and once, when we were talking about what it would take to get tenure, he told me only half in jest that he hoped to see the day when publishing an article in *PMLA* (the journal of the Modern Language Association) counted against a candidate. Another time, on the occasion of his first conversation with the person hired to be the department's new chair, Floyd made it a point to tell him he had voted against him. The statement was so coarse, so gauche—and Floyd so characteristically unconcerned with anything but telling the truth—that it might have been spoken by Hamlet: not the stagey, indecisive Hamlet, but the real Hamlet, courageous and purposeful even in spite of his own best interests, as Lytton Strachey once wrote, "who called his father's ghost old truepenny, who forged his uncle's signature, who fought Laertes, and ranted in a grave, and lugged the guts into the neighbor room."

> *There was a direct relationship between his fondness for a person and the spiciness of his wit. When I first introduced my wife to Floyd, he turned to me, feigning bewilderment: "But Bill," he said, "this isn't the woman who was with you when you came down for your interview."*

At the same time Floyd was the most generous and considerate of men; he took great pleasure in talking with his neighbors in Ball Ground as well as with colleagues in the English Department (he told me more than once that he preferred the former). Each year he took his students in Southern Literature on tours of North Georgia so they could experience firsthand some of the landscapes that gave rise to writers and their work. Twice I was invited to go on these excursions. We went to Tallulah Falls near the southern end of the Appalachian Trail, we toured the marble quarries Floyd had known growing up near the town of Ball Ground, and we drove blue highways through James Dickey country. Driving through hills whose features were hidden beneath drifts of kudzu, foliage so deep and lush you could almost sense the plants growing, Floyd told me stories about his ancestors ("The Watkinses don't have easy deaths," he said, with almost no conversational run-up) and quoted from Dickey's poem about the invasive vines: "Up telephone poles, / Which rear, half out of leafage / As though they would shriek, / Like things smothered by their own / Green, mindless, unkillable ghosts."

Those who tried to catch Floyd and pin him down always failed. His conversation was full of humor and vitality, untouched by any trace of snobbery or affectation. He loved to tease people he liked; there was a direct relationship between his fondness for a person and the spiciness of his wit. When I first introduced my wife to Floyd, he turned to me, feigning bewilderment: "But Bill," he said, "this isn't the woman who was with you when you came down for your interview." Another time, a female colleague whose office was next door to Floyd's stopped by with a male companion. Floyd's door was open, and so she knocked politely and stepped into the doorway with her friend, saying, "Floyd, you remember X, don't you?" Floyd swiveled slowly in his chair and looked up: "I don't know," he said, "I see so many men in your office." Floyd and Lore Metzger, another member of the department faculty, were longtime antagonists, and on the day that Emory announced her election to a Candler Professorship I happened to run into Floyd in the library. I knew that he had just learned the news about Lore, and I thought I'd see if I could needle him: "Floyd," I said, "what did you think when you heard about Lore's promotion?" "I bubbled with glee," was his marvelously cryptic response.

Behavior like this was not always well received by people who knew Floyd only superficially. At about the time when Emory had begun to think it needed a national identity, I sometimes heard people speak of Floyd as the last Southern Agrarian. With its unsubtle hints of regressive politics if not actual bigotry, the comparison was not meant to be flattering. As he grew near the end of his career there was in Floyd's conversation a persistent gloominess. He once told me about a minor surgical procedure. Thinking I could cheer him up, I responded with a thoughtless platitude to the effect that "it could have been worse." But Floyd always chose his words carefully, and his reply still stands in my mind as the single best retrospective on the phenomenon of tragedy that I have ever heard: "Most things could." His conversation in those years was as lively, simple, and witty as ever. Yet on campus he seemed, increasingly, an anachronism; it was as if he had become a stranger to his own household. Floyd didn't change or swerve; only the surroundings did. Overnight there was a shift in America's idea of its workplaces: eccentricities had become abrasive, conversations with colleagues and staff had become sanitized, humor like Floyd's was officially déclassé.

It's hard for me to believe that I have now spent almost as many years at Emory as had Floyd Watkins when I first came to Atlanta, but such is the chronology. Floyd began his career teaching at Emory in 1949, and I joined the faculty of the Department of English in the fall of 1980. I came to campus for a job interview in May of that year, and after I spent the day meeting with department faculty and representatives of the administration, I was taken out to dinner. In those days spouses were considered to be an essential part of any social event—it was my first real glimpse into southern hospitality—and so the dinner party that evening consisted of the department chair, Bill Dillingham; his wife, Elizabeth; Floyd and Anna Watkins, and me. We met at what was then one of the few good places to eat in downtown Decatur, a building that had been converted into a restaurant from an old department store. The dinner was not actually an interview, but it was clear that I was still being tested, and at about the time the entrées arrived the women dropped out of the conversation as if on cue. There was nothing awkward or sexist about this; Anna Watkins and Elizabeth Dillingham were good friends, and they clearly preferred to ignore the men in preference to their own subjects of interest.

The three of us moved through light academic conversation to more personal topics. By the time the waiter brought the pecan pie, Floyd had begun to tell jokes. The evening might well have ended there; later that night, back in my hotel room, replaying in my mind the events of the day, I remember thinking that the sharing of jokes meant that whatever test I had been given, I had apparently passed. But after the pie there was one more bourbon and some more small talk about departmental business, and then Floyd, who had known Bill ever since he was a student in his classes in the 1950s, asked Bill how he wrote. That was in an era when many faculty still gave their handwritten letters and manuscripts to secretaries for typing. Floyd always composed everything on a Royal manual typewriter, and he was curious to know whether his department chair wrote in longhand or on a machine. Bill said he didn't like to use a typewriter; he did all of his writing with a pen, on a tablet. "Then what do you do," Floyd said in that frustrating, retarded drawl, "when the words come too fast for you to keep up?"

It was the first of what would be countless times when I would be shocked at the disjunction between the slowness of Floyd's speech and the quickness of his mind. In a heartbeat he had moved from asking an apparently trivial question about pens and typewriters to a subject of the most profound mystery. The writer caught up in the moment of inspiration is literature's holiest image of itself. Floyd described how Thomas Wolfe scrawled his novels on the top of his refrigerator. Bill Dillingham told about Hemingway traveling the world in search of environments where he felt the words flowed best. We talked about Keats, who once wondered in what bodily position Shakespeare had composed Hamlet's most famous soliloquy, and about Frost's composition of "Stopping by Woods on a Snowy Evening," the words of which came to him in a rush early one summer morning after he had stayed up all the previous night trying to write something else.

Since that day I have thought many times about the sequence of events that brought me to a job teaching literature at Emory. The truth is that in early March of 1980 I responded like one of Pavlov's dogs to an advertisement for a drama specialist in the Department of English at Emory University in Atlanta, a school at that time I had never heard of, only because during the previous week I had been refused the job I thought I wanted at Illinois State. I cannot put my finger on the exact moment when I began to see that what looked at first like misfortune turned out to be Fortune's largesse, much less when I understood that the episode of joke telling in the restaurant had been a necessary component of the architecture of that day's events, but from a distance of almost thirty years that dinner party in Atlanta now seems to me to have been one of the most extraordinary experiences of my life. A conversation that had begun with Floyd teasing me about an old church pew in the lobby of the restaurant ("Dr. Gruber," he had said, "do you think this is a Baptist pew or a Methodist pew?") came finally to rest with three people who loved literature paying rapt homage to Plato's account of the mind in the moment of its greatest triumph, suddenly possessed "like a light kindled by a leaping spark [that] comes to be in the soul and at once becomes self-nourishing."

In May 1988, the Department of English held a retirement celebration for Floyd Watkins. After the food, the wine, and the speeches, and after we had presented him with a geode almost the size of a basketball—Floyd was a knowledgeable collector of rocks and gemstones—we asked him to say a few words of reflection on his retirement. Characteristically blunt and characteristically making his point by telling a story, he told this joke:

One day a long time ago, when people's manners were more refined than they are now, a country schoolteacher named Miss Johnson climbed atop a chair in her classroom to reach some books on a high shelf. All of a sudden she lost her balance and fell ungracefully to the floor in a cascade of stockings, undergarments, and youthful laughter. Deeply embarrassed, she quickly rose to her feet and attempted to regain her dignity and authority with her students.

Jimmy, she said, what did you see?

I saw your stockings, Miz Johnson, Jimmy replied.

Very well, Jimmy, you go home for a day.

She then turned to the next child: And what did you see, Bobby Joe?

I saw your knees, Miz Johnson.

Then you must go home for a week.

Just as she was about to question the next person, Miss Johnson noticed that one of her students, a shy little boy named Billy, had left his desk and gone to the wardrobe at the back of the classroom, where he was picking out his coat, hat, and lunchbox.

Just what do you think you're doing, Billy? she asked.

Oh, Miz Johnson, he replied, I heard the way you were punishing everybody for what they were looking at, and I know that after what I saw, my school days now are over.

Surely the story was parabolic. The story of the little boy who was both jubilant and fearful at the prospect of the end of his school days must have been Floyd's way of expressing his own mind, weighed down at the time with thoughts of retirement and mortality and yet answering them with the one thing short of eternal salvation that can ease the sting of death—a joke. Take away the sexism and the stereotyping, make the language more politically sensitive, and you destroy both story and storyteller. Perhaps it is nostalgic of me to think that something is missing from a university with no room for the complex, contradictory nature of a person like Floyd Watkins. Still I am committed to the belief that Floyd's presence once was a natural manifestation of the genius of this institution, and I sometimes worry that we may have grown too priggish to be comfortable with the likes of his sprawling, irreverent spirit. The great drag on our humanity, as novelist and essayist Marilynne Robinson has said, might not be our jokes but our humorlessness.

CHAPTER 31

A FORTUNATE LIFE
William B. Dillingham
— GREG JOHNSON —

The life and career of William B. Dillingham have constituted a uniquely American blend of high intelligence, good fortune, natural talent, and hard work. The Emory University English Department had the luck to find Dillingham early in his career, and the University had the good sense to keep him for close to forty years, awarding him its highest accolades for teaching and scholarship: in 1984 he received the University Scholar/Teacher Award and was appointed as the Charles Howard Candler Professor of American Literature. A charismatic and gifted teacher, Dillingham likewise pursued his scholarly endeavors with remarkable energy and success. During his long and still-flourishing career, he published numerous books, including seminal works on Herman Melville and Rudyard Kipling. Equally important, he developed a reputation as an affable and admired colleague among his academic peers and as a valuable friend and mentor to his students.

A**N ATLANTA NATIVE,** the young Dillingham did not find his career path until stints in the army and in an insurance firm made it clear that he was suited neither for lifelong military service nor for the drudgery of a nine-to-five position that would oblige him to care deeply about the insurance company's "profit and loss ratio." His upbringing had not necessarily dictated an academic career, however. Born in 1930, the youngest of seven children, he was the son of loving parents who considered him "a blessing"; his mother was a homemaker, and his father worked as a superintendent of a nonenforcement branch of the Atlanta police department. The times were not easy—his childhood coincided with the Great Depression—but his parents remained supportive even though, as he now admits, his early school career was less than stellar. His elementary school years were "undistinguished," he says, and he went on to attend Hoke Smith Junior High and Atlanta's best high school at the time, Boys High. "It was a demanding school attended mostly by students bound for college," Dillingham remembers, "whereas I had no such intention."[1] He had unsympathetic teachers who rewarded his efforts with a D in English and Fs in chemistry, geometry, and ROTC (the last of which, he notes, was not easy to fail). These academic vicissitudes mattered little, however, once he began dating, near the end of his high school career, a girl named Marion Elizabeth Joiner. Dillingham sums up this early, dramatic rise in his fortunes: "Confusion ceased, grades improved, clarity dawned, and the world sang. Later I married her, and I am still married to her."

During Dillingham's senior year, Boys High was abolished and he returned to Hoke Smith, where he and Elizabeth graduated together in January 1948. "That was my eighteenth year," he says, "the best year of my life by a long shot. Everything after that has been somewhat anticlimactic and of less magic intensity." While this may be true of his personal life, his academic career continued to be anything but "anticlimactic." Rather, it has been a study in consistent, brilliant achievement in teaching and scholarship, both of which were surely bolstered by the fact that the world continued to "sing," thanks to his long and happy marriage.

First, however, there was the matter of that insurance company, the Hartford. Dillingham's mother, who was "dear and bold," simply called up the personnel manager one day and insisted that he hire her son, which the manager promptly did. Bill Dillingham was all of seventeen. Once again his efforts were not particularly memorable: he was a "poor worker," he says, though the women in the office treated him with maternal solicitude in view of his extreme youth. Nonetheless he felt alienated, owing to his inability to care whether the company made money or not. Soon enough another major life change saved him from considerations of profit and loss: his country came calling in the form of the Selective Service System. At age twenty he was drafted in order to serve in what was then called the Korean Conflict. He never went to Korea, instead becoming a tank crewman stationed in Louisiana, but after some time at his assignment, he says, "I discovered why I had failed ROTC at Boys High. My affinity for forced discipline and subservience to lesser sorts (as I then perceived the situation) was but thin at best and was wearing thinner." Once again his determined mother took action and precipitated another turn of good fortune in Dillingham's life: she simply phoned the Georgia governor and insisted that he be transferred to Fort McPherson, near Atlanta, and he was. He spent the rest of his army service in a safe office job near his parents and home.

During this period, on July 3, 1952, Dillingham married the woman "who made the world sing," and he began taking evening courses at the Atlanta division of the University of Georgia (now Georgia State University). He recalls it as a "grubby place," but one of the classes he took there had a strong effect: it was a literature course, and in retrospect it seems remarkable that this experience represented another fortunate turning point, for the professor "was not a sparkling teacher," and Dillingham "had never been a literature-loving person" up until then. Moreover, he learned that the academic world was not necessarily the easeful ivory tower that some people imagine it to be. One evening he visited his professor during office hours: "He was in a closetlike office sitting at his small desk eating a sandwich, which he had taken from a brown bag. I asked him what it was like to be a college teacher. He said, 'What is it like?' Then he swept one arm around his small office and back to his desk and to the sandwich, and he said, 'This is what it is like.'" But Dillingham was not discouraged, for dealing with literature seemed infinitely more appealing than the insurance company's daily grind of profit and loss.

After being discharged from the army in December 1952, Dillingham did return to his old job at Hartford, but soon enough he made a life-changing decision: he applied to Emory University for admission as a transfer student. He and Elizabeth were now expecting their first child and had little money, so the decision to return full-time to school was "a risky business," Dillingham recalls. But good fortune came calling once again: Emory not only admitted him, with full credit for the courses he had already taken, but also awarded him a scholarship that enabled him to complete his undergraduate degree, with a major in English, in 1955. Soon afterward he entered the graduate program in English and won a nonteaching assistantship. At first he decided to pursue a master of arts in teaching degree and become a high school teacher, but his graduate adviser, he says, had other ideas. That adviser, Floyd C. Watkins, who was to become a lifelong friend and colleague, was "then a rather young and obviously brilliant, different kind of assistant professor. At first I believed him to be some sort of good-natured but highly eccentric crank." Eccentric or not, the young Watkins took the even younger Dillingham in hand, guiding him toward completing a master's thesis on Nathaniel Hawthorne. Then came yet more strokes of good fortune, both personally and professionally: Dillingham's wife was again pregnant, with the couple's second daughter, and the English Department chair took him aside one day and said simply, "Would you like to teach at Emory?" When the stunned Dillingham managed an affirmative, the chairman said he would take him over to see the dean. "That's how I was hired at Emory," Dillingham remembers. "No competition. No interviews at the Modern Language Association convention. No campus visits. No papers to deliver. I was hired on the spot. It was astonishing. It was miraculous." Dillingham is surely modest in this recollection, however, for the English Department faculty must have been acutely aware that they had an extraordinarily gifted young man in their midst, one with a great career ahead.

> *As time passed, he no longer felt "fraudulent" as a teacher and, as anyone who has known him in the classroom can attest, became a true master.*

For two years, 1956–58, Dillingham taught at Emory with his master's degree, and after a summer of graduate work at Vanderbilt University, he enrolled in the PhD program in English at the University of Pennsylvania, where he completed his course work in three semesters. He returned to Emory in the fall of 1959, teaching a heavy load of three courses per quarter, while somehow finding time to work on his dissertation on the novelist Frank Norris.

He was making significant headway as a teacher. Early in his professorial career he had imitated the effective Socratic method of his mentor Floyd Watkins, but now he developed his own more informal, looser style of teaching that emphasized classroom discussion. As time passed, he no longer felt "fraudulent" as a teacher and, as anyone who has known him in the classroom can attest, became a true master. With his doctorate conferred in 1961, he began to distinguish himself in the scholarly arena as well, publishing articles in well-known journals, editing a volume on the humor of the Old Southwest in 1964, and in 1969 producing an expanded version of his dissertation as a book, *Frank Norris: Instinct and Art*. Clearly, he was on his way.

Through the 1960s and 1970s Dillingham secured his position in the English Department as a colleague of uncommon integrity, clarity of mind, and congeniality. Hired as an instructor, Dillingham was swiftly promoted through the ranks and became a full professor in 1968. During this same period he was awarded a Fulbright Fellowship, and taught at the University of Oslo, in Norway, during the academic year 1964–65.

Perhaps most important for his scholarly career, Dillingham had found his great subject. He had always been drawn, he once said, to literary artists who struggled with profound questions of universal significance, especially "the timeless question of the shaping of truth—chaotic as one sees it at first—into order and art." One of the preeminent authors who confronted these questions, he thought, was Herman Melville, and Dillingham began publishing articles on Melville's work as early as 1965. He then calmly embarked on what was to become a decades-long project: a systematic, orderly, multivolume study of the great nineteenth-century writer's entire career. The first volume to appear was *An Artist in the Rigging: The Early Work of Herman Melville* in 1972. This was followed by *Melville's Short Fiction: 1853–1856* in 1977 (this book was nominated for the 1978 Christian Gauss Award) and *Melville's Later Novels* (again nominated for the Christian Gauss Award) in 1986. His fourth and presumably final book on Melville, *Melville and His Circle: The Last Years*, arrived in 1996.

To read through Dillingham's books on Melville is an awe-inspiring experience, so broad is the scope, so diligent the research, and so precise and graceful the prose. Anyone who happens to be a teacher has an added boon: when teaching a particular story or novel by Melville, one has only to look up the relevant chapter in Dillingham to find a synthesis of all previous scholarship and an exhaustive, original interpretation of the work.

Dillingham's prolific writing on Melville was rewarded with a National Endowment for the Humanities Fellowship in 1978–79 and by a Guggenheim Fellowship in 1982–83. He also earned accolades from his fellow scholars in nineteenth-century American literature and from his Emory colleagues. One of these, the playwright and Renaissance scholar Frank Manley, Emory's Charles Howard Candler Professor of Renaissance Literature, Emeritus, observed in 1983 that Dillingham was becoming "the major interpreter of Melville for our generation,"[2] an opinion borne out by the reprinting of much of Dillingham's work in major Melville editions and anthologies, such as *Herman Melville*, edited by Harold Bloom, and *Herman Melville: Critical Reassessments*, edited by A. Robert Lee. Amazingly, during the years Dillingham spent on these complex, seminal works on Melville, he also found time to publish articles on Frank Norris and Stephen Crane; to write essay-reviews in such distinguished journals as *Modern Fiction Studies* and the *Sewanee Review*; and to coauthor, with Floyd Watkins, the popular *Practical English Handbook*, which has sold nearly 2 million copies worldwide.

Anyone so prodigiously active as a scholar might be excused for limiting his teaching and engagement with students, but through the decades Dillingham remained both a devoted teacher and a popular one. Like all good professors he developed a personal theory about excellent teaching. A good teacher, he once said, "is one who is first of all committed not to the art of teaching but to the material that he or she is teaching. Second, a good teacher has a keen sensitivity to the presence of the student and is aware of the nature of the learning process, so that the material is not made boring, uninteresting. A person who has no commitment to the material but is a good actor will be a flashy teacher but not really a good teacher. A person who has a commitment to the material but no sensitivity to the students' presence and interests will become a scholarly teacher but a boring one." The late Floyd Watkins once wrote of Dillingham's teaching excellence, "He has a good many students who think his perception and depth are unequaled as a teacher."

One such student was the author of this essay. I had the privilege of taking two courses with Dillingham—a graduate survey of nineteenth-century American literature and a seminar on Melville's short stories—in the late 1970s, and of working with him on a dissertation focused on Emily Dickinson's poetry. At the time I was teaching my own initial courses as a graduate teaching fellow, and like most apprentices I looked to my own professors as exemplars of the teaching art. In the classroom, Dillingham was always cordial and informal, putting sometimes-tense graduate students at ease, but at the same time he did not suffer fools gladly. I well remember the first meeting of the Melville course, when a loquacious male student tried to commandeer the class discussion by veering off topic to make vague but grandiose pronouncements about "these nineteenth-century writers." Dillingham politely but decisively cut him off, observing that we were there to discuss the writing of Herman Melville. Miffed, the student tried to pollute the atmosphere by making further irrelevant statements, but Dillingham again stopped him. I noticed, with much relief and gratitude, that this potentially troublesome student dropped the course, leaving the rest of us at peace to consider what the class was really about.

As a reader of my seminar papers and as a dissertation director, Dillingham showed a similar combination of congeniality and tough-mindedness. He could administer both gratifying praise and crisply worded critiques with the same precision, clarity, and grace. And his helpfulness far exceeded the call of duty. After my dissertation was complete he guided me in shepherding an expanded manuscript to publication, and likewise advised me as I sought teaching positions. Through the years, whenever I visited Emory's English Department or the stacks of Woodruff Library, where he worked tirelessly in his study, he was always a welcoming presence and an advocate, even hiring me as a visiting professor of English in 1985. Now, more than thirty years after I first enrolled in one of his classes, I am proud and grateful to have been his student and still to be his friend. No doubt my story is multiplied many times over, in the lives of countless former students who consider themselves lucky indeed to have benefited from his wisdom and guidance.

> *As in his work on Melville, Dillingham is extraordinarily adept in the Kipling books at sifting through and assimilating past criticism on the author, even as he develops fresh and valuable insights of his own.*

During his many years at Emory, Dillingham graced the University not only with thoughtful teaching and prolific scholarship but also by serving—during the years 1979–82, 1985–86, and 1990–91—as a successful and well-liked chair of the English Department. During his first stint as chair, roughly one-third of the faculty positions at both junior and senior levels were filled, influencing the future of the department in important ways. He told *Emory Magazine* in 1983 that "this was a time of extreme importance to the English Department as well as to the University. It was a time of almost constant introspection and goal-establishing." Frank Manley gave Dillingham's performance as chair the highest praise, insisting that he was "the best we have had in many, many years. . . . I think his real contribution was to bring the department together and make it harmonious and peaceful. He was able to do that by the strength of his personality; by not forcing issues down people's throats; by being a human, kind, gentle person; by knowing how to handle people; by knowing when to back off and when to push on; and by the strength and clarity of his mind. He has a very clear vision of things."[3]

Another colleague, John Sitter, who taught at Emory for more than two decades before moving to the University of Notre Dame, has also spoken highly of Dillingham's work. Noting that after his four decades with the University Dillingham had been both "a child of Emory and a founding father of Emory," Sitter writes, "What a scholar-teacher he has been. His courses at all levels have across the decades been not only among the most popular but among the most highly respected for, like the man himself, their rigor and high standards. Bill Dillingham is a man of so many talents, so many achievements, and such virtues as to resist our summation and adequate recognition."[4]

During these decades of superb teaching, scholarship, and service, Dillingham continued to have a happy personal life, anchored by the woman who still "made the world sing." His family had been made complete by a third child, a son, born in 1960, and as the years passed the Dillinghams began dividing their time between their home in Decatur and a place he named "Hope House" in Daytona Beach Shores, Florida. He has also for many years pursued a major avocation, bass fishing—one he shared with his son and, eventually, with his grandson. He retired in 1996, and at such a happy and fulfilled place some professional careers might have come to a serene stopping place.

Not so with Bill Dillingham. Though his teaching career had concluded, he not only continued to pursue his scholarly work but, having surveyed Melville's entire career, turned to yet another major subject, the British poet and novelist Rudyard Kipling. His first book on this author, *Rudyard Kipling: Hell and Heroism*, appeared in 2005 and was selected by CHOICE as the Outstanding Academic Title for 2006. A second major study, *Being Kipling*, appeared in 2008, and he immediately embarked on yet a third work on Kipling. As in his work on Melville, Dillingham is extraordinarily adept in the Kipling books at sifting through and assimilating past criticism on the author, even as he develops fresh and valuable insights of his own.

And so the fortunate life and career of William B. Dillingham continue in a pleasant and productive way. In the mornings he keeps at his work in the same library study where he has toiled for so many years, and in the afternoons, after lunch with Elizabeth, he works at home. And despite all the achievements and the accolades, he remains a modest, unassuming, and always cheerful man, whom any of his friends and former colleagues are always happy to see. Clearly, for Bill Dillingham, the world is still singing.

CHAPTER 32

RUSSELL MAJOR
Candler Professor of Renaissance History
— ALEXIS VICTORIA HAUK —

Through four decades J. Russell Major helped to shape Emory as a modern research university through his scholarship, rigorous teaching, and exemplary service in many capacities. Along with his wife, Blair Rogers Major, he embodied both the graciousness of an older Emory and the intellectual excellence of an emerging institution of the highest quality.

JAMES RUSSELL MAJOR landed at Emory seemingly by chance, without ever having seen the campus. In fact, the only face-to-face encounter he had with anyone from Emory prior to his appointment as an instructor in history, in 1949, was when he rode his bike through the snow-covered streets of Princeton, New Jersey, the previous winter to speak with Emory's registrar, J. Gordon Stipe, who was in Princeton on other Emory business. Apparently Stipe's report on the budding historian radiated enough conviction in Major's abilities that Emory offered him thirty-four hundred dollars a year to come teach.[1] At that time, the History Building, now Bowden Hall, had just been built—a happy parallel with Major's own career, which was just in building stages of its own.

Major would spend his entire career at Emory—more than forty years—earning appointment as the Candler Professor of Renaissance History in 1980 and the University's Thomas Jefferson Award in 1986. (The Jefferson Award recognizes "significant service through personal activities, influence and leadership."[2]) Along the way, Major chaired the History Department three times, built up the Woodruff Library's archives in French history, and guided fifteen doctoral students through their dissertations to tenure-track positions elsewhere. Over the years, he rejected several appealing offers from other universities. For instance, writing to Dean Lester G. Crocker at Case Western Reserve University in 1967, he said, "My situation at Emory is as near ideal as one can imagine. The University has done so much for me that I always try to resist such tempting suggestions as the one you have made." The next year, the University of Virginia tried its hand at coaxing him back to his native state, but UVA, too, received a polite letter of decline. His colleague Irwin Hyatt recalled,

> In the late 1960s he was offered chaired professorships at other schools three times that I know of (a Kenan chair twice at NYU and an unnamed chair at the University of North Carolina), and each time he decided to stay with his longtime colleagues and guide the development begun by Professors Mathews and Young at Emory.[3]

While he became a star in academia, his students often recalled "an authentic humbleness and even a bit of shyness."[4] Frank Williams (Graduate School 1992) recalled that Major would take his lunch break in the library, poring over materials, an aspect of the disciplined routine rooted in books and reading that he carried out for most of his career.[5] Indeed, the pragmatic Major often turned down preferred writing gigs and speaking engagements, in favor of keeping his nose in the books of the Woodruff Library. These offers included an invitation from the *Encyclopedia Britannica* in 1970 to write the entry on France from 1490 to 1715. Major rejected it out of eagerness to make progress on another project that he had long been working on. When he was invited in 1990 to give the Joseph Mathews Address at Emory for the second time, he reminded the organizer that he had already accepted the honor ten years earlier and that people would "probably prefer to see a new face."

This fastidious approach to lifelong scholarship made him intolerant of lazy scholarship by others. Albert Hamscher (Graduate School 1970, PhD 1973, later a distinguished professor of history at Kansas State University), one of Major's so-called scholarly progeny, described in a letter two characteristic encounters with his mentor:

> Shortly after I had passed preliminary examinations and was preparing for my "dissertation year" in France, I asked to borrow some of his microfilm (those dreadful peasant *cahiers* [notebooks], if I remember correctly) in order to practice reading the challenging handwriting of the 16th and 17th centuries. Russell's response: "get over to France and read your own documents . . . why are you still here?"
>
> Years later, when I was beginning to get serious about my third book project . . . I explained to Russell that in order to do the project properly I would have to visit at least thirty provincial

archives and expand the chronological scope of my research from the reign of Louis XIV to the entire period, 1670–1789. At least a decade of fresh archival research lay before me. I guess I was fishing for some sympathy, something along the lines of, "Well, Al, you could get by, and probably fairly well, with a handful of provinces and a shorter time period." I should have known better. Russell's two-word response to my predicament: "You're young." (Implied addendum: "get to work.")[6]

Born in Riverton, Virginia, on January 7, 1921, to a long-established Virginian family (Stonewall Jackson evidently sat on the Majors' porch once), Russell grew up shy. He loved reading but hated hunting and didn't dance. His mechanical ability, according to his friend Dan Kilbourn, was "best served by finer dexterity on the phone, calling for help when anything need[ed] fixing." Major was a "rat" (freshman) at Virginia Military Institute when he first met the young woman—then a high school sophomore—who would later become his wife of fifty-two years, Blair Rogers. They were living near each other in Front Royal, a pretty town along the Shenandoah River, where her father was commander of an army post that was used to raise horses for the cavalry, and Russell's family owned a jelly factory. Their first date was at a roller rink, after which they went to a drugstore for ice cream sodas. "Our activities seem amazingly innocent by current standards," Major remarked in his memoir.[7]

Over the next several years, in the midst of both personal and national change, the couple would separate and reunite several times. Blair wanted to graduate from college (Vassar) before settling down, and by the time her graduation day arrived in 1944, World War II was in full swing, and Russell was "over there."

Ten days after Russell graduated from the Virginia Military Institute in 1942 he entered the service, training at Fort Monroe in Virginia, Fort Bragg in North Carolina, and Fort Sill in Oklahoma. In Patton's Third Army, from 1942 to 1946,[8] in the dangerous position of artillery forward observer, Major recalled later that he was transformed from a "bookish recluse who knew nothing of firearms and war, woefully lacking self-confidence . . . into a decorated officer with highest possible combat efficiency rating."[9] The metamorphosis into decorated soldier—he brought home a Silver Star for Gallantry, Bronze Star and Purple Heart with two oak clusters—was "dictated by chance," Major wrote in the memoir about his war years. (*The Memoirs of an Artillery Forward Observer, 1944–1945* was published less than a month after Major died of complications from abdominal surgery in December 1998.)

That Major had fought in the Battle of the Bulge and become a highly decorated officer proved revelatory to many of his students. One of Major's closest doctoral students, Mack Holt (PhD 1980, later professor of history at George Mason University), said Major "never talked about this experience with students" but that it clearly "shaped his feelings on responsibility, duty, citizenship . . . It did not transform him politically so much as professionally. . . . I just thought he was a workaholic. Now I realize it was because of his upbringing, service."[10]

When Blair's father, a general, went home from Paris in June 1945 for the wedding of his older daughter, Blair's sister, he asked to have Russell assigned to him as an aide so that Russell could come home for the wedding as well. That weekend, Blair and Russell took a drive through the Blue Ridge Mountains below Skyline Drive and decided to get married the next weekend. She wore her sister's wedding dress, and her sister wore Blair's bridesmaid's dress from the previous week.

Like many young men who fought in World War II, returning to regular life for Major meant the end of "the one exciting period in my life."[11] Even with the inherent danger all around him, he had seen an entirely different part of the world. He had purposefully taken a "wrong turn" into Czechoslovakia when the war was over, just to see it, and when he was stationed in England, he managed to see *A Midsummer Night's Dream* at Stratford-upon-Avon. Perhaps it was his experience in France that inspired him to spend so much of his life—both literally and cerebrally—in Europe, poring though dusty volumes of Renaissance history. And perhaps it was his annoyance and anger at the hierarchy he witnessed on the front lines that made him focus specifically on the idea of monarchal power in French history.[12]

With $106 a week on the GI Bill, the Majors moved to Princeton, where Blair had been working as a bacteriologist, and where Russell began work on a PhD. He had been influenced by medievalist Joseph Strayer and the Reformation historian Elmore "Jinks" Harbison. Soon they were also supporting an ever-growing family of three daughters and a son. In his acknowledgment for his last book, which he dedicated to Blair—"the one who has shared the glorious adventure with me from the very start"—Major wrote, "It began at 11 Dickenson Place at Princeton, where we shared a tiny kitchen and all other facilities with five other families."

> *Major argued with President Sanford Atwood over the need for better tenure criteria, which he thought varied and did not work sufficiently to ensure excellence in new faculty appointments.*

Major submitted his dissertation, "The Estates General of 1560," for publication in 1949. He would put a capstone on this work forty-five years later, when he published his final scholarly work, released in 1994, at age seventy-three, three years after retiring from Emory. That book, *From Renaissance Monarchy to Absolute Monarchy: French Kings, Nobles, and Estates*, was the culmination of his life's work—the intentions he had mapped out initially as his dissertation topic. It won the Leo Gershoy Award of the American Historical Association. Thomas I. Crimando, reviewing the book in the *Renaissance Quarterly*, called it a "masterfully written narrative" against the idea of the formation of an absolute monarchy.[13]

Major's arguments, according to his former student Mack Holt, "did not become the new orthodoxy. He was too modest to proclaim that . . . ; however, even if scholars did not agree with his entire schema, various components of it had become part of a growing consensus on the need to reevaluate the nature of the early modern state."[14]

When the Majors arrived at Emory in 1949 they moved to Emory Court Annex, a circle of twelve faculty homes formerly on the site of what is now Clinic B and the Clinic Parking Garage. James Harvey Young, the late Candler Professor of History, remembered that period as essential in forming a community of faculty and their families. "In its day the Annex played an important University role; inhabited mostly by fairly new additions to the faculty its structure made for close association," he wrote. "Children played together safely, adults became close friends. Professors talked shop."[15] Other new faculty members who lived there and later became prominent leaders of the faculty in their own right were Floyd Watkins (English), Will Beardslee (theology), and Jack Boozer (religion). Parties were plentiful, and, according to Blair Major, "despite the Methodist atmosphere of the campus booze flowed amply."[16]

Eventually, the Majors moved to a house on Houston Mill Road, where they lived for the next thirty years. They bought the house from former theology dean Burton Trimble, who had built three houses on his property and lived in one himself. He also apparently had a cow and chickens on the property for many years. The Majors' house was transformed into the Ben Franklin School.

During the early years, Major regularly taught "History of the Renaissance and Reformation" in the fall and a course on the Enlightenment in the spring. But in 1952 Major had a break from routine, when a yearlong Fulbright Research Fellowship and a Guggenheim Fellowship allowed him to pack up his family (all four kids were six years and under) and return to France and the fields he had first discovered in battle. Living in Montmorency, outside Paris, for nine months, they then spent three summer months traveling some ten thousand miles throughout England. (Ten years later they would be back in France, tearing from one French provincial archive to another, mostly staying in hotels with no private baths, cooking food in city parks, and camping in the Bois de Boulogne.) "We enjoyed gypsying around the world together," Blair Rogers Major later said.[17]

Putting the gypsy lifestyle aside when he returned to Emory, Major became known as an immensely dedicated teacher, famous for getting comments back to students within twenty-four hours. Even with the repetitive semesters, former doctoral student Donna Bohanan (Graduate School 1979, PhD 1982, later professor of history at Auburn University) said that Major would prepare meticulously for each lesson. "There was nothing stale about Russell Major's performance in the classroom; each time he taught a class he introduced new literature and new ideas, and each time he taught from a classic like Huizinga's *Waning of the Middle Ages* he took the time to review a much-loved work."[18] Major even assigned himself to teach introductory courses when he was chair of the History Department—classrooms full of eighty to ninety freshmen and sophomores. As Irwin Hyatt, emeritus professor of history and former associate dean of Emory College, recalled,

> For a senior faculty member of Russell's distinction to do such a thing now would, I'm afraid, be unimaginable. The regard that we in the department had for Professor Major [was] a combination of several factors. As a scholar and for his organizational work at national level, he had our great respect as a leader in the profession. Beyond that, his leadership abilities and traits of character had for a number of years made him a special colleague. . . . Very importantly, . . . Professor Major conveyed a sense of unselfish loyalty to the job of building the department and the school rather than building individual reputation.[19]

As a scholar, Major flourished, winning two Guggenheim fellowships, in 1953 and 1967, and being named Outstanding Educator in America in 1973.

He could also be a nitpicky professor, revealing a generational gap at times. He once wrote to Professor Robert Lambert, in 1969, in regard to a recommendation of a former student for a teaching position at Clemson, "My reservation concerning him stems primarily from the fact that he is a sloppy dresser on campus, to put it mildly. Perhaps a shift from student to member of a faculty would produce a sufficient change in that regard."[20] In rapidly changing times for Emory during the 1960s Major revealed a conservative reluctance to shape the curriculum toward "relevance." Recalling faculty debate over demands of black students, he wrote to a fellow faculty member, "I don't think the *Emory Wheel*'s report on our confrontation was very accurate. It totally missed the point that on Tuesday the faculty refused to accept the Black demands by a 2-to-1 vote and also avoided a motion that would have, in effect, censured [then–University president Sanford] Atwood. . . . However, we will undoubtedly be faced with very strong pressure to do far more than we are doing. For the moment at least the faculty still controls the curriculum and faculty appointments."[21]

On July 7 the same year, Major wrote to Joy Hoffman, "I don't think anybody in an academic institution ought to make demands on anybody about anything, however reasonable. The *Wheel*, as usual, missed the boat."[22]

Major saw himself as continuing a sharp advocacy for faculty interests. In a memo to Dean John Palms in the fall of 1977, he notes that the first priorities for the College should be student scholarships and faculty salaries, and that the renovation of the history building should be "lower" on the list. Major argued with President Sanford Atwood over the need for better tenure criteria, which he thought varied and did not work sufficiently to ensure excellence in new faculty appointments. He also struggled with Atwood when Professor Bell Wiley was denied space to carry on research and hold his library during retirement. In the existing correspondence, Major chastises the administration for not recognizing the value of keeping research faculty.

His impact on the History Department was powerful and lasting. According to Hyatt,

He raised the graduate program to its highest level by securing a $300,000 Ford Foundation development grant, greatly increased undergraduate courses and enrollment, and added . . . valuable members to our faculty. He was instrumental in securing the Kenan and Mellon chairs, . . . and in his second term he added a new dimension to the department by outstanding junior appointments in the history of Africa, Latin America, and the Middle East.[23]

Nor was Major contained by the academic interests at Emory. When he found out that the University System of Georgia was considering putting a law school in Atlanta (eventually founded at Georgia State in 1982), he wrote to William S. Morris III, vice chair of the Board of Regents, "It is neither a favor to them [prospective students] nor to the taxpayer to provide this opportunity unless there is a demonstrated need for more lawyers. Apparently there is none." Morris wrote back in agreement, "I have serious doubts it would be wise use to taxpayers' money."[24]

"Clearly Russell had never been greatly influenced by [Roosevelt's] soft-speaking manner," former colleague Thomas Burns, the Samuel Candler Dobbs Professor, Emeritus, joked in a letter. "None of us thought of our chats with Russell as in any way 'Fireside Chats.' He let you know that there was something greater depending upon your success—the department."[25]

On the day Burns received an advanced copy of his first book, he ran into Major's office to show it off, thinking that "at last he would stop prodding me. . . . Russell smiled a particularly wry grin, congratulated me, shook my hand, and without pause, asked, 'How's the next one coming?' After several such lessons, I finally got the point."

Blair Rogers Major continues to work on her and her late husband's "fifth child"—the Blair Rogers Major and James Russell Major Fellowship for one student each year writing about European history in the period of 1350 to 1700. This munificent gift permits the student to travel in Europe for ten months while completing research. The gift was inspired by Russell Major's last year of his dissertation, when he received the Elias Boudinet Fellowship, a seven-hundred-dollar gift that allowed him to finish his own dissertation research.

Major is buried along the Shenandoah River outside Front Royal, where his tombstone notes the three facets of his life that formed his self-identity, "Soldier, Historian, Educator."

CHAPTER 33

RICHARD ELLMANN AT EMORY, 1976–1987

— RONALD SCHUCHARD —

In 1980 Richard Ellmann joined the Emory faculty as one of the University's first two Robert W. Woodruff professors; by then he had already been captivating the Atlanta community for several years with lectures that packed Glenn Memorial. After Ellmann's death, English professor Ron Schuchard persuaded President James Laney to establish a lecture series in Ellmann's memory, now one of the premier sets of lectures about literature anywhere in the world. A good friend as well as colleague of Ellmann, Schuchard himself is the best person to tell the story of Ellmann at Emory.

WHEN RICHARD ELLMANN (1918–1987) began a decade of annual visits to Emory in 1976, he was a preeminent literary biographer and one of the foremost scholars of modern literature. He had taught readers worldwide how to read Yeats, Joyce, and other difficult authors. He had a reputation for writing clearly, elegantly, and urbanely about serious literature, and he had created a large audience for modern writers through his books and anthologies. His *James Joyce: A Biography* (1959) had won the National Book Award for nonfiction, and thousands of students had discovered their favorite authors in his *Norton Anthology of Modern Poetry* (1973), still the primary teaching anthology in America twenty-two years after his death. A Guggenheim Fellow and a member of the American Academy of Arts and Sciences, he was also a member of the British Academy and the Royal Society of Literature. His academic career had taken him from Northwestern University to Harvard, from Harvard to Yale. When, in 1970, he announced his plans to write a biography of Oscar Wilde, Oxford University elected him to its Goldsmiths Professorship of English at New College, one of the highest chairs in academe. So how did it come about, many have asked, that Ellmann soon chose to begin his annual association with Emory and assist the rise of the Woodruff Library and the humanities to international prominence?

On Sunday night, September 28, 1976, I received a call out of the blue from David Farmer, a former classmate who was then an assistant director of the Harry Ransom Center at the University of Texas, Austin. He confided that Ellmann would be in Atlanta the next day and asked whether Emory would like to have him give a lecture. "Of course!" I replied, delighted by the prospect. "How long will he be in Atlanta?" "Just tomorrow, Monday," said Farmer, aware of the absurdity of the challenge. "Don't say I didn't give you a chance!" On his return to Oxford, Ellmann was passing through Atlanta for a one-day layover to see his son, Steven, who, after graduating from Harvard Law School, had just taken a clerkship in Atlanta's U.S. Court of Appeals with Federal Judge Elbert P. Tuttle. "Thanks for the information," I said, after a long pause. "I'll get back to you."

"I know I shouldn't call the dean at home on Sunday night after 9:00 p.m.," I said to my wife, "but tomorrow morning will be too late." I knew John Palms, former chair of the Physics Department and then dean of Emory College, better as a squash opponent than as a dean. "You're not going to believe this," I explained to Palms, "but I need your support for a lecture by a distinguished scholar tomorrow evening. I've never met him, I don't have his title, and I haven't reserved a lecture room, but if you'll provide an honorarium I'll see that it comes off." With a doubtful "yes," Palms took a fortuitous chance. Phone lines buzzed all evening, flyers flew the next morning, and Ellmann was met at the airport in the afternoon. That evening, in Tull Auditorium, before an audience of 350 hastily gathered lovers of literature, Richard Ellmann gave an electrifying lecture on "Oscar Wilde: A Late Victorian Love Affair." Dean Palms, who had come to witness the result of his blind investment, told me afterward, "That was the best lecture I've ever heard. Wouldn't it be great to have him at Emory?"

Driving Ellmann to his son's flat after the lively reception with a long-lingering audience, I asked him if he ever thought of returning to America from Oxford. "Yes," he said, "but I can't. I'm dependent on the National Health Service in England for my wife." And then he recounted how his wife, Mary, the former Mary Donahue, a pioneer of feminist literary criticism and author of *Thinking about Women* (1968), had suffered a cerebral aneurysm, followed by botched surgery, just before they left Yale for Oxford. Her condition required extensive treatment and rehabilitation, he explained, and no American university would provide him with Blue Cross/Blue Shield or other insurance coverage.

"Would you be interested in coming back if a good university offered to provide such coverage?" I asked.

"Yes."

The next day I called Dean Palms and asked him if he was serious about wanting Ellmann on the faculty. "Yes." "Could you get him Blue Cross/Blue Shield?" "I think so."

And that was all it took—a positive response to a personal need—to bring Dick, as he preferred to be called, and Mary to Emory every spring for six weeks between the Hilary and Trinity terms at Oxford. They came first in the spring of 1978, after health insurance coverage had been successfully negotiated, and immediately immersed themselves in the intellectual, cultural, social, and teaching life of Emory. They were famous in Oxford for hosting a few guests most afternoons for drinks, water biscuits, and Greek taramasalata in their sitting room at 39 St. Giles, and at Emory they held a similar court at the newly built Clifton Towers, later in their Harwood condominium on Houston Mill Road. They were Emory royalty, and Dick exercised kingly care and patience as he helped Mary move about with braced legs and tripod cane. He brought with him another new lecture, "James Joyce and the Uses of Decadence," and he filled the lecture hall with faculty and students and citizens of literature from every corner of the University, as he would every spring for the next nine years.

> *One could sense that a seismic shift of energy and possibility had begun to take place throughout the University, and that autumn it became clear that Dick was part of the energizing force.*

Each spring, first on the quarter system, then on the semester, he offered an intensive mini-course for advanced undergraduates and graduate students—on Joyce, Yeats, Auden, Beckett, Stevens, and others. He was not a dynamic lecturer, but what the students heard in his classrooms was heard in no other: they heard him recount his conversations and interviews with Maud Gonne, Mrs. Yeats, Joyce's heirs and friends, each story enhancing his close readings of works with his firsthand knowledge of literary contexts and anecdotes. His Emory students felt not only amazement at his textual explications but the privilege of having an extraordinary scholar share forty years of biographical research with them. Such were his gentlemanly, polite, and considerate ways that in controversial meetings of the English Department no one would dare speak impatiently, dismissively, or discourteously to other colleagues in front of him. His presence brought and maintained an atmosphere of respect, civility, and courtesy always.

In April 1978, during Ellmann's first visiting appointment, James T. Laney was inaugurated as Emory's seventeenth president, and the friendship that developed between the two men was to have a significant impact on the future of the University, especially after Robert and George Woodruff's munificent gift of $105 million in Coca-Cola stock that year made possible previously unimagined areas of development and growth. Ellmann's arrival at that time could not have been a happier triangular coincidence for the future of Emory. He was aware that Laney had helped negotiate the purchase of the Hartford Theological Library in the mid-1970s, an acquisition that made the Pitts Theology Library second in holdings only to those of Union Seminary in New York, and he suggested to Laney that if he wanted to build a university "of the first rank," as he had stated in his inaugural address, that the Woodruff Library must also be developed into a major research library. In December 1978, as an act of encouragement toward that distant goal, Ellmann placed his own extensive collection of the works of W. B. Yeats in the library.

When the Ellmanns returned in the spring of 1979, an appreciative Emory had determined to award Dick an honorary degree at Commencement. Again, a large University audience took great pleasure in his newest lecture, "W. B. Yeats's Second Puberty." One could sense that a seismic shift of energy and possibility had begun to take place throughout the University, and that autumn it became clear that Dick was part of the energizing force. He sent word from Oxford to Ted Johnson, then the director of libraries, and Marella Walker, the indefatigable and inimitable director of collection management (and recipient of the Thomas Jefferson Award), that a major two-part auction of modern literature, including Lady Augusta Gregory's papers and her private collection of Yeats's work from her Coole Park library, would take place at Sothebys in London in July and December. With President Laney's approval, and with lists of preferences from Ellmann and me, Emory's agents bid strategically and came away from both auctions with the lion's share of books, manuscripts, letters, and other materials by Yeats and Lady Gregory. "I thought it would be a good strategy to bid on the first two items and try to discourage the competition from even coming to the afternoon sale," Walker wrote to me of Emory's success on December 20:

> Ted appears to be pleased with the outcome and I am very happy over it. Dr. Laney is also well pleased.... I talked to Dick Ellmann after your letter came. Then it was decided that I would go to London for the sale. I called Dick from London because he told me that he would come up for the sale and he met me at Sothebys for the afternoon session. I went to look at the manuscripts and books in the morning and sat through the morning session which was a most interesting experience. Afterwards we rode by his apartment and had a drink and chatted for an hour—about Mr. Woodruff's gift . . . and the English Dept. in general. I bit my tongue several times because I could not mention how much Emory wants him to come full time. He is *such* a nice person; and oh how lightly he wears his learning.[1]

With the astonishing successes at the Sotheby auctions, in combination with Dick's own Yeats collection, the Woodruff Library now had set in place the cornerstone for building a major research collection in modern literature. Dick was now fully committed not only to the library enterprise but to his long-term relationship to Emory, even if it could not be full-time. His friendships across the University increased rapidly, and he helped with the recruitment of new faculty. In the English Department, the administrative secretary, Trudy Kretchman, and other members of the staff eagerly awaited his refreshing annual return. Lee Ann Lloyd began to enter chapters of his Wilde biography into the Lanier word-processing machine as he submitted them to her, and the entirety of the book was prepared at Emory rather than Oxford.

"When Trudy introduced me to him I was very awed," Lee Ann recalled. "I called him Dr. Ellmann, and he replied, 'Oh, call me Dick.' It made a great impression on me (especially after working in the medical field for years when all the docs insisted on being called 'Doctor,' no matter how long one had worked with them)."

He enjoyed the increasing flow of writers who were coming to Emory, and in March 1981 he helped welcome Seamus Heaney for his first reading. My wife, Keith, and I held a party in honor of Heaney, the Ellmanns, and the classical scholar William Arrowsmith, all of whom were treated to sips of the finest South Carolina moonshine (Heaney thought it better than Irish poitin) to seal their new southern bonds. At the end of the following academic year, on June 21, 1982, the trustees named both Ellmann and Arrowsmith the first Robert W. Woodruff professors at Emory, effective that September. The Ellmanns bought a condo in the Harwood complex and made Emory their permanent second home.

When the Ellmanns were back in Oxford, their home was a port of call for visiting Emory faculty. Emory's British studies program, situated at University College, Oxford, had begun in the summer of 1979, and each year members of the teaching staff looked forward to drinks, taramasalata, and new Oxford acquaintances at 39 St. Giles. In 1984, when Heaney came to read and conduct a poetry workshop for the Emory program, the Ellmanns hosted a rare dinner party for the Heaneys and an Emory group that included Dr. John Stone and his wife, Lou. A photograph of that memorable gathering is in the Emory archives. The friendships and camaraderie had increased from year to year, but at the end of that summer Dick retired, as required, at age sixty-five, from his Goldsmiths professorship and took up a research position as an Extraordinary Fellow at Wolfson College, Oxford, where he continued to write the Wilde biography and prepare his annual lectures for Emory.

The Ellmanns made their last journey to Emory in the spring of 1986, Dick having just published *Four Dubliners: Wilde, Yeats, Joyce, and Beckett*, comprising lectures that he had given before Emory audiences. That summer I was elected to a visiting research fellowship at Wolfson College, and when I arrived for the academic year in September I found that Dick's speech had become slurred. Dick explained that he had made a self-diagnosis of motor-neuron disease (Lou Gehrig's disease), medically confirmed in October, fourth stage. As the disease took its rapid toll, I wrote to President Laney, proposing that Emory honor Ellmann by establishing a lecture series in his name. Laney soon flew to Oxford to visit Dick and inform him personally that Emory would indeed establish the Richard Ellmann Lectures in Modern Literature. Asked whom he would like to inaugurate the lectures, Dick replied softly, "Seamus."

> *For the past twenty years the Ellmann name has attracted the world's finest writers and critics to Emory.*

For the remaining months of his life Dick struggled valiantly to complete his Wilde biography, finished just before his death on May 13, 1987. Published posthumously later that year, *Oscar Wilde* won a Pulitzer Prize and the National Book Critics Circle Award. At the memorial service in Cannon Chapel, members of the Emory community celebrated his extraordinary presence at Emory and his personable nature. President Laney shared a lighter side of his relationship with Dick, as witnessed and recounted by Trudy Kretchman:

President Laney told of bumping into Dick in the early morning in Lullwater, while Dick was jogging and he [Laney] was walking to pick up the morning paper by the gate. Actually, Laney said, Dick's jog was more like a heavy trudge. After meeting this way for several days, Dick began to pick up the paper at the gate and Laney would see him come trudging up his driveway, a smile on his face and paper in hand. Was there ever such a paper boy, Laney mused. Very nice.

Thus, in April 1988 Dick's friend Seamus Heaney came to Emory to inaugurate the Richard Ellmann Lectures in Modern Literature, delivering three lectures before packed audiences in Glenn Auditorium. The lectures, which he followed with a reading of his poetry, were published as *The Place of Writing* (1989), with a frontispiece photograph of Seamus and Dick walking and talking together in 1982 on the Hill of Howth above Dublin Bay. Heaney's summary of Ellmann's special gifts in his prefatory remarks to the audience stands as a lasting tribute:

Ellmann was a scholar and biographer of unparalleled scope and meticulousness, one who possessed a commanding sense of the whole outline of his subjects and delicate capacity for eliciting fully fledged meaning by brooding upon details. He was also a critic with a unique double gift: his illuminations were as felicitous as his judgments were authoritative. He could maintain subtle, receptive vigilance over a text and explicate it within the idiom of his profession; but he could also produce a kind of Johnsonian meditation that considered what the text was worth to the fuller enjoyment or better enduring of our unspecialized lives.

This was because his writing, like his conduct, came out of that place from which, according to the poet Ted Hughes, the truest poetry also comes: the place in us where our ultimate capacity for suffering and decision is lodged. To meet Richard Ellmann was to encounter a gathered force. I was always moved by a feeling that innate gifts of fortitude, tenderness and fairness had been consecrated to a discipline, one which placed immense intellectual and personal demands upon him but which rewarded him with a rock-bottom emotional verity. In Keats's terms, he was an intelligence who had been schooled into a soul, and the good consequences for all who knew him are palpable here this evening.

When Heaney then donated the manuscripts and correspondence of his Ellmann Lectures to Special Collections (now the Manuscript, Archives, and Rare Book Library, or MARBL), Dr. Linda Matthews, who as director played a key role in developing the modern collection after 1979, determined that MARBL should begin developing its strengths in contemporary as well as modern literature. The full story of the extraordinary growth of MARBL's development as the major research library that Ellmann, Laney, and others envisioned in 1978 has yet to be told. In September 2003, however, after Emory had honored Nobel Laureate Heaney with an honorary degree at Commencement the previous May, Heaney announced that he would place his correspondence at Emory. That generous act, which also honored his relationship with former President William Chace, was yet another part of the Ellmann legacy that continues to expand into the future, especially through the Ellmann lecturers, two of whose other participants—Anthony Hecht and Salman Rushdie—have also placed their papers at Emory.

For the past twenty years the Ellmann name has attracted the world's finest writers and critics to Emory, including, most recently (2008), the Italian novelist Umberto Eco. When Eco was invited to give the Ellmann lectures he responded at once with alacrity, "Yes!"—saying that he had long wished to pay homage to the man who had not only helped him immensely with Joyce but who had written a major review of his first novel, *The Name of the Rose*, in the *New York Review of Books*, a review that catapulted him into recognition and prominence in America. How could we have known that a scholar who came to Emory for Blue Cross/Blue Shield would play such a prominent role in shaping the University that we know today, and that twenty years after his death he would still have the power to draw great writers for our enjoyment and their papers for our keeping?

CHAPTER 34

IN PRAISE OF A LEGAL POLYMATH
Harold J. Berman, Emory's First Woodruff Professor of Law
— JOHN WITTE JR. *and* FRANK S. ALEXANDER —

Harold J. Berman is one of the great polymaths of American legal education. He has molded an enviable array of legal disciplines—legal history, Russian law, international trade, legal philosophy, and law and religion. His twenty-five books and hundreds of articles, together with the contributions of his numerous students, stand as monuments to his enlightened pedagogy. The critical acuity and catholic influence of his legal thought have earned him a place alongside such twentieth-century legal giants as Roscoe Pound, Karl Llewellyn, and Lon Fuller.
—James T. Laney, president, Emory University (1993)

Harold Berman is a giant, whose work defies the banalities of the age and allows us to take their measure. In a scholarly world drifting toward the particularistic exploration of "unique" contexts, Berman points in a different direction—toward holistic descriptions of entire systems of legal thought. . . . Berman's work, and especially his Law and Revolution, will endure when almost everything is forgotten. He is the only American who might be paired with Max Weber in the depth of his historical and comparative understanding of the remarkable character of legal modernity.
—Guido Calabresi, dean, Yale Law School (1996)

ON NOVEMBER 13, 2007, Emory University lost its first Robert W. Woodruff Professor of Law, Harold J. Berman. He left a scholarly legacy of 25 books and 458 articles, translated into 18 languages. He left some 8,000 students and 500 public lectures delivered throughout North America, Europe, Russia, and China. And he left his beloved wife of sixty-two years, Ruth Harlow Berman, and their four children, seven grandchildren, and two great-grandchildren.

Born in 1918 in Hartford, Connecticut, Berman—"Hal" to all his friends—received his BA from Dartmouth College in 1938, a certificate of graduate studies from the London School of Economics and Political Science in 1939, and an MA in history from Yale in 1942. He served in the U.S. Army in the European Theater of Operations from 1942 to 1945, and received the Bronze Star. He then took his JD degree in 1947 from Yale Law School.

Fresh from law school, Berman began his teaching career at Stanford Law School in 1947, then moved back east in 1948 to Harvard Law School, where he taught until 1985—for eight years as the Joseph Story Professor of Law, for sixteen more as the James Barr Ames Professor of Law. During those remarkable decades at Harvard he also served as founding director of Harvard Law School's Liberal Arts Fellowship in Law, fellow of the Russian Research Center of Harvard University, and member of the Legal Committee of the U.S.-U.S.S.R. Trade and Economic Council.

Not one to accept Harvard's mandatory retirement demurely at age sixty-five, he happily received a visit from James T. Laney, then president of Emory University, who traveled to Cambridge, Massachusetts, to recruit Berman to the Emory faculty. Devoted to teaching, deeply engaged in new research, Berman did not require much persuading. He joined the Emory Law School faculty in 1985 and accepted simultaneous appointment as fellow of Russian Studies in the Carter Center at Emory. He was the founding director of the American Law Center in Moscow, founding director of the World Law Institute at Emory Law School, and senior fellow in Emory's Center for the Study of Law and Religion.

The expanding reach of Professor Berman's thought gives an impressive symmetry to the six decades of his career. For the first three decades, his principal scholarly energies were focused on the Soviet legal system and the law of international trade. He developed new courses, testified frequently before courts, commissions, and Congress, and traveled regularly to Europe and the Soviet Union—fifty-five times to Russia alone. He spent the 1961–62 academic year studying at the Moscow Institute of State and Law, where he encountered a rising young star named Mikhail Gorbachev. In 1982 he returned to Russia for another year of teaching, this time as Fulbright Professor of Law at Moscow State University.

He produced a massive body of scholarship in this early period. His *Justice in the U.S.S.R.* (1950; rev. ed. 1963) and *The Russians in Focus* (1953; rev. ed. 1969) will long endure as classics, as will several of his lengthy law review articles on the *lex mercatoria*, the medieval law of commerce. In these first decades of teaching, Berman also developed a keen interest in bringing legal education into college courses and into the public mainstream. These interests he distilled in two other signature titles, *On the Teaching of Law in the Liberal Arts Curriculum* (1956) and *The Nature and Functions of Law* (1958; 6th ed. 2004). Extending the classroom to the world, he orchestrated a series of public lectures on the fundamentals of public, private, penal, and procedural law that were broadcast throughout the world on Armed Forces Radio, and then published in multiple languages as *Talks on American Law* (1961).

In the last three decades of his career, Berman shifted the main focus of his legal scholarship to legal philosophy, legal history, and law and religion. His series of pathbreaking volumes included, most notably *The Interaction of Law and Religion* (1974), *Faith and Order: The Reconciliation of Law and Religion* (1993), and his monumental legal history series: *Law and Revolution: The Formation of the Western Legal Tradition* (1983) and *Law and Revolution II: The Impact of the Protestant Reformations on the Western Legal Tradition* (2003). The final volume in this series—on the American, French, and Russian revolutions—was on his writing desk when he died.[1]

Throughout his career, Professor Berman had the remarkable ability to think above, beyond, and against his times. In the 1950s and 1960s the dominant Cold War logic in the West taught that the Soviet Union was a lawless autocracy. Berman argued to the contrary, that the Russians would always honor contracts and treaties that were fairly negotiated. His view prevailed and came to inform various nuclear treaties and East-West accords. In the 1970s the conventional belief persisted that the Middle Ages were the dark ages as the West waited impatiently for renaissance, enlightenment, and modernization. Berman argued the contrary, that the medieval era was the first modern age of the West, and the founding era of our Western legal tradition. This view is now standard.

> *"First it was Russian law, then it was Western law, now it is world law. What's next, cosmic law?"*

In the 1980s and 1990s jurists fought fiercely over whether legal positivism or natural law or some other perspective offered the best understanding of our modern legal system. Berman called for an integrative jurisprudence that reconciled these views with each other and with other perspectives on law. This view now prevails in a world dedicated to interdisciplinary legal study. And, in the past decade, with the world hell-bent on waging "a clash of civilizations," Berman called for a world law, grounded in global structures and processes, universal customs and principles of peace, cooperation, and reconciliation. This view holds so much more promise than the jingoism and jihadism of the past decade.

"First it was Russian law, then it was Western law, now it is world law. What's next, cosmic law?" This is how Professor Berman's beloved wife, Ruth, once summarized (with a blend of exasperation and astonishment) the stages of Berman's storied legal career. There is keen insight in this statement. For Berman, every legal system—even the budding legal system of the world—must be founded upon cosmic commandments and contemplation, divine examples and exemplars. Berman has long prophesied that those legal systems that build on secular and material foundations alone will ultimately fail. The spectacular failure of the Soviet legal system in the later twentieth century was ample vindication of his insight into the essential religious foundations of law.

Berman repeated this message in China, too, where he gave a series of resounding lectures on law and religion the year before he died. One of his Chinese respondents asked whether one needed to believe in God in order to have a just legal order. "It would certainly help!" Hal quipped immediately. "But no," he went on diplomatically, "you don't necessarily have to believe in God, but you have to believe in *something*. You have to believe in law at least. If you can't accept God, then just focus on the law that God has written within on all of our hearts. Even children intuitively sense this law within us. Every child in the world will say, 'That's *my* toy.' That's property law. Every child will say, 'But you *promised* me.' That's contract law. Every child will say, 'It's not my fault. He hit me first.' That's tort law. Every child will say, too, 'Daddy said I could.' That's constitutional law. Law comes from our human nature." And our human nature is an image of God.

Such views reflect Berman's lifelong effort to integrate his religious faith with his legal learning. In his dozens of chapel talks delivered in the Harvard Memorial Church over the years Berman contrasted "the wisdom of the world" with "the wisdom of God." The wisdom of the world, he declared, "assumes that God's existence is irrelevant to knowledge, and that truth is discoverable by the human mind unaided by the Spirit." Jewish and Christian wisdom, by contrast, "seeks God's guidance . . . in order to discover the relationship between what we know and what God intends for us." Knowledge and intellect are "intimately connected with faith, with hope, and with love." "God does not call us to be merely observers of life; rather he calls all of us—even the scholars in all that we do—to participate with him in the process of spiritual death and rebirth which is fundamental religious experience."

Berman also preached a deep theology of reconciliation. Jewish and Christian theologies, he reminded his listeners, teach that persons must reconcile themselves to God, neighbor, and self. For Berman, building on St. Paul, this meant that there can be "no real division between Jew and Gentile, slave and free, male and female"—or, for that matter, black and white, straight and gay, old and young, rich and poor, citizen and stranger. For every sin that destroys our relationships, he emphasized, there must be grace that reconciles them. For every Tower of Babel that divides our voices, there must be a Pentecost that unites them and makes them coherent.

> *At the turn of this new millennium, Berman believed, the Western legal tradition is undergoing a profound integrity crisis, graver and greater than any faced in the past millennium.*

Such spiritual sentiments could shackle the narrow-minded. They liberated Berman from conventional habits of mind and traditional divisions of knowledge. He challenged Max Weber on his separation of fact and value, is and ought. He criticized Alexander Solzhenitsyn for his contradistinction of law and morals, law and love. He fought against the divisions of the very world itself into East and West, old and new. His favorite jurists were the medieval canonist Gratian, the English jurist Matthew Hale, and Supreme Court Justice Joseph Story, all of whom wrote concordances of discordant canons. His favorite philosophers were Peter Abelard, Philip Melanchthon, and Michael Polanyi, who developed integrative holistic philosophies.

"The era of dualism is waning," Berman declared in *The Interaction of Law and Religion*. "We are entering into a new age of integration and reconciliation. Everywhere synthesis," the overcoming of false opposites, is "the key to this new kind of thinking and living." Either-or must give way to both-and. Not subject versus object, not fact versus value, not is versus ought, not soul versus body, not faith versus reason, not church versus state, not one versus many, "but the whole person and whole community thinking and feeling, learning and living together" —that is the common calling of humankind, Berman wrote.

Berman applied this gospel of reconciliation and integration most vigorously to his legal studies. He called for the reintegration of the classic schools of legal positivism, natural law theory, and historical jurisprudence—which, in his view, had been separated since God was cast out of the legal academy. He called for the integration of public law and private law, of common law and civil law, of Western law and Eastern law. He urged that law be given a place among the humanities and enrich itself with the ideas and methods of sundry humane disciplines. And he urged most strongly that the subjects and sciences of law and religion be reconciled to each other. Their separation was, for him, a theological "heresy" and a jurisprudential "fallacy" that cannot survive in the new era of synthesis and integration. "Law and religion stand or fall together," he wrote. "If we wish law to stand, we shall have to give new life to the essentially religious commitments that give it its ritual, its tradition, and its authority—just as we shall have to give new life to the social, and hence the legal, dimensions of religious faith."

Berman's talk of the death of dualism and the birth of an age of synthesis points to another example of how he manifested his religious faith in his legal works. Berman held a providential view of history. Both Jewish and Christian theologies teach that time is continuous, not cyclical, that time moves forward from a sin-trampled garden to a golden city, from a fallen world to a perfect end time. Berman was convinced that slowly but surely all the peoples of the world would come into contact with each other, and ultimately, after revolutionary struggle and even apocalyptic explosion, would seek finally to be reconciled with each other forever.

Berman's grand account of evolution and revolution in Western history, set out in his monumental *Law and Revolution* series, is rooted in this basic belief about the nature and pattern of time. There is a distinctive Western legal tradition, he argued, a continuity of legal ideas and institutions, which grow by accretion and adaptation. The exact shape of these ideas and institutions is determined, in part, by the underlying religious belief systems of the people ruling and being ruled. Six great revolutions, however, have punctuated this organic gradual development: the Papal Revolution of 1075, the German Lutheran Reformation of 1517, the English Puritan Revolution of 1640, the American Revolution of 1776, the French Revolution of 1789, and the Russian Revolution of 1917. These revolutions were, in part, rebellions against a legal and political order that had become outmoded and ossified, arbitrary and abusive. But, more fundamentally, these revolutions were the products of radical shifts in the religious belief systems of the people—shifts from Catholicism to Protestantism to Deism to the secular religion of Marxist-Leninism. Each of these new belief systems offered a new eschatology, a new apocalyptic vision of the perfect end time, whether that be the second coming of Christ, the arrival of the heavenly city of the Enlightenment philosophers, or the withering away of the state. Each of these revolutions, in its first radical phase, sought the death of an old legal order to bring forth a new order that would survive the Last Judgment. Eventually, each of these revolutions settled down and introduced fundamental legal changes that were ultimately subsumed in and accommodated to the Western legal tradition.

At the turn of this new millennium, Berman believed, the Western legal tradition is undergoing a profound integrity crisis, graver and greater than any faced in the past millennium. The old legal order of the West is under attack both from within and from without. From within, Western law is suffering from the critical and cynical attacks relentlessly issued by jurists and judges—a "form of lawyerly self-loathing," he once called it. These legal skeptics, particularly Berman's former Harvard colleagues who led the "critical legal studies" movement in American law schools, have dismissed legal doctrine as malleable, self-contradictory rhetoric. They have depicted the law as an instrument of oppression and exploitation of women, of minorities, of the poor, of the different. They have derided the legal system for its promotion of the political purposes of the powerful and the propertied. This assault from within the law, from within the legal academies and within the courts—devoid as it is of a positive agenda of reconstruction—reflects a cynical contempt for law and government, a deep loss of confidence in its integrity and efficacy. The "secular priests of the law," its officials and its educators, no longer seem to believe in what they are doing.

From without, the radical transformation of economic life and the rapid acceptance of new social forms and customs, many born of Eastern, Southern, and new-age thinking, have stretched traditional Western legal doctrines to the breaking point. Complex new legal issues surrounding, say, the fresh rise of polygamy, arranged marriages, and primogeniture, or the new insistence on creating public schools, public library, and public media that cater to the linguistic, religious, and cultural needs of local transplanted communities, are just the tip of an iceberg. All of the major branches of Western law—contract, property, tort, family, criminal, commercial, and constitutional—have transformed several times over in the past two generations. Many of these changes may well be necessary to modernize the law, to conform it to contemporary social needs and ideals, to purge it of its obsolete ideas and institutions. But as a consequence, Western law—always something of a patchwork quilt—has become more of a collection of disjointed pieces, with no single thread, no single spirit holding it in place and giving it integrity and direction. This also has led to profound disillusionment with and distrust of the law.

For Berman, these are signs of end times. We are reaching the end of an age and the end of the Western legal tradition, as we have known it. "Western law is dying," he wrote, "a new common law of all humanity is struggling to be born" out of the counterforces of violent balkanization, radical fundamentalism, and belligerent nationalism that now beset us all. Western law, rooted in the soils and souls of Christianity, Judaism, and their secular successors, will have a place in this new common law of humanity. But so will the laws of the East and the South, of the tribe and the jungle, of the country and the city, each with its own belief system.

What needs to be forged in this new millennium, Berman challenged his readers, is a comprehensive new religious belief system, a new pattern of language and rituals, a new eschaton, that will give this common law of humanity cohesion and direction. We need a new common law and a new common faith on a world scale, a new *ius gentium* and *fides populorum* for the whole world. We need global structures and symbols, global processes and principles. These cannot be found only in worldwide science and commerce, or in global literature and language. They must also be sought in a new "world law" and a new "world religion." For law and religion are the only two universal solvents of human living that can ultimately bring true peace, order, and justice to the world. We have our work cut out for us.

SECTION 4

Religions and the Human Spirit

CHAPTER 35

Day Chapel at Oxford, circa 1940

EMORY AND METHODISM
— RUSSELL E. RICHEY —

Russell Richey, professor of Methodism at Candler School of Theology, explores the unique ties between Emory and the Methodist denomination that founded it. Growing out of the educational ideals of John Wesley (the founder of Methodism), Emory has matured from a small college where religion, community, and education would coexist into a university where Methodist leaders hoped to help shape a Christian America, and then into an institution shaped in turn by the age of professionalism and a dynamic variety of subgroups, professions, and disciplines within both the church and the University. Within this context, Emory and the church have forged and reshaped a relationship that reflects their shared heritage and honors the nuances of change and diversity.

INSTRUCTION, FORMATION, TRAINING, education, and dissemination of knowledge lay at the very heart of the popular religious movement headed by John and Charles Wesley in the eighteenth century. Once it matured, American Methodism, too, made education central to its enterprise, to its mission, to its connectional life. And Emory—founded early in Methodism's college-launching era—has typified both the church's vital commitment to education and the connection-foundational role played by colleges and universities. Unusual in the saga of Methodist higher education has been Emory's crucial contributions at local (Oxford/Atlanta), conference (Georgia), and connectional (national) levels.[1] Unusual as well, though a topic beyond the scope of this chapter, has been Emory's part in defining Methodist race relations at the highest as well as the most personal levels of connectional life—from Bishop James O. Andrew's slaveholding in the nineteenth century, to Bishop Warren Candler's part in the creation of a segregated but reunified Methodism, to Emory University's late-twentieth-century leadership in helping to forge a new South. But first a word or two about connectionalism and education.

Connection | To speak of "connection" and to reflect on higher education in relation to the Methodist connection is to mine a semantic vein with peculiarly Wesleyan theological and organizational layers. Early Methodism on both sides of the Atlantic referred to itself, informally and formally, as a connection. Following British precedent, early minutes of American Methodist conferences bore the title, "Minutes of Some Conversations Between the Preachers in Connection with the Rev. Mr. John Wesley." In its first gathering in 1773 the little American movement made commitments to remain loyal to John Wesley, referring to themselves individually and collectively as "in connection with Mr. Wesley."[2] As John Tigert explains, "connection" came to have specific significance for Methodists.

> Connectionalism is of the essence of the system, equally opposed to congregationalism in the churches and to individualism in the preachers. Mr. Wesley, in America no less than in England, was, at the first, the center of union. Connection with him was the living bond which held incipient American Methodism together.[3]

Methodists have used the word "connection" to affirm their bond with Wesley; to identify themselves; to specify ministerial status and conference membership; to refer to episcopal, conference, or agency governing authority; to recognize actions, measures, or processes that bond the denomination together; and in various ways to describe the Methodist institution, organization, or polity. Methodists have never given it precise theological or ecclesiological force. Its peculiar and specifically Wesleyan character may have prompted the MEC General Conference in 1816 (after the death of Bishop Francis Asbury) to substitute throughout Methodism's book of order, the *Discipline*, the more catholic word "church" for the Wesleyan terms "society" and "connection." That action undercut whatever motivation American Methodists might have had to add "connection" to the theological lexicon of the larger Christian church. Instead, Methodists have employed the term and its variants descriptively, speaking of "our connection," or "the connection" or "connectional agencies," or "Methodism as a connectional church."

That usage of the word as a form of organizational classification has been picked up in the press and in some surveys of American religion, where "connectional" is used to distinguish denominations with centralized authority, governance, and structure from those that lodge such prerogatives in the congregation. Property holding is one key discriminator. Does bishop, judicatory, or conference own church and parsonage, or does a local board of trustees or deacons?

Recently, United Methodism has been using the term more consistently, with ecclesiological as well as structural import. The current *Discipline* references connectionalism in some thirty-two paragraphs. The church is now creating similar connectional authority structures at conference and local levels. Increasingly, Methodism, United Methodism at least, recognizes itself as a connectional church, and in connectionalism it offers Christianity a distinctive theology of the church.

Connectional and Educational Phases | If Methodist connectionalism has changed and evolved over two and a half centuries, no less so have Methodist patterns of education. They fall into five distinct phases—popular, collegiate, bureaucratic, professional, and post-Christian. Each phase witnessed a new way of providing general and ministerial education. Each succeeding education system taxed Methodism's existing connectional pattern, yielded distinctive modes of governance and control, and thereby played a key part in creating a new denominational connectional pattern. As each educational system institutionalized itself, it altered the fabric of Methodist life, imposing itself on patterns already in place, adding ever-greater complexity and structure. Later phases did not so much supplant as augment their predecessors. Consequently contemporary United Methodism lives with a complex of educational systems and a layered connectional apparatus.

Established along with other Methodist colleges in the second phase of Methodist education, Emory has made distinctive contributions in the periods since, helping to shape Methodism's connectional patterns and to keep education at the heart of Methodist connectionalism. Emory's story shows that what it means for a college or university to be related to a religious institution has also evolved.

Emory's history also illustrates some constants in Methodist higher education. Methodism has sought consistently to educate its people and ministers together or in tandem. Its approach to education has been nonsectarian, community-oriented, and civic spirited. With notable exceptions, it has not cramped its institutions theologically, subjected faculty to dogmatic tests, or veered toward fundamentalist or other authoritarian controls. Unlike other denominations, Methodism founded universities and located its theological schools there, becoming thereby a university-founding denomination and leader in higher education. Perhaps uniquely, Emory has positioned itself to exercise leadership in understanding and structuring a fresh relation between a church and a complex research university appropriate for a highly pluralistic society.

The Inherited Popular Pattern

Methodism's educational imperative, the nonsectarian character and centrality of education in Methodism, and the style of Methodist education all derive from John Wesley. His educational and teaching experience at Oxford University and the school he founded at Kingswood come most immediately to mind.[4] Both figure in American Methodism's aspirations and eventually become idealized within its agenda. Georgia Methodists evoked such a commitment to Wesleyan educational ideals by naming the site for their new college Oxford. Lest anyone mistake their intent, they named main streets after John Wesley, John's lieutenant the Reverend John Fletcher of Madely, and the Reverends Adam Clarke and Richard Watson, important successors to Wesley. More immediately relevant, however, to the American movement that began spontaneously in several places in the 1760s and achieved formal ecclesial status in 1784, were provisions for education that John and Charles Wesley built into the fabric of Methodism.

Virtually the entire Wesleyan system functioned educationally and permitted John Wesley a teaching role. In open fields and small rooms, in addresses for rustic auditors and discourses aimed at the university trained, in texts suited to the meanest intelligence and in selections from the best of the tradition, in items for private study and in hymns for public praise, the Wesleys taught pervasively and systematically. John was Methodism's teacher, Charles its muse.

John's genius lay in creating a literature and media for instruction. His correspondence, tracts, sermons, magazine, societies, rules, libraries, Sunday schools, conferences, training of assistants and helpers—indeed the entire structure of Methodism—reveal a remarkable drive to educate people in the faith. From John, Methodists learned how to say what they believed; from Charles, how to sing it. Both Wesleys consistently taught.

The Wesleys, then, created popular literature but also social systems—classes, bands, societies—within which education in the faith could take place, all to the purpose of reforming the church and the nation. Similarly, Wesley taught his preachers, most of them not university educated. Through meetings with preachers in conference, he established standards, encouraged them in reading, and provided guidelines for belief and practice. These instructions, published as *The Large Minutes*, became the *Discipline* of early American Methodism. It functioned as the syllabus for education in ministry, just as the standards that Wesley provided for the American movement functioned as a curriculum. His *Explanatory Notes on the New Testament*, *Standard Sermons*, and modified version of the Anglican *Articles of Religion*, along with the *Discipline*, became the touchstones of American Methodism.[5]

> *The little college established in 1836 was webbed into Methodism's popular connectional educational enterprise at every level.*

Wesley exercised what theologians call the teaching office. He made Methodism into a giant classroom, and the activities and structures by which he taught connected Methodists to him and to one another. The educational was connectional; the connectional was educational. At the heart of both was Mr. Wesley.

The first two American bishops, Thomas Coke and Francis Asbury, endeavored with much more modest resources, under frontier conditions and with little success, to make comparable provision for American Methodists, to deliver nonsectarian instruction, and to connect the movement through education. They did succeed in founding a few Sunday schools and in overseeing modest publishing—of hymnbooks, *Minutes*, a *Discipline*, and guides to the spiritual life. More tellingly, under their guidance American Methodism failed twice to make a magazine go and twice to establish a college.[6]

After Asbury's death in 1816 and under the leadership of Joshua Soule, Nathan Bangs, and others, Methodists gradually implemented the Wesleyan system. They put in place connectional (national) magazines, newspapers (the *Christian Advocate*), Sunday school organization, missionary societies, reading expectations for preachers, and other templates for Wesley-like delivery of education. One can see the full flowering of that in the Georgia Annual Conference's implementation of various teaching resources. In the 1850s, for instance, the *Minutes* evidence an impressive educational infrastructure within which Georgia Methodists had situated their new college. The 1854 *Minutes* list the officers and recommendations of the Sunday School Society, the course of study for preachers, examining committees for ministerial education, visiting committees for Emory, five female colleges, the Collingswood Institute, and organization of the Georgia Tract Society. The 1856 *Minutes* add a "Report of the Committee on the Education of the Children of Preachers," a "Report of the Committee on Education," and a "Form of Statistical Report."[7]

This last report specified the conference's expectations from every charge in matters of communication, resources, or instruction—that is, education. Such mandates, replicated across the conferences of southern and northern Methodism, held the church together, made it genuinely connectional. The little college established in 1836 was webbed into Methodism's *popular* connectional educational enterprise at every level. The school, whose president and faculty were initially all preachers, conducted itself like a church, complete with revivals and commitment to the missionary cause. The faculty members were tied to the Georgia Annual Conference, and the school received annual inspections from the conference visiting committee. Unusual were Emory's national ties, symbolized in the residence of bishops James O. Andrew and William Capers in Oxford. Unusual were the number of Emory alumni (and, in the next century, alumnae) whom the church would elect to the episcopacy. Unusual were roles that Emory leaders would play in national Methodist politics.

Gradually, then, in the years after 1816, a maturing Methodism put in place the popular educational scheme featuring

- Robust Sunday schools with elaborate systems of leaflets, catechisms, and lesson plans.
- Local, conference, and national Sunday school, Bible, tract, missionary, and reform societies that delivered goods and services, raised money, and webbed the church in communication around its causes.
- Mandates for preachers to push these educational products (they actually received commissions) and put the Sunday schools and organizational systems in place.
- Reporting expectations that measured preachers' performance in relation to the educational enterprise as well as by conversions and membership.

Wesley would have envied what his modeling had produced. Methodism established colleges to cap off this extensive enterprise.

Collegiate Methodism

After the deaths of bishops Coke and Asbury, in 1814 and 1816, respectively, Methodism oversaw its interests and launched new ventures under the guidance of its conferences, the regional judicatories organized largely along state lines. They, rather than the bishops, carried through on Asbury and Coke's dream of Methodist schools. Under the mandate of General Conferences of 1820 and 1824, the annual conferences undertook to establish schools, literary institutions, and colleges (as well as Sunday schools and missionary societies).

Kentucky Methodists established Augusta College (1822), Virginia Methodists Randolph-Macon (1830), New Englanders Wesleyan University in Connecticut (1831), Georgia Methodists Emory College and Wesleyan College (for women) in 1836.[8] By the Civil War, Methodism had created or acquired some two hundred such institutions. Lacking adequate funding, staffing, and clientele, many did not survive. But some thirty-four founded before 1861 did.[9]

Why were these fragile institutions entrusted to conferences? In that period, conferences managed Methodism's enterprises. The single dominant bishop of Asbury's day had given way to a small cadre of bishops who worked together only partially successfully.[10] Alongside the bishops, the *Christian Advocates* (Methodism's widely circulated newspapers) channeled resources and focused the church's attention on connectional objectives. So did the Missionary Society. But even these depended on conferences to do the work. So conferences undertook missions, fund-raising, evangelism, and education. Methodism functioned, then, with a highly decentralized system, connected through a network of regular conferences—quarterly, annual, general—with annual conferences playing the key administrative roles.

The college served a vital function within this decentralized system. Primary was its role in educating the church's leadership, both lay and ministerial. To that end, Methodist conferences appointed their very best talent to the colleges, as presidents and faculty. From the colleges came much of the church's literary production. If faculty members or a president left, they often went to a national teaching office, as editor of the *Advocate* or as bishop. Emory contributed lavishly to the church's leadership and especially to the episcopacy, as the following presidents or deans were elected to the church's highest office: George Foster Pierce, Atticus Greene Haygood, Warren Akin Candler, James Edward Dickey, William Ragsdale Cannon, and Mack B. Stokes.

Emory-related individuals played exceptional parts in the division of the Methodist Episcopal Church. President Ignatius A. Few submitted the "scarlet letter" resolution to the 1840 General Conference prohibiting testimony in disciplinary cases of "colored persons" in states "where they are denied that privilege in trials of law."[11] Anger at that moral compromise, the Few amendment, fueled abolitionist sentiment at the following General Conference, in 1844, but Emory's symbolic and substantive roles there were even more dramatic. Central was Bishop James O. Andrew, whose slaveholding became the cause around which the division of 1844 occurred. Not surprisingly, other Emory people supported Andrew. President A. B. Longstreet delivered the key "Declaration of the Southern Delegates" and drafted the rules for the 1845 southern conference that organized the Methodist Episcopal Church, South (MECS). Future president George F. Pierce made important speeches in defense of Andrew. Longstreet, along with George and Lovick Pierce, represented Georgia at the first General Conference of the new MECS, in 1846. Both Pierces served in later General Conferences, as did former president Alexander Means.

So an Emory very much at home in little Oxford contributed out of its life to the Methodist connection, to national and then to southern Methodism. It did so because the Georgia Annual Conference entrusted Emory faculty and presidents with key roles that often led to the episcopacy. Georgia Methodists identified the college with national Methodism, naming it after the recently deceased and highly respected John Emory, who had presided over the conference. In addition to identifying the college with Wesley, Oxford, and British Methodism, the streets of the town bore the name of every MEC bishop elected through 1816, save for Robert Roberts, and added Joshua Soule for good measure. A walk around town took students back into Methodist history. Emory had a high view of its future place within Methodism.[12]

If Asbury-the-bishop incarnated Methodist connectionalism in the early years, the college president did so in the pre–Civil War decades, knitting the church together on education's behalf. During the period of the founding of these institutions especially, from the 1830s to the Civil War, conferences made the colleges a primary benevolence, appointing agents to solicit funds, and raising modest funds themselves. The conferences pressed for educational institutions out of their sense of Methodism's capacity to take part in the larger endeavor to shape a Protestant America. They also did so mindful that, without their own institutions, many of their own college-bound youth would find an educated home in another denomination. Presidents, founders, and benefactors sounded this "denomination" alarm loudly. Stephen Olin, president of Wesleyan University, previously president of Randolph-Macon and faculty member at the University of Georgia, asserted in 1844,

> No Christian denomination can safely trust to others for the training of its sons. . . . History has too clearly demonstrated that, without colleges of our own, few of our sons are likely to be educated, and that only a small portion of that few are likely to be retained in our communion.

Olin complained that, of the Methodists who had attended others' colleges, three-quarters had been "lost" to other denominations.[13]

On behalf of the next generation of lay leadership—female as well as male—Methodist conferences created colleges. In the men's colleges, the conferences trained their preachers. Emory, Wesleyan, Dickinson, and Randolph-Macon constituted the seminaries of their day. Of the students graduated from Wesleyan, for instance, in its first forty years, a third entered the Methodist ministry—three-quarters of the northern Methodist preachers who earned college degrees.[14] Northern Methodists by the 1870s could call Wesleyan "the mother of our denominational institutions" and "the crown and glory of our Church" and "mother of us all."[15]

Were these institutions sectarian? Scholars divide on this question, but Methodist schools, like those of most denominations, were state-chartered, imposed no religious tests, and welcomed students from various denominations (Protestant). Like Emory, they generally took seriously the imperative of religious and moral character formation, which they undertook through formal instruction, regular worship, revivals, and moral codes. Such formation was understood in relation to a classical, liberal arts curriculum and capped by moral philosophy. The Methodist, indeed the denominational, college was, according to one historian, "a curious hybrid"—a public, incorporated institution controlled by administration and trustees accountable in some fashion to a denomination.[16] Through the colleges, the denominations carried on the larger mission of reforming the nation, a common endeavor to instill Protestant commitment, republican ideals, and civic virtue in the nation's rising leaders.

Bureaucratized Support and Governance

Methodist aspirations for Christianizing the nation and the world increased dramatically as a consequence of the Civil War. Both the Methodist Episcopal Church (MEC) and Methodist Episcopal Church, South (MECS) had learned from their war efforts what mobilization on a national, connectional scale could do for denominational enterprise—for funding, coordination, quality control, uniformity, efficiency, and wise distribution of time and resources. Both churches recognized that enterprises previously overseen by conferences could be rendered more accountable and supported better on a denominational level. So in 1872 (1874 in the MECS),[17] Methodism transformed what had been voluntarily supported associations into national denominational agencies legally accountable to the General Conference.[18] In the South such organization focused on rebuilding a war-torn society. The northern church modeled what connectional organization might achieve programmatically.

The point of this organizational revolution and bureaucratization was to make Methodism a force, a world player, in missions, communications, and education. Better organization would give muscle to the church's effort to make disciples—by conversion, publishing, and instruction. Motivation for this nationalization came as much from the ground up as from the top down. Methodist schools, south and north, wanted national exposure and support. Methodist leadership craved for their institutions the prestige and clout enjoyed by counterpart universities. Out of such aspirations came efforts to make some Methodist colleges into genuine universities. So the southern church founded Vanderbilt.

Various developments illustrate the new national patterns of connectionalism. Within both northern and southern churches, the gearing up of the missionary enterprise dramatically evidenced what could be accomplished if businesslike principles of nationally centralized structure, training, fund-raising, communication, strategy, and deployment were applied to evangelization. The WCTU represents a comparable example of women's connectional enterprise. Northern Methodism, not saddled with the war's devastation and subsequent rebuilding, could bring corporate principles of promotion to education and did so by establishing the Board of Education to oversee and support higher education,[19] by mounting a campaign for an American (Methodist) university, and by creating the Freedmen's Aid and Southern Education Society (1866) to coordinate northern Methodist educational ventures in the South, especially for African Americans.[20]

No enterprise more visibly exhibits national efforts for education than those channeled into southern African American communities through the MEC's Freedmen's Aid and Southern Education Society. With monies raised nationally and an army of educator-missionaries, Freedmen's Aid created over the next quarter-century a "thoroughly unified system of schools, . . . including professional, classical, academic, and industrial schools."[21] By 1892 it was distributing funds to and overseeing the educational welfare of Bennett College, Central Tennessee College, Claflin University, Clark University, Gammon Theological Seminary, George R. Smith College, Little Rock University, Morgan College, New Orleans University, Philander Smith College, Rust University, Samuel Huston College, U. S. Grant University, and Wiley University.

Centralized, standardized, efficient, and purposive, this national system modeled post–Civil War Methodist connectionalism, channeling the church's missionary aspirations, its commitment to education, its print and publishing strengths, its effective fund-raising.

The organizational genius displayed in Freedmen's Aid expressed itself in all educational ventures. Methodists transformed the Sunday school from a recommended but local initiative into a national enterprise, with a uniform lesson plan, graded instruction and literature to suit age levels, teacher academies topped off with Chautauquas, and building designs to accommodate congregations organized for education. The Akron Plan educational complex, the Family Life Center of its day, gave local architectural expression to Methodism's educational connectionalism.

No enterprise more visibly exhibits national efforts for education than those channeled into southern African American communities through the MEC's Freedmen's Aid and Southern Education Society.

Southern Methodism lagged in centralizing its enterprises, but Emory contributed to the first order of postwar business, rebuilding church and society. Georgia Methodists routinely elected Emory presidents to the MECS General Conference. From the church's beginning in the 1844 division to reunification in 1939, ten of the twelve men who served as president of Emory from in those years served as delegates to General Conferences, often multiple times (the exceptions were James R. Thomas and Luther M. Smith).

Southern Methodism's future commitment to a new day was well signaled in Emory President Atticus Haygood's courageous 1880 vision of a New South.[22] The founding of Vanderbilt as a central university for the MECS in the 1870s and of the Scarritt Bible and Training School (Kansas City) in 1892 as a comparable institution for deaconesses indicate southern appreciation for the importance of connectional (or national) education institutions. Nothing, however, illustrates that commitment to connectional educational policy more than the establishment of Emory University (1915) and Southern Methodist University as the two connectional universities, when the MECS lost Vanderbilt.

As they created these new research universities, southern and northern Methodists put religion at their very heart, symbolizing that commitment architecturally with a chapel and programmatically with a theology school. At Emory the Durham Chapel within the Theology Building served school, university, and community, eventually yielding Glenn Memorial. Methodism envisioned the university as *the* place to educate its ministry. Emory, Boston, Drew, Duke, and Southern Methodist universities all had divinity schools or seminaries as a constitutive part. Methodists also located separately chartered theological schools adjacent to major universities (typically then denominationally related)—Garrett (Northwestern), Iliff (Denver), Claremont (University of Southern California), Gammon (Atlanta), and Wesley (American). Methodism in its university-founding phase made a statement about education as formational of the national connection.

Much of this work was animated by a vision that through education Methodism could shape a Christian America. Denominational structures—the University Senate, the Board of Education (now Board of Higher Education and Ministry), the Board of Global Ministries, and NASCUMC (The National Association of Schools and Colleges of the United Methodist Church)—effectively served the Methodist interest in higher education.[23] The research universities, Emory included, charted their own path toward national prominence.

A Professional Stage

The research university came to dominance only gradually and through a variety of social forces. Paramount were ideals of and passion for knowledge and the techniques, pedagogies, and media of specialized research—experimentation, seminars, journals, and the like. Noteworthy as well were the huge investments, much of it inspired by the Cold War, that the federal government made in technology, science, and medicine; creation of funding agencies; increased regulatory intrusion of government; growing preference for specialized knowledge; the erosion of the liberal arts ideal; loss of an integrative curricular principle; increased pressure to market education and to produce career-ready graduates; recognition of the pluralism of American society in admissions policies; and new academic fields.

Professionalism reinforced these patterns of disaggregation. A long trend in American life, professionalism served particularly well in the late twentieth century university to provide coherence and identity amid pluralism, complexity, and specialization. It did so *not* by uniting those within the university into common perspective and endeavor, but by joining specialists from across the country, indeed across the globe, into professional organizations. In translocal professional societies—through meetings, journals, credentialing, and research—administrators and members of departments or specialists within departments found community and identity.[24] Professionalism became the new mode of connection, of kinship within universities, as in American society generally. Such community, in uniting academics by guild globally, fragmented the university locally.

Professionalism also fragmented the denominational identity of the university, in at least two ways. First and most clearly, professionalism privileged within the university the values and agendas of the professions and the disciplines.[25] Paramount for each field was its own methodology, its procedures of inquiry, its standards for truth. Professionalism fragmented faculties and curricula into specialized fiefdoms. The liberal arts ideal that once unified higher education, and within which religious study had once been central, gave way amid the plethora of new fields, interdisciplinary programs, special degrees, and preprofessional emphases.

Religion, too, became but one guild among many. Professionalized religion, like everything else, finds its place in niches—in religious studies, divinity schools, prayer groups, chaplaincies, volunteer networks, and parachurch organizations. In this second way professionalism eroded the place of a shared denominational identity within the university. Religious life itself has been professionalized and thereby segmented into separate roles or offices that do not always cooperate. Consequently there is often no overarching religious presence or policy on campus.

In an earlier day, the university or college president would have been an ordained minister, as were Emory presidents until 1920. He (and it was a "he") presided over the religious life as over the institution as a whole, performing the role of chaplain and counselor, preaching regularly, and probably teaching. He led revivals, advised those headed into ministry, conferred with bishops, toured conferences on the school's behalf, raised money from Methodists, was elected to General Conference, and helped to shape denominational educational policy. He hired faculty, some of whom would themselves be ordained, and many of whom would be Methodists. He married graduates, buried trustees, and in general represented Methodism. And when he needed assistance, he turned to faculty who played these roles consummately and readily themselves.

Today in the research university, Methodism has no such embodied presence and unified leadership. Denominational affiliation falls to those who work interstitially—the theology dean, chaplains, denominational executives, the president, some board members. A portion of the latter would be expected to be United Methodist and include some bishops, as Emory's board illustrates. In selection of a president, Methodist board members seek someone capable of leading the institution who at least understands and affirms the school's denominational affiliation. Thereafter the president's attention and cooperation are sought by denominational and conference officials only occasionally. The president networks primarily not with the church but with other presidents, board members, prospective donors, and business and governmental leaders.

Religious ethos and community are not the president's responsibility, nor the faculty's. Instead, those roles belong to the chaplain and religious life professionals, who care for students emotionally and spiritually, counsel, intercede, refer, conduct worship. They may run volunteer programs and share functions with student life professionals. Like student life personnel generally, chaplains have professional networks and separate confessional relations. Chaplains labor on the margins of university life, in the realm of the extracurricular. No longer privileged with a religious emphasis week, they live in the clash of calendars, of sacred times, of religious identities. In a Balkanized university, relations between Serbia and Kosovo belong to them. To them falls campus peacekeeping, a role of immense importance, especially after September 11. So chaplains and campus ministers find common cause with one another and increasingly take an ecumenical or interreligious direction, well evidenced in the model Emory programs led by Susan Henry-Crowe.

> *Emory can be United Methodist without for a moment qualifying its pride in the Rabbi Donald A. Tam Institute for Jewish Studies, in its powerful Catholic constituency, in its growing Islamic and Buddhist studies programs.*

Denominational affiliation is strongest and most coherent in the divinity or theology school. But even there the patterns of professionalization and pluralism pertain. Faculty have strong orientation to their fields and must work hard to build coherence into the curriculum. Some have additional professional identity as clergy; others do not. Many divide their attention between professional and graduate studies. Divinity faculty and schools are pulled in various directions—toward disciplinary guilds, toward the denomination, toward religious studies, toward other professional schools in the university. So within the theology school, some faculty and administrators— the dean, admissions director, development officer, and field educators— take special care for Methodist connections.

The professionalism that fragments the university's capacity to speak clearly and univocally to the church has its denominational counterpart. Methodist connectionalism takes professional form. The denomination holds itself together and does its work through professional and quasiprofessional networks (elders, deacons, business administrators, Christian educators, church musicians, chaplains, youth ministers, conference directors). But what holds the church together also divides it. Each of these groups or professions wires together its own. Ideally, these separate wires would twist together into cable, the whole stronger than the parts. More typically, however, these separate wires jumble, cross, wear, crimp, and short one another.[26]

A Methodism so professionally united and fragmented relates to universities and to the world in chaotic fashion, with many faces and agendas. Each party speaks for the church, oblivious to the partiality of its message and the cacophony to which it contributes.

Professionalism, then, greatly complicates the university's relation to the church. It does so because the university fragments internally along professional, disciplinary, role, and group lines, allowing no interest—religion included—a privileged unitive place. It does so because religious life within the university fragments along professional, disciplinary, confessional, and group lines, offering no coherent religious witness. It does so because the denomination fragments along professional, ideological, ethnic, and role lines, presenting no single face to the school.

It should come as no surprise, then, that interpreters have focused on religion in higher education and the church-related college as questions, problems, and challenges. What remains of church relationship, they ask? In denominational identity? In religious ethos? In curricular coherence? In faith community? In leadership sensitive to the church? In the shaping of persons for church professions?[27]

An Emergent Post-Christian Stage

The once-cozy connection between college chapel, Emory, surrounding Methodist community, annual conference, and denomination has fractured and fragmented. Can the denomination and the university find a new basis for relating, a new way of connecting—a direction that respects the concerns of the church and the special genius, the immense diversity, and the incredible complexity of the research university? And how might that connection be achieved? Who will be the agents on the church's side? What texture, program, or dimension of university life will give expression to that church relation? Will it be something familiar or something new that the university generates? Where might leadership for the new directions be found?

Emory shows signs of being best equipped and positioned to forge a new relation of church and university, to chart the next stage of church relations, to find coherence amid the diversity and complexity of research and instruction. First, Emory possesses leaders on all levels—among trustees, throughout the administration, in the schools, in the Religion Department, across the faculty, among chaplains, at Candler, in Oxford—sensitive to and appreciative of the Methodist connection. Second, it enjoys relatively positive relations with United Methodism, though at times it has to remind the church of its own historic commitments to open, inclusive, nonsectarian education. Third, it boasts, across the University, hundreds of faculty in diverse departments with research interests in religious topics. Many of these research agendas take their own course, but, fourth, some are institutionalized and given programmatic and curricular expression through the Center on Myth and Ritual in American Life, at Candler, in the Religion Department, in the Pew Center for the Interdisciplinary Study of Religion, and in the Center for the Study of Law and Religion.

Fifth, various multidisciplinary, multischool centers and special projects pursue related agendas in ethics, ritual, advocacy, outreach, public health, and global and political policy. Sixth, the diverse, vibrant religious communities at Emory cooperate through common programming and collaborative leadership and through official chaplaincies, which draw support from the campus and interpret the campus to wider religious publics. Seventh, the chaplaincies support and draw support from faculty and students in the top-flight graduate, professional, and undergraduate programs. Eighth, other bonds grow through shared research in religion, spirituality, and healing and through joint degree programs between Candler and other professional schools. Ninth, the University enjoys leadership on religious policy and practice from individuals, groups, and schools in external forums, on public platforms, in the media, and within foundations.

Such patterns suggest that Emory has the capacity to weave the various strands that constitute its many programs, disciplines, and concerns into some new connective fabric. It will never have the small compass of a cable (as in Bishop Andrew's day). For such a tight weave, Emory's religious life and religious studies, indeed the interests of the research university, remain too diverse and dynamic. But some loose weave, some netting, can hold together the university's religious impulses *and* can be extended to United Methodism and other communities. The church, as well, seeks postprofessional connective fabric, something that would hold it together and connect its endeavors into common purpose. The church may look to Emory for this new fabric, this new connective style. In one way or another, university and church can bind the cords of their respective and diverse lives. Emory, out of the vibrancy and richness of its religious studies and activities, can fashion a new Methodist connection, and it can refashion this new Methodist identity without giving up other Emory descriptors.

Emory can be United Methodist without for a moment qualifying its pride in the Rabbi Donald A. Tam Institute for Jewish Studies, in its powerful Catholic constituency, in its growing Islamic and Buddhist studies programs. Nor by enhancing Methodist relations does Emory compromise its Coca-Cola heritage, its partnerships with the Centers for Disease Control and Prevention, its national prominence as a health-care center, its federal contracts, its role as a major Georgia employer, its other corporate and various foundation connections, its platform for the arts, its commitment to ethical animal research.

Secure in Methodism's place within its immense diversity and complexity, Emory can help the church—and religious communities generally—learn what it means to function in a world where confessions and ideologies jostle one another. Emory can extend the loose weave of its intellectual life so that United Methodism, and Roman Catholicism, Judaism, Islam, and Buddhism can recognize and claim the loose weave that will provide civility and coherence in interaction and within.

CHAPTER 36

The steeple of Cannon Chapel

STUDYING RELIGION AT EMORY
Continuing Tradition, New Directions
— PAUL B. COURTRIGHT —

As an educational institution, Emory has engaged in a long and admirable tradition of the scholarly study of religion, as well as in the discipline of training ministers. Paul Courtright observes in his essay, however, that the study of religion at Emory has seen dramatic growth in new directions over the past several decades. Since 1988–89, the Religion Department has broadened its perspectives beyond Christianity to other major world religions, beyond the study of religious texts to ethnographic study, and beyond the categorization of particular traditions to a wider understanding of religion as a common human experience. In addition to this growth within the department itself, strong partnerships with Candler School of Theology, the law school, the American Academy of Religion, and the Tam Jewish Studies Institute, along with an innovative scholarship exchange program with Tibetan institutions, have contributed to the status Emory now holds as a national leader in the field of religion.

THE STUDY OF religion at Emory is as old as Emory itself. As a college formed in the nineteenth-century American landscape, Emory placed the study of the Bible, theology, and Christian thought and ethics at the core of its pedagogical mission. When the Atlanta campus and the Candler School of Theology were established in 1915, Emory extended its reach into the study of religion at the professional level in preparing young adults for ministry and leadership in the Methodist tradition.

Over the past half-century, and with dramatic acceleration over the past two decades, the study of religion at Emory has expanded in a number of directions that have deepened its roots in the Christian tradition and ventured into new areas. During the past twenty years I have been privileged to be one of many at Emory who have witnessed this process and participated in it. What follows here are my own recollections of my two decades in the flow of this remarkable process.

Emory College and the Department of Religion | Like most of its peers in American colleges and universities, Emory College's undergraduate Department of Religion for most of its existence offered courses mainly in the area of Christian studies: Bible, Christian thought, and ethics, with only general survey courses in world religions. Many Emory students who majored in religion through much of the twentieth century went on to careers in a variety of professions, especially ministry and law.

In 1954 the faculties of the Department of Religion and the School of Theology jointly launched a PhD program in the academic study of religion under the umbrella of the Graduate School, a program now known as the Graduate Division of Religion. For more than three decades the GDR curriculum ran largely parallel to the curricula of both the School of Theology and the Department of Religion, focusing on biblical studies, theology, ethics, and pastoral studies. Along with other universities like Harvard, Yale, Princeton, Duke, Vanderbilt, and the University of Chicago, Emory sent its graduates into teaching and research professions in colleges, universities, and seminaries around the country.

As in so many areas at Emory, the dramatic increase in the University's resources arising from the Woodruff gift in 1979 made possible more ambitious planning in the study of religion. In the 1980s, Emory College expanded considerably, establishing new departments and programs, and revisioning and expanding existing ones. President James T. Laney laid down a vision for Emory to grow from a good regional university to an internationally distinguished research and teaching institution. During this same time, the city of Atlanta was undergoing its own transformation from a "southern" city to an international center for commerce, transportation, and culture.

In the fall of 1988 the dean of Emory College, David Minter, announced that the Department of Religion was looking for a new chairperson. In addition, he committed to adding four new faculty positions to the department, with the expectation that the department would expand its curricular reach into new areas. I was most fortunate to be invited to fill the post of chairperson, and when I arrived on campus in the summer of 1989 I took up the challenge of rethinking the department's mission and recruiting new colleagues.

After I settled into my office on the third floor of the well-worn Physics Building (since renovated into the sparkling Callaway Center) I called a meeting of the faculty. There were ten of us around the table at that first meeting. As I looked around I felt lucky to be among them—all fine scholars and teachers, well recognized in their fields: biblical studies, theology, philosophy of religion, Judaic Studies, comparative religion—the core areas of most religion departments around the country at that time. There were also newer areas of inquiry: African American religion and feminist studies in religion. As we sat there together, imagining what a nearly 50 percent increase in our faculty might look like, we felt like we had just won the lottery. It was our turn to enter into the expansion that we had seen other departments at Emory undertake.

I began the meeting with a question: "Who's not here?" It was not a question about whether any one current faculty member was absent from the meeting; everyone in fact *was* there. But who was not there *yet*? What areas of inquiry within the study of religion did we need to add that would complement and extend what we could offer our students, colleagues in other parts of the university, and ourselves? What sort of vision of whom we wanted to become could we articulate together that would guide our recruiting of new colleagues over the next several years?

What emerged over many meetings during that first year, supplemented by our own research into the state of the academic study of religion, consulting with colleagues in other universities, and calling on colleagues from many fields within Emory, were a few principles that have guided the remarkable expansion of the department over the past two decades.

First, we agreed that we needed to have enough expertise in several religious traditions to draw from in thinking about religion as a category of human meaning and formation across the world. The department already had considerable strength in Christian tradition; what it needed was additional focus on other religions. We concluded it would be wiser to attend to a few religions in greater depth, rather than to spread ourselves thinly across all the major (and some minor) religions. We decided to go against the trends of many departments around the country of having one colleague in each of many religions, and we planned instead to build the kind of depth that comes from two or three colleagues working together on a particular religion. We wanted each new colleague to have conversation partners either within the department or close by in cognate fields (for instance, history or Middle Eastern studies). We wanted to develop courses taught by two faculty members, each with expertise in a different tradition, teaching together in introductory courses that would make it possible for our students to engage in comparative study at the highest level. Hence, we have built depth in Judaism, Islam, Hinduism, and Buddhism in addition to Christianity.

A second response we made to the "who's not here?" question grew out of our recognition that we all studied texts: sacred texts, philosophical texts, and historical texts. We realized that we needed someone at the table whose research and approach to understanding religion came from face-to-face engagements with oral traditions, someone who studied what people do when they are "being religious" in oral and performative settings, through storytelling, dance, song, and ritual. The next year (1990), we advertised for a position in the ethnographic study of religion. We were less concerned about which religion would show up than about how someone might approach her or his subject in an oral context. We expected that such a colleague would also offer natural connections to disciplines such as anthropology, ritual studies, and dance.

As it turned out, the person we brought on board, Joyce Burkhalter Flueckiger, focuses her research in India, supplementing my own study of the religion in India, giving us two "India people." Joyce grew up in India, the daughter of Mennonite missionaries, and earned her doctorate at the University of Wisconsin in South Asian languages and literature. Her research now focuses on performance studies and anthropology of religion, with a special interest in gender. What we have seen over the years has been a multiplier effect: we are all more aware of the limits and opportunities that texts extend, because there is someone at the table paying attention to religion that does not come in texts.

The third principle that guided our era of expansion was the importance of looking at religion outside the boundaries of the category of any particular tradition or religion. For example, we were eager to bring on board a colleague who looked at the general phenomena of religion, apart from any particular tradition, in the context of a broad set of cultural categories such as arts, politics, and media, in ways that called our attention to areas where religion moves beyond the boundaries of its own institutions, doctrines, and practices. This process led to Gary Laderman, who studies religion and American public culture. With a doctorate in religious studies from the University of California-Santa Barbara, Gary has published books on the cultural history of death and burial in America, celebrity worship, and science and religion.

Where Courageous Inquiry Leads: *The Emerging Life of Emory University*

With each new faculty member taking her or his seat at the table, our conversation about the study of religion evolved, and our curriculum of courses, majors, and joint majors with other departments reflected our shared vision. At the end of my six years as chair, in 1996, our department had successfully launched and nourished what has become an ongoing conversation over additional years of expansion within the department and new links to other parts of the University under the very able leadership of successive chairs.

Emory's Department of Religion has now emerged as one of the largest in the country. Including some colleagues in cognate departments, Emory College has at least three faculty members studying each of the major religions of the world.

Expanding Emory's Traditions in the Study of Religion | While the teaching of undergraduates in Emory College is the core project of the department, one-fourth of the faculty's course offerings are in the Graduate Division of Religion, Emory's PhD program in the academic study of religion. During the years our department was rethinking its own project we also participated in rethinking the graduate program with our colleagues in the Candler School of Theology. Consequently the doctoral program expanded its reach into studies in Jewish, Hindu, Islamic, and Buddhist traditions. Along the way new synergies emerged in comparative studies. Increasingly, doctoral candidates wrote dissertations in comparative theology and studies in religious practices that added new resonances to long-standing emphases in theology, ethics, and the study of religious communities.

During the 1990s expansion took place in many related areas across the University simultaneously. The law school, for instance, established a research institute in the study of law and religion under the direction of John Witte, the Jonas Robitscher Professor of Law. The Law and Religion Program supports research seminars, lectures, and publications in the comparative study of law, especially Christian, Islamic, and Jewish traditions and their relation to areas of contemporary life, such as family, marriage, sexuality, and childhood. The Center for the Interdisciplinary Study of Law and Religion has evolved into a local and international focal point where the study of religion and the study of law converge.

Another major development in the study of religion during this decade was the University's affiliation with the American Academy of Religion (AAR), the largest professional association of academics in the study of religion at colleges and universities in North America. Under the directorship of Barbara DeConcini, who also held an appointment in the Department of Religion, the AAR expanded dramatically in size and mission. Within a few years it put down its organizational roots with the construction of the Luce Center, adjacent to the Miller-Ward Alumni House, on Houston Mill Road. With a membership of nearly ten thousand scholars, the AAR sponsors an annual national conference and a number of regional conferences, conducts research on the study of religion in American higher education, provides services for young scholars seeking jobs and departments searching for new colleagues, and publishes the *Journal of the American Academy of Religion* along with a number of other publication series in collaboration with Oxford University Press. The presence of the AAR and the Society of Biblical Literature in the same building has created a widespread sense that Emory is at the center of what is going on nationally, and increasingly internationally, in the study of religion.

Another vital area that has emerged powerfully during the last decade has been Emory's Jewish Studies Program. Drawing upon faculty in the Department of Religion and several other departments, the Tam Institute for Jewish Studies coordinates undergraduate and graduate instruction, sponsors lectures and symposia, and has expanded considerably the University's library resources in print and electronic media.

The most recent addition to Emory's initiatives in the study of religion is the Emory-Tibet Partnership. Initiated in 1998 with the support of the Dalai Lama and the Institute of Buddhist Dialectics in Dharamsala, India, and the Drepung Loseling Monastery in Atlanta, the partnership has been instrumental in strengthening curricular offerings at undergraduate and graduate levels in the study of Tibetan language, religion, and culture. The Dalai Lama has personally visited Emory three times during this period, accepting appointment in 2007 as Presidential Distinguished Professor, and a number of scholar-monks have come from India to teach seminars.

The Carlos Museum and the Schatten Gallery have sponsored major exhibitions of Tibetan art and photography. The Center for International Programs Abroad sponsors both a semester study program and a summer program in Dharamsala for Emory undergraduates and students from other universities, in collaboration with the Institute for Buddhist Dialectics, near the residence of His Holiness. Additional faculty appointments and vigorous expansion of library collections have placed Emory as an internationally recognized center for the study of Tibetan religion, philosophy and culture. New research initiatives are under way among colleagues in psychiatry and religion on the effectiveness of meditation in preventing or mitigating the effect of depression or emotional stress on the body.

As these academic areas for the study of religion have evolved, the Office of the Dean of the Chapel and Religious Life has expanded its own mission by embracing and nurturing the religious diversity of Emory students. This office supports some thirty different student religious organizations representing many traditions. The Religious Life Office also sponsors the Journeys Program (originally called "Journeys of Reconciliation"), which enables students to travel to other countries and regions within the United States to engage with groups involved in the work of conflict resolution through community development, health care, and culture. These two-week journeys, taken at the end of the spring semester to places as diverse as Bosnia, Cuba, South Africa, and Appalachia, have proven to be life changing for many of the participants.

Consolidations and Futures | The study of religion at Emory today is a major growth industry. Building on its formative focus on the study of Christianity and Christian ministry, Emory has nourished the study of religion in a variety of locations: undergraduate and graduate instruction, research institutes, and academic support of diverse religious communities. At the same time, it has supported the interconnections among multiple disciplines in the study of religion. Emory has encouraged scholars to view the complex interplay between the study of religion and the practice of religion itself as a focus of inquiry and appreciation. Along with Emory's distinctive strengths in medicine and health care, law, business, and the arts and sciences, the study of religion broadly defined today takes its place as one of Emory's signature emphases.

Emory may now be moving into a phase of consolidation of all the expansions it has undertaken over the past two decades. As each location around the campus for the study of religion pursues its particular goals, the challenge of effective coordination and mutual support remains part of the ongoing work. No one at Emory needs to be persuaded that religion matters. Religion is a powerful and important part of the global landscape. It has never been more urgent to understand and appreciate the roles religion plays in our global cultures and politics. Emory harbors a sense of collective ownership of the study of religion, an ownership that embraces the differences between traditions and the importance of inquiring into areas of resemblance as well. The roots for the study of religion at Emory are deeply planted and well watered. What lies ahead as these various initiatives mature is further collaboration and collegial networking, both within Emory and around the world. In the study of religion, Emory has become an important and respected center of a global network. Much has been built over the past decade; there is plenty more to be accomplished.

CHAPTER 37

Arri Eisen demonstrates lab techniques for Tibetan monks in Dharamsala, India.

UNITING "THE PAIR SO LONG DISJOINED"
Science and Religion at Emory
— ARRI EISEN —

As a university with long-standing strengths in the sciences and religion, Emory has long fostered the growing interrelationship between the two.[1] Arri Eisen, senior lecturer in biology, describes the emergent voices at Emory in this interdisciplinary conversation and details achievements in the arenas of faith, health, and healing. Emory has played a significant role on the global stage in this dialogue, as evidenced by the collaboration between the University and Tibetan Buddhists to develop a five-year science curriculum for Tibetan monastics in exile.

I deeply appreciate that Emory University has accepted my invitation, and has made a commitment to fully collaborate with the Library of Tibetan Works and Archives to develop and implement a comprehensive and sustainable science education program for Tibetan monastic institutions. I have long believed in and advocated a dialogue and cross-fertilization between science and spirituality, as both are essential for enriching human life and alleviating suffering on both individual and global levels. The Emory-Tibet Science Initiative has a unique opportunity to fulfill this need, and thus make a contribution not only to the Emory and Tibetan communities but to the world at large, by expanding the horizons of human knowledge and wisdom.
—His Holiness the Dalai Lama

Scene I | On January 7, 2008, the Dalai Lama, seated in a throne at the top of a high stairway of a new prayer hall, is addressing more than fifteen thousand Tibetan Buddhist monks and nuns at the Drepung Loseling Monastery, near Mundgod, in southern India. Pageantry and a rich sense of anticipation are in the air among the monastics, draped in saffron and maroon, sitting outdoors in their traditional cross-legged position, attention focused on their revered leader. His Holiness stands as Emory dignitaries officially present him with *A Handbook of Science*. The handbook—in both English and Tibetan—is the synthesis of more than two years of work by Emory scientists to develop a comprehensive modern science curriculum for all Tibetan monastics in exile.

The Dalai Lama graciously accepts the gift and makes the official announcement of the Emory-Tibet Science Initiative. Emory physicists, biologists, neuroscientists, and physicians have worked for two years to develop an intensive course in cosmology, life sciences, math, Western philosophy, and neuroscience. The ambitious goal is to work with one hundred monks and nuns each year for five years, as they come from the many Tibetan monasteries in India to gather in Dharamsala, India, home of the Tibetan government in exile. Through these first learners, the aim is to reach all monks and nuns with a rigorous curriculum in modern science that will become part of their regular learning cycle.

The unveiling of the initiative in 2008 marks both a culmination and a new beginning, and further establishes Emory as an international center for engagement at the nexus of science and religion.

Scene II | In April 2009, distinguished interdisciplinary scholars from around the world gather at the Emory Conference Center Hotel at the invitation of the Ford Foundation. Scott Atran, whose intellectual breadth spans anthropology, psychology, and evolution, is here. His work explores issues ranging from Middle East terrorism to the natural history of Mayans, and he holds positions in group dynamics, anthropology, psychology, and public policy at the University of Michigan and the Centre National de la Recherche Scientifique in Paris.

Atran is joined by Lori Alvord, associate dean for student and minority affairs at Dartmouth Medical School and the first woman Navajo surgeon; her experiences of being raised on a reservation amid traditional medicine and then trained as a Western physician are notably recounted in *The Scalpel and the Silver Bear* (Random House, 2000). She is at Emory for the second time. Edward Larson, Pepperdine Professor of Law and Pulitzer Prize winner for his 1998 book on the Scopes trial, is also here. There is Andrew Lustig, from Davidson College and author of numerous books in bioethics, theological ethics, and health-care policy, including, most recently, *Altering Nature: Religion, Biotechnology, and Public Policy* (Springer, 2008).

The Ford Foundation has asked Emory—specifically Gary Laderman, chair of the Religion Department in Emory College—to host this special roundtable of leading thinkers in identifying key issues in science and religion for the twenty-first century. The foundation's inviting the

University and Emory's own scholars—including, among others, Laderman; David Lynn, chair of chemistry; Robert McCauley, philosopher and director of the Center for Mind, Brain, and Culture—to host and lead this conversation is again a symbolic landmark of the University's role in science and religion teaching and research.

Scene III | The audience grows hushed as Sherwin Nuland grows reflective. Nuland, the author of the National Book Award–winning *How We Die: Reflections on Life's Final Chapter* (Vintage, 1995), has come to Emory as part of a 2006 project that includes an undergraduate seminar on mind, medicine, and healing. Students in the course have hosted three renowned surgeon/writers working at the borders of mind, belief, and medicine—Nuland, Lori Alvord, and Richard Selzer (a former Yale surgeon whose writings on medicine and the spirit have gained a wide audience). In a two-day public symposium, the students have presented their research projects from the course and the three surgeons have given talks. This is Nuland's.

After a few jokes and insightful comments on what he sees as humans' natural tendency toward using superstition and religion to explain the unexplained, the audience quiets as Nuland tells a story.

Unbeknown to the organizers of the conference, Nuland and Selzer have known each other for more than fifty years. They were part of the same surgery residency at Yale, decades ago, and were the only two left standing at the end of the experience; in the meantime they had become close friends. Now, Nuland, giving a talk on science and religion, relates a story he says he believes even Selzer, sitting next to him, has never heard.

Years before, when both were practicing at the same hospital, Nuland heard that Selzer was suddenly taken mysteriously and drastically ill. Nuland hadn't seen his friend in some months and was shocked to discover this. He went to visit Selzer in intensive care, where he lay unrecognizably swollen and near death from an ailment his doctors could not identify. Selzer was unconscious and unaware of the presence of his friend. Nuland, overcome with shock and disbelief, leaned down and kissed his dying friend on the cheek.

Then, Nuland continues to tell a rapt audience, he did something he had not done in many years—having long since given up the Judaism in which he was raised. Nuland went to synagogue and prayed for his friend, Richard Selzer.

A week later, Nuland heard that Selzer was out of ICU, and nearly completely recovered.

Scene IV | In a 2008 paper published in the well-respected science journal *Psychoneuroendocrinology*, Emory psychiatrist Charles Raison and Emory senior lecturer in religion Lobsang Tenzin Negi, a Tibetan and former Buddhist monk, demonstrate that compassion meditation positively affects stress levels and the immune system. The results are striking. Subjects who meditate as little as ten minutes a day have decreased stress levels and inflammation/immune response as measured at the performance level and at the molecular level.

This research linking mind and body, connecting what originated as a Buddhist meditation technique with modern scientific molecular measurement, is at the cutting edge of the East/West collaboration. The work is supported by the Emory Strategic Initiatives, an integrated collection of transdisciplinary themes identified out of a University-wide self-evaluation. Several of the initiatives engage science and religion, including the Religion and Health Initiative and the Emory Collaborative in Contemplative Studies, which helped support the meditation study.

What are the backstories behind these scenes and Emory's emergence as an intellectual center in science and religion, mind and body, religion and health?

Emory has long had all the pieces in place for such a development: strength in the basic and medical sciences (with departments and programs in biology, chemistry, physics, and neurobehavioral biology, and schools of medicine, nursing, and public health) along with strength in the humanities and social sciences (with departments in anthropology, psychology, and religion, and schools of theology and law). But pieces do not necessarily a whole make, and, as is typical of any history, the real story lies in the people behind the scenes.

The history of science and religion in the West goes back at least to the Enlightenment, Descartes, and Francis Bacon, and the emergence of science as we know it. But other than writing about and wrestling with the controversies between the two worldviews, it is telling that until the last few decades, relatively little teaching and research has been done into how science and religion can work together, into understanding the underpinnings and positive overlap between the two. The reasons behind this are beyond the scope of this chapter, but clearly have to do with the historical moment in which we now live. Emory has a rich and long history in science and religion separately, an emerging and strong history in the two together, and now a clear opportunity to lead the conversation integrating the two into the future.

Foundation Builders | The foundation of Emory's leadership in science and religion can be viewed, for simplicity, through three lenses: faith, health, and healing; science and religion in dialogue; and, call it a new synthesis, a third lens that integrates the first two for a greater understanding of the human condition. The three share many elements but allow a convenient structure through which to examine Emory's history in these areas.

Faith, Health, Healing
Gary Gunderson is a national leader at the interface of public health and faith. He leads the Interfaith Health Program (IHP), which was launched at the Carter Center (now part of Emory) in 1992 and then moved to the Rollins School of Public Health at Emory. Through his well-known books—including *Leading Causes of Life* (Methodist LeBonheur Healthcare, 2007) and *Boundary Leaders* (Augsburg Fortress, 2004)—and extensive coalition-building across local and government agencies, Gunderson and the IHP have effected positive health change through partnership with religious institutions. IHP has worked with the Centers for Disease Control and Prevention and developed the Institute for Public Health and Faith Collaborations, which has trained many teams of leaders from across the United States.

At the international level, Gunderson and the IHP, together with colleagues at the universities of Cape Town, Kwazulu Natal, and Witswatersrand, led the World Health Organization in mapping religion and health connections in Africa. Gunderson, now also working as a leader of Methodist LeBonheur Healthcare in Memphis, Tennessee, envisions the collaboration of health care and religious institutions making for healthier communities overall.

In 2002 the momentum generated by IHP and others working from Emory outward to the local, national, and international communities was gathered to enrich the scholarship inside the University through a combination faculty seminar/undergraduate course/public symposium. This project also harnessed momentum of two previous public symposia featuring diverse Emory scholars focusing on science and religion themes. These symposia were initiated by myself and Gary Laderman, now chair of religion in the Emory College of Arts and Sciences. The first symposium was "Science and Religion: Perspectives on Suffering and Healing," and the second "Science and Religion: Perspectives on Death and Prolonging Life." Like most work at the interface of science and religion, the symposia gathered participants and knowledge from strong interdisciplinary scholars—from the College, the Center for Ethics, the law school, and the nursing school, among others—to address diverse public audiences.

Growing from these symposia, the new project on health and spirituality also involved resources and scholars from many disciplines. The Center for Theology and the Natural Sciences at Berkeley and Emory's own Center for the Study of Health, Culture, and Society and the Program in Science and Society joined forces for an integrated program that began with a semester-long faculty and graduate student seminar on religion, healing, and public health. The effort was led by Gunderson, Peter Brown in anthropology, and Howard Kushner in public health and the Institute for Liberal Arts. This seminar laid the foundation for an undergraduate course taught by two seminar participants the following semester. Based on a successful model for building interdisciplinary community pioneered at Emory by former Luce Professor James Gustafson (himself a leader in bridging disciplines; some call him the "father of bioethics"), the seminar also included participants from theology, religion, psychiatry, epidemiology, music, and the United States Centers for Disease Control and Prevention.

The seminar for faculty and graduate students and the undergraduate course ("Mind, Medicine, and Healing") have been offered several times since and use readings, discussion, guest lectures from faculty who participate in the seminar, and research projects.

> *Exciting Emory research has been done over the past quarter-century in religion and health, primarily at the level of public health and sociology—that is, looking at faith as a variable in people's health, and how they view their health or interact with the health-care system.*

The focus is on these questions: What role do religion and spirituality play in healing? What does the role of religion and spirituality in healers' lives have to do with their approach to healing? What role have religion and spirituality played historically in Western medicine? How are modern biomedical investigations into mind/body connections challenging conventional views about religion in the West? How do religion and issues of mind and body fit into the broad social context of particular communities' understanding of illness and health? How do we best develop educational instruments to integrate these issues into public discourse?

As a culmination of the project, the students in the course presented their research at a public symposium, where they hosted the three surgeons—Nuland, Selzer, and Alvord—discussed in an opening scene of this chapter. The project also resulted in a special issue on the topic of religion and health in the *Academic Exchange*, Emory's scholarly faculty newsletter.

While most early discussions centered understandably on Judeo-Christian ideas and their interaction with science/health and religion/spirituality (Emory is, after all, related to the United Methodist Church and has a large Jewish student population), Eastern religions began to enter the conversation soon after—notably through Lori Alvord's talk on traditional Navajo medicine, physics professor P. V. Rao's talk on Hinduism, and the burgeoning scholarship in Buddhism at Emory. Dating to the mid-1990s, Emory's program in Tibetan Buddhism, especially, was finding a place in the intellectual pursuits of Emory scholars. Much of this work (as we will see below) has blossomed into a major partnership, catalyzed by a quiet Buddhist monk sent by the Dalai Lama to study at Emory.

Lobsang Negi, the son of a Tibetan sheepherder, was recruited from the foothills of the Himalayas by Tibetan monastics and went on to attain the highest intellectual level—that of *geshe*—in that community. Coming to America with only a scant knowledge of English, Negi earned a PhD from Emory and is a senior lecturer in religion and director of the Emory-Tibet Partnership.

Negi helped spearhead one of the first of what will surely be more studies looking at the health/spirituality connection at the physiologic and molecular levels—discussed in an opening scene above. Exciting Emory research has been done over the past quarter-century in religion and health, primarily at the level of public health and sociology—that is, looking at faith as a variable in people's health, and how they view their health or interact with the health-care system. Among others doing such work at Emory, William Branch, professor of medicine, explores the role of spirituality in the dying process of African Americans; Corey Keyes, in sociology, looks at the role of spirituality in mental health in the aged; and professors Ralph DiClemente and Gina Wingood, both in the Rollins School of Public Health, do similar work with African Americans affected by HIV. Negi, working with Charles Raison in Emory's Psychiatry Department, takes such work one step further.

Negi took to heart the Dalai Lama's charge to test in a Western medical model the traditional ancient approaches to healing. Negi and Raison have been measuring the effects of Buddhist meditation on health and response to stress in people previously untrained in meditation—thus, the striking connections noted at the beginning of this chapter between meditation and more effective management of stress and immune responses as measured at the behavioral and molecular levels. Negi and Raison are now extending their research by applying their findings to help children in distress.

Science and Religion in Dialogue | Distinct from, but clearly connected to, Emory's history in health and spirituality has been the development of a broader scholarship in science and religion, scholarship that also underlies much of Emory's current status and accomplishment in the meeting of the two areas.

Since the late 1990s Emory professors and students have been deeply engaged in basic science research that explores foundational elements of religion. The complex human emotions that undergird religion—such as love and altruism—are thought by scientists to have evolved in organisms much the same way all biological traits have evolved. Emory's Larry Young, in the Psychiatry Department, and Frans de Waal, in psychology and Emory's Yerkes National Primate Research Center, along with Thomas Insel, former director of Yerkes and later director of the National Institute of Mental Health, have long been at the forefront of research in such traits.

Insel and Young discovered the biologic mechanisms of pair bonding in voles—the endocrinology of love, if you will—by studying the behaviors and brains of two closely related species of this little furry animal, one of which is monogamous and the other not.

De Waal has become world famous at the Yerkes Primate Center for his groundbreaking research into the evolution of altruism and other complex traits in nonhuman primates. He is as well known among a general audience for his popular books and lectures in this area as he among scientists for his striking research.

In the realm of human culture, Gary Hauk, editor of this volume, has been a key player in many of the signal events enriching the science-and-religion dialogue at Emory. Active in cultivating Emory's relationship with the Dalai Lama, he was present at the Dalai Lama's landmark announcement of the Emory-Tibet Science Initiative in India, highlighted above. In addition, Hauk is a leader, with Dr. Steven Darsey, director of music at Glenn Memorial United Methodist Church on the Emory campus, and other Emory faculty, of a nonprofit organization called Meridian Herald. Recognizing that a gap in conversation existed between the "church side" of campus and the "academic side"—a gap symbolized by the Baker Woodlands—Emory and Meridian Herald collaborated on a series of programs bridging the gap by bridging science and theology. Bringing leading international scholars in science and religion to campus for symposia with Emory scholars and the public, these programs, begun in 2000, featured the likes of Sir John Polkinghorne, the renowned physicist and Anglican priest; Ian Barbour, famous for his work on integrating science and religion; Harold Koenig, a leader in health and faith research at Duke; and Emory's Presidential Distinguished Professor, Emeritus, William Foege, who, among many other public health feats, helped eradicate smallpox from the earth.

Before Meridian Herald, before Gary Gunderson began his work with the Interfaith Health Program, and before the publication of any of the fifty Emory health-and-religion studies listed on Medline (the major American health and science database), Hoyt Oliver, a religion professor at Emory's Oxford College for decades, began teaching a course in science and religion.

Oliver was one of the first at Emory to address the science-and-religion dialogue and expressly commingle science and religion in a course. From 1987 until his retirement in 2006, he taught different versions of "Science and Religion: Starting with Wonder" with colleagues from astronomy, biology, and physics. Oliver focused on five central areas: (1) an understanding and comparison of scientific and religious worldviews; (2) historical development of the scientific worldview and religious responses; (3) introductory material about several areas in science with a connection to religion—cosmology, physics, biology, evolution, complexity, and chaos theory; (4) a sampling of insights from world spiritual traditions with emphasis on the mystical and contemplative; and (5) exploration of areas like ecology, ethics, and healing, where science and religion can work together for human and planetary health.

> *The Emory-Tibet partnership, formalized in 1998, took on its most significant challenge to date in 2006: responding to the Dalai Lama's request for Emory to develop a comprehensive modern science curriculum for all the thousands of Tibetan monks in exile.*

The initial development of Oliver's course was supported by one of the first nationally competitive Templeton Foundation course grants in 1987. The John Templeton Foundation is credited with (or accused by, depending on one's perspective) reinvigorating scholarship in science and religion. John Templeton made millions investing in the stock market. Knighted by Queen Elizabeth, Templeton was still going to work every day when he died in 2008 at the age of ninety-six on his private island in the Bahamas. His foundation has supported innumerable courses and scientific investigations around the world and at Emory, at the borders of science and topics that in the West have not typically lent themselves to scientific exploration, topics like that of de Waal's research: love, faith, creativity, healthy aging, and curiosity.

Templeton funding also helped support the public health and healing project described above, as well as physicist P. V. Rao's course "Science and Religion in Dialogue," which he has taught for several years since winning an initial award in 2000. Emory philosopher Robert McCauley teamed up with Luther Martin of the University of Vermont, with support from Templeton, through a project titled "Modes of Religiosity: Psychological and Cognitive Foundations of Religiosity." McCauley has worked for a number of years on his thesis that, put simply, religion "comes naturally" to humans, while science does not and, instead, takes significant intentional investment. His project with Martin included two workshops and catalyzed research that appeared in *Theorizing Religions Past: Archaeology, History, and Cognition* (AltaMira Press, 2004) and in *Mind and Religion: Psychological and Cognitive Foundations of Religion* (AltaMira Press, 2005).

Timothy Jackson, in the Candler School of Theology, enters the scholarship and conversation in science and religion from the perspective of Christian ethics. He has debated the (in)famous atheist Christopher Hitchens, author of *God Is Not Great* (Hachette Book Group, 2007), in the public arena; offered courses in science and religion at Candler; and in 2006 was a visiting fellow in the Program for Evolutionary Dynamics at Harvard, where he worked on "The Evolution and Theology of Cooperation" project, which has resulted in publications at the interface of evolution, genetics, and religion.

With John Witte in the Center for the Study of Law and Religion (see chapter 38) and Philip Reynolds in the Theology School, Jackson is also working on another Templeton-supported project, "The Pursuit of Happiness: Scientific, Theological, and Interdisciplinary Perspectives on the Love of God, Neighbor, and Self." This five-year project, begun in 2008, involves twenty fellows from Emory and other institutions collaborating, writing, and lecturing on the intricacies of happiness from many trans-disciplinary angles. The project is a collaboration with the Institute for Research on Unlimited Love at Case Western Reserve University.

From 2005 to 2007 Gary Laderman and I, with support from the Program in Science and Society at Emory, developed a series of public events and scholarship projects to synthesize the wide array of work going on at Emory. We first hosted a series of faculty seminars on science and religion as a lead-in to another version of our undergraduate course, this time taught with

Lobsang Negi, on mind, medicine, and healing. This faculty seminar discussion featured Emory experts in origin-of-life chemistry, contemplative practice, neuropsychology, Buddhist philosophy, internal medicine, genetics, medical anthropology, depression, the history of psychiatry, theological studies, interfaith health, public health of women and children, religions of India, oncology, Tibetan Buddhism, and the psychology of religion.

Following the seminar series and the course, an analysis of the work, "Bridging 'the Two Cultures': A Comprehensive Interdisciplinary Approach to Teaching and Learning Science in Societal Context," by Laderman and me, appeared in the *Journal of College Science Teaching*. We then went on to synthesize some of the scholarship in science and religion at Emory and around the world as editors of *Science, Religion, and Society: An Encyclopedia of History, Culture, and Controversy* (M. E. Sharpe, 2007). The collection of essays features many Emory scholars and other collaborators from over the years and addresses general and diverse worldviews from science and different religions. It includes sections in areas of study (reminiscent of Hoyt Oliver's course topics) where the interplay of science and religion are most evident and most promising: creation and the cosmos, ecology and evolution, mind and consciousness, healers and healing, death and dying, and genetics and religion.

The work opens with a preface from the Dalai Lama. He begins, "Today, our world requires us to accept the oneness of humanity. In the past, isolated communities could afford to think of each other as fundamentally separate. But nowadays, whatever happens in one region eventually has repercussions elsewhere. Within the context of the new interdependence that globalization has brought about, self-interest clearly lies in considering the interests of others."[2]

He goes on to say that different cultures, whether the "two cultures" of science and religion or the many different religions and cultures of the world, must work together for all of us to be able to achieve peace and happiness. In this typically elegant and straightforward appeal, the call is for science and religion to collaborate, not war, but it is more than that: this collaboration of science and religion is vital to making the world a better place and improving the human condition.

I close with a brief Emory history of this approach, using science and religion as a lens through which to better ourselves and to better understand ourselves.

In the early 1990s Robert Paul, the Charles Howard Candler Professor of Anthropology and later dean of the Emory College of Arts and Sciences, began what was to become a transformative relationship between the Dalai Lama, the spiritual leader of Tibetans in exile. In the years since, the relationship has become richer and more significant, from the Dalai Lama speaking at Commencement in 1998 to His Holiness's accepting appointment as a presidential distinguished professor in 2007. Now Emory undergraduates can spend a semester in Dharamsala, India, the home of the Tibetan government in exile, learning about Buddhism, and Tibetans, including Lobsang Negi, have come to Emory to teach and learn, as well as to earn undergraduate and graduate degrees.

The Emory-Tibet partnership, formalized in 1998, took on its most significant challenge to date in 2006: responding to the Dalai Lama's request for Emory to develop a comprehensive modern science curriculum for all the thousands of Tibetan monks in exile. His goal was that eventually this would become a regular part of the centuries-old Tibetan monastic curriculum.

After much planning and discussion with Buddhist and Tibetan scholars in education, philosophy, medicine, and science, the initiative was announced, and the first edition of a five-year version of the course was taught to thirty-eight monks and nuns in Dharamsala in the summer of 2008. The six-week course covered topics taught by Emory scholars in philosophy, math, cosmology and physics, evolution and biology, and the neurosciences. In 2009 the project expanded to include another sixty-five monks and nuns, taught by fifteen Emory professors. In addition, a dozen Emory undergraduates joined the experience to complement courses in science and Buddhism that they took simultaneously.

Not surprisingly, the learning goes both ways, from the Emory professors to the student monastics, but as much from the monastics to the professors. As we hiked the Himalayan foothills in June 2008, one monk told me he was studying modern science because it was helping him understand his Buddhism better. This seemed a hint of what the Dalai Lama was speaking of in the quotation opening this chapter, perhaps the ultimate aim of studying and teaching science and religion: enriching human life.

Emory's deep history of scholars working in the field of science and religion goes well beyond Emory's strength in the basic and health sciences and in religion and theology. It points to the more profound emergent property of their collaborative engagement, the willingness to risk crossing boundaries that often keep us unnecessarily and counterproductively apart—both in the academy and in the greater American and global societies.

CHAPTER 38

Visiting Woodruff Professor Desmond Tutu

THE CASE FOR LAW AND RELIGION
— APRIL L. BOGLE —

Building on interdisciplinary strengths at Emory, the Center for the Study of Law and Religion began to take shape in 1982. April Bogle, director of communications for the center, recounts how a triad of renowned leaders—Hal Berman, Frank Alexander, and John Witte—built a program of international reputation by concentrating on topics like the intersection of Christianity and democracy, the interplay of religion and human rights, and proselytism in the "new world order." These led to a huge array of publications and law and elevated the program into a full-fledged center of international reputation and unique distinction.

Opening Statements | One could say that the modern study of law and religion had its beginning when a vision of Jesus Christ appeared to future legal scholar Harold J. Berman, a Jew, as he fled for his life on a German train in 1939. Hitler had just invaded Poland, and Berman feared the imminent end of civilization. In his despair, he saw the scarred and tragic face of Jesus. "I suddenly realized that I was not entitled to such despair, that it was not I but another, God himself, who bore the burden of human destiny, and that it was rather for me to believe in him even though human history was at an end."[1]

Berman used this life-changing experience to inform and shape his scholarship—and a modern field of study. He believed that "law and religion are two different but interrelated . . . dimensions of social experience—in all societies. . . . Despite the tension between them, one cannot flourish without the other."[2]

Fast-forward seventy years, and this field of study is well ensconced and world renowned at Emory University in the Center for the Study of Law and Religion (CSLR), owing in large part to Berman's influence and presence. Not only was he the mentor of CSLR's founding director, Frank S. Alexander, and the scholar who succeeded Alexander as director, John Witte Jr., but Berman also spent the last twenty-two years of his life teaching at Emory Law School and serving as the CSLR's preeminent senior fellow. (See pages 343–348 for a biography of Berman.)

Cocounsel Frank S. Alexander | At Harvard in 1974, Berman met Alexander, a graduate of the University of North Carolina at Chapel Hill and newly enrolled in both Harvard's divinity and law schools. "A mutual friend introduced me to Hal, and a small group got together to talk about law and religion," recalls Alexander. The keystone of the discussions, Alexander said, was Berman's Lowell Lectures, delivered at Boston University in 1971, and the 1974 publication of the lectures as *The Interaction of Law and Religion*, which became the seminal publication in the field. "It was Hal's ability to read across religious traditions and draw upon historical traditions, and his conviction about the future, that gave us the opportunity for discussion."

This was no ordinary small group. Members included the nation's leading theologians and legal scholars—among them James Luther Adams, William Stringfellow, Tom Porter, Doug Sturm, and Robin Lovin. In 1975 they formally became the Council on Religion and Law (CORAL), and with Alexander leading the way, they took the conversation to a larger audience. It was a defining experience for Alexander. The young graduate student led CORAL to produce a national symposium, "Law and Theology: Towards a Deeper Understanding of Vocation," and a lecture series featuring discussions between distinguished divinity and law faculty.

Soon the group was facilitating law-and-religion conferences in other schools, including the University of California Hastings College of the Law, Mercer University School of Law, and the University of Notre Dame. To further legitimize the field of study, CORAL pushed for acceptance by two prominent associations, the American Association of Law Schools, which added a Law and Religion section, and the Society of Christian Ethics, which added Law, Ethics, and Religion to its roster. CORAL also orchestrated creation of a scholarly journal. Steven Young, who left Harvard to become dean of Hamline University School of Law, agreed to edit the journal, and the inaugural issue of the *Journal of Law and Religion* rolled off the press in 1982.

With his Harvard law and divinity degrees in hand, in 1980 Alexander headed to Atlanta to work for a law firm. Little did he know that a friendship he had established at Chapel Hill and maintained while at Harvard would guide his career in Atlanta. He had met that friend, James T. Laney, then dean of Emory's Candler School of Theology, when Laney delivered a lecture at Chapel Hill in 1973. Impressed with the lecture, Alexander approached Laney to see if he would serve as an informal adviser and review his senior thesis. It was Laney's counsel that Alexander sought when trying to determine whether to attend law or divinity school. "He told me, 'Both,' so I did," said Alexander. Enrolled the next year at Harvard, in August 1974 Alexander was delighted to learn that Laney was teaching there while on sabbatical from Emory. Alexander added Laney's class to his schedule.

In Atlanta, Alexander and Laney stayed in touch. Having become Emory's president in 1977, Laney challenged each division of the University to start an interdisciplinary program, and Alexander was invited to teach a course in law and theology at Emory Law. Despite his heavy workload as a practicing attorney, Alexander happily taught in the spring semesters of 1981 and 1982. In 1982 the law school asked him to join the faculty full-time and create a program in law and religion, with new joint-degree programs between the law school and theology school.

"Frank's interests intersected in many ways with mine," recalled Laney in a 2007 interview. "He had a passion for religion, for commitment, for values, for meaning in life. And he had such a marvelous sense of the discipline of law itself, both its practice and its potential: not just as a vehicle to be exploited for aggrandizement, but as a promotion of the larger public good. He was determined to see that law worked for the good of society."

Laney had long held the vision of creating an interdisciplinary university, and it became feasible when Emory received the Woodruff Fund gift of $105 million in 1979. He reflected,

> My deep conviction—in fact, my passion—was that the University should be a scene of fertile intellectual conversation, where different disciplines fortify each other's imagination and thought. The University of Chicago had initiated a cross-disciplinary approach, resulting in a climate of intellectual ferment. I wanted to re-create that at Emory.
>
> The university, I think, also has a moral calling to work toward the larger good. That role includes unmasking the hidden assumptions and accepted wisdom from the past, to help us better understand what's going on in the present. From there, our responsibility is to educate the public and thus to inform decision making.
>
> My role as president was to plant a seed for such work and to provide some resources, which arrived with an infusion of . . . funds from the Woodruff gift. Since there were no restrictions on that gift, we were able to be innovative. And one of the innovations I was most interested in was the conversation between law and religion.[3]

True to his leadership style, Laney pursued the very best talent for the University, using Woodruff funds to create distinguished professorships named for Robert W. Woodruff. Alexander recommended that Laney appoint Berman as the first Robert W. Woodruff Professor of Law, with joint appointments in the Department of Soviet and East European Studies in Emory's College of Arts and Sciences and at the Carter Center, where Berman served as senior fellow in Soviet studies.

Nearing retirement age, Berman resisted Harvard's rule that at age sixty-five professors received emeritus status but had to leave the classroom. "I was determined to keep teaching. I knew that I still had many books to add to the shelf," he told an interviewer in 2007.[4] In 1985 Laney made the offer; Berman accepted.

The young Law and Religion Program acquired national status overnight, and Berman was able to keep teaching, writing, and lecturing until one month before his death in November 2007. While at Emory, Berman published ten books and one hundred–plus articles.

"Hal Berman brought a great historical perspective, establishing our program's legitimacy within the legal order and among the faculty. He was able to interpret the interaction of law and religion in a way that won enormous support across the University, across the nation, and throughout the world," said Laney.[5]

Cocounsel John Witte Jr. | While engaging Berman was certainly a coup that gave the new Law and Religion Program instant credibility, Laney had no idea that the research assistant Berman planned to bring along, a brilliant new Harvard Law graduate named John Witte Jr., would quickly elevate the CSLR to international prominence.

"I came to Emory in 1985 as a stowaway in Hal Berman's briefcase," Witte said with a chuckle during a 2007 interview.[6] An admirer of Berman's as an undergraduate student at Calvin College, Witte followed a whim and cast a long letter to the esteemed professor, explaining his interests and aspirations and asking whether, as his next step, he should attend law school at Yale or Harvard, or pursue graduate work in philosophy. Within three days, Berman sent Witte a two-page, handwritten reply counseling him to come to Harvard and offering him a research assistantship.

It was the start of a deep friendship that would last for twenty-five years. With his new law degree from Harvard and a growing list of scholarly publications, Witte accompanied Berman to Emory. After serving as a research fellow in legal history for a year, he entered legal practice. Nine months later came the windfall. Witte recalled,

> President Laney called and said, "We have the unique opportunity to make religion a legitimate part of serious discourse in any profession, any discipline, any department on the Emory campus. I would like you to help lead the discussion of religion in the law school."
>
> I was still a youngster and recognized my inadequacies. But I thought, here's a crack in the door, a chance for me to prove myself. Teaching. Scholarship. Advancing new areas of research. Dazzled, I didn't hear what the salary was. I didn't hear what the responsibilities were. I just said "yes."[7]

From Laney's vision and discerning choices, something unique had arisen at Emory: a rich and groundbreaking interdisciplinary exchange, anchored in three uncannily well-matched leaders: Alexander, with his ardent mission of combining law and activism into a law-based ministry; Berman, with his trailblazing, panoramic scholarship on the Western legal tradition and its underlying belief systems; and Witte, with what Laney called "his laser-like mind, sweeping historical and legal perspective, galvanizing vision, and soaring standards for scholarship, teaching, and collegiality."[8]

Presentation of Evidence | To the founders of the Law and Religion Program, the need for focused scholarship and teaching in the field was paramount:

- *Where else could students and scholars learn the fundamentals of church and state, faith and order?*
- *How could they learn to balance justice and mercy, rule and equity, discipline and love in their work as legal and religious professionals?*
- *Where could they come to understand Jewish, Christian, and Islamic laws and their respective places in the modern nation-state and emerging global order?*
- *How could they explore the essential religious foundations and dimensions of law, politics, and society?*

According to Alexander, "We based the joint-degree program in the legal academy, to boost legal education's receptivity to the idea of linking religion and law. At that time virtually no law school in the country was doing serious scholarship or teaching related to religion. Indeed, most law schools were hostile to the study of theology, religion, and issues of church and state."[9]

There was also healthy skepticism about the wisdom of this new venture among the Emory law faculty, according to Witte.

There's a burden of proof against any new area of interdisciplinary discourse, especially in a law school. Interdisciplinary legal study needs to enhance the study of law, to open up new understanding of how law works in context and in concert with other disciplines. In the face of healthy suspicion, that's exactly how we had to portray the Law and Religion Program and to shape its projects.

We are not proselytizing our faith.... Instead, we genuinely seek to sponsor a deeper and richer understanding of law, by increasing understanding of the fundamental role religion has played in shaping law, politics, and society.[10]

Intent on asserting the field's legitimacy, Alexander, Berman, and Witte began a prodigious push toward productivity. The most visible proving ground was a series of multiyear, interdisciplinary research projects that culminated in international conferences and dozens of new scholarly books.

Exhibit Number One:
"Christianity and Democracy in Global Context" | As evidence of the need for their program, Witte and Alexander posited the tumultuous world events of the 1980s. The Berlin Wall had crumbled. The Soviet Union was dissolving. African autocrats were flinching. Apartheid was fading. Latin American dictators were falling. Fundamentalist Islamic factions were emerging. Since 1973, thirty new democracies had been born, and democratic agitation had reached even Tiananmen Square. Surely these events proved the need to understand how law and religion interact.

The two men launched "Christianity and Democracy," their first major international research project, securing participation from fifty scholars around the globe. They would demonstrate how Christianity had influenced democracy throughout history, and determine what it could—and should—contribute in the future. The project culminated in 1991 in an international conference, "Christianity and Democracy in Global Context," attracting eight hundred scholars, lawyers, theologians, clergy, and laypersons from five continents and more than five hundred additional Emory participants. Former President Jimmy Carter opened the conference, and Archbishop Desmond Tutu closed it. In between, some forty distinguished authorities took up the contributions of Christianity to democratic ideas and institutions in their respective homelands. Protestants and Catholics, Africans and Americans, freedom fighters and prime ministers shared the same stage and compared views on conditions in Europe, Latin America, North America, Africa, and Asia. It was a conference to set the standard. According to Witte, "The conference put the discourse of law and religion on the map. It demonstrated . . . that there was a thirst . . . to deal with these hard questions . . . about what contributions religious communities . . . could make to the new democratic revolution that was breaking out around the world."[11]

Witte spun the conference findings into a new volume, *Christianity and Democracy in Global Context* (1993) that was eventually published in four languages. Witte and Alexander also developed a series of follow-up projects on the place of Christianity in modern law and politics. Together, they published a prize-winning, three-volume work, *The Teachings of Modern Christianity on Law, Politics, and Human Nature* (2005–07). Witte followed with two additional prize-winning volumes, *Law and Protestantism: The Legal Teachings of the Lutheran Reformation* (2002) and *The Reformation of Rights: Law, Religion, and Human Rights In Early Modern Calvinism* (2007).

Exhibit Number Two:
Religion and Human Rights, Proselytism, and Beyond | The Law and Religion Program had demonstrated the capacity to lead the discourse on a major world issue, and it continued immediately to the next major project, "Religion and Human Rights in Global Perspective." This project was codirected by Witte and a distinguished new faculty member,

Johan D. Van der Vyver, Emory's I. T. Cohen Professor of International Law and Human Rights, and senior fellow for human rights at the Carter Center. Formerly a professor of law at the University of the Witwatersrand, Johannesburg, Van der Vyver was one of the doyens of human rights discourse in his native South Africa who had actively participated in efforts to end apartheid and bring constitutional reform. Drawing on a team of twenty-five human rights scholars and activists, the project sought to map the field of religious rights theoretically, legally, and in the activist communities—and to identify the major problems and pressure points.

> *"We are not proselytizing our faith. . . . Instead, we genuinely seek to sponsor a deeper and richer understanding of law, by increasing understanding of the fundamental role religion has played in shaping law, politics, and society."*

In 1994 the CSLR hosted its second major global conference to inform the public of its findings. Archbishop Tutu returned as a keynote speaker, joined by the University of Chicago's Martin E. Marty and Ninth Circuit Court of Appeals Judge John T. Noonan. The event drew 750 participants and 50 speakers, generated important media coverage, and inspired a surge of new scholarship that continues today.

Witte and Van der Vyver integrated the wisdom gained from the conference into *Religious Human Rights in Global Perspective* (1996), a two-volume anthology presenting religious perspectives and legal perspectives of leading scholars and activists in the field. That work became one of the anchor texts of the budding industry of scholarship on religion and human rights around the world, and portions of these volumes were translated into French, German, Italian, Romanian, Russian, Spanish, and Ukrainian, and widely circulated.

Among the conference participants were three scholars who would eventually join the Emory Law School faculty and become CSLR senior fellows. One was Abdullahi Ahmed An-Na'im, internationally recognized scholar of Islam and human rights, who had just published his pathbreaking volume, *Toward an Islamic Reformation: Civil Liberties, Human Rights and International Law* (1990). A second was Michael J. Broyde, a world-renowned Jewish law scholar and eventual coeditor of *Human Rights in Judaism* (1998). The third was Michael J. Perry, one of the world's leading authorities on constitutional law and religious morality, who had already contributed a series of volumes on the religious and moral foundations of human rights, including *The Idea of Human Rights: Four Inquiries* (1998) and *Under God? Religious Faith and Liberal Democracy* (2003).

With the ink not yet dry on the 1994 conference findings, Alexander and Witte drew An-Na'im, Broyde, and Van der Vyver into a new project on the issue of proselytism in the new world order. The five project leaders assembled teams to undertake investigations of proselytism in Russia, Eastern Europe, Ukraine, Africa, and Latin America. Ultimately more than 160 scholars, religious leaders, and activists from around the world participated in twelve regional conferences. Results were published in a series of volumes, symposia, and articles.

An-Na'im and Van der Vyver then sharpened their focus on human rights issues in non-Western cultures. With funding from the Ford Foundation, they launched "Cultural Transformation in Africa: Legal, Theological, and Human Rights Perspectives," an exploration with particular emphasis on improving women's rights to, and control over, land as an economic resource and vindication of second-generation rights. The project generated two volumes, *Cultural Transformation and Human Rights in Africa* (2002) and *Women and Land in Africa: Culture, Religion, and Realizing Women's Rights* (2003).

With additional Ford Foundation backing, An-Na'im launched two more endeavors: the Islam and Human Rights Fellowship Program, a residential program for scholars and activists from various parts of the Islamic world to explore the relationship between human rights and Islam, and the Islamic Family Law Project, a comprehensive analysis of the sources and scope of Islamic family law around the world, and of possible reforms in light of international and domestic human rights norms. Three volumes resulted: *Islamic Family Law in a Changing World: A Global Resource Book* (2002), *Islam and Human Rights: Advocacy for Social Change in Local Contexts* (2006), and *African Constitutionalism and the Role of Islam* (2006).

In 2008 An-Na'im published the book he believed would be his legacy, *Islam and the Secular State: Negotiating the Future of Shari'a*. Written from a compassionate insider's point of view, he analyzes the relationship of religion, state, and society in its specifically Islamic context, paying particular attention to the ongoing interpretation of ancient texts and the postcolonial condition of Islamic countries.

In 2009 An-Na'im was named a Carnegie Scholar by the Carnegie Corporation of New York and launched a new effort, "Enhancing Citizenship: American Muslims and American Secularism." In this project, he began investigating the theoretical and practical underpinnings of American secularism as the basis for encouraging American Muslims to participate more actively in civic life. His methodology included conducting workshops, discussion groups, and interviews, with plans to convey his findings in a website and blog as well as in a new volume.

The Verdict: From Program to Center

By the year 2000 the Law and Religion Program had proven its legitimacy, thanks to the financial support of several benefactors. After awarding the program some $1.25 million of project funding in the prior decade, the Pew Charitable Trusts awarded Emory a $3.2 million grant to establish the Center for the Study of Law and Religion (initially called the Center for the Interdisciplinary Study of Religion), elevating it from an academic program to a "Center of Excellence," one of ten such centers Pew was funding throughout the country.

It was only the beginning of generous affirmation and benefaction. Unflagging support came from Emory itself, particularly the law school, the theology school, Emory College, and the Office of the Provost. Extremely generous external support flowed also from the Ford Foundation, the Lilly Endowment, the Alonzo L. McDonald Family Foundation, the John Templeton Foundation, the Henry Luce Foundation, and many other individual and institutional benefactors. By 2010 the CSLR had raised more than $12 million in grant funding.

Discussions of Justice

With its intellectual and financial worth confirmed, the center had realized its full potential—dozens of new volumes were rolling off the presses, world-renowned scholars were taking part in international conferences and other public forums, the very best students were enrolling in the joint-degree program (which had graduated some seventy-five students through 2009), and hundreds of students were taking its cross-listed courses each year. The CSLR had become the place where students and faculty could indeed find discussions of justice.

The CLSR took those discussions to matters of the heart, launching projects on marriage, children, the poor, and religious minorities. Much of the Pew funding was used to host two multiyear research projects on the legal and religious issues swirling around the family: Sex, Marriage, and Family & the Religions of the Book, and the Child in Law, Religion, and Society.

Sex, Marriage, and Family & the Religions of the Book

The CSLR inaugurated its Sex, Marriage, and Family project in 2001 amid grim statistics about the family. Between 1975 and 2000 in the United States a quarter of all pregnancies were aborted, one-third of all children were born to single mothers, half of all marriages ended in divorce, two-thirds of all juvenile offenders came from broken homes, three-quarters of all African American children were raised without fathers. The previous four decades had seen a doubling of divorce rates in the United Kingdom, France, and Australia. And while marriage rates had decreased dramatically, illegitimacy, domestic violence, and sexually transmitted diseases had increased around the globe.

Fall 2001 brought the project's kickoff seminar, an assembly of twenty-one experts from varied disciplines across the Emory campus, who were appointed as CSLR senior fellows and charged with examining issues of marriage, sex, and family in relation to the religions of the Book: Judaism, Christianity, and Islam. The field was wide open, welcoming explorations of interfaith marriage, American divorce laws, same-sex unions, Islamic family law, child custody, sexual identity, intergenerational relations, abortions, euthanasia, contraceptive practices, cloning, the depiction of women in scripture, and more.

Witte tapped Don S. Browning of the University of Chicago to codirect the project and serve as Robert W. Woodruff Visiting Professor of Interdisciplinary Religious Studies. Browning and Witte guided the project's shape, commissioning new monographs and anthologies from each senior fellow, and organizing three retreats, thirteen intensive seminars during the semester, and a series of public lectures.

There was no shortage of public forums on the subject. Lectures included "An Apt and Cheerful Conversation on Marriage" (Witte's Distinguished Faculty Lecture), "The Perils of Celibacy: Clerical Marriage and the Protestant Reformation" (Witte's Kessler Reformation Lecture), "Sex and American Catholics" (by Luke T. Johnson of the Candler School of Theology), and the Decalogue Lecture by Mark Jordan, later published as *Blessing Same-Sex Unions: The Perils of Queer Romance and the Confusions of Christian Marriage* (2005). In a public lecture and panel discussion, Atlanta family law attorney John C. Mayoue and three scholars from the project—Broyde, Hogue, and Timothy P. Jackson—shared a conversation on "Legal and Ethical Issues Surrounding Frozen Embryos." Through these forums and others—which were webcast, published as DVDs, and reported on the CSLR website—the center heightened public awareness and highlighted the complexity of profound questions surrounding sex, marriage, and family.

In March 2003 the project's ambitious international conference—Sex, Marriage, and Family & the Religions of the Book: Modern Problems, Enduring Solutions—offered answers to many of the questions. Martin Marty, who keynoted the event, called the gathering "a cosmic conference,"[12] and it is easy to see why. The roster of distinguished presenters reads like an honor roll of public intellectuals, policy makers, and scholarly leaders. Anthropologists, economists, ethicists, historians, jurists, primatologists, psychologists, sociologists, theologians, and public health experts, these eighty speakers represented a multitude of religious, academic, and political perspectives. The conference attracted more than 750 participants during its three days of sessions on topics from covenant marriage to in-vitro fertilization, contraception, adoption, same-sex marriage, divorce, unwed mothers, African American fathers, and interreligious marriages. Yielding a lavish library of video and electronic resources, scholars at the conference eventually produced twenty-nine new volumes and hundreds of new scholarly articles, essays, and op-eds.

The Child in Law, Religion, and Society

When Martin Marty delivered the closing keynote of the Sex, Marriage, and Family conference, he did not try to argue away the gloomy version of the future the conference had outlined. Instead, he posed new questions: "Where do all the good kids come from? And what do you mean by 'good'? And if you find out, what do you do with the knowledge?"[13]

Marty himself decided to pursue this "mystery" and codirect with Browning and Witte the CSLR's next project, The Child in Law, Religion, and Society. The Child project arose naturally from the conference on Sex, Marriage, and Family, whose wide-ranging sessions on family life had often ended with the almost-overlooked question, "What does this mean for children?" The project came at a critical time. *Newsweek* magazine had reported that more than 15 million children were projected to be "lost" in America—born in poverty and in broken households, and more likely than not to drop out of school and out of society altogether.

Marty, in residence for the 2003–04 academic year, stated from the outset his intention to raise big, multifaceted questions that scholars of all disciplines would find relevant to their research. Participants gathered around the seminar table once again, and the weekly buzz of querying, exchanging, and refining resumed. The project's emerging roster of topics stretched across academic disciplines and forged some intriguing new alliances: Alexander's interest in children and housing and the impact of laws on the housing of America's families; Broyde's study of Jewish tradition and the technological selection of embryos and designer babies; an in-depth inquiry by Mary E. Odem, associate professor of history and women's studies, on how Central American and Mexican children fare in migrant families.

Public sharing of the scholars' projects was quickly followed by the launch of the Family Forum Series lectures and panel discussions, which addressed crises that afflict the lives of twenty-first-century children. Marty served variously as interviewer, moderator, and respondent. For each event, the law school's Tull Auditorium attracted a full house.

> *In 2009 the CSLR launched a website that provides full bibliographic information on more than one thousand books, journals, articles, and chapters.*

"Who Cares for the Children?" in September 2003 featured Browning and Martha A. Fineman, newly arrived at Emory as Robert W. Woodruff Professor of Law and an acclaimed expert in family law and feminist theory. In October that year, "Children: Will We Ever Get It Right?" featured William H. Foege, former director of the United States Centers for Disease Control and Prevention, past executive director of the Carter Center, Presidential Distinguished Professor Emeritus at Emory, and a fellow and adviser to the Bill and Melinda Gates Foundation. The following February, Millard Fuller, founder of Habitat for Humanity International, addressed the question, "Where Do the Children Live?"

Conversation led to a momentous challenge during the season's showpiece, the visit of former President Jimmy Carter in October 2003. A huge crowd jammed into Tull Auditorium, listening to Carter and interviewer Marty explore what proved to be a volatile question: "What Happens to Children in Peril?" Carter pointed to the ever-growing chasm between the world's rich and poor as the most profound threat to children today. Extreme poverty, he said, causes "despair and hopelessness, and eventually alienation and anger that sometimes leads to violence."[14]

Carter called to account the United States—"the wealthiest and the greatest nation in the world"—for its low ranking in foreign aid; for its criminal justice system, "grossly biased" toward rich, white, affluent people such as himself; and particularly for its refusal to sign the United Nations Convention of the Rights of the Child. Seriously but without rancor, Carter persisted, "What is the Emory Law School going to do about these problems? What are its individual deans or students going to do? I would guess, nothing. . . . I hope and pray that out of this forum will come not just advice and analysis, but some tangible means to alleviate the problems of the children of the world. If that were done, it would send reverberations throughout the legal profession."[15]

Plans for the Child project had always intended a major conference, but Carter's challenge decided its direction. In October 2005 a crowd of some five hundred conferees gathered at Emory Law School to debate the question, "What's Wrong with Rights for Children?"—specifically to exchange perspectives on the failure of the United States to ratify the UN Convention on the Rights of the Child. Although American scholars and diplomats had played a leading role in drafting the Children's Convention, and although early signs had suggested that the U.S. Senate might provide its consent, it was never sent to the Senate for a vote. By 2010 the United States and Somalia were the only countries that had not ratified the Convention.

Marty summed up the conference proceedings. "Most of the contributors to the October conference regarded the United States' failure to ratify to be a diplomatic mistake, a misreading of the document, or the product of an overheated domestic atmosphere, all of which combined to derail the intended result: the ratification and employment of the Convention in domestic life and international affairs. . . . Meanwhile, if the United States keeps erring by failing to support [the Convention], Carter and most conference participants will keep pointing at all that can be accomplished in its generous name and spirit."[16]

The proceedings of the conference were published in a symposium issue of the *Emory International Law Review*, the first of more than a score of books on children to emerge. But how were the books, forums, and conference of the Child project going to generate change? In a 2007 CSLR interview, Marty offered a confident response: "If Frank Alexander goes back to Flint, Michigan, where he studies the laws for the homeless and draws together ten or twenty people who deal with homeless children and families elsewhere, they're going to change the world. And if our books are ones that teachers read and then teach, or that parents read and then talk about with their friends, these books will change the world, too."[17]

Affordable Housing and Community Development | Changing the world at the ground level is where several CSLR scholars have focused their energy. Although the CSLR itself does not exist for advocacy, it fosters the work of individual scholars impassioned by social inequities and the abuses of human dignity. Frank Alexander uses his law and divinity degrees to help people in need by working for better laws and support systems. The homeless, the down-and-out, the chronically mentally ill, the victims of credit loans, foreclosures, and evictions: these people and their suffering are never far from Alexander's awareness, even when he is in legislative overdrive. Besides teaching his law classes at Emory, he has made the rounds at local homeless shelters, housing projects, and housing facilities for chronically mentally ill adults. He has drafted ordinances and bills, testified before legislative committees, met with attorneys and public policy experts on strategies, and served a major advisory role to the U.S. Congress and the Obama administration.

Child Advocacy | Each year, a million children in the United States are abused or neglected, and on any given day, between fourteen thousand and sixteen thousand of those children are in the legal custody of the state of Georgia. These two facts continually sharpen the zeal of CSLR Senior Fellow Karen L. Worthington, who called herself "a strident child advocate."[18] Founding director of the Barton Child Law and Policy Clinic, housed in Emory Law School, Worthington received the 2009 Outstanding Legal Advocacy Award from the National Association of Counsel for Children (NACC) for her efforts. Georgia State Representative Mary Margaret Oliver (D-Decatur) nominated Worthington, whom she described as a "pioneer in children's law in Georgia." Since its founding in 2000 the Barton Clinic has helped Georgia serve neglected and abused children by providing multidisciplinary, child-focused research, training, and support for practitioners and policy makers charged with protecting these vulnerable ones. As part of her work with the Child project, Worthington, along with Martha Fineman, edited *What Is Right for Children? The Competing Paradigms of Religion and Human Rights* (2009), which examines the state of "rights-talk" about children in the United States compared with that in other countries.

Law, Religion, and Human Rights | As the CSLR entered its third decade, Witte and Alexander decided it was time to return to history—and in some cases, reach outside Emory—for answers to current and future questions of law and religion. For more than twenty years, the CSLR had explored the contributions of Christianity, Judaism, Islam, and other faith traditions to the cultivation—and abridgement—of human rights and democratic norms within international law and domestic constitutional law. The work probed hard issues of religious persecution and bigotry, religious proselytism and discrimination, women's and children's rights and their abuse by religious groups, among other topics. In view of the ongoing religion-inspired conflict throughout the world, the time was right to make the CSLR's research more visible.

With a grant from the Henry Luce Foundation, the CSLR explored ways to make this work more accessible to activists, public policy leaders, and media experts, and to use historical data to inform and help assess the current state and future questions of religion and human rights issues in different legal communities around the world. The conversation expanded first to Durban, South Africa, in the spring of 2008, with thirteen participants from nine African countries. Convened by Van der Vyver and CSLR Senior Fellow M. Christian Green, it probed issues of separation of church and state in Africa. Findings from the event and other research have been compiled in a volume by Witte and Green, *Religion and Human Rights: An Introduction* (2011).

The Internet became the host of further discussions. In 2009 the CSLR launched a website that provides full bibliographic information on more than one thousand books, journals, articles, and chapters. Most titles link to an individual page providing more information about the work, including access to related material—from video lectures to news articles—available on the site. In 2010 the website hosted religious human rights issues of the new millennium, compiled by Green (Law 1995), who returned to Emory Law in 2008 as the Alonzo McDonald Family Senior Lecturer and Senior Research Fellow in the CSLR.

Christian Legal Studies
In 2004 Witte and Alexander developed a project to probe the role of Christianity in shaping law, politics, and society in the twenty-first century. Designed to retrieve, reconstruct, and reengage some of the best Catholic, Protestant, and Orthodox learning on law, politics, and society, it "serves to equip the modern Church to deal with modern legal, political, and social questions with doctrinal rigor, biblical authenticity, and cogency for a pluralistic world," said Witte.

With funding from Alonzo L. McDonald, an Emory alumnus (College 1948) and Emory trustee emeritus, and chairman of the McDonald Agape Foundation, the project assembled a team of two dozen Catholic, Protestant, and Orthodox scholars who met annually to discuss how they could: (1) help the church and individual Christians reengage responsibly in the public square in the great legal, social, and political issues of our age; and (2) work out a "comprehensive new ecumenical 'concordance of discordant canons' that draws out the best of the Catholic, Protestant, and Orthodox Christian traditions, that is earnest about its ecumenism, and that is honest about their greatest points of tension."

Thirty new books were commissioned. Impressed with the team's approach and productivity, McDonald selected Witte as the Alonzo L. McDonald Family Foundation Distinguished Professor and provided funding for a new project, the Christian Foundations of Religious Freedom and Rule of Law, which was complemented by Law, Religion, and the Reformed Tradition, a project sponsored by the Lilly Endowment. For these projects Witte committed to produce five new volumes, fifty articles, and eighty public lectures on fundamental questions of law and religion, church and state, marriage and family, and Christian jurisprudence.

From Silver to Gold:
The Next Twenty-Five Years of Law and Religion
Suddenly, a quarter of a century had gone by. The Law and Religion Program and its successor, the Center for the Study of Law and Religion, had accomplished a great deal, but the world needed much more conversation and understanding about the interaction of law and religion. To celebrate its first twenty-five years, CSLR asked twenty-five distinguished scholars to help formulate the hardest questions of law and religion to be addressed in the next quarter century. During its anniversary conference, "From Silver to Gold: The Next 25 Years of Law and Religion" (October 2007),

scholars applied their prophetic voices in a series of keynotes, lectures, and panel discussions. Emory President Emeritus Laney delivered the opening keynote address, calling for universities to be places of not only instruction but inspiration, preparing students for a life of purpose beyond self-profit, and noting that the CSLR has done much to support this ideal.

"All of us [who were there at the beginning] are simply astounded at the range of its influence on the University, the nation, and the world," Laney said, noting that thirty interdisciplinary law and religion programs have emerged around the country since Emory's program was established in 1982.[19]

CSLR senior fellows An-Na'im and Perry also spoke, as did Berman via video broadcast. It was to be Berman's last public address before his death. Anxious to take part in the commemorative celebration for an interdisciplinary center he had so richly inspired, Berman prepared his lecture text early in the fall and gladly agreed to videotaping interviews in advance. As the event approached, however, he fell ill and was unable to attend. Instead, excerpts from his video interviews were shown during his lecture slot, and the full text of his lecture was published in the CSLR's commemorative book, *When Law and Religion Meet: The Point of Convergence* (2007). It also is permanently posted on the CSLR website.[20] Berman died the month following the conference. Though saddened by the passing of their great mentor, Witte and Alexander continued to be buoyed by his great teachings. Said Alexander, "I was emboldened by Hal's convictions of things to come, of the ways things ought to be."

The Way Forward

One of "the way things ought to be," according to Berman, was for the CSLR to expand its reach globally and into Eastern religions. Various CSLR leaders have concurred. Said Witte,

> The fundamental questions of faith, freedom, and family, and the fundamental questions of human rights and religious liberty are going to continue to be perennial contests in the culture wars domestically and internationally. . . . There are three other areas we'll need to consider: first, the great contests today between religion and science; second, the issues of environmental stewardship and the world's concerns about a growing biological holocaust; and, third, given the rapidly globalizing understanding of religion, law, commerce, and society altogether, we must incorporate the richness of Confucianism, Buddhism, Taoism and Hinduism into our work.[21]

Alexander's viewpoint was similar:

> We're going to have to confront two new sets of issues in ways we haven't before. First is the interplay of multiple religious traditions on tough questions of international policy. Looking at the Middle East, the Indian subcontinent, and the Far East, we're going to have to broaden our understandings both of Western common law and of religious traditions. I also think it will be time to take on contemporary social and political issues. . . . For example, our immigration policies have to deal with what it means to be a member of this community, and we can no longer go forward in law and religion if we don't begin to talk about who belongs in the community.[22]

An-Na'im approached the issue differently:

> When we look deeply enough and thoughtfully enough we will find that all human societies and human persons share the same basic qualities, concerns, needs, desires, and so on. . . . So my question for the future phase of the Center is how to appeal to and respond to the human in all of us globally.[23]

Broyde's focus remained on the family:

I believe over the next several years that issues of family—marriage, divorce and children, and sexuality—will be front and center in the interplay between law and religion in the United States. This is a central issue that our secular society needs to come to grips with, and we as a Center should lead that scholarly conversation.[24]

When Law and Religion Meet | A first outcome of all the thinking about the future was the lecture series "When Law and Religion Meet," established in 2008. The series opened a forum for religious leaders to discuss difficult legal and moral issues facing international religious communities. The first year featured the three Abrahamic religions: Wilton D. Gregory, archbishop of Atlanta, discussed the Catholic Church's viewpoint and the death penalty; Irwin Cotler, Canadian parliamentarian and former minister of justice, warned of Iran's threat to annihilate Israel with nuclear weapons; Mona Siddiqui, professor of Islamic Studies and Public Understanding at the University of Glasgow, challenged the West to grasp a greater understanding of Islamic law; and V. Gene Robinson, bishop of the Episcopal Diocese of New Hampshire, told an overflowing crowd why religion matters in the quest for gay civil rights.

The success of the lecture series, along with the CSLR's emerging pursuit of international issues of law and religion and Eastern faiths, converged with the success of another large CSLR research project, the Pursuit of Happiness, which had been launched a year before the silver anniversary. The impact of this convergence would lead the CSLR to produce the most visible and widely appealing work in its history.

The Pursuit of Happiness | Soon after the start of the new millennium, developments in positive psychology and a flurry of books brought the idea of happiness back to public attention. The CSLR responded in 2006 with a research project designed to analyze the concept of "the pursuit of happiness" using the methods and insights of science, theology, ethics, law, politics, and the behavioral sciences. "Most famously formulated in the American Declaration of Independence," Witte said, "the theme is an ancient and enduring Western ideal grounded in various Hebrew, Greco-Roman, Christian, and Enlightenment sources." The new project was funded in part by a grant from the John Templeton Foundation.[25]

Leading the project was CSLR Senior Fellow Philip Reynolds, a historian and scholar of medieval theology and the family. With a team of eighteen distinguished scholars collaborating as senior fellows, the project considered happiness at the intersection of two axes: (1) the relationship between personal well-being and unselfish love, and (2) the relationship between the religious tradition and science. The topic promised wide-ranging conversation across historical periods, religious traditions, and academic disciplines in the arts and the sciences.[26] Reynolds sparked those conversations during a series of roundtables exploring charity and forgiveness, equality and virtue. Some twenty new volumes are expected to result from the project.

The biggest and most well-attended conversation about happiness was yet to come: an interfaith dialogue among His Holiness the XIV Dalai Lama and representatives of the Abrahamic faiths in October 2010. It was a first for the CSLR: giving center stage to an Eastern religion for an event with nearly universal appeal and significance, to be attended by an audience of some four thousand.

Witte, Alexander, and hundreds of distinguished scholars successfully proved the case for the *study* of law and religion. But the *trial* of its interaction—inspired by Jesus Christ in the life of Harold Berman, energized by God and Allah, and expanded by the Buddha—continues.

SECTION 5

Frontiers in Science and Medicine

CHAPTER 39

THE MAKING OF THE WOODRUFF HEALTH SCIENCES CENTER

— SYLVIA WROBEL —

In 1915, when Emory University planted roots in Atlanta, the city already had a plethora of programs to train doctors, nurses, and dentists, as well as hospitals to provide care. Some were well established; others struggled, uncertain of their future. Emory offered a new vision of strength through partnership.

Over the next half-century, the University incorporated and transformed existing schools of medicine, nursing, and dentistry, and two hospitals, while creating affiliations with others—ties that continue unbroken. Emory also, somewhat surprisingly, accepted an offer from Yale University to take ownership of Yale's primate research institute, which was then located in Florida. With help from Atlanta's best-known business leader and philanthropist of the second half of the twentieth century, Emory built what was missing and needed in Atlanta: the area's first cancer clinic for nonindigent patients and a general clinic where Emory physicians could practice while setting aside time to teach. These schools, hospitals, centers, and clinics were the components of the city's first medical center, named after Robert Woodruff, the legendary leader of The Coca-Cola Company.

At its birth in 1966 the Woodruff Medical Center already had a cumulative age of more than four and a half centuries represented in its components, yet the next four decades saw a maturing whose speed, breadth, and impact would have astonished the center's progenitors. The Robert W. Woodruff Health Sciences Center (WHSC), as it is now called, includes Georgia's largest, most comprehensive patient-care system, and the center has gained dizzying momentum as a research institution, characterized by interdisciplinary approaches and a growing globalization. The only public health school in the state—together with the Centers for Disease Control and Prevention (CDC), located next door to the Emory campus, and other national, state, and local public health organizations—has made Atlanta the city of public health. What has not changed with the growth and sophistication of the WHSC is its involvement with the community.

Building Blocks of a Medical Center for Atlanta
The School of Medicine

The promise of a new university in Atlanta was a godsend for the Atlanta Medical College. Like hundreds of small, proprietary medical colleges scattered throughout the country in the early 1900s, it needed to respond to the Carnegie Foundation's no-holds-barred "Flexner Report," which in 1910 had lambasted the four privately owned schools in Atlanta along with other for-profit medical schools around the country. Following Abraham Flexner's advice, Atlanta's two strongest schools had merged into the Atlanta Medical College, the original name of the oldest, chartered in 1854. That move alone earned the new school an A from the American Medical Association's new accreditation system.

But the Flexner report also called for all privately owned medical schools to align themselves with a university, in order to ensure both a financial and a scientific foundation. Flexner recommended that the Atlanta Medical College join the well-established University of Georgia. Instead, school leaders cast their lot with the new university being planned in the Druid Hills suburbs. In 1915 the medical college transferred its holdings—property worth twenty-two thousand dollars near Grady Memorial Hospital—to Emory University. Faculty also dug into their own pockets to support the alliance. In turn, Emory's founders, including Coca-Cola magnate Asa Candler, gave the medical school a quarter of a million dollars for an endowment and built the pink-marble, red-tile anatomy and physiology laboratories that today make up the wings of the school's modern education building.

The newly named Emory University School of Medicine maintained its facilities across from Grady and its commitment to the public hospital, founded in 1892 to serve the city's poor. Grady depended on those Emory doctors to provide free treatment for both black and white indigent patients, and the Emory medical school depended on Grady as a training site for teaching its medical students and residents.

A Hospital of Its Own: The Origin of Emory University Hospital

School leaders also wanted a hospital for the new campus. Why not repeat the success of adopting a medical school and adopt, also, a hospital? Asa Candler knew Wesley Memorial Hospital well. He personally had paid, on behalf of the North Georgia Conference of the Methodist Episcopal Church South, to renovate a downtown antebellum mansion to house the hospital, and he proposed merging the hospital with the new university.

Opened in 1905, the 50-bed hospital had outgrown its historic quarters by 1920. Candler brokered the agreement with Emory and, again using his own resources, built a new, 275-bed facility on the Emory campus. In 1922, patients staying in the hospital at the corner of Auburn and Courtland were driven the five miles from downtown to new quarters at Emory in vehicles provided by Atlanta's funeral homes. Already rich with teaching opportunities at Grady, the medical school now could provide additional experiences for students—and care for Atlantans—at the hospital soon to be renamed Emory University Hospital, on Clifton Road.

Although some doubters had feared that patients would not be willing to drive to the "countryside" for care, the hospital was a great success, requiring frequent expansion, including the 1946 addition of the Whitehead Surgical Pavilion and later additions and remodeling to fit changing medicine—advances that Emory doctors embraced and increasingly helped shape.

Nursing: Where the Nell Hodgson Woodruff School of Nursing Began

When it opened in 1905 Wesley Memorial Hospital launched a training program to prepare its own nurses. When the hospital moved, so did the nurses' training program; faculty and students lived and studied in the new Florence Candler Harris Home for Nurses (now Harris Hall), named in memory of Asa Candler's older sister and funded by her nieces and nephews to honor their aunt's volunteer service to the hospital.

As in most hospital-based schools of the time, nursing students earned diplomas in largely hands-on programs. But nursing was changing. In the 1920s the Wesley program was chosen by the U.S. government as one of eight schools to explore university-based education in nursing. In the early 1940s the U.S. Public Health Service looked at the feasibility of such a school at Emory. But first, there was the war. Nursing faculty and alumni joined their medical school colleagues in the reactivated Emory Unit, which had been created during World War I to care for the wounded in France, and they headed for Europe and North Africa. On the home front, Nell Hodgson Woodruff (who had dropped out of nursing training to marry Robert) recruited Red Cross volunteers like herself to fill in for staff nurses serving in the military.

In 1944 the nursing school officially became the Emory University School of Nursing, phasing out its diploma program in favor of the new degree of bachelor of science in nursing (BSN).[1] The school barely paused to celebrate before making plans for a master's degree program. Begun in 1954 it was the first MSN program in the Southeast.

The nursing school has a special place in University history for having admitted—indeed, having gone out and recruited—the first two African American students to graduate from Emory. When those two students—Verdelle Bellamy and Allie Saxon—arrived at the run-down former army barracks that then housed Emory's nursing school (near the site where the Schwartz Center for Performing Arts was later built), they found the entire nursing school faculty and student body waiting to welcome them.

In 1967 the school was renamed the Nell Hodgson Woodruff School of Nursing after one of its most devoted supporters. Shortly before her death Woodruff attended the groundbreaking of the school's new home behind Emory Hospital, where it would stay until 2001, when the current building was completed at the corner of Clifton and Houston Mill roads.

The State's First Dental School

Like medical schools at the end of the nineteenth century, proprietary dental schools abounded, with little oversight. When Atlanta Medical College joined Emory in 1915, the two competing dental schools in the city (one established in 1887, the other in 1892) must have considered the possibility of a similar move. Instead, in 1917 they merged to form the Atlanta-Southern Dental College, continuing on their own, with volunteer faculty who became leaders in emerging national dental organizations.

But discussions continued about becoming part of Emory, especially after both the Carnegie Foundation and the American Dental Association strongly recommended that all schools affiliate with a university. In 1944 the school became the Emory University School of Dentistry. It was then the only dental school in Georgia and surrounding states. But not for long.

Demand for dentists grew quickly with the baby boom. In 1969, just as Emory's largest dental class entered its sleek new home on Clifton Road, paid for in part by federal dollars, the first class of students entered the new, state-supported Medical College of Dentistry in Augusta, Georgia. Over the next decade, things began to change. Surrounding states built their own dental schools. The advent of fluoride in public water supplies meant fewer cavities. Diminishing demand for general dentists, together with emerging concern over newly recognized blood-borne diseases like HIV, caused applications to plummet at dental schools everywhere.

In 1985, when the number of applicants to Emory's School of Dentistry barely exceeded the number of slots available, raising concerns over quality, Emory's trustees approved the administration's recommendation to phase out the training of general dentists and to transform the school into the Emory University School of Postgraduate Dentistry, the nation's only institution devoted entirely to training specialists (orthodontists and oral surgeons, for example) and to research.

There were protests from faculty and alumni, but the postgraduate school was a smashing success. Young dentists from across the region clamored for admission, and research grants poured in, more per faculty member than in any other unit in the University. But the school's success did not translate into financial stability, as the school required an annual $1 million subsidy from the University. The noble experiment was closed in 1992, with programs in oral surgery and oral pathology moving into the medical school.

Another Hospital Adopted: The Road to Emory University Hospital Midtown

In 1908, two Atlanta doctors—Edward Campbell Davis and Luther C. Fischer—used their own resources to open a private, twenty-six-bed hospital called the Davis-Fischer Sanatorium, near where Turner Field now stands. Three years later, to meet growing demand, they built a larger facility, with eighty-five beds, on Peachtree Street in what is now Midtown Atlanta. Adding still more beds in 1931 and rechartering their enterprise as a not-for-profit hospital, they renamed it in honor of Georgia's Dr. Crawford W. Long, the first physician to use ether as anesthesia during surgery.

The hospital boomed. In 1945, beds were more than doubled again, to six hundred, and during the postwar baby boom, more than one of every three Atlanta babies was born at Crawford Long. The hospital brought to Atlanta such medical advances as the city's first postoperative hospital recovery room, the first blood bank with complete Rh testing, and the first nursery for premature infants in the Southeast.

When Davis died in 1931, Fischer decided to assure the hospital's strong momentum forever by deeding it to Emory, enabling the University to continue its tradition of reaching into the community for strong institutions to further its missions of teaching and patient care. With Fischer's death in 1953, ownership passed to Emory, and the hospital went through several name changes—and enormous growth—over the next half-century. Today it is called Emory University Hospital Midtown, but the Crawford Long name remains on the 1931 hospital building at Peachtree and Linden streets.

Ahead of the Research Curve, the Decision to "Buy" a Primate Research Center

In 1956 Emory took Yale University up on its offer to sell Emory the primate research center established in 1928 by Robert Yerkes, one of the first scientists to understand that primates, because of their evolutionary closeness to humans, could provide vast amounts of information on the roots of human behavior and, perhaps, much more of interest to medical science and practice. In 1930, after one winter in Connecticut, Yerkes had moved his collection of more than two dozen chimpanzees and apes to Florida, where he and other Yale scientists could observe the animals' behaviors in a climate closer to that of their native habitats. Throughout the 1930s and 1940s Yale researchers traveled back and forth from New Haven, an increasingly impractical and costly process. In 1956, after Yerkes's death, Emory paid Yale one dollar to transfer ownership.

The original center had focused exclusively on behavioral research, but at midcentury, comparative medicine—the study of animals to understand the mechanisms of human disease—was gaining credence in the research world, especially after primate research made possible the development of the polio vaccine. In 1960 the National Institutes of Health (NIH) created a primate research program to provide the scientific community with the specialized resources needed for primate research; seven facilities around the country, including Yerkes, were designated NIH regional primate research centers. Using federal funds to create a building on the edge of the Emory campus and a 117-acre field station in nearby Lawrenceville, Emory brought the center "home" in 1965. In the years ahead, as chapter 40 and the research section of this chapter describe, the Yerkes Center would continue, even expand, its behavioral research and become one of the most interdisciplinary parts of the entire University in areas such as vaccines, neurosciences, and neuro-imaging.

What Was Missing?

Thanks to the incorporation, redirection, and expansion of well-established community programs, by midcentury Emory had a medical school full of doctors, and two hospitals where they could practice—one on campus, staffed only by Emory faculty, the other in midtown, where faculty and community doctors worked side by side.

Emory physicians also provided—and continue to provide—the majority of physician care in many of the city's biggest public/private hospitals. As Grady grew, so did Emory's involvement. In 1946 the Veterans Affairs Medical Center asked Emory doctors to be responsible for patient care in exchange for allowing the medical school to use VA facilities for teaching and research. In 1952 it was the first VA hospital in the nation to affiliate with a medical school. When the VAMC built its new hospital on Clairmont Road in 1966, on land that had been part of Emory's Lullwater preserve, specifically chosen for its nearness to Emory doctors, the medical school and the VAMC also shared a backyard.

In 1954 the sixty-four-acre Wesley Woods campus, founded to meet housing and healthcare needs of the elderly, also was built adjacent to the Emory campus, opening the door for Emory to become a hub for pioneering advances in geriatric care and research. At the other end of the patient spectrum, the Henrietta Egleston Hospital for Children (now Children's Healthcare of Atlanta at Egleston) relocated to the Emory campus in 1959, after thirty years downtown, again to be closer to the Emory faculty. Emory provided the land, on Clifton Road, for one dollar.

Clinical care also took place in two small clinics. In 1937, annoyed that Atlantans suffering from cancer had to travel out of state to the Johns Hopkins University hospital and elsewhere for care, Robert Woodruff had built the Winship Clinic for Neoplastic Diseases, named after his maternal grandfather who, like Woodruff's mother, had died of cancer. ("Cancer" then had a stigma attached to it, so the term "neoplastic disease" was used to ensure that patients would actually come to the clinic.) It was the first cancer clinic for non-indigent patients in Atlanta.

The Birth of the Emory Clinic

Also missing in the swatch of health-related institutions at Emory was an organization where Emory medical faculty could maintain private practices, earning a living while still teaching and conducting research. In 1949 Emory faculty had established a small private diagnostic clinic in Emory University Hospital so they could be closer to their patients at the hospital. The medical school dean, Dr. Hugh Wood, and Woodruff's handpicked director of the Winship Clinic for Neoplastic Diseases, Dr. Elliott Scarborough, lobbied Woodruff to build the school a more substantial and free-standing clinic. They promised it would be good for health care *and* a smart business decision.

Woodruff knew better than anyone how desperately a good business plan was needed. In the mid-1940s, the medical school still had only two paid faculty members and relied heavily on volunteer doctors to teach. Woodruff gave the nod for Emory to recruit full-time faculty, as other schools around the country were doing, with the tacit understanding that he would foot the bill. Salaries were not the only cost, however. As the school grew, so did its deficits. Each year the Emory president would go, hat in hand, to ask Woodruff to cover the shortfall from the Emily and Ernest Woodruff Foundation, then wait to see if Woodruff would. He always did. By the early 1950s, the annual check was around a quarter of a million dollars.

Some other medical schools had started faculty clinics to help cover costs. Convinced that this would work at Emory, Woodruff provided $1 million to build the first half of the Scarborough Building that still stands across the street from Emory Hospital on Clifton Road. When Woodruff pointed out the new building was "lopsided," Scarborough assured him that it would look just fine when Woodruff provided money for the other half. (See pages 447–455 for an account of this development by Emory alumnus and administrator Boisfeuillet Jones.)

In January 1953, backed by Woodruff's generosity, the Emory Clinic was founded as a for-profit partnership agreement. The seventeen initial physicians promised to spend at least 25 percent of their time teaching students and residents. Not only would they cover their own salaries through their clinical practice, they also would pay rent to the University, which would in turn use the money to cover costs in the medical school. Clinic partners also would contribute money to the medical school.

What was not to like? For community doctors, plenty. They feared that the Clinic gave Emory physicians an unfair competitive advantage. At the same time, some faculty members feared that it would weaken Emory's long-time commitment to Grady. These fears soon were allayed. Clinic doctors would accept patients only by referral, a practice maintained for the next forty years. As for Grady, the solvent medical school poured even more resources into its long-time affiliate, further enhancing the school's reputation as an extraordinary teaching institution.

Putting It All under an Expanding Center Umbrella

By mid-century, some forty years after Emory University was chartered, the family of institutions and programs focused on health professional education and patient care had grown rapidly. The units operated largely on their own, but beginning in 1953 they were overseen and coordinated by a Health Services Board—essentially a committee of the University Board of Trustees—with a chief administrator running the complex operation (Boisfeuillet Jones, 1953–64, and Orie Myers Jr., 1964–73).

In 1966 the trustees created the Woodruff Medical Center (now the Woodruff Health Sciences Center) as a more formal umbrella organization for the three schools, two hospitals, clinic, and primate research center, as well as the relationships with Atlanta's public/private hospitals and other organizations.

There was never any question that the center would be named for Robert Woodruff, whose involvement and support had often built and often bailed out center components; however, the famous "Mr. Anonymous" would consent only to the use of his last name. Not until 1983, when he was ninety-four years old, was it renamed the Robert W. Woodruff Health Sciences Center. Woodruff's modesty did not mean he was not deeply immersed in the affairs of the center, both big and daily. The first director of center after its naming in 1966, and first vice president for health affairs at Emory, was Dr. Garland Herndon, Woodruff's personal physician. Herndon was on call twenty-four hours a day for Mr. Woodruff, and the two men met for breakfast daily.

In 1983 Herndon's declining health made it impossible for him to continue directing the center (he died in 1984), and Emory President James Laney turned for help to one of the Emory Clinic's medical, administrative, and financial superstars. Cardiothoracic surgeon Charles R.

Hatcher Jr. was responsible for many surgical firsts in Georgia, including the first operations on so-called blue babies, valve replacements, and coronary bypasses. As chief of cardiothoracic surgery, he had made Emory one of the country's largest, most respected, and, not incidentally, most economically successful centers for open-heart surgery, a place where the best young surgeons vied for jobs, and to which other physicians sent their hardest, sickest cases. As director of the Emory Clinic, Hatcher had quadrupled billings, clinical dollars that fueled the medical school's growth.

Hatcher was not so sure he wanted to be interim director of the Health Sciences Center. The zero salary did not much bother him, but he already held arguably the most powerful job on the health sciences campus. But Laney was persuasive. For a year, Hatcher rose at dawn, performed surgery, taught young surgeons, handled the division of cardiothoracic surgery and the clinic, and then walked across Clifton Road to the medical center. Until this point, the medical center had been the loosest of confederations, with the real power located in the units. Afternoons were sufficient to do what needed doing. Now, as the University started planning how to use most effectively the 1979 gift of $105 million from Robert and George Woodruff, Hatcher began to see interesting centerwide potential. Following Herndon's death in 1984, Hatcher gave up directorship of the clinic to become the second center director and vice president for health affairs.

> *For years, as the only medical school in town, Emory had the entire responsibility for physician care at Grady. Then, in 1978 the new Morehouse School of Medicine was founded.*

He would prove to be the right man for the right time—as would another 1984 appointment. James B. Williams (College 1955), former chairman and CEO of SunTrust Banks, was named chair of the Woodruff Board, that committee of the Emory Board of Trustees that oversees the health sciences components of the University. Over the next sixteen years, the center headed in directions that continue today. Four things in particular marked this period.

First was the establishment in 1991 of the first system to align the center's patient-care components, making it easier for patients to enter and move among them, and to gear up to address changes in health-care contracts and reimbursement. The Emory Clinic gave up its forty-year policy of accepting only referrals and began to establish small primary-care practices in addition to the specialized care for which it was known. The cumbersome Emory University System of Health Care name (even more disharmoniously nicknamed EUSHC, rhyming with whoosh) was chosen to emphasize what medical leaders of the time, like the founders, saw as their strength and differentiation: the relationship with Emory University.

Second was the creation of a structure for the medical school's rapidly expanding programs to train doctors not only at Emory's own hospitals but also at the affiliated hospitals—Grady, VAMC, Egleston Children's Hospital, and Wesley Woods Center, each an institution with its own mission and needs. The relationship with Grady was both the oldest—faculty in the Atlanta Medical College and later Emory School of Medicine had cared for Grady patients since the public hospital opened in 1892—and the most complex. A handshake relationship became contractual in 1930 and again in 1951: the medical school would train doctors at Grady, and these young residents (MDs learning specialty medicine) would help with patient care under Emory faculty supervision. The complexity and sheer quantity of patient care at Grady simply would not have been possible without these residents. The wide range of care provided at Grady clinched Emory's reputation as a teaching institution and enhanced care across Georgia, where one of every four practicing physicians could boast of having learned hands-on medicine at the hospital.

For years, as the only medical school in town, Emory had the entire responsibility for physician care at Grady. Then, in 1978 the new Morehouse School of Medicine was founded in Atlanta to train family-care physicians for practice in medically underserved inner-city and rural areas. Hatcher and Emory were instrumental in getting the new school off the ground, providing clinical training for its earliest students until Morehouse began granting its own MD degrees in 1985. The 1984 Emory/Grady contract, the first in more than three decades, reflected Emory's voluntary sharing of work at Grady with this newer medical school. It was believed to be the first such arrangement in the country.

The third big change in the Hatcher era was the new commitment that the Woodruff center, like the University itself, would become a leading research institution.

Fourth, following the difficult decision to close the dental school, was the creation of the first school of public health in Georgia.

Helping Make Atlanta the City of Public Health | The Rollins School of Public Health may have been a latecomer, but Emory's efforts toward public health had begun early and reached far, with the help of the ubiquitous Robert Woodruff. His first interest in public health was piqued by malaria, because of its impact on South Georgia, where he had a hunting preserve, Ichauway Plantation. Always a man of action, he hired nurses, bought quinine to treat everyone in the county, and gave Emory faculty members money to study how malaria was transmitted. In 1942 the federal government established on Peachtree Street, in Atlanta, the Office of Malaria Control in War Areas, to train experts to control mosquitoes in areas of military importance. When the war ended, this program was converted into a permanent institution dedicated to the control of communicable diseases, then called the Communicable Diseases Center. To forestall the government's possible relocation of this center to Washington, D.C., Woodruff bought fifteen acres next door to Emory and gave the property to the University to "sell" to the government. (See next chapter for a fuller account of this development by one of the participants, Boisfeuillet Jones.) CDC employees pitched in the $10 needed to make the arrangement legal, although it would take another decade before construction began on new headquarters. With access to CDC professionals as adjunct faculty, and with triumphs like the defeat of polio bringing the value of public health to the public eye, the medical school's small Department of Community Health began to expand, eventually becoming a division.

The public health neighborhood along Emory's Clifton Road campus became even stronger in 1988 with the arrival of the headquarters of the American Cancer Society, one of the largest nonprofit organizations in the world. Cities across the country had competed to become the ACS's new home when it announced its decision to leave New York City for more cost-effective space. Atlanta's bid surely was helped when the Robert W. Woodruff Foundation bought and donated four and a half acres on Clifton Road across from the CDC. (When the ACS moved again, to downtown Atlanta in 2007, the University had the right of first refusal on this property and acquired the headquarters building at 1599 Clifton Road.)

Other public health giants in town included CARE International and the Carter Center. Founded in 1982 by former president Jimmy Carter, in partnership with Emory, the Carter Center has become renowned not only for its work to improve human rights around the world but also for its leadership in prevention and control of diseases like Guinea worm and river blindness.

Given this constellation of public health strengths, including strong local and state heath departments, Emory leaders seized the opportunity to create a school of public health, the first new school created at Emory since the dental school had come to campus in 1944.

The School of Public Health opened in 1990 with thirty-some faculty, many with joint appointments elsewhere, working in rented quarters in the ACS building and in small 1950s-era ranch houses scattered nearby. Student applications poured in. That same year, as the O. Wayne Rollins Research Center was being dedicated, Mr. Rollins himself offered to make the lead gift for a new public health building. After his sudden death, his sons, Randall and Gary, stepped forward as the major supporters of the building, named after their mother, Grace Crum

Rollins, and for programs, professorships, scholarships, and other elements in the growing school. Soon afterward, the school itself was named for the family. Within five years, the young Rollins School of Public Health had become one of the top schools nationwide.

Transition | In 1996, when Charles Hatcher retired as head of the WHSC, the job he once did in an afternoon after surgery had become so broad, so complex, so visible, and so necessary not only to Emory but to the city, that the *Atlanta Journal-Constitution* bid him farewell and welcomed his successor, Dr. Michael M. E. Johns Jr., as "Atlanta's health czar."

Johns arrived from Baltimore just as Atlanta went into Olympics fever. An ear, nose, and throat surgeon, he had served as dean of the Johns Hopkins School of Medicine and vice president of the medical faculty at Johns Hopkins University. The selection of Johns by President William Chace and his ratification by the Emory trustees were themselves a sign of Emory's commitment to teaching, patient care, *and* research. Under Johns's leadership, Hopkins had revamped its medical teaching, moved the sponsored-research program to the ranking of first in the nation, and built the number-one clinical practice. Johns chose Emory because it was one of the few institutions where health sciences schools and clinical entities operated under one umbrella, making integration of activities possible at the highest level.

As the torch was passed from Hatcher, Johns was given an amazing opportunity, just as his predecessors had been in 1979—and from the same folks. The Woodruff, Whitehead, and Evans foundations—together sometimes referred to as "the Woodruff interests"—created a new Woodruff fund from a two-hundred-ninety-five-million-dollar gift of stock, the income of which was to benefit the WHSC and, especially, its Winship Cancer Institute. Additional gifts enabled construction of the Whitehead Biomedical Research Building. With Johns in place as executive vice president for health affairs and director of the Woodruff Health Sciences Center, and with James B. "Jimmy" Williams (College 1955, Honorary 2004) as chair of the Woodruff Health Sciences Center Board, the University had not only strong leadership in place in the health sciences but also a commitment toward targeted growth and the funds to begin it. Strategic planning began in both health care and research. The WHSC began the most extensive facilities improvement plan at Emory since the end of World War II, investing more than $579 million to create more than 2 million square feet of new clinical, research, and teaching space over the next decade.

Emory Healthcare: "Making People Healthy" | When it came to changing Emory's health-care system, Johns faced both the best and worst of times. Emory doctors provided the majority of health-care in Atlanta, most notably in specialized care, in its own facilities and those of its clinical partnership. Everyone in Georgia knew that if you were really sick, you needed to go to Emory, where doctors often had pioneered state-of-the-art treatments. The challenges lay in the growing market realities nationwide: managed care, competition, and declining federal and state reimbursement.

After a year of planning, Johns and his team introduced Emory Healthcare in 1997. Designed to be a tightly unified yet flexible organization, Emory Healthcare enabled its various components to respond with one voice to those market realities, especially to the managed care companies that were making up an increasing share of "covered lives." (Today, such managed care contracts, whether commercial, Medicare, or Medicaid, account for approximately 60 percent of revenue.) Emory Healthcare also included more than its predecessor, EUSCH. The independent Emory Clinic, the largest, most comprehensive group practice in Georgia, was legally and financially moved under the new Emory Healthcare umbrella that encompassed Emory University Hospital, Crawford Long Hospital, and the Emory Children's Center, the largest pediatric multispecialty group practice in the state. The following year, when the Wesley Woods Center also joined Emory Healthcare, bringing with it the ten-year-old Wesley Woods Geriatric

Hospital (the first freestanding geriatric hospital in the nation), Emory Healthcare included the full continuum of care, from fetal to geriatric medicine.

By 1999, when John T. Fox was named the first president and CEO of Emory Healthcare, Emory's healthcare umbrella extended further into the community. Emory-Adventist Hospital, owned jointly by Emory and Adventist Health System, was located in rapidly growing Cobb County. EHCA, a joint venture with HCA-The Healthcare Company, added eight community hospitals, many of which would close or return to HCA. (As of 2010 Emory retained responsibility for clinical management and quality assurance in two EHCA hospitals: Emory Eastside Medical Center and a completely restructured Emory Johns Creek Hospital that opened in 2007.)

> *The integration of care with the advances made possible by research was what would distinguish Emory medicine from the excellent health facilities across the state, often staffed by well-prepared Emory graduates.*

The next decade was a steady progression of construction and redevelopment aimed at better serving metropolitan Atlanta. Like Emory University Hospital, Crawford Long Hospital had expanded in the 1970s and 1980s, but $270 million redevelopment project completed in 2002 was the largest private hospital project—and one of the largest hospital constructions of any kind—ever seen in Georgia: a six-story, 511-bed hospital, topped by a fourteen-story medical office tower. A joint venture partnership with developer (and Emory trustee) Thomas G. Cousins, the plan supported the city's revitalized midtown. The hospital already had added "Emory" to the front of its name. In 2009 it was renamed again, becoming Emory University Hospital Midtown, to strengthen the visibility of its Emory relationship and the importance of its midtown location. (The name "Crawford Long" was retained in the 1931 building that had housed that hospital for more than seven decades.) During this time, while planning was under way for a huge makeover of Emory University Hospital and the Emory Clinic, EUH also underwent extensive renovation of some older patient-care units.

In 2002, with the dedication of the new $75 million Winship Cancer Institute (WCI) building, Robert Woodruff's ambition for Georgia to have a gateway to cancer care and a discovery accelerator for cancer research took further material shape. Constructed with funds from the Woodruff Foundation, the facility, where clinicians and researchers could come together in one location, provided one of the missing pieces in Emory's quest to become Georgia's first National Cancer Institute Cancer Center. Gaining this designation in 2009 WCI joined an elite group of sixty-four cancer centers nationwide. The coveted NCI designation would have pleased Woodruff, and it also pleased, and was a tribute to, the Woodruff Foundation, the Georgia Cancer Coalition, and the Georgia Research Alliance, all of whom had helped support the WCI and the push for NCI designation.

This kind of community partnership characterized much of the WHSC's growth. In keeping with its commitment to Grady, the WHSC opened a new four-story Emory Clinical Training and Faculty Office building in 2004, providing space for the Emory physicians who work at Grady. The $15 million for construction came from Emory University, the School of Medicine, and the Emory Medical Care Foundation, the nonprofit organization through which all money that Emory doctors receive for patient care at Grady is reinvested into programs to benefit the hospital.

That same year, 2004, the Emory Children's Center opened a new building next to Children's Healthcare of Atlanta at Egleston. (Egleston and Scottish Rite hospitals had earlier joined to form CHOA, then had taken on further responsibility for Hughes Spalding Hospital in downtown.) The long-awaited building was viewed as a visible bridge—along with a shared medical directorship and the Emory physicians who are the primary staff—between Emory's academic pediatrics program and CHOA's top-rated hospital. (In 2006 the two organizations added a hyphen to Emory-Children's Center to symbolize their increasingly integrated relationship.)

The following year, 2005, the Emory Orthopaedics & Spine Center consolidated all components of outpatient orthopaedics under one roof, near campus, and in 2008 opened the six-story, 120-bed Emory University Orthopaedics & Spine Hospital, an extension of Emory University Hospital, about seven miles north of the Emory campus.

The momentum in health care had been strategically planned to allow Emory to remain the leading delivery system for high-quality health care, in the most challenging environment academic health care had ever known. That meant growth, modernization of current facilities and programs, and a continuing shift toward becoming a geographically dispersed multispecialty group practice. But the WHSC also had to accomplish this clinical mission while continuing to strengthen its teaching and research missions. In fact, the integration of care with the advances made possible by research was what would distinguish Emory medicine from the excellent health facilities across the state, often staffed by well-prepared Emory graduates. The health sciences center continued to pioneer discoveries, changing medicine through new approaches, such as predictive health, and through a greatly expanded clinical trials program to increase access to new treatments. As Emory Healthcare grew, it did so in tandem with an ever-expanding research direction.

Joining the Ranks of the Country's Leading Research Institutions

In its youth and adolescence, Emory did not think of itself as a research institution. In the WHSC, the goals were preparation of new generations of doctors and nurses and providing and constantly improving health care for Atlanta and the region. That seemed enough. True, the Woodruff Memorial Research Building had been constructed in 1952 to help basic and clinical departments do some research, and the incorporation of the Yerkes Primate Research Center in 1956 added more research, even if the center itself did not move to campus for another nine years. True, in 1960, Emory University Hospital was chosen as one of eight national clinical research centers, a distinction it still holds (and one that Emory doctors also later would get funded at Grady Hospital as well). The medical school's basic science PhD programs were strong, and the first joint MD/PhD degree was granted in 1964, another sign of appreciation for research in clinical care. But in the late 1950s and throughout the 1960s, when the newly formed National Institutes of Health began pouring out Cold War–era research dollars on willing institutions, Emory held back. Other medical schools rushed to the spigot; Emory's decided instead to further expand its teaching and care missions.

When the longtime medical dean Arthur Richardson retired in 1979, he admitted that the school's research record was not as great as it ought to be. But that record was about to change. That same year, the Woodruff gift offered Emory a chance to grow in new directions, and in the WHSC Hatcher and Williams were ready. New research-minded medical deans in turn looked for research-minded faculty. Recruitment and retention, not to mention the work itself, required research facilities, and both the Woodruff Foundation and other donors stepped up.

Businessman and philanthropist Holland Ware, for example, funded the first cancer laboratories, professorships, and graduate programs. When trustee O. Wayne Rollins saw plans for a major research building where researchers from the WHSC and the other side of the campus could work together on biomedical research, Rollins—previously a generous donor to the theology school—wanted to be part of the research promise. The O. Wayne Rollins Research Center, opened in 1990, doubled the amount of research space on campus. Then a $50 million renovation to the Woodruff Memorial Research Building more than trebled it. With these spaces, together with the faculty recruitment they made possible, no one could ignore Emory as a research institution.

Emory had never bothered adding up any research dollars won from NIH and other agencies until 1986, when the University's tally was $50 million, a mere fraction of the $484 million in 2010, 90 percent of it in the WHSC. By 1990 the medical school had set a national record with the fastest-rising increase in research income over the previous five years of any U.S. medical school. It would maintain this pace right through the first decade of the new century, bypassing schools that had a half-century head start in the research race to rank.

The School of Medicine had some extraordinary partnerships, all aimed at what research could do for patients and the community, now and in the future. Clinicians in Emory Healthcare, Grady, CHOA, the VAMC, and other community partners were eager to become involved in multidisciplinary research programs. The Wallace H. Coulter Department of Biomedical Engineering was established jointly between Emory and the Georgia Institute of Technology in 1997. In addition to joint MD/PhD degrees and research in biomedical engineering, the Coulter Department includes the Emory/Georgia Tech Predictive Health Institute, an innovative model of health care that uses the new tools of bioscience to identify and measure risks and deviations from health, thus intervening at the very earliest indication, based on an individual's personal profile, to restore normal function.

> *By 2010 the economic impact of the Woodruff Health Sciences Center on Atlanta and Georgia was more than $5 billion yearly.*

Emory also continues to garner support from two powerful organizations for research efforts. The Georgia Research Alliance, a partnership of business, research universities, and state government committed to helping Georgia become a leader and encouraging working partnerships between industry and academy, supports research professorships and programs such as molecular screening for new drugs and nanotechnology. The Georgia Cancer Coalition, the first statewide cancer initiative of its kind, initially built with Georgia's share of funds from the 1998 Tobacco Master Settlement Agreement, also provides the WHSC important support, especially in the Winship Cancer Institute and cancer programs at Grady.

Perhaps just as important as these outside partnerships and funding sources has been the determination throughout the past twenty years of all the research-oriented WHSC components to work together. One of the biggest research growth areas throughout the 1990s and early 2000s was at Yerkes. Behavioral research took place at a growing field station campus near Lawrenceville, while the main campus, tucked away in the woods near Emory's main campus, became increasingly biomedical, with Yerkes, WHSC, and University researchers (often individuals with multiple appointments) working hand in hand. The combination was powerful, perhaps unique: expertise to do precise physiological studies—through imaging and hormonal assays, for example—coupled with large groups of monkeys living in a natural environment. The other power was the ability to combine research in both nonhuman primates and humans. Vaccines were one of the most promising research areas, especially after 2001, when the new Emory Vaccine Center opened at Yerkes. The growing trend of moving discovery quickly from bench to patient care could be seen in the development and testing of vaccines for HIV/AIDS and other diseases in nonhuman primates at Yerkes, with clinical human trials at Emory's Hope Clinic. This new clinical research facility, in nearby Decatur, is home to one of the largest basic and preclinical vaccine research programs at any university worldwide. Emory's well-established clinical and research strengths in neurological diseases—movement disorders, Alzheimer's, and others—also moved forward with the opening in 2004 of a new neuroscience research building on the Yerkes campus or, as Yerkes leaders preferred, the Yerkes science village.

The Nell Hodgson Woodruff School of Nursing conducted its own strategic research plan in 1996, aimed at quickly becoming one of the top nursing schools in NIH funding. Establishing a doctoral program, the school began overcoming barriers to this aspiration. Focused largely on bio-behavioral determinants of health, the program also helped with recruitment of faculty prepared to function as independent researchers. In 2001 the school also moved into a new building, designed to make possible both research and teaching of new nurses (for example, simulation laboratories allow nursing students to "treat" robotic patients, sometimes in tandem with medical students). The school's partnerships with the School of Public Health became increasingly significant as the School of Nursing sought to become a strong and influential lead in global health international nursing, working through the Lillian Carter Center for International Nursing to support nursing and improve the health of vulnerable people worldwide. By 2009 it ranked twenty-sixth among nursing schools.

By its fifth birthday, in 1995, the Rollins School of Public Health already had quintupled its research funding to become the second-most heavily funded school in the University (second only to medicine), a rank it would trade back and forth with Yerkes. Partnership was paramount, in research as in teaching, in a school where faculty members often shared appointments, programs, or research projects with the CDC (half of all adjunct faculty), the Carter Center, the American Cancer Society, CARE, the Arthritis Foundation, the Task Force for Child Survival (now the Task Force for Global Health), and state and local public-health agencies. Students reveled in the research opportunities, as they did in the possibility of earning joint MPH/MD degrees; joint MPH and master's degrees in business, law, nursing, and theology; and MPH and doctor of physician assistant and physical therapy degrees. One price of success, however, was that its sleek building, designed for a once ambitious target of six hundred students, was bursting at the seams. The Rollins family once again stepped forward with support. The new Claudia Nance Rollins Building, named for O. Wayne Rollins's mother and Randall's and Gary's grandmother, was completed in 2010 and doubled the school's physical space and teaching, research, and partnership opportunities.

Back to the Future | The WHSC began another new leadership cycle in 2007, when President James Wagner named Michael Johns chancellor of Emory University (a senior advisory position) and appointed Fred Sanfilippo, MD, PhD, as executive vice president for health affairs, CEO of the Woodruff Health Sciences Center, and chair of Emory Healthcare. A former professor at Duke and former chair of the pathology department at Johns Hopkins, Sanfilippo had most recently served as executive dean for health sciences at Ohio State University. Doug Ivester, former CEO of the Coca-Cola Company and current president of Deer Run Investments, LLC, had already taken office, in 2003, as chair of the WHSC board.

Sanfilippo arrived at Emory impressed by the Woodruff Health Sciences Center's strengths and collegiality (what he called "a differentiating strength, especially in leveraging Emory's incredible internal and external partnerships"), and immediately set about seeking ways to refine its vision and accelerate its already terrific momentum.

Two of his first initiatives were to add to the Center's growing list of comprehensive centers in cancer, neurosciences, transplant, and heart and vascular disease. The new Emory Center for Critical Care was charged with standardizing and harmonizing care across all of Emory's ICUs, while the Center for Comprehensive Informatics aggregates expertise from several disciplines across the university and in partnership with Georgia Tech, Children's Healthcare of Atlanta, Grady Memorial Hospital, CDC, and others.

As of 2010, the Woodruff Health Sciences Center had roughly twenty-five hundred faculty, plus another fifteen hundred adjunct or volunteer faculty and collaborative scientists, and some eighteen thousand employees. Its economic impact on Atlanta/Georgia was more than $5 billion yearly. Its scientists received more than $400 million in research funding, and its clinicians were responsible for nearly 5 million patient services at Emory's own hospitals and clinics and those in the community—Grady, Children's Healthcare of Atlanta, and Veterans Affairs—where Emory doctors provide the bulk of physician care. In 2008–9, Emory Healthcare physicians provided nearly $50 million in charity care in its own hospitals, and millions more in uncompensated care provided by Emory physicians practicing at Grady and other affiliated institutions.

Its schools and centers continue to rise in the ranks and to have an impact worldwide.

The early founders of the first components of what would become the Woodruff Health Sciences Center—perhaps even Robert Woodruff and Garland Herndon, talking over goals and challenges in those daily breakfast meetings in the 1970s—might well be astonished by what the center has become, what it has accomplished, and the ambitious plans it has for the future. What would not surprise them is that the WHSC continues its deep immersion into the community from which so much of it sprang. The hope for a healthier community that animated those early Atlantans to charter a medical school in 1854 continues to flourish, even as it is realized in more powerful ways each year.

HUMANS AND OTHER PRIMATES
Yerkes since 1979
— FREDERICK A. KING and STUART M. ZOLA —

When Yale University approached Emory in 1956 with an offer to sell some property in Florida for a dollar, the New England school was selling a treasure at a bargain price.[1] Since their establishment at Orange Park, Florida, in 1930, the primate laboratories named for their founding director, Robert M. Yerkes, PhD, had allowed that distinguished psychologist to study, for the first time, the reproductive and developmental processes of chimpanzees, and had prepared the way for a systematic investigation of nonhuman primates that would lead to deeper understanding of the social behavior of humans.

With the retirement of Yerkes from Yale in 1941, the distance between New Haven and Orange Park became an obstacle for the university's continued development of the laboratories for research and teaching of Yale faculty and students. Following the death of Yerkes in 1956, Yale sought to convey the facility to a southern university that could carry on his distinguished legacy. Emory agreed to receive the transfer of the facility. Four years later the U.S. Congress enacted the National Institutes of Health's (NIH) Primate Research Centers Program to provide the specialized resources needed for primate research. The following year the NIH designated the Yerkes facility in Orange Park as a Regional Primate Research Center, and the NIH funding that came with that designation enabled Emory to transfer the center to the Druid Hills campus. Twenty-five acres carved out of the north side of Lullwater provided the home for the new Yerkes Primate Research Center, which was completed in 1965; a 117-acre field station opened the following year, some twenty-five miles away, in Lawrenceville, Georgia.

Since then, Yerkes has grown rapidly to become one of the nation's leading research centers for the study of neurodegenerative diseases, development of vaccines, and neurobehavioral science, as well as continuing study of primate biology and behavior.

This chapter collects some of the reminiscences of the scientists who have led the development of Yerkes for more than three decades.

Frederick King

Frederick A. King, PhD, became director and professor of neuroscience at Yerkes in 1978 and held those positions until his retirement, in 1994. King also served as professor of anatomy and cell biology, associate dean of the Emory University School of Medicine, and adjunct professor in the Department of Psychology in the College of Arts and Sciences. He is now director and professor emeritus.

Following an undergraduate program at Stanford and doctoral studies in behavioral and neurological sciences at Johns Hopkins, King completed postdoctoral work in neurophysiology at the Institute of Human Physiology at the School of Medicine of the University of Pisa. He also has studied medicine at the Universidad de San Carlos of Guatemala and the University of Florida. Prior to coming to Emory, King was professor, chair of the Department of Neuroscience, and founding director of the Center for Neurobiological Sciences at the University of Florida College of Medicine.

With wide-ranging research interests, King studied brain mechanisms and behavior, human and animal epilepsy, tropical medicine, and parasitology. He was the codiscoverer of Zeman-King Syndrome, a neurological and behavioral syndrome in humans that occurs during growth of cerebral tumors in certain deep structures of the forebrain. He has published in the fields of neuroscience, behavior, and primatology and served on editorial boards of scientific journals and books, as well as on major committees of the National Institutes of Health, the National Science Foundation, and the National Academy of Science.

As a leader for the humane care of animals in research, as well as for the importance and necessity of animal studies to improving human and animal health, King has received commendations from the NIH and the American Medical Association, among others. During his directorship, the

Dr. Frederick King

Yerkes Center experienced a remarkable growth and expansion in scientific programs. Yerkes was one of the first research facilities in the United States to use both monkeys and great apes in the study of AIDS (SIV and HIV) and to build a strong, continuing program that has helped to advance the field. The primate colony increased to over three thousand animals, and for the first time in its history Yerkes received full accreditation from the American Association of Laboratory Animal Care—the gold standard in excellence in laboratory and animal care.

Dr. King, tell us about your work before you came to Emory.
I was at the University of Florida School of Medicine as chair of the Department of Neuroscience, which I had founded with the support of the university. Before that I was performing neurosurgical research at the University of Florida School of Medicine. We founded the first accredited medical school neuroscience department in the country, I believe. A few other schools were offering mixes of neurology, behavior, pharmacology, neuroanatomy, but ours was probably the first full-fledged, accredited neuroscience department.

What kind of primate research did you do at the University of Florida?
Brain research. My focus was the interaction between cognitive and so-called limbic functions, that is, functions having to do with drive and basic processes in organisms, such as eating, drinking, and emotion, including aggression, hostility, pleasure—all of those things that fall into the motivational realm rather than the cognitive, knowing realm. I also had a special focus on temporal lobe epilepsy, primarily human research and clinical work.

Do you consider yourself a primatologist?
A real primatologist is usually a field scientist who understands more of the basic habits, the sexual behavior, and other fundamental natural activities of the animal. I'm not a primatologist but a neuroscientist who specialized in research with primates, including humans, apes, and monkeys.

What was your first encounter with Yerkes?
At that time Yerkes belonged to Yale. The center had become famous but an inconvenience for them because it was so distant from their campus. Governance of it was increasingly difficult from afar. They came down to Florida and tried to sell us the whole thing—monkeys, faculty, buildings, and everything in Orange Park. At that time we at the University of Florida were a brand-new medical school, not yet equipped or staffed to manage another operation of that large a scale. We didn't have many research programs in primatology. At first we had only a handful of primates at the University of Florida, and most of those were the ones I worked with. So we had to say no to Yale.

The National Institutes of Health were planning to establish seven regional primate centers to serve the primate research needs of the nation, however, and they received applications and eventually selected seven universities strong enough to give good all-around support to centers devoted to the study of primates. While we had done primate research at Florida, we were not selected because of the general limited size and scope of primate research there. NIH, however, did provide the University of Florida funds to build a modest structure and equip it for primate research and housing.

Meanwhile the NIH awarded Emory a regional primate center for the Southeast. I was asked to serve on the board of directors of the new primate center they had built in Atlanta. I served on the board for eight years.

We were evaluating and making recommendations on a number of matters, including innovations in research projects, employment of senior faculty, personnel, species of animals, and other facets that go naturally with primate research. NIH usually took our recommendations.

What attracted you to the directorship of Yerkes?

I was enthusiastic about Yerkes for two reasons. First, they had a unique colony that included not only several species of monkeys, especially rhesus, but great apes as well. They had the largest collection of great apes research subjects anywhere. I also wanted to work with great apes. I saw some opportunities here for evolutionary inferences. Yerkes had a good reputation. It was the second primate center established in the world. The first had been Russia's National Primate Center in Sukhumi on the Black Sea in 1925.

Russia had a prominent reputation in the 1920s through 1950s in primatology. They specialized in behavioral, Pavlovian, and neurological research. In the beginning, it was the only primate center. It was very large but not as broad in concept and scope of work as American primate centers. I thought Yerkes could outstrip many of Sukhumi's in technology and creativity, which would permit Yerkes to do studies in areas that weren't being done in Russia.

I also saw an opportunity to build a more active neuroscience program here at Emory. Emory had no department or division of neurosciences then. Emory had no center for neurosciences, and as I look back, I think that was in part because each department pretty much had its own building and a tradition in which interdisciplinary studies were not especially encouraged.

Did you apply for the directorship of Yerkes, or were you recruited?

I was asked if I wanted to apply, perhaps because I was on the board of directors. Yerkes was nearby. I knew a lot of people here and knew the work they had done. Yerkes seemed an ideal place to do primate research, and Emory was beginning to be increasingly an up-and-coming university. They had just gotten $105 million from the Woodruff Fund, and I thought some of those funds might be available, in addition to the NIH contributions.

Geoffrey Bourne was the director prior to you.

Yes, and although he was retiring, he next went down to the Caribbean and was a main force in establishing what became the best English-language medical school in the Caribbean, St. George's University School of Medicine.

Anyway, Geoffrey was leaving, and he said to me, "Would you like to be the next director of Yerkes?" I said, "Sure." Later the head of the board I was on asked me if I would be interested in being a candidate, and I said that would be an honor, and I would like to be considered.

The search came down to the last three candidates, and I was one of them. I never thought I would get the directorship because I'm not really a primatologist, but neither were some of the other people who had already been appointed directors of the Oregon Primate Center, the Washington Primate Center, the California Primate Center—seven of them all together.

Then I came down here on a visit. In my interview with President Laney, I remember I said that I think I know what to do here to strengthen the program and make it what it should be—an integral part of Emory's science programs, and the premier center in the United States. The next thing I knew, I was named director.

What was your vision for Yerkes?

One vision I had was that neurosciences should be strengthened, and that the way to strengthen them was not simply to hire highly competent neuroscientists, and a lot of updated equipment, which we did also, but to unite them more with the University departments that had neurosciences in them, and we did this: neurology, neurosurgery, neurophysiology, neuroanatomy, psychology, neuropharmacology, neurochemistry, and ophthalmology, among others.

Emory already had these programs, but they tended to be entities unto themselves. In fact, we did learn how those sciences fit together and why it's essential not to stay isolated in a rapidly changing scientific world. But I found it difficult to achieve here. Emory was a bit isolationistic and occasionally defensive. Department chairmen were somewhat territorial. They worried about it.

We received the first training grant here in neurosciences.

I wanted to see Yerkes rise up to where it had been years ago. It had declined because of many, many factors, including the attitude of the School of Medicine toward Yerkes, which tended to be negative in certain regards.

When you came into the directorship, what needed to be changed?

We needed a better spirit of cooperation and a feeling that we were in this together, all putting our scientific efforts together, not isolating the intimately close biological fields which comprise the neurosciences, both within the center and between the University and the center.

The chairmen had a good deal of power, as they should. Some of them were cooperative. If they could get something from me, they would. If I told them, look I'll give you half a position, I'll pay for half of one of your tenured faculty members, if you'll give him half-time appointment at Yerkes, plus laboratory space (the sine qua non for lab scientists), and equipment and assistants. That's what I did to get things going—give a little, get a little. Eventually we had a large number of medical school joint appointments with Yerkes, and these I chose for collaborative research, or I set them up in labs at Yerkes because that was about the only place they could study primates at Emory in those times.

What other challenges did you face, and how did you address them?

The former director often had hired people to achieve particular ends in his interests in anatomy and related fields, which were legitimate interests. I wanted to build a neuroscience institute, without damaging other programs. So I took special pains to seek out good people with different and varied interests across the disciplines, people in other areas that we were active in. Endocrinology, for example—sexual behaviors are very important in primates—and hormone studies.

A primate center, especially one sponsored by the national government, should bring together the various disciplines—and that's what I set out to build. If there is any big mistake I made at Yerkes, it was overdoing it and not building neurosciences within the centers strongly enough to strengthen the University's neural programs more fully. Eventually we were able to do that, helping the University with its neuroscience and behavior-related programs, to gain [other departments'] trust.

So my goal was to see a well-balanced primate center with the neurosciences as perhaps preeminent or at least very high.

What other areas you did build?

Reproductive biology and contraception, in vitro fertilization, and so on, which is good to work on with primates because they are more similar to humans than other species are. We built reproductive biology quite strongly with Dr. Ken Gould as head of the reproductive biology division.

Pathology. You couldn't find a more direct, honest, down-to-earth guy than Dr. Harold McClure, and he was a very good general pathologist.

We did infectious disease research, especially tropical disorders, pretty well.

We had students from twenty different universities at any one year at Yerkes who came to work for varying periods of times. We gradually had more and more postdocs. We had more and more graduate students come and want to do their work at Yerkes. We had 29 core scientists when I retired, 21 associate scientists, and 170 science faculty with affiliate, collaborative, or visiting relationships, including appointments in the CDC. We had them from all over the world, everywhere from Asia, Africa, Europe, Latin America. I believe we put Yerkes quite strongly on the modern scientific map.

Were these new appointments core or affiliated faculty?

Some became core. Sometimes, in the case of ophthalmologists who wanted to practice ophthalmology but also do research, the Ophthalmology Department didn't have the space and the equipment—or the monkeys—for them to do it. So we invited them to come to Yerkes, if they brought their grants with them. Often a chair of the department would go through the ceiling when he heard that, and I would say, "Well, hey, give a little, get a little. We're making our facilities, our technology, our atmosphere, everything we have available to you, and all we ask is that you pay your way in what you would normally pay for out of the grant anyway." That began to sink in. We were getting more and more sharing on a fair basis. It had a payoff on both ends, for both sides.

This collaboration occurred not only in medical school departments [but also in College departments like] psychology, sociology, anthropology, and biology and biomedical engineering that we did with Georgia Tech. Many times individual scientists would bring in unique but appropriate projects.

What other research highlights occurred while you were director?

Especially in ophthalmology we hired some very good young people. We did some AIDS research, and we did some Simian Auto-Immune Deficiency, or SAIDS research on primates, as well as eye surgery, prosthetics, and pharmacological treatments.

Was Yerkes the first division to do AIDS research at Emory University?

Yes, I believe that Yerkes was the first, and there were some objections from the administration. It wasn't a "respectable disease." There was a social stigma attached even to conducting research. That has always been so for various kinds of research. The public thought of [AIDS as primarily affecting homosexuals and thought of] homosexuals as aberrant people. But AIDS is a disease, and if it's a disease, cure it. We treat typhus and smallpox and others, but these do not have a moral stigma. We even treat a whole spectrum of sexually transmitted disease.

You encountered resistance in the administration.

Sometimes. We proceeded nonetheless, and now Emory has one of the largest programs and grant funding in AIDS research in the country. Now they aren't embarrassed by it and have made significant contributions to the development of the vaccine and treatment.

How did you begin AIDS research?

Primarily [with grants] from NIH. The fullest understanding requires the knowledge, skills, and talents of pharmaceutical companies, federal labs, and field studies on humans and a highly sophisticated level of knowledge of biochemical microbiology. To do this work takes an enormous understanding of the steps in metabolism through which the AIDS virus passes, and what occurs when a virus mutates. These classes of viruses that caused AIDS were little understood and required, in a sense, starting from scratch to understand their nature and their transformation. We have found out a lot about AIDS, and we are finally, hopefully, close to a serviceable vaccine. We still don't have a cure, but we have developed treatments that have extended life from months to many years. AIDS is a true pandemic, however, in the sense that it exists in virtually all parts of the world and causes millions of deaths and parentless children throughout countries that do not have developed science and medicine.

Did you personally want to see AIDS research done at Emory, or were the core scientists interested in it initially as well?

Both. Our pathology and microbiology departments were extremely interested, and the CDC [Centers for Disease Control] was highly desirous of collaborating with us, and we with them. We had to construct protective facilities to ensure that the vaccine would not escape into the human population of Yerkes or the CDC.

Did you hire Harriet Robinson, who has been at the fore of developing an AIDS vaccine?
She came just before I left and was a great asset to the vaccine program.

What other hires are you proud of?
Frans de Waal. He is a highly individualized scientist who takes a unique approach to the social behavior of primates and their relationship to human society. Kim Wallen, who was jointly appointed with psychology, became a superb biobehaviorist. I could name several others: Mark Wilson in behavioral physiology.

What other research highlights occurred while you were director?
We did a good job on Parkinsonism research. Pathology research we did mainly in the pathology of malaria, of AIDS, and a number of infectious diseases and some noninfectious diseases, some of them obscure diseases that exist only in a few places in the world but are very serious and have a high mortality rate—ebola and other esoteric African and Latin American fevers.

We set up a mini–language center and helped fund it at Georgia State University. Dwayne Rumbaugh and his wife, Sue Savage Rumbaugh, and cohorts were very interested in symbolic representation in animals and in primates, and of evolution of language, particularly, and it looked as though it might be useful in human therapy for people with speech or language problems. Chimpanzees could communicate by the exchange of symbols about as well as a three- or four-year-old human. Children would come into the language center and learn how to use a keyboard with simple symbols in place of spelled-out words. But limitations impeded this landmark research, although from the seventies through the nineties it attracted a great deal of attention.

The center also studied the comparison of conflict resolution between subhuman primates and humans. We looked at ways to correct vision and prevent partial and total blindness in humans.

What was the relationship of Yerkes to the Woodruff Health Sciences Center when you came, and how did it change during your tenure?
Gradually the relationship between Yerkes and the health sciences center grew. Some departments pretty quickly gained trust in us. Psychology was one of them, perhaps because I had gotten my original degree in physiological psychology, so they thought of me as a psychologist and gave me an adjunct appointment. I had also been chair of anatomy at the University of Florida for a period of time, and the Anatomy Department here awarded me a tenured appointment.

Overall I would say that we strengthened the Center's relationships with the campus, through reciprocal or joint faculty appointments as well as undergraduate, graduate, and medical students working in collaboration with Yerkes scientists, who also may have served as their mentors. We developed models for understanding animal-human biological functions and behavior.

Did NIH shape the research agenda of the scientists, or did the scientists shape their own agenda, or both?
Certain primate centers tend to be somewhat specialized in particular areas of research. So a primate center might start exploring in that area, but with the approval of NIH, it had the privilege of branching off on its own and starting new projects and working in new areas of science. Generally the scientists, of course, came committed to an area, and they would do work in that area, and we could start new areas of research at our university that way. We chose scientists from Yerkes and other units of the University to assist in critically evaluating

grants before submission to Federal agencies to be certain we were producing a product of scientific usefulness.

How did you begin to work with Zoo Atlanta?

Zoo Atlanta viewed me as a primatologist. Consequently I was asked to serve on the primate committee of the zoo. The zoo was coming under criticism for its care of animals, and we finally came to the conclusion that we should either move the zoo or rebuild the zoo. Moving the zoo to Stone Mountain was under consideration, but that would have deprived city residents without transportation of access to it. I was opposed to that, and so were most of the people [involved in the decision]. Then they pointed out that they did not have a variety of primates at the zoo, and only one great ape.

Terry Maple was becoming director then. He had worked at Yerkes, although his primary appointment was at Georgia Tech, and he asked if Yerkes could provide them with some apes.

After much consideration, I said, "Yes. We'll have to go through our inventory because we have orphans that need mothers, and we could put a mother with an orphan out at the zoo. We can do it but it would have to be under this condition—that our scientists, subject to approval of both our and your animal care committees, would be permitted to carry out behavioral noninvasive research."

Then we also had to get the new zoo facility built. The Ford Foundation paid for the physical development, and Yerkes gave them thirteen gorillas and a dozen orangutans—several million dollars worth, which I placed on permanent loan, along with chimps. They wanted those orangutans. One reason we gave them was that we do not wish to do any invasive work on them. Also, we wouldn't want to take a species like that that's so rare and scarce and use it invasively or in a way that would damage or impair the sexual reproductivity of the species.

I also gave animals to Busch Gardens with the same agreement, although they donated a million dollars to Yerkes.

Speaking of millions, we then wanted to build a neuroscience building at Yerkes, but I was seventy years old. I figured that would be a good starting point from which to begin soliciting additional money to fund a neuroscience building at Yerkes. So when I retired I left additional money specifically to be assigned to the new neuroscience building, and I understand it was used for that purpose, in addition to large grants from NIH and elsewhere.

What do you see as some of your main achievements at Yerkes?

Expansion of research programs, growth in the number of affiliate and collaborative scientists, and interaction with regional, national, and international institutions. We set up programs in Kenya, Indonesia, and Borneo, and did some interesting projects in China and Japan.

I was director from 1978 to 1994; during that time we significantly expanded and improved research labs, isolation space, and animal care facility space, strengthened the center's research and educational relationship with the University, increased four-fold the number of scientists on the Yerkes faculty, as well as students representing twenty other universities and institutions worldwide who were involved in research at Yerkes, and increased the primate colony to almost four thousand animals. The basic and applied biomedical research program expanded significantly, and we strengthened the programs in the behavioral sciences. For the first time in its history Yerkes earned accreditation and was the first primate lab to earn full accreditation from the American Association for the Accreditation of Laboratory Animal Care.

That accreditation was an enormous achievement, because I was told upon my arrival that the primate center would never get accredited, no matter what I did. Even the head veterinarian said we couldn't. I said, "Yes, we can," and we worked for a year. We were the first major primate center to receive this accreditation.

We increased significantly the research on medical problems that might someday have practical applications. We also improved vastly the Yerkes field station at Lawrenceville by constructing new, modern compounds with recreational facilities for the animals and new interior buildings for sleeping quarters. We established a much stronger breeding program of primates so we would not have to take animals from the wild.

Stuart M. Zola | Stuart Zola, PhD, arrived at Emory in 2001 as director of the Yerkes National Primate Research Center and professor of psychiatry and behavioral sciences in the School of Medicine. He is also co-director of the Emory Alzheimer's Disease Research Center, a senior research career scientist at the Atlanta Veterans Administration Medical Center, the highest honor the V.A. bestows, and a fellow of the American Association for the Advancement of Science.

As one of the nation's leading neuroscientists, Zola has contributed valuable insights into how the brain organizes memory, and how this process relates to memory problems. He is also regarded as a leader in how to better communicate science and research to the general public. His own research focuses on memory formation, consolidation, and retrieval. He is perhaps best known for developing an animal model of human amnesia in nonhuman primates that conclusively identified brain structures critical to memory function. His research has contributed significant insights into the memory loss in humans that results from head trauma and characterizes progressive diseases such as mild cognitive impairment and Alzheimer's disease. His research also has provided knowledge about less severe memory problems that often accompany depression, chronic stress, and normal aging.

You arrived at Emory and Yerkes in 2001 from the University of California at San Diego, where you had spent most of your career.

September 11, 2001, as a matter of fact. My first staff meeting was on that morning, and we had just started it when news came of the attacks in New York.

What attracted you to Yerkes?

I saw the energy and potential and growth here. I actually came here—Tom Insel invited me—under the cover story of giving a talk. And then as the day grew closer, he said, as long as you're going to be here, would you mind if we set up some appointments for you with other people in the University? He said, we're looking for a new director, and since you have experience with primates at UCSD, it might be useful for people here to see somebody like you, the kind of person we'd be looking for.

I said I'd be glad to do that as long as you know I am not movable. I then had a chance to meet a lot of people, including [then–executive vice president for health affairs] Michael Johns, and for me that was a turnaround. So, although I had met the chair of the search earlier that day and had told him I was not available, I called him back that evening and said, You know, I think I'd like to change my mind and put my hat into this ring. It took about nine months for

Stuart Zola

them to do the search, and in the end I was the last person standing.

There was a real issue, though. Yerkes had at the time two major components. One was neuroscience, and the other was vaccines and immunology. The question was, where would the director sit? The immunologists, of course, wanted to have somebody in that field, and the neuroscientists wanted somebody in that field.

As I became more and more a candidate, I decided to spend two weeks at Smith College taking a microbiology course. It was a whole year in two weeks, and we spent twenty hours a day for fourteen straight days working in the labs and listening to lectures. This is an internationally known course made up of people from the CDC and people like me who were trying to get a good sense of what molecular biology and immunology were all about. I did that so I could talk to the immunologists on my next visit to Yerkes. I had a little bit of the jargon that I could toss around and make clear that I really had an interest and understanding of this. I actually was heavily invested in it intellectually.

Yerkes center

I think that helped turn the corner for the immunologists. I seemed to be somebody who could bridge both camps. In fact, I thought that the immunologists and the neuroscientists ought to be talking to each other a lot more, because one of the most promising developments in neuroscience is the possibility of vaccines for neurodegenerative diseases like Alzheimer's, using strategies that include neuromodulation of the immune system. That came about with this idea of smudging those sharply defined borders between infectious and noninfectious diseases. One of the first things I did here was organize a small conference that brought together immunologists and neuroscientists to imagine a convergence of those areas. That actually has paid off well for us.

When you were in California, you were working with primates.
  We had a small primate facility for my research—probably about thirty animals. There was one other researcher there, Gordon Baylis, who was in the Psychology Department and did research in primates, so the two of us shared this small facility in the basement of the science center at UCSD.
  We worked with cynomolgus monkeys, a macaque species. At the time I started my work, there was a shortage of rhesus monkeys, so we did some comparative behavioral testing and found that cynomolgus monkeys performed at about the same level as rhesus in our critical tasks, so we were able to switch to the cynos. At Yerkes, rhesus macaques are the major animals used for vaccine research as well as other kinds of studies.

When you came to Yerkes, how did you go about getting a sense of appropriate priorities and strategy for the center?
  I actually came in with a very clear vision of the future for us. The search process took quite a long time, and I had some time to think about these things. The first thing was to develop the neuroscience area. There was a small group in neuroscience, but how could we harness all that potential? Part of the negotiation for my coming was a building to house our neuroscience program. That was part of the inducement for me to come. It became clear to me during the search that the building they were envisioning was not going to suffice; I knew we would fill that building literally in the first week—enough people would want to come

here. We needed something bigger and better. Tom Gordon, then the associate director of Yerkes for scientific programs, and I went through long negotiation with the Woodruff Health Sciences Center to ensure that we would have what I thought would be adequate.

Now, in truth, I underestimated even that, but we moved from a thirty-thousand-square-foot building to a ninety-four-thousand-square-foot building. To the credit of Emory, the neuroscience research building became such an attractive entity for so many people, not just at Yerkes but in psychology and other departments, that that building literally was filled before it was even completed. We found ourselves immediately back in the same space crunch that I saw when I first got here, but at least we had a great program under way, brought in some terrific people who have blossomed, and furthered scientific careers for the center's more experienced researchers. As an administrator you try to get stable investigators who you know are going to do great work and bring in solid grants, and then complement this with junior researchers who may be untested but who you are certain are going to be stars.

Who are some of the people you brought in?
Jocelyne Bachevalier is one. She's in the Psychology Department but lives and works at Yerkes. She is a renowned behavioral and cognitive neuroscientist who was recently elected to the American Association for the Advancement of Science for her "exemplary work on the role of specific brain structures in the regulation of social and cognitive behaviors in humans and in animal models."

Anthony Chan is another. He was the first person I recruited to Yerkes. He developed the first transgenic monkey, literally the only transgenic monkey in the world at the time. With the extensive resources at Yerkes he has developed a transgenic monkey model of Huntington's disease, which is key to advancing our understanding of neurodegenerative diseases.

One other high-level recruit was Lary Walker, who is one of the most eloquent speakers on science, and whose work is directed toward understanding the causes of Alzheimer's disease and developing immunization therapy for the disease.

Thanks to Rafi Ahmed, there was already a well-developed immunology and vaccine group with Harriet Robinson and others. Harriet developed a leading AIDS vaccine candidate while at Yerkes, but the time came that she needed to move to the private industry to further advance the vaccine. A couple of other people departed around the same time, and that left us with the opportunity to revitalize our vaccine program, which had been the foundation at Yerkes for some time. The focus of our recruiting has been to draw together neuroscientists and immunologists with the idea that we ought to be sharing strategies with each other. Guido Silvestri, whom we just recruited back to Yerkes to further his HIV/SIV work, is one such researcher who has the right idea about scientific collaboration. Presumably there are some overlapping strategies that nature has found to make the immune system work and the brain work, and with leaders like Guido, we will figure those out and bring them together.

It's interesting, given Emory's history in cardiology, that Yerkes does not focus on that.
We focus on what is going to be best for us based on the researchers and resources we have. Every morning I think about what we're going to discover today. In addition to our immunology and neuroscience programs, we have a solid program in transplantation. In fact, we have just been awarded a $15 million grant to build a new facility, a major portion of which will be dedicated to research in transplant medicine. Another area we are developing is stroke research. We're looking at ways to intervene to prevent continued growth of the stroke once it has happened, and even to prevent the onset of a stroke. Nonhuman primates serve as a great model because their middle cerebral artery is very much organized in the same way ours is. Monkeys are also greatly suitable for imaging because of their large brains, and

we can do behavioral assessments with nonhuman primates in much the same way we do with our patients, in terms of both motor assessments and cognitive assessments. The nonhuman primate is now seen as necessary to move stroke and stroke intervention technology forward. While we do not have direct programs in cardiology, per se, we are heavily involved in aspects linked to cardiovascular research.

What do you see for the Yerkes of the future?

I think there are a few things. One place where the action is clearly going to be is genetics, and we have just redeveloped the Yerkes field station in that regard. We have a brand-new building for genetic research. We recruited an incredible geneticist, Zack Johnson, who is leading our efforts to genotype our entire colony. We need to understand the interaction between genetics and the environment for disease vulnerability and, ultimately, for human health. We have only begun to scratch the surface on that.

How does the environment affect genetic expression? How does genetic expression affect what happens to us and how we behave, and, more important, how proteins behave and create vulnerabilities or protection. Those are the real mysteries for young scientists coming up in the field.

Transgenics is going to be another big field. The fact that we have demonstrated a proof in principle with our first-in-the-world transgenic model of Huntington's disease in a nonhuman primate is important for the future. The next real step is going to be determining how to use these founder animals to create populations that will be sufficient for meaningful research. For example, right now we have only four animals that are Huntington's disease models. That's not enough to carry out a program, but it's enough during the next three to five years to develop a colony of forty to fifty animals. Those animals will be available to the entire nation for research in Huntington's disease. The same will be true for Alzheimer's animals and others. Even for AIDS one can imagine developing transgenic models for research. It opens up remarkable new areas that we simply never could have accomplished before without nonhuman primates as a model.

A third area is imaging technologies. These technologies are going to provide a better way for us to look into the brain and other bodily organs. We can map nerve fibers of the brain and look noninvasively at where nerves connect with each other. This means we could use animals over and over again, thus having a very efficient and important way to accelerate the pace of research.

These are three technologies where our strengths lie. We have some of the best people in the country in these fields, and we're going to move forward swiftly and effectively.

Animal rights protests seem to have died down a bit in recent years.

I credit our proactive outreach to Emory and the local community. When I got to Yerkes, we began sending researchers to speak with local groups, and we began inviting people to tour our two facilities. Today, because of this first-hand experience approach, there is a much better understanding about our research programs, why they are so important, and how they are advancing science and improving health. I'm pleased with the support we have from the community, and I look forward to furthering our outreach, especially when it comes to educating and inspiring the scientists of tomorrow.

CHAPTER 41

Heart and Soul
What makes the Emory Heart Center tick?

A LEGACY OF HEART
The Evolution of Cardiology at Emory
— J. WILLIS HURST —

Cardiology at Emory University has a decades-long tradition of excellence and a record of top national rankings. Willis Hurst, who was personally involved in much of the growth in cardiology over the last half-century, details the achievements of the division in this essay. His story begins in 1950, when he first joined the Emory faculty. The decades following saw tremendous growth in the field of cardiology and sweeping changes at Emory.

I **AM SOMETIMES** asked why Emory cardiology is consistently ranked in the top ten of the nation's heart centers. Here is the story. Note that the story, involving patient care, excellent teaching, and groundbreaking clinical and basic research, would not exist without the contributions of Emory faculty members in many departments, including medicine, pediatrics, surgery, pathology, radiology, anesthesiology, pharmacology, as well as the nursing staff. Likewise, the story unfolds in many settings: Emory University Hospital, Grady Memorial Hospital, Atlanta Veterans Affairs Medical Center (VAMC), Emory Crawford Long Hospital (now Emory Midtown), Egleston Children's Hospital, the Emory Clinic, dozens of satellite locations, and several research buildings. Since the beginning of cardiology at Emory, our faculty have shared what they know not only between departments but also with colleagues at other universities worldwide, creating unusual collaborations where one usually finds competition.

The Early Decades | We all stand on the shoulders of those who came before us. In the early years, when cardiology was being midwifed at Emory, several cardiologists started our story off right. In 1915, when Emory University took over the Atlanta Medical College, Jean George Bachmann served as the first chair of physiology. (He discovered Bachmann's bundle in the atria of the heart.) In the late 1920s Carter Smith Sr., a volunteer faculty member, introduced electrocardiography to Grady Hospital. Stewart Roberts Sr., known as the "Osler of the South," worked at Emory Hospital and later served as president of the American Heart Association (see chapter 24).

In those early decades Daniel C. Elkin, who became chair of Emory's Department of Surgery, began his nationally known work with patients with traumatic arteriovenous fistula. He continued this work in the U.S. Army during World War II, and after the war he and Frederick W. Cooper Jr. achieved national prominence for their work in peripheral vascular disease.

In 1942 Eugene Stead Jr. became Emory's first full-time professor and chair of the Department of Medicine. Although he began as the sole cardiologist at Grady Hospital, Jim Warren, John Hickson, Jack Myers, Paul Beeson, and others soon joined him. Stead and Warren created the famous cardiac catheterization laboratory at Grady, one of only four such laboratories in the world at that time. Supported by the army, the doctors studied circulatory shock in the laboratory and later turned to studies of the altered physiology of heart failure. Heinz Weens, chair of the Department of Radiology, aided the creative research effort (see chapter 42). In 1945 the research of Warren, Weens, and Emmet Brannon led to the first use of cardiac catheterization for diagnostic purposes.

Stead and his coworkers catapulted a struggling department of medicine into international prominence. When Stead accepted the chair of medicine at Duke in 1946, he handed the reins to Paul Beeson, who, while chairing the Department of Medicine at Emory, continued his research, making many original observations on patients with infective bacterial endocarditis.

Growing: 1940s and 1950s | Stead's recruitment of R. Bruce Logue to Emory in 1946 marks an important chapter in our history of cardiology. A man of vision, a superb clinician, a charismatic teacher, and an excellent writer, Logue had the right combination of abilities to develop a comprehensive cardiology center. He developed the Private Diagnostic Clinic (the forerunner of the Emory Clinic) in Emory Hospital and taught cardiology at Emory and Grady hospitals and the Atlanta VAMC. Much loved by all who knew him, Logue deserves the credit for the development of clinical cardiology at Emory. He also founded the Georgia affiliate of the American Heart Association.

Robert Grant, already on the scene, was a creative genius. He joined the Emory faculty at Grady in 1947 and developed a method of analyzing electrocardiograms by using basic principles and vector concepts.

Paul Beeson, chair of medicine, recruited me to join Emory in 1950. My job was to teach house staff and fellows at Emory and Grady hospitals, to help build a consulting referral practice, to engage in clinical research, and to write. My cardiology training with Dr. Paul White at the Massachusetts General Hospital prepared me for just such a position. Because pediatric cardiology was not yet a discipline, Logue and I also served as pediatric cardiologists.

During my first years at Emory I encouraged collaborations between cardiology and cardiac surgery. In 1951, for example, I urged our surgeons to operate on one of my patients who had severe mitral valve stenosis. They did so in probably the first operation of that type performed in the South, and set a precedent for future collaboration between cardiologists and cardiac surgeons at Emory. I also worked with a cardiac fellow to develop a new standardized type of digitalis for children, a preparation still used today.

With the support and guidance of Robert Grant I published my first book on electrocardiography in 1952. Along with Logue I edited the cardiovascular sections of J. C. Meakins's well-known textbooks of medicine.

Meanwhile, our ranks were growing. Eugene Ferris, who replaced Beeson as chair of the Department of Medicine, recruited Nobel Fowler to direct the Stead-Warren cardiovascular laboratory, in the Steiner building on the Grady campus. Beeson had left Emory to become chair of medicine at Yale in 1952. Edward R. Dorney, a superb clinician and teacher, joined Emory cardiology in 1954.

Keeping pace with the expanding faculty was a growing enterprise. The Emory Clinic, in which Logue and I were founding members, was formed in 1953 by the merger of the Private Diagnostic Clinic and several other units in Emory Hospital. This development was of utmost importance, because it created a superb method for growth and financial support.

Changing: Through the 1960s | In 1954 I was drafted by the military for the second time and was assigned to the cardiology service of the U.S. Naval Hospital in Bethesda, Maryland. While there, I attended cardiology conferences at the National Heart Institute, across the street, and made contacts with many of the future leaders in cardiology. Near the end of my tour of duty, in 1955 I became chief of cardiology. In that role, I attended Senate Majority Leader Lyndon Johnson when he experienced his first heart attack. Johnson convalesced at his ranch in Texas in the early fall of 1955, and he was admitted to Emory Hospital for examination before returning to the Senate. We became friends, and I served as his cardiologist for the next eighteen years. This long relationship introduced the public at large to Emory cardiology.

Meanwhile, in 1955, upon my return to Emory I discovered an alarming situation. The chairs of medicine, surgery, and obstetrics were embroiled in a heated disagreement with Dean Arthur Richardson, ultimately leading to their release. In the early fall of 1956, at the request of the dean and his search committee I agreed to become chair of the Department of Medicine; I was thirty-five years old.

My work as chair began on February 1, 1957, a year in which the story of Emory cardiology had progressed to include three cardiologists at Emory Hospital and one at Grady Hospital. No research space and no hard-core budget for the Department of Medicine yet existed. The National Heart Institute gave a twenty-five-thousand-dollar annual stipend to every medical school in the nation for the teaching of cardiology. But we obviously needed more than that to support our programs. We needed many more talented people, research space, and a budget.

One of the talented people who joined us in 1957 was Sam Poole, who organized and taught physical diagnosis to sophomore medical students. Garland Perdue, another young talent, became director of the division of vascular surgery in 1957 and served in that capacity until 1984.

In 1958 I recruited Brigham-trained Robert Schlant to direct the Stead-Warren cardiac-catheterization laboratory. Destined to become a world-class master cardiologist, Schlant took over as director of the Division of Cardiology in 1962, a capacity in which he served until 1986. As a part of his responsibilities, he expanded the cardiology fellowship training program. He also served as chair of the American Heart Association's Council of Cardiology.

An important financial commitment by the Robert W. Woodruff Foundation allowed us to build new cardiac laboratories within the new Grady Hospital. They were completed in 1958. Gordon Barrow was the first director of the cardiac clinic at Grady, followed by Freeman Cary, both volunteer faculty members. In 1960 Nanette Wenger, who had just completed her cardiac fellowship with us, became the clinic's director. A polished speaker and writer, she was a true pioneer, being one of the first women cardiologists.

> *Emory cardiac surgeons became leaders in coronary bypass surgery, with patients being referred from other states and other countries.*

In another development, the Crippled Children's Service of Georgia donated funds to build a cardiac catheterization laboratory in the relatively new Woodruff Memorial Research Building, attached to Emory Hospital. This laboratory became the first cardiac catheterization laboratory in a private hospital in Atlanta. I appointed Robert Franch, who was finishing his fellowship at Grady, to direct the lab.

Others also flocked to our ranks in the 1950s and 1960s: Woofin Cobbs Jr., who brought creative research in phonocardiolography; William Rawles, who contributed to the further development of the Stead-Warren laboratory; William Logan and Robert Smith, who developed vascular surgery; Charles Gilbert, who developed stress testing; Paul Robinson, who became a superb clinician and teacher; Don Nutter, an excellent teacher/researcher and one of our former fellows, who later directed the Stead-Warren cardiovascular laboratory; Alan Paulk, who helped develop the coronary care unit at Grady; and Joel Felner, an American Heart Association teaching scholar, who helped develop the software for the cardiac mannequin used to teach examination of the heart and later developed echocardiography at Grady.

We were experiencing growth at the Atlanta VAMC, too. The first full-time Emory faculty member in cardiology at the Atlanta VAMC was Joseph Lindsay Jr., appointed in 1966. An excellent teacher and clinical researcher, he became a national authority in dissection of the aorta. Sylvia Crawley joined the staff at the Veterans Hospital in 1967 and became chief of cardiology in 1970. Later, Paul Wallis joined the group at the Atlanta VA hospital. His interest in cardiac electrophysiology eventually led to his moving to Emory Hospital, where he developed the first electrophysiology laboratory.

At Crawford Long Hospital, which became part of Emory in 1963, Linton Bishop (Medicine 1947), a devoted volunteer faculty member, was the moving force in the development of cardiology.

Cardiology at Emory flourished during the sixties for several reasons. Each year Emory offered the only postgraduate courses in cardiology in the Southeast. We invited internationally renowned experts to help present these courses. Hundreds of practicing physicians attended, and Emory became recognized around the world as a major teaching center for cardiology. We organized the first postgraduate course in cardiology for the American Heart Association in 1963, followed a year later with the first postgraduate course in cardiology for nurses. The internationally known speakers and the participants learned what was happening at Emory and liked what they saw. These courses in cardiology led to the creation of the Continuing Medical Education Program at Emory.

Logue and I created the textbook *The Heart* in the early sixties. The book brought further acclaim to our cardiology efforts. It was becoming clear that textbooks in cardiology needed redoing. When single individuals wrote, they took too long to finish. The first chapter would be out of date by the time the last chapter was finished. So I proposed a multiauthored book, and with significant contributions from Robert Schlant, Nanette Wenger, and others, the first edition of *The Heart* was published in 1966. Subsequently, a new edition was created every four years. Now translated into six languages, and ten editions later, it has brought international recognition to Emory cardiology. After the seventh edition, I passed the editor-in-chief responsibilities to Schlant and Wayne Alexander, at which time the publishers renamed the book *Hurst's The Heart*. Although there are many books on cardiology today, the Emory book continues to be popular and used worldwide.

Several other pioneering developments accompanied the sixties. Emory physicians at Grady were the first in Atlanta to use cardiac defibrillation to treat atrial fibrillation, and the first in Atlanta to use a cardiac pacemaker. Schlant performed the first coronary arteriogram in Atlanta in the Grady cardiac laboratory. Franch, working in the cardiac catheterization laboratory on the Emory campus, performed the first atrial septotomy in the South in 1967.

Catherine Edwards, appointed director of pediatric cardiology in 1960, was given free access to the cardiac catheterization laboratory in the Woodruff Memorial Building. When she later entered the field of pediatric radiology, Dorothy Brinsfield became director of the Division of Pediatric Cardiology. These two pediatric cardiologists laid the groundwork for what was to become a nationally known pediatric heart center at Egleston.

Grady Hospital became even more famous because the national examination in cardiology was often given there. I was a member of the Board of Cardiology for a few years before becoming chair of that board. In 1967 I became a member of the advisory council of the National Heart Institute. The council funded development of clinical training programs in cardiology throughout the country. I believed that research was paying off, but we needed more clinicians to deliver the advances to patients. As a result Emory was awarded a large grant to train cardiology fellows. This granting process by the National Heart Institute is the reason for the dramatic increase in the number of cardiologists in the country.

The arrival of Charles Hatcher to the Division of Cardiothoracic Surgery in the early sixties adds another chapter to our story. By 1971 Hatcher was director of the division, and his leadership was a major force in the development of cardiac surgery at Emory. Emory cardiac surgeons became leaders in coronary bypass surgery, with patients being referred from other states and other countries. Hatcher continued as division director until 1995, also serving as director of the Emory Clinic from 1976 to 1984 and leading the Robert W. Woodruff Health Sciences Center from 1984 to 1996.

Rounding out the recruitments of the 1960s, Gerald Fletcher joined the faculty of the Department of Medicine in 1969. He created a superb, nationally recognized cardiovascular rehabilitation program in the physical educational building on the Emory campus.

Onward and Upward: Roll Call of the 1970s | During the 1970s Emory's cardiology group experienced extraordinary growth.

Hatcher assembled an excellent team of cardiac surgeons, which by the end of the decade could perform any cardiac surgery needed in adults and children. These surgeons quickly became leaders in coronary bypass surgery, so patients from distant states and abroad were referred to Emory University Hospital for cardiac care.

In 1970, at the request of several devoted Emory volunteer faculty members at Piedmont Hospital, I selected Mark Silverman to head medical education there. Silverman, an excellent cardiologist, teacher, clinician, writer, and organizer, performed beautifully in that role. In addition to being a valuable Emory faculty member, he developed a reputation as one of the nation's best cardiac historians.

Steve Clements joined the Cardiology Division; he was destined to become an outstanding addition who helped develop electrocardiography. That same year, Michael Gravanis became chair of the Department of Pathology. As a cardiac pathologist he contributed significantly to the teaching and research program. Cardiac pathology also was highlighted by the annual two-month visit of Reginald Hudson, the internationally known cardiac pathologist at the National Heart Hospital in London.

I became president of the American Heart Association in 1972. The same year Spencer King, one of our former trainees, returned to Atlanta from Denver to further develop the cardiovascular laboratories in Emory Hospital and to develop coronary arteriography. He designed four cardiac laboratories in the new addition to Emory University Hospital in 1974. John S. Douglas Jr. joined King to create first-rate diagnostic laboratories.

Several construction projects propelled cardiology at Emory onward, upward, and literally outward. For example, we added a new wing and connector to Emory University Hospital in the early 1970s, providing space for medical cardiology and cardiac surgery to be located on the same floor of the hospital. The design of the coronary care unit was so successful that it was published and copied by other institutions. We also created the Carlyle Fraser Heart Center at Crawford Long Hospital through the generosity of the Fraser family in 1976.

Leaps to the Top: The Early 1980s | The year 1980 marked a milestone in our history. Bruce Logue retired from his duties at Emory Hospital and the Emory Clinic and became director of the Carlyle Fraser Heart Center at Crawford Long.

That same year brought Andreas Gruentzig to the Emory faculty. Just three years before, at a hospital in Zurich, Switzerland, Gruentzig had made history by inserting a catheter into a patient's clogged coronary artery and inflating a tiny balloon. The procedure restored blood flow to the heart, and angioplasty was invented. Through his acquaintance with Spencer King, John Douglas, and others at Emory, Gruentzig accepted my invitation to join our team. I originally gave him adequate office space in Emory Hospital and later added an entire floor in the connector for his use, one-half of the entire space allotted to the Department of Medicine.

When Heinz Weens retired, William Casarella stepped up as chair of the Department of Radiology and, being greatly interested in Gruentzig's work, assisted us in accommodating Gruentzig's needs. Gruentzig was a genius. While he loved life and lived on the edge, he was a tender, honest, and compassionate advocate for his patients. During his five years at Emory, before he and his wife were killed in a tragic plane accident in 1985, he performed more than twenty-four hundred coronary angioplasties, sponsored an annual postgraduate course attended by hundreds, and propelled cardiology at Emory to the top ranks of world medicine. After his death we created the Andreas Gruentzig Center of Interventional Cardiology in Emory Hospital. Steve Clements was selected to develop the outpatient cardiac catheterization laboratory.

The cardiac surgery program was keeping pace, with the rise of Robert Guyton, Kirk Kanter, and Willis Williams to national prominence. The first cardiac transplant performed at Emory Hospital came in 1985, followed by the first transplant in children at Egleston in 1988. Quite simply, the transplant service became recognized as one of the best in the country.

A Changing of the Guard | After serving as chair of the Department of Medicine for thirty years, I retired from that position in November 1986 and passed the job to Juha Kokko, who appointed Wayne Alexander as director of the Division of Cardiology in 1988. Alexander greatly expanded cardiology research at Emory. During these years a large amount of research space became available in the enlarged Woodruff Memorial Building. A new electrophysiology laboratory opened at Emory Hospital. New space also was provided for a heart-failure service as well as a congenital heart disease clinic for adults.

Alexander was promoted to professor and chair of the Department of Medicine in 1999. To fill the job he was leaving as director of the Division of Cardiology, he appointed David Harrison, the Bernard Marcus Professor of Medicine, without argument one of the top researchers in the world in vascular biology.

The Emory Heart Center was created in 1994. This new organization, including the Andreas Gruentzig Cardiovascular Center at Emory Hospital, the Carlyle Fraser Heart Center at Emory Crawford Long, and outpatient cardiology at the Emory Clinic, was designed to be the umbrella under which clinical cardiology would thrive, fostering collaboration and coordination among the many aspects of heart disease treatment and diagnosis. Each year since, *U.S. News & World Report* has ranked the Heart Center in the top ten in the nation. In 2003 Emory's program in heart and heart surgery was ranked seventh, the only heart program in Georgia included in the nation's top fifty.

These distinctions are well earned, and the first four years of the new century continued to see growth in every area. Patient care at Emory has become increasingly sophisticated and sought after. The teaching programs for students, house officers, and fellows is increasingly popular. Taking stock in 2004 was rewarding because the audit of faculty talent, space, and funds assures continued excellence in patient care. Emory patients likewise benefit from an ambitious research agenda with studies ranging from women's cardiology to basic science.

Emory can now boast of adequate research space for cardiology in the enlarged Woodruff Memorial Building on the Emory campus, the Atlanta VAMC, and at Emory Hospital Midtown. The funding of such a large group of people comes from the money our cardiologists earn by caring for patients at the Emory Clinic or a similar facility, from endowments, and from research grants. The annual research budget from grants awarded to the Division of Cardiology of the Department of Medicine alone is more than $10 million (2009).

Our teaching program remains one of the best in the nation. In addition, all categorical interns and residents in general internal medicine rotate through the cardiology service at Emory Hospital, and the Emory cardiac fellowship program is one of the largest programs in the country. A large number of cardiac fellows leave Emory to populate the hospitals of Atlanta and other cities throughout the nation and world. Many of them practice cardiology, and a significant number join academic research institutions. In fact, Emory has trained 85 percent of practicing cardiologists and heart surgeons in Georgia.

From a fledgling effort in 1915 Emory cardiology has evolved into the top ten of the nation's best heart centers. And that is the story.

A Personal Note of Acknowledgment | Given the limitation of space, I could not include the names of everyone who participated in nurturing the growth of cardiology at Emory. I regret this. The article on which this chapter was based was originally written in 2004; much has happened since then.

Bruce Logue retired and lived with his wife in a retirement facility. A few years after his wife, Coraline, died, he himself died, in 2007.

During his retirement I would often have lunch with him. We talked about the time when there were only five or six cardiologists in Atlanta and the fun we had creating cardiology at Emory. Later, after my wife, Nellie, died, I moved into Lenbrook, the same facility where Bruce lived, while I continued my work at Emory. So we saw each other frequently. I discontinued teaching cardiology at Emory on January 1, 2009. The house staff asked me if they could come to Lenbrook once a month for teaching sessions. That I viewed as my greatest award (reward). So now, in 2009, at age eighty-eight, I continue to teach.

CHAPTER 42

PIONEERING IN RADIOLOGY
Heinz Stephen Weens
— PERRY SPRAWLS —

Under the tutelage of Heinz Stephen Weens, the Radiology Department at Emory University grew from a fledgling science to an extensive discipline in the practice of medicine. In recounting Dr. Weens's career, Perry Sprawls chronicles the rapid and extensive advancement of a new field as Weens and his colleagues fine-tuned the arts of pediatric radiology, X-raying major vessels, gastrointestinal radiology, mammography, and above all, education in radiology as medicine. Emory remains a significant teaching hub in the field and continues to advance radiology practice and care.

FOR CENTURIES ONE of the great challenges in the practice of medicine was to see into the human body without cutting it open. Like so many breakthroughs in medicine this ability had to wait on advances in scientific knowledge and developments in technology. The revolutionary window into the human body opened up with the discovery of a new kind of rays—X-rays, as we know them today—in 1895 in a physics laboratory in Wurzburg, Germany. When the news of this discovery and the ability to produce pictures of the interior of the human body spread around the world, a great revolution in medicine began. Even after 115 years the revolution continues, as more advanced forms of imaging provide a foundation for modern medicine and health care. The early years of radiology at Emory offer a perspective on how this new technology not only served the Atlanta community but also provided academic leadership for the country. For more than forty years, radiology at Emory and Grady Memorial Hospital took root and flourished under the leadership of Heinz Stephen Weens, MD.

Like X-ray technology itself, which would be his life's work, Weens was born in Germany, on May 12, 1912, in Berlin. He studied at the universities of Berlin, Heidelberg, and Berne, receiving his MD degree from the University of Berne in 1937. Perhaps a life-defining event was the opportunity to take an elective course in roentgenology (radiology) early in his medical education in Germany. Weens came to the United States in 1938 for an internship in Chicago and then moved to Piedmont Hospital in Atlanta for additional medical training. It was at Piedmont Hospital that the radiologist with whom he was working stimulated his interest in radiology. In 1940 Weens left Piedmont and joined Grady Hospital as Atlanta's first X-ray resident, in training under Dr. Paul Elkin.

A Rapid Immersion into Atlanta X-Ray

Early in Weens's residency program, Elkin left Grady for private practice, and the sole radiologist at Piedmont Hospital went into military service, leaving only the young resident to provide all of the X-ray coverage at both Grady and Piedmont. The long days and nights—sometimes eighteen to twenty hours—that he devoted to this work demonstrated his commitment to ensuring that patients received appropriate medical service. This work ethic prevailed throughout his long career.

At the time—the 1940s—radiology was in its infancy and consisted of rather basic X-ray procedures, so it was possible for a young physician with limited training to provide quality service for so many patients. Recognizing that there was much more to learn, however, especially if the field were to move into the future, Weens arranged to go north to Boston for a couple of summers for additional training—first at the Brigham and then at Massachusetts General Hospital—completing his residency in 1944.

Radiology Comes into Its Own

In the early days at Emory, X-ray technology was an activity within the Surgery Department. In 1946, however, Weens was given the appointment of associate in the newly formed Radiology Department, where in 1947 he became professor and chair of the department. In 1960 he was appointed the Charles Howard Candler Professor of Radiology.

Now with radiology established as a department and recognized as a significant medical specialty, the new department chair was in a position to develop an Emory department with national significance. This he did during the next three decades through a comprehensive program emphasizing education and training, research and development, and high-quality clinical medicine.

The Elements of Radiology

Radiology is a synergistic composite of two major elements, one human and the other technological. Radiology differs from other medical specialties because of its dependence on technology and equipment to produce images. The advances in radiology over more than a century have depended on scientific discoveries, inventions, and the development of technology that would open up more of the human body for noninvasive exploration by physicians. The discovery of X-radiation and its immediate application to imaging the human body was one of the major landmarks in medical diagnosis. Even as remarkable as the early X-ray images were, though, there was much within the body, especially signs of disease, that remained invisible. What was needed, and what continues today, is a variety of imaging methods using emerging technologies to make more and more of the body's interior, its anatomical conditions and function, visible to the physician. Weens's insight into what was needed and what was possible led Emory in its innovations in radiology.

The second element of radiology is physicians with the education and training to use the growing scope and complexity of imaging methods. If Heinz Weens were able to share today his thoughts on what brought him the greatest satisfaction throughout his distinguished career, no doubt it would be the education and training that the department has provided—one of the major Emory contributions to medicine, especially in the Southeast.

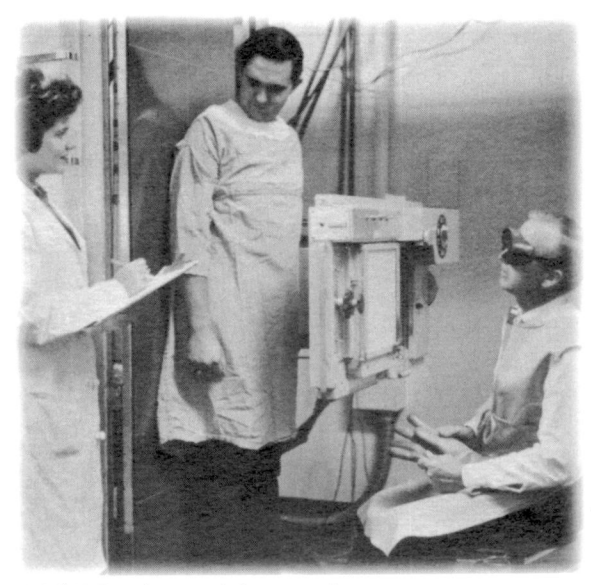

Ted F. Leigh examining a patient.

Weens also made it his aim to develop a faculty that would lead the evolution of radiology both on the Druid Hills campus and at Grady, and who would thereby gain national recognition. Among those on that journey with him was Ted F. Leigh, MD. Born in Oxford, Alabama, in 1911 and a graduate of the Emory University School of Medicine (1938), Leigh was a true partner in the development of radiology at Emory. He joined the Emory faculty in 1948 for a career that saw his formal retirement from Emory in 1980, but then extended another nineteen years as a part-time radiologist, mentor, and teacher at Grady Memorial Hospital. During this fifty-year career Leigh served as director of radiology at Emory Hospital until 1973, when he became director of residency training until his retirement in 1980. Nationally he served as either president or vice president of the three major radiological societies.

The parallel careers of Drs. Leigh and Weens were a true partnership for the development of radiology at Emory. Leigh was directing clinical radiology at Emory Hospital while Dr. Weens was directing at Grady. Upon their formal retirements in 1980 and 1981, respectively, the Radiology Department honored this partnership by establishing the Weens-Leigh Radiology Library and the Weens-Leigh Endowment Fund to support education.

James V. Rogers Jr., MD, was a son and father of physicians. Growing up in Cairo, Georgia, he entered Emory's junior college at Valdosta and then graduated from Emory College (1943) and Emory School of Medicine (1945). After an internship in New York it was back to Grady Hospital in 1947 and then to Emory in 1948, where he had a long career as chief of radiology service, vice chair of radiology, and acting chair from 1978 to 1980 following Weens's retirement. Rogers earned the distinction of being the "physician's radiologist" before retiring in 1991. He was the one so many other doctors consulted, especially with some of the most difficult clinical cases and to learn what could be achieved with radiological procedures. In 1950 these three—Drs. Weens, Leigh, and Rogers—were the full-time Radiology Department faculty. Dr. Richard Elmer was part-time faculty but also served on the Grady Hospital staff.

A turning point in radiology was the realization that children are not just small adults when it comes to X-ray imaging, and that they require special equipment, techniques, and radiologists with extensive training and experience in this special clinical activity. This realization gave birth to the specialty of pediatric radiology.

Brinton B. Gay Jr., MD, was a major leader in that development. He came to Emory in 1952, joining the Radiology Department at Emory Hospital. In 1963 Weens asked him to move over to Egleston, the pediatric hospital on the Druid Hills campus, to direct and develop the Radiology Department there. After returning from service in World War II, Dr. Gay had had an interest in pediatrics and applied for a residency in that field. All of the pediatric resident positions were already filled, but a vacancy in the radiology program beckoned, and he applied and was accepted. This proved fortunate for the future of pediatric radiology, not only at Emory but nationally.

In 1958 Egleston Hospital for Children moved to the Emory campus to become the pediatric teaching hospital for the School of Medicine. In 1962 Gay became the first full-time director of the department, a post he held until 1986. Even though "Brit" officially became professor emeritus in 1992 he continued to work four mornings a week and give his ever-popular conferences for residents. In 1995 the board of trustees at Egleston Hospital named the Radiology Department the Brit B. Gay Department of Radiology and Diagnostic Imaging. The radiology residents at Emory give an annual award for excellence in teaching. He won the award so many times that he was finally retired from consideration, and the award is now designated as the Brit B. Gay Award for Excellence in Teaching and given to other faculty members each year.

Among his many honors, one of the most significant is the Katherine Dodd award given by the Greater Atlanta Pediatric Society. The award is given only occasionally, for exceptional service to children, and Brit is the only nonpediatrician to have received it. In 2003 he received the Gold Medal of the Society for Pediatric Radiology, the most distinguished honor to a pediatric radiologist for a lifetime of service and contributions to this very specialized field, which provides something special for the little ones.

Grady Hospital has always offered outstanding learning opportunities for physicians because of its many patients with a variety of diseases and injuries. For many years the rich learning experience for medical students, interns, residents, and fellows was provided by two who joined Dr. Weens there: Drs. Wade H. Shuford and James L. Clements Jr.

Shuford, a native of North Carolina, attended the University of North Carolina and then received the MD degree from the University of Rochester. He began his practice of radiology as a captain in the U.S. Army and then continued at Duke University. In 1957 he joined Weens at Grady, and the two of them were the radiology department there. Grady proved to be the ideal clinical setting for Shuford to develop and refine X-ray methods for the examination of the major vessels, and he became one of the national authorities and leading teachers on the topic. His textbook, *The Aortic Arch and Its Malformations with Emphasis on the Angiographic Features*, published in 1974 with Dr. Robert Sybers, served as a major reference for many years. He also shared his experience and expertise with the world through the two chapters he authored in *The Heart*, 4th edition, by Dr. Willis Hurst. He later transferred from Grady to the Emory campus and retired as professor emeritus in 1999.

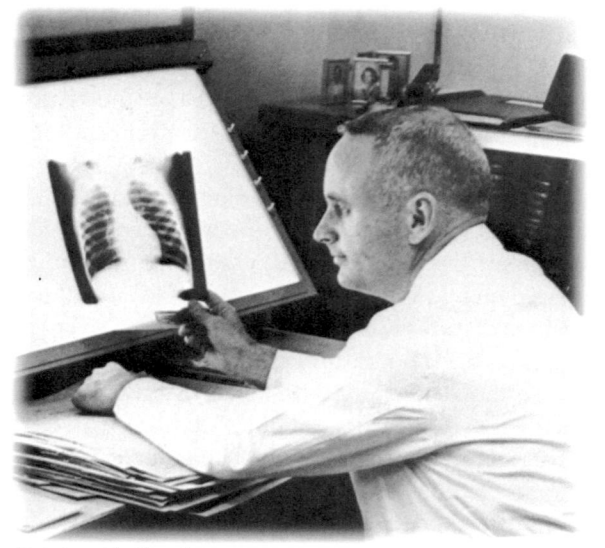

Brinton B. Gay Jr.

An Emory radiology clinical conference in 1963

Clements, born in 1924 in Eatonton, Georgia, was a 1947 graduate of the Emory School of Medicine. After military service he completed his radiology residency in the Emory and Grady program. After some years in private practice in community hospitals he joined the Emory faculty in 1968 at Grady Hospital. There his extensive research and publications established him as one of the nation's most respected authorities in the field of gastrointestinal radiology. This dual team of Shuford and Clements joined Weens in the early days to make radiology at Grady one of the great learning experiences for many physicians.

Weens recognized that, to advance in radiology, Emory would require a strong scientific capability. In 1956 he recruited William B. Miller Jr., an engineer working in surgery, and then, part-time, Robert H. Rohrer, PhD, from the Emory College Physics Department, to work with him on some research projects.

In 1960 I joined the Emory faculty for what was to become a forty-five-year tenure, concluding with retirement as professor emeritus in 2005. During this time I served as director of the Division of Radiological Sciences and Education that was being developed to include scientists working in the many evolving methods of medical imaging. Seeing one of my major roles as that of educator, I developed educational methods and materials now used around the world to enrich radiology education. In addition to publishing several textbooks, in more recent years I have focused on Web-based educational resources, especially for developing countries, provided as an open and free source through the Sprawls Educational Foundation.

In 1964 another step in building Emory radiology into an even more significant clinical and teaching resource took place with the coming of Robert Sybers, PhD, MD, to the Emory faculty and the radiology staff at Grady. Sybers, a native of Wisconsin, was the first nonsoutherner to come into the department; he had graduated from the University of Wisconsin with two BS degrees, MD and PhD degrees, and an internship and a residency in radiology. With the PhD in physiology-cardiology he became the first clinical scientist to join Weens's expanding team. This added a new dimension to the research, especially in collaboration with Shuford in radiology and several of the thoracic and vascular surgeons. His caring personality and warm sense of humor made working with Bob, or being one of his students or residents, a special experience. In 2001, when he lost the battle with cancer, his memorial service fittingly was held in the chapel of Grady Memorial Hospital, where he had dedicated his career to patient

Robert L. Egan

service, education, and moving Emory radiology forward.

Definite challenges to imaging the different parts of the human body arise from the unique anatomical characteristics of each. The breast has proved to be one of the most difficult. Unlike most other parts of the body, which contain bone matter or air (as in the lungs), the breast consists of all soft tissue and very little difference in tissues to form X-ray images. Adding to the challenge is the need to image cancers in their very early stages of growth, when they are the most treatable. The signs of these early cancers are just not visible with conventional X-ray imaging. Over the years there were attempts to image breast cancers, but these efforts produced very little in the early and effective diagnosis of breast cancer, when lives can be saved.

What was required was a revolutionary approach to the X-ray imaging of the breast, the technique now known as mammography. One of the major leaders in that revolution was Robert L. Egan, MD, who joined the Emory faculty in 1965 from the M. D. Anderson Cancer Center in Houston, where he began his pioneering work in mammography while still in residency training. He brought several major research grants and teaching programs along with his extensive work in the development of modern mammography. With his coming, Emory developed as one of the major medical centers leading the way with research and education in the effective clinical application of modern mammography.

Perhaps his greatest contribution was the promotion of mammography as an effective method of cancer diagnosis that could save many lives. It was his development of "the Egan technique" for performing X-ray examinations and conducting clinical studies to demonstrate its diagnostic capabilities that convinced the medical profession of its value in the battle against breast cancer. His many national and international recognitions and awards included the American Cancer Society's Distinguished Service Award in 1975 and the Gold Medal of the American College of Radiology in 1992. In 2001, at the age of eighty, he lost his personal battle with cancer, apparently initiated by years of exposing his unprotected arms and hands to X-rays during his investigations to develop new methods to save lives. Perhaps Dr. Gerald Dodd, his former professor at M. D. Anderson when he was completing his residency in 1955, described it best: "Egan was the man who developed a smooth-riding automobile compared to a Model T. He put mammography on the map and made it an intelligible, reproducible study. In short, he was the father of modern mammography."

Upon Weens's retirement in 1980 the Weens era came to an official conclusion. Rather than being an end, however, it was actually the commencement of many major developments that would move Emory radiology to among the nation's outstanding departments. Radiology today is the result of extensive innovations and developments in technology and a large faculty of radiologists and scientists with expertise in many specialized fields. At Emory, it is built on the foundation and values established by Heinz Weens:

> High-quality patient care—always the first priority; a vision of the future and of what can be achieved with advances in science and technology; and education, education, education . . . to develop the future generations of physicians and scientists. There is no greater legacy.

CHAPTER 43

PARTNERING FOR HEALTH CARE IN TBILISI, GEORGIA

— H. KENNETH WALKER *and* ARCHIL UNDILASHVILI —

For more than two decades, faculty members and administrators at Emory University have fostered relationships with institutions in the capital city of Georgia—not the Georgia that is the largest state east of the Mississippi River, but the former Soviet republic on the eastern shore of the Black Sea. One of the principal craftsmen in forging these relationships has been Ken Walker (Oxford 1956, College 1958, Medicine 1963), and one of the beneficiaries of the relationships has been Archil Undilashvili (Public Health 2006), who now, in turn, is helping to direct the training of nurses in his home country while serving on the medical staff at Grady Hospital.[1]

FOR PERSONS WHO learn for the first time of the relationship begun in 1988 between Emory and the Republic of Georgia, one immediate question often is, why Emory and Georgia? Since the answers to this question form the axis of the rest of this chapter, it is important to give them at the beginning. Here are the reasons as we see them:

- *The tradition of public health at Emory.* Beginning with Robert Woodruff's support of malaria research in South Georgia in the 1930s this focus has extended to the gift by Emory and Woodruff of land for the Centers for Disease Control, the creation of the Rollins School of Public Health, the Carter Center's efforts to eradicate disease, and the unique partnership between Georgia and Emory.
- *The belief in the importance of human relationships.* Evident in the culture of Georgia, this ethos is reflected in Emory's focus upon the worth and value of the individual active in community.
- *The accumulated knowledge and wisdom of Emory's people in dealing with other cultures and religion.* Emory can apply such experience in dealing with cultures in other countries in transition. Emory and its partners from other countries are working together to produce new knowledge and make it available to others.
- *The insights gained from Emory's partnership with Georgia.* The Emory-Georgia relationship can serve as a basis for Emory to broaden immeasurably the University's global footprint with beneficial results. The partnership has discovered that, in transitional countries, certain microsectors have a disproportionate influence on cultural and societal stability. These microsectors include nursing, emergency medical care, health-care administration, libraries, university curricula, and agricultural education. Knowledge gained by Emory and its Georgian partners can now be applied to other transitional countries.
- *Emory's role in education.* Emory has educated more Georgians than any other university in the United States in disciplines of business, law, arts and sciences, medicine, public health, nursing, and graduate education. In a reciprocal fashion, there are now five Georgians on the faculty at Emory.

Introduction: Georgia

Georgia is an indescribably beautiful country in the South Caucasus, on the eastern shore of the Black Sea. A verdant land of six microecological systems produces a cornucopia of vegetables, fruits, and wine. Slightly smaller than the state of South Carolina, the country has a population of 4.6 million. Tbilisi, the capital, has a population of 1.25 million.[2]

Georgia's strategic location at the crossroads of Europe and Asia has had important consequences. Four skulls discovered in Dmanisi, a small village in Southwest Georgia, belong to *Homo erectus* and are the oldest skulls found outside of Africa, implying that early human beings came out of Africa through Georgia. Conquerors of Georgia constitute a litany of the empires of the world: Greeks, Romans, Mongols, Arabs, Turks, and Russians. Modern history begins with the "friendly ally" treaty with Russia in 1783 followed by the takeover of the country by Tsar Alexander I in 1801. Georgians took advantage of the chaos in Russia during the Bolshevik revolution and declared Georgia independent in 1918, only to find their nation occupied by the Bolsheviks in 1921. Two giants of Communism, Joseph Stalin and Lavrenti Beria, were Georgians. In 1990 Georgia became the second USSR republic, after Lithuania, to declare independence.

Georgia shares the core values of the West, but its geographical position has for centuries created ongoing interactions with groups and individuals from other religions, ethnicities, and cultures, including Islam, Communism, and separatism. Georgia is thus a fertile environment for broadening the scope of cultural and practical knowledge crucial for establishing collaborative, sustainable programs in regions characterized by diversity and instability. Georgia is also noteworthy for its extraordinary attitude toward human relationships, which Georgians have elevated to be the highest good of society through unique traditions of friendship, hospitality, and feasting.

Georgia is also, unfortunately, a classic example of the difficulties occurring during transition after independence: the gross domestic product dropped precipitously from 1989 to 1994, with health-care spending alone decreasing from the equivalent of 95 U.S. dollars per capita per annum to 90 cents. Health expenditure per capita for Georgia in 2002 was 123 U.S. dollars, compared to more than $5,000 in the United States. Income for both physicians and nurses is quite low.

The Beginnings

The first contact between Emory and Georgia occurred when Ellen Mickiewicz, then dean of the Graduate School and a political science professor, visited Tbilisi in the summer of 1988 while doing research on Soviet media. That contact led to a visit to Tbilisi by Emory University Secretary Thomas Bertrand, acting on behalf of President James Laney, during Tbilisi State University's seventieth anniversary celebration in October 1988. An exchange program was established in the spring of 1989, and Bertrand hosted a visit to Emory in December by Tbilisi State University Rector Nodar Amaglobeli and international relations director Zurab Zhvania. The visitors met with scholars and administrators of Emory and the Carter Center, including former president Jimmy Carter.

In the spring of 1990 Bertrand and Stephen Strickland (College 1956), president of the National Peace Foundation, arranged a visit and lectures by the Georgian philosopher Merab Mamardashvili. Strickland, whose late wife, Tamara, was of Georgian ancestry, guided many Georgian visitors to Emory and opened his house in Washington, D.C., to them. Also in the spring of 1990 Laura Hardman (College 1967), a trustee of Emory, and her husband, John, now president of the Carter Center, took their family to Tbilisi on a two-week Friendship Force visit. In the summer and fall of 1990 Lynn Newman, chair of Emory's Music Department, participated in the Georgian Summer Language Institute in Tbilisi and did extensive research on medieval Georgian music. Newman developed a close friendship with Georgian President Eduard Shevardnadze's daughter Manana, and Manana's daughter, Tamuna Mosashvili, entered Emory College as a Woodruff Scholar in 1991. She subsequently went to Emory Law School and became a specialist in international law.

Such increasing, though informal, visits developed into more formal exchanges. Goizueta Business School has had an extensive relationship with Georgia, beginning with the entrance of Lado Gurgenidze into the 1993 MBA class. Gurgenidze went on to a distinguished career in finance in London and Moscow before becoming chair of the Bank of Georgia in 2006 and prime minister of Georgia in 2007–08. Levan Vasadze received his MBA in 1995, then went on to play a prominent role in the Sistema holding company in Moscow before starting his own venture capital company. Ten Georgians received MBAs from Goizueta from 1992 to 2005.

Georgia's health-care system was characterized by crumbling facilities, poorly trained personnel, little modern technology, and emerging epidemics of infectious diseases when the U.S. Department of State in the spring of 1992 invited Emory to start a relationship with Georgia. The State Department was starting a Hospital Partnership Program, pairing U.S. institutions with institutions in the former Soviet Union. (The name "Georgia" undoubtedly had much to do with the pairing of Emory with the Republic of Georgia.) The idea for the partnerships came from the U.S. Agency for International Development (USAID), which, as the Soviet Union was breaking up, conceived the hope that providing support to a number of sectors might stabilize an urgent situation.

Jim Smith, executive director of the American International Health Alliance (AIHA), which had been given a $13.5 million grant from USAID to implement the partnerships between U.S.

medical institutions and hospitals in the former Soviet Union, approached Emory, Grady, and Morehouse about establishing a relationship with a hospital in Georgia. This overture led to a visit to Tbilisi in August 1992 by professors Susie Buchter of pediatrics, Roger Foster of surgery, and Ken Walker of medicine, accompanied by Don Snell, then associate administrator of Grady Hospital, and Nelson McGee and Dewitt Alfred of Morehouse School of Medicine. The beginning for Walker was a late-afternoon call from Dean of Medicine Jeffrey Houpt, asking if Walker would go to Tbilisi the next week. "Sure," was the answer. "Where is Tbilisi?"

This trip formed the basis of an enduring partnership in health care between Georgia and Emory. The initial Memorandum of Understanding was signed on August 19, 1992. Archil Kobaladze, the guiding inspiration behind this partnership, met the first group on the tarmac when they arrived at 2 a.m., and he quickly became the Georgian leader of the partnership. Born in 1944, he was a leader of medicine in Georgia, as his father had been.[3]

In Tbilisi the group assessed the state of Georgian health care. William Casarella, chair of the Department of Radiology at that time, did a survey of radiologic resources in Georgia, capturing the essence of the country in the early nineties:

> The overall medical situation in Tbilisi was surprising. There is a massive surplus of physicians, and six thousand students attend the Georgian Republican Medical Institute. The physician glut is potentially worsened by the recent founding of no [fewer] than twenty-two brand-new post-revolutionary private medical schools in Tbilisi. . . . Physician unemployment is extensive, especially among women graduates, who account for 75 percent of the students. The glut is partially offset by a shortage of nurses, technicians, and other personnel. This shortage requires physicians to perform nursing, technical, and clerical duties. . . .
>
> The hospital was a shock: no heat, no hot water, no plumbing, no supplies, no surgical pathology, no auxiliaries, no volunteers, no central transportation, and, perhaps not a failing, no administrators. The radiology department at City Hospital #2 consists of three rooms located in a freezing basement. The temperature was 45 degrees F (7 degrees C) outside and 40 degrees F (4 degrees C) inside. . . . One airless closet contained the manual developing system and hangers for drying the films. Another small room served as the site of the generator control for an ancient Czechoslovakian fluoroscope. The generator also supplied a radiographic tube and table in the same main room as the fluoroscope. . . . A broken sewer pipe leaked foul-smelling liquid along one wall. Boxes of exposed films sorted by size rather than by patient name served as a film file room. . . .
>
> All fluoroscopy was done with the patient in the upright position. The last time the ancient table was placed in the horizontal position, it refused to return upright for several weeks. Of course, no spot films were taken as almost no film or developer was available, and the spot film device was inoperative. The patient gagged repeatedly on the noxious barium that had been scooped out of the top bag in the reading room and mixed with water. Examination of the esophagus, stomach, and duodenum was over in two min[utes]. However, through the haze and blur of the fluoroscopic television screen a posterior duodenal ulcer could be seen. . . . The patient's physician wandered into the room and discussed the case for a few seconds, a one-line note was made in the log book, and the patient walked out. This patient was followed immediately by the next patient, who had been standing in the room throughout the previous examination along with several members of her family and other patients, and the process was repeated. . . .
>
> Radiology is broken in the Republic of Georgia. So is the rest of medicine. The causes of the breakdown are many. First is the rigid bureaucratic control of medicine that led to a lack of investment and an insistence on a false economy that deprived the people of health care in the name of cost efficiency. Second is the gross oversupply of physicians who are willing to work for the equivalent of twelve dollars a month. . . .
>
> The medical school library has a million volumes, but about [half] are irretrievable. This does not matter, as most of the material . . . was published before 1990. No western books or journals

have arrived since 1978. Medicine stopped developing here in 1921, when the Bolsheviks annexed Georgia to the Soviet Union. . . . What was a poor centralized system under Soviet control has now collapsed, leaving a vacuum. The system is broken without the skills, tools, knowledge, or capital to get it started again. The only thing keeping it going is the talent, hard work, humaneness, and dedication of the highly intellectual Georgian physicians. They are looking for help, begging their new-found American friends to reverse the consequences of seventy years of incompetent Soviet government.[4]

Since that report, the work of nearly two decades has effected a considerable difference both in the country overall and in the health sector. The economic situation has changed greatly for the better, with significant foreign investment after the "Rose Revolution" in 2004. The United States and the European Union contributed additional aid after the Russian invasion in August 2008. In 1992 there were few cars and enormous numbers of large and deep potholes in Tbilisi. Today many cars, most of recent vintage, travel over new pavement and produce daily gridlocks. Georgia has been ranked among the top countries in the world with respect to ease of doing business.

The health-care sector offers a number of oases of excellence: five new hospitals throughout the country with the latest technology, a few excellent private clinics, and increased quality of rural health care owing to governmental emphasis on primary care. The partnership between Emory and Georgia has had a part in this improvement. The Georgian partners have been the Ministry of Health, the Ministry of Education, Tbilisi State University, Tbilisi State Medical University, Chavchavadze State University, and four hospitals. The Atlanta partners have been Emory University, Georgia State University, Morehouse School of Medicine, and Grady Hospital. The initial goal was to connect the Atlanta partners with one Georgian hospital each. After the first two visits I determined to enlarge this goal to encompass the entire health-care sector of the country.

Goals and Achievements | *Education in medicine and public health* was a core part of the first thirteen years of the program. During the first six years, twenty-one students from Tbilisi State Medical University spent four to six months on clinical clerkships at Emory. In exchange, seventeen Emory students spent an elective month during the summers in Tbilisi, each with a project—for example, prevalence of HIV in patients with tuberculosis, analysis of trauma in Tbilisi, and support for the legal basis of medicine by a student with a law degree. One student, working with Professor Glenn Maberly of the Rollins School of Public Health, collected placental blood on five hundred newborns, which was analyzed for thyroid-stimulating hormone back at Emory. Over 60 percent of the specimens were found to be deficient. This critical finding led to interventions by the government of Georgia and international organizations.

Richard Krause, former dean of Emory School of Medicine, and then, as now, a senior scientist at the National Institutes of Health, went to Tbilisi and developed an assessment and suggestions for future plans for biomedical research in the country. His successor, Dean Jeffrey Houpt, and three associate deans of Emory visited Tbilisi, and several deans/rectors from Tbilisi visited Emory.

Almost fifty Georgian medical school graduates received U.S. residencies with the help of the partnership. Thirty of these were at Emory in internal medicine, radiation oncology, neurology, and psychiatry. Five of these Georgians later joined the faculty of Emory School of Medicine: Andro Kacharava, Koba Lomashvili, and Valery Akopov in medicine; Natia Esiashvili in radiation oncology; and Marina Demetrashvili in psychiatry.

Another early goal was to reform health policy, as the Georgian health system moved from the Soviet model to a more sustainable system predicated on social insurance models of health financing. Professors Deborah McFarland and James Setzer of the Rollins School of Public Health were key players, making numerous trips to Georgia from 1993 to 2002 to consult and conduct workshops. Sherry Carlin (Nursing 1985, Public Health 1993) was the on-site representative of the partnership during 1993–94, and worked with the Georgian government to create Decree 400, issued by President Eduard Shevardnadze in December 1994. The decree established the State Health Care Fund, ensured licensure of medical facilities, created registration and quality control of medications and supplies, and provided for certifying and licensing health-care providers.

The partnership participated extensively in the National Health Policy Workshops in 1995–96 that resulted in World Bank funds for health projects in Georgia. David Delozier (Oxford 1990, College 1993, Public Health 1996) also made many trips to Georgia while a student, collecting key documents and writing some of the background papers needed to move forward health-system reform.

Reform of the health-care system inevitably has gone through fits and starts, as the economic situation of the country has changed. The commitment to a social insurance model continues to be the cornerstone of health reform efforts.

Twenty students from Georgia have completed their MPH, MsCR, and short-term programs as Muskie and Fogarty fellows in the Rollins School of Public Health. Of those, Drs. Tata Chanturidze, Tea Akaladze, and Archil Undilashvili are actively involved in health reform in Georgia. The focus of the Rollins School in health reform since the late 1990s has been to support training of graduates now involved in health-systems reform rather than in direct consultation with the Ministry of Health or the State Health Fund in Georgia.

Access to information was identified early as a huge need. There was no current medical literature at all; what was available was ancient Russian literature of no scientific value. The National Medical Library was filled with decaying, musty Russian literature, much of it stacked on floors and stairs. The library of the Regional Medical Center of Western Georgia in Kutaisi had acres of empty shelves. Internet access was almost nonexistent, and there was no knowledge of electronic medical databases.

Health-care professionals in Georgia were not accustomed to consulting recent medical literature: they focused on books and periodic stays in postgraduate training hospitals. They did have, however, an unlimited appetite for new information and a remarkable capability for digesting and applying any information they obtained. The partnership initiated its Health Information and Medical Literature Accessibility project under the leadership of Carol Burns, then-director of Emory's Woodruff Health Sciences Center Library, with the objective of providing "access to the world's biomedical literature via the Internet and an on-site collection of print and CD-ROM resources":

> In 1994, at the request of the partnership, the Woodruff Health Sciences Center Library (WHSCL) at Emory University developed a proposal for library services. A review of the current situation in Georgia and the status of various development projects in Tbilisi revealed significant challenges: what type of library could be established in a country with no mail service, extremely limited Internet access, no negotiable currency, no banks, irregular electrical service, intermittent telephone service, and no established government? Given these challenges, the WHSCL team proposed a nontraditional library for Tbilisi. Rather than a collection of print resources, the team envisioned an electronic library that would essentially bypass the problems of delivering print materials to a country with no reliable postal service. This strategy was developed in consultation with faculty at Tbilisi State Medical University and Georgian medical students and residents who had visited Emory over the previous two years. . . . The proposal . . . relied most heavily on networkable CD-ROM products and access to resources available on the Internet. . . . Two goals for this electronic library were established:

—To provide biomedical institutions and health professionals in Georgia with consistent and cost-effective access to the global information resources . . . , and

—To bring about in Georgia a major transition from the traditional practices in information management and education to the emerging multimedia modes of communication and education.[5]

The National Information Learning Centre (NILC), under the direction of Zviad Kirtava, was opened on December 12, 1996, by President Shevardnadze and U.S. Ambassador William Courtney. Walker had this to say at the dedication:

What you see today has been accomplished through the efforts of many Georgians and Americans. It is truly a joint venture. The capital of the new age we are entering is information. Information is to our age what gold, diamonds, and oil were to previous generations. Georgia is uniquely suited to take full advantage of this new wealth. . . . This library will supply the raw material, the capital, that Georgians will use to attain a new golden age.[6]

The NILC operated quite successfully for many years. In addition to four large rooms and an auditorium, it had twenty-two computers, a high-speed connection to the Internet, and servers. Pat McGahan, of the Cummins Company in Atlanta, donated a fifty-thousand-dollar diesel generator that was a lifeline during the usual 30 percent of the day when electricity was unavailable. The NILC staff received extensive training from Emory, and the partnership also provided on-site professional assistance. In 1997 Emory medical librarian Karen Marsh spent four months as NILC codirector for library operations and returned for two weeks in 1998 to follow up on operational and sustainability initiatives. In 2002 Caron Fraser served as an intern from the Canadian Society for International Health and helped develop a comprehensive three-year business plan for the NILC.

Tbilisi library

In addition to providing on-site materials, reference services, document delivery, and training in the use of MEDLINE and Internet resources for students, faculty, practitioners, and government officials, the NILC offered classes to health-care workers and the general public in techniques for email and Internet searching of medical and other electronic databases. Staff of the NILC participated in training courses at Emory, and Emory librarians went to Tbilisi to offer on-site courses.

The NILC continued to thrive until about 2006, when it declined, becoming the victim of its own success. Launched when almost no one and no institutions had Internet access, the NILC classes demonstrated the Web's usefulness, and many other medical institutions and libraries began offering Internet access. Many individuals also now have Internet access at home. The NILC is currently being resuscitated in a different model, with a focus upon telemedicine and distance learning.

Clinical practice and diagnostic capabilities required much effort during the early years of the partnership. Documentation of substandard radiology care led the partnership to supply a library of fifteen hundred teaching films. Emory donated X-ray equipment and an endoscopic laboratory. Georgian gastroenterologist Vladimir Shengelidze trained for a month at Emory. A Georgian cardiologist, Alex Aladashvili, spent a month at Emory Hospital and returned to become a leading interventional cardiologist in Georgia. Echocardiographic training and equipment were supplied. David Vroon of Grady Hospital's clinical laboratory provided assessment, training, and equipment. Crawford Long Hospital, now Emory University Hospital Midtown, donated a mammography unit, establishing the first modern mammography unit in the Caucasus. The National Mammography Project was set up for the early detection of breast cancer.

The high number of amputees in Georgia creates significant challenges. The number has grown because of minefields left from the separatist wars, and as a result of peripheral vascular disease owing to high incidence of smoking, poorly treated hypertension, and diabetes. Through the partnership a prosthetics lab from Fitzsimmons Army Hospital was donated to the Traumatology Hospital in Tbilisi. An Emory orthopedist, Robin DeAndrade, visited Tbilisi and assessed prosthetics production and made suggestions for development of the field. Mark Geil, of Georgia Tech and Georgia State University, an expert in the design and manufacture of prostheses, visited Tbilisi and drew up plans (not yet realized) for modern CAD-CAM prosthetic production.

Maternal and child-health training was provided to Georgian health-care workers in Atlanta under the leadership of Susie Buchter and Al Brann of the Department of Pediatrics. In 1997 Buchter and Brann had the Neonatal Resuscitation Program book translated into Georgian and established an outreach training group, Neonatus. Efforts included training exchanges, donation of electronic fetal monitoring equipment, physician training, and three train-the-trainers courses over three years on neonatal care and resuscitation.

Nursing reform began with the visit of the first American nurse to go to Tbilisi for the partnership, Catherine Futch, assistant vice president for nursing at Grady. She immediately saw the need and potential for help and recruited other nurses: Judy Wold, then undergraduate director of nursing at GSU and later a visiting professor at Emory's Woodruff School of Nursing; Laura Hurt, director of medical-surgical nursing at Grady; and Lila Gunter, director of in-service nursing education at Grady. Kim Crawford, a family nurse practitioner and emergency room nurse at Children's Healthcare of Atlanta, soon joined the group. In every year since the partnership began, nurse participants have advised Georgian nursing leaders and the Georgian government on nursing affairs. The partnership has made an extensive effort to improve the expertise and professional acceptance of nursing in Georgia by a three-pronged approach: enhancement of nursing skills, strengthening of the political base of nursing, and implementation of a university-based program for nursing education. Regime upheavals, economic challenges, and changing political players have made lasting changes difficult.

The professional level and training of nurses in Georgia, as in the rest of the former Soviet Union, is very low. Physicians outnumber nurses. In 2003 there were nearly 21,000 physicians, or 400 per 100,000 population in Georgia, and 18,000 nurses, or 347 per 100,000 population. The ratio of nurses to physicians in Europe varies from 0.7 in Greece to 7.2 in Ireland. Georgia, at 0.9, ranks near the bottom.

Nursing education in Georgia was and is carried out by both the government and private schools as "middle and higher technical medical education." No nursing education takes place in institutions of higher education; therefore, no graduates from these programs have the degree that would allow them to teach in a university-level baccalaureate nursing education program. Nursing is taught by physicians, and nursing education is carried out in schools with little funding and low expectations of their graduates. State-run nursing school facilities in 1992 were in advanced disrepair, used out-of-date Russian texts, and had few resources available. After 1992 many private for-profit schools of nursing sprang up. Most of these had even fewer resources than the state colleges of nursing. In the Soviet era thirteen state nursing institutions were functioning in Georgia. After the declaration of independence the number of nursing schools increased by a hundred. Thirteen remained state-owned, and one hundred were private secondary-level professional institutions whose principal function was enrichment of the owners. About twelve hundred students graduate yearly from the current state-owned institutions, and about a thousand from the private institutions.

Introducing well-trained nurses into the health-care sector has significant implications for all the people of Georgia, but especially for those at the bottom of the income scale and those in rural areas. The role of the nurse or nurse practitioner in these areas can be lifesaving at a number of levels: primary health clinics, public health offices, hospitals, midwifery, and schools.

For these reasons the partnership decided early to devote every effort to improving the quality and expanding the role of nurses. In the beginning, nursing delegations from Georgia completed intense train-the-trainer sessions at Grady Hospital. In 1997 fifty-four nurses were trained in nursing leadership and thirty in advanced nursing skills. Four nurses spent one month at Grady in an advanced leadership and teaching course. The partnership encouraged and helped in establishing the Georgian Nursing Association, the first of its kind in the former Soviet Union, in 1996, leading to creation of the position of chief nurse in the Ministry of Health.

Beginning in 1995 the partnership exerted multiple efforts to establish a baccalaureate nursing school, without success. A major step was taken in 2005, when a grant from the Soros Foundation and from USAID funded four Tbilisi nurses for six months at the Emory School of Nursing. The four participants undertook individual faculty development programs that led to their developing a curriculum for upgrading the skills of practicing nurses, and another curriculum for a baccalaureate-degree nursing school. The latest steps in the formation of a nursing school are described at the end of this chapter.

Emergency services in the former Soviet Union are primitive, the specialty of emergency medicine almost unknown. Emergency care is virtually unknown in most transitional countries, although it is high on the list of expectations of communities, who identify it as a key need of their health-care system. In Georgia, emergency rooms were often on the higher floors of hospitals and unreachable much of the time owing to electricity outages.

The partnership, under the leadership of Gail Anderson, then chief of staff at Grady, opened the National Emergency Medical Services Training Center (EMSTC) in October 1995, and immediately commenced extensive training in prehospital care and life support. By 1998 numerous training activities had occurred: the partnership had trained five instructors, held sixty training courses, and trained fifteen hundred people, most of them physicians and nurses, but also mountain guides, government guards, rescuers, high school students, and pipeline company workers. A webpage was created; EMS staff prepared three different manuals for healthcare professionals, nonphysicians, and children; and an illustrated textbook, *First Aid*, was prepared in Georgian and Russian.

The next large step in the partnership's development of emergency medicine in Georgia occurred in 2004, with a project to change the admitting room in the Iashvili Children's Central Hospital in Tbilisi to a true emergency room, thereby establishing the first emergency department (ED) in the former Soviet Union. The ED at Iashvili replaced the Soviet concept of an admitting room, which had no triage (resulting in increased morbidity and mortality), ineffective and inefficient diagnosis and care (resulting in longer hospital stays), unnecessary hospitalization of patients who could be treated and discharged, and patient and provider dissatisfaction. The new ED yielded significant improvements in patient care and use of hospital services. From 2003 to 2004, patient visits more than doubled, to seventeen thousand, owing to a reputation for excellent care and revisions in insurance financing. Hospitalization of ED patients decreased from 73 percent to 47 percent of arrivals as a result of better diagnosis and outpatient treatment. Length of stay decreased by 50 percent, thanks to more rapid diagnosis and initiation of treatment. Utilization rates of subspecialists for ED patients decreased from 42 percent to 17 percent. Hospital costs thus were reduced by $430,000.

USAID recognized the paradigm shift in the Iashvili ED, by awarding the 2006 USAID Outstanding Citizenship Achievement Award to Drs. Sasania and Walker.[7] Steve Lanski and David Goo and their colleagues in the Emergency Medicine Division of the Department of Pediatrics of Emory led this program, working with Irakli Sasania, the chief doctor of the hospital. This experience resulted in the development of a large proposal to train emergency medicine specialists in Georgia.

Health-care administration as a career for professionals was absent in the former Soviet Union. The health-care system functioned on the *Semashko* model, named for the Russian physician who devised it; the central government in Moscow totally controlled every aspect. All facilities were owned by the state. Hospitals and clinics received a budget and were managed by chief doctors with no administrative training. The concepts of budgeting, costing, marketing, resource allocation, quality assurance, performance measurement, and human resource management were unknown. The situation was worse in the regional and municipal hospitals, which were headed by chief doctors who had been unsuccessful as physicians and were therefore transferred to administration. The state set mandatory norms for manpower, hospital beds, purchasing, and billing. The chief doctors were consequently unable to do program management or financial accounting of the cost of services.

In 1991, weaned off the Soviet system, Georgia faced the difficult transition of its health sector. Unable financially to support inherent inefficiencies, the hospitals and medical technology rapidly deteriorated. Access to even basic medical care came to depend on the old system of patient gratuities. Consequently, Georgia inadvertently established a two-tiered privately funded health-care system with, by many estimates, "gray market" payments composing up to 80 percent of all expenditures.

In 2000 the partnership faced the fact that health-care administration needed to be reformed, and added faculty in health-care administration from Georgia State University—Andy Sumner, the chief of the health-care division in Georgia State's Robinson College of Business; David Harrell, the former CEO of Georgia Baptist Hospital with faculty positions at Emory's School of Public Health and the Robinson School of Business; and Brue Chandler, a former executive at St. Joseph's Hospital in Atlanta on the GSU faculty.

Harrell and Chandler made multiple trips to Tbilisi, working with the management teams at Gudashauri and Children's hospitals, and brought the managers to Atlanta to observe hospital management in excellent hospitals. It was clear that contemporary hospital administration could not be taught in a limited and short-term fashion: it required either certificate or university-level programs for senior and middle management. The partnership identified six Georgians who had business training and were in health care and brought them to GSU in 2005 for one-month intensive training to prepare them to teach the Certificates in Health Services Management course at the Caucasus School of Business (CSB).

In 2009 Chavchavadze State University invited the partnership to set up a health-care management division in its new business school. Dr. Undilashvili is overseeing this effort, working with Chandler, Harrell, and Sumner and colleagues from Goizueta. The curriculum provides basic theoretical knowledge; understanding of pragmatic applications of theoretical concepts to operations; technical skills necessary to success as a health-care manager; understanding of the values, traditions, ethics, and attitudes basic to excellence in health-care leadership; and awareness of a need to continue lifelong learning. The concepts of business administration and health administration are being applied in the context of Georgian practices, regulations, and culture.[8]

HIV/AIDS and tuberculosis programs have been a big success of the partnership, with the leadership of Carlos Del Rio and Henry Blumberg of the Emory Department of Medicine, joined a few years ago by Michael Leonard. The first case of HIV in Georgia was diagnosed in 1989, and more than six hundred cases were reported through December 2004. The World Health Organization estimated that the true number of infections might be closer to three thousand. Seventy percent of reported cases were in injection-drug users. With a dire economic environment, increased trafficking and use of illicit drugs, a large prison population, rise in sexually transmitted infections, increased migration and internally displaced populations, rising incidence of HIV infection in neighboring countries, and a burgeoning commercial sex trade, the stage is set in Georgia for a devastating HIV/AIDS epidemic. In addition, hepatitis C is widespread, and tuberculosis is epidemic and could prove to be as destructive as it is in Africa.

> *At one time or another, Georgians educated at Emory or with strong Emory ties have served as prime minister of Georgia; deputy prime minister; minister of the regions; minister of the environment; minister of health, labor, and social affairs; minister of culture; ambassador to the United States; and rector of Caucasus University.*

The Emory-Georgia TB Research Training Program and the Emory AIDS International Training and Research Program in Georgia began in 1997, in collaboration with Tengiz Tsertsvadze of the AIDS Institute, and Giorgi Khechinashvili, followed by Archil Salakaia, of the Tuberculosis Institute. Since then Emory has worked closely with the Infectious Diseases, AIDS, and Clinical Immunology Research Center as well as with the National Center for Tuberculosis and Lung Diseases to build capacity for high-quality research and to enhance the public-health infrastructure for TB and HIV control and prevention. The U.S. National Institutes of Health (NIH) through the Fogarty International Center has provided the primary support for this collaboration. Additional funding has come from the World AIDS Foundation, the Civilian Research and Development Foundation, the Biotechnology Engagement Program, and the Emory Global Health Institute for research projects on HIV, hepatitis, and tuberculosis in Georgia.

Working closely with Dr. Tsertsvadze to put together a successful National AIDS Plan, which has resulted in funding from the Global Fund to Fight AIDS, Tuberculosis, and Malaria, Emory collaborators helped Georgia become the first former Soviet republic to offer universal access to antiretroviral treatment. The partnership also worked with Dr. Salakaia to develop a comprehensive National TB Control Plan to conduct annual in-country training workshops on a variety of topics, including grants and manuscript preparation, TB/HIV co-infection, implementation science research, blood-borne infections and injection drug use, and infectious diseases.

Scholarly activities and biomedical research have received great emphasis. The collaboration has resulted in twenty-four articles published and one in press in peer-reviewed journals, including eleven first-author publications from the Georgian trainees. The training environment has enabled fourteen Emory medical students, one internal medicine resident from Cornell University, and one infectious diseases fellow from Emory to work on collaborative research projects on HIV, TB, and Hepatitis B/C in Georgia, with funding from grants and from Emory.

Women and children's health has been of great concern to the partnership. Laura Hurt and Selma Morris of Emory Midtown Hospital and Grady Hospital have led in focusing on perinatal medicine with an emphasis on public health. Neonatal mortality in the 1990s was five to seven times that in the European Union. Fetal monitoring during gestation or labor was rudimentary. A group of Emory physicians, comprising an obstetrician and several neonatologists, assessed care practices in the maternity houses throughout Georgia, while educational exchanges focused on obstetric monitoring and neonatal care.

The Atlanta/Kutaisi Partnership, led by Hurt and inaugurated in 1999, established the first Women's Wellness Center (WWC) in western Georgia, including a project promoting breast health. In 2000 the center was opened in a renovated building. The WWC provides gynecological screenings and preventive care; education about contraception, nutrition, prenatal care, and breast health; and reproductive counseling. (Thirty-six thousand women have received instruction in breast self-examination.) The partners established a community health council, a project in secondary schools on reproductive and psychiatric assessment of teenage girls, and community classes on childbirth, prenatal health, breast self-examination, and breast-feeding. William Eley (College 1979, Medicine 1983, Public Health 1990), an oncologist and executive associate dean of the Emory School of Medicine, was a key participant.

Conclusion | The work in Georgia would not have happened without enormous support from many people at Emory. Jeffrey Houpt, who was dean of the School of Medicine in 1992, had the insight to understand what the invitation from USAID could lead to, and he provided guidance and significant supplementary funds during the first years. Dean Thomas Lawley has continued the support in many ways. His encouragement and wisdom have been of incalculable value. Juha Kokko and Wayne Alexander, successive chairs in the Department of Medicine, went out of their way to push the projects forward. Presidents Jim Laney, Bill Chace, and Jim Wagner provided an encouraging environment, in addition to meeting and inviting to campus Georgians such as Eduard Shevardnadze. The Global Health Institute has provided funds for many projects, especially for those involving students.

The personal relationships have been remarkable, just as the influence of Emory on Georgia has been pervasive. At one time or another, Georgians educated at Emory or with strong Emory ties have served as prime minister of Georgia; deputy prime minister; minister of the regions; minister of the environment; minister of health, labor, and social affairs; minister of culture; ambassador to the United States; and rector of Caucasus University. President Shevardnadze gave an address at Emory, and President Saakasvili and his wife, Sandra Roeloffs, have visited Emory.

This connection between a university and a country outside its own, between Georgia and Emory, is perhaps unique in history. The influence of each upon the other has been substantial and continues to grow.

CHAPTER 44

Boisfeuillet Jones, far left, talks with trustees (left to right) Roberto Goizueta, James B. Williams, and Chairman Robert Strickland.

CLINICS, KENNEDY, AND MR. WOODRUFF:
Looking Back with Boisfeuillet Jones

In 1986, as Emory prepared to celebrate its sesquicentennial, someone had the good idea to gather the oral history available in the persons of men and women who had helped shape the institution through much of the twentieth century—persons like alumnus Boisfeuillet Jones (College 1934, Law 1937). Students who come to campus for admissions tours or pay their bills at the Bursar's Office probably know Boisfeuillet Jones as a building—the center that houses those offices. In this interview Jones comes to life as much more than a building name. The quite-long interview, conducted by the late James Harvey Young, a professor of history in Emory College from 1941 until his retirement in 1987, ranged from Jones's undergraduate years through his service in the Kennedy administration and later work as president of the Robert W. Woodruff Foundation. The parts of the interview presented here focus on his work in developing the Woodruff Health Sciences Center at Emory.

Postwar Beginning

Young: How did you end up at Emory after [serving in the United States Navy during World War II]?

Jones: About a year before the war was over I had a note from [President Goodrich C.] White. He said, "When the war is over, I want you at Emory. Please do not make a commitment until we have an opportunity to talk." . . .

I had looked at some other [opportunities]. One was the new [federal] housing program, as a deputy. . . . The one that was sort of appealing was a call about a month before I was to leave, from . . . [President] Truman's chief White House aide. He said, "You have been recommended for a position on the White House staff, and I would like to talk with you about it." I went over and duly reported. I didn't get exactly what [the position was] but I think they just needed more help than they had. I finally decided that wasn't for me. . . .

In any event, I came as assistant to the president, which was the title he [White] decided on. . . . Dr. White said that one thing I want you to do as a specific assignment is to set up a personnel system for the University. The University had hired and fired the same fellow three different times over a period of some months in three different divisions of the University. It was just so diverse, growing so, and there wasn't any organization in the University.

The first thing we did was to establish a [University] budget procedure because nobody, including Dr. White, knew where the resources of the University were except Mr. [George] Mew, and he kept it to himself. If there was something he thought ought to be done, then the money could be found; if it was something which he thought was not necessary, you couldn't find the money anywhere. And that just couldn't continue. It wasn't fair to the president; it wasn't fair to the University.

I tried to establish categories of the budget, by schools; and then to relate the anticipated expenses of those units to a plan of action. Then, just because I'd started it, I became the equivalent of the budget officer as dean of administration.

Enter Mr. Woodruff

Young: Robert C. Mizell became the University's first development officer, I believe.

Jones: He was an Emory-Oxford graduate. Very unusual individual, very thoughtful and very quiet. Emory had a capital funds campaign in 1936 connected with the [University's] centennial. And Mr. Mizell went to see Mr. Robert Woodruff in connection with that. Somehow or other they seemed to just hit it off.

Mizell and Mr. Woodruff went to New York and talked to the administrator of Memorial Hospital [now Memorial–Sloan Kettering], which was then the leading cancer medical facility in the country. They told him they were looking for a young doctor, a southerner, who could come to Emory and set up a cancer clinic. He recommended J. Elliott Scarborough, a graduate of the University of Alabama, a native of Alabama. He went to Harvard Medical School and then had been through the program at Memorial Hospital. They employed Dr. Scarborough, and he came. And they set up a place for him on the ground floor of the Emory University Hospital, and that became the Winship Clinic [the cancer clinic named for Woodruff's maternal grandfather]. Dr. Scarborough came in 1937 on a salary of thirty-six hundred dollars a year, and eventually hired one or two associates. Mr. Woodruff later provided some money to support indigent patients who came in for cancer treatment, and then became very good friends with Dr. Scarborough, and Dr. Scarborough really became Mr. Woodruff's personal physician.

Young: How did you get to know Woodruff?

Jones: I didn't meet Mr. Woodruff until 1952, when I became involved with the medical school. I'd worked six years as the assistant to the president and dean of administration. The summer of 1952 Mr. Mizell and Dr. White went down to The Coca-Cola Company for lunch with Mr.

Woodruff, and when they came back from the luncheon, Dr. White or Mr. Mizell drafted a one-page memorandum of the luncheon conversation that they showed to Mr. Woodruff, and he approved it.

Dr. White came in my office and handed me the memorandum. It started off, "The Emily and Ernest Woodruff Foundation would be interested in reviewing a blueprint of Emory's plans for development of its health services, including the schools of medicine, dentistry, nursing, Emory Hospital and Crawford Long, and related activities." And it said, "If the plan commends itself, the Emily and Ernest Woodruff Foundation will consider underwriting it."

[White] gave it to me and said, "Boisfeuillet, you prepare the plan." And I said, "Yes, sir."

I spent the next two or three months working on it pretty hard with the deans of the respective schools, and the dean of the Graduate School and then with some of the principal professors and principal clinicians. Eventually we came up with a rather simple statement of what was needed and how things would be organized, and what it would cost. The whole idea was that the Woodruff Foundation wanted to put up a sum of money, which would get them and the University out of the situation where Mr. Woodruff was picking up the deficit of the medical school every year. He and two other members of the board had agreed to split it three ways.

One was Mr. T. K. Glenn [president and chairman of Atlantic Steel and later of Trust Company of Georgia], and the other was Mr. Preston Arkwright [first president of Georgia Power]. But they dropped out after several years and left Mr. Woodruff holding the bag, and the University never knew until about the middle of the year whether Mr. Woodruff was going to pick up the deficit. Mr. Woodruff was always confronted with a fait accompli: It was there, and he didn't have much choice, so it wasn't a very happy situation.

One thing we recommended was that the University determine how much it could put from its general revenues into the medical school budget. It had been around $240,000; we whittled it down to $160,000, and this was the commitment of the University to medical education. If the medical school balanced its budget, fine. If it went into a deficit situation, they would have to overcome it themselves; the University would be obligated only to the $160,000; if they underspent their income they could retain as a credit the difference, including the $160,000 from the University. What it did was make the medical school financially autonomous—not independent but autonomous.

We set up a Division of Basic Health Sciences. The nursing school, the dental school, and the medical school were competing with each other for money and strength in the same basic health sciences. They couldn't successfully do this. All of the deans agreed [to establish] University departments: anatomy, bacteriology, biochemistry, physiology, and microbiology. . . . And then we established the clinic plan for the full-time members of the clinical faculty who were based in the Emory Hospital for the most part. We had a lot of practitioners coming in from the community, bringing patients to the Emory Hospital, and they were the real backbone of Emory's competency in clinical medicine, and they contributed to Grady, which was the major center of Emory's teaching program in clinical medicine. The plan was relatively simple. It was tailor made, I may add; we looked at plans all over the country.

Young: Didn't the Mayo Clinic have an influence?
Jones: No. There were two extremes. One was the University of Chicago, where the clinical members of the faculty were full-time employees of the school and the departments, and the departments had full responsibility for the clinic operation. They sent bills, they determined what to charge the patients, and what the income from the doctors would be. This was socialized medicine in the minds of the AMA [American Medical Association], because they were on salaries and others determined what those salaries were, and others. . . .

The other [extreme] was Duke. Duke had virtually given concessions to groups of specialists, that in return for using the Duke Hospital facilities, those holding a specialty concession would carry full responsibility for the teaching load in that specialty.

Young: And you were the diplomat planner who carried the ball and met with the various factions and drew up the precise blueprint?
Jones: I didn't do it by myself; I had plenty of people to help me, but that was my job, and we accomplished it.

What we did was to create a private partnership for the group practice of medicine among the clinicians who would be geographically [on campus] full-time, and then a contract between that partnership and the University, that in return for the privileges of the University hospital and facilities in which to see patients, they would devote at least 25 percent of that time, on assignment by the school, to teaching duties either on this campus or at Grady, and that teaching was the reason why they were here; they wanted to be in a medical school setting. If they weren't, then they shouldn't be in this situation. . . .

I brought the leaders in a meeting and said, "We cannot go any further until we know what the membership of the clinic should look like by specialties and by numbers, and there are three criteria: one is the teaching needs of the medical school, the second is a balanced group practice in the clinic, and the third is the capacity of the Emory Hospital to serve these people."

Our [plan] was a compromise. The clinic partners had their own director, and their own business officer; they would set their own fees, collect their own bills, pay their basic cost, and then pay their drawing accounts. Money that was left over after these things would be divided three ways, [among the physicians, the clinic, and the University]. The University would get paid . . . a percentage of the earnings, [and] that would come into the medical school to offset the costs of the basic sciences.

There were some other ramifications, too. The Medical Association of Georgia didn't like it; some of the doctors in the town thought it was unfair competition, and the Medical Association of Georgia engaged a law firm to ferret out instances of corporate practice of medicine in Georgia, which was against Georgia law.

The only thing they could find to take issue was the fact that the University controlled the practice of the doctors through [a governing board]. When we changed [its name] to Coordinating Council, that satisfied them.

We readied it and Dr. White agreed to the proposition and had me present this to the Emory Board, and they listened very carefully, and then finally voted to approve the plan in principle and authorize its presentation to the Woodruff Foundation. That was in November 1952, and we presented it to the Woodruff Foundation in December.

The plan called for the creation of a position of administrator of health services, who would be a deputy to the president. . . . Then we set up a health services board, which was nothing but a committee of the board of trustees. Mr. Woodruff had wanted the whole medical deal to be completely separate from the University, and I wouldn't agree to that, and I didn't think the University would [agree]. But we did the same thing by giving [the health sciences] their financial autonomy and setting up this health services board, which was called a board and served under that name but was really a committee of the board of trustees. They represented the trustees on policy matters connected with this whole medical center, and the administrator represented the president in the administration of it; it was a perfectly legitimate and proper academic exercise.

I recommended to Dr. White someone to be [the administrator who] happened to be an Emory graduate at the National Institutes of Health. I think they'd set the job up at ten thousand dollars, and this person had just been promoted to a job for twelve thousand dollars. I asked Dr. White to let me offer him the twelve thousand, and Dr. White wouldn't go beyond that ten thousand. He said, "I don't want to pay them any more than you're getting." I said, "Well, . . . a lot of people in the medical school make a whole lot more than I [do]; that's not a factor."

Anyway, he said, "Boisfeuillet, I'd like for you to get this plan started the first of January, '53, even though the Woodruff Foundation has not reacted." . . .

Dr. White spent an awful lot of time with me and others investigating every possible aspect of [the plan]. . . . The end result was that we limited the University contribution to $160,000. We asked for $4 million of endowment to [pay out] the equivalent of $160,000 that would be for the basic health sciences, essentially. . . . Then we asked for a million dollars to build an office building for the clinicians to see patients, and that was the $5 million we asked for.

In December of '53 Mr. Woodruff had Jimmy Carmichael and James D. Robinson—who were on the Health Services Board as members of the Emory board—meet him in Dr. Scarborough's office. He told them that the Woodruff Foundation would provide this money. He really set the $4 million up as a trust at the Trust Company, income coming to the clinic, and gave Emory the $1 million to build a clinic building. Then he pointed out the window and said, "The building ought to be built right here." That was between the hospital and the nursing dormitory [Harris Hall]. I said, "We can't build it there, it will give us no room for development or expansions. It ought to be across the street." We went through a lot of trauma on that one.

We did put it across the street, a long, narrow building with a corridor with examining rooms and offices on either side of it. We put the entrance down at one end deliberately, because we knew the building was [eventually] going to need a comparable wing going out the other way. Mr. Woodruff was driven by to see the construction, and he asked, "Why's the entrance down there?" Dr. Scarborough told him that that was so that they could build another wing and have the entrance in the middle and service both ways. And then Mr. Woodruff provided the additional money to shell in the other wing, so it would not look unbalanced when it was completed.

Mr. Woodruff was very generous through the years in providing for the capital needs, and I think the clinic became his favorite operation because it was making money being earned by the doctors, going back into the medical center program, and that suited his entrepreneurial spirit just fine. . . .

Because of the medical relationship, I more and more represented the medical center with Mr. Woodruff. That's how I came to know him, by explaining things we were trying to do. One of these was Egleston Hospital; we had made arrangements for affiliated units to locate around the center. It took five years of negotiation with Egleston before they were prepared to move. . . . But it was clear, then, that a children's hospital had to be affiliated with a medical center, or it couldn't exist.

Young: Mr. Woodruff was also involved in bringing the CDC to Atlanta.
Jones: I was still dean of administration. Dr. Glenville Giddings, who was the Coca-Cola physician in charge, was a good friend of Dr. Tom Parran, who was then the surgeon general of the United States. Dr. Elkin was also a good friend of theirs, and they said it would be a shame to move out of Atlanta the Office of Malaria Control in War Areas. This very fine group of scientists had done a lot to eliminate malaria in the areas of the world where troops were involved. And there were other communicable diseases that needed attention: why not keep this group together for that purpose?

So Mr. Woodruff talked with Senator [Walter] George before President Eisenhower was in office. The Communicable Disease Center, or CDC, was set up in some of the surplus buildings at the naval air base, which is now the DeKalb airfield, and had people in buildings all around the town. They wanted to build a facility but couldn't; the Korean War had come along.

Emory bought fifteen acres of land for a thousand dollars an acre and gave that to the federal government on which to build a CDC facility.

I made the request, through Bob Mizell, to use fifteen thousand dollars of money Mr. Woodruff had given to Emory for a program at Grady Hospital which was no longer needed for the purpose intended. He agreed, so it was Woodruff money that bought the original site of CDC. This was in '49, I think. Then they could not get appropriations to build the building. I worked with the respective directors of CDC over a period of time, and we worked with Senator George and Senator [Richard] Russell. President Eisenhower came into office in '53, and Mr. Woodruff talked to Eisenhower about it, and then they eventually received approval of a public works program that would permit construction under a building lease.

It was 1959 when it was completed, and the Emory board had a dinner for the secretary of HEW, who was then Dr. Arthur Flemming. The top people in NIH and Public Health Service came.

As time went on I became increasingly involved in dealing with Mr. Woodruff for new activities in the medical center. . . . Mr. Woodruff [had a complex relationship with] the University. When Dr. White became president, Charles Howard Candler was chairman of the board. Mr. Candler was a very staunch supporter of the University and followed in the footsteps of his father [Asa Candler], but Mr. Candler had rather narrow views of what should and shouldn't be. He measured the development of the University too much in terms of what he remembered [of his years in Emory College] at Oxford.

Boisfeuillet Jones

Mr. Woodruff became president of Coca-Cola in 1923, after his father had led a syndicate that bought control of Coca-Cola from the Candler family in 1919 for $25 million. Robert Woodruff was with the White Motor Company in Cleveland. He'd come to high position in the company, having to do with marketing, primarily, because that was his main strength. He had borrowed money in Atlanta and Cleveland and in New York to buy into the syndicate personally, and the stock went down over a period of four years from forty to eighteen [dollars a share], and the company was virtually bankrupt. Charles Howard Candler was still running it, as he'd been doing under his father, but it wasn't doing too well. So the [Coca-Cola] board wanted Mr. Woodruff to come down and run the company over the objections of his father, with whom Robert Woodruff was at odds very often because he didn't want to do what his father told him to do. He was pretty independent.

Mr. Woodruff pretty well restricted his interest in Emory to the medical field and let Mr. Candler go ahead with the other aspects of the University. He didn't have confidence in Candler as chairman of the board of Emory in view of the lack of confidence he had in him in running The Coca-Cola Company. Furthermore, there was some feeling that developed on the part of the Candlers after Mr. Woodruff took over and had the company completely solvent in four years.

This would have been 1927 when he was able to straighten things out with the company and decided to stay on. He was a very loyal man, very sentimental man, but also very positive about what he thought was right and a very principled person. He was a man of very great integrity. He was very demanding, very rough, but he wanted everybody that had anything to do with Coca-Cola to make money. I never had anything to do with Coca-Cola, so I didn't make any.

In the 1930s and 1940s there were seven members of the executive committee of the [Emory] board, and Mr. Candler dominated it. With Mr. Mizell's help, Mr. Woodruff's encouragement, and the help of several other members of the board, Emory authorized the increase of the Executive Committee from seven to eleven. They put on the Executive Committee younger people, . . . who took control in the sense that they would do things without any trauma that would reinforce their responsibility as [stewards] of Emory's interests. This reinstated Mr. Woodruff's confidence in the management of the University.

Young: That was all indispensable, leading to his greater benefactions.
Jones: Mr. Woodruff was a member of the Executive Committee of Emory's board in 1944. The question arose whether to accept the offer of the Atlanta Southern Dental College as a dental school of Emory University. They debated whether to do this or not, and they finally turned to Mr. Woodruff, and he nodded, and they voted unanimously to accept it, and that was the origin of the Emory School of Dentistry.

Eventually he went off the board [because] he thought he wasn't needed; he had representatives who could report to him, and he wanted to be able to sit back and have objectivity. He didn't need the recognition, didn't want it, shied away from it.

Presidential Transition
Years in the Kennedy Administration
Young: Tell us about your going to Washington from Emory and becoming involved both with the congressional and the executive branches of government there, especially with respect to national health.
Jones: I became the administrator of the health program at Emory in 1953. In 1955, after we had made a good bit of progress and had attracted some attention nationally, I was invited to serve as a member of the National Advisory Health Council, which was a statutory body to advise the Public Health Service. . . . I came to know some of the scientists and people in NIH and the Public Health Service.

In 1959 Senator Hill, from Alabama, was chairman of the Health Subcommittee of the Senate Appropriations Committee; he asked me to chair a committee to study medical research in terms of whether the NIH programs particularly were adequate funded and efficiently run.

While I was working on this . . . the surgeon general asked that we expand this committee and experts on environmental problems, radiology, atmospheric pollution. That's how I became involved, and things just snowballed. Once you get started, if you get along with people then you're asked to do [more].

Young: How did you become involved in the Kennedy administration?
Jones: When there was a change in administrations and Kennedy was coming in, I had a phone call from [HEW secretary-designate Abraham] Ribicoff about the middle of December of 1960. He said, "We have this job and we wanted to let you know about it, special assistant to the secretary for health and medical affairs." Four different physicians had held the job since 1953, when the department was created.

I met Mr. Ribicoff, and we spent a few hours together. He offered me the job in about thirty minutes, and I told him I'd have to think it over and talk to my family and to Emory and see what to do. I did not want to make a career of government and did not want to be dependent on a presidential appointment. I came back home and . . . talked to a good many people

I called Mr. Ribicoff on December the thirtieth, a Friday. On December the thirty-first, the middle of the day, we received a phone call. [My wife,] Ann, called me to the phone and said it was Mr. Kennedy calling from Palm Beach. I told the children to please be quiet because the president-elect was calling Daddy, and so they kept quiet by going to the other telephone and listening to the whole conversation. He said, "Mr. Jones, Governor Ribicoff tells me that you're willing to come to Washington to help us with the health program, and I want you to know how much we appreciate it." And he said, "I'd like to make the announcement in the next thirty minutes. Mr. Pierre Salinger will call you shortly to confirm several things." And that was that.

Young: It involved you with the total health situation in the nation.
Jones: Yes. Mr. Ribicoff said, we either want to make this position significant or abolish it. So he really gave me line responsibility, policy-wise, over the health activities of the department, including the Public Health Service, the Food and Drug Administration, maternal and child health program, and the rehabilitation program. . . .

I might say that when I was invited to do this and was trying to decide what to do, I talked to board members, talked to friends, as many as I could. I talked to Mr. Woodruff. The only person who said, "You should do this," was Mr. Woodruff.
Young: Do you think he saw ahead, knowing you and what you'd been doing, to the kind of impact you might have for the benefit of the nation when you were in such a responsible position?
Jones: I just assumed he felt I would be coming back and I would have had this broader experience, and it would be helpful. . . . My impression was that he was much more oriented toward a bigger picture than so many of our people, including me. We were provincial for the most part.

Young: What were the circumstances of your transition back to Atlanta?
Jones: I'd planned to stay [in Washington] about two years in the first place. I did not want to make a career out of it. Then, after [Kennedy's] assassination I couldn't leave. I had not known Mr. Kennedy beforehand, but I had known Mr. Johnson. He asked me to stay. You just could not run out in a situation of that kind. But after a total of three years I was ready to give it up.

Without advertising the fact that I was leaving, I was offered six jobs, three of them connected with medical affairs, one of them with starting a brand-new medical school under a state university with private money. I'd already said I was not going back to Emory; that was before all this happened. I thought it would not be fair to Sandy Atwood. . . . Before I could [make a decision], I had the offer of the presidency of the Emily and Ernest Woodruff Foundation, and this just suited me to a tee. I accepted that pretty quickly.

The position was never defined—just to be president of the Emily and Ernest Woodruff Foundation. I didn't know what my duties would be; I didn't know where the office would be. I didn't even know what they were going to pay me; I didn't ask, and they didn't volunteer. They just dealt that way, and with Mr. Woodruff I was perfectly prepared to deal that way.

I came back to Atlanta in late June of 1964 to head the Emily and Ernest Woodruff Foundation.

Young: When you were involved with creating the medical center, were there any things happening that related to Grady worth mentioning?
Jones: One of the problems between Emory and Grady had to do with who was going to pay for what. The care of the indigent in the city and the care of emergency victims was a public responsibility, and yet, with Emory providing the professional services, they expected Emory to provide all the professional services for all the care that was needed at Grady. And there was way more patient need than was important to Emory's teaching program. . . . This was resolved eventually by a contract that Dr. Richardson negotiated with Grady that provided that once a year a trustee group of Emory's Health Services Board and a committee of the trustees of Grady would sit together and, with the professional people making the case one way or another, agree on the budget for the next year. This began to regularize the process and made it possible to be effective partners in an increasingly difficult situation. . . . Other hospitals that treat indigent patients did get state support, but Grady didn't, on the theory that Atlanta was rich and could afford to support its own. People gravitated toward Atlanta when they

were out of jobs, and the Atlanta metropolitan area, Fulton and DeKalb counties in particular, became heavily responsible for care beyond that which represented their own citizens.

Young: Have you, Boisfeuillet, thought of things about Emory people that reveal them in a vivid light, or matters that might embellish the historical record?

Jones: I don't know how to respond to that. I do know from my own personal experience that having been at Emory has been a very great asset in my appreciation for quality people and understanding of what people given responsibilities, with a proper background, can accomplish. It gives one a choice of what's important and what isn't. Emory made it possible for me to do things in what I hope has been an acceptable fashion. Since I'll be seventy-five years old next week I look back on these days with great, great pleasure. Thank you for letting me participate in a totally inadequate recitation of a part of Emory's history.

ACKNOWLEDGEMENTS

We are grateful to the members of the editorial board for their judicious stewardship of this project through the generous contribution of their time and knowledge of Emory. To the faculty members, alumni contributors, and friends of Emory whose essays fill this volume, we extend both praise for splendid work and our thanks for patience with our editing: your excellence and expertise bring renewed vigor and insight to the study of the history of Emory. To the staff of the Manuscript and Rare Book Library and at Emory University—especially Naomi Nelson, Susan McDonald, Elizabeth Chase, and Kathy Shoemaker—we offer thanks for consistently helpful advice and, especially, retrieval of forgotten or overlooked materials, as we prepared drafts and prepared the manuscript. We owe a huge debt of thanks to Ann Borden and the staff of Emory Photo/Video for their cheerful help in locating photos and digitizing them for our use. We heartily applaud our student assistants—Samantha Reid, Susanna Sierra, Kanisha Billingsley, Jennifer Wang, Whitney Pierce, and Salvador Rizzo—for their dedication to the project and assistance in preparing the manuscript. To our spouses, Sarah Haigh Hauk and Frederick King, we offer thanks and love in return for your great patience, love, and support.

CONTRIBUTORS

Delores P. Aldridge is the Grace Towns Hamilton Professor of Sociology and African American Studies at Emory. She was the first African American woman on the faculty at Emory and founded the first African American studies degree program in the South, in 1971.

Frank S. Alexander is professor of law, director of the Affordable Housing Project, and founding director and codirector of the Center for the Study of Law and Religion at Emory. He has served as interim dean of Emory Law and in 2007 received the University's Thomas Jefferson Award for distinguished service.

Maximilian Aue is associate professor of German studies at Emory and director of graduate studies in the Department of Comparative Literature. He holds a PhD from Stanford University.

Mark Auslander is director of the interdisciplinary master's program in cultural production and assistant professor of anthropology at Brandeis University. He also serves as coordinator for the Greater Boston Anthropology Consortium. His anthropological interests focus on Africa and the African diaspora.

Beth Dawkins Bassett is a freelance writer and editor and formerly served as associate editor of *Emory Magazine*.

Herbert Benario, professor emeritus of classics, came to Emory in 1960 and retired in 1987. He served as president of the Classical Association of the Middle West and South.

April Bogle is director of public relations for the Center for the Study of Law and Religion. Her research interests focus on law, religion, and human rights from an international perspective.

David Bright served as dean of Emory College for six years before returning to teaching in the Department of Classics. He is currently professor emeritus of classics and comparative literature and professor of medieval studies at Emory.

Martine Watson Brownley is the Goodrich C. White Professor of English and the Winship Distinguished Research Professor. She is the founding director of the Fox Center for Humanistic Inquiry at Emory and an associated faculty member in comparative literature and in the Institute for Women's Studies.

Rudolph P. Byrd is the Goodrich C. White Professor of American Studies in the Graduate Institute of the Liberal Arts and the Department of African American Studies at Emory. He is the founding director of the James Weldon Johnson Institute for Advanced Interdisciplinary Studies.

Candace Coffman is a 2009 graduate of Emory College of Arts and Sciences.

David Cook is professor and head of the Department of Broadcasting and Cinema at the University of North Carolina at Greensboro.

Paul Courtright joined the Emory faculty in 1989 as professor of religion and chair of the Department of Religion. He is a senior fellow for the interdisciplinary study of religion and serves on the editorial board for the *Journal of the American Academy of Religion*. He specializes in Hinduism and in religious history in India.

Ali P. Crown, founding director of the Center for Women, served for three years as chair of the Women's Center Division of the National Association of Women in Education. A Phi Beta Kappa graduate of Emory, she served twice as president of the Emory chapter, most recently from 2005 to 2009.

Nancy Diamond is research associate professor in the College of Education and Social Services at the University of Vermont, where she also is special assistant to the vice president for research and graduate studies. She specializes in the study of research institutions and serves as a reviewer for the National Research Council.

William Dillingham served on the faculty of Emory's English Department from 1956 to 1996, including three stints as chair. The University appointed him Charles Howard Candler Professor of American Literature in 1984 and named him professor emeritus in 2004.

Peter W. Dowell is professor emeritus of English. He taught American and African American literature and taught American studies in the Graduate Institute of Liberal Arts. His special teaching interests in recent years have been baseball and American culture.

Marshall Duke is the Charles Howard Candler Professor of Personality and Psychopathology at Emory. He joined the faculty at Emory in 1970 and chaired the Psychology Department from 1994 to 1997. He is a licensed clinical psychologist and a reviewer for several academic journals. He received the University's Thomas Jefferson Award in 2001.

Arri Eisen is senior lecturer in the Biology Department and director of the Emory College Program in Science and Society. His research interests include genetics and molecular biology of life processes. He is committed to the interdisciplinary connection of science with history, medicine, sociology, psychology, ecology, and religion.

Michael Evenden, associate professor of theater studies and resident dramaturg for Theater Emory, earned a doctorate from Yale, where he served as assistant literary manager at the Yale Repertory Theater. He has worked on productions for the Alliance Theater, the Georgia Shakespeare Festival, Actors Express, and Theater Gael.

Martha Fagan is senior director of the Emory Alumni Association. She has worked in the law school administration to provide career services and fund-raising for scholarships, building projects, and academic programs. The University presented her with an Award of Distinction in 2001.

William H. Fox, who came to Emory in 1971 in pursuit of a doctoral degree, became the first dean and vice president of Campus Life. In 1991 he became vice president for institutional advancement (now the Office of Development and Alumni Relations), and in 2003 became senior vice president for external affairs before retiring in 2005.

Ralph Freedman is professor emeritus of comparative literature and English. He directed the Comparative Literature Program at Emory from 1988 to 1991.

Billy E. Frye earned one of the first doctorates granted by the Emory Biology Department. In 1986 he returned to Emory as vice president of research and dean of the Graduate School. He later served as the first provost of the University, interim president, and chancellor. Frye retired from Emory in 2001.

Jerry Gentry earned his MDiv and doctoral degrees from Southern Theological Seminary in Louisville, Kentucky. He currently works as a hospice chaplain.

Jan Gleason, executive director of marketing at Emory, chaired the President's Commission on the Status of Women in 1990–91 and served on the Executive Committee of the Center for Women at Emory Advisory Board since 1992, serving as chair in 1997 and, recently, as cochair of its Long-Term Planning Committee.

Nathaniel Gozansky is professor of law and director of international programs at Emory Law. He joined the faculty in 1967 and served as associate dean for academic affairs at Emory Law from 1985 to 1989 and again in 1993. His areas of academic interest are family law and legal education.

William Gruber is professor and former chair of the English Department at Emory. He also serves as an adjunct professor in the Department of Theater Studies. His interests include British and European drama of the twentieth century as well as creative nonfiction.

Carole L. Hahn is the Charles Howard Candler Professor of Comparative Education and Social Studies Education. She joined the Emory faculty in 1973 in the Division of Educational Studies, which she directed from 1986 to 1992. She has served on many advisory and governance bodies of the University.

Alexis Hauk graduated with a BA from Emory University in 2006 after majoring in creative writing and Italian studies. She worked as a teacher and journalist for two years, then completed an MA degree in publishing and writing from Emerson College. She works as a newspaper reporter in the Boston area.

Gary Hauk is vice president and deputy to the president of Emory University. He is the author of *A Legacy of Heart and Mind: Emory since 1836*. Hauk chairs the Emory Traditions and History Committee, which he founded to foster development of a stronger sense of history at the University.

J. Willis Hurst joined the faculty of Emory in 1950 and became a founding member of the Emory Clinic. He served as chair of the Department of Medicine from 1957 to 1986. He authored the textbook *The Heart*, which has become a foundational resource for students of cardiology.

Irwin Hyatt, an Emory College alumnus, is professor emeritus of history and taught East Asian history at Emory for thirty-six years. He also served as senior associate dean for faculty development for thirteen years before retiring in 2002. Upon his retirement, the University honored him with the Thomas Jefferson Award for his significant leadership.

Thomas H. Jackson Jr., vice president for public affairs at the University of Georgia, earned his PhD degree in history from the University of Georgia. He is a descendant of former Emory president James Edward Dickey.

Greg Johnson earned his PhD degree in English from Emory University and teaches at Kennesaw State University. He is a frequent contributor of book reviews to various publications.

George Jones joined the Emory faculty in 1989 as dean of the Graduate School and vice president for research. He also served as interim dean of Emory College for the 1990–91 school year. He currently holds the position of Goodrich C. White Professor of Biology. His research interests include the biochemistry and evolution of RNA processes.

Melissa F. Kean is centennial historian at Rice University, working with archivists to piece together details of the history of the university that would otherwise remain unknown. Her doctoral dissertation, on the desegregation of five private southern universities, including Emory, reflects her love for southern history and academic culture.

Frederick King served for sixteen years as director of the Yerkes National Primate Research Center. He is now director emeritus and professor emeritus of anatomy and cell biology and former associate dean in the Emory University School of Medicine. His areas of research include behavioral neuroscience and tropical medicine.

Sally Wolff King has taught Southern literature, Native American literature, and writing for more than twenty years at Emory, where she has also served as associate dean of Emory College of Arts and Sciences and as assistant vice president.

Rosemary Magee is vice president and secretary of Emory University. Before her current appointment, she served as a senior associate dean in the College of Arts and Sciences. The University awarded her the Thomas Jefferson award in 2008.

David Minter was vice president for arts and sciences and dean of Emory College from 1980 until 1990. Before coming to Emory, Minter was professor of English at Rice University. His area of academic specialty is American literature, and he has written a biography of William Faulkner and works of literary criticism and literary history.

Eric Nitschke, Robert W. Woodruff Librarian Emeritus, retired from the Emory University Libraries in 2006 after a thirty-three year career as reference librarian and librarian for European History.

Marie Nitschke retired from the Emory University Libraries in 2003 after thirty-seven years of service. She was named distinguished emerita by the Emeritus College in 2006.

Mary E. Odem, associate professor of women's studies and history and associated faculty in Latin American and Caribbean studies at Emory, studies gender, sexuality, immigration, race, and ethnicity in American history. Her book *Delinquent Daughters: Protecting and Policing Adolescent Female Sexuality* won several awards, and she has coedited two additional volumes.

Clyde "Doc" Partin served the Emory University Physical Education Department for over fifty years. He founded the Emory Sports Fitness Camp and coached baseball and softball. He retired in 2002. In 2007 Emory endowed the athletics director position in his name. Dr. Partin died in June 2009.

Contributors

Russell Richey is the William R. Cannon Distinguished Professor of Church History in the Candler School of Theology at Emory. His scholarship centers on American Methodism, comparative denominational studies, and American civil religion.

Charles Stewart Roberts, who earned his MD degree from Emory University in 1986, is the grandson of Dr. Stewart Roberts and one in a long family line of Emory graduates. He is section chair of thoracic and cardiovascular surgery at Winchester Medical Center in Virginia.

Steven Sanderson was vice president for arts and sciences and dean of Emory College from 1997 to 2001. He is now president and chief executive officer of the Wildlife Conservation Society in New York and a member of the Council on Foreign Relations.

W. Ronald Schuchard is the Goodrich C. White Professor of English at Emory. Specializing in British and Irish literature, he serves as faculty adviser for the Manuscripts, Archives, and Rare Books Library at Emory and is the founder and former chair of the Richard Ellmann Lectures in Modern Literature.

Nancy Seideman, associate vice president of communications and executive director of media relations at Emory, made a commitment to stewardship of Emory's natural environment on the day in 1999 when she stood in Lullwater and observed the beginning of the Lullwater shuttle road construction and its impact on the land.

Catherine Howett Smith is associate director and director of academic services for the Michael C. Carlos Museum. She has served on the President's Commission on the Status of Women and on the disability/accessibility committee for the University.

Gayatri Chakravorty Spivak is professor of English and comparative literature and director of the Institute for Comparative Literature and Society at Columbia University. She specializes in nineteenth- and twentieth-century literature, Marxism, feminism, deconstruction, poststructuralism, and globalization.

Perry Sprawls, professor emeritus of radiology, served on the Emory faculty for forty-five years, beginning in the Physics Department and then joining the medical school. He retired in 2005, and in 2009 the Emeritus College honored him as distinguished emeritus. The School of Medicine has created a special lecture series in his name.

John Stone was an accomplished doctor, teacher, and poet. Coming to Emory for a fellowship in cardiology, he served on the medical school faculty for forty years. He developed the first course on medicine and literature at Emory. In 2007 he was inducted in the Georgia Writers Hall of Fame. He died in 2008.

Archil Undilashvili graduated from Tbilisi State Medical University in 2003. He completed an MPH degree at the Rollins School of Public health and earned MBA and MHA degrees from Georgia State University. He is now leading programs to develop emergency medicine, healthcare administration, and nursing education in his native Republic of Georgia.

H. Kenneth Walker is professor of medicine and neurology at the Emory School of Medicine and codirector of the Atlanta-Tbilisi Healthcare Partnership. In 2004 he was named an honorary citizen of the Republic of Georgia for his work with the exchange program between Tbilisi and Emory.

Richard Ward, professor emeritus of psychiatry, came to Emory in 1960. Since retiring in 1986 he has maintained a private practice in medical psychotherapy and is active in the Emeritus College at Emory. His interest in languages has taken, in recent years, the form of a long struggle with mandarin Chinese.

Dana F. White, Goodrich C. White Professor of the Liberal Arts at Emory, focuses on urban studies and has written *The Urbanists: 1865–1915*. He has served as consultant for exhibitions at the Atlanta History Center, the Braves Museum, and Woodruff Library at Emory. He wrote and co-narrated an award-winning documentary, *The Making of Modern Atlanta*.

John Witte Jr. is the Jonas Robitscher Professor of Law, the Alonzo L. McDonald Distinguished Professor, and director of the Center for the Study of Law and Religion. Specializing in legal history, marriage law, and religious liberty, he has published 180 articles and 23 books, and he lectures around the world.

Sylvia Wrobel came to Emory in 1982 as practitioner of public relations and communications in the Woodruff Health Sciences Center. She led Health Science Communications until retiring in 2004, and she now spends much of her time writing about science and medicine.

Stuart Zola, director of the Yerkes National Primate Research Center since 2001, is also professor of psychiatry and behavioral sciences at the Emory University School of Medicine, associate director of the Emory Alzheimer's Disease Research Center, and senior research career scientist at the Atlanta Veterans Affairs Medical Center.

EDITORIAL BOARD

Susan Ashmore, associate professor of history at Oxford College, specializes in the history of the American South. In 2008 the University of Georgia Press published her prize-winning book *Carry It On: The War on Poverty and the Civil Rights Movement in Alabama, 1964–1972*. She has been honored twice by Oxford College for exemplary teaching and service.

Virginia (Ginger) Cain (Emory College 1977, Graduate School 1982) was the first Emory University archivist and currently serves as interim director of the Manuscript, Archives, and Rare Book Library at Emory.

Rose B. Cannon is professor emerita of the Woodruff School of Nursing. In addition to specializing in maternity nursing, she has extended her research interests to the history of nursing; she holds a PhD from Emory in American Studies.

Peter W. Dowell taught at Emory for forty-five years in the English Department and the Graduate Institute of Liberal Arts. He became professor emeritus in 2009.

Thomas E. Frank, formerly professor of religious leadership and administration in the Candler School of Theology, is now University Professor at Wake Forest University.

David Goldsmith is professor emeritus in chemistry at Emory. He earned his PhD from Columbia University and completed postdoctoral research at Harvard.

Eric Goldstein (College 1992) is associate professor in the Department of History with a joint appointment in the Institute for Jewish Studies. His areas of interest include the issues of race and Jewish identity, Jewish history and culture, and the cultural and social history of America.

Leslie M. Harris is associate professor of history and African American studies at Emory University. She cofounded and directed the Transforming Community Project, which examines the role of race in the history and current experience of Emory. Her research focuses on pre–Civil War African American history, slavery, and urban history.

Irwin Hyatt (College 1957), professor emeritus, taught East Asian history at Emory for thirty-six years. Upon his retirement, the University honored him with the Thomas Jefferson Award for his significant service and leadership.

Consuelo Kertz (Law 1975), professor of accounting in the Goizueta Business School, teaches taxation and the legal environment of business. Her research focuses on the effects of federal tax policy. She is a member of the State Bar Association of Georgia.

Richard M. Levinson is Charles Howard Candler Professor and executive associate dean for academic affairs at the Rollins School of Public Health. He also serves as adjunct professor of community and preventative medicine in the School of Medicine.

Clyde Partin Jr. (College 1978, Medicine 1983) is associate professor of general medicine in the Department of Medicine at Emory and writes extensively about medical and local history.

Polly J. Price (College/Graduate School 1986) is professor of law at Emory and an associated faculty member of the Department of History. She earned her JD degree from Harvard. Her research interests include American legal history, property law, Latin American legal systems, and the judiciary.

NOTES

Chapter 1: "Emory Are Here"
1. Personal communication from one of the culprits.
2. Bradd Shore has documented this meeting in a video available through MARIAL at http://www.marial.emory.edu/exhibitions/familyrevival.html.
3. Both quotations from Guy Lyle, *Beyond My Expectation: A Personal Chronicle* (Metuchen, NJ: Scarecrow Press, 1981), 174–75.

Chapter 2: "Dreams Deferred"
1. Bishop Emory freed at least some of his slaves posthumously. His last will and testament includes this passage: "To the colored servants now in my possession, for terms of years, viz. Alexander, Maria, William, Mary and Nathan, I will their freedom, the males on the twenty fifth day of December next after attaining the age of twenty-one, and the females on the same day of December after attaining the age of eighteen years, respectively, provided they take with them any child or children which either of them may have, which I will to be free at the same time." Last Will and Testament of John Emory, witnessed June 22, 1834, testated January 2, 1836, Baltimore County Registry of Wills: 436-7. Maryland State Archives.
2. Published accounts by white authors of the Kitty story are largely derived from Rev. J. O. Andrew, *Miscellanies: Comprising Letters, Essays and Addresses* (Louisville, KY: Morton & Griswold, 1854), and George G. Smith, *Life and Letters of James Osgood Andrew*, 1883. Subsequent accounts of the story are found in: Henry Morton Bullock, *A History of Emory University* (Nashville: Parthenon Press, 1936); Webb Garrison, "Emory's Role in the Methodist Civil War," *Emory Alumnus*, 1960; Charles C. Jarrell, *Oxford Echoes*, 1967; A.O.A., "Enigma," *Emory Magazine*, Spring 1997; Gary S. Hauk, *A Legacy of Heart and Mind: Emory since 1836* (Atlanta: Emory University, 1999). I offer a provisional analysis of the Kitty narrative in "The Myth of Kitty: Narratives of Slavery and Kinship in a Georgia Community" (MARIAL Working Paper, 2000). I am currently completing a book-length study of the cultural history of the Miss Kitty narrative in white and African American memory.
3. McCord was strongly influenced in these actions by Bishop Warren Candler, former president of Emory College and first chancellor of Emory University. McCord and Candler, committed segregationists, were deeply concerned that the reunification of the Methodist Church would lead to the appointment of Negro bishops in the South and to the desecration of Kitty's Cottage, which Candler described as "the most interesting building in Georgia."
4. Typescript in the possession of Virgil Eady Jr., Oxford, Georgia.
5. Brown was killed in the Civil War; the Lackey Funeral Home in Covington now occupies the site of the old Coleman Brown house.
6. Mark Auslander, ed., "Remembering the Founders: Early Trustees of Rust Chapel, United Methodist Church in Oxford, Georgia," Paper #3 of the Newton County African American Family Research Project, Emory Center for Myth and Ritual in American Life, n.d.
7. **Acknowledgments:** Field research with African American families in Newton County, Georgia, was supported by the Emory Center for Myth and Ritual in American Life: A Sloan Center for Working Families. I also wish to acknowledge the generous assistance of Virginia Cain, Randall Burkett, and other staff members at Woodruff Library's Manuscript, Archives, and Rare Book Library. I am deeply grateful to the many families of Oxford and Covington, Georgia, for sharing their memories, documents, and photographs. My research has received invaluable support from the congregations of Rust Chapel and Mount Zion Baptist churches in Oxford, as well as the Newton County Afro-American Historical Society.

I am especially grateful for the guidance and insights of J. P. Godfrey Jr., Marty Gaither McKlurkin, Emogene Williams, and Sarah Francis Hardeman. This essay emerges in part out of exhibition projects undertaken with my students at Oxford College of Emory University, 1999-2001.

Chapter 3: Lynching, Academic Freedom, and the Old "New South"

1. Emory University, "Emory History," http://emoryhistory.emory.edu/people/index.html (accessed March 19, 2006).
2. Ignatius A. Few's father, Ignatius Few, was brother to Dickey's great-great-grandfather, Benjamin Few. Ignatius Few's wife, Mary Candler, was sister to Daniel Candler, grandfather to the brothers Warren, Asa, and John Candler. Jessie Munroe Dickey to the Emory Library, 1938, James Edward Dickey Collection; Manuscripts, Archives and Rare Book Library, Emory University.
3. Dickey family papers held by the author.
4. Terry L. Matthews, "The Voice of a Prophet: Andrew Sledd Revisited," *Journal of Southern Religion* 6 (December 2003).
5. Ralph Reed Jr., "Emory College and the Sledd Affair: A Case Study in Southern Honor and Racial Attitudes," *Georgia Historical Quarterly* 72 (Fall 1988): 484. Reed relies upon many of the same original letters and college records as others who have examined this issue but interprets them differently, arriving at unique conclusions that Dickey was ill prepared to handle the crisis, that he and Candler were in "icy silence" for years following the Sledd Affair, and that the scandal cost the college financially. These differing interpretations become evident as this chapter unfolds.
6. Ibid., and Matthews, "Voice of a Prophet."
7. For further scholarship on the lynching of Sam Hose, see W. Fitzhugh Brundage, *Lynching in the New South: Georgia and Virginia, 1880–1930* (Urbana: University of Illinois Press, 1993), and Darren E. Grem, "Sam Jones, Sam Hose, and the Theology of Racial Violence," *Georgia Historical Quarterly* 90, no. 1 (Spring 2006): 35–61.
8. Reed, "Emory College and the Sledd Affair."
9. W. J. Cash, *The Mind of the South* (New York: Knopf, 1941), 35, 87–89.
10. Brundage, *Lynching in the New South*, 33–34.
11. Rebecca Felton would in time have her own destiny with Congress, when Georgia's Senator Tom Watson died in office in 1922. Governor Thomas Hardwick, who intended to run for the seat in the November special election, appointed the aged Mrs. Felton to serve when the Senate reconvened. On November 21, 1922, she became the first woman sworn into the Senate, serving only one day before Walter George, who had defeated Governor Hardwick in the special election, was sworn in to serve his term. Hers was the shortest Senate term in history. At age eighty-seven she was the oldest freshman senator ever. See Biographical Directory of the United States Congress, "Felton, Rebecca Latimer," http://bioguide.congress.gov/scripts/biodisplay.pl?index=F000069 (accessed December 29, 2008).
12. *Atlanta Journal*, August 12, 1897; Brundage, *Lynching in the New South*, 198.
13. John E. Talmadge, *Rebecca Latimer Felton: Nine Stormy Decades* (Athens: University of Georgia Press, 1960), 115.
14. Dickey shared Candler's view on this point. In an undated baccalaureate address he said, "I beg you, therefore, as you take your part in the governmental affairs of our nation, that you refrain from any action that will thrust woman into the political maelstrom where man's regard for her will be destroyed" (James E. Dickey, "The Value of True Estimates," undated baccalaureate address, James Edward Dickey Collection; Manuscripts, Archives and Rare Book Library, Emory University, box 1, folder 7).

15. Talmadge, *Rebecca Latimer Felton*, 110. See also LeeAnn Whites, "Rebecca Latimer Felton and the Problem of 'Protection' in the New South," in *Visible Women: New Essays on American Activism*, ed. Nancy A. Hewitt and Suzanne Lebsock (Champaign-Urbana: University of Illinois Press, 1993), 41–52.
16. W. A. Candler to Felton, October 1, 1924. W. A. Candler Collection, Manuscripts, Archives and Rare Book Library, Emory University. For more scholarship on the running conflict between Felton and Candler, see Mark K. Bauman, *Warren Akin Candler, the Conservative as Idealist* (Metuchen, NJ: Scarecrow Press, 1981), 72–74.
17. *Atlanta Constitution*, November 2, 1902.
18. Cited in Brundage, *Lynching in the New South*, 199.
19. Andrew Sledd, unpublished autobiography (1905), 40–41, Department of Special Collections, George A. Smathers Libraries, University of Florida; Matthews, "Voice of a Prophet"; Reed, "Emory College and the Sledd Affair."
20. Sledd autobiography, 2–3.
21. Ibid., 35–36.
22. Ibid., 48.
23. Ibid., 66–67.
24. Matthews, "Voice of a Prophet."
25. Sledd autobiography, 3–4.
26. Ibid., 6–9.
27. Although media reports and scholarly accounts refer to the accused as "Sam Hose," the name is a pseudonym for Samuel Wilkes. See Grem, citing Ida B. Wells-Barnett, *Lynch Laws in Georgia* (Chicago, 1899), 13.
28. *Atlanta Constitution*, April 16, 1899; Brundage, *Lynching in the New South*, 34.
29. Wells B. Whitmore to Rebecca Latimer Felton, April 25, 1900, Rebecca Latimer Felton Papers, Hargrett Rare Books and Manuscripts Library, the University of Georgia, cited in Brundage, *Lynching in the New South*, 83 (emphasis in original).
30. Brundage, *Lynching in the New South*, 82–83. Brundage refers to the employer as "Cranford" throughout, but all other sources cited have him as "Crandall."
31. Talmadge, *Rebecca Latimer Felton*, 116.
32. Ibid.
33. Sledd autobiography, 75; Matthews, "Voice of a Prophet"; Reed, "Emory College and the Sledd Affair."
34. Andrew Sledd, "The Negro—Another View," *Atlantic Monthly*, July 1902, 65.
35. Ibid.
36. Ibid., 68 (emphasis in original).
37. Ibid.
38. Ibid., 69.
39. Ibid. (emphasis in original).
40. Ibid., 71 (emphasis in original).
41. *Emory College Board of Trustees Minutes*, June 6, 1902.
42. J. W. Renfroe to Rebecca Latimer Felton, July 5, 1902, Rebecca Felton Papers, Special Collections, University of Georgia.
43. *Emory College Board of Trustees Minutes*, July 8, 1902.
44. "Another Light that Falls," *Atlanta Constitution*, July 11, 1902, 6.
45. Ibid.
46. Madison Bell to Rebecca Felton, July 29, 1902, Rebecca Felton Papers, Special Collections, University of Georgia.
47. "The Negro as Discussed by Mr. Andrew Sledd," *Atlanta Constitution*, August 3, 1902, B4.
48. Ibid.

49 Ibid.
50 Ibid.
51 Sledd autobiography, 76.
52 Ibid., 77–78; *Atlanta Journal*, August 4, 1902.
53 Reed, "Emory College and the Sledd Affair," 479.
54 Ibid.
55 "Leaders of the Race Differ in Their Views," *Atlanta Constitution*, August 6, 1902, 7.
56 Sledd autobiography, 78–79.
57 Ibid., 83–84.
58 Dickey to W. A. Candler, December 1, 1902, W. A. Candler Collection, Manuscripts, Archives and Rare Book Library, Emory University, box 11.
59 Sledd autobiography, 81.
60 Ibid., 84–88. Also, Warren Candler to Dickey, January 5, 1903, W. A. Candler Collection, Manuscripts, Archives and Rare Book Library, Emory University.
61 "To Protect Emory, Sledd Will Leave," *Atlanta Constitution*, August 9, 1902, 1.
62 Ibid., and *Emory College Board of Trustees Executive Committee Minutes*, August 12, 1902, contained within the *Emory College Board of Trustees Minutes*, annual meeting, June 6, 1903.
63 John S. Cohen (editor, *Atlanta Journal*), to Felton, August 8, 1902, Rebecca Felton Papers, Special Collections, University of Georgia.
64 "Trustees Have Taken No Action," *Atlanta Constitution*, August 10, 1902, 4.
65 "Committee Is to Meet Today," *Atlanta Constitution*, August 12, 1902, 7.
66 "The Passing Throng," *Atlanta Constitution*, August 12, 1902, 6.
67 Dickey to W. A. Candler, November 26, 1902, W. A. Candler Collection, Manuscripts, Archives and Rare Book Library, Emory University, box 11.
68 "Sledd Is to Leave Emory," *Atlanta Constitution*, August 13, 1902, 7.
69 Sledd autobiography, 88–89.
70 Dickey to W. A. Candler, November 26, 1902.
71 Andrew Sledd to W. A. Candler, August 16, 1902, W. A. Candler Collection, Manuscripts, Archives and Rare Book Library, Emory University, box 11.
72 Dickey to W. A. Candler, August 27, 1902, W. A. Candler Collection, Manuscripts, Archives and Rare Book Library, Emory University, box 11.
73 "Conference Next Week, Methodist Preachers and Laymen to Gather at Epworth Church," *Atlanta Constitution*, July 18, 1902, 7; "District Conference Opens," *Atlanta Constitution*, July 24, 1902, 7. "Dickey Takes Charge as President of Emory," *Atlanta Constitution*, July 18, 1902, 3. "Brilliant Addresses at LaGrange Conference," *Atlanta Constitution*, July 18, 1902, 6. "Masons Lay Corner Stones," *Atlanta Constitution*, July 30, 1902, 4.
74 *Emory College Board of Trustees Executive Committee Minutes*, September 3, 1902, contained within the *Emory College Board of Trustees Minutes*, annual meeting of June 6, 1903; "Arnold Will Succeed Sledd," *Atlanta Constitution*, September 6, 1902, 7.
75 Andrew Sledd to W. A. Candler, October 7, 1902, W. A. Candler Collection, Manuscripts, Archives and Rare Book Library, Emory University, box 11.
76 Bauman, *Warren Akin Candler* (n. 21).
77 Dickey to W. A. Candler, November 26, 1902, W. A. Candler Collection, Manuscripts, Archives and Rare Book Library, Emory University, box 11.
78 W. A. Candler to Dickey, November 28, 1902, W. A. Candler Collection, Manuscripts, Archives and Rare Book Library, Emory University, box 11.
79 Dickey to W.A. Candler, January 3, 1903, W.A. Candler Colletion.
80 W. A. Candler to Dickey, January 5, 1903, W. A. Candler Collection, Manuscripts, Archives and Rare Book Library, Emory University, box 11.

81 Reed, "Emory College and the Sledd Affair," 485.
82 Dickey family papers.
83 Elam Franklin Dempsey, *Life of Bishop Dickey* (Nashville: Publishing House of the Methodist Episcopal Church, South, 1937), xi–xii.
84 Reed, "Emory College and the Sledd Affair," 483; Henry Y. Warnock, "Andrew Sledd, Southern Methodists, and the Negro: A Case History," *Journal of Southern History* 31, no. 3 (August 1965): 251–71.
85 Mark A. Bauman, "Warren Akin Candler: Conservative Amidst Change" (Ph.D. diss., Emory University, 1975), 317.
86 W. J. Cash, *The Mind of the South* (New York: Alfred A. Knopf, 1941), 323.
87 C. Vann Woodward, *Origins of the New South, 1877–1913* (Baton Rouge: Louisiana State University Press, 1971).
88 Sledd autobiography, 81.
89 Earl W. Porter, *Trinity and Duke* (Durham, NC: Duke University Press, 1964): 96–121.
90 Bauman, *Warren Akin Candler*, 158, citing Warren Candler letter to "My Dear Brother Southgate," November 30, 1903, Kilgo papers, Duke Special Collections.
91 Porter, *Trinity and Duke*, 122–25.
92 Ibid.
93 Warnock, "Andrew Sledd, Southern Methodists, and the Negro," 264.
94 Laurence R. Veysey, *The Emergence of the American University* (Chicago: University of Chicago Press, 1965), 382.
95 Ibid., 386.
96 Ibid., 385.
97 J. Victor Baldridge, David V. Curtis, George Ecker, and Gary L. Riley, *Policy Making and Effective Leadership* (San Francisco: Jossey-Bass, 1978), 254–55.
98 Henry M. Bullock, *A History of Emory University* (Nashville: Parthenon Press, 1936), 240; Dempsey, *Life of Bishop Dickey*; Warnock, "Andrew Sledd, Southern Methodists, and the Negro."
99 Emory University, Media Advisory, "Emory MLK Week Keynote Event Jan. 22: Opening Celebration of Exhibits on Emory's Early Black History and Anti-Lynching Activity," January 18, 2001, http://www.emory.edu/WELCOME/journcontents/releases/MLKmediaadvisery.html; and a review of the exhibit and program by Daryl White, "Without Sanctuary: Lynching Photography in America," *Public Historian* 25, no. 1 (Winter 2003): 123–25.
100 Sledd autobiography, 105.
101 Andrew Sledd to W. A. Candler, December 20, 1906, June 18, 1907, Sledd Collection, University of Florida; Reed, "Emory College and the Sledd Affair," 490–91; Albert Edward Barnett, *Andrew Sledd: His Life and Work*, pamphlet, Duke University Library, 1956 (?).
102 W. A. Candler to Andrew Sledd, July 17, 1914, Sledd Collection; Bullock, *History of Emory University*, 356; Reed, "Emory College and the Sledd Affair," 491; Matthews, "Voice of a Prophet," 12–13.

Chapter 4: National Ambition, Regional Turmoil
1 Thomas H. English, *Emory University 1915–1965: A Semicentennial History* (Atlanta: Emory University, 1966).
2 Emory University Archives (hereinafter EUA), biographical files; Sam M. Shriver and Robert F. Whitaker, "The 14th President's 15 Years," *Emory Alumnus*, April 1957, 5–23.
3 Calvin Kytle and James Mackay, *Who Runs Georgia?* (Athens: University of Georgia Press, 1998); Ivan Allen Jr., *Mayor: Notes on the Sixties* (New York: Simon and Schuster, 1971), 30–31.

4   White reviewed the then-current historical literature on the era of his youth in the South and compared his own childhood experiences to the observations of several historians. Box 31, White Papers, EUA.

5   See V. O. Key, *Southern Politics in State and Nation* (New York: Vintage Books, 1949), chap. 6, and Numan Bartley, *From Thurmond to Wallace: Political Tendencies in Georgia, 1948–1968* (Baltimore: Johns Hopkins Press, 1970).

6   See Key, *Southern Politics,* 117–19; Numan Bartley, *The Creation of Modern Georgia* (Athens: University of Georgia Press, 1983), 161, 166, and 202–3 for how the county unit system thwarted coherent politics in the vitriolic 1946 election. Earl Black points out that Georgia was unusual in the extent to which race was a campaign issue in the 1940s in *Southern Governors and Civil Rights* (Cambridge, Mass.: Harvard University Press, 1976), 29.

7   Even in the late 1940s, the presence of a large, educated, and prosperous black community in Atlanta moderated white racism through its ability to exercise limited political power. See Jack L. Walker, "Protest and Negotiation: A Case Study in Negro Leadership in Atlanta, Georgia," *Midwest Journal of Political Science* 7 (May 1963): 99–124. Clarence A. Bacote, "The Negro in Atlanta Politics," *Phylon* 16 (Fourth Quarter, 1955): 349.

8   Ellis Arnall, a lawyer from Newnan, Georgia, was a classic progressive reformer. See Harold P. Henderson, *The Politics of Change in Georgia: A Political Biography of Ellis Arnall* (Athens: University of Georgia Press, 1991), and R. L. Patton, "A Southern Liberal and the Politics of Anti-Colonialism: The Governorship of Ellis Arnall," *Georgia Historical Quarterly* 74 (Winter 1990): 599–621. Arnall gives his own interpretation in *The Shore Dimly Seen* (Philadelphia: J. B. Lippincott, 1946).

9   *Smith v. Allwright*, 321 U.S. 649 (1944). On this case, see Richard Kluger, *Simple Justice: The History of Brown v. Board of Education and Black America's Struggle for Equality* (New York: Knopf, 1976), 235–37. On Georgia's 1946 and 1948 elections, see Harold P. Henderson, "The 1946 Gubernatorial Election in Georgia" (MA thesis, Georgia Southern College, 1967), and Bartley, *Creation of Modern Georgia,* 197–207. Robert C. Mizell to John A. Griffin, February 8, 1946, Box 2, Robert C. Mizell Papers, EUA. Like White, Mizell worked vigorously to improve black higher education in Atlanta. Morris Brown College was his particular interest.

10 Harry Truman, "Letter of Appointment," reproduced in the commission's report, *Higher Education for American Democracy: The Report of the President's Commission on Higher Education* (Washington, DC, 1947). White gave a speech to a meeting of church-related colleges in July 1948 and explained the workings of the Commission in great detail. He made clear that the report was no "rubber stamp," but that every section had been thoroughly debated and redrafted repeatedly both in subcommittee and by the entire commission. Goodrich White, "Speech to Meeting of Church Related Colleges," July 26, 1948, Box 25, White Papers, EUA.

11 White to George F. Zook, October 27, 1947, Box 17, White Papers, EUA.

12 Ibid.; *Higher Education for American Democracy,* 29.

13 White to George F. Zook, October 27, 1947, Box 17, White Papers, EUA; *Higher Education for American Democracy,* 29.

14 Report of the Commission Meeting, Nov. 3–4, 1947, Box 17, White Papers, EUA.

15 White, draft of reminiscences, Box 31, White Papers, EUA.

16 On the Atlanta black elite, see Floyd Hunter, *Community Power Structure: A Study of Decision Makers* (Chapel Hill: University of North Carolina Press, 1953): 116–17 and August Meier and David Lewis, "History of the Negro Upper Class in Atlanta, Georgia, 1890–1958," *Journal of Negro Education* 28 (1959): 128–39. Also see Gary M. Pomerantz, *Where Peachtree Meets Sweet Auburn: The Saga of Two Families and the Making of Atlanta* (New York: Scribner, 1996).

17. Goodrich White Biographical Files, EUA.
18. See, for example, "Announcing a Series of Forums on Human Relations," Fall Quarter 1945, Box 17a, EUA. Dr. Rufus Clement, president of Atlanta University, spoke in this series.
19. No explanation for the failure to consider them was offered. Dean J. Gordon Stipe of the Graduate School merely noted that "while Emory has no racial clause of any kind in its admissions regulations, it has, as a private institution, the prerogative of accepting or rejecting any application." *Emory Wheel*, October 19, 1950; *Atlanta Journal*, February 15, 1950.
20. *Emory Wheel*, February 28, 1948.
21. Memo, Boisfeuillet Jones to Goodrich White, February 21, 1948, Box 6, Mizell Papers, EUA.
22. "In re: Emory Christian Association Racial Equality Meeting set for Monday, February 23, 1948," John A. Dunaway to Goodrich White, February 20, 1948, Box 6, Mizell Papers, EUA. "In re: Separation of Races," John A. Dunaway to Goodrich White, February 20, 1948, Box 3, Henry L. Bowden Papers, EUA; copy of letter, John A. Dunaway to Boisfeuillet Jones, March 19, 1948, Box 22, Rufus Harris Papers, Tulane University Archives.
23. *Emory Wheel*, January 27, 1948; February 28, 1948. The "Resolution" is found in "A Brief Documentary Account of the Integration of Emory University." This is a collection of copies of key documents gathered from many sources relating to Emory's struggle with integration. Norman Smith and his colleagues in Emory's Development Office compiled it in 1966. Box 10, EUA. Copy of letter from White to Robert A. Young, April 1, 1948, Box 22, Rufus C. Harris Papers, Tulane University Archives.
24. See Numan V. Bartley, *The New South, 1945–1980* (Baton Rouge: Louisiana State University Press, 1995), esp. chap. 4; Allan P. Sindler, ed., *Change in the Contemporary South* (Durham, NC: Duke University Press, 1963); and J. Milton Yinger and George E. Simpson, "Can Segregation Survive in an Industrial Society?" *Antioch Review* 28 (March 1958): 15–24.
25. See, for example, Aldon Morris, *The Origins of the Civil Rights Movement: Black Communities Organizing for Change* (New York: Free Press, 1984). The best account of the genesis and history of the *Brown* cases is Kluger, *Simple Justice*.
26. *Emory Wheel*, January 27, 1950; October 12, 1950.
27. *Emory Alumnus*, December 1957; English, *Emory University*, 76; Henry Bowden, "The Christian University in a Scientific Age (A Board Chairman's View)," speech given to Emory faculty group, April 5, 1959, Box 4, Bowden Papers, EUA.
28. *Emory Wheel*, February 5, 1953; November 5, 1953.
29. "First Atlanta Conference on The Churches and World Order, April 6–7, 1953"; Charles Howard Candler to Goodrich White, March 26, 1953, Box 1, Robert F. Whitaker Papers, EUA.
30. White to Charles Howard Candler, March 30, 1953, Box 1, Robert F. Whitaker Papers, EUA.
31. Ibid.
32. Geoffrey Perret, *Eisenhower* (New York: Random House, 1999), chap. 41, presents a nuanced but ultimately negative portrayal of Eisenhower's actions (and lack thereof) on civil rights. See also Dwight D. Eisenhower, *The White House Years: Mandate for Change, 1953–1956* (Garden City, NY: Doubleday, 1963), 234; Robert Frederick Burk, *The Eisenhower Administration and Black Civil Rights* (Knoxville: University of Tennessee Press, 1984), 151–73.
33. *Southern School News*, September 3, 1954; Numan Bartley, *The Rise of Massive Resistance: Race and Politics in the South during the 1950s* (Baton Rouge: LSU Press, 1969), 41–42, 54–55.
34. Bartley, *Rise of Massive Resistance*, 68–72. See Joseph L. Bernd, *Grass Roots Politics in Georgia: The County Unit System and the Importance of the Individual Voting Community in Bifactional Elections, 1942–1954* (Atlanta: Emory University Research Committee, 1960), for a sophisticated and detailed analysis of Georgia politics in this period.

35 See Donald R. Matthews and James W. Prothro, "Negro Voter Registration in the South" in *Change in the Contemporary South*, ed. Allen P. Sindler (Durham, NC: Duke University Press 1963), 119–49; Margaret Price, *The Negro Voter in the South* (Atlanta: Southern Regional Council, 1957), 1–5. This influence was largely exercised behind the scenes, negotiated privately by leaders of the black community. See Clarence Stone, *Regime Politics: Governing Atlanta, 1946–1988* (Lawrence: University of Kansas Press, 1989), 46–50, 52–55.

36 Bartley, *Rise of Massive Resistance*, 22–24, discusses the position of the urban businessmen who were the major spokesmen for the South's cities. In *Inside Agitators*, David Chappell analyzes the ideology of the southern civic-commercial elite and their economic motivations for acting as peacemakers. See David L. Chappell, *Inside Agitators: White Southerners in the Civil Rights Movement* (Baltimore: Johns Hopkins University Press, 1994). For a cogent discussion of the Atlanta business community and its agenda, see David Andrew Harmon, *Beneath the Image of the Civil Rights Movement and Race Relations: Atlanta, Georgia, 1946–1981* (New York: Garland, 1996), esp. 45–82.

37 Report of the President to the Board of Trustees, October 26, 1954; Report of the Dean of the Graduate School, October 1954, EUA.

38 *Emory Wheel*, May 20, 1954.

39 Phi Beta Kappa Address, May 21, 1954, Box 26, White Papers, EUA.

40 Report of the President to the Board of Trustees, October 26, 1954, EUA; Notes on Meeting of Committee of One Hundred at Emory University, November 10, 1954, Box 14, Arthur J. Moore Papers, EUA.

41 "The Segregation Question: Some Points of Information," *Emory Alumnus*, October 1954.

42 Ibid.

43 Report of the President to the Board of Trustees, Minutes, Board of Trustees Meeting, November 1, 1955, EUA.

44 Randy Fort, "Cutting the Throat to Cure the Cancer," *Emory Alumnus*, April 1956; Albert W. Stubbs to Randy Fort, May 8, 1956; Charles Howard Candler to Albert W. Stubbs, May 11, 1956, Box 3, Henry Bowden Papers, EUA.

45 *Emory Wheel*, 1955–56, contains a great many articles, editorials, and letters on these topics.

46 Boone M. Bowen, *The Candler School of Theology—Sixty Years of Service* (Atlanta: Emory University, 1974), 112–13. Statement of the Faculty on the School of Theology and Race, n.d. but April 1957; White to Members of the Board of Trustees, n.d. but April 1957, Box 90, Robert Woodruff Papers, EUA.

47 *Emory Alumnus*, May 1957; Emory University Press Release, April 18, 1957, Box 69, Walter S. Martin Papers, Valdosta State University Archives (VSUA).

48 Minutes of the Meeting of the Board of Trustees, April 18, 1957; Faculty Group to Charles Howard Candler, April 3, 1957, Box 86, Robert Woodruff Papers, EUA.

49 G. B. Connell to Martin, April 23, 1957, Box 61, Martin Papers, VSUA.

50 Dean Rusk to Martin, May 23, 1957, Box 62, Martin Papers, VSUA; Report of the President to the Board of Trustees; Minutes of the Meeting of the Board of Trustees, November 14, 1957, EUA.

51 Interview with S. Walter Martin, April 28, 1999. Notes in possession of the author. In response to a student column in the *Wheel* that suggested Emory faculty members had simply given in to the administration's views on segregation, there came explicit denials from the faculty that they had been pressured to conform in any way.

52 S. Walter Martin, "Civilization's Need: The Moral Touch," April 9, 1958, Box 68, Martin Papers, VSUA; "Washington Alumni Talk," October 7, 1959, Box 4, Martin Papers, VSUA.

53 Hartsfield was elected mayor in 1936 and, apart from a brief interruption during World War II, held that office until Ivan Allen Jr. replaced him in 1961. Dependent on black votes and the goodwill of the white business elite, Hartsfield preserved a sense of racial calm and

progress, providing new services and facilities to black neighborhoods, hiring black police officers, and generally doing a masterful job of preserving segregation while allowing change to proceed. See Pomerantz, *Where Peachtree Meets Sweet Auburn*, 161–64, 184–88. A good biography of the colorful Hartsfield is Harold H. Martin, *William Berry Hartsfield: Mayor of Atlanta* (Athens: University of Georgia Press, 1978).

54 *Vivian Calhoun et al. v. A. C. Latimer et al.*, 188 F. Supp. 401 (1959).

55 Jeff Roche, *Restructured Resistance: The Sibley Commission and the Politics of Desegregation in Georgia* (Athens: University of Georgia Press, 1998), is an excellent study that pulls together the strands of the extended and very complicated political conflict over the state's school desegregation.

56 Statement by Emory Faculty, *Atlanta Journal and Constitution*, November 30, 1958.

57 In the fall of 1962 history professor Harvey Young, who gathered many of the signatures, acknowledged the "thrill that came from the awareness that there was some slight hazard in the venture." Faculty Orientation Talk, September 25, 1962, Box 15, James Harvey Young Papers, EUA.

58 On Bowden, see "From 'Mr. Alumnus' to Top Trustee," *Emory Alumnus*, December 1957. His response to the faculty statement is at Bowden, "The Christian University in a Scientific Age (A Board Chairman's View)," talk given to Emory faculty group, April 5, 1959, EUA.

59 *Emory Wheel*, February 6, 1959. The *Wheel* was now regularly editorializing on the need for racial liberalization on campus and for keeping the public schools open. "Crisis in the Schools," *Emory Alumnus*, February 1959.

60 Walter R. Davis [alumni director] to Emmet B. Cartledge Jr., February 27, 1959, Box 4, Henry Bowden's Papers, EUA, contains numerous letters from Davis, Bowden, Judson Ward, and other Emory officials defending the right of students and faculty to discuss these issues openly in any forum at all.

61 *Emory Wheel*, March 31, 1959.

62 Roche, *Restructured Resistance*, 76–80. See also Charles Boykin Pyles, "S. Ernest Vandiver and the Politics of Change," in *Georgia Governors in an Age of Change: From Ellis Arnall to George Busbee*, ed. Harold P. Henderson and Gary L. Roberts (Athens: University of Georgia Press, 1988), and Bartley, *Creation of Modern Georgia*, 213–17.

63 Roche, *Restructured Resistance*, 78–95.

64 *Atlanta Constitution*, March 9, 1960; Pomerantz, *Where Peachtree Meets Sweet Auburn*, 251–58; Harvard Sitkoff, *The Struggle for Black Equality, 1954–1980* (New York: Hill and Wang, 1981), 69–73. Emory students were divided on racial matters, with most preferring segregation or espousing an empty "moderation." An active and vocal minority, though, participated in demonstrations and sit-ins, and condemned the student paper for spinelessness.

65 President's Report to the Board, November 1959, EUA; *Emory Alumnus*, February 1960.

66 Minutes of the Faculty of the College of Arts and Sciences, March 16, 1960, Box 2, Emory University Faculty Papers, EUA.

67 S. Walter Martin, Remarks to Selected Faculty Members Concerning Race Relations at Emory, March 31, 1960, Box 86, Robert Woodruff Papers, EUA.

68 Harvey Young to Martin, May 6, 1960, Box 1, Emory University Faculty Papers, EUA; copy of letter, Henry Bowden to Martin, May 12, 1960; Martin to William C. Archie, May 17, 1960, Box 1, Emory Faculty Papers, EUA.

69 Minutes of University Senate Meeting, April 6, April 27, May 25, 1960, Box 4, Emory University Senate Papers, EUA; William C. Archie to Martin, May 26, 1960, Box 3, Bowden Papers, EUA.

70 Roche, *Restructured Resistance*, 162–75.

71. On the Atlanta demonstrations see David Garrow, *Atlanta, Georgia, 1960–1961* (Brooklyn, NY: Carlson Pub., 1989); Jack L. Walker, "Protest and Negotiation: A Case Study of Negro Leadership in Atlanta, Georgia," *Midwest Journal of Political Science* 7 (May 1963): 99–124.
72. Bowden to Harlee Branch, January 13, 1961, Box 4, Bowden Papers, EUA.
73. Bowden to Tim Adams, January 24, 1961, Box 4, Bowden Papers, EUA.
74. Minutes of Meeting of Special Committee of the Executive Committee of the Board of Trustees of Emory University, February 1, 1961, Box 4, Bowden Papers, EUA.
75. Martin to Harlee Branch, February 3, 1961; draft report, n.d. but February 1961; Bowden to Ernest Colwell, April 13, 1961, Box 4, Bowden Papers, EUA.
76. Ben Johnson to Henry Bowden, October 21, 1961, Box 4, Bowden Papers, EUA.
77. Report of Special Committee to Review University Policy on Admissions, May 1, 1961, Box 9, Bowden Papers; Minutes of the Board of Trustees Meeting, May 4, 1961; Charles D. Hounshell to Martin, May 24, 1961, "Brief Documentary Account," Manuscript Box 10; Minutes of the Faculty of the College of Arts and Sciences, May 25, 1961, Box 2, Emory Faculty Papers, EUA.
78. Roche, *Restructuring Resistance*, 178–88; Taylor Branch, *Parting the Waters: America in the King Years, 1954–63* (New York: Simon and Schuster, 1988), 395–97. Goodrich White wrote a friend, "The mob spirit that has manifested itself in Little Rock, New Orleans, Athens, and elsewhere can, I think, be kept under control by the kind of planning and public appeals that went on in Atlanta" (White to Everett Case, November 2, 1961, Box 11, White Papers, EUA).
79. Report of Special Committee, adopted by the Board of Trustees, May 3, 1961, Box 9, Bowden Papers, EUA. At least one trustee (probably several more) was unhappy with this decision.
80. *Emory Wheel*, November 30, 1961. Martin's statement is in "A Brief Documentary Account," Box 10, Emory University Manuscripts, EUA. Letters from faculty, staff, and alumni are in Boxes 3 and 4, Bowden Papers, EUA. *Atlanta Constitution*, November 4, 1961.
81. *Emory University et al. v. Nash*, 218 Ga. 317 (1962). Emory's legal briefs are in "A Brief Documentary Account," Box 10, Emory Manuscripts, EUA. The May 1962 issue of the *Emory Alumnus* contains both a reprint of the petition and an explanation of the suit by law dean Ben Johnson. Johnson stressed that "it is not necessary in this action for Emory to champion the rights of Negroes, and this action does not do so; we champion the rights of Emory, and every other private educational institution in Georgia, to choose its own admission policy in this regard." The reception of the students is discussed in the *Emory Wheel*, October 18, 1962, and Judson C. Ward to Roland P. Mackay, January 18, 1963, Box 4, Bowden Papers, EUA.
82. Bowden to Spencer Walden Jr., February 27, 1961; Bowden to Hugh Comer, March 8, 1961, Box 4, Bowden Papers, EUA.
83. Harris Purks to Martin, May 9, 1961, Box 4, Bowden Papers, EUA.

Chapter 5: Putting Black Blood and White Blood on the Same Shelf
1. Jerry Gentry, *Grady Baby: A Year in the Life of Atlanta's Grady Hospital* (Jackson: University Press of Mississippi, 1999). This essay is adapted from the chapter, "Black Appendicitis White Appendicitis," revised and published with permission.
2. Dr. Roy C. Bell, interview by author, November 1, 1994.
3. Charles Black, interview by author, July 9, 1996.
4. Jondelle Johnson, interview by author, February 10, 1996.
5. Bell, interview by author. "Hospital Is Picketed in Segregation Plaint," *Atlanta Inquirer*, November 18, 1961, 1.
6. Bell, interview by author, April 4, 1995. "Dentist Appears before Hospital Authority," *Atlanta Inquirer*, August 12, 1961, 1.

7. Pete Page, interview by author, January 19, 1996.
8. "Hospital Is Picketed in Segregation Plaint," *Atlanta Inquirer*, November 18, 1961, 1.
9. "Activist Dentist Wants to Be Heard," *Atlanta Constitution*, October 10, 1961, 5.
10. "Dr. Bell Blasts Leaders on Bonds," *Atlanta Inquirer*, August 11, 1962.
11. Ernestine Kelsey, interview by author, February 5, 1996.
12. Dr. Joseph Wilber, interview by author, May 15, 1995.
13. "Hospital Authority to Hear Grady Workers' Pay Demands," *Atlanta Inquirer*, September 21, 1963, 1.
14. Kelsey, interview by author. "Hospital Authority to Hear Grady Workers Pay Demands," *Atlanta Inquirer*, September 21, 1963, 1.
15. Bernice Dixon, interview by author, September 20, 1995.
16. Dr. Joseph Wilber, interview by author, May 15, 1995.
17. Howard Zinn, *SNCC: The New Abolitionists* (Cambridge, MA: South End Press, 1965), 25.
18. "Protest Renewed on Naming Nurses Dorm Mississippi," *Atlanta Inquirer*, September 25, 1961, 3.
19. Charles Gerkin, interview by author, February 8, 1996.
20. Charles Black, interview by author, July 9, 1996.
21. "Ask Quick Action on Grady Bias," *Atlanta Inquirer*, October 7, 1961, 1.
22. "Eight Sue Grady Over Race Bias," *The Atlanta Inquirer*, June 23, 1962, 1.
23. "Civil Action #7966," National Archives and Records Administration, College Park, Georgia.
24. Personal papers of Dr. Thomas Blasingame.
25. Bell, interview by author, April 4, 1995.
26. "Civil Action #7966."
27. "The Civil Rights Act of 1964," *Hospitals* 38 (November 16, 1964): 51–54.
28. "Civil Action #7966."
29. Leroy Johnson, interview by author, May 10, 1995.
30. Kelsey, interview by author, February 5, 1996.
31. Jondelle Johnson, "Undercover Segregation at Grady," *Atlanta Inquirer*, June 19, 1965, 1.
32. Gerkin, interview by author, February 8, 1996.
33. Bell, interview by author, April 4, 1995.
34. Bernice Dixon, interview by author, September 20, 1995.
35. Gerkin, interview by author, February 8, 1996.
36. Pete Page, interview by author, January 19, 1996.
37. "Dr. Roy C. Bell Tells HEW," *Atlanta Inquirer*, August 13, 1966, 4. "Atlanta Negro Physicians Threaten Drastic Action," undated *Atlanta Constitution* clipping in personal papers of Dr. Thomas Blasingame.
38. Xernona Clayton, interview by author, March 13, 1995.
39. Ibid.; "Atlanta Doctors Urge Hospital Integration," *Atlanta Constitution*, July 27, 1966, 4.
40. Personal papers of Dr. Thomas Blasingame.

Chapter 6: Lullwater and the Greening of Emory

1. Thomas H. English, *Emory University, 1915–1965: A Semicentennial History* (Atlanta: Higgins-McArthur, 1966), 23–24.
2. Ibid., 24.
3. Woolford B. Baker, "Campus Development at Emory: A Historical Perspective," transcript of remarks prepared for Campus Development Committee, Emory University Senate, 1980, 1.
4. John Gladden, interview with author, February 21, 2009; Office of the President, University Senate Campus Development Committee minutes, November 14, 1974, Series 029, Box 9, Folder 6, Emory University Manuscript, Archives and Rare Book Library, 1.

[5] Office of the President, University Senate Campus Development Committee minutes, October 11, 1962, Series 029, Box 8, Folder 6, Emory University Manuscript, Archives and Rare Book Library, 2.

[6] William H. Murdy and Eloise Carter, *A Report on the Status of Forested Land of Emory University*, July 1986, 2. (Emory University Manuscript, Archives, and Rare Book Library.)

[7] The Emory University Senate adopted the following position statement on forest use at its November 11, 1993, meeting:

Sustaining Emory's existing Forests is central to maintaining the quality and character of Emory's environment. Mounting evidence over the last thirty years supports preservation of urban forest areas as a primary means of sustaining local environmental quality. Preserving forest provides numerous values directly benefiting Emory University.

Emory's policy on forest areas must address the conflicting issues of property development and natural area preservation. Traditional institutional property ownership means development of all property, a belief that is in direct conflict with the forest preservation. Creating a sustainable human and natural environment at Emory requires balancing property use between new construction and forest preservation.

The following policy derives from the recommendations of the Murdy-Carter report (W. H. Murdy and M. E. B. Carter, A Report on the Status of Forested Land of Emory University, July 1986, p. 5 and Fig. 1, Approved by the University Senate, February 4, 1987).

1) Near-pristine forest lands delineated in the Murdy-Carter report shall be preserved undisturbed in perpetuity. Emory's near-pristine forests will be designated as named preserves. Endowment gifts will be sought for these forests, and the resulting funds in part will be used to support the establishment of these preserves, including development of long-term management plans to sustain them. The management plans will address at least the following: educational and recreational programs and opportunities, rare species populations, recovery and possible enhancement of natural values, and routine operations, where appropriate.

2) Mature hardwood forests delineated in the Murdy-Carter report shall not be disturbed, neither in whole nor in part, without an environmental assessment and the development of an ecologically sound land-use plan. The Committee on the Environment (COE) will evaluate requests for development within these forests and an assist with the procurement of assessments and land-use plans.

3) Second-growth pine forests may be suitable for new construction siting if the best available environmental precautions and sound land-use management measures are taken. These include but are not limited to avoiding wetland and rare species populations, maintaining buffer zones, and preventing sediment runoff during construction. The Committee on the Environment will review and respond to requests for development within second-growth pine forests.

Acknowledging the beauty and value of forests, Emory University espouses a policy of no net loss of forest. Emory will seek to maintain connections between existing parcels in an effort to promote natural corridors for the protection of wildlife.

At the April 18, 1995, meeting of the University Senate, University Secretary Gary Hauk (according to an *Emory Report* story published May 1, 1995), stated that "the Program and Budget Committee (of the Board of Trustees) has reviewed the proposed (forest use) policy and agrees with the Senate Environmental Policy Committee that Emory should conduct environmental impact estimates for all future construction. The policy has been forwarded with a favorable recommendation to the Trustees' Real Estate, Buildings and Grounds Committee with two comments: a) The Program and Budget Committee hopes the land use plan would not automatically prohibit development in any mature hardwood forest. While forest areas classified as pristine are off limits for development, Hauk said the administration needs the 'active engagement' of the trustees in considering development policy for mature hardwood forests; and b) The committee wonders if the policy's call for 'no net loss of forest' will be a tenable policy down the road. Hauk said Emory currently follows a practice of allowing no net loss of trees, but that is different from having no net forest loss. He said the administration is also asking the trustees' engagement on this issue."

In the April 5, 1999, issue of *Emory Report*, the following revised forest use policy, which had been approved by the Board of Trustees, was published:

> University policy governing forest on Emory's Druid Hills campus
>
> Recognizing the scientific, educational and aesthetic value of sylvan habitats, Emory University espouses a goal of no net loss of wooded acreage and will take appropriate measures to preserve for future generations the forests on Emory property. At the same time, the University recognizes that creating a sustainable human and natural environment at Emory requires balancing the need for new construction and the need for preservation. In striving to harmonize these sometimes competing goods, the University will follow the guidelines enumerated here.
>
> 1. The University will take all practical measures to preserve near-pristine forest lands delineated in the report of W. H. Murdy and M. E. B. Carter ("A Report on the Status of Forested Land of Emory University," July 1986). These properties may be considered irreplaceable and should be disturbed only when their loss may be outweighed by other environmental goods or mitigated by exchange of other properties.
>
> 2. Mature hardwood forests identified in the Murdy-Carter report should not be disturbed without an environmental assessment of the impact of their development.
>
> 3. Second-growth forests suitable for construction sites should be developed only after appropriate environmental precautions have been taken. These precautions include avoiding wetlands and habitats for rare species, maintaining buffer zones, and preventing sediment runoff during construction.
>
> 4. Whenever possible, Emory will maintain connections between existing wooded parcels of land in order to promote natural corridors for wildlife habitat.

[8] The following Emory University Environmental Mission Statement was approved by the Emory University Senate on March 27, 2001:

We, the Emory University community, affirm our commitment to protect and enhance the environment through our teaching, research, service, and administrative operations. We seek to foster a community that sustains ecological systems and educates for environmental awareness, local action, and global thinking. We seek to make environmentally sound practices a core value of the University. Our fundamental principles are to:

* Incorporate environmental concerns as a significant priority in university decision making.
* Seek alternative practices and procedures to minimize negative impacts on the environment.
* Conserve natural resources and restore environmental quality.
* Protect the biodiversity of our region and serve as a living library and habitat for local species.
* Consider the social and economic impacts of Emory's environmental policies and foster a participatory process in developing these policies.

Our decisions and actions will be guided by the University's Mission Statement, reflective of the University's resources, and informed by the University's Campus Master Plan. As a learning institution, we recognize that planning for sustainability will be an evolving practice.

Vision:
Emory University seeks to be a campus:

- Where part of the University's mission is to be an environmental leader in all aspects of university functioning, including buildings, operations, planning, and purchasing;
- Where we live responsibly as part of a forested ecosystem;
- Where all students, faculty, and employees are provided opportunities to become environmentally literate and where environmental leadership is seen as a continuous, participatory process of learning;
- Where environmental studies are available through strong undergraduate programs, graduate-level and professional specializations in environmental issues, and diverse opportunities for environmental learning across the curriculum;
- Where environmentally oriented faculty and student research is encouraged and supported;
- Where environmental efforts encourage cross-university ties and multi-unit collaboration;
- Where university leadership and expertise contribute to local and regional environmental efforts, fostering links with other regional institutions; and
- Where environmental understanding and concern contribute to a dynamic sense of campus cohesion and community.

Chapter 7: Shaped by a Crucible Experience

[1] F. Stuart Gulley Jr., *The Academic President as Moral Leader: James T. Laney at Emory University 1977–1993* (Macon, GA: Mercer University Press, 2001), 7.

[2] *Campus Report*, October 9, 1989, 11.

[3] *Emory Wheel*, February 2, 1990, 1, 3.

[4] *Campus Report*, February 12, 1990, 3.

[5] **Acknowledgments:** The authors wish to thank the dedicated and caring staff of the Manuscripts, Archives, and Rare Book Library, Emory University, for their assistance in locating original source materials for this article. Portions of this essay first appeared in the Fall 2007 *Women's News & Narratives*, the CWE's newsletter.

Chapter 8: Catching Up

[1] An earlier version of this chapter appeared in *History of Higher Education Annual 1999*. The author thanks Roger Geiger and the late Hugh Davis Graham for invaluable intellectual insights and perspectives.

[2] See, for example, Hugh Davis Graham and Nancy Diamond, *The Rise of American Research Universities: Elites and Challengers in the Postwar Era* (Baltimore: Johns Hopkins University Press, 1997).

[3] Beth Dawkins Bassett, "The Path to Preeminence," *Emory Magazine* 65, no. 2 (June 1989): 10.

[4] John M. Palms, interview with the author, March 1, 2000. Dr. Palms, an Emory Graduate School alumnus, joined the Emory physics faculty in 1966. Later he served as department chair, dean of the College of Arts and Sciences, and vice president for academic affairs. In 1988 he was appointed Charles Howard Candler Professor of Physics. He served as president of Georgia State University (1989–91) and president of the University of South Carolina (1991–2002), and retired from the USC Department of Physics and Astronomy in 2007.

[5] Emory University, *A Self-Study of Emory University, 1960–61* (hereafter *Self-Study 1960–61*), 13–14.

[6] See Edgar W. Knight, *A Documentary History of Education in the South before 1860* (Chapel Hill: University of North Carolina Press, 1950); Howard W. Odum, *The Way of the South: Toward Regional Balance of America* (New York: MacMillan, 1947); Wilson Gee, *Research Barriers in the South* (New York: Appleton-Century Crofts, 1932); Mary Bynum Pierson, *Graduate Work in the South* (Chapel Hill: University of North Carolina Press, 1947); and Edith Webb Williams, *Research in Southern Regional Development* (Richmond, VA: Dietz Press, 1948).

7. At the outbreak of World War I, the region could claim only sixty thousand of the nation's four hundred thousand college students.
8. Odum, *Way of the South*, 6.
9. Gee, *Research Barriers in the South*, 166.
10. Raymond B. Fosdick, *Adventure in Giving: The Story of the General Education Board* (New York: Harper & Row, 1962), 27.
11. Ibid., 277–78.
12. National Emergency Council, *Report on Economic Conditions of the South* (Washington, DC: U.S. Government Printing Office, July 5, 1938), 1; David R. Goldfield, *Promised Land: The South since 1945* (Arlington Heights, IL: Harlan Davidson, 1987), 1.
13. See, for example, Roger L. Geiger, *Research and Relevant Knowledge: American Research Universities since World War II* (New York: Oxford University Press, 1993), and Numan V. Bartley, *The New South, 1945–1980* (Baton Rouge: Louisiana State University Press, 1995), 1–37.
14. Pierson, *Graduate Work*, 188; Williams, *Research in Southern Regional Development*, 9–10.
15. In 1949, only five southern schools were members of the Association of American Universities (AAU)—Duke, Vanderbilt, and the Universities of North Carolina, Texas-Austin, and Virginia (Fosdick, *Adventure in Giving*, 288).
16. Thomas N. Bonner, "Sputnik and the Educational Crisis in America," *Journal of Higher Education* 29, no. 2 (1958): 105.
17. Cameron Fincher, *Research in the South: An Appraisal of Current Efforts* (Atlanta: Georgia State College, 1964). In this discussion southeastern states included Alabama, Arkansas, Florida, Georgia, Kentucky, Louisiana, Mississippi, North Carolina, South Carolina, Tennessee, and Virginia.
18. Eighteen percent of faculty at private campuses, as compared with 25 percent in other regions, earned fourteen thousand dollars or above (Peggy Heim, "Academic Compensation in the South: Its Present and Future," *Southern Economic Journal* 29, no. 4 [April 1963]: 345). Nevertheless, Peter G. Blau has argued that lower salaries did not necessarily lead to difficulty in recruiting faculty at southern universities (Blau, *The Organization of Academic Work* [New York: Wiley, 1973], 43).
19. Alan M. Cartter, "Qualitative Aspects of Southern University Education," *Southern Economic Journal* 32 (July 1965): 48–49.
20. Ibid., Table II, 44.
21. Hayward Keniston, *Graduate Study and Research in the Arts and Sciences at the University of Pennsylvania* (Philadelphia: University of Pennsylvania Press, 1959), 115–50.
22. There were no southern institutions in Berelson's category 1 ("the top 12 universities") or category 2 ("the next 10 universities"). In category 3 ("other AGS universities"), there were eight (of twenty-five total) southern schools: Duke, Emory, North Carolina, Rice, Texas, Tulane, Vanderbilt, and Virginia. Emory and Rice were included because they had received Ford accomplishment grants. Bernard Berelson, *Graduate Education in the United States* (New York: McGraw-Hill, 1960), 280–81.
23. See J. Merton England, *A Patron for Pure Science: The National Science Foundation's Formative Years, 1945–1957* (Washington, DC: National Science Foundation, 1982), chap. 12.
24. Southern Regional Education Board, Commission on Goals for Higher Education in the South, *Within Our Reach* (Atlanta: SREB, 1961), 21.
25. Southern Regional Education Board, *Statistics for the Sixties: Higher Education in the South* (Atlanta: SREB, 1963).
26. William H. Nicholls, *Southern Tradition and Regional Progress* (Chapel Hill: University of North Carolina Press, 1960), 162.

[27] For examples, see Peter Wallenstein, ed.. *Higher Education and the Civil Rights Movement: White Supremacy, Black Southerners, and College Campuses* (Gainesville: University Press of Florida, 2008), Appendix 1.

[28] Richard Kluger, *Simple Justice: The History of Brown v. Board of Education and Black America's Struggle for Equality* (New York: Knopf, 1976), 280–89. See also George Tindall, *The Emergence of the New South, 1913–1945* (Baton Rouge: Louisiana State University Press, 1967), 561–64; Bartley, *New South*, 154–55.

[29] The Council of Southern Universities was organized in 1952, incorporated in 1954, and decommissioned in 1985. In 1954 the council created the Southern Fellowship Fund to administer $3 million donated by the General Education Board for a system of graduate scholarships and fellowships. See Robert M. Lester, *A Summing Up, 1954–1964* (Chapel Hill, NC: Southern Fellowship Fund, 1964). Council and Southern Fellowship Fund documents are housed in the Southern Historical Collection, University of North Carolina–Chapel Hill, Accession No. M-3779. See also Clarence Mohr and Joseph E. Gordon, *Tulane: The Emergence of a Modern University, 1945–1980* (Baton Rouge: Louisiana State University Press, 2001).

[30] National Board of Graduate Education, *Science Development, University Development, and the Federal Government* (Washington, DC: NBGE, June 1975), Table 6, 33–37.

[31] Cameron Fincher, *The Closing System of Academic Employment* (Atlanta: Southern Regional Education Board, 1978), 14.

[32] John K. Folger, *The South's Commitment to Higher Education: Progress and Prospects* (Atlanta: Southern Regional Education Board, 1978), 3–14.

[33] See Bradley Rice, "If Dixie Were Atlanta," in *Sunbelt Cities; Politics and Growth from World War II*, ed. Richard M. Bernard and Bradley Rice (Austin: University of Texas Press, 1983), 31–57.

[34] Ivan Allen with Paul Hemphill, *Mayor: Notes on the Sixties* (New York: Simon and Schuster, 1971), 145–46.

[35] See Henry Morton Bullock, *A History of Emory University, 1836–1936* (Nashville: Parthenon Press, 1936).

[36] The story of Vanderbilt's break with the Methodist Church is told by Paul K. Conkin, *Gone with the Ivy: A Biography of Vanderbilt University* (Knoxville: University of Tennessee Press, 1985), chap. 8. For Emory University's first fifty years, see Thomas H. English, *Emory University, 1915–1965* (Atlanta: Emory University, 1965).

[37] For more information about Asa Griggs Candler, "The Million Dollar Letter" (July 16, 1914), see Emory University, "History," http://www.emory.edu/home/about/history/.

[38] English, *Emory University*, 15.

[39] Ibid., see chap. 2.

[40] Nick Taylor, "Emory on the Rise," *Atlanta Magazine*, May 1982, 76.

[41] See Nancy Diamond, "New Models of Excellence: Rising Research Universities in the Postwar Era, 1945–1990" (PhD diss., University of Maryland Baltimore County, 1999), for more documentation.

[42] By 1947 Emory's thirty-six hundred students included twenty-two hundred veterans. See English, *Emory University*, chap. 3.

[43] See David R. Levine, *The American College and the Culture of Aspiration, 1915–1940* (Ithaca, NY: Cornell University Press, 1986), 78–82.

[44] Taylor, "Emory on the Rise," 77.

[45] Dumas Malone, "Report to the President on the Development of the Graduate School," *Bulletin of Emory University* 31, no. 15 (October 1, 1945): 3.

[46] Ibid., 5.

[47] Ibid., 9.

[48] In the late 1930s and early 1940s the GEB had supported creation of a regional academic center in Atlanta involving Emory, Agnes Scott, Georgia Tech, the University of Georgia, Columbia Theological Seminary, and Oglethorpe University. This effort led to formation of the University Center in Georgia, whose descendant organization is the Atlanta Regional Council for Higher Education (ARCHE). GEB interest in a few key southern universities continued until the liquidation of its assets in the late 1950s. See Fosdick, *Adventure in Giving*, 293.

[49] Expenditure and endowment data from Emory University (hereafter, EmU), Annual Administrative Report of the President to the Board of Trustees (hereafter, Annual Administrative Report of the President), 1966–67, 57, Emory University, Manuscript, Archives, and Rare Book Library (hereafter MARBL). Presidential reports, Minutes of the Board of Trustees, and other unpublished documents cited below are available from MARBL.

[50] For the decision to admit women to the College, see EmU, Minutes of the Board of Trustees, 1953. Women had been enrolled in other Emory divisions—in law (1917), the Graduate School (1919), theology (1922), and medicine (1943).

[51] EmU, Annual Administrative Report of the President, 1966–67, 57.

[52] English, *Emory University*, 80.

[53] In 1940 Luther C. Fischer deeded the Crawford Long Memorial Hospital to Emory, the gift to become effective at the time of his death. (He died in 1953.)

[54] For the history of Yerkes and its role at Emory, see chap. 45.

[55] English, *Emory University*, 91.

[56] EmU, Faculty Senate, Report to the Trustees Committee for the Selection of the President for the University, May 1956, Series I, Box 18, Goodrich C. White Papers.

[57] EmU, Board of Trustees, Minutes of the Board of Trustees, April 18, 1957, MARBL. For faculty opposition to Martin, see Department Chairs Letter to Charles Howard Candler, April 3, 1957, Henry L. Bowden Papers.

[58] A substantial literature discusses the "golden" years that spanned 1958–68. See especially Geiger, *Research and Relevant Knowledge*, chaps. 4–6.

[59] *Self-Study 1960–61*, EU Box Series, Box 37, Folder 4, Item 1, 2–3, 6.

[60] *Self-Study 1960–61*, "Emory and the Community," EU Box Series, Box 37, Folder 4, Item 2, 8.

[61] In 1955–56, there were 121 full-time Emory College faculty, a number that grew to 199 a decade later. Campuswide, there were 430 full-time university faculty, 90 part-time faculty, and 563 volunteers in the Schools of Medicine and Dentistry. EmU, *Self-Study 1960–61*, "The Faculty," EU Box Series, Box 37, Folder 6, Item 8, 1.

[62] Ibid., 9.

[63] Ibid., 10–11.

[64] *Self-Study 1960–61*, "Committee on Graduate Faculty Report," EU Box Series, Box 37, Folder 9, Item 9, 7.

[65] *Self-Study 1960–61*, "The Faculty," 12.

[66] Gordon N. Ray, "Report on the English Department of Emory University," May 2, 1961, *Self-Study 1960–61*, Box 37, Item 11, n.p.

[67] *Self-Study 1960–61*, "An Appraisal of the Department of Biology of Emory University and Its Program," EU Box Series, Box 37, Item 10, 58.

[68] John S. Toll, "Visitor's Evaluation of the Department of Physics of Emory University," June 15, 1961, 1, EU Box Series, Box 37, Item 15, 9.

[69] *Profile of Emory University*, Report to the Ford Foundation, 1966, Part II, A-1-a, 71.

[70] See William A. Emerson Jr., "Where the Paper Clips Jump," *Newsweek*, October 19, 1959, 94–96. For race relations in Atlanta, see Ronald H. Bayor, *Race and the Shaping of Twentieth-Century Atlanta* (Chapel Hill: University of North Carolina Press, 1996), and Gary M.

Pomerantz, *Where Peachtree Meets Sweet Auburn: The Saga of Two Families and the Making of Atlanta* (New York: Scribner, 1996).

71. Although they were hardly at the forefront of the civil rights movement, some southern businessmen concluded that racial harmony was profitable and therefore preferable. See Elizabeth Jacoway and David R. Colburn, eds., *Southern Businessmen and Desegregation* (Baton Rouge: Louisiana State University Press, 1982), and David R. Goldfield and Blaine A. Brownell, *Urban America: A History* (Boston: Houghton Mifflin, 1990).

72. Georgia's "private school plan" threatened the loss of state funds for any school attempting to integrate. For Atlanta's school integration crisis, see pages 50–52, this volume.

73. EmU, Board of Trustees, Minutes of the Board of Trustees, November 1961.

74. EmU, Board of Trustees, Minutes of the Board of Trustees, November 1963; Minutes, November 1964. See also Paige B. Parvin, "Life after Brown," *Emory Magazine*, Spring 2009, http://www.emory.edu/EMORY_MAGAZINE/2009/spring/prelude.html.

75. "In Racial Diversity Emory University Stands Tall," *Journal of Blacks in Higher Education* (Summer 2009): 26. In *JBHE*'s 2007 survey, 9.4 percent of the first-year class was black, an enrollment second only to Duke among southern universities. African Americans constituted 12 percent of Emory's medical students.

76. *Self-Study 1960–61*, "Financial Resources," Box 37, Item 16, 7.

77. Southern Association of Colleges and Schools (hereafter SACS), Progress Report on the Recommendations of the Visiting Committee of the SACS, April 15, 1962, 3.

78. Several respondents, who chose to remain anonymous, agreed that Martin, "a nice gentleman handpicked by the board," was a mistake from the first.

79. "New Broom for Emory," *Time*, July 19, 1963, 36–37.

80. From 1960 to 1965, five private universities in the South appointed new presidents.

81. EmU, Board of Trustees, Minutes of the Board of Trustees, July 8, 1963.

82. "New Broom for Emory," 36. Charles Lester, interview with the author, March 1, 1995.

83. A version of Atwood's statement appeared in the *Time* article cited above, but an anonymous respondent recalled this version.

84. EmU, Office of the President, Annual Administrative Report of the President to the Board of Trustees, 1963/64, 8.

85. EmU, *Profile of Emory University*, Part II, A-1, 71–72.

86. EmU, Office of the President, Annual Administrative Report of the President, 1966–67.

87. Henry L. Bowden, interview with the author, February 24, 1995.

88. Judson C. Ward, interview with the author, February 13, 1994. Clarence Stone, interview with the author, June 15, 1999. Stone, an assistant professor at Emory during the late 1960s, confirmed that Atwood was able to attract faculty from other regions.

89. Respondent wished to remain anonymous.

90. See discussion at Emory University, Emory History, "Controversies and Enigmas," http://emoryhistory.emory.edu/enigmas/GodIsDead.htm.

91. Alan Cartter, vice president of the American Council of Education, identified the four as Vanderbilt's Alexander Heard, Emory's Sanford Atwood, Tulane's Herbert Longenecker, and Duke's Douglas K. Knight. "On the Move in the South," *Time*, December 17, 1965, 94.

92. *Profile of Emory University*, Part II, A-1, 94.

93. For a list of universities receiving NSF Development Funds, see Geiger, *Research and Relevant Knowledge*, Table 15, 207.

94. By the mid-1960s, there were eighteen PhD programs at Emory (EmU, *Profile of Emory*, Part II, A-1, 7–9).

95. Ibid., 9.

96. In 1957, half of incoming graduate students had scored below the 50th percentile on standardized tests; in 1965–66, only 10 percent in math and 3 percent in verbal tests scored below

the 50th percentile. Fellowship information, Alan M. Cartter, "Qualitative Aspects," 53.

97 EmU, Office of the President, Annual Report of the President, 1963/64, 55.

98 EmU, Annual Administrative Report of the President, 1965–66; Annual Administrative Report, 1966–67; Annual Administrative Report, 1967–68.

99 In 1960, the U.S. Congress mandated an NIH Regional Primate Centers Program to provide resources for primate research across the nation. Emory received NIH Center status for the Yerkes Laboratories in 1961. NIH funding supported transfer of the labs to Atlanta in 1965.

100 Allan M. Cartter, *An Assessment of Quality in Graduate Education* (Washington, DC: American Council on Education, 1966).

101 English, *Emory University*, ix.

102 The years from 1968 to 1978 have been called "the stagnant decade," "the age of survival," and "the age of adjustment" for U.S. higher education. See Earl Cheit, *The New Depression in Higher Education* (New York: McGraw-Hill, 1970); Roger L. Geiger, "The Dynamics of University Research in the United States, 1945–90," in *Research and Higher Education: The United Kingdom and the United States*, ed. Thomas Whisten and Roger Geiger (Buckingham, UK: Society for Research in Higher Education, 1992), 3–17; and Graham and Diamond, *Rise of American Research Universities*, chap. 4.

103 EmU, Office of the President, Annual Administrative Report of the President, 1971–72, 3.

104 Ibid.

105 EmU, Board of Trustees, Minutes of the Executive Committee of the Board of Trustees of Emory University (hereafter, Minutes of the Executive Committee), September 16, 1971, 2.

106 EmU, Board of Trustees, Minutes of the Executive Committee, January 21, 1971, 3.

107 "Two African Americans Who Integrated the Faculty at Emory," *Journal of Blacks in Higher Education* (Spring 2001): 60. Another African American could rightly claim to be Emory's first black faculty member. In 1958 Dr. Asa G. Yancey Sr. became the first black doctor at the Hughes Spalding Pavilion, the hospital for paying African Americans at then-segregated Grady Memorial Hospital. Yancey became chief of surgery at Hughes Spalding and associate dean of the medical school in 1964 and served as medical director of Grady from 1972 until his retirement in 1989.

108 Boisfeuillet Jones, Letter to Sanford Atwood, July 18, 1972, Sanford S. Atwood Papers. The grant was in the form of thirteen hundred shares of Coca-Cola stock.

109 "The Atwood Years," 18. Despite fluctuations in the stock market, Emory's endowment increased to $177 million by 1977 (EmU, Office of Institutional Research, "Selected Highlights of Growth," 1994). In fact, other private campuses also rebounded from the decade's first difficult years. See Earl Cheit, *The New Depression in Higher Education—Two Years Later* (Berkeley, CA: Carnegie Commission on Higher Education, 1973).

110 EmU, *A Self-Study of Emory University, 1972* (hereafter *Self-Study 1972*), "Report of the Committee on the Graduate Faculty," EU Box Series, Box 37.1, Item 17, 12.

111 In 1960–61, the six most heavily enrolled departments (chemistry, psychology, biology, history, English, and political science) employed forty-eight at the upper ranks, and the remaining departments had only thirty-seven. Ten years later, the "big six" had fifty-three professors and associate professors, while the other departments totaled seventy in these ranks. Ibid.

112 Ibid., 14.

113 EmU, Office of the President, Annual Report of the President, 1966/67, 7.

114 *Self-Study 1972*, "Report of the Committee on the Graduate Faculty," 15. This was the trend at campuses across the nation. See Alan C. Bayer, *Teaching Faculty in Academe 1972–73* (Washington, DC: American Council on Education, 1973), 17.

115 *Self-Study 1972*, "Report of the Committee on the Graduate Faculty," 4.

[116] EmU, University Senate, Remarks by Sanford Atwood to the Emory University Senate, Minutes of the Regular Meeting October 16, 1973, n.p., EUA Series, Faculty Senate, Box 16.
[117] *Self-Study 1972*, "Report of Committee on the Graduate Faculty," Appendix A.
[118] *Self-Study 1972*, "Self-Study Report of the Graduate School of Arts and Sciences," Box 37.1, Item 17, 10–11.
[119] Faculty publication and award data from ibid., 20. Programs rated by the ACE for the first time were French, philosophy, psychology, botany, population biology, zoology, and chemistry (Kenneth D. Roose and Charles J. Andersen, *A Rating of Graduate Programs* [Washington, DC: American Council on Education, 1970]).
[120] EmU, Office of the President, Annual Report of the President, 1971/72. For the impact of federal programs on admissions at a southern medical school, see Randolph Batson and F. Tremaine Billings, "The Leavening of a Private Medical School," *Southern Medical Journal* 66, no. 1 (January 1973): 159–64.
[121] A Ford Foundation Challenge Grant also contributed to this increase. See Geiger, *Research and Relevant Knowledge*, Tables 15 and 16, 207, 209.
[122] *Self-Study 1972*, "Graduate School Self-Study of Research and Training," EU Box Series, Box 37.1, Item 18, 8.
[123] Moses Abramovitz, "Catching Up, Forging Ahead, Falling Behind," *Journal of Economic History* 46 (1986): 385–406.
[124] EmU, Office of the President, *Five-Year Planning Report, 1976–77—1980–81*, November 11, 1976, 56–57.
[125] Ibid., 60.
[126] See, for example, Roger Geiger, "Research Universities in a New Era: From the 1980s to the 1990s," in *Higher Learning in America, 1980–2000*, ed. Arthur Levine (Baltimore: Johns Hopkins University Press, 1993), 67–85.
[127] EmU, Board of Trustees, "Guidelines for the Selection of Emory University's President," May 1976. Author's copy.
[128] EmU, Board of Trustees, Minutes of the Board of Trustees, March 17, 1977. Some faculty speculated that Laney, who had not come up through traditional academic ranks that included experience as a provost, was an unusual choice.
[129] "A New Era—A New President," *Emory Magazine* (Summer Quarter 1977): 10. Laney earned three degrees at Yale—a BA in economics, a divinity degree, and a PhD. Yale awarded him an honorary doctorate in 1992.
[130] Ibid., 13.
[131] EmU, Office of the President, Annual Report of the President, 1977/78.
[132] James T. Laney, "A Future for Research," *Emory Magazine* (Fall Quarter 1977): 13.
[133] Laney had received a copy of a directive from the Carter administration that urged federal agencies to consider the long-range implications of basic research. See "OMB Memorandum to the Heads of Executive Departments and Agencies on the Funding of Basic Research, August 15, 1977," reprinted in National Science Foundation, *Basic Research in the Mission Agencies* (Washington, DC: National Science Foundation, 1978), Appendix B, 371.
[134] For a discussion of national economic conditions, see William C. Berman, *America's Right Turn: From Nixon to Bush* (Baltimore: Johns Hopkins University Press, 1994).
[135] EmU, Office of the President, "The State of Emory University, 1979," November 1979, 5–6.
[136] Elizabeth Coe, "Laney Announces Fund Drive," *Emory Wheel*, October 9, 1979, 9.
[137] Emory alumnus, trustee, and CEO of the Trust Company Bank James B. Williams chaired the campaign, and Robert Woodruff served as honorary chairman.
[138] Trustees of the Emily and Ernest Woodruff Fund decided that "the resources committed to their care [would have] greatest potential for service in the South, their area of special interest, if concentrated in Emory University." Robert W. Woodruff, Letter to James Laney, n.d., Robert

W. Woodruff Papers, Collection 10, Box 7, Folder 2. The Woodruff Fund's assets consisted of 15,707 shares of Coca-Cola International corporate stock with a market value of more than $100 million and an annual income of more than $5 million. EmU, Board of Trustees, Minutes of the Executive Committee, November 8, 1979, 3.

[139] See F. Stuart Gulley, *The Academic President as Moral Leader: James T. Laney at Emory University, 1977–1983* (Macon, GA: Mercer University Press, 2001). Charles Lester also observed that Atwood could not have obtained the Woodruff gift. Lester, interview with the author, March 1, 1995.

[140] James Laney quoted in Beth Dawkins Bassett, "The Path to Preeminence," *Emory Magazine* 65, no. 2 (June 1989): 15.

[141] John M. Palms quoted in Smith, "Self Portrait for the Future," *Emory Magazine* 58, no. 1 (October 1981): 14.

[142] EmU, Board of Trustees, Minutes of the Executive Committee, November 8, 1979.

[143] Palms quoted in Smith, "Self Portrait for the Future," 15.

[144] About 70 percent of the faculty endorsed Palms's promotion, but others criticized Laney because he did not actively solicit faculty opinion before suggesting the appointment. See Jack S. Boozer, Letter to James T. Laney, September 6, 1979, James T. Laney Papers, Box 17, Folder AAUP, 1, MARBL.

[145] Billy E. Frye, Interview with the author, December 15, 1999.

[146] Smith, "Self Portrait for the Future," 16.

[147] James T. Laney, Letter to the Emory Faculties, March 13, 1980, 1.

[148] EmU, *University Self-Study 1981* (hereafter *Self-Study 1981*), "Report of the Natural Sciences Review Committee," EU Box Series, Box 19, Item 8, 102.

[149] For example, biological sciences faculty at Hopkins won thirty-nine NIH training grants, while Emory faculty had received only five such grants. Ibid., Table 44, 22.

[150] *Self-Study 1981*, "Report of the School of Medicine," EU Box Series, Box 19, Item 6, 15.

[151] *Self-Study 1981*, "Report on the Division of Social Sciences," 145. The division included three service departments—Physical Education, Educational Studies, and Librarianship. Economics was based in the business school. The nationally ranked history program was an exception to the findings.

[152] *Self-Study 1981*, "Report of the Humanities Division," 166.

[153] James T. Laney, Letter to the Faculty of Arts and Sciences, April 27, 1982.

[154] The comparison with Stanford was made in *Self-Study 1981*, "Law School Self-Study," 39.

[155] The NRC assessment placed six Emory departments (English, history, biochemistry, microbiology, psychology, physiology) in the "Good" category, and ranked pharmacology among the nation's top programs. See Lyle V. Jones, Gardner Lindzey, and Porter E. Coggeshall, eds., *An Assessment of Research-Doctorate Programs in the United States*, 5 vols. (Washington, DC: National Academy of Sciences Press, 1982).

[156] Laney, Letter to the Faculty of Arts and Sciences. The committee included Stanley Cavell, a philosopher from Harvard; Robert Bellah, a Berkeley sociologist; Eliot Stellar, physicist and provost at the University of Pennsylvania; Martin Glicksman, biologist and provost at Brown; and Judith Shklar, a feminist scholar from Harvard.

[157] EmU, "Report of the Emory University Visiting Committee for the Arts and Sciences to President James Laney," April 2, 1982 (the "Lamar Report"), EU Box Series, Box 37.9, Folder 8, Item 8, 33.

[158] Ibid., 34.

[159] Ibid., 33.

[160] Ibid., 40.

[161] Ibid. The ILA, supported by generous federal and foundation funding, grew in size and vigor in the 1960s and early 1970s, but then struggled to overcome a reputation for modishness.

162 Ibid., 7, 41.

163 Ibid., 5.

164 Ibid., 13.

165 SACS, Report of the Reaffirmation Committee Visit to Emory University, April 24–27, 1983.

166 Ibid. Quotes from pages 6, 34, 12.

167 Ibid., 33. Vanderbilt had established an Office of Sponsored Programs in 1971. At Emory, grants and contracts were reviewed by an associate dean, the Graduate School dean, and the Controller's Office.

168 Palms, interview with the author, March 3, 2000; Minter, interview with the author, February 4, 2000.

169 The Woodruff gift made possible an 80 percent increase in the Graduate School budget despite a 7 percent decrease in enrollment. An Emory–Georgia Tech Biomedical Research Center established in 1984 enabled the campus "to assume a significant role" in the bioscience revolution "for economic development of the region." EmU, Annual Report of the President, 1983/84, 11.

170 EmU, "The State of the University 1984" (November 1984). Salary data from EmU, "The State of the University 1982" (November 1982). Nationally prominent faculty—William Arrowsmith (classics), Richard Ellmann (English), Ulric Neisser (psychology), and Harold Berman (law)—were among the first Woodruff Professors.

171 On the Carter appointment, see "Celebrity Professors: Do They Pay Off for Colleges and Students?" *Newsweek on Campus*, September 1987, 9.

172 According to one calculation, Emory's R&D dependency (a ratio of federal R&D expenditures divided by total expenditures) was 88.5 percent, fourth behind Stanford, Boston University, and UC San Diego. Emory's "institutional ratio" (percent of federal grants and contracts to total 1979 E&G revenues) was 26.3, compared to Caltech (62.0), Duke (33.5), University of North Carolina–Chapel Hill (25.2), and Alabama-Birmingham (23.7). See Marilyn McCoy, Jack Krakower, and David Madowski, "Financing at the Leading 100 Research Universities: A Study of Financial Dependency, Concentration and Related Institutional Characteristics," *Research in Higher Education* 15 (1981): 334.

173 Emory ranked sixty-ninth in 1981 and 1982 (with about $18 million); seventy-first in 1983 ($20.6 million); sixty-fourth about $33 million) in 1986; and forty-ninth in 1987 (about $47.3 million). National Science Foundation, *Federal Support to Universities, Colleges and Other Non-Profit Institutions*, FY 1981 and various years (Washington, DC: FY 1981, 1982, 1983, 1986, 1987).

174 EmU, Office of the President, "The State of the University, 1979" (November 1979).

175 Billy E. Frye, interview with the author, December 15, 1999. See William C. Richardson, "The Appropriate Scale of the Health Sciences Enterprise," in *Research University in a Time of Discontent*, 253–69; William G. Rothstein, *American Medical Schools and the Practice of Medicine* (New York: Oxford University Press, 1987). See also Graham and Diamond, *Rise of American Research Universities*, 209–10.

176 Vice President for Health Affairs Charles Hatcher recalled with good humor that it was no surprise that Laney, a minister, would want a tithe on the earnings. See Gulley, *Academic President as Moral Leader*, 126, 157.

177 Minter, interview with the author, February 4, 2000.

178 EmU, Transcription of Remarks Presented at the Trustee Retreat, Sea Island, Georgia, March 13–14, 1987. Box 10, Trustee Retreat Folder, James T. Laney Papers, 72.

179 The University Athletic Association is a National Collegiate Athletic Association (NCAA) Division III athletic conference established in 1985.

180 Emory ranked tenth in federal funds, but eighty-sixth in the nation, thirty positions behind Vanderbilt, the next lowest in the comparison group (James T. Laney, "Emory 2000: An Address to University Faculties," *Emory Wheel*, May 4, 1987, 6).

181 For data on tuition and endowment, see ibid. Federal R&D data compiled from National Science Foundation, *Federal Support to Universities, Colleges and Other Nonprofit Institutions, Fiscal Year 1986* (Washington, DC: National Science Foundation, 1987).
182 Laney, Transcription of Remarks Presented at the Trustee Retreat, 9.
183 EmU, Transcription of Remarks Presented at the Trustee Retreat, 10. In 1986 Georgia received six dollars per capita in research support, while Massachusetts and Connecticut received more than sixty dollars per capita. Laney observed that U.S. Senator Sam Nunn, an Emory alumnus and former trustee, would find it intolerable if military spending in the South reflected a similar ratio.
184 Ibid., 13.
185 This decision was made in 1987. Gulley, *Academic President as Moral Leader*, 143. Gulley counted the number of faculty listed in the Academic Catalog to derive this figure.
186 EmU, Office of Institutional Research, *Selected Indicators of Growth, 1977, 1984, 1992* (Atlanta: Emory University, 1994). By the early 1990s the faculty included eleven from Stanford, twelve from Berkeley, and twenty-three from Yale. In 1977 there had been only one faculty member from Stanford and none from Berkeley (EmU, Office of the President, Annual Report of the President, 1990/91, 6).
187 Minter, interview with the author, February 4, 2000.
188 Don Wycliff, "Emory Raises Its Status," *New York Times*, August 23, 1990, A18.
189 Laney, Transcription of Remarks at the Trustee Retreat, 47.
190 James T. Laney, Letter to Robert Strickland, May 3, 1989, Box 6-8, James Laney Papers, 3.
191 O. Wayne Rollins, an Atlanta business executive, donated $10 million for the Center (EmU, *Self-Study of Emory University*, February 1993).
192 Ibid., 41–42. Opened in 1960, U.S. Centers for Disease Control and Prevention programs complemented Emory's biomedical research agenda.
193 Ibid., 39-40.
194 Of this amount, some $570 million belonged to the Woodruff endowment. EmU, Office of Institutional Research, Selected Indicators of Achievement.
195 Frye, interview with the author, December 15, 1999.
196 "Research Funding Posts Another Record Year," *Emory Report*, September 9, 1995.
197 "University Sees Record-Breaking Totals for Sponsored Research in '97 Fiscal Year," *Emory Report*, September 29, 1997.
198 "Sponsored Research Funding's Modest Growth," *Emory Report*, October 19, 1998.
199 "Faculty Town Hall Focuses on Current and Future Research," *Emory Report*, March 2, 1998. Quote, Dennis Liotta, vice president for research.
200 "Moving Research From the Lab to 'Reality,'" *Emory Report*, September 11, 1995.
201 For 1998 data, see "Sponsored Research Funding's Modest Growth"; for earlier data, see "Research Funding Posts Another Record Year," *Emory Report*, September 10, 1995.
202 Palms, interview with the author, March 3, 2000.
203 Laney, Transcription of Remarks at the Trustee Retreat, 72.
204 Dewey W. Grantham, *Southern Progressivism: The Reconciliation of Progress and Tradition* (Knoxville: University of Tennessee Press, 1983), chap. 8.

Chapter 9: How it Came to Pass
David Minter Interview

1 Readers who recall David Minter's lucid prose, incisive wit, and brilliant lectures will note in this interview the effects of health problems that he has suffered in retirement.
2 *Emory Magazine* records that "Laney had met Minter and his family in August [1980] and had talked with him again in early fall, but shortly after receiving the [search] committee's list [in which Minter had been recommended as the first choice for dean] [Laney] boarded a plane and flew to Houston for another round of discussions. Laney was attracted

by the candidate's blend of intellectual curiosity and academic distinction. He also found it intriguing that Minter shared his ideas about undergraduate education, especially the notion that a university must do whatever possible to encourage 'intellectual aggressiveness, vitality, and confidence' among its students. That was a goal Laney had tried to promote at Emory for several years. He felt that in Minter he had found a kindred spirit. And he offered him the job" (Jeffrey Smith, "The Education of David Minter," *Emory Magazine*, April 1983, 13).

3   Dr. Minter noted elsewhere that "the faculty had gone through a long period without growth; during the whole decade of the seventies it remained within one or two [faculty positions] of the size it was ten years earlier. It needed to grow in order to spread the teaching load and to diversify and improve" (ibid., 15).

4   In addition to the development noted above, Minter, as dean, was responsible for increasing support for faculty travel and summer research grants for junior faculty, establishing a faculty committee to advise the dean on budget and planning, increasing faculty involvement in policy formation, establishing the College Staff Consortium, working to restructure the guidelines for promotion and tenure, and revising procedures for choosing members of the Faculty Council to make the group more directly representative of the arts and sciences faculty. Members were to be elected directly by the faculty instead of appointed by the dean, based on the results of a nonbinding faculty referendum. The Emory University Museum of Art and Archaeology was also established (ibid.).

George Jones Interview

5   This interview was conducted on November 12, 2008, and edited by Gary Hauk and Sally Wolff King.

6   Teaching Assistant Training and Teaching Opportunity is a four-stage program required by the Graduate School for doctoral students, to prepare them in the art of teaching.

Steve Sanderson Interview

7   This interview was recorded on February 4, 2009, and edited by Gary Hauk and Sally Wolff King.

Peter Dowell and Irwin Hyatt Interview

8   This joint interview was conducted on October 1, 2008, and edited by Gary Hauk and Sally Wolff King.

Rosemary Magee Interview

9   Interview conducted March 25, 2009, and edited by Gary Hauk and Sally Wolff King.

10 In 1982 President James T. Laney appointed the Emory University Visiting Committee for the Arts and Sciences, chaired by Emory alumnus and Yale College dean Howard Lamar. For more about the impact of this committee's report, see Nancy Diamond's chapter in this volume, pages 93–99.

Chapter 10: Campus Life

1   This interview was recorded on October 24, 2008, and edited by Gary Hauk and Sally Wolff King.

2   In April 1990 Sabrina Collins, an Emory College freshman, reported that she had found racist epithets scrawled in her room in Longstreet Hall. Later she reported receiving death threats. A long and thorough investigation by police and the Georgia Bureau of Investigation determined that the threats and epithets had been the work of Collins herself.

Chapter 11: The School of Theology as a Prelude
1. This interview was conducted by Robert Carr and was recorded on May 2, 2008. It has been edited by Gary Hauk.

Chapter 14: "If You Build It, [They] Will Come"
1. Since most of the principals involved in this part of the story are—one way or another—gone, I can write about it now without stepping on too many toes. Because I was the only full-time faculty member teaching film at Emory during these years, much of my perspective on these events is naturally personal. A more "objective" third-person voice would sound clumsy and, worse, would probably obscure the truth. So the first part of this essay is inevitably about the English Department and me, with my apologies for talking so much about myself.
2. Mulvey, in her 1973 essay "Visual Pleasure and Narrative Cinema," had reoriented film theory toward a psychoanalytic and feminist framework by claiming that the apparatus of classical Hollywood cinema forced the spectator into a masculine subject position that is simultaneously voyeuristic and sadistic. Studlar argued the opposite: that visual pleasure for all spectators derives from a masochistic perspective in which a passive audience is overwhelmed by the cinematic image. This thesis became the subject of her foundational book published by Columbia University Press in 1988, *In the Realm of Pleasure: Von Sternberg, Dietrich, and the Masochistic Aesthetic*.

Chapter 15: Guy Redvers Lyle and the Birth of Emory's Research Libraries
1. Emory University Library Annual Report, 1954–55, Manuscript, Archives, and Rare Book Library, Emory University (MARBL).
2. "Library Needs," September 2, 1954, Guy Redvers Lyle Papers, MARBL.
3. "Emory Faces Its Library Problem, Prepared for Presentation to the Faculty of Arts and Sciences and the Graduate School," December 29, 1954, Guy Redvers Lyle Papers, MARBL; *Emory Wheel*, January 27, 1955; "We've a Long Way to Go," *Emory Alumnus*, March 1955, 12–16, 50.
4. Emory University Library Annual Report, 1954–55, MARBL.
5. Guy Lyle, *Beyond My Expectation: A Personal Chronicle* (Metuchen, NJ: Scarecrow Press, 1981), 175.
6. *Emory Wheel*, May 24, 1956.
7. Letters of Guy R. Lyle to Ivan Allen Jr., Henry L. Bowden, Charles Howard Candler Jr., et al., September 29, 1958, Guy Redvers Lyle Papers, MARBL.
8. Lyle, *Beyond My Expectation*, 194.
9. "Lamont Library History," Harvard College Library, September 3, 2008, http://hcl.harvard.edu/libraries/lamont/history.html.
10. "First in the South—The Library for Advanced Studies," Report to the Campus Development Committee, January 12, 1961, Guy Redvers Lyle Papers, MARBL.
11. Lyle, *Beyond My Expectations*, 195.
12. Ibid., 201.
13. Emory University Library Annual Report, 1971–1972, MARBL.
14. Guy R. Lyle, "What Education Is All About," *Emory Alumnus*, October 1964, 11.
15. For a bibliography of Lyle's writings up to the time of his retirement, see Ruth Walling, "Guy R. Lyle: Publications," *The Academic Library: Essays in Honor of Guy R. Lyle*, ed. Evan Ira Farber and Ruth Walling (Metuchen, NJ: Scarecrow Press, 1974), 162–71.
16. *American Libraries*, September 1972, 921–22.
17. Lyle's autobiography, *Beyond My Expectation*, and Walling's biographical essay, "Guy Redvers Lyle," are the major sources for the facts of Lyle's life. See also Philip Dare, "Guy R.

Lyle," *Leaders in American Academic Librarianship: 1925–1975*, ed. Wayne A. Wiegand (Pittsburgh: Beta Phi Mu, 1983), 149–66, for another interpretation of his career.

[18] "Hollywood Comes to the Library; and Introduces It to College Freshmen Through a Film Called 'Found in a Book,'" *Christian Science Monitor*, October 13, 1936.

[19] "Crow's Nest," *Wilson Library Bulletin*, September 1935 through October 1942, an entertaining and informative column about library publicity, which was also the subject of his second book, *College Library Publicity* (Boston: Faxon, 1934).

[20] *The Administration of the College Library* (New York: Wilson, 1944).

[21] *A Bibliography of Christopher Morley* (Washington: Scarecrow, 1952) updated an earlier work by Alfred P. Lee, *A Bibliography of Christopher Morley* (Garden City, NY: Doubleday, 1935).

[22] *I Am Happy to Present: A Book of Introductions* (New York: Wilson, 1953), coauthored with Kevin Guinagh.

[23] The last article he published was about horseback riding: "Pleasure Trail Riding," *Georgia Horse Trader*, February 1988, 1–4.

Chapter 16: Emory Law and the Formation of a University

[1] Letter from H. W. Arant to Warren Candler, January 11, 1916, Warren Candler Papers, Manuscript, Archives, and Rare Book Library, Emory University.

[2] Letter from Warren Candler to Paul Bryan, March 2, 1916, Warren Candler Papers, Manuscript, Archives, and Rare Book Library, Emory University.

[3] Letter from Warren Candler to Paul Bryan, March 25, 1916, Warren Candler Papers, Manuscript, Archives, and Rare Book Library, Emory University.

[4] There is some question about the number of students enrolled on the first day of classes. The Emory Law School Register Book has twenty-eight entries. Marc Miller puts the number at twenty-seven. See Marc Miller, "Georgia's Historic Law Schools: Part III—Emory: The Creation of a National Law School," *Georgia State Bar Journal* 27, no. 2 (November 1990).

[5] *Bulletin of Emory University* (1916): 192.

[6] *Bulletin of Emory University* 8, no. 4 (June 1922): 7.

[7] *Bulletin of Emory University* 8, no. 6 (June 1927): 5; *Bulletin of Emory University* 37, no. 14 (August 1951): 6.

[8] *Bulletin of Emory University* 7, no. 5 (August 1921): 31.

[9] *Emory Law School Register*, 1918, 2–4.

[10] *Bulletin of Emory University* 5, no. 3 (May 1919): 6.

[11] Annual Reports to the President, 1929–1930, 100, Manuscript, Archives, and Rare Book Library, Emory University.

[12] *Bulletin of Emory University* 8, no. 4 (June 1922): 8.

[13] *Bulletin of Emory University* 11, no. 7 (July 1925): 4

[14] Miller, "Georgia's Historic Law Schools: Part III—Emory": 88.

[15] *Bulletin of Emory University* 12, no. 5 (May 1926): 5.

[16] Annual Reports to the President, 1935–1936, 104, Manuscript, Archives, and Rare Book Library, Emory University.

[17] Annual Reports to the President, 1927–1928, 114, Manuscript, Archives, and Rare Book Library, Emory University.

[18] Annual Reports to the President, 1931–1932, 105, Manuscript, Archives, and Rare Book Library, Emory University.

[19] Annual Reports to the President, 1930–1931, 122, Manuscript, Archives, and Rare Book Library, Emory University.

[20] Annual Reports to the President, 1937–1938, 84, Manuscript, Archives, and Rare Book Library, Emory University.

[21] Annual Reports to the President, 1938–1939, 127, Manuscript, Archives, and Rare Book Library, Emory University.
[22] Annual Reports to the President, 1945–1946, 32, Manuscript, Archives, and Rare Book Library, Emory University.
[23] *Bulletin of Emory University* 34, No. 14 (August 1948): 7
[24] *Bulletin of Emory University* 34, No. 14 (August 1948): 6
[25] *Bulletin of Emory University* 35, No. 14 (August 1949): 23.
[26] *Bulletin of Emory University* 36, No. 14 (August 1950): 5.
[27] See Annual Reports to the President, 1951–1952 to 1958–1959, Manuscript, Archives, and Rare Book Library, Emory University.
[28] Miller, "Georgia's Historic Law Schools," 91.
[29] Ibid., 92.
[30] Ibid., 93.
[31] Ibid.

Chapter 17: Feminist Activism and the Origins of Women's Studies at Emory

[1] Mari Jo Buhle, "Introduction," in *The Politics of Women's Studies*, ed. Florence Howe (New York: Feminist Press, 2000), 3.
[2] Danielle Service, "Emeritae Faculty Cite Changes, Urge Continued Concern," *Emory Report*, April 8, 1996.
[3] Martine Brownley, personal interview, December 9, 2008.
[4] Peggy Barlett, personal interview, November 3, 2008.
[5] Service, "Emeritae Faculty Cite Changes."
[6] Carole Hahn, personal interview, November 21, 2008.
[7] Emory Women's Caucus, letter to Sanford Atwood, September 1974, Emory Women's Caucus papers, Series 1000, Box 36b, Folder 4, Manuscript, Archives and Rare Book Library, Emory University.
[8] Emory Women's Caucus, letter to Sanford Atwood, November 6, 1975, Emory Women's Caucus papers, Series 1000, Box 36b, Manuscript, Archives, and Rare Book Library, Emory University.
[9] President's Commission on the Status of Women, "Report on the Status of Women at Emory University," September 1977, Emory Women's Caucus papers, Series 1000, Box 36b, Folder 9, Manuscript, Archives, and Rare Book Library, Emory University.
[10] Ibid.
[11] Barlett, personal interview.
[12] Emory Women's Caucus, newsletter, February 16, 1977; March 14, 1977, Emory Women's Caucus papers, Manuscript, Archives, and Rare Book Library, Emory University.
[13] Emory Women's Caucus, newsletter, January 1978, Emory Women's Caucus papers, Manuscript, Archives, and Rare Book Library, Emory University.
[14] Barlett, personal interview.
[15] Ibid.
[16] Ibid.
[17] President's Commission on the Status of Women, "Report on the Status of Women at Emory University," September 1977.
[18] Peggy Barlett et al., "Proposal for a Program in Feminist Studies," January 31, 1984, Peggy Barlett personal papers.
[19] Peggy Barlett et al., "Proposal to Establish Programs in Women Studies and Critical Theories," May 10, 1985, Peggy Barlett personal papers.
[20] Ibid.
[21] Ibid.

[22] Barlett, personal interview.
[23] Hahn, personal interview.
[24] G. P. Cuttino, "Secret Committee Promotes Shibboleth," *Emory Wheel*, November 1, 1985.
[25] Polly Price, "Cuttino Editorial Is Wrong on Program," *Emory Wheel*, November 12, 1985.
[26] Melvin Konner, "Cuttino's Editorial Is Medieval," *Emory Wheel*, December 6, 1985.
[27] Mechal Sobel *New York Times Book Review*, January 8, 1989.
[28] Emory University Institute for Women's Studies Self-Study, Fall 1992, 3.
[29] Ibid.
[30] Carol Iannone, "How Politicized Studies Enforce Conformity: Interviews with Julius Lester and Elizabeth Fox-Genovese," *Academic Questions* (Summer 1992): 56.
[31] Emory University Institute for Women's Studies Self-Study, Fall 1992, 5.
[32] Ibid.
[33] Ibid., 16.
[34] Ibid., 8.
[35] Emory University Institute for Women's Studies Self-Study, Spring 2006, n.p.
[36] "Best Colleges 2010—Historically Black Colleges and Universities Ranking," *U.S. News & World Report*, September 25, 2009, http://colleges.usnews.rankingsandreviews.com/best-colleges/hbcu-rankings.
[37] Emory University Institute for Women's Studies Self-Study, 1992 Self-Study, 5.
[38] Ibid.
[39] Tina Brownley, personal interview, December 9, 2008.
[40] Ibid.
[41] Emory University Institute for Women's Studies Self-Study, 1992 Self-Study, 8, 12.
[42] Scott Heller, "Emory U.'s Director of Women's Studies Quits, Describing Complaints as 'Political Power Play,'" *Chronicle of Higher Education*, February 12, 1992, A13.
[43] Ibid.
[44] Norah Vincent, "Spread 'Em: Pro-Choice Is No-Choice on Campus," *Village Voice*, April 25, 2000, http://www.villagevoice.com/content/printVersion/159447.
[45] Iannone, "How Politicized Studies Enforce Conformity," 61.
[46] Emory University Institute for Women's Studies Self-Study, Spring 2006, n.p.
[47] Brownley, personal interview.
[48] Emory University Institute for Women's Studies Self-Study, Spring 2006, n.p.
[49] Brownley, personal interview.
[50] Emory University, "Professor Received Governor's Award in the Humanities," May 6, 2009, http://www.emory.edu/home/news/releases/2009/04/fox-centers-brownley-receives-governors-award.html.
[51] Robyn Fivush, personal interview, November 13, 2008.
[52] Ibid.
[53] Ibid.
[54] Ibid.
[55] Ibid.
[56] Patricia Owen-Smith, personal interview, November 11, 2008.
[57] Ibid.
[58] Letter from the Graduate Students of Women's Studies to Dr. Frances Foster, May 2, 2000, personal collection of Dr. Foster.

Chapter 20: Lore Metzger

[1] The Dora Helen Skypek files in the library contain the newsletters and some further information about the caucus. See also chap. 18.

Chapter 21: "Athletics for All Who Wish to Participate"
1. Personal correspondence to the author from Mrs. Herman L. Donovan, March 11, 1967.

Chapter 22: Richard A. Long
1. Amalia Amaki, "Being Richard A. Long: The Life, The Odyssey," *International Review of African American Art* 22, No. 3: 13.
2. Maya Angelou, *Even the Stars Look Lonesome* (New York: Random House, 1997), 53.

Chapter 23: A Century of Vitality
1. In writing this piece, the author relied heavily on the transcript of an interview of Pat Butler by Mary Loftus, of the Emory Creative Group, in 2008, for the Emory University Women's Oral History Project. This project celebrated the achievements of women at Emory as part of the thirtieth anniversary of the President's Commission on the Status of Women and the fifteenth and twentieth anniversaries, respectively, of the Center for Women and the Women's Studies Department.

    The author also acknowledges the article "A Pioneering Spirit" by Wendy Cromwell, which appeared in the Summer 2008 issue of *Emory Lawyer* magazine, and "A Stentorian Life" by Jennifer Bryon Owen in the Spring 2004 issue of *Agnes Scott The Magazine*.

    The primary source for the article is the author's own recollection of several conversations with Mrs. Butler over the course of their acquaintanceship, which began in 1995 during a memorable breakfast at the Mayflower Hotel in Washington, DC.

Chapter 24: The Osler of the South
1. PBS Online, "A Science Odyssey: People and Discoveries—Pellagra Shown to Be Dietary Disease," http://www.pbs.org/wgbh/aso/databank/entries/dm15pa.html.
2. Emory University, Beck Center, "Emory's Creed," http://beck.library.emory.edu/oxfordexperience/document.php?id=oeJarrell428EmoryCreed.

Chapter 25: The Classicist
1. For brief sketches of his life and career, see *National Cyclopedia of American Biography* 52 (1970): 288, with a fine photograph (coincidentally, the biographical sketch on the facing page is that of Edith Hamilton, also a great popularizer of classical literature and culture); W. M. Calder III, *Dictionary of American Biography Supplement* 8 (1988): 235–37; G. Highet, "Moses Hadas 1900–1966," *Classical World* 60 (1966–67): 92–93; H. W. Benario, in *Biographical Dictionary of North American Classicists*, ed. W. W. Briggs Jr. (Westport, CT: Greenwood Press,1994), 244–45.
2. The OSS (Office of Strategic Services) was founded and commanded by General William J. Donovan. For an example of his activities, see R. W. Winks, *Cloak & Gown: Scholars in the Secret War, 1939–1961*, 2nd ed. (New Haven, CT: Yale University Press, 1996), 213–14.
3. *Journal of Hellenic Studies* 83 (1963): 192.
4. *American Historical Review* 66 (1960–61): 1005–6.
5. *Terzo Contributo alla Storia degli Studi Classici e del Mondo Antico* (Rome: Edizioni di storia e letteratura, 1966), 765.
6. Indianapolis: Bobbs-Merrill, 1965.
7. Herbert W. Benario, *Tacitus. Agricola, Germany, Dialogue on Orators* (Indianapolis: Bobbs-Merrill, 1967).

Chapter 26: Emory Historical Minds and Their Impact

1. Also joining the history faculty that year, with a freshly signed and sealed PhD from Princeton, was Russell Major, who would burnish Emory's legacy in a career lasting more than four decades (see chap. 33).
2. C. Vann Woodward, *Thinking Back: The Perils of Writing History* (Baton Rouge: Louisiana State University Press, 1986), 21.
3. Ibid.
4. John Herbert Roper, *C. Vann Woodward, Southerner* (Athens: University of Georgia Press, 1987), 5.
5. See, for example, "Emory University: Highlights of Excellence and Achievement 1997," at http://www.emory.edu/PROVOST/IPR/documents/selectedacademichighlights/1997_highlights.htm.
6. Roper, *C. Vann Woodward*, 56.
7. Woodward, *Thinking Back*, 31.
8. Ibid., 105.
9. Ibid., 113.
10. Ibid., 82.
11. Quoted in ibid., 92.
12. Marcus Cunliffe and Robin W. Winks, eds., *Pastmasters: Some Essays on American Historians* (New York: Harper & Row, 1969), "Introduction."
13. Sir Denis Brogan, "David M. Potter," in *Pastmasters*, 316.
14. Ibid., 332.
15. For a more recent interpretation of this story, see Annette Gordon-Reed, *The Hemingses of Monticello* (New York: W. W. Norton, 2008).
16. Ibid., 252.
17. Quoted in the "Introduction" to *The Bell Irvin Wiley Reader*, ed. Hill Jordan, James I. Robertson Jr., and J. H. Segars (Baton Rouge: Louisiana State University Press, 2001), 2.
18. Henry T. Malone, "Bell Irvin Wiley: Uncommon Soldier," in *Rank and File: Civil War Essays in Honor of Bell Irvin Wiley*, ed. James I. Robertson Jr. and Richard M. McMurry (San Rafael, CA: Presidio Press, 1978), 3.
19. Bell Irvin Wiley, *The Life of Billy Yank, the Common Soldier of the Union* (Indianapolis: Bobbs-Merrill, 1952), 14.
20. Malone, "Bell Irvin Wiley," 18.
21. Quoted in ibid., 12.
22. Krista Reese, "The Uncommon Common Man," *Emory Magazine* 76, no. 4 (Winter 2001): 35.

Chapter 27: The Charles Howard Candler Professorships

1. "Awards Banquet Program Booklet," May 30, 1960, Manuscript, Archives, and Rare Book Library, Emory University.
2. Ibid., 2.
3. Eric Rangus, "Irvine schools teachers in diversity," *Emory Report*, May 30, 2000, V. 52, No. 34.

Chapter 29: Medievalist Extraordinary

1. This chapter is adapted from Hyatt's tribute to Cuttino in J. S. Hamilton and Patricia J. Bradley, eds., *Documenting the Past: Essays in Medieval History Presented to George Peddy Cuttino* (Wolfeboro, NH: The Boydell Press, 1989): 239–42. Used with permission.

Chapter 31: A Fortunate Life

1. For this essay, Professor Dillingham composed his own charming recollections, from which I draw heavily.

[2] Quoted in Andrew W. M. Beierle, "An Artist in the Rigging," *Emory Magazine* (December 1983): 29.
[3] Ibid., 30.
[4] Quoted in "Minutes of Emory College Faculty Meeting," April 17, 1996. Emory University, Manuscript, Archives, and Rare Book Library.

Chapter 32: Russell Major

[1] James Russell Major, *The Memoirs of an Artillery Forward Observer, 1944–1945* Manhattan, KS: Sunflower University Press, 1999), 140.
[2] Emory University, "Awards: The Thomas Jefferson Award," http://www.emory.edu/PROVOST/facultydevelopment/awards/thomasjefferson.php.
[3] Letter from Irwin Hyatt to Vice President John M. Palms nominating Russell Major for named chair, June 6, 1980. In personal collection of Blair Rogers Major.
[4] Personal correspondence to Blair Rogers Major from Wytch Stubbs, a history major (College 1952, Theology 1955, Medicine 1966), December 15, 1998, personal collection of Blair Rogers Major, Decatur, GA.
[5] Personal correspondence to J. Russell Major, from Frank Williams, a student in Major's "Early Modern French History" course, September 29, 1998, personal collection of Blair Rogers Major, Decatur, GA.
[6] Personal correspondence from Albert Hamscher to Blair Rogers Major, February 10, 1999, personal collection of Blair Rogers Major, Decatur, GA.
[7] Major, *Memoirs of an Artillery Forward Observer*, 20.
[8] Rachel Tobin, "Russell Major, Historian, War Hero," *Atlanta Journal Constitution*, December 14, 1998.
[9] Major, *Memoirs of an Artillery Forward Observer*, xviii.
[10] Mack P. Holt, Society for French Historical Studies, "News: Recent Deaths," 1999, personal collection of Blair Rogers Major, Decatur, GA.
[11] Major, *Memoirs of an Artillery Forward* Observer, 134.
[12] Ibid.
[13] Thomas I. Crimando, "Review of *From Renaissance Monarchy to Absolute Monarchy: French Kings, Nobles and Estates*," *Renaissance Society of America: Renaissance Quarterly* 50, no. 1 (Spring 1997): 290–91.
[14] Mack P. Holt, *Societies and Institutions in Early Modern France, Festschrift for J. Russell Major* (Athens: University of Georgia Press, 1991.
[15] James Harvey Young, from Russell Major Memorial Service, January 23, 1999, personal collection of Blair Rogers Major, Decatur, GA.
[16] Interview with Blair Rogers Major, November 20, 2008.
[17] Tobin, "Russell Major."
[18] Letter from Donna Bohanan to Blair Major, January 11, 1999, personal collection of Blair Rogers Major, Decatur, GA.
[19] Letter from Hyatt to Palms.
[20] Letter from J. Russell Major to Robert Lambert, 1969, Russell Major papers, Manuscript, Archives, and Rare Book Library, Emory University.
[21] Letter from J. Russell Major to Charles Strickland, June 11, 1969, Russell Major papers, Manuscript, Archives, and Rare Book Library (MARBL), Emory University.
[22] Letter from J. Russell Major to Joy Hoffman, July 7, 1969, Russell Major papers, MARBL.
[23] Letter from Hyatt to Palms, MARBL.
[24] July 10/19, 1972, MARBL.
[25] Letter from Thomas Burns to Blair Rogers Major, in personal collection of Blair Rogers Major, Decatur, GA.

Chapter 33: Richard Ellmann at Emory, 1976–1987
1. Marella Walker, personal correspondences, in possession of the author.

Chapter 34: In Praise of a Legal Polymath
1. Professor Berman was a member of both the American Academy of Arts and Sciences and the Russian Academy of Sciences. He received more than a hundred prizes and awards for his scholarly achievements, including the prestigious Scribes Award from the American Bar Association, and honorary doctorates from the Catholic University of America, the Virginia Theological Seminary, the University of Ghent, and the Russian Academy of Sciences. He received three *Festschriften*: *The Weightier Matters of the Law: Essays on Law and Religion in Tribute to Harold J. Berman* (1988); *Law after Revolution: Essays on Socialist Law in Honor of Harold J. Berman* (1988); and *The Integrative Jurisprudence of Harold J. Berman* (1996). The *Emory Law Journal* (2008) published a series of memorial tributes to him written by his students and colleagues. A full collection of his articles, in both printed and digital forms, is available through the Emory library. A comprehensive collection of his writings from 1948 to 1985 is included in the "Red Set" of faculty publications in the Harvard Law Library. The newly dedicated Harold J. Berman Library in the Emory Center for the Study of Law and Religion houses some of his personal books and effects. The newly established Harold J. Berman Lecture Series at Emory Law School offers regular lectures on the many legal topics that Professor Berman long championed.

Chapter 35: Emory and Methodism
1. This chapter depends especially on Gary S. Hauk, *A Legacy of Heart and Mind: Emory since 1836* (Atlanta: Bookhouse Group, 1999); Wilbur A. Carlton, *The Oxford Church, North Georgia Conference* (Oxford, GA: n.p., 1973); Thomas H. English, *Emory University, 1915–1965: A Semicentennial History* (Atlanta: Emory University, 1966); Henry Morton Bullock, *A History of Emory University* (Nashville: Parthenon Press, 1936); Boone M. Bowen, *The Candler School of Theology: Sixty Years of Service* (Atlanta: Candler School of Theology, Emory University, 1974); Herchel H. Sheets, *Methodism in North Georgia: A History of the North Georgia Conference* (Milledgeville, GA: Boyd Publishing Company under sponsorship of Commission on Archives and History and Bishop and Cabinet of the North Georgia Annual Conference, 2005); James W. May, *The Glenn Memorial Story: A History of the United Methodist Church on the Emory University Campus* (n.p., 1985); and Mark K. Bauman, *Warren Akin Candler: The Conservative as Idealist* (Metuchen, NJ: Scarecrow Press, 1981). It also reworks portions of my *University and Church: Notes on the Methodist Experience* (Atlanta: Office of the President, Emory University, 2002). Related excursions on Methodism and higher education and on Methodist connectionalism with fuller documentation can be found in two fall 2009 Richey volumes, tentatively titled *Methodist Connectionalism: Historical Perspectives* (General Board of Higher Education and Ministry), and *Doctrine in Experience: A Methodist Theology of Church and Ministry* (Abingdon).
2. *Minutes*/Methodist Episcopal Church 1773, 5. Pitts Theology Library, Emory University.
3. John J. Tigert, *A Constitutional History of American Episcopal Methodism*, 3rd ed., rev. and enlarged (Nashville: Publishing House of the Methodist Episcopal Church, South, 1908), 58–59.
4. On the former, see Richard P. Heitzenrater, *Wesley and the People Called Methodists* (Nashville: Abingdon Press, 1995). On the latter, see several essays in Sharon J. Hels, ed., *Methodism and Education: From Roots to Fulfillment.* (Nashville: General Board of Higher Education and Ministry, 2000).
5. Controversy continues over what constitute United Methodist standards. See Scott J. Jones, *United Methodist Doctrine: The Extreme Center* (Nashville: Abingdon, 2002); Ted A.

Campbell, *Methodist Doctrine: The Essentials* (Nashville: Abingdon, 1999); Thomas C. Oden, *Doctrinal Standards in the Wesleyan Tradition* (Grand Rapids: Zondervan, 1988); Thomas A. Langford, ed., *Doctrine and Theology in the United Methodist Church* (Nashville: Kingswood Books/Abingdon, 1991); Walter Klaiber and Manfred Marquardt, *Living Grace: An Outline of United Methodist Theology* (Nashville: Abingdon, 2001); W. Stephen Gunter et al., eds., *Wesley and the Quadrilateral: Renewing the Conversation* (Nashville: Abingdon, 1998); and Dennis M. Campbell, William B. Lawrence, and Russell E. Richey, eds., *Doctrines and Discipline: Methodist Theology and Practice* (Nashville: Abingdon, 1999).

[6] On this venture and Methodist education generally, see Francis I. Moats, *The Educational Policy of The Methodist Episcopal Church Prior to 1860* (PhD thesis, Graduate College of the State University of Iowa, 1926), 38–56; A. W. Cummings, *The Early Schools of Methodism* (New York: Phillips & Hunt, 1886); Slyvanus M. Duvall, *The Methodist Episcopal Church and Education up to 1869* (New York: Bureau of Publications, Teachers College, 1928); Robert H. Conn with Michael Nickerson, *A Handbook for Higher Education and Campus Ministry in the Annual Conference*, foreword by F. Thomas Trotter (Nashville: Division of Higher Education/GBHEM, 1989).

[7] *Minutes of the North Georgia Annual Conference of the Methodist Episcopal Church, South*, 1854, 1856.

[8] Hauk, *Legacy of Heart and Mind*; Samuel Luttrell Akers, *The First Hundred Years of Wesleyan College, 1836–1936* (Macon, GA: Wesleyan College, 1976). "Greensboro College . . . was chartered by the Methodist Church in 1838 as a women's college" (*Handbook of United Methodist-Related Schools, Colleges, Universities and Theological Schools* [Nashville: GBHEM/UMC, 1996], 89).

[9] Donald G. Tewksbury, *The Founding of American Colleges and Universities before the Civil War* (New York: Arno Press & The New York Times, 1969), 103–11. By contrast, Tewksbury estimates (102) that the Presbyterians founded forty-nine. Beth Bowser portrays this stage of Methodist education as characterized by disarray, inconsistent standards, poor planning, misuse of and inadequate resources, isolation, and unnecessary competition (Beth Adams Bowser, *Living the Vision: The University Senate of the Methodist Episcopal Church, the Methodist Church, and the United Methodist Church, 1892–1991* [Nashville: Board of Higher Education and Ministry of the United Methodist Church, 1992], vi–viii).

[10] On this point, see James E. Kirby, Russell E. Richey and Kenneth E. Rowe, *The Methodists* (Westport, CT: Greenwood Press, 1996), 24–42.

[11] Donald G. Mathews, *Slavery and Methodism* (Princeton, NJ: Princeton University Press, 1965), 201–4, 213–15.

[12] Bullock, *History*, 57–58.

[13] "Christian Education," in *The Works of Stephen Olin, D.D., LL.D., Late President of the Wesleyan University* (New York: Harper & Brothers, 1852), 2:240–53, citations from 249 and 251.

[14] Duvall, *Methodist Episcopal Church and Education*, 39–40. James Edward Scanlon, *Randolph-Macon College: A Southern History, 1825–1967* (Charlottesville: University Press of Virginia, 1983).

[15] Cited by David B. Potts, *Wesleyan University, 1831–1910: Collegiate Enterprise in New England* (New Haven, CT: Yale University Press, 1992), 76, 73.

[16] Glenn T. Miller, *Piety and Intellect: The Aims and Purposes of Ante-Bellum Theological Education* (Atlanta: Scholars Press, 1990), 127–39. Charles Coleman Sellers, *Dickinson College: A History* (Middletown, CT: Wesleyan University Press, 1973), 195–99; James Henry Morgan, *Dickinson College: The History of One Hundred Fifty Years, 1783–1933* (Carlisle, PA: Dickinson College, 1933); Scanlon, *Randolph-Macon College*; Potts, *Wesleyan University*.

Compare the estimate of John O. Gross: "While both Wesleyan and Randolph-Macon were under the control of the Methodist Church, neither required religious tenets for the admission of students" (John O. Gross, *Methodist Beginnings in Higher Education* [Nashville: Division of Educational Institutions, Board of Education, The Methodist Church, 1959], 39).

[17] See Quentin Charles Lansman, *Higher Education in the Evangelical United Brethren Church: 1800–1954* (Nashville: Division of Higher Education/UMC, 1972).

[18] See "The Report of the Special Committee on the Relation of Benevolent Institutions to the Church," *Journal of the General Conference*/MEC (1872): 294–99.

[19] Bowser, *Living the Vision*, i, 7–43. She affirms, the Senate "was the first body in the United States to establish and apply standards for educational institutions on a nationwide basis," a fact appreciated, she notes, by neither the regional accrediting associations nor other denominations. See also Myron F. Wicke, *A Brief History of the University Senate of the Methodist Church* (Nashville: Issued by Dept. of Public Relations and Finance, Division of Educational Institutions, Board of Education, The Methodist Church, 1956), and Gerald O. McCulloh, *Ministerial Education in the American Methodist Movement* (Nashville: United Methodist Board of Higher Education and Ministry, 1980). The prior sentence and the paragraph that follow appear in my "Connectionalism and College," and this section's claims echo those of that essay.

[20] *Journal of the General Conference*/MEC, 1872, 300–302. The adopting resolution described the Freedmen's Aid Society "as a regular constituted Society of the Methodist Episcopal Church" (300).

[21] *Journal of the General Conference*/MEC, 1892, "Report of the Freedmen's Aid and Southern Education Society," 692-704, and "On Freedmen's Aid and Southern Education Society," 479–81. The statements, including the heading, are from 696–97. See William Wilson, "The Methodist Episcopal Church in Her Relation to the Negro in the South," *Methodist Review* 76 (1894): 713–23.

[22] Atticus Haygood, *The New South: Gratitude, Amendment, Hope. A Thanksgiving Sermon* (Oxford, GA: Published by the author, 1880).

[23] See the treatment in Robert H. Conn with Michael Nickerson, *United Methodists and Their Colleges*, foreword by F. Thomas Trotter (Nashville: United Methodist Board of Higher Education and Ministry, 1989), esp. chap. 5.

[24] Professionalism interacted with various other long-term trends in American life—the nationalization of culture; the prominence of new media (radio and then television) and of advertising in setting cultural standards; the subsuming of economic life under huge national and international corporations; the growth of the military as employer and purchaser; gradual shifts in gender roles and race relations; secularization; the increasing diversity, individualism, and pluralism of society; the growing prominence of technology and science; and the general commodification of life.

[25] The theme that looms largest in treatments of religion and higher education is secularization and what are seen as attendant developments—the increasing role of the federal government, the dominance in higher education generally of the research university and its values, the consequent displacement of the liberal arts ideal as an integrative principle, and the effective marginalization of religion (in religious studies, student groups, chaplaincies, and the Christian college). See the trilogy of 1994 items: Merrimon Cuninggim, *Uneasy Partners: The College and the Church* (Nashville: Abingdon Press, 1994); George M. Marsden, *The Soul of the American University: From Protestant Establishment to Established Nonbelief* (New York: Oxford University Press, 1994); and Douglas Sloan, *Faith and Knowledge: Mainline Protestantism and American Higher Education* (Louisville, KY: Westminster John Knox Press, 1994). Also pertinent is Conrad Cherry, *Hurrying toward Zion: Universities, Divinity Schools, and American Protestantism* (Bloomington: Indiana University Press, 1995).

26. On the groups within denominations—caucus or struggle groups—especially and their effect on denominations, see Robert Wuthnow, *The Restructuring of American Religion* (Princeton, NJ: Princeton University Press, 1988), and *The Struggle for America's Soul* (Grand Rapids: Wm. B. Eerdmans, 1989). The fault lines created by the struggle, especially between armies that line up left and right, led Wuthnow in the 1980s to wonder about the future of denominations.
27. The substantive questions and the pursuit of the several components thereof—pursued so resolutely by Merrimon Cuninggim in *Uneasy Partners*—remain terribly important. See also George M. Marsden and Bradley J. Longfield, eds., *The Secularization of the Academy* (New York: Oxford University Press, 1992), especially the Marsden and Robert Lynn sections, 3–45 and 170–94.

Chapter 37: Uniting "The Pair So Long Disjoined"

1. Charles Wesley, along with his brother John one of the founders of Methodism and, indirectly therefore, a spiritual progenitor of the founders of Emory, is famous for saying, "Unite the pair so long disjoined—knowledge and vital piety." Perhaps the same can be said of Emory's approach to science and religion, an approach that has historical antecedents as old as the institution. One of the first faculty members of Emory College, and its fourth president, Alexander Means (1801–83), embodied something of this intention to join the two realms of knowledge, as he pursued all of his life his twin passions of religion and science. He was both an ordained Methodist clergyman and a medical doctor and later in life was elected to the American Academy for the Advancement of Science.
2. Arri Eisen and Gary Laderman, eds., *Science, Religion, and Society: An Encyclopedia of History, Culture, and Controversy* (Armonk, NY: M. E. Sharpe, 2007).

Chapter 38: The Case for Law and Religion

1. Kelly Monroe Kullberg, *Finding God at Harvard: Spiritual Journeys of Thinking Christians* (Downers Grove, IL: InterVarsity Press, 2007), quoted in Matt Sieger, "Answering to a Higher Authority: The Life and Legacy of Harold J. Berman," *Issues: A Messianic Jewish Perspective* 17, no. 9: 2.
2. Harold J. Berman, *The Interaction of Law and Religion* (Nashville: Abingdon Press, 1974), 11.
3. Portions of this chapter are excerpted from April L. Bogle and Ginger Pyron, *When Law and Religion Meet: The Point of Convergence* (Grand Rapids: Wm. B. Eerdmans Publishing Co., 2007), 4.
4. Ibid., 5.
5. Ibid.
6. Ibid.
7. Ibid.
8. Ibid., 7.
9. Ibid., 19.
10. Ibid.
11. Center for the Study of Law and Religion, "Interview with John Witte Jr.," Center for the Study of Law and Religion, Emory University, October 2007, http://cslr.law.emory.edu/fileadmin/media/Silver_Anniversary/Q___A_with_the_Experts/Q___A_with_the_Experts_-_John_Witte__Jr..pdf.
12. Bogle and Pyron, *When Law and Religion Meet*, 75.
13. Ibid., 79.
14. Ibid., 85.
15. Ibid.
16. Martin E. Marty, "What We Can Do for Children," *Emory Report*, November 28, 2005.

17. Bogle and Pyron, *When Law and Religion Meet*, 88.
18. Ibid., 59.
19. Mary J. Loftus, "Laney Opens Conference with Appeal to Universities: Address Larger Questions of Life and Purpose," Center for the Study of Law and Religion, Emory University, October 25, 2007, http://cslr.law.emory.edu/news/news-story/headline/laney-opens-conference-with-appeal-to-universities-address-larger-questions-of-life-and-purpose/.
20. Berman, "Law and Religion in the Age of the Holy Spirit," Center for the Study of Law and Religion, Emory University, October 25, 2007, http://cslr.law.emory.edu/people/in-memorium/harold-j-berman/interview-webcasts-and-lectures/.
21. "Q&A: Why Bring Law and Religion Together?" *Emory Report* Special Insert, September 10, 2007.
22. Ibid.
23. "Law and Religion: The Next 25 Years, What CSLR Senior Fellows Are Saying . . . ," *Emory Report* Special Insert, September 10, 2007.
24. Ibid.
25. April L. Bogle and Elaine Justice, "Templeton Grant Awarded to Emory's Center for Study of Law and Religion," Center for the Study of Law and Religion, Emory University, April 18, 2006, http://www.emory.edu/news/Releases/TempletonGrant1145380791.html.
26. Ibid.

Chapter 39: The Making of the Woodruff Health Sciences Center

1. In 1988, the Crawford Long Hospital nursing school also ended the granting of diplomas when it merged with the Nell Hodgson Woodruff School of Nursing.

Chapter 40: Humans and Other Primates

1. For a history of the Yerkes Primate Research Center from its founding through its move to Emory, see Donald A. Dewsbury, *Monkey Farm: A History of the Yerkes Laboratories of Primate Biology, Orange Park, Florida, 1930–1965* (Lewisburg, PA: Bucknell University Press, 2006).

Chapter 43: Partnering for Health Care in Tblisi, Georgia

1. The authors express their gratitude and appreciation to the help they received in preparing this chapter from many colleagues in the partnership.
2. The origin of the name "Georgia" comes from the Greeks, who believed the Georgians were the oldest indigenous land farmers in the ancient world. The Greeks' word for earth or land was *gheos*; hence the "people of their land" or "land workers" were Georgians. This fits with the legend that Kartlos, one of Noah's grandsons, was the only one of Noah's family who never traveled after the flood, but settled near the Ark's landing spot in the Caucasus. Contrary to popular belief, the name does not come from St. George, a saint from the third century of the common era, who was from Cappadocia but is believed to have had Georgian ethnic roots—hence his name. The native Georgian word for the country is *Sakartvelo*: the root *kartvel-i* comes from Kartlos. Georgians call themselves *kartvelebi*.
3. In the 1980s Kobaladze translated and published the Declaration of Independence so his fellow citizens could begin to understand what democracy was about. He was intelligent and wise, and always had a twinkle in his eyes. He developed severe headaches in October 2001 and was brought to Emory Hospital, where a diagnosis of a malignant brain tumor was made. He died at Emory on Christmas Eve, 2001. His son Sergo had been brought to Emory by Professor Tom Burns of the History Department as a college student a year earlier. Sergo had a brilliant but short two-year career at Emory, dying, in Tbilisi, of a motor vehicle accident in the summer after his father's death.

[4] W. J. Casarella, " Radiology in Tbilisi: The Legacy of 70 Years of Soviet Government," *American Journal of Radiology* (1993): 23–25.

[5] Carol Burns, Zviad Kirtava, and H. Kenneth Walker, "The Role of Information Access in Sustainable Healthcare in Georgia: The Atlanta-Tbilisi Health Partnership Model," *Information Services and Use* 25 (2005): 125–35.

[6] H. Kenneth Walker, "Georgia: Saturday Dec. 14, 1996–Thursday Jan. 2, 1997," http://medicine.emory.edu/atl_tbl/PDF/trip_reports/Dec_96-jan_97.pdf.

[7] USAID, "Outstanding Citizen Achievement Citation: USAID Honors Atlanta, Tbilisi Partners with Outstanding Citizen Citation," June 5, 2006, http://www.usaid.gov/locations/europe_eurasia/press/pub_rec/oca_ws.html.

[8] Business education in Georgia was spearheaded by Bijan Fazlollahi of Georgia State University's J. Mack Robinson College of Business. He is director of the Center for Business Development in Transitional Economies. In 1997 he approached the partners about the feasibility of starting a Western business school in Georgia. The need was obvious and desperate: there was no knowledge at all of a market economy in Georgia, economic development was at a standstill, and poverty and discouragement were pervasive. This overture led to establishment of one of the highest-ranked business schools in the former Soviet Union. In 1998, after obtaining grants from the Department of State Bureau of Educational and Cultural Affairs and USAID through the Eurasia Foundation, Fazlollahi led the Consortium of Georgian Universities—a partnership between Robinson College of Business, Tbilisi State University, and Georgian Technical University—to establish the Caucasus School of Business (CSB) in Tbilisi. The school offers BBA and MBA degrees patterned after Robinson's own programs.

The role of the woman in Georgian business was not prominent during Soviet Union times, in contrast to her role in medicine. Seeing the need for a greatly expanded role of women in business, Georgia State University in partnership with CSB developed and managed a Businesswoman's Leadership Training Program in 2002. Georgian women were taught how to manage small businesses as well as serve as leaders and managers in larger ones. The program contributed to the development of the business environment in Georgia through development of small and medium enterprise empowerment of women and building a more gender-sensitive society.

Dr. Fazlollahi was made an honorary citizen of Georgia in 2008 by President Saakashvili in recognition of his efforts.

INDEX

Page numbers in *italics* indicate photographs.

Abraham, Julie. 229, 231
Abrams, Howard. 221
Academic Affairs, Vice President for. 94, 105, 116
academic freedom, historical aspects of. 37
academic health center. 138, 143
Ad Hoc Productions. 155
Administration Building. 74, *93*, 210, 294
administrator of the health program. 453
affirmative action plan, university-wide, and gender discrimination. 225, 226, 253
African American and African Studies Program. 180, 181, 183. *See also* African American Studies Department; African Studies, Institute of
African American literature. 151, 232
African American Reading Room. 180, 182
African American students. 101, 151, 160, 173, 174, 175, 179, 180
African American studies. 134, 135, 265–267
   defined. 174
   history. 174, 175
   PhD degree in. 151
African American Studies Department. 151, 173–185
   community relations. 176, 179, 180, 184
   courses. 176–183
   department, status as. 175, 177, 178, 181, 184
   enrollment. 178, 179, 181
   faculty. 177, 179–184
   funding. 177–179
   and the Graduate Institute of Liberal Arts. 151, 178, 181
   as interdisciplinary field. 178
   internships. 176
   and libraries. 177, 179, 181, 182, 184
   relations with other departments. 180
   sponsored programs of. 179–183
   study abroad. 176, 177
African American Studies Program. *See under* African American Studies Department
African Americans, education of. 299
African Studies, Institute of. 124
Agnes Scott College. 268, 270, 272, 303–305
Agnor, William. 218
Ahmed, Rafi. 419
AIDS. *See under* HIV/AIDS
Air Force ROTC. *See under* Reserve Officers Training Corps.
Akopov, Valery. 439
Aldridge, Delores. 151, 175–177, *177*, 182–184, 253
   first black female faculty member of Emory College.103, 176
   full professor. 183
Alexander, Frank S. 219–221, 379–384, 387–391
Alexander, Wayne. 425, 426, 446
Alkaladze, Tea. 440
Alonso, Carlos. 126, 153
Altizer, Thomas J.J. 102
alumni. 11, 24, 40, 48, 50, 51, 53, 54, 79, 85, 101, 108, 110, 149, 155, 160.
Alumni House (Miller-Ward). 160
Alumni Memorial University Center (AMUC). 10

Coca-Cola Commons. 10
Alvord, Lori. 370, 371, 373
Alzheimer's disease. 406, 417–420
American Academy of Religion. 363, 367
American Association for the Accreditation of Laboratory Animal Care. 416
American Association of Anatomists. 301
American Association of Laboratory Animal Care. 411
American Association of University Professors, Emory Chapter. 253, 254
    Committee W (on women's issues). 253
American Bar Association. 217
    Administrative Law Section. 271
American Cancer Society. 402, 407, 434
American College of Physicians. 298
American Council of Learned Societies. 304
American Council on Education.
    report on Emory (Cartter Report, 1966). 102, 104
American Dental Association. 397
    and segregation. 63–65
American Heart Association. 274, 298, 300, 422, 424, 426
American Historical Association. 288, 334
American Hospital Association.
    and segregation. 64, 65
American Library Association. 213, 214
American literature. 143, 151, 301, 316, 320, 325, 328
American Medical Association. 396, 449
    and segregation. 64, 65
    and scientific membership. 64
American studies. 143, 144, 148
An-Na'im, Abdullahi Ahmed. 384, 385, 390
Anatomy Building. 10, 396
Anatomy Department. 114, 301
Anderson, Maxwell L. 154
Andrew, James Osgood. 355, 356, 361
    as slave owner. 15, 16, 352, 356
Andrews, Dwight. 133
angioplasty. 426
animal rights protests. 420
Annex B. 154, 204, 246–248
Annex C. 205
Anthropology Department. See under Sociology and Anthropology Department
Apkarian, Juliette Stapanian. 152, 253
applied sciences. 138
Arant, Hershel W. 216
Archie, William. 52, 54

area studies. 133, 153
Arkwright, Preston. 449
Arnall, Ellis. 42
Arnold, Ben. 154
Arp, Bill. 25
Arrowsmith, William. 152, 340
Art History Department. 177, 182, 245–249
    art collection. 246, 247
    masters program. 247
Arthritis Foundation. 407
Arthur, Thomas. 220, 221
arts and sciences. 98, 108, 110, 118, 124, 125, 128, 131, 135, 138, 140, 142
    faculty growth. 108
Arts and Sciences, Vice President for. 123, 130, 131, 135, 137, 140
Arts and Sciences Council. 131
arts center. 80, 134, 135, 154, 155, 159, 205. See also Schwartz (Donna and Marvin) Center for Performing Arts
Asbury, Francis. 352, 354–356
assistant to the president. 448
Association of American Law Schools. 45, 217, 295, 380
Association of American Universities. 93, 94, 128
Association of Anatomy Chairmen. 301
Association of College and Research Libraries. 214
Association of Southeastern Research Libraries (ASERL). 213
athletics. 257–263
    educational characteristics. 259, 262
    facilities. 258, 260–263. See also Woodruff (George W.) Physical Education Center
    intercollegiate sports. 257, 259, 260–262
    intramural sports. 259–262
    staff. 261, 262
    student participation. 260–262
    and women. 262
Atlanta, Ga.
    economic conditions. 96
    growth. 96, 364
    public schools. See under Atlanta public schools
    race relations. 47, 50, 51, 58, 59
Atlanta College of Physicians and Surgeons. 274
Atlanta Constitution and the "Sledd Affair." 29–34
Atlanta Inquirer. 60, 61, 63, 66
Atlanta Journal and the "Sledd Affair." 30, 33
Atlanta Legal Aid Society. 218, 270
Atlanta Medical College. 58, 274, 396, 397, 401, 422

becomes Emory University School of Medicine. 58
Atlanta public schools. 164, 183
   desegregation of. 48, 51–54
   and Emory faculty. 48. 51, 52
   Georgia law and closing of. 51
Atlanta Regional Consortium for Higher Education (ARCHE). 483–48
Atlanta-Southern Dental College. 397, 453
Atlanta Theological Association.
   origins of. 165
Atlanta University. 151, 266–268
   joint programs with Emory University. 267
Atlanta University Center. 228, 229, 267, 268
Atran, Scott. 370
Atticus Haygood Professor. 265, 268
Atwood, Sanford Soverhill 76, 77, 84, 101–105, 109, 170, 175, 210, 225, 247, 292, 335
   achievements of. 101, 109
   Five-Year Planning Report. 104

Bachevalier, Jocelyne. 419
Bachman, Jean George. 422
Baer, Kenneth. 176
Bijaj, Krishan. 154
Baker, Woolford B. 73, 74, 81, 114
Bancroft (Frederic) Prize. 304, 306
Bangs, Nathan. 354
Barksdale, Marcellus. 183
Barlett, Peggy. 81, 224, 226, 227, 253
Bartleby the Scrivener affair. 199
Barton Child Law and Policy Clinic. 388
Bassett, John Spencer. 36, 37
Beard, Charles. 284
Beardslee, William A. 297, 334
Beaty, Jerome. 146
Beeson, Paul. 422, 423
Bell, Roy. 58–60, 63, 64, 66–68
   suit against Grady Hospital. 64, 65
Bellamy, Verdelle. 397
Ben-Dor, Immanuel. 165
Bennington, Geoffrey. 134
Benston, Alice. 126, 154
Berman, Harold Joseph. 219, 220, *343*, 343–348, 379–383, 390
   research on Russian legal systems. 344, 345
   views on religion and law. 345–347
   views on Western legal traditions. 346–348
Bernstein, Matthew. 202
Bertrand, J. Thomas. 86, 122, 158, 437

Billingslea, Mary E. 180
Biochemistry Department. 114, 297
biography (genre). 305, 307, 309
Biology Department. 96, 99, 106, 114, 129, 138, 150, 294
Biomedical Engineering Department (Wallace H. Coulter). 406
biomedical research. 98, 104, 106, 109
biophysics. 138
Biostatistics Department, women faculty. 224
Bishop, Linton. 424
Bishops Hall. 246, 247
Black, Charles. 59, 60, 63
black colleges (in Atlanta). 20, 44, 46, 47, 52, 54, 60, 151, 229
Black Student Alliance. 174, 178, 179
Black Studies Ad Hoc Review Committee. 177
"The Black Rose" (theater). *187*, 189, 192
Blaetz, Robin. 203, 206
Blankenship, Mark. 190
Board of Trustees (Emory College, 1836–1915). 15, 29, 35
   and Andrew W. Sledd. 31–35
Board of Trustees (Emory University). 41, 45, 46, 48, 50–52 71, 96, 102, 110, 119, 128, 151, 155, 198, 206, 207, 210, 211, 225, 260, 293, 359, 398, 450
   Executive Committee. 46, 54, 452, 453
   and integration. 50–55
   Health Services Board. 400, 450, 451, 454
   membership characteristics. 41, 48
   Real Estate, Buildings, and Grounds Committee. 155
   special committee on admitting blacks. 53, 54
   Woodruff Board. 401
Boers, Hendrick. 167
Bohanan, Donna. 335
Boozer, Jack. *161*, 334
Bourne, Geoffrey. 412
Bowden, Gloria. 177
Bowden, Henry Lumpkin. 44, 47, 51–55, 101, 210, 211, 218, 294
   as chair of Board of Trustees. 51, 294
   views on segregation. 55
   and tax exemption suit. 54
Boys High School (Atlanta). 326
Branch, Harlee. 270
Branch, William. 373
Brannon, Emmet. 422
Brewer, Earl D. C. 164, 297, 298

Bright, David. 126, 128, 130–137, *131*, 147, 148, 153, 154, 204–206, 229, 230
Brinsfield, Dorothy. 425
Brogan, Donna. 224
Brotherhood Week. 46, 51
Brown, Elizabeth Barkley. 182
Brown, Frank Clyde. 260
Brown, Peter. 372
Brown v. Board of Education. 46, 95
    and Georgia politics. 46, 47
    reaction to by Emory administration. 47
Browne, Irene. 229, 231
Browning, Don S. 386, 387
Brownley, Martine ("Tina"). 224, 229–231, 253
Broyde, Michael J. 384, 386, 387, 390
Buchter, Susie. 438, 442
Buddhists. 369
Burbank, William. 114
Burkett, Randall. 183
Burns, Carol. 253, 440
Burns, Thomas S. 292, 336
Busch Gardens. 416
Butler, Patricia Collins. 269, 269–272
Byrd, Rudolph. 133, 183

"Campaign for Emory." 105
Campus Development Committee (University Senate). 74–77, 79
Campus Life, dean of. 157–162
Campus Life, dean of (Oxford College). 151
Campus Life, Division of. 84, 87 140, 149, 153, 158–162
    and food service. 161
    priorities. 159, 160
    relations with College. 135, 149, 153
Campus Life, Vice President for. 135, 157
Campus Master Plan. of 1970. 75, 76
cancer treatment facilities. 395, 399, 403–407, 448
Candler, Asa Griggs. 26, 31, 34–36, 38, 45, 96, 97, 110, 293, 396, 452
    endowment for Medical School. 396
Candler, Charles Howard, Sr. (Howard). 45, 46, 48–51, 97, 210, 261, 293, 294, 452
    and "The Church and World Order" Conference (1953). 45, 46
    and the election of president S. Walter Martin. 49, 50
    views on race. 45, 46
Candler, Flora Glenn (Mrs. Charles Howard.). 294
Candler, John S. 26, 31, 270

Candler, Walter, T. 71, 72, 263
Candler, Warren Akin. *23*, 24–26, 45, 46, 96, 216, 283, 352, 355, 467n3(Ch.2)
    and the "Bassett Affair." 37
    and James E. Dickey. 34–36
    and the "Sledd Affair." 29, 31, 33–36
    view of women in politics. 25
Candler Lake. 77
Candler (Asa Griggs) Library. 8, 9, 9, 11, 180, 184, 200, 202, 203, 210, 211, 246, 294
    reading room. 8, 210
Candler Professorships. *See under* Charles Howard Candler Professorships
Candler School of Theology. *See Under* School of Theology
Cannon, William Ragsdale. 49, 164, 166–169
    and academic excellence. 166, 168
Cannon Chapel. 248, *363*
Capers, William. 355
cardiac surgery. 423–427
cardiac transplants. 426
Cardiology, Division of. 421–427
    courses in. 424
    training of cardiology fellows. 424, 425, 427
cardiology, pediatric. 423, 425
cardiovascular disease. 274, 275, 419, 420
cardiovascular research. 420, 423, 424, 426
CARE International. 402, 407
Carlin, Sherry. 440
Carlos Hall. *223*. *See Also* Law School Building
Carlos (Michael C.) Museum. 7, 9, 75, 247, 249, 368
    John Howett Works on Paper Gallery. 247
Carlyle Fraser Heart Center. 426, 427
Carmichael, Jimmy. 451
Carnegie Foundation. 47, 385, 396, 397
Carney, William J. 221
Carter, Dan. 292
Carter, Eloise. 77, 81
Carter, Jimmy. 107, 111, 383, 387, 388, 402, 437
Carter, Rosalynn. 229, 232
Carter Center. 344, 372, 381, 384, 402, 407, 436, 437
Cary, Freeman. 424
Casarella, William. 426, 438
Caucasus School of Business. 444
Cauley, Troy J. 284
cell biology. 301
Center for Comprehensive Informatics. 407
Center for Ethics. 372

Center for Faculty Development and Excellence. 154.
Center for Federalism and Intersystemic Governance. 221
Center for Humanistic Inquiry (Bill and Carol Fox). 224, 231
Center for International and Comparative Law. 221
Center for International Nursing, Lillian Carter. 407
Center for International Programs Abroad (CIPA). 133, 153, 368
Center for Mind, Brain, and Culture. 371
Center for Teaching and Curriculum. 138, 153, 154
Center for the Study of Health, Culture, and Society. 372
Center for the Study of Law and Religion. 220, 344, 361, 367, 375, 379–391. *See also* Law and Religion Program
  and child advocacy. 388
  and Christian legal studies. 389
  establishment of. 385
  research programs on children. 386–388
  research programs on housing and the homeless. 388
  research programs on marriage and the family. 384–387, 389–391
  research programs on the pursuit of happiness. 391
Center for the Study of Myth and Ritual in American life (Alfred P. Sloan) (MARIAL). 5, 195
Center for Transactional Law and Practice. 221
Center for Women at Emory. *83*, 83–89, 234
  facilities. 88
  opens. 88
  programs. 88, 89
  strategic plans. 89
Centers for Disease Control, Atlanta GA. *See under* U.S. Centers for Disease Control and Prevention
Ceremonies Committee. 313
Chace, William Murdough. 79–81, 119, 120, 128, 137, 139, 154, 342, 403, 446
Chan, Anthony. 419
Chancellor of the university. 38, 96, 97, 119, 120, 407
Chanturidze, Tata. 440
Chapel and Religious Life, Office of the Dean of. 368

Charles Howard Candler Professorships. 154, 227, 233, 293, 301, 303, 304, 315, 316, 322, 325, 328, 430
chaplains (college and university). 359–361
Chemistry Department. 77, 97, 104, 106, 107, 138, 139, 150, 294, 299
Chief Environmental Officer. 81
Chief Marshal (of the University). 313
child health and Georgia (country). 442–444, 446
Children's Healthcare of Atlanta at Egleston. 397, 401, 404, 405, 407, 442. *See also* Egleston (Henrietta) Children's Hospital
Chirinko, Robert S. 139
CHOICES (student group). 84, 86
Choices and Responsibility (Frye). 89, 120, 121
Chopp, Rebecca. 120
Christian Advocate. 354, 355
Christianity and democracy. 379, 383
Clairmont Campus. 79, 80, 159, 161
Clark Atlanta University. 175
Clark College. 44, 175
classical studies. 124, 278–280
Classics Department. 130
Clayton, Xernona. 67, 68
Clement, Anthony Calhoun. 115
Clements, James L., Jr. 432, 433
Clements, Steve. 425, 426
clinical practice and Georgia (country). 442
Cloud, Morgan. 221
Coalition Against Rape at Emory (CARE). 84, 88
Cobbs, Woofin, Jr. 424
Coca-Cola Company. 96, 97, 395, 396, 448, 451, 452
Coke, Thomas. 354, 355
Cole, Johnnetta. 184, 229
colleges and universities. 40, 102, 109, 110. *See also* research universities
  desegregation of. 45, 54
  federal funding of. 40, 53, 55, 95, 97, 99, 102, 104
  "golden age." 95, 99
  southern states. 40, 94–96, 103, 111
Collins, Sabrina. 84, 160
Colquitt, Alfred H. 285
Commission on Teaching. 298
Committee of One Hundred. 47, 98
Committee on Implementation (doctors for civil rights). 67, 68

Committee on the Appeal for Human Rights. 60
Committee on the Environment (University Senate). 77, 79
Communist Party (USA). 284
comparative literature. 134, 255
Comparative Literature Department. 134
"Comprehensive Master Plan for a Quality Natural Environment" (Platt). 76
computer technology. 124
computing, academic. 118, 119
Congress of Racial Equality (CORE). 51
Contemplative Studies, Emory Collaboration on. 371
Cook, David A. 154, 197–207, *200*
Cooper, Frederick W. 422
corporate law. 295
Counseling Center. 161
Council of Colleges of Arts and Sciences. 134
Council of Southern Universities. 96
Council on Legal Education Opportunity (CLEO). 215, 218
Council on Religion and Law (CORAL). 380
county unit system. 42, 46
Courtright, Paul B. 364, 365
Covington, Ga. 20, 30, 31
Cox, Harvey Warren. 73, 97, 119
Crawford Long Hospital. 98, 398, 403, 404, 422, 424, 426, 427, 442, 449
   renamed Emory University Hospital Midtown. 404
Crawley, Sylvia. 424
Crelly, William. 246
Crim, Alonzo. 183
Crippled Children's Service of Georgia. 424
Croaker, John. 203
Crooks, Joe. 119
Crown, Ali P. 85, 87, 89
Culp, Maurice. 218
Curran, James W. 138
Curriculum Committee (Emory College).
   and film studies. 203
   Report on Black Studies. 175
   subcommittee on Afro-American Studies. 175
Cutler, Anthony. 246
Cuttino, George Peddy. 147, 298, *311*, 311–314
   and students. 313, 314
   and women's studies. 227, 228
Cuttino (George P.) medal for distinction in mentoring. 130, 143

Daffin, Julianne. 253
Dalai Lama. 366, 366–368, 370, 373, 374, 376, 377, 391
   Presidential Distinguished Professor. 376
   on science and religion. 376
Dance Program. 142, 155
Darsey, Steven. 374
Davis, Albert M. 67
Davis, Edward Campbell. 398
Davis, Ted. 232
Davis-Fischer Sanatorium. 398
de Man, Ariel. 190
de Waal, Frans. 374, 375, 415
dean of administration. 448, 451
DeAndrade, Robin. 442
DeConcini, Barbara. 367
Deinhard, Charlotte. 253
del Ray, Pat. 232
Delozier, David. 440
Demetrashvili, Marina. 439
Dennis, Michael. 155
Dental School. *See under* School of Dentistry
Dental School Building. 154
Desai, Snehal. 191
Detweiler, Robert. 158
Devito, Michael. 218
Dezhbaksh, Hashem. 139
Dickey, James Edward. *23*, 24, 29, 34, 355
   and Andrew W. Sledd. 31–33
   and Warren A. Candler. 34–36
   view of women in politics. 468–14
Dickinson College. 356
DiClemente, Ralph. 373
Dictionary of American Biography. 289
Dillingham, Elizabeth (Marion Elizabeth Joiner). 323, 326, 330
Dillingham, William B. 323, *325*, 325–330
   research on Herman Melville. 328
   teaching style. 328, 329
Director of Libraries. 209, 210
disabled. *See under* people with disabilities.
Distinguished Faculty Lecture. 299
Division of Basic Health Sciences. 449
Dobbs (Samuel Candler) Professor. 5, 139
Dobbs (Howard R., Jr.) University Center. 10, 160
doctoral programs. *See under* PhD programs
Doernberg, Richard. 219
Dooley (Emory mascot). 145, *157*
Dorney, Edward R. 423
Dougherty, Richard. 118

Douglas, John. 426
Dowell, Peter W. 138, 143–151, *144*, 175, 180
Dowman, Charles E. 24, 29
Drepung Loseling Monastery (Atlanta). 367
Drepung Loseling Monastery (India). 370
Druid Hills. 7, 8, 38, 72, 96
Drummond, Margaret. 225, 253
Duck Bowl. 262
Dudley, Charles. *39*
Duffus, Dwight. 154
Duke University. 24, 36, 41, 95, 96, 98, 107, 108, 161, 164, 358
Dunaway, John A. 44
Durham Chapel. *163*, 358

ecological concerns. 75, 81
Economics, Department of. 139, 296
Educational Studies, Division of. 139.
Edwards, Betty. 253
Edwards, Catherine. 425
Edwards, Kay. 253
Egan, Robert L. *434*, 434
Egleston (Henrietta) Hospital for Children. 399, 401, 404, 422, 425, 426, 432, 451. *See also* Children's Healthcare of Atlanta at Egleston
Eisen, Arri. 369, 372, 375
Eisenman, Peter. 134, 154, 155
Elkin, Daniel C. 422, 451
Ellison, J.B. 67
Ellmann, Richard. 337, 337–342
Ellmann (Richard) Lectures in Modern Literature. 337, 341, 342
Elmer, Richard. 431
emergency medical services in Georgia (country). 443, 444
emergent properties (concept). 10
Emerson (Cherry Logan) Hall. 154
Emory, John. 14, 356
    as anti-abolitionist. 14
    as slave owner. 14, 467n1(Ch.2)
Emory Alumnus. 51, 52
    article on plan to close public schools. 48, 49
    article on integration. 48
Emory Center for Critical Care. 407
Emory Children's Center. 403–405
Emory Christian Association. *See under* Freshman Emory Christian Association
Emory Clinic. 98, 107, 298, 395, 399–401, 403, 404, 422, 423, 425–427, 449–451. *See also* Private Diagnostic Clinic

Emory College (1836–1915). 96, 274, 281, 282, 288, 355, 452
    and African-Americans. 13–21
    Board of Trustees. *See under* Board of Trustees (Emory College, 1836–1915)
    curriculum. 40
    financial affairs. 36
    law department. 24, 26
    as Methodist institution. 355–357
    move to Atlanta. 7, 8, 11, 58, 97, 257
    president of. 355, 356, 359. *See also* Candler, Warren Akin; Dickey, James Edward; Dowman, Charles E.; Few, Ignatius A.; Haygood, Atticus G.; Hopkins, Isaac S.; Longstreet, Augustus Baldwin; Means, Alexander; Smith, Luther M.; Smith, Osborn L.; Thomas, John D.
    and slaves. 14–18
    and the "Sledd Affair." 23–38
Emory College (1915–present). 114, 278, 364, 367, 372, 385
    administration. 127, 129, 146–148
    budget. 124, 127, 132, 140, 146, 153
    and computer technology. 124
    curriculum. 129, 131, 133, 138, 139, 142, 145, 147
    Curriculum Committee. *See under* Curriculum Committee (Emory College)
    dean of. 116 122–148, 297. *See also*, Lester, Charles; Palms, John; Minter, David; Jones, George; Bright, David; Sanderson, Steve; White, Goodrich C.
    dean of juniors and seniors. 146
    dean of sophomores and freshmen. 146
    deans, associate/assistant. 122, 128, 131–133, 138, 143, 145, 146, 148–151, 153
    enrollment. 103, 107
    executive committee. 132
    faculty. *See under* faculty (Emory College)
    Freshman Seminar Program. 124, 138
    fund raising. 125, 135, 136
    growth. 125, 131, 364
    Honors Committee. 313
    lecturers. 141
    in the 1960s. 146–148
    priorities. 123, 124, 127, 131–133, 147, 148, 152
    relations with the graduate school. 123, 124, 127, 128, 140, 148
    relations with the University. 138
    scholarships. 107, 123, 152

students. *See under* undergraduate students
tuition. 101, 107, 117, 124
women enrolled. 98
and Yerkes National Primate Center. 414
Emory Court Annex. 334
Emory Creed. 275
Emory/Georgia Tech Predictive Health Institute. 406
Emory Healthcare. 403–407. *See also* Emory University System of Health Care
Emory Heart Center. 427
Emory Hope Clinic. 406
Emory Hospital. *See under* Emory University Hospital
Emory Junior College at Valdosta. 431
Emory Medal. 272
Emory Orthopaedics & Spine Center. 405
Emory Orthopaedics & Spine Hospital. 405
Emory Scholars Committee. 145
Emory Scholars Program. 147
"Emory 2000" speech. 125
Emory Unit. 397
Emory University.
   and academic freedom. 102, 110
   admission of blacks. 44, 45, 54, 101
   black students, first admitted. 54
   Board of Trustees. *See under* Board of Trustees (Emory University)
   budget. 99, 101–103, 105, 109, 110, 117, 140, 448
   capital campaigns. 72, 102, 105, 108, 129, 448. *See also* Emory University, fundraising
   character of. 5, 7, 85, 142
   compared to other institutions. 94, 99, 103, 108
   dean of students. 282
   diversity. 84, 85, 98, 101, 123, 130, 137, 160
   and education. 211
   endowment. 98, 101, 105, 108–110
   environmental issues. 71–81
   faculty. *See under* faculty (Emory University)
   finances. 41, 47, 48, 50, 101, 103–105, 107, 109, 110
   founding of. 96, 358
   funding, external. 45, 47, 50, 97, 98, 102–105, 109, 110, 125, 167
   fundraising. 45, 47, 50, 84, 101, 161. *See also* Emory University, capital campaigns
   Georgia (country), relations with. 435–446
   graduate education. 47, 97–99, 103–106, 108, 109
   growth of. 94, 97, 98, 102, 109–111, 258

   as "hotbed of iniquity." 284
   integration of. 39–55, 101, 103, 174
   joint programs with Atlanta University. 267
   and the Methodist Church. 40, 41, 47–49, 99, 109, 351–362
   "old" Emory/"new" Emory. 7, 8, 11
   origins of. 40, 96, 97
   as plural. 12
   president of. 136, 359. *See also* Atwood, Sanford S.; Chace, William M.; Laney, James T.; Martin, Sidney Walter; Wagner, James W.; White, Goodrich C.
   priorities. 54, 101, 104–106, 108
   progress. 7, 8, 10
   race relations. 42–55
   regional characteristics. 40, 47, 94, 104, 146, 147
   as research university. 97–99, 107–109, 111, 353, 358, 361
   Senate. *See under* University Senate
   since 1945. 40, 93–111
   sponsored research. 87, 99, 109
   strategic initiatives. 371
   student aid. 104, 107–110, 152. *See also* graduate students, financial aid; undergraduate students, financial aid
   student responsibilities. 6, 7
   students. *See under* graduate students; undergraduate students
   and tax exempt status. *See under* tax-exempt status and integration
   tradition. 7, 10
   University Budget Committee. 117
Emory University Award of Distinction. 316
Emory University Hospital. 298, 396, 397, 399, 403–405, 422–427, 430–432, 449, 450. *See also* Wesley Memorial Hospital
   national clinical research center. 405
   segregation of. 59, 64, 67, 68
Emory University Hospital Midtown. 404, 422, 427
Emory University Legal Service. 299
Emory University Museum (Bishop's Hall). 246, 247. *See also* Carlos (Michael C.) Museum
Emory University System of Health Care. 401. *See also* Emory Healthcare
Emory Vaccine Center. 406
Emory Visiting Committee for the Arts and Sciences. 106, 107
Emory Wheel. 335
   and admission of black students. 44, 45, 49

and *Brown v. Board of Education*. 47
Emory Williams Distinguished Teaching Award. 249, 292, 300, 302, 316
Emory Women's Caucus. 223–227, 252, 253
Emory Women's Center. *See under* Center for Women at Emory
Emory-at-Oxford. *See under* Oxford College of Emory University
Emory-Georgia Partnership. 435–446
    child health. 442, 446
    clinical practice. 442
    emergency medical services. 443, 444
    health policy reform 439, 440
    and HIV/AIDS. 445
    information access. 440, 441
    medical education. 439
    nursing education. 442, 443
    tuberculosis. 445
    women's health. 442, 446
Emory-Tibet Partnership. 367, 368, 373, 376
Emory-Tibet Science Initiative. 370, 374
endowment. *See under* Emory University, endowment
English, Department of. 99, 102, 104, 106, 107, 143, 144, 147, 150, 254, 255, 316, 317, 320, 322, 325, 327, 329
    and Film Studies. 198–201
    growth. 150
    teaching methods of. 317
    undergraduate major in literature. 255
    women faculty. 224
environmental concerns. 71–81
environmental studies. 134, 139
Epstein, David G. 220
Esiashvili, Natia. 439
Evans, Arthur. 237–243
Evans, Mercer G. 284
Evans (Lettie Pate) Foundation. 403
Evenden, Michael. 154
External Affairs, Senior Vice President for. 157

Fabrick, Jen. 81
faculty (Emory College). 123, 124, 126, 129, 131–133, 135, 137, 140, 148, 149, 490–3
    diversity of. 130, 160, 182. *See also* women faculty
    feminist movement. 253
    grants. 490–4
    growth. 103, 107, 124, 131, 134, 483–61

promotion and tenure. 107, 134, 135, 141, 150, 490–4
    regional characteristics. 147
    salaries. 107, 125, 126, 141, 152
    teaching load. 106, 131, 132
    teaching *versus* research. 125, 131, 132, 138
faculty (Emory University). 99, 101, 103, 107, 483n61. *See also* women faculty
    integration of. 103
    regional characteristics. 47, 101
    salaries and benefits. 90, 98, 99, 101, 103
    support of integration. 52–54
    teaching load. 99
    views on segregation. 47
faculty job security, historical aspects of in the U.S. 37
Faculty Council. 201, 204, 206, 252, 490–4
FAME. *See under* Freshman Advising and Mentoring at Emory
family law. 299
family narratives. 5, 6
Family Narratives Project. 5
Faulkner, William. 290, 318, 321
Felner, Joel. 424
Felton, Rebecca Latimer. 24, 25, 27, 29–31, 33, 34, 468–11
    and Warren A. Candler. 24, 29
Feminist Legal Theory Project. 220
Fenton, John. 175
Ferris, Eugene. 423
Few, Ignatius Alphonso. 24
    "scarlet letter." 356
field house. 261
Film Studies, Department of. 197–207
    cost of renting/acquiring films. 199, 200
    and the Department of English. 198–201
    and the Department of Theater (and Film Studies). 201, 202, 204
    and film theory. 200, 202, 206
    and the Graduate Institute of Liberal Arts. 202–205
    major in. 203–205, 207
    masters degree in. 203–205
    as program versus department. 198, 204–207
    and 35mm projectors. 201
Finance and Administration, Executive Vice President for. 140
fine arts. 132
Fineman, Martha Alberton. 220, 387.
Fischer, Luther, C. 398

Fitts, Ralph L. 261
Fivush, Robyn. 5, 6
   director of Women's Studies Program. 231, 232
Flannery, James. 123, 126, 188, 201, 204
Fletcher, Gerald. 425
Flexner, Abraham. 396
Flexner report. 396
Flueckiger, Joyce Burkhalter. 365
Foege, William. 117, 374, 387
Ford Foundation. 98, 102, 183, 370, 384, 385
forested land report. 77, 78
forests. 72, 73, 77–81
Fort, Randy. 48, 49, 51
Foster, Frances Smith. 133
   director of women's studies. 232
Foster, Roger. 438
Fowler, Nobel. 423
Fox, Carol. 158
Fox, John T. 404
Fox, William H. ("Bill"). 85, 149, 153, 158–162, *161*
Fox-Genovese, Elizabeth. 123, 223, 224, 228, 229
   director of women's studies. 228–230
   lawsuit against. 230
   resignation from Institute for Women's Studies. 229, 230
Franch, Robert. 424, 425
fraternities. 144, 145, 149. *See also* Kappa Alpha
   and alcohol. 144, 145
   skits. 145
   student participation. 144
Freedman, Ralph. 251
Freedmen's Aid and Southern Education Society. 20, 357, 358
   colleges and universities supported by. 357
Freeman, Carla. 229, 231, 233
Freer, Richard. 221
Freshman Advising and Mentoring at Emory (FAME). 124
Freshman Advisory Committee. 313
Freshman Emory Christian Association. 44
freshman orientation. 149
freshman seminars. 138, 142
Fritz, Michael E. 298
Frye, Billy. 84, 105, 111, 113–121, *115*, 126, 131, 154
   and graduate education. 116, 117, 128
Frye, Elisa. 115
Fulbright Fellowship. 266, 296, 297, 327, 334, 344

Fuller, Buckminster. 248
Fullerton, Randy. 154
Fulton County (Ga.) Commissioners. 59
Fulton-DeKalb Hospital Authority. 60, 64
Funk, Robert. 165

Gaines, J. W. 31
Gambrell, E. Smyth. 217, 219
Gambrell Hall. 217, 219, 270
Gardner, Clinton. 164
Garland-Thompson, Rosemarie. 233
Garrett, David. 190
Gay, Brinton B., Jr. *432*, 432
General Conference of the Methodist Episcopal Church. 352, 355–357
General Conference of the Methodist Episcopal Church, South. 96, 354–359
General Education Board (Rockefeller Foundation). 45, 47, 50, 94, 98
General Education Requirements (GER). 132, 133
Geological Society of America. 296
Geology Building. 296
Geology, Department of. 104, 118, 295, 296
Georgia (country). 436, 437. *See also* Emory-Georgia Partnership
   economic conditions. 439
   medical facilities. 437–439
   relations with Emory University. 435–446
Georgia (state).
   hearings on desegregation. 52
   influence of Atlanta business community on. 41, 47, 55, 99
   racial politics of. 42, 46, 47
Georgia Baptist Hospital.
   and segregation. 67
Georgia Cancer Coalition. 404, 406
Georgia Conference Manual Labor School. 14, 96
Georgia Annual Conference, Methodist Episcopal Church, South. 96, 354–359
Georgia Heart Association. 298, 300
Georgia Institute of Technology. 284, 406, 407, 414
Georgia Research Alliance. 404, 406
Georgia State University. 268, 415
   relations with Georgia (country). 439, 444
Georgia State University Law School. 218, 336
Gerkin, Charles. 62, 63, 66, 169
Giddings, Glenville. 451
Gilbert, Charles. 424

Gilbert, John ("Jack"). 161
Giles, Micheal W. 141
Girls High School (Atlanta). 303
Gladden, John. 74
Gleason, Jan. 86
Glee Club; cancellation of trip to Tuskegee Institute. 52
Glenn, T. K. 449
Glenn Memorial United Methodist Church. 294, 337, 358
Global Health Institute. 445, 446
"God is Dead" controversy. 102
Godfrey, Israel. 19, 20
Godfrey, John Pliny, Jr. 20
Goizueta, Roberto C. *447*
Goizueta (Roberto C.) Business School. *See under* School of Business
Goldstein, Eric. 11
Goldstein, Jacob. 294
Goo, David. 444
Goodchild, Chauncey G. 294, 295
Goodpastor, Larry. 171
Goodrich C. White Professor. 5, 124, 224, 231
Gosnell, Cullen B. 281
Gotwals, Joan. 119
Gould, Kenneth. 413
Gould, Virginia. 230
Gozansky, Nathaniel E. 215, 218, 221
graduate education. 40, 94–97
Graduate Institute of Liberal Arts. 106, 144, 148, 151, 158, 265, 266, 268, 297, 302, 304, 308, 312
 and African American studies. 151, 178, 181
 and art history. 246, 247
 and film studies. 202–205
 and women's studies. 228, 231
Graduate School. 97, 98, 106, 108–110, 116, 117, 126, 128, 138, 148
 administration. 126–129
 budget. 116, 117, 148, 488–169
 growth. 47, 116, 117, 128, 148, 296
 dean. 116, 124–126, 148, 296, 437
 faculty. 126, 148
 relation to the College. 128, 140, 148
graduate students. 88, 127, 128, 138
 financial aid. 47, 107, 110, 116
 housing. 151
 and women's studies. 85, 229
Grady, Henry. 58, 285

Grady Memorial Hospital. 57, 58, 298, 396, 399–402, 404–407, 422–425, 430–433, 435, 449–451, 454
 black staff of and segregation. 59–62
 desegregation of. 66, 67
 Emory Clinical Training and Faculty Office Building. 404
 and Emory Medical Care Foundation. 404
 and Georgia (country), relations with. 438, 439, 442, 443, 446
 integration of. 58–69
 nurses and segregation. 61, 62
Grant, Robert. 422, 423
Gravanis, Michael. 425, 426
Graves, Iverson, as slave owner. 15
Graves, Michael. 248
Green, M. Christian. 389
Griffin, Marvin. 46
Gruentzig, Andreas. 426
Gruentzig (Andreas) Cardiovascular Center. 427
Guggenheim Fellows. 289, 296, 304, 306, 307, 312, 316, 328, 334, 335, 338
Gunderson, Gary. 372, 374
Gustafson, James. 169, 170, 373
Guy-Sheftall, Beverly. 229
Guyton, Robert. 426

Hadas, Moses. 277, 277–280
Hahn, Carole. 225, 227, 253, 254
Hall, Annie. 207
Hall, Joan. 150
Hall, Pam. 229, 231
Hall, Robert. 218
Hamilton (Grace Towns) Professor. 173, 183
Hammond, Bob. 20
Hammonds, Bennie. 177
Hamscher, Albert. 332
Hansell, Granger. 270
happiness, research on. 375, 391
Hardman, Laura. 155, 437
Hardman, John. 437
Harlan, Louis R. 281, 288
Harris, Leslie. 183, 184
Harris (Florence Candler) Home for Nurses. 397
Harrison, David. 426, 427
Hartford Theological Seminary Library. 104, 118, 339
Hartsfield, William B. 50, 52, 53
Hartshorne, Charles. 295
Hartsock, Ernest. 283

Harvard University Press. 289
Hascall, Robert. 80, 81
Hatcher, Charles R. 108, 128, 401–403, 405, 425
Hauk, Gary. 374
Hay, Peter. 220
Haygood, Atticus Greene. 8, 24, 355, 358
Haygood (Atticus) Professor. 265, 266, 268
Haygood-Hopkins Memorial Gateway. 7, 8, 10
   dedication address. 8
   restoration. 10
HCA-The Healthcare Company. 404
Health Affairs, Executive Vice President for. 108, 128, 138, 400, 401, 403, 407, 417
health care administration in Georgia (country). 444, 445
health care information, access to in Georgia (country). 440, 441
health policy reform in Georgia (country). 439, 440
health sciences. 135, 401, 403
   federal funding of. 99, 102, 104, 107, 109, 110
Health Sciences Library. *See under* Woodruff (Robert W.) Health Sciences Center Library
Health Services Board. 400, 450, 451, 454
Healy, Sarah. 225
Heaney, Seamus. 340–342
The Heart (Hurst). 298, 424, 425, 432
Henry-Crowe, Susan. 171, 360
Hepburn, William M. 218
Heritage Ball. 160
Herndon, Angelo. 284
Herndon, Garland. 400, 401, 408
Hesla, David. 158
Hickson, John. 422
higher education. *See under* colleges and universities
Hilkey, Charles Joseph. 217
History Building (Bowden Hall). 332, 335
History, Department of. 102, 104, 106, 107, 132, 134, 150, 281, 282, 292, 296, 301, 302, 313, 332, 335, 336
   doctoral program. 281
   growth. 150
A History of Emory University (Bullock). 37
history of medicine. 301
A History of Narrative Film (Cook). 198, 200
HIV/AIDS. 373, 398, 406, 411, 414, 415, 419, 429
   Georgia (country). 445
Hochman, Steven. 290
Hoffman, Joy. 335
Hoffmann, Manfred. 166–171
Hogue, Carol J. Rowland. 386

Holt, Mack. 333, 334
Homiletics. 295
Hooper, Frank A. 51, 53, 65, 66
Hope Lodge. 79
Hopewell, Jim. 166, 169
Hopkins, Isaac Stiles. 8, 24
Hornbostel, Henry. 216
Hose, Sam (Samuel Wilkes). 24, 27, 28, 30, 469–27
hospitals, private in Atlanta; desegregation of. 67–69
Houpt, Jeffrey. 438, 439, 446
housing. 159
Howett, Catherine. 248
Howett, John. 175, *245*, 245–249
   awards. 249
   community service. 248, 249
Hudson, Reginald. 426
Huff, Matt. 191
Huffer, Lynne. 234
human rights, research on. 383–385, 388, 389
humanities. 98, 106, 141, 148
Humanities Building (Callaway Center North). 204
Humanities Department. 158
Hunt, Earl. 170
Hunter, Hannah. 19
Huntington's disease. 419, 420
Hunter, Howard O. (Woody). 207, 220
Hurst, J. Willis. 298, 421, 423, 426, 427
Hurst's The Heart (Hurst). 298, 425
Hyatt, Irwin. 125, 133, 138, 141, 143–151, *145*, 292, 335

imaging technology. 420
immunology. 418, 419
Inclusive Instruction, Assistant Dean for. 150
Insel, Thomas. 374, 417
Institute for Comparative and International Studies. 153
Institute for Jewish Studies (Rabbi Donald A. Tam). 361, 363, 367
Institute for Public Health and Faith Collaborations. 372
Institute for Women's Studies. 206, 223, 224, 228–233. *See also* Women's Studies, Department of; women's studies
   becomes Department of Women's Studies. 233
   doctoral program. 228, 229, 231–233
   established. 224
   growth of. 229, 231, 233, 234
   honorary fellows program. 229
   honors program. 229

minor and major in. 228, 232
  relations with other universities. 229
  undergraduate courses. 228
Institute of Buddhist Dialectics. 367, 368
Institute of Ecumenical and Cultural Research. 297
Institute of Liberal Arts. *See under* Graduate Institute of Liberal Arts.
Institutional Advancement, Senior Vice President for. 157, 160, 161
instruction, changes in. 145
insurrection, law against. 284
integration of Emory University. 39–55
Interdenominational Theological Center. 164, 165
  and interracial exchange with Candler School of Theology. 164, 165
interdisciplinary education. 106, 134, 147, 148, 158, 381
interdisciplinary studies major. 158
Interfaith Health Program. 372, 374
intergenerational self. 6, 7, 11
Interinstitutional Program in Social Change. 267, 268
International Philosophical Association. 295
internationalization. 132–134
interseminary movement. 165
interseminary seminar. 170
Irvine, Jacqueline Jordan. 298, 299
Islam. 382–386, 388, 391
Italian studies program. 133, 153
Ivester, Doug. 407
Ivey, Adrienne. 232

Jack, Theodore H. 281
Jackson, Timothy P. 375, 386
Japanese language courses. 127
Jefferson, Thomas; biography of, by Dumas Malone. 288, 289
Jefferson (Thomas) Award. *See under* Thomas Jefferson Award
Jenkins, Helen. 161
Jewish Studies Program. *See under* Institute for Jewish Studies (Rabbi Donald A. Tam).
Johns, Michael M.E. 138, 403, 407, 417
Johnson, Ben F., Jr. 54, 75, 218, 219
Johnson, Edgar H. 281
Johnson, Jondelle. 59
Johnson, Lyndon Baines. 68, 298, 423, 454
Johnson, Luke T. 386
Johnson, Ronald. 153
Johnson, Ted. 339
Johnson, Zack. 420
Johnston, Thomas P. *100*, 100
Jonas Robitscher Professor of Law. 367
Jones, L. Bevel. 164
Jones, Boisfeuillet. 44, 400, 402, *447*, 447–455, *452*
Jones, George. 124–130, *125*, 153, 203
Jones, Robert Tyre ("Bobby"). 270
Jordan, G. Ray. 295
Jordan, Mark D. 386
Joseph, Richard. 184
Joslin, G. Stanley. 218, 295
Journeys Program (Journeys of Reconciliation). 368
Junior College at Oxford. *See under* Oxford College of Emory University

Kanter, Kirk. 426
Kappa Alpha. 144
Kacharava, Andro. 439
Keck, Leander. 167
Kennedy, John F. 447, 453, 454
Keyes, Corey. 373
Kilgo, John C. 37
Kimbrough, Calvin. 171
Kimbrough, Nelia. 170, 225, 253
King, Frederick A. *410*, 410–417
King, Martin Luther, Jr. 52, 53
King, Martin Luther, Sr. 63, 165
King, Spencer. 426
Kirkpatrick, Dow. 165, 166
Kitty (Miss). 16, 17
Kobaladze, Archil. 438
Kokko, Juha. 426, 446
Konner, Melvin. 228
Krause, Richard. 439
Kresge Foundation. 155
Kretchman, Trudy. 340, 341
Kushner, Howard. 372

Laderman, Gary. 365, 370–372, 375, 376
Lamar, Howard R. 94, 106, 111, 287
Lamar, Lucius Quintus Cincinnatus (L.Q.C.). 216
Lamar Committee Report. 106, 107, 152
land use classification plan. 81
Lane, George W., as slave owner. 15
Laney, James T. 104–108, 111, 115–120, 122, 123, 125, 128, 131, 145, 152, 158–161, 182, 183, 226, 247, 294, 337, 339–344, 380, 381, 390, 400, 401, 412, 437, 446
  achievements of. 110

as Dean of Candler School of Theology.
  168–171
and Center for the Study of Law and Religion.
  381, 383
and the Center for Women at Emory. 84–87
and diversity. 86
fiscal policy. 105–107
goals for Emory. 85, 104–106, 108, 364, 381
and graduate education. 106, 128
and graduate student aid. 107, 116
named University president. 104
on conflict. 87
recruited to Candler School of Theology. 169, 170
and Robert W. Woodruff. 105
ties with Atlanta business community. 110
and undergraduate student aid. 107
and University budget. 117
language education. 138
Lanski, Steve. 444
Larson, Edward. 370
Latin American and Caribbean Studies Program.
  124, 133
Law and Economics Program. 219
Law and Religion Program. 367, 381, 383, 385,
  389. *See also* Center for the Study of Law and
  Religion
  becomes Center for the Study of Law and
    Religion. 385
  goals. 382, 383
Law School. *See under* School of Law
Law School Building. *215*, 216, 218, 248. *See also*
  Carlos Hall; Gambrell Hall
Lawley, Thomas J. 138, 446
Lawson, George. 270
Leadership in Energy and Environmental Design
  (LEED). 81
learning disabilities. 149
Leigh, Ted F. *431*, 431
Lesbian, Gay, Bisexual, and Transgender Life,
  Office of. 161
Lester, Charles Turner ("Charlie"). 101, 148, 149,
  200, 307, 308
Lester, James G. 261, 295, 296
Lewis, Earl. 184
liberal arts education. 4, 5, 105, 108, 109
libraries. 98, 103, 107, 118, 119, 210, 368. *See
  also* Candler (Asa Griggs) Library; MacMillan
  (Hugh F.) Law Library; Pitts Theology Library; Woodruff (Robert W.) Health Sciences
  Library; Woodruff (Robert W.)Library

collections. 106, 209, 292
and education. 211
growth. 210
needs. 98, 106, 210, 211
undergraduate library. 211
research library. 210, 211
Library School (Division of Librarianship). 118.
Liebeskind, Lanny S. 139, 141
Liebniz, Gottfried Wilhelm von. 296
Lillian Carter Center for International Nursing. 407
Lilly Endowment. 385, 389
Lindsay, Joseph J., Jr. 424
Linguistic Atlas of the Gulf States (Pederson). 150
Liotta, Dennis. 123, 138, 139, 154
Lipstadt, Deborah. 11
literature.
  undergraduate major in. 255
Littell, Franklin. 165
Liu, Robert. 129
Lloyd, Lee Ann. 340
Loemker, Leroy. 283, 296
Logan, William. 424
Logue, R. Bruce. 422–424, 426, 427
Lomashvili, Koba. 439
Long, Crawford W. 398
Long, Richard A. 151, 184, *265*, 265–268
  publications. 266, 267
  as teacher. 267
Longstreet, Augustus Baldwin. 356
  as anti-abolitionist. 14
Loridans Foundation. 155
Lowrey, Gerald B. 308
Lucas-Tauchar, Frances. 135, 140
Luce (Henry) Foundation. 385, 389
Lucchesi, John. 154
Lullwater. *71*, 72, 74, 77, 78, 79–81
  sale of property to Veterans Administration
    Hospital. 76, 77
  shuttle road. 79–81
  and toxic chemicals. 77
Lullwater Farms. 72
  purchase by Emory. 72, 77
Lullwater House. 77
Lullwater Management Task Force. 81
Lullwater Study Committee. 77
Lustig, Andrew. 370
Lyle, Guy Redvers. 8, *209*, 209–214
Lyman, Thomas. 246–247
lynching. 20, 24, 25, 27, 28, 30
Lynn, David. 133, 139, 371

Maberly, Glenn. 439
MacMillan (Hugh F.) Law Library. 220, 270
Magee, Rosemary. 125, 134, 138, 151–155, *152*
Magnolia League. 161, 162
Main, Eleanor. 139, 140, 146, 153
Major, Blair Rogers. 331, 333–336
Major, J. Russell (James Russell). 292, *331*, 331–336
Major (Russell and Blair Rogers) Scholarship. 336
malaria. 402, 415, 436, 445, 451
Mallard, William. 164–171
Malone, Dumas. 97, 98, 109, 111, *281*, 288–290
 and Jefferson biography. 288, 289
 report on graduate studies at Emory. 97, 98, 109
Malone, Henry T. 290
Malone, Kemp. 288
mammography. 429, 434
Manchester College (Oxford, England). 146
Mandel, Leon. 299, 300
Manne, Henry. 219
Manley, Frank. 328, 329
Manual Labor School. *See under* Georgia Conference Manual Labor School
Maple, Terry. 416
MARIAL. *See under* Center for the Study of Myth and Ritual in American Life
Markle (John and Mary R.) Foundation. 199, 200
Marquis, Harold. 219
Marr, Thomas. 219
marriage and the family, research on. 384–391
Marsh, Karen. 441
Marshall Scholarship. 152
Martin, Edwin T. 316, 320
Martin, Nina. 206
Martin, Sidney Walter. 39, 41, 49, 50, 52–54, 99, 101, 105, 210, 263, 293, 294
 opposition to by faculty. 50, 52, 53
 views on integration. 50, 52–54
Martin Luther King Jr., Scholarship Program. 124, 178, 183
Marty, Martin E. 384, 386–388
Mathematics and Science Center. 154
Matheson, Mrs. William. 8
Mathews, Joseph J. 296, 332
Matthews, Linda. 342
Mayoue, John C. 386
Mays, Benjamin. *161*
Mayton, William T. 221
McCauley, Robert. 371, 375
McClure, Harold. 413
McCord, H.Y. 16, 467n3(Ch.2)

McCord, Jeff D. 258, 261
McDonald, Alonzo L. 389
McDonald Agape Foundation. 389
McDonald (Alonzo L.) Family Foundation. 385
McDonough, Thomas Edwin. 257–263
McDonough, Tim. 189
McFarland, Deborah. 440
McGough, Lucy S. 299
McMains, Harrison. 44
Means, Alexander, as slave owner. 15, 18
Means, Louisa. 17, 18
Means, Sam. 17, 18
Medical Association of Georgia. 298, 450
Medical College of Dentistry. 398
Medicare.
 influence on desegregation. 69
Medicine, Department of. 298, 422, 423, 425–427
Medieval Academy of America. 298, 312
meditation and health. 368, 371, 374
Medlin, Ed. 85
Meier, Richard. 249
Melion, Walter. 126
Meridian Herald (organization). 374
MERIT (Mobilizing Educational Resources and Ideas for Tomorrow) campaign. 102
Methodism.
 connection/connectional defined. 352, 353
 on racial discrimination. 48
Methodism and education. 351–362
 and African Americans. 357, 358
 bureaucratic phase. 357, 358
 collegiate phase. 355–357
 non-sectarian aspects of. 353, 356, 357, 361
 popular phase. 353–355
 post-Christian phase. 361, 362
 professional phase. 358–360
 research universities. 353, 358, 359, 361
 role of conferences in. 354–356
 role of university presidents in. 354–356, 358–360
 theological schools. 353, 358
Methodist Episcopal Church. 14, 352, 357. *See also* United Methodist Church
 Board of Education. 357
 division over slavery. 356
 and Emory faculty. 354–356
 Freedmen's Aid and Southern Education Society. 357, 358
 General Conference. 352, 355–357
 Georgia Conference. 354, 356

Methodist Episcopal Church, South. 19, 40, 96, 356–358. *See also* United Methodist Church
   and education. 354
   and Emory faculty. 356, 358
   General Conference. 96, 354–359
   Georgia Conference. 354, 356
   North Georgia Conference. 40, 396
   universities. 358
Methodists.
   Georgia. 353–356, 358
Metzger, Lore. 225, 227, 250–256, 322
   committee activity. 253, 254
   first female full professor. 251
   and status of women at Emory. 225, 253
   and women's studies. 227, 253, 254
Mew, George. 261
Mickiewicz, Ellen. 254, 437
Microbiology, Department of. 414
Miller, William B. 433
Minter, David. 105, 107, 108, 116, *122*, 122–124, 130, 132, 136, 146–148, 151–153, 181, 188, 254, 364
   as advocate for faculty. 147
   and faculty recruitment. 107, 147, 148, 152
   and film studies. 201, 202
   and undergraduate recruitment. 152
   and women's studies. 227, 231
Mitchell, Henry ("Billy"). 15, 20
Mizell, Robert. 42, 448, 449, 451, 452
molecular spectroscopy. 294
monks, Tibetan. *366, 369*, 379, 376
Moon, Joseph. 151, 162
Moran, Neil C. 300
Morehouse College. 44, 46, 151
Morehouse School of Medicine. 401, 402, 438, 439
Morgan, E. Phil. 175
Morgan, Thomas D. 219, 220
Morris, Holly J. 190
Mosashvili, Tamuna. 437
Mosley, Diane. 171
multicultural education. 299
Multicultural Programs and Services. 160, 178
Murdy, William. 77, 78, 81
Murdy-Carter report. 77–79
Murphy, Vincent. 154
Music, Department of. 155
Myers, Jack. 422
Myers, Orie, Jr. 75, 400

National Association for the Advancement of Colored People (NAACP). 45, 50, 62, 64
   Atlanta Chapter. 58, 59, 61
National Book Award. 304
National Council of Black Studies. 179–183
National Dental Association. 63
National Endowment for the Humanities. 304, 312, 316, 328
National Heart Institute. 423, 425
National Information Learning Centre, Georgia (country). 441
National Institute of Dental Research. 298
National Institutes of Health. 295, 297, 299–301, 399, 405, 406, 445, 452, 453
   and primate research. 410–412, 414–416
National Primate Research Center (Soviet Union). 412
National Science Foundation. 95, 114, 299
National Science Foundation Academic Year Institute. 115
Navarro, Emilia. 229, 230, 239, 253, 254
Negi, Geshe Lobsang Tenzin ("Lobsang"). 371, 373, 374, 376
neighborhood law office. 218, 299
neurosciences. 370, 376, 399, 407
   and Yerkes National Primate Research Center. 412, 413, 418, 419
   characteristics of at Emory. 412, 413
Neurosciences Building. 406, 416, 419
Neville, Gwen Kennedy. 225, 226, 253
New Testament scholarship. 297
Newby, Wendy. 150
Newman, Lynn. 437
No Strings Attached. 155
nonhuman primates. *See under* primates, nonhuman
North Georgia Conference, Methodist Episcopal Church, South. 396
Norton (W.W.) & Company. 198
Nowicki, Stephen. 4
Nuland, Sherwin. 371
nursing education. 397. *See also* School of Nursing
   Georgia (country). 442, 443
Nutter, Don. 424

O'Connor, Flannery. 254, 255
Odem, Mary E. 229, 231, 387
Oeler, Karla. 206
Office of Equal Opportunity Programs. 149, 150
Office of Multicultural Programs and Services. 178
Office of Sponsored Programs. 125

Oglethorpe University. 268
Olin, Stephan. 356
Oliver, Hoyt. 374, 376
Oliver, Mary Margaret. 388
The Omni. 146
O'Neal, Sondra. 84, 182
"One Percent Plan." 98, 164
Ordover, Abe. 219
Organic chemistry. 299, 300
Organization of American Historians. 288
Orr, Gustavus John.
    as slave owner. 15
    and ex-slaves. 19
Osler, William. 275
Owen-Smith, Patricia. 232
Oxford, Ga. 356
    and African-Americans. 17–21
    Kitty's Cottage 16
    Oxford City Cemetery. 16, 17, 21
    race relations. 17, 19–21
    street names. 356
    town plan. *3*
Oxford College of Emory University. 7, 14, 15, 20, 97, 283
    and African-Americans. 19–21
    Day Chapel. *351*
    and women' studies. 232
Oxford (England) summer program. 146

Page, Peter. 60, 67
Palms, John M. 94, 105, 146, 147, 199, 226, 308, 335, 338, 339
parasitology. 294
parking. 74, 75, 80
Parran, Tom. 451
Partin, Clyde, Sr. 159
Pathology, Department of. 414, 422, 426
pathology, research in. 413, 415
Patterson, Barbara A.B. ("Bobbi"). 85, 86
Patterson, Cynthia. 229
Patterson, L. Ray. 219
Patton, Laurie L. 154
Paul, Robert. 207, 376
Peavine Creek. 72, 74
Pederson, Lee. 150
pedestrian campus. 75, 80
Pediatric Cardiology, Division of. 425
Peirce, Charles. 295
pellagra. 274
Penn, Ojeda. 178

people with disabilities. 149
Perdue, Garland. 423
performing arts. 134, 135
Perry, Michael J. 220, 384, 390
Petroleum Research Fund. 299
Pew Charitable Trusts. 385
PhD. programs. 41, 45, 98, 102, 108, 128 148, 211
    first, in chemistry. 98, 100
pharmacology. 102, 104, 106, 300, 422
Phillips, Ulrich B. 284, 287
Philosophy, Department of. 295, 296
physical chemistry. 294
Physical Education and Athletics, Division of. 257, 258
Physics Building (Callaway South). 154
Physics Department. 99, 106, 124, 138
Physiology Building. 10, 396
Pickett's Charge on the Quadrangle. 144
Pierce, George Foster. 355, 356
Pierce, Lovick. 356
Pierce Hall cornerstone laying. *13*
Pinkston, William. 63, 66, 67
Pitts Theology Library. 37, 118, *163*, 339
Platt, Robert B. 75, 76, 81
Platt report on Emory's natural environment. 75, 76
Playwriting Center of Theater Emory. 192, 193
Poetry Month. 143
Poling, Clark. 248
Poole, Sam. 423
Political Science, Department of. 132, 281
Potter, David M. 281, 283, 286–288, *287*
    publications, 287, 288
Practical English Handbook (Watkins and Dillingham). 319, 320, 328
President's Advisory Council. 150
President's Commission on Higher Education (1953).
    recommendation on elimination of segregation. 43
President's Commission on the Status of Women. 84–87, 225, 226, 234, 253
Price, Polly. 228
primate research centers. 399, 410–420
    nonhuman primate population of. 411, 416, 418
    Soviet Union. 412
primates, nonhuman.
    research involving. 399, 410, 411, 413–420
Prince, Astrid. 129
Private Diagnostic Clinic. 399, 422, 423. *See also* Emory Clinic

professional schools. 98, 118, 125, 138, 210, 215, 216, 360, 361
proselytism, research on. 383, 384
Provost and Vice President for Academic Affairs. 84, 88, 105, 113, 116–120, 131, 135, 136, 385
Psychology Department. 104, 132, 150
public health. 372–374, 376, 402, 439, 445, 446
Public Safety, Department of. 182
Pulitzer Prize. 281–283, 288, 289, 304
Pushkin Institute. 152

the Quadrangle. *xii*, 1, 2, 7, 9, 12, 73, 144
quarter system. 145
Quillian, Henry Milton. 217

"Race Relations Sunday." 165
Radell, Sally. 135, 154
radiology. 429–434
   and breast cancer. 434
Radiology, Department of. 422, 426, 429–434, *433*
radiology, pediatric. 425, 432
Raggi-Moore, Judy. 153
Ragsdale, Larry. 75, 81
Rainey, Glenn Weddington. 283, 284
Raison, Charles. 371, 373, 374
Randolph-Macon College. 355, 356
Ransom, William. 154
Rao, P.V. 373, 375
Raoul, Eléonore. 215, 217
rape. 85, 87
the ravine. 74–76, 248.
Rawles, William. 424
Ray, Linda. 150
Real, Leslie. 139
Reconstruction (of the South). 284, 285
Reed, Walter L. 154, 155
Reeves, Geoffrey. 201
Reingold, Beth. 229, 231
religion.
   and democracy. 383
   and health/healing. 372–374
   and human rights. 383–385, 388–390
   and science. *See under* science and religion
   research programs on. 374, 375
   study of at Emory. 363–368
Religion, Department of. 104, 132, 297, 363–368
   curriculum. 364, 367–368
   faculty. 364, 365, 367, 368

joint PhD. program with School of Theology. 364
   non-Christian religions, study of. 365
   undergraduate courses. 364, 367
Religion, Graduate Division of. 364, 367
   PhD. program. 367
Religious Life, Office of. *See under* Chapel and Religious Life, Office of the Dean of
Religious Research Association. 298
research universities. 94, 104, 107, 136, 137. *See also* colleges and universities
   characteristics of. 353, 358, 359, 361
Religion and Health Initiative. 371
Research, Vice President for. 124, 125, 138
Reserve Officers Training Corps. 147, 247
Reynolds, Philip. 375, 391
Rhodes Scholarship. 152, 312
Rice University. 123, 150
Richardson, Arthur. 405, 423, 454
Richmond, Garland. 122, 145, 151
Roberts, James William. 274
Roberts, Clifford Rebecca Stewart. 274
Roberts, Stewart R. 273, 273–275, 422
Roberts Clinic. 274, 275
Robeson, Linton B. 7
Robinson, Cornelius and Ellie. 15
Robinson, Henry and Milly. 18
Robinson, Harriet. 415, 419
Robinson, James D. 451
Robinson, Jontyle. 180, 182
Robinson, Paul. 424
Rockefeller Foundation. 40, 101, 289, 304, 307. *See also* General Education Board (Rockefeller Foundation)
Rogers, James V. 431
Rohrer, Robert H. 433
Rojas, Carlos. 300, 301
Rollins (Claudia Nance) Building. 407
Rollins (Grace Crum) Building. 402
Rollins, Howard. 139, 146, 151, 153
Rollins, O. Wayne. 402, 405
Rollins (O. Wayne) Research Center. 108, 154, 402, 405
Romance Languages, Department of. 237–239
Rosenwald School, Oxford, Ga. 20
Roy, Deboleena. 234
Rudolph, Paul. 248
Rumbaugh, Dwayne. 415
Rumbaugh, Sue Savage. 415
Runyon, Theodore. 165–171
Rusk, Dean. 50

Russell, Jane A. 297
Rust Chapel Methodist Church (Oxford, Ga.). 19
Rust, Richard. 20
Salem, Ga. 6, 7, 16
Salem Camp Meeting. 6, 7, 16
Salmon, Marla. 140
Sanders, Kimberly Wallace. 233
Sanders, Mark. 183, 184
Sanderson, Steven. 134, 136–143, 147, 150, 153, 154, 206, 207, 233
Sanderson, Rosalie. 137
Sanfilippo, Fred. 407
Sawyer, Forrest Jr. 20
Saxon, Allie Frances. 397
Scarborough, Elliott. 399, 400, 448, 451
Scarritt Bible and Training School. 358
Schatten Gallery. 368
Schlant, Robert. 424, 425
Scholar/Teacher Award. *See under* University Scholar/Teacher Award
scholarships. 67, 107, 110, 123, 124, 152
School of Business (Goizueta Business School). 117. *See also* School of Economics and Business.
   relations with Georgia (country). 437
School of Dentistry. 97, 298, 397, 398, 449, 453. *See also* Atlanta-Southern Dental College; School of Postgraduate Dentistry
   phased out. 108, 398, 402
School of Economics and Business. 97
School of Law. 97, 215–221, 270, 272, 295, 299, 344, 363, 367, 372, 380–385, 387, 388
   admission requirements. 216
   curriculum. 216, 218–221
   deans. 216–221
   diversity. 218, 220, 221
   enrollment. 216–219
   evening program. 217, 218
   faculty growth. 218–220
   and Georgia integration law. 218
   integration of. 218
   JD degree. 217
   joint degree programs with Theology. 381, 382
   journals. 219
   LLM program. 219
   library. 216, 219, 220. *See also* MacMillan (Hugh F.) Law Library
   named for L. Q. C. Lamar. 216
   regional characteristics. 217–219
   women students. 270

School of Medicine. 57, 58, 96, 98, 99, 106–108, 110, 125, 274, 300, 301, 396, 398–402, 404–406, 408, 432, 449
   budget. 99, 102, 449, 450
   Department of Community Health. 402
   faculty growth. 108, 400
   funding sources. 98, 99, 102, 107, 400, 405, 406, 449
   and Georgia (country). 438, 439, 444, 446
   and Grady Hospital. 396, 399–402, 404, 405
   PhD. program. 405
   sponsored research. 405, 406
   and Yerkes National Primate Research Center. 413–415
School of Medicine Building. 10
School of Nursing (Nell Hodgson Woodruff School of Nursing). 66, 80, 97, 128, 140, 372, 397, 406, 407, 443, 449
   Crawford Long Hospital Nursing School merges with. 502n1(Ch.39)
   degree programs. 397, 407
   integration of. 54, 101, 397
   named for Nell Hodgson Woodruff. 397
School of Postgraduate Dentistry. 298, 398
   closed. 398
School of Public Health (Rollins School of Public Health). 108, 109, 117, 371–373, 396, 402, 403, 407
   dean. 138
   degree programs. 128, 407
   funding. 407
   and Georgia (Country). 439, 440, 444
   joint programs. 407
School of Theology (Candler School of Theology). 38, 96, 98, 107, 108, 163–171, 297, 363, 364, 385
   academics *versus* service to church. 166, 170
   clinical pastoral education movement. 169
   early reputation. 164, 166
   faculty characteristics. 167, 168, 171
   faculty petition on integration. 49, 164
   graduate program, establishment of. 166, 167, 171
   growth of. 170, 171
   and interracial exchange with the Interdenominational Theological Center. 165
   and the issue of racial discrimination. 49, 164–166
   joint PhD. program with Department of Religion. 364

joint program with School of Law. 381, 382, 385
student characteristics. 171
supervised ministry program. 169
women students. 170, 171
Schuchard, Ronald. 146, 338–341
Schwartz, Donna. 155
Schwartz, Marvin. 155
Schwartz (Donna and Marvin) Center for Performing Arts. 155
Science and Society, Emory College Program in. 372, 375
science and religion. 369–377
   and Emory. 372–377
   courses. 373–376
   programs. 375, 376
   research programs on. 374
   symposia. 372, 374
Science 2000. 138, 139, 154
sciences. 135, 138, 139, 154
   curriculum for Tibetans. 374, 376, 377
Scully, Pamela. 234
Seale, Bobby. 179
Seefried, Monique B. 247
segregation, racial. 42, 44, 46–48, 52, 53, 55, 58, 60, 63, 64, 68, 69, 95, 109
Selzer, Richard. 371
semester system. 145
Setzer, James. 440
Shanor, Charles. 221
Sharp, Henry. 175
Shayne, Julie. 233
Shea, Ed. 262
Shelton, William. 246
Shevardnadze, Eduard. 437, 440, 441, 446
Shockley, Grant. 103
Shore, Bradd. 5, 123
Shuford, Wade H. 432, 433
Shure, Donald. 75, 81
Sigma Delta Psi. 261
Silverman, Mark. 425
Silvestri, Guido. 419
Simian Auto-Immune Deficiency. 414
Singer, Valerie. 232
Sitter, John E. 329
Size, William. 79, 81
Skypek, Dora Helen. 177, 225, 225, 253, 254
Sledd, Andrew Warren. 23, 24–38
   article in *Atlantic Monthly*. 26–29
   criticism of Emory College. 26
   letter of resignation. 32–33

on faculty of (Candler) School of Theology. 38
views on James E. Dickey. 31, 32
and Yale University. 34
Sledd, Florence (Candler). 25, 32
Sledd, James Hinton. 37
"Sledd Affair." 24–38
   historical treatment of. 37
   role of public relations in. 36, 37
Sloan (Alfred P.) Foundation. 195
Smathers, Ray K. 261
Smith, C. Miles. 61
Smith, Carter, Jr. 422
Smith, Gary. 221
Smith, James. 158
Smith, Luther M. 24
Smith, Osborn L. 24
Smith, Otis. 67
Smith, Robert. 427
Smith, Ruby Doris. 64
Smyke, Ed. 262
social sciences. 106
Society of Biblical Literature. 297, 367
Sociology and Anthropology Department. 224, 226
sororities. 149
Soule, Joshua. 354, 356
"Source Route." 248
Southeastern Library Network (SOLINET). 213
Southern Association of Colleges and Schools. 77, 107
Southern Literary Renaissance. 282, 286
Southern Medical Association. 274
Southern Medical College. 58
Southern Methodist University. 96, 158, 161, 162, 358
Southern Regional Education Board. 95
Southern Society for Philosophy and Psychology. 296
Southern Society for Philosophy of Religion. 296
southern states. 45,
   economic growth. 96
   population growth. 45, 96
southern studies. 124
Soviet and East European studies (Center for Russian and East European Studies. 124, 133
Soyinka, Wole. 183, 184
Spanish and Portuguese, Department of. 153, 300
Sparks, Holloway. 234
Spelman College. 229
Spencer, Margaret. 178
Spivak, Gayatri Chakravorty. 201, 251, 255, 256

Sprawls, Perry. 433
Stead, Eugene Jr. 422
Stead-Warren Cardiovascular Laboratory. 423, 424
Stein, Donald G. 140
Stephens, John C., Jr. ("Jack"). 145, 146, 246, 307, 308
Stevenson, Elizabeth. *303*, 303–309
    publications. 304, 306–9
stewardship. 11, 72, 75, 77, 79, 81
Stewart, Joseph Spencer. 274
Stinson, R.D. 31
Stipe, J. Gordon. 332
Stokes, Mack. B. 355
Stone, Albert E. ("Al"). 151
Stone, John. 2
Strickland, Robert. *447*
Strickland, Stephen. 437
Student Environmental Action Coalition. 79
Student Government Association. 77
studio art program. 246, 247
Studlar, Gaylen. 202, 205
study abroad. 4, 133, 139, 146, 151–153, 176, 177
    funding. 152, 153
summer school. 151, 153
Sutin, Jerome. 301
Sybers, Robert. 432, 433

Talmadge, Eugene. 42
Talmadge, Herman. 42, 46, 49
Task Force for Global Health. 407
Task Force on Security and Responsibility. 85–87
TATTO (Teaching Apprenticeship, Teacher Training Opportunity) program. 127, 129
tax-exempt status and integration.
    and Emory. 47, 48, 53, 54, 99, 101, 215, 218
Taylor, Jo. 253
television history. 199, 200, 204
Temple, John. 117, 140
Templeton (John) Foundation. 375, 385
Terrell, Timothy. 221
Thanksgiving dinner, all university. 160
Theater Emory. 187–196, 201, 247
    and adaptations. 193, 194
    and anthology productions. 193
    growth. 189
    interdisciplinary aspects. 195, 196
    Playwriting Center. 192, 193
    productions. 190–195
    relation to Theater Studies Department. 187, 188
    repertory. 191, 192
    resident artists. 189, 191
    and site-specific productions. 191, 194, 195
    and undergraduate education. 191
Theater Studies, Department of. 124, 126, 187–196
    courses. 189–191
    and film studies. 201, 202, 204
    growth. 189
Theology Library. *See under* Pitts Theology Library
theology schools. 353, 356–358, 360
Theory Practice Service Learning (TPSL). 232
Thigpen, Carol. 146
Thomas, James R., as slave owner. 15
Thomas, John D. 7
Thomas Jefferson Award. 113, 144, 151, 292, 299, 302, 316, 332
Thompson, Gordon. 170
Thomson, William Danner. 216
TIAA-CREF. 253
Tibet. 367, 368, 370, 373, 374, 376
Tbilisi State University. 437, 439
Tbilisi State Medical University. 439, 440
traffic. 75–77, 80
Trakas, George. 248
transgenics. 419, 420
transplantation, medical. 407, 419, 426
Trimble, Burton. 46, 164, 334
Trinity College (Durham N.C.). 36, 37
Troutman, Robert. 202, 203
Trust Company of Georgia. 97, 451
tuition. 103, 104, 107, 109, 117, 124, 152
tuition, undergraduate. 101, 117, 124
    benefiting Graduate School. 117
Turman, Pollard. 202
Turman Residential Center. 159
Turner, Henry M. 31
Tutu, Desmond. 183, *379*, 383, 384

undergraduate education. 116, 127, 128, 133, 138
undergraduate students. 124, 133, 135
    advising of. 131, 153
    diversity of. 123, 130, 160
    enrollment. 103, 107, 123, 150
    financial aid. 107, 110, 123, 152
    and identity. 6, 7
    majors. 131
    quality of. 145
    regional characteristics of. 94, 123, 146, 147, 149
    social activities. 149, 282
Undilashvili, Archil. 440, 444

United Methodist Church. 295, 298. *See also* Methodist Episcopal Church; Methodist Episcopal Church, South
United Nations Convention on the Rights of the Child. 387, 388
U.S. Centers for Disease Control and Prevention. 97, 117, 272, 373, 396, 402, 407, 413, 414, 418, 438, 451, 452
U.S. Department of Health, Education, and Welfare. 67–69, 453, 454
    Atlanta Office. 60, 67
U.S. Department of Justice. 270–272
    Board of Immigration Appeals. 271
    Office of Legal Counsel. 271
    Office of the Attorney General. 271
U.S. Food and Drug Administration. 301, 454
U.S. Public Health Service. 102, 397, 452–454
U. S. Supreme Court Historical Society. 271, 272
University Apartments (Clairmont Road). 79, 80, 161
University Athletic Association. 108, 161
University Center in Georgia. 485n48
University College (University of Oxford). 146
University of Florida. 38
University of Georgia. 24, 42, 49, 50, 53, 54
University of Michigan. 115, 116, 118
University of Oxford. 146
University of St. Andrews. 139
University of Virginia. 285, 286, 289
University Priorities Committee. 84, 117
University Scholar/Teacher Award. 237, 293, 301, 325
University Senate. 79–81, 296, 297, 313. *See also* Campus Development Committee; Committee on the Environment
    and integration. 53

V-12 training program. 259
Valdosta Junior College. *See under* Emory Junior College at Valdosta
Van der Vyver, Johan D. 384, 389
Vance, Rupert. 282
Vandall, Frank J. 221
Vanderbilt University. 25, 40, 41, 96, 98, 107, 108, 137, 161, 357, 358
Verene, Don. 123
Veterans Affairs Hospital (Veterans Administration) Hospital. 76, 77, 399, 407, 417, 422, 424, 427
    affiliations with School of Medicine. 399, 401
Vice President for Academic Affairs. 94, 105, 116
Vice President for Arts and Sciences. 105, 122, 123, 130, 131, 137, 140
Vice President for Campus Life. 135, 157
Vice President for External Affairs, Senior. 157
Vice President for Finance and Administration, Executive. 140
Vice President for Health Affairs, Executive. 128, 138, 407, 417
Vice President for Institutional Advancement, Senior. 157, 160, 161
Vice President for Research. 124, 125, 138
Vietnam War. 103, 147, 247
Vision for Emory (Frye). 120, 121
Visual Arts Department. 246

Wagner, James W. 81, 407, 446
Waits, James. 166, 171
Walker, Ken. 435, 438, 441, 444
Walker, Lary. 419
Walker, Marella. 339, 340
Wallace (Henry) For President Club, Emory. resolution on admission of blacks. 44, 45
Wallen, Kim. 415
Walters, James. 114
Ward, Judson C. ("Jake"). 101, 149, 261
Ward, Richard S. 238–242
Ware, Holland. 405
Warner, Clinton. 64
Warner, Isiah. 123
Warren, Jim. 422
Warren, Robert Penn. 282, 318, 321
Washington, Paula. 86
Watkins, Anna. 323
Watkins, Floyd. 147, *315*, 315–324, 327, 328, 334
    and "New Criticism." 318, 320
    research interests. 320, 321
    and students. 318–320, 322
    teaching style. 317–319, 321
    and writing. 319, 320
Watson, Tom. 284, 285
Weber, Theodore. 163–171
Weens, Heinz Stephen. 422, 426, *429*, 429–434
Wegner, John. 80, 81
wellness center. 79
Wenger, Nanette. 424, 425
Wescoat, Bonna. 253
Wesley, Charles. 352–354
Wesley, John. 351–354
Wesley Fellowship, Emory. 46
Wesley Memorial Hospital. 97, 396

Wesley Woods Center. 399, 401, 403
Wesley Woods Geriatric Hospital. 403, 404
Wesleyan College (Georgia). 355
Wesleyan University (Connecticut). 355, 356
Westminster Fellowship. 49
White, Dana. 151, 204
White, Goodrich C. 8, 41–48, 50, 97–99, 101, 109, 210, 293, 448–452
　and admission of Blacks. 45, 49
　and black colleges. 44
　and Charles Howard Candler. 45, 46
　and graduate studies. 97, 98
　and the President's Commission on Higher Education (1953). 43
　and interracial meetings. 45, 46
　and sports. 258, 259, 261
　views on race. 42–44
　views on segregation. 42–45
White, Toni. 170
White Hall. *113*
White (Goodrich C.) Professor. *See under* Goodrich C. White Professor
Whitehead (Lettie Pate) Foundation. 403
Whitehead Biomedical Research Building. 81, 403
Whitehead Surgical Pavilion. 397
Whitman, W. Tate. 296, 297
Wilber, Joseph. 61, 62
Wildlife Conservation Society. 137, 143
Wiley, Bell Irvin. 281, 290–292, *291*, 335
　and integration. 290
　and his Civil War trilogy. 291
　and the Civil War centennial (1961). 291
　and students. 291, 292
Wilhelmi, Alfred E. 297.
Williams, Frank. 332
Williams, James B. ("Jimmy"). 401, 403, 405, *447*
Williams, Samuel C. 217
Williams, Willis. 426
Wilson, Elizabeth. 234
Wilson, Frank. 61, 62, 64, 65, 67
Wilson, Jack. 167
Wingood, Gina. 373
Winship Cancer Institute. 403, 404, 406
　named National Cancer Institute Cancer Center. 404
Winship Clinic for Neoplastic Diseases. 399, 448. *See also* Winship Cancer Institute
Winship Hall. 258
Witte, John, Jr. 220, 367, 375, 379, 380, 382–384, 386, 388–391

Wolfe, Thomas. 316, 320, 323
women faculty. 255
　Emory College. 226
　first full professor. 251
　and gender discrimination. 224–226
　salaries, hiring, tenure, and promotion. 225, 226
Women's Caucus, Emory University. 84, 224–227, 252, 253
women's centers. 87. *See also* Center for Women at Emory
women's health in Georgia (country). 442, 446
women's studies. 124, 224, 253, 254. *See also* Women's Studies Department; Institute for Women's Studies
　committee to establish. 227
　courses. 226–229
　at Oxford College. 232
　proposal for. 227, 228
Women's Studies, Department of. 128, 134, 135, 206, 207, 223, 224, 233, 234, 252, 253. *See also* Institute for Women's Studies; women's studies
　becomes department. 233
　program *versus* department. 227
Wonderful Wednesday. 6, 145
Wood, Hugh. 399
Wood, James. 150
Woodruff, Ernest. 97
Woodruff, George W. 84, 97, 105, 158, 303, 339, 401
Woodruff, Nell Hodgson. 397
Woodruff, Robert Winship. 42, 97–99, 105, 110, 395, 399–401, 408, 448–454
　and malaria research. 402
　Woodruff Health Sciences Center named for. 400
Woodruff Board. 401
Woodruff Endowment for Medical Education. 102
Woodruff (Emily and Ernest) Foundation. 105, 110, 400, 448, 450, 451, 454
Woodruff (Robert W.) Foundation. 98, 103, 155, 161, 402–405, 424, 447
Woodruff gift. 84, 94, 105–107, 109, 110, 117, 121, 158, 229, 340, 364, 381, 401, 405, 412
Woodruff (Robert W.) Health Sciences Center. 97, 395–408, 425, 447–454
　Board. 403, 407
　charity care. 407
　created. 400
　economic impact. 407

as research institution. 396, 402, 403, 405–407
and Yerkes National Regional Primate Center. 415, 419
Woodruff (Robert W.) Health Sciences Center Administration Building. 74, *395*
Woodruff (Robert W.) Health Sciences Center Library.
relations with Georgia (country). 440, 441
Woodruff (Robert W.) Library. 4, 74, 76, 118, 206, 209–211, *212*, 246, 321, 329, 332, 338–339
Great Library Book Turnaround. 4, 5
manuscripts and rare books. 184, 268, 340, 342
Woodruff Medical Center. 396, 400. *See also* Woodruff (Robert W.) Health Sciences Center
renamed Robert W. Woodruff Health Sciences Center. 400
Woodruff Memorial Research Building. 405, 424–427
Woodruff (George W.) Physical Education Center. 159.
Woodruff (Robert W.) Professors. 183, 219, 337, 340, 343, 344, 381
Woodward, C. (Comer) Vann. 36, 281–287
publications. 285, 286
Woodward, Hugh A. (Jack). 282
Woolford B. Baker Award. 245
Woolford B. Baker Woodlands (Antoinette Gardens). 74, 75, 248.
World Law Institute. 344
Worthingon, Karen L. 388

X-rays. 430–432, 434
Yale Divinity School. 122
Yale University. 283, 284, 286–288, 290, 398, 409–411
Yarbrough, Dona. 89
Year of Reconciliation. 120, 299
Yerkes, Robert M. 398, 409
Yerkes National Primate Research Center. 372, 395, 398, 399, 405–407, 409–420, *418*
accredited in animal care. 411, 416
behavioral research. 399, 406
and biomedical research. 406, 416
cardiovascular research. 419–420
and Emory College. 414
community outreach. 420
faculty. 406, 413, 416
field station, Lawrenceville, Ga. 399, 406, 410, 417
genetic research. 420

growth of. 416, 417
and NIH funding. 410–412, 414, 416
non-human primate population of. 411, 416
and the Woodruff Health Sciences Center. 415, 419
research activities. 413–415, 419, 420
and the School of Medicine. 413–415
transfer to Emory. 398, 410
Young, James Harvey ("Harvey"). 151, 292, 301, 302, 334, 447
Young, Larry. 374
Ziegler, Peggy. 225
Zola, Stuart. *417*, 417–420
Zoo Atlanta.
and Yerkes National Primate Research Center. 416